Learning WCF

Michele Leroux Bustamante

Beijing · Cambridge · Farnham · Köln · Sebastopol · Tokyo

Learning WCF
by Michele Leroux Bustamante

Copyright © 2007 O'Reilly Media, Inc. All rights reserved.
Printed in the United States of America.

Published by O'Reilly Media, Inc., 1005 Gravenstein Highway North, Sebastopol, CA 95472.

O'Reilly books may be purchased for educational, business, or sales promotional use. Online editions are also available for most titles (*safari.oreilly.com*). For more information, contact our corporate/institutional sales department: (800) 998-9938 or *corporate@oreilly.com*.

Editor: John Osborn	**Cover Designer:** Karen Montgomery	
Production Editor: Lydia Onofrei	**Interior Designer:** David Futato	
Proofreader: Reba Libby	**Illustrators:** Robert Romano and Jessamyn Read	
Indexer: Ellen Troutman Zaig		

Printing History:

May 2007:	First Edition.

ISBN: 978-0-596-10162-6
[LSI]   [2011-02-07]

For my dad

Table of Contents

Forewords

Hi, I'm Steve Swartz. Michele asked me to write the foreword for her new book, *Learning WCF,* because I was one of the two breadth architects for WCF V1. That shows how easy it is to be overimpressed by a title. I am just a pawn in the game of software development. The architect who conceived of WCF and guided our team's technical work was Brad Lovering, our division's Technical Fellow. The architect who designed and implemented the core of WCF was Eric Christensen, one of our division's Distinguished Engineers. Breadth architects like Steve Millet and me were responsible for shaping the parts of WCF into a coherent whole. Each of the parts of WCF was guided by a depth architect and built out by a team of developers, product managers, testers, and documentation engineers. How well you know any one of these 200-plus people has nothing to do with their relative technical impact on WCF. The plain truth is, most Microsoft product team people don't get out much. We're a shy bunch overall. The ones you end up knowing are simply the ones who are outgoing enough to become involved with community.

Microsoft product teams think a lot about community. I haven't counted, personally, but I'm sure the WCF team alone had several million active customers as we developed WCF: people using COM, DCOM, COM+, and MSMQ; people using ASMX, .NET Remoting, Enterprise Services, and System.Messaging; people using WSE; and people using early releases of WCF. Try as we might, it turns out to be impossible to interact with all these people and do our day jobs at the same time. Our strategy, instead, is to spend a lot of time with a core group of influential members of the community, and count on them to pass that knowledge along to the rest of you. We spend time with our RDs, the Microsoft "Regional Directors," professionals around the world who have established good relationships with both the Microsoft employees and the developer community in their areas. We spend time with our MVPs, the Microsoft "Most Valuable Professionals," the best, brightest, and most active people in the community. Most profoundly, we spend time with the WCF Digerati, a secret society of the ten or twenty wisest and most dapper customers on the planet.

Since I was the first person on the product team to recognize the existence of the WCF Digerati, I'm in a good position to tell you more about this mysterious bunch. The full membership of the WCF Digerati is not known, even to the management of the WCF team. Those who claim to be Digerati often are not; those who are silent on the subject often are. Official lists, when they exist at all, are misleading. It's true that you can tell a Digerati because they hold one of the WCF Staffs of Power because they know the Dance of the Seven Channels, and because they have had the Service Oriented Mandala tattooed onto an unmentionable part of their bodies. But these are all secret signs hidden even from their friends and families. The rest of us have to examine more subtle signs: the contacts in industry, the activity in the community, the speaking at conferences, the trips to Redmond, the publications.

Which brings me around to my point. In your hands (or on your computer, or in whatever other form you've found), you are holding a book that was written by a person who is an MVP **and** an RD **and** (I dare reveal to you now) a member of the WCF Digerati. You are holding a book written by someone with the rich practical experience, the excellent communication skills, and the deep connection to the product team you would expect of a Digerati. That makes for a great book, which is what this is. The only thing that could improve this book is if it included a life-size poster of Michele herself. Absent that, this book is a gateway into the realm of WCF expertise. Buy it. Take it home. Profit from it. If you are ever to have the Service Oriented Mandala tattooed onto an unmentionable part of your body, you will look back at that painful moment and realize that reading this book was one of the springboards that sent you on your way. You will be grateful.

—Steve Swartz
Architect, Connected Systems Division,
Microsoft Corporation

At TechEd 2004 in San Diego, I was privileged to be among a handful of non-Microsoft employees who were introduced to a new, very hush-hush technology code-named Indigo. It was to be a complete reinvention of distributed programming on the Microsoft platform, part of a suite of managed technologies that would ship at some distant point in the future. We sat through a few lectures (punctuated by questions and discussions—after all, this group could hardly just sit back and not comment on things we felt weren't quite sound decisions), did a few code examples, ate some catered food, drank a lot of soda, then we trudged back to the here-and-now that TechEd focuses on.

Fast-forward about twelve months. Indigo was released to the world as a Community Tech Preview. I was sitting around a table with other speakers at a conference in Amsterdam, and one of those speakers (who later joined Microsoft) leaned over to me and complained bitterly that Indigo—now given the moniker of Windows Communication Foundation—was too easy, that it would represent a bad thing for those of us who did articles and books and training for a living. I can clearly remember thinking, "No, I don't think so," but at the time there was no time to debate—more beer was being served.

Fast-forward a bit more. Vista was announced, and with it the release of what was then called "NetFX3," now christened the .NET Framework 3.0. Indigo and her sister technologies were given named by the folks in Marketing at Microsoft: Indigo was called Windows Communication Foundation or WCF, Avalon was called Windows Presentation Foundation or WPF, and WinOE was called Windows Workflow Foundation, or WWF, leaving many developers to scratch their head and wonder, "WTF?"

Windows Communication Foundation represents something of a quandary to the trainer or presenter: conceptually, WCF is a simple technology, with its emphasis on the "ABCs" of endpoints: Addresses, Bindings, and Contracts. What makes WCF so infernally intimidating is the huge number of details that go along with those concepts. There are a near-infinite number of possible combinations of contract and binding options that can be applied to a given endpoint, and each of them has implications about that endpoint's usage and availability, not to mention the implications about the options in combination with one another. By the time a prospective WCF user finishes just a cursory overview of the System.ServiceModel namespace, the sheer number of classes is usually enough to frighten off the timid or faint-of-heart.

Fast-forward just a touch more. Michele approached me about six months ago with a simple request: have a look over the chapters, and offer up any feedback I might have on the material therein. She apparently felt that I, as someone who's been speaking and teaching about WCF almost since its inception, could not only make sure there weren't any obvious technical errors (there weren't), but could also help bounce around a few ideas about how best to present the vast amount of WCF material to readers. For reasons that were multifaceted, including my desire to help out someone I considered a friend, I agreed.

Turned out, I was really glad I did, and not just because I get my name in the book.

I expected the book to be well-written, and it was. I expected Michele's explanation of WCF to be well done, and it was. What I hadn't expected was to be drawn into it, to feel that the step-by-step lab-based approach she took was, in fact, arguably the best way to present WCF to the working programmer. Much of that is due to how she does it, in a clean, practical, no-nonsense style.

As Virgil to your Dante, Michele will walk you through WCF, from its simplest beginnings to the depths of its options, keeping one eye on what's practical and what's real, and avoiding the arcane or the simply weird. And should you stay with your guide through the journey, as did Dante, when you emerge, you will have seen the best WCF has to offer you—and your clients and customers—in building distributed, service-oriented communication layers.

Enjoy. When you're done, you will be one among a very few—those who can use WCF the way it was intended.

—Ted Neward
http://www.tedneward.com

Preface

My entire career has been about learning and applying new technologies. It has also been about taking on new challenges related to technology and business. I enjoy learning new things, and I like to share things that I have learned through writing and public speaking. I like to help others learn challenging subjects, in particular related to building distributed enterprise systems—one of my favorite subjects. I was serious about writing another book for a few years leading up to this book, but I was waiting for something that I could get really passionate about: something that solved the kinds of problems that architects and developers face when they build enterprise systems; something that was worth giving up sunlight for months on end. Windows Communication Foundation (WCF) was that something.

There are many reasons why WCF excited me enough to write a book on the subject. Undoubtedly my focus on web services and interoperability is a driving factor, given that WCF has deep support for emerging web service standards (WS*) and can evolve with those standards through its extensibility. Another quality about WCF that impresses me is that it is a pure SOA platform—making the "service" artifact a first-class citizen and decoupling the development of services from downstream business components. Possibly the most compelling reason why WCF is attractive is that when you build a service, it can be used to perform classic client-server calls across process and machine boundaries on the intranet, to expose queued calls and delivery assurances, and to expose interoperable web services using the full WS* protocol stack. In short, WCF unifies earlier technology stacks, namely .NET Remoting, Enterprise Services, ASP.NET web services (ASMX), and Web Services Enhancements (WSE).

Before WCF, developers were forced to couple the distribution of functionality to a technology that would deploy that functionality. Meaning that you had to know in advance if you were deploying remote objects, serviced components, or web services because they were all represented by different constructs. I'm not sure which aspect of this is worse—that developers would have to learn possibly all three technologies in order to satisfy different communication requirements, or that developers would use whichever of the three they understood, for all communications. With WCF, these problems go away because developers can learn a single programming model, then design services based on required contracts and decide on the required protocol requirements and policy at deployment. Furthermore, developers are shielded from the underlying plumbing and messaging protocols.

I believe that anyone designing or developing enterprise systems today should be using WCF, period. There isn't another platform on the market today that encapsulates the value proposition of SOA, wraps the long list of WS* protocols, and provides features that can support different types of distributed communication with full support for security, transactions, delivery guarantees, and other system services. WCF is an enabler of sound system design and secure, reliable, and scalable deployments.

I wrote this book to educate system designers and developers on the elegance and power of WCF, to provide recommendations for specific scenarios, to express the importance and relevance of WS* protocol support, and to help them to be productive quickly with the platform. Even more, I wrote this book for myself—because I was so excited about WCF that I wanted to dive into every nook and cranny of the platform, its underlying architecture, and its rich feature set.

In this book, I share my own deep exploration of the WCF platform, as I apply past experiences and knowledge about building large-scale, distributed and service-oriented systems to this new platform. I also include details gleaned from discussions with numerous Microsoft product team members. I worked closely with the CardSpace product team during the Beta 1 phase of .NET 3.0, where I worked directly with the underlying code base, with a special focus on federated security features, to integrate CardSpace with Portable Security Token Service (PSTS) devices. I also had direct contact with WCF team members during regular Software Design Reviews (SDRs) and through other frequent communications. In addition, the benefits of detailed Q and A sessions throughout my own journey are reflected in this book.

Who This Book Is For

The primary target audience for this book is the intermediate-to-advanced developer looking for a comprehensive introduction to WCF for building a Service Oriented Architecture (SOA)—which implies the need for an enabling technology for building distributed enterprise systems. This book starts with a backgrounder on the evolution of SOA and a discussion about the four tenets of SOA and how WCF satisfies those tenets. After this, I dive into a top-to-bottom overview of core WCF concepts that all readers should know about before proceeding to specific features related to contract design, hosting, bindings, instancing and concurrency, throttling, reliability, security, and error handling.

My goal is to leave you with a deep understanding of each feature and its purpose, to provide you with hands-on practice to solidify your understanding, and to discuss practical usage and recommended practices. I try to answer the questions related to each feature based on design scenarios that I frequently encounter so there is an element of architecture and design discussion, mixed with explanations for the purpose of each setting.

WCF can be applied to many problem domains, including distributed communication, messaging, and web services—all of which are discussed for relevant scenarios in the book. I try to capture the beauty of the fact that you can apply the programming model of WCF to each of those domains. This book does not attempt to teach you everything about distributed communication, and yet I do give you some background as I discuss scenarios for WCF services on the intranet. This book does not provide a comprehensive discussion on messaging systems, but I do show you how to apply WCF and MSMQ to messaging scenarios. This book also does not teach you everything there is to know about web services, although I definitely provide you with insight into the standards applied and how they work, how to control the wire, and how to enable interoperability on many levels.

If you are a beginner with very little experience building systems that rely on distributed communications or web services, you should plan to read the book from beginning to end, in order. By following the hands-on labs in order of appearance, you will be introduced to successively more difficult scenarios that should help you to grasp not only how WCF works, but what problems it is trying to solve.

Although comprehensive, to keep the scope reasonable, this book does not cover all aspects of WCF in detail, specifically:

- Throughout the book I use several extensibility points of WCF; however, I do not have a chapter dedicated to extensibility or custom channels.

- I do not cover peer-to-peer communications, which would require several chapters to provide an adequate introduction. Before you can implement solutions with peer channel, you need to understand the fundamentals discussed in this book.

- The next release of Visual Studio, code-named "Orcas," will include many productivity tools for building WCF applications. I touch on some of these tools at least once, but since they are not yet released, I am using interim versions that may change.

How This Book Is Organized

This book includes detailed discussions, code samples, and hands-on labs. While the first chapter provides an important overview of the fundamentals, subsequent chapters each discuss more-specific related features. I recommend that you read Chapter 1 first, and after that, you can freely jump between chapters as your interest carries you. That said, I have organized the book such that each chapter uncovers another layer of complexity, so it can be helpful to read them in order.

Chapters Overview

Here's a brief look at what you'll take away from each chapter.

Chapter 1, *Hello Indigo*

Having started working with the platform very early on I became quite attached to the code name for WCF, Indigo. Alas, we all have to give up code names for product names eventually...but that doesn't stop me from paying homage to it in Chapter 1. In this chapter, you will be introduced to WCF and the problems it solved for distributed enterprise systems, and learn how it supports Service Oriented Architecture. In addition, you'll learn many fundamental concepts that will make you immediately productive with WCF, including creating service contracts and services, hosting services, and generating proxies to invoke services.

Chapter 2, *Contracts*

This chapter focuses on contracts and serialization. It teaches you how to design service contracts, how to create data contracts for complex type serialization, and how to work with other serializable types to solve specific challenges, including contract-first design approaches. You'll learn how services expose metadata to clients for proxy generation and how metadata exchange supports this. In addition, the chapter provides you with guidance for versioning service contracts and data contracts.

Chapter 3, *Bindings*

Bindings are the heart of WCF. Through bindings, you configure the communication protocols supported by services, including those related to interoperable messaging. This chapter explains practical uses for each of the core bindings: how to customize those binding configurations for intranet and Internet applications, for one-way messages and callbacks, and for handling large message payloads. You'll also learn how bindings configure communication channels for clients and services, and learn how and when to apply custom bindings to handle special situations.

Chapter 4, *Hosting*

This chapter explores the various hosting options for WCF services, including Windows applications, Windows services, IIS and the Windows Activation Service. You'll learn about the hosting features and protocols supported by each environment, about the underlying hosting architecture they share, and practical reasons for selecting each hosting environment.

Chapter 5, *Instancing and Concurrency*

Instancing and concurrency modes control the allocation of services to support requests and have a real impact on application scalability. This chapter explains how to configure services to run as singletons, to provide support for application sessions and concerns they introduce, or to run as scalable sessionless services. Concurrency modes that impact the number of concurrent requests and other service throttling behaviors are also discussed. You'll learn the scalability implications of each option and take away recommendations related to load balancing services.

Chapter 6, *Reliability*

WCF features such as reliable sessions, distributed transactions, and queued messaging improve the overall reliability of an enterprise system. Reliable sessions based on interoperable protocols make it possible to overcome transient network interruptions, transaction support over TCP and HTTP improve system consistency, and queued messages provide durable and transacted reliability. This chapter explores how you apply these features with WCF, with guidance on when to use each feature.

Chapter 7, *Security*

This chapter covers a lot of ground since security features run deep in WCF. I first describe the fundamental security concepts as they are implemented by WCF, including identities, mutual authentication, and message protection as it is implemented for key WCF bindings. Then, in an attempt to simplify this otherwise daunting subject, I provide you with scenarios for intranet, Internet, partner or machine authentication with certificates, and federated security. I provide you with guidance on how you would configure these scenarios while reducing the noise of features that don't apply to it. What you should take away from this chapter is an understanding of several rich security scenarios with samples that can serve as starting templates for your applications.

Chapter 8, *Exceptions and Faults*

Although I do talk about exceptions and faults in appropriate places earlier in the book, this chapter focuses solely on error handling concepts, including debugging techniques, fault contract design, and error handling components. I put this chapter last because you will have more context from earlier chapters related to the types of things that can go wrong, and because I cover some advanced extensibility features of WCF.

Appendix A, *Setup Instructions*

This appendix provides detailed setup instructions for database configuration and setup, for ASP.NET membership provider model setup, and for working with certificates. You will be directed to this chapter periodically for support in setting up labs and code samples.

Appendix B, *ASP.NET Meets CardSpace*

This appendix includes an article I wrote for *asp.netPRO* on Windows CardSpace to provide additional background on the technology that is explored briefly in Chapter 7.

Labs and Code Samples

Each chapter contains several hands-on labs to help you walk through scenarios and related code samples that illustrate finer points and advanced scenarios. The labs and code samples have been written in C#, but the concepts covered in this book are the same for VB development. For labs, any setup instructions are presented inline, while for code samples you'll find a "Read Me" file indicating required setup for each (if applicable). The detailed setup instructions in both cases will be provided by Appendix A.

Required files for labs and code samples can be downloaded from *www.oreilly.com/catalog/9780596101626*. For updates, keep an eye on my blog dedicated to this book at *http://www.thatindigogirl.com*.

Assumptions About the Reader

This book assumes that you are familiar with .NET 2.0 and Visual Studio. Lab instructions earlier in the book will provide detailed steps the first time you perform an action such as adding a project reference. In subsequent labs, the step will be more generally stated, assuming that you are familiar with the process. Thus, if you are a beginner to these technologies, it is best if you read the book front to back.

Some of the labs and code samples will also use Windows Forms, ASP.NET, and Windows Service applications. You are not required to know these technologies in detail since the labs provide instructions, but it does help.

System Requirements

This section describes the supported operating systems, database engines, and software you need to complete the labs and run code samples from this book. You should install these requirements in the order of their appearance in this list:

- Windows XP with SP2 or higher, Windows Vista, Windows Server 2003 or Windows Server 2008 with IIS and MSMQ enabled.
- Microsoft SQL Server 2000, Microsoft SQL Server 2005, or Microsoft SQL Server 2005 Express Edition (SQL Express).
- Microsoft Visual Studio 2008.
- Microsoft .NET 3.0 Framework Runtime. This is installed with Visual Studio 2008.
- Microsoft Windows Software Development Kit for Windows Vista.

Your Working Directory

The ZIP file provided with this book contains labs, sample code, and other supporting files such as database scripts, certificates, and media. I suggest that you unzip the file to a directory named *c:\LearningWCF*, or some equivalent on a different drive. This directory will be referred to throughout the book as *<YourLearningWCFPath>* as I reference directories and files.

After you unzip the file you will end up with the following subdirectories:

Path	Contents
\Labs\Chapter1, *\Labs\Chapter2*, etc.	Each chapter has a subdirectory where in many cases initial solutions for labs have been provided. At the beginning of each lab, you will be instructed as to which solution should be opened to begin.
\Labs\Chapter1\CompletedLabs, *\Labs\Chapter2\CompletedLabs*, etc.	The completed version of each lab is located beneath the *\CompletedLabs* directory for each chapter. These samples may not run until you complete setup steps that are provided in the associated lab instructions.
\Samples	This folder contains samples referenced throughout the book. These are organized by topic heading rather than by chapter.
\SupportingFiles\Certificates	Contains the certificates to be installed to support labs and samples. Instructions for installing certificates can be found in Appendix A. Each lab and code sample will specify its certificate requirements.
\SupportingFiles\DatabaseScripts	Contains database scripts to support labs and sample code. Each lab and code sample will specify its database requirements.
\SupportingFiles\SampleImages	Contains sample images to support labs and code samples.
\SupportingFiles\SampleMedia	Contains sample media to support streaming labs and code samples.

Conventions Used in This Book

The following typographical conventions are used in this book:

Italic

> Used for new terms, URLs, filenames, file extensions, pathnames, and directories.

Constant width

> Used for code samples, statements, namespaces, assembly names, types, method names, parameters, values, XML tags, HTML tags, or the output from commands.

Constant width bold

> Used for emphasis in code samples and to show text that should be typed literally by the user.

Constant width italic

> Used for text that should be replaced with user-supplied values.

 This icon signifies a tip, suggestion, or general note.

 This icon indicates a warning or caution.

This book is here to help you get your job done. In general, you may use the code in this book in your programs and documentation. You do not need to contact us for permission unless you're reproducing a significant portion of the code. For example, writing a program that uses several chunks of code from this book does not require permission. Selling or distributing a CD-ROM of examples from O'Reilly books *does*

require permission. Answering a question by citing this book and quoting example code does not require permission. Incorporating a significant amount of example code from this book into your product's documentation *does* require permission.

We appreciate, but do not require, attribution. An attribution usually includes the title, author, publisher, and ISBN. For example: "*Learning WCF* by Michele Leroux Bustamante. Copyright 2007 O'Reilly Media, Inc., 978-0-596-10162-6."

If you feel your use of code examples falls outside fair use or the permission given above, feel free to contact us at *permissions@oreilly.com*.

Comments and Questions

Please address comments and questions concerning this book to the publisher:

O'Reilly Media, Inc.
1005 Gravenstein Highway North
Sebastopol, CA 95472
800-998-9938 (in the United States or Canada)
707-829-0515 (international or local)
707-829-0104 (fax)

We have a web page for this book, where we list errata, examples, and any additional information. You can access this page at:

http://www.oreilly.com/catalog/9780596101626

To comment or ask technical questions about this book, send email to:

bookquestions@oreilly.com

For more information about our books, conferences, Resource Centers, and the O'Reilly Network, see our web site at:

http://www.oreilly.com

I have also provided a blog for this book where follow on discussions and code samples related to chapter content, references to errata, and other WCF-related content can be found:

http://www.thatindigogirl.com

Safari® Enabled

 When you see a Safari® Enabled icon on the cover of your favorite technology book, that means the book is available online through the O'Reilly Network Safari Bookshelf.

Safari offers a solution that's better than e-books. It's a virtual library that lets you easily search thousands of top tech books, cut and paste code samples, download chapters, and find quick answers when you need the most accurate, current information. Try it for free at *http://safari.oreilly.com*.

Acknowledgments

I started planning this book with John Osborn of O'Reilly during the Beta 1 period of WCF in May 2005. Initially we discussed a short and simple book to help readers learn the basic features of WCF; however, as the book evolved and as my own experience with the platform deepened, I thought it would be important to provide a well-rounded and detailed perspective on the platform, consistent with my areas of expertise and interest. I have unending gratitude to John for his support in letting this book "evolve" to the published work it is today. Without his support and dedication to a quality product, the end product would not be the same. I'd also like to thank Brian MacDonald, who is one of the best editors in the business, and who helped significantly in the organization, quality, and consistency of this text, not to mention fast-tracking the final review cycle.

As I began the book, I was commissioned by Microsoft to contribute to the CardSpace (then "InfoCard") Beta 1 code to integrate portable devices with the identity provider. Thanks to John Shewchuk (my WS* idol) and Arun Nanda for the opportunity to work with the CardSpace team. This isn't a CardSpace book (although I touch on it) but through that project and my interaction with the team, I gained invaluable insight into the underlying WCF code base in particular that related to security (incidently, my longest chapter). Many thanks also to the members of the CardSpace team for their support, including Richard Turner, Andy Harjanto, and Rich Randall.

While I embarked on the CardSpace project, I also became involved with the Strategic Design Review process for WCF, which provided me with direct contact with so many wonderful members of the Connected Systems team including (in no particular order): Doug Walter, Doug Purdy, Clemens Vasters, Steve Swartz, Alex DeJarnatt, Alex Weinert, Brett Hill, Brian McNamara, Craig McLuckie, Craig McMurtry, Daniel Roth, Ed Pinto, Elliot Rapp, Eugene Osovetsky, Ford McKinstry, Jan Alexander, Hervey Wilson, John Justice, Kenny Wolf, Kirill Gavrylyuk, Krish Srinivasan, Laurence Melloul, Madhu Ponduru, Martin Gudgin, Nicholas Allen, Ramesh Seshadri, Shy Cohen, Sowmy Srinivasan, Steve Maine, Steve Millet, T. R. Vishwanath, Vijay Gajjala, and Yasser Shohoud. In particular, thanks to Steve Swartz for his early support and generous IM sessions, and for connecting me to the rest of the team. Without the support of these "WCF Friends" and the details they provided on the inner workings of the platform as it evolved, I would certainly have required years of research and rework to complete this book and soon matched Truman Capote's infamous four-year tour de force.

Many of my friends and colleagues have helped with this book. I am very grateful to Juval Löwy, not only for encouraging me to write this book and connecting me to

John, but also for his generosity in offering support and insight, and for the years of mentoring and friendship he has given me. Thanks to my other good friend and colleague Ted Neward, who also recommended me to John and who has been the primary reviewer for this text providing invaluable insight and guidance throughout. To brian Noyes, a great sounding board for general advice and support. Thanks to the many reviewers who offered of their time to this book including Sam Gentile, Peter Young, Marc Charbonneau, Mike Fox, Morten Abrahamsen, John Spadafora, and Blair Shaw. Special thanks to Peter Young and Sam Gentile for their detailed review of the entire book and invaluable feedback. Thanks to Peter also for walking through labs and code samples in great detail and agreeing to perform the initial conversion of all code to VB.

During the final review cycle, several people stepped up to perform a quick review and final test on each lab for accuracy, including John Hidey, Mike Bird, Eric Stump, George McDonald, Siji Varghese, Steve Figore, Kiran Tvarlapati, Jesus Rubio, Steve Valenzuela, Daniel Egan, Jay Lazzaro, and Simon Morgan.

On a personal level, the most important person to thank is my husband, Andres, whose love, encouragement, support, and cooking skills have helped me get through many periods of hibernation to (try to) meet deadlines. I'd also like to thank my dad for his general encouragement and advice, and my mom for being such a great listener. Thanks also to my brother Paul and his band for contributing images for the sample code. Last but not least, to my very good friends for their patience—thanks for waiting, and yes, I'm free for dinner again!

CHAPTER 1

Hello Indigo

Windows Communication Foundation (WCF), formerly code-named "Indigo," is Microsoft's platform for Service-Oriented Architecture (SOA), designed for building distributed service-oriented applications for the enterprise and the web. WCF was released with Windows Vista as part of the .NET Framework 3.0 (.NET 3.0) which includes four core technologies: Windows Presentation Foundation (WPF), Windows Workflow Foundation (WF), Windows Communication Foundation (WCF), and Windows CardSpace. As Figure 1-1 illustrates, .NET 3.0 relies on the .NET Framework 2.0 (.NET 2.0) and is supported on Windows XP, Windows Vista, Windows Server 2003, and Windows Server 2008 platforms.

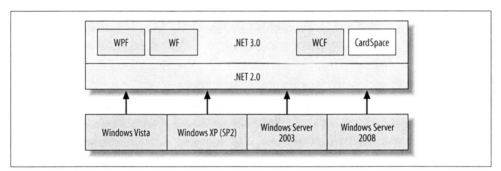

Figure 1-1. Platform support for WCF

Why release yet another technology for building distributed applications? Unlike its predecessors, WCF is a truly service-oriented, loosely coupled, and interoperable platform. It simplifies service-oriented system design by removing the design dependencies that traditionally exist between how you access business functionality and the actual implementation of that business functionality. WCF promotes loose coupling not only between services and the functionality they expose, but also for choice of protocol, message encoding formats, and hosting environment. For example, services can be accessed over a variety of supported protocols, including named pipes, TCP, HTTP, and MSMQ. WCF also supports all of the core and emerging web service standards, which makes it a highly interoperable platform. Messages can always be represented in a format consistent with a set of well-adopted standards to communicate with other platforms.

Besides these modern characteristics, what's even more interesting is that you can now choose a single communication stack to gain access to the system services necessary to build a distributed system. WCF unifies the disparate programming paradigms you have previously used on the Windows platform to achieve similar goals—namely .NET Remoting, ASP.NET Web Services (ASMX), and Enterprise Services. WCF provides all of the plumbing for security, transactions, and reliable messaging over any protocol. Only Enterprise Services came close to providing all of these features in a single stack, but your component design was coupled to the technology and limited to TCP communication (thus, not interoperable).

This chapter will be your introduction to the programming model of WCF. I'll start by reviewing the principles of a Service Oriented Architecture and how WCF supports those principles. I'll also describe some practical deployment scenarios for WCF in distributed enterprise systems and then summarize some of the fundamental WCF concepts that will be discussed first in this chapter and then elaborated on throughout this book.

After introducing core WCF concepts, I'll walk you through labs that exercise certain techniques and features. Instead of boring you with a bunch of "Hello World" examples, I plan to kick things up just a notch in this introductory chapter by enforcing good practices from the start while I teach you core concepts. Each of the labs you complete in this chapter will become successively more complex, and each will expose a new layer of detail. After each lab I will explain the relevant techniques and features you applied, discuss their relevance, and comment on recommended practices.

The labs in this chapter will cover the following topics:

- Manually creating and consuming WCF services without the help of Visual Studio templates and related tools. This will provide you with a picture of the bare necessities you need to create, host, and consume a WCF service so that you understand the underlying programming model.
- Creating WCF services using various Visual Studio project and service templates, leveraging configuration tools, and generating code to consume services.
- Approaches to assembly allocation and service hosting over various protocols.
- The importance of service metadata for publishing and consuming services.

By the end of this chapter you will be familiar with many core concepts including service contracts, endpoints, bindings, behaviors, hosting, metadata, channels, and proxies. Of course, throughout this book, the same concepts as well as additional ones will be discussed at length as you dive more deeply into specific WCF features.

Service Oriented Architecture

What is *Service Oriented Architecture* (SOA)? There have been so many interpretations of this throughout the years that it seems important to establish a common understanding before I discuss WCF as an SOA platform. The Organization for the Advancement of Structured Information Standards, better known as *OASIS* (*http:// www.oasis-open.org*), provides this official definition in its Reference Model for Service Oriented Architecture:

> Service Oriented Architecture (SOA) is a paradigm for organizing and utilizing distributed capabilities that may be under the control of different ownership domains.

 You can find the OASIS SOA Reference Model documentation at *http:// www.oasis-open.org/committees/tc_home.php?wg_abbrev=soa-rm*.

You might add to this definition by stating that SOA relies on the ability to access chunks of business functionality, potentially owned by different applications, departments, companies, or industries. Notice that this description does not specify the mechanism through which those chunks of functionality are accessed. In fact, the term "service" isn't even mentioned, although it is implied.

From OOP to SOA

The road to SOA has been a progressive one—driven by the need to improve how developers build complex enterprise systems. The principals behind enterprise system design are far-reaching: from object-oriented programming to component-oriented programming to service-orientation. All three approaches share the common goal of encapsulation and reuse. With *object-oriented programming,* classes encapsulate functionality and provide code-reuse. To share classes between distinct applications or binaries, however, you have to copy the code, as shown in Figure 1-2.

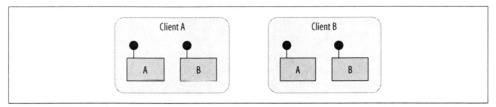

Figure 1-2. Duplicating types between components

Component-oriented programming introduces the concept of sharing binaries that encapsulate reusable classes. Initially, this was limited to the same machine until distribution was made possible with technologies like COM and DCOM, CORBA, and later Enterprise Java Beans (EJBs) and .NET Remoting. Although these technologies accomplish distribution in different ways the result is the same—binary components are activated over process and machine boundaries (see Figure 1-3).

Component-oriented programming has many limitations, but the most obvious is tight coupling to a specific technology. How can a Java client call a COM component? How can a .NET assembly invoke an EJB? It all boils down to protocols and messaging formats. Invoking a remote component of any kind requires serializing a message and passing it across applicable process or machine boundaries. Bridge technologies and adapters exist to transform messages from one technology into another, so that when the message arrives it can be understood and processed. The reverse happens as responses are fed back to the caller. This approach is cumbersome, however, sometimes introducing multiple transformations between clients and components—and sometimes not even possible. Instead of exposing components directly, components can be accessed through service boundaries to alleviate some of this pain (see Figure 1-4).

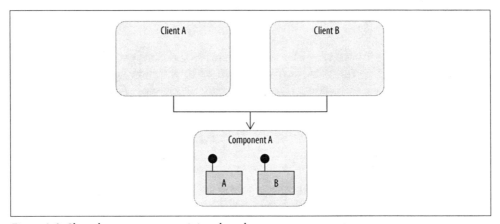

Figure 1-3. Shared component containing shared types

So, does service-orientation solve the problems inherent to component-oriented programming? It depends on where you sit on the meaning of service-orientation. I would definitely agree that in its purest form, *service-orientation* delivers a solution to these problems by introducing (via web services) the concept of contracts, policies, and interoperability. In that respect, applications can communicate with one another's services, as shown in Figure 1-5, without concern over the technology each employs. But you could also argue that service-orientation is an approach to development that implies the encapsulation of business components, data access, and data storage such that access is controlled through a top-level entry point. The package is a service, accessible over whatever protocols are supported, even if it lacks interoperability.

No matter how you define a service, the underlying point here is that to build an enterprise system, developers must be able to distribute chunks of functionality across process and machine boundaries to deal with performance bottlenecks, to introduce security boundaries, and to facilitate reuse. In addition, these chunks of functionality may be important to expose to other applications in a corporate ecosystem—which implies the potential need for interoperability on top of the rest.

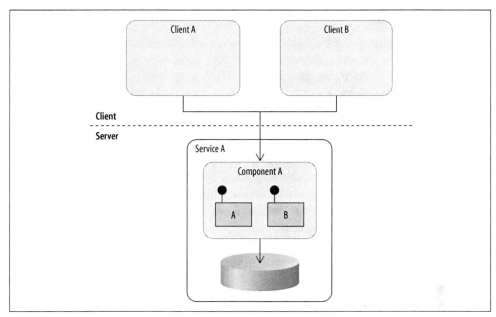

Figure 1-4. Exposing functionality through a service boundary

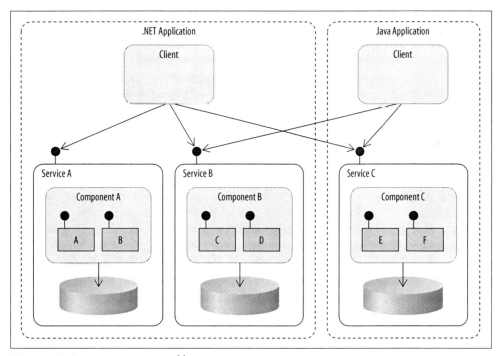

Figure 1-5. Consuming interoperable services

What Is a Service?

This is an important question—and the answer varies depending on the context of the discussion. For example, a service is a logical term to SOA, but it has physical meaning to WCF. I'll focus on the former in this section. According to the high-level definition of SOA, business functionality must be distributable and accessible in some way. The term *service* in this case refers to the entry point or "window" through which business functionality can be reached. Consider the application architecture illustrated in Figure 1-6. The client application represents an Agency Management System that includes many chunks of business functionality such as Certificate Issuance, General Ledger, CRM, and Reporting. In Figure 1-6, the client application coordinates access to these features by consuming business components directly. In this case, components are not distributable in such a way that they can be location transparent, thus they are not services.

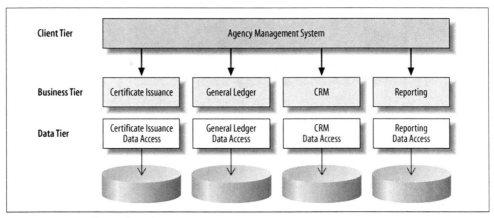

Figure 1-6. Directly invoking business components

So, what constitutes a service in SOA terms? It could be a serviced component exposed using Enterprise Services, a .NET Remoting component, an ASMX web service, or a WCF service. Any of these technologies can be useful in exposing the business logic in such a way that the client can reach that functionality at remote locations in a distributed environment, without communicating directly with business components. Figure 1-7 illustrates the same services beneath the Agency Management System example from Figure 1-6, but this time each feature is exposed via one of the aforementioned technologies. Serviced components are reached using DCOM over TCP, .NET Remoting components via RPC over TCP, ASMX web services via SOAP over HTTP, and WCF services via SOAP over any protocol.

The point is that services are not necessarily web services—they are merely chunks of business functionality exposed in some way such that they respect the tenets of SOA.

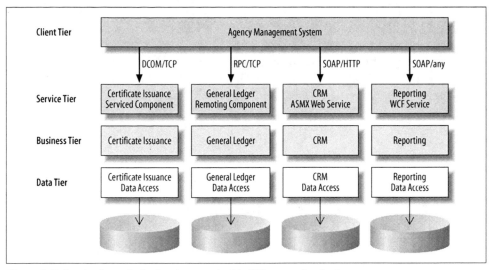

Figure 1-7. Service boundaries implemented with different technologies

Tenets of SOA

Although there is no official standard for SOA, the community seems to agree on four basic tenets as the guiding principles for achieving an SOA. They are:

- Service boundaries are explicit.
- Services are autonomous.
- Clients and services share contracts, not code.
- Compatibility is based on policy.

Let's look at each of these in greater detail.

Service boundaries are explicit

Services are responsible for exposing a specific set of business functionality through a well-defined contract, where the contract describes a set of concrete operations and messages supported by the service. Services completely encapsulate the coordination of calls to business components in response to operations it exposes to clients, as Figure 1-8 illustrates. Implementation details behind the service are unknown to clients so that any technology platform could be invoked behind the service without impact to the client. In addition, the location of the service isn't important to the client as long as the client knows where to reach it.

Enterprise Services, .NET Remoting, ASMX, and WCF all support this tenet. With Enterprise Services and .NET Remoting, the boundary and contract are defined by the public operations of the serviced component or remote component, respectively.

In the case of Enterprise Services, the contract is described as a type library, while with .NET Remoting the contract is a shared CLR interface. As for ASMX and WCF, contracts are described in Web Services Description Language (WSDL), an interoperable standard. All of these technologies also support location transparency in one respect or another. That is, the contract is independent of the location of the service in all cases.

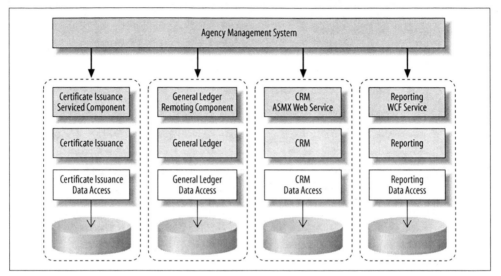

Figure 1-8. Services encapsulate business components and data access

 Where WCF improves on earlier technologies in support of explicit boundaries is in the way contract design and deployment are handled. With WCF, you explicitly define the contract and opt-in every operation and data element that you intend to expose publicly. WCF also goes beyond location transparency with protocol transparency, meaning you can expose services over any number of protocols.

Services are autonomous

Services encapsulate business functionality, but they must also encapsulate other dependencies of the business tier. In this way the entire service should be moveable or even replaceable without impact to other services or system functionality as illustrated in Figure 1-9. As I mentioned before, a service represents a major chunk of business functionality that owns its own business components, data access components and data storage if applicable. It should be able to perform key functions without external dependencies. This is what is meant by *atomicity*.

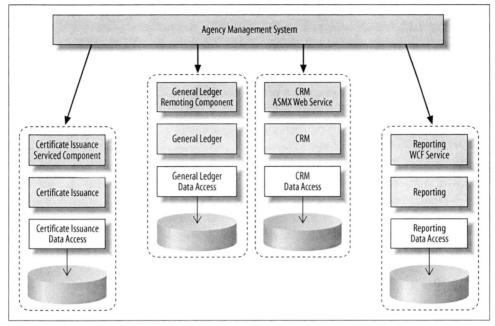

Figure 1-9. *Services are location transparent*

Part of atomicity also dictates the following:

- The service boundary must act as an independent unit for versioning. Changes to business components may require versioning the service contract, for example.
- The service boundary is the deployment boundary for callers.
- The service must operate in isolation and be fault-tolerant. That is, exceptions behind the service tier should not impact other services.

> Atomicity is largely influenced by design, but WCF does enable atomicity by providing a clear approach to contract versioning, a flexible approach to deployment, and certainly handles fault isolation if services are hosted by the same process.

Clients and services share contracts, not code

Given the first SOA tenet, that service boundaries are explicit, it only makes sense that this boundary be the law as far as how clients interact with services. That means that the contract must not change once published, or must at a minimum remain backward compatible to existing clients—and this requires discipline.

In theory, contracts are not tied to a particular technology or platform, but this is not actually an official requirement of SOA—only a strong tendency. Thus, you could say that serviced components, ASMX web services, and WCF services all support this tenet since they all are capable of publishing a contract that is consumed by clients without sharing code (type libraries or WSDL, respectively). This is where .NET Remoting falls down, since it relies on sharing CLR types, a .NET-specific construct.

 The beauty of WCF is that it uses interoperable contract definitions (WSDL) for all types of services—regardless of the communication protocols used to reach those services.

Compatibility is based upon policy

While contracts describe the business functionality available at a service boundary, policy describes other constraints, such as communication protocols, security requirements, and reliability requirements. Enterprise Services and .NET Remoting don't really have a way to publish such policy requirements, but ASMX with Web Services Enhancements (WSE) and WCF do. Policy is actually an extension to WSDL that can describe access constraints in a way that clients can be aware of them and invoke services in a compatible manner.

 WCF support for policy is completely hidden from the developer—it is automatically included with the WSDL document based on how you configure WCF service for features such as security and reliability.

Big SOA, Little SOA

The problem with discussing the tenets of SOA in the strictest sense is that levels of compliance may vary based on the scenario. On the one hand, SOA is a big business buzzword tossed into conversations at board meetings, at executive briefings, and in hallway conversations between C-level executives. At this level, however, SOA really refers to connecting disparate systems across application, department, corporate, and even industry boundaries. This is what I call *Big SOA*. The other use for the term SOA is to describe how applications are designed as chunks of business functionality that are isolated behind explicit service boundaries. I call this *Little SOA*.

Big SOA is an Enterprise Architect (EA) activity. The EA cares about connecting heterogeneous systems that may originate from different vendors. For example, you can connect HR, Payroll, CRM, and possibly other applications across the organization to achieve a business goal. In some cases, it is even useful to control messaging between systems and track usage with an *Enterprise Service Bus* (ESB)—a term that also means many things, but in this case I refer to the ability to pass all messaging through a common service for tracking and routing purposes. In short, Big SOA is about connecting entire systems through their respective service boundaries.

Little SOA is a Software Architect (SA) activity. The SA cares about designing a system that may encapsulate functionality behind service boundaries to achieve reuse, maintainability, version control, visibility, orchestration, and other benefits. These services may never see the light of day outside the application to which they belong. On the other hand, some internal application services may also be exposed for public access to facilitate communications and interoperability with other applications. If applications don't expose public services, it becomes a challenge to connect applications.

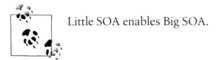 Little SOA enables Big SOA.

The distinction between approaches in SOA is important because of the level of strictness in applying SOA tenets. For example, it isn't always possible to completely isolate business components, business entities, and data tiers between services in the same system. Data is usually highly relational within a system, such that different areas of business functionality share common data stores and entities. Figure 1-10 illustrates an application with three services: Accounts, Customers, and Reporting. Accounts Service and Customers Service each expose operations to their respective types, but Accounts data is related to Customers in the system; thus, there isn't a pure separation between the tables required to support each service. At the same time, both Accounts and Customers also provide access to business functionality and CRUD operations (Create, Read, Update, Delete) that can be considered completely independent of one another—thus the need for separate services. The Reporting Service, in fact, needs to access all tables to aggregate results.

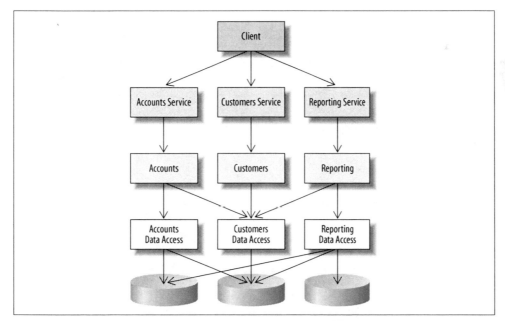

Figure 1-10. Sharing data between services is sometimes unavoidable

In a pure SOA play, each service would have sole ownership over its data tables, and services would have to communicate with one another to access those tables, even for reporting. This can create unnecessary overhead and complexity within a system. Instead, Figure 1-10 illustrates a way to support sharing relational tables behind the service boundary by coordinating relational results at the database, possibly via stored procedures. This way, the vertical assemblies associated with a service are completely owned by the service, and if a particular service, such as Reporting, requires access to multiple relational tables that are also accessed by other services, the data access layer coordinates this result for the service. While serialized business entities may be shared between services, business and data access components are not. Services can always call other downstream services to share functionality when service isolation is clear cut and the overhead of the service call makes sense—for example when services provides core functions such as document generation or messaging.

The point is that not all four tenets of SOA can be followed to the letter when designing services within an application. When application services are exposed to Big SOA in most cases the entire application is deployed with the service, thus the shared entities and data stores are implied parts of the atomic service.

 In this book, I'll be focusing on how you deploy WCF services as part of an enterprise application. In other words, Little SOA.

WCF Services

WCF services are the new distributed boundary in an enterprise application—with an emphasis on SOA. In the past, you had to deliberate between Enterprise Services, .NET Remoting, or ASMX to distribute and reuse functionality, WCF provides you with a single programming model to satisfy the needs of any equivalent distribution scenario. With WCF, you can cross process, machine, and corporate boundaries over any number of protocols; you can expose interoperable web services; and you can support queued messaging scenarios. I'll take you through a few examples where WCF is deployed in lieu of earlier technologies.

Figure 1-11 illustrates an intranet scenario where a WCF service is invoked within an application domain over TCP protocol. In this scenario, the client needed to reach remote services and authenticate with Windows credentials, and didn't require interoperability. As such, the service is accessible over TCP using binary serialization for better performance, and supports traditional Windows authentication using NTLM or Kerberos. In the past, this may have been achieved using Enterprise Services (or possibly .NET Remoting although security features are not built-in).

Figure 1-12 illustrates an Internet scenario where multiple web services are exposed—one supporting legacy protocols (Basic Profile), another supporting more recent protocols (WS*). With WCF, a single service can be defined and exposed over multiple endpoints to support this scenario.

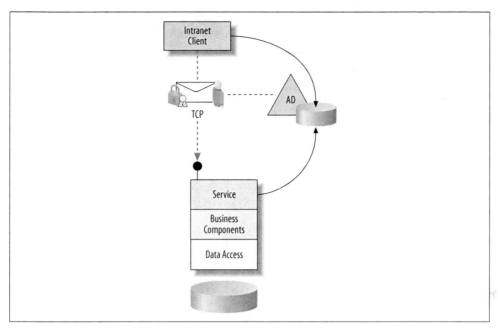

Figure 1-11. Deploying WCF services on the intranet

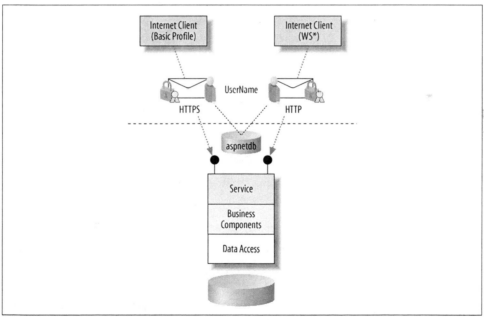

Figure 1-12. WCF services exposed on the Internet

In Figure 1-13 you can see WCF implemented at several tiers—behind the firewall to support an ASP.NET application, and outside the firewall for smart client applications. Again, the same service can be exposed over multiple protocols without duplicating effort or switching technologies.

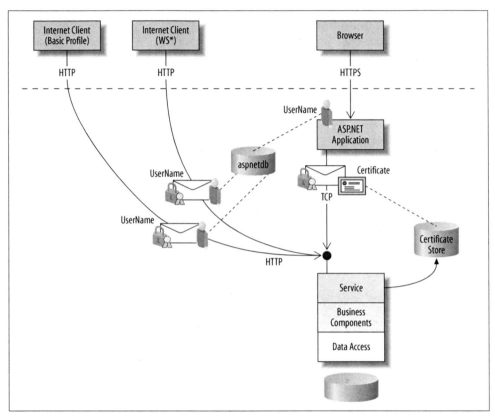

Figure 1-13. WCF services deployed at several tiers over multiple protocols

Throughout this book, I'll be exploring these and other scenarios while discussing specific features of the WCF platform.

Fundamental WCF Concepts

At its core, WCF is a development platform for service-oriented applications. As I mentioned earlier, WCF is part of the .NET Framework 3.0, which comprises a set of new assemblies that rely on the .NET Framework 2.0. System.ServiceModel is the assembly that contains core functionality for WCF, which explains why the WCF platform is often called the *service model*. Any project that exposes or consumes WCF services must reference the System.ServiceModel assembly, and possibly other supporting assemblies.

Before you can begin to do interesting things with the service model, it helps to understand the core features that make it possible to create, host, and consume services. In this section, I will briefly summarize some of the concepts that will be elaborated on in this chapter, to help you on your way.

Message Serialization

All enterprise applications at some point must make remote calls across process and machine boundaries. This is handled by sending messages between applications. The format of the message is what determines an application's ability to communicate with other applications. Remote procedure calls (RPC) and XML messaging formats are two common ways for applications to communicate.

RPC calls are used to communicate with objects (components) across boundaries—for example, calls from a client application to a remote object living in another process. RPC calls are marshaled by converting them to messages and sending them over a transport protocol such as TCP. When the message reaches its destination, it is unmarshaled and converted into a stack frame that invokes the object. This is all usually handled transparently through a client proxy and stub at the destination. Both proxy and stub know how to construct and deconstruct messages. This process is known as serialization and deserialization.

Figure 1-14 illustrates the serialization and deserialization process (often just called serialization) from a high level. As I mentioned, the transport carries a message according to the agreed-upon format of both the client and remote application. As far as the client is concerned, it is usually working with a proxy that looks like the remote object. When a method is invoked at the client, the proxy invokes underlying plumbing of the technology (for example, Enterprise Services or .NET Remoting) to serialize the outgoing message. The remote application usually listens for messages on a particular port, and as they arrive, deserializes those messages (using the same technology) to build a stack frame and invoke the appropriate method on the remote object. The method return is likewise serialized by the underlying plumbing and returned to the client, at which time the plumbing deserializes the message and constructs a stack frame for the response. RPC communication like this comes in many flavors, and each flavor is generally not compatible with another—that's why RPC is not interoperable.

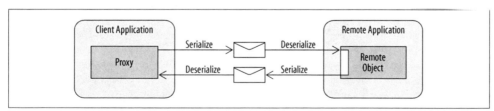

Figure 1-14. RPC serialization and deserialization

To achieve interoperability, systems rely on a standard format for messages understood by both ends of the communication. Applications still exchange messages, but they are formatted in XML according to known protocols. The technology used to support this is traditionally associated with web services such as ASMX, WSE, or WCF. As Figure 1-15 illustrates, the serialization process is consistent with RPC, the key difference being the underlying plumbing, the format of the message, and the target object, which is usually a web service. The other difference is in the lifetime of the service. While remote objects are frequently kept alive for the duration of a client session, web services are typically constructed anew for each call.

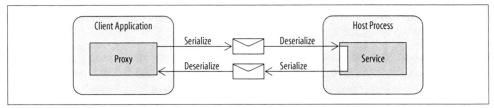

Figure 1-15. Web service serialization and deserialization

WCF can be used to achieve both RPC-style messaging and web service messaging. In both cases, the type that ultimately processes messages is a service type, but its lifetime can be controlled to behave like traditional client-server components or like web services without the notion of a session. The service model handles all serialization activities based on configuration settings.

Services

WCF applications expose functionality through services. A *service* is a Common Language Runtime (CLR) type that encapsulates business functionality and exposes a set of methods that can be accessed by remote clients. In order for a regular CLR type to be considered a service it must implement a service contract.

A *service contract* is defined by applying the ServiceContractAttribute to a class or interface. When applied to a class, the class becomes a service type. When applied to an interface, any class that implements the interface becomes a service type. In either case, methods exposed by the class or interface must be decorated with the OperationContractAttribute to be considered part of the service contract. Methods with this attribute are considered service *operations*.

A service type must be hosted before clients can invoke service operations.

Hosting

Service functionality is made available at runtime through a host process—any managed process will do the trick. Many hosting options are available for WCF services, including:

Self-hosting
> This includes console applications, Windows Forms or WPF applications, or Windows services.

Internet Information Services (IIS)
> Services can be hosted alongside other ASP.NET applications, for example.

Windows Activation Service (WAS)
> This is similar to IIS hosting but is only available to IIS 7.0.

 Each hosting environment has its benefits and appropriate uses, which will be discussed in Chapter 4.

Although a host process is important, ultimately it is the service model that knows how to process messages targeting a service. For this a ServiceHost instance is associated with each service type. ServiceHost is part of the service model and is responsible for initializing communication channels that receive messages to a service. Basically, to host any service, you construct a ServiceHost, provide it with a service type to activate for incoming messages, provide it with one or more addresses where the service can be located along with the service contract supported by each address, and provide it with the supported communication protocols.

You can think of the ServiceHost as responsible for managing the lifetime of the communication channels for the service.

Endpoints

When the ServiceHost opens a communication channel for a service, it must expose at least one endpoint for the service so that clients can invoke operations. In fact, endpoints are the key to invoking service functionality. An *endpoint* describes where services can be reached, how they can be reached, and what operations can be reached. Thus, endpoints have three key parts:

Address
> Refers to the URI where messages can be sent to the service.

Binding
> Bindings indicate the protocols supported when messages are sent to a particular address.

Contract
> Each address supports a specific set of operations, as described by a service contract.

The ServiceHost is provided with a list of endpoints before the communication channel is opened. These endpoints each receive messages for their associated operations over the specified protocols.

Addresses

Each endpoint is associated with an address, identified by a URI. An address has a scheme, domain, port, and path in the following format: *scheme://domain*[*:port*]/ [*path*].

The *scheme* indicates the transport protocol being used, such as TCP, named pipes, HTTP, or MSMQ. Respectively, the schemes for these protocols are net.tcp, net.pipe, http, and net.msmq. The *domain* refers to either a machine name or web domain. Sometimes localhost is used for communications on the same machine. The *port* can be specified to use a specific communication port other than the default for the protocol identified by the scheme. For example, HTTP defaults to port 80. Here are some examples of valid base addresses before specifying a path:

```
net.tcp://localhost:9000
net.pipe://mymachinename
http://localhost:8000
http://www.anydomain.com
net.msmq://localhost
```

A *path* is usually provided as part of the address to disambiguate service endpoints. The path does not usually include a filename for self-hosting, but with IIS (as you will see later in this chapter) a physical file is implicitly included in the address. These are valid self-hosting addresses that include paths:

```
net.tcp://localhost:9000/ServiceA
net.pipe://mymachinename/ServiceB
http://localhost:8000/Services/ServiceA
http://www.mydomain.com/ServiceA
net.msmq://localhost/QueuedServices/ServiceA
```

When you add endpoints to a ServiceHost instance, you must specify a unique address for each endpoint. That means that you must vary at least one of the scheme, domain, port, or path specified.

Bindings

A *binding* describes the protocols supported by a particular endpoint, specifically, the following:

- The *transport protocol,* which can be TCP, named pipes, HTTP, or MSMQ
- The *message encoding* format, which determines whether messages are serialized as binary or XML, for example
- Other *messaging protocols* related to security and reliability protocols, plus any other custom protocols that affect the contents of the serialized message

There are a number of predefined bindings (called *standard bindings*) provided by the service model. These standard bindings represent a set of typical protocols representative of common communication scenarios. Bindings are discussed in detail in Chapter 3.

Metadata

Once the ServiceHost is configured for one or more endpoints, and communication channels are open, service operations can be invoked at each endpoint. This is according to the protocols supported by each endpoint. Clients invoke service operations at a particular endpoint. To do so, they need information about the endpoint, including the address, the binding, and the service contract. Information about service endpoints is part of the *metadata* for a particular service. Clients rely on this metadata to generate proxies to invoke the service.

Metadata can be accessed in two ways. The ServiceHost can expose a metadata exchange endpoint to access metadata at runtime, or it can be used to generate a WSDL document representing the endpoints and protocols supported by the service. In either case, clients use tools to generate proxies to invoke the service.

 You'll explore different ways to work with service metadata throughout this chapter, and Chapter 2 discusses metadata in further detail.

Proxies

Clients communicate with services using proxies. A *proxy* is a type that exposes operations representative of a service contract that hides the serialization details from the client application when invoking service operations. For WCF applications, proxies are based on the service contract, so if you have access to the service contract definition, you can create a proxy instance to invoke the service. Before the proxy instance can be used to call service operations, it must be provided with information about one of the endpoints exposed for that service contract—there is a one-to-one relationship between proxy and endpoint.

Tools also exist to generate proxies and endpoint configurations from metadata. In this chapter, you will learn how to create a proxy manually, without generating metadata, and how to use proxy generation tools. In either case, the client must open a communication channel with the service to invoke operations. This channel must be compatible with the channel exposed by the ServiceHost for communications to work.

Channels

Channels facilitate communication between clients and services in WCF. The ServiceHost creates a *channel listener* for each endpoint, which generates a communication channel. The proxy creates a *channel factory*, which generates a communication channel for the client. Both communication channels must be compatible for messages between them to be processed effectively. In fact, the communication channel is comprised of a layered channel stack—each channel in the stack is responsible for performing a particular activity while processing a message. The channel stack includes a transport channel, a message-encoding channel, and any number of message processing channels for security, reliability, and other features. Without getting into specifics, the binding controls which channels participate in the channel stack, as shown in Figure 1-16. (The details of channels and bindings are explored in Chapter 3.)

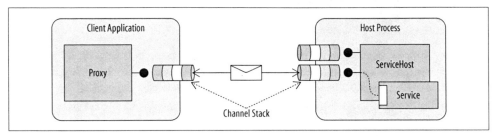

Figure 1-16. Messages are processed by equivalent channels at the client and service

Behaviors

Behaviors also influence how messages are processed by the service model. While services and endpoints determine the core communication requirements and metadata shared with clients, a *behavior* modifies the way messages are processed as they flow through the channel stack. Behaviors are local to the client or service—thus, they are not included in metadata.

There are behaviors to control many service model features such as exposing metadata, authentication and authorization, transactions, message throttling, and more. Behaviors are enabled either in configuration or by applying behavior attributes to client proxies and services.

 In this chapter, you'll learn how to apply the metadata behavior to a service, but other behaviors will be explored throughout this book as they relate to each feature.

Creating a New Service from Scratch

You're about to be introduced to the WCF service. This lab isn't your typical "Hello World"—it's "Hello Indigo"! In this lab, you will learn how to build a new WCF service and in the process learn the minimum requirements of service development and consumption. Here's a short list of things you'll accomplish:

- Create a new service contract and service implementation
- Programmatically configure a service host, its endpoints, and bindings
- Create a client application and open a client channel proxy to invoke the service

Now, before you start thinking "been there, done that," this simple lab will be slightly different because I'm going to give you some practical design tips that ensure configurability and appropriate decoupling of service, host, and client. In addition, I'll be diving deeper into basic concepts such as services, service contracts, endpoints, bindings, ServiceHost, and channels.

Lab: Creating Clients and Services Programmatically

In this first lab, you will create a new solution with three projects: a service, a host, and a client. When you run the service host, you'll expose a single service endpoint. The client application will access service operations through that endpoint. You'll host the service in a console application and invoke the service using a manually constructed proxy. This lab will teach you the basic requirements for creating, hosting, and consuming a service with WCF.

Creating a new service

The first thing you will do is create a new service contract with a single operation and implement this contract on a new service type.

1. In this lab, everything begins from scratch, so you'll start by creating a new Visual Studio solution. Open a new instance of Visual Studio 2008. Select File → New → Project, and from the New Project dialog, create a new Blank Solution in the *<YourLearningWCFPath>\Labs\Chapter1* directory. Name the solution ServiceFromScratch. Verify that the .NET Framework version selected in the dropdown list is set to .NET Framework 3.0 or .NET Framework 3.5. Click OK to create the empty solution.

2. Create the service project. From Solution Explorer, right-click on the solution node and select Add → New Project. Select the Class Library template, name the project HelloIndigo, and make sure the location path matches the solution at *<YourLearningWCFPath>\Labs\Chapter1\ServiceFromScratch*. Click OK to create the new project.

3. Now you will create your first service contract. From Solution Explorer, rename the project's only class file to *Service.cs*. Open this file in the code window.

    Add a new interface named IHelloIndigoService in *Service.cs*. Add a single method to the interface, HelloIndigo, with the signature shown here:

    ```
    public interface IHelloIndigoService
    {
        string HelloIndigo();
    }
    ```

4. Add a reference to the System.ServiceModel assembly. From Solution Explorer, right-click References and select System.ServiceModel from the list. You'll also need to add the following using statement to *Service.cs*:

    ```
    using System.ServiceModel;
    ```

5. To turn this interface into a service contract, you'll need to explicitly decorate the interface with the `ServiceContractAttribute`. In addition, each method should be decorated with the `OperationContractAttribute` to include it in the service contract. In this case, you'll make `IHelloIndigoService` a service contract and expose `HelloIndigo()` as its only service operation by applying these attributes as shown here:

```
[ServiceContract(Namespace="http://www.thatindigogirl.com/samples/2006/06")]
public interface IHelloIndigoService
{
    [OperationContract]
    string HelloIndigo();
}
```

 Providing a namespace for the `ServiceContractAttribute` reduces the possibility of naming collisions with other services. This will be discussed in greater detail in Chapter 2.

6. In the same file, create a service type to implement the service contract. You can modify the existing class definition, renaming it to `HelloIndigoService`. Then add the `IHelloIndigoService` interface to the derivation list and implement `HelloIndigo()` with the following code:

```
public class HelloIndigoService : IHelloIndigoService
{
    public string HelloIndigo()
    {
        return "Hello Indigo";
    }
}
```

7. Compile the service project.

At this point, you've created a service contract with a single operation and implemented it on a service type. The service is complete at this point, but to consume it from a client application, you will need to host it first.

Hosting a service

Next, add a new console application to the solution. This will be the host application. You'll instantiate a `ServiceHost` instance for the service type and configure a single endpoint.

1. Go to the Solution Explorer and add a new Console Application project to the solution. Name the new project Host.

2. Add a reference to the `System.ServiceModel` assembly, and add the following using statement to *Program.cs*:

```
using System.ServiceModel;
```

3. You will be writing code to host the `HelloIndigoService` type. Before you can do this, you must add a reference to the `HelloIndigo` project.

4. Create a ServiceHost instance and endpoint for the service. Open *Program.cs* in the code window and modify the Main( ) entry point, adding the code shown in Example 1-1. This code initializes a ServiceHost instance specifying the service type and a base address where relative service endpoints can be located. It also adds a single relative endpoint for the service. In this case, a base address is provided for HTTP protocol, and the relative endpoint uses one of the standard bindings, BasicHttpBinding, based on HTTP protocol.

5. Compile and run the host to verify that it works. From Solution Explorer, right-click on the Host project node and select "Set as Startup Project." Run the project (F5), and you should see console output similar to that shown in Figure 1-17.

6. Stop debugging and return to Visual Studio.

Example 1-1. Code to programmatically initialize the ServiceHost

```
static void Main(string[] args)
{
  using (ServiceHost host = new ServiceHost(typeof(HelloIndigo.HelloIndigoService),
new Uri("http://localhost:8000/HelloIndigo")))
  {
    host.AddServiceEndpoint(typeof(HelloIndigo.IHelloIndigoService),
new BasicHttpBinding( ), "HelloIndigoService");
    host.Open( );

    Console.WriteLine("Press <ENTER> to terminate the service host");
    Console.ReadLine( );
  }
}
```

Figure 1-17. Console output for the host application

You now have a host application for the service. When it is running clients will be able to communicate with the service. The next step is to create a client application.

Creating a proxy to invoke a service

Now you will create a new console application to test the service. To do this, the client requires metadata from the service and information about its endpoint. This information will be used to initialize a client proxy that can invoke service operations.

1. Go to Solution Explorer and add a new Console Application to the solution. Name the new project Client.

2. As you might expect, this project also requires a reference to System.ServiceModel. Add this reference and add the following using statement to *Program.cs*:

   ```
   using System.ServiceModel;
   ```

3. Copy the service contract to the client. First, add a new class to the Client project, naming the file *ServiceProxy.cs*. Open this new file in the code window and add the IHelloIndigoService contract metadata as shown in Example 1-2. This service contract supplies the necessary metadata to the client, describing namespaces and service operation signatures.

4. Now you can add code to invoke the service endpoint. Open *Program.cs* and modify the Main( ) entry point by adding the code as shown in Example 1-3. This code uses the ChannelFactory to create a new channel to invoke the service. This strongly typed channel reference acts as a proxy. The code also initializes an EndpointAddress with the correct address and binding expected by the service endpoint.

5. Test the client and service. Compile the solution and run the Host project first, followed by the Client project. The Client console output should look similar to that shown in Figure 1-18.

Example 1-2. Service contract metadata for the client

```
using System.ServiceModel;

[ServiceContract(Namespace = "http://www.thatindigogirl.com/samples/2006/06")]
public interface IHelloIndigoService
{
    [OperationContract]
    string HelloIndigo( );
}
```

Example 1-3. Code to invoke a service through its generated proxy

```
static void Main(string[] args)
{
  EndpointAddress ep = new
EndpointAddress("http://localhost:8000/HelloIndigo/HelloIndigoService");

  IHelloIndigoService proxy = ChannelFactory<IHelloIndigoService>.
CreateChannel(new BasicHttpBinding( ), ep);
  string s = proxy.HelloIndigo( );
  Console.WriteLine(s);
  Console.WriteLine("Press <ENTER> to terminate Client.");
  Console.ReadLine( );
}
```

In the next few sections, I will explain in more detail the steps you completed and the features you explored in the lab.

Figure 1-18. Output from the Client application

Assembly Allocation

The first thing I'd like to touch on is the allocation of assemblies when you create a new solution that includes services. For example, in this lab you created a new solution with three projects: one for the service, another for the host, and another for the client. Note that the service definition is decoupled from the host project. This is an approach I always recommend because it allows you to host the same service in multiple environments. For example, you may need to expose a service behind the firewall over TCP, and yet also allow remote, interoperable clients to consume it over HTTP. These two approaches require distinct hosting environments (specifically, a Windows service and IIS, as I will discuss in Chapter 4 at length). For simplicity, many examples may couple service and host, but this is merely a convenience—not a practical approach. As such, at a minimum I recommend that you always create a separate project for service contracts and services.

Services are the window through which business functionality is invoked, but business logic has no place in the service assembly. Business functionality should never be coupled with the service implementation because it is possible that multiple services and applications may need to reuse the same business logic. Furthermore, while you may use services to reach that functionality in most cases, what if you needed to expose an Enterprise Service component to interoperate with a particular application or system? If business logic is stored in its own assemblies, this type of sharing is made easy.

Another reason to decouple business logic from service implementation is to improve manageability and versioning. The service tier may need to coordinate logging activities and exception handling around calls to business components, and the service tier may need to be versioned, while business components and associated functionality have not changed. For this reason, I always recommend that business components, data access components, and other dependencies of the business tier also represent a separate set of assemblies in your solution. Figure 1-19 illustrates this breakdown from a high level.

There may be times when it is desirable to share the service contracts with client applications. In that case, service contracts and service implementations may also be decoupled. This makes it possible to share the metadata of the service without sharing the implementation.

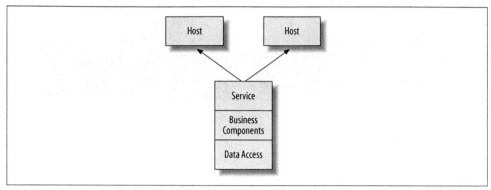

Figure 1-19. Assembly allocation for services, hosts, business components, and data access

 Later in this chapter, you'll see a scenario in which the service contract and service are decoupled.

Defining a Service

The first step in creating a service is to define a service contract. You create a service contract by applying the ServiceContractAttribute to an interface or type. Methods on the interface or type will not be included in the service contract until the OperationContractAttribute is applied. In a typical service contract, all methods will be included in the contract—after all, the entire reason for defining a service contract is to expose operations as part of a service. Business interfaces should not be directly converted into service contracts. Likewise, business components should not be directly converted to services. The service tier should instead be explicitly defined with the sole purpose of exposing public functionality and should internally consume business components, rather than embed business logic with the service implementation.

When you implement a service contract as an interface, the service type implements this interface. In this lab, the service implements a single service contract, IHelloIndigoService. This contract exposes a single operation, HelloIndigo( ).

An alternative to this approach is to apply both the ServiceContractAttribute and the OperationContractAttribute directly to the service type. Example 1-4 shows the changes you would make to the lab to achieve this. Here is a summary of those changes:

- When you apply the ServiceContractAttribute to the service type, the service type name becomes the official name of the service contract. Thus, this is the name that must be provided when you create a new endpoint (see AddServiceEndpoint( )).

- On the client side, the service contract can still be represented as an interface (the client only requires metadata) but the name of that interface (the service contract) must match the new service contract name, HelloIndigoService—instead of IHelloIndigoService. To update the lab, you can rename the interface at the client, or specify a value for the Name property of the ServiceContactAttribute as shown in Example 1-4. Service contracts are discussed in Chapter 2.

 The following sample illustrates the coupling of service contracts with service type: *<YourLearningWCFPath>\Sample\ServiceContracts\ServiceContractOnServiceType.*

Example 1-4. Changes that support defining the service contract with the service type

```
// HelloIndigo Project - Service.cs

[ServiceContract(Namespace = "http://www.thatindigogirl.com/samples/2006/06")]
public class HelloIndigoService
{
  [OperationContract]
  public string HelloIndigo( )
  {
    return "Hello Indigo";
  }
}

// Host Project - Program.cs

host.AddServiceEndpoint(typeof(HelloIndigo.HelloIndigoService), new BasicHttpBinding( ),
"HelloIndigoService");

// Client Project - ServiceProxy.cs

[ServiceContract(Name="HelloIndigoService", Namespace = "http://www.thatindigogirl.com/
samples/2006/06")]
public interface IHelloIndigoService
{
    [OperationContract]
    string HelloIndigo( );
}
```

Hosting a Service

Any managed process can host services. Within that process, you can create one or more ServiceHost instances, each associated with a particular service type and exposing one or more endpoints for that type. This lab shows you how to host a service by creating an instance of the ServiceHost type for the HelloIndigoService type within a console application.

Before opening the ServiceHost instance, you can also provide it with base addresses if you are planning to create relative endpoints. In order to reach the service, at least one endpoint is required. To programmatically supply base addresses to the ServiceHost, you can pass them to the constructor. The ServiceHost type also provides an AddServiceEndpoint() method to create endpoints as shown here (from Example 1-1):

```
using (ServiceHost host = new ServiceHost(typeof(HelloIndigo.HelloIndigoService),
new Uri("http://localhost:8000/HelloIndigo")))
{
  host.AddServiceEndpoint(typeof(HelloIndigo.IHelloIndigoService),
new BasicHttpBinding( ), "HelloIndigoService");

  // other code
}
```

In a simple scenario, the ServiceHost need only know its service type and associated endpoints where the service can be reached. This information is used to create a server channel that can receive and process messages. The channel is created when you call the Open( ) method on the ServiceHost instance. This creates a channel listener to receive messages for the service through its associated endpoints. The receiving channel processes incoming messages, invokes service operations, and processes responses. When the Close( ) method is called, the channel is gracefully disposed of after processing any remaining requests. In Example 1-1, Close( ) is automatically called when code block associated with the using statement ends.

The using statement can be applied to any type that implements IDisposable. At the end of the statement, Dispose( ) is called within a try...finally block to ensure cleanup even in the case of an exception. Dispose() calls Close()—but if the channel has faulted (faults are discussed in Chapter 8) Abort() should be called instead of Close(). Thus, the using statement is convenient for simple code samples, but not a general best practice.

Exposing Service Endpoints

Endpoints expose service functionality at a particular address. Each endpoint is associated with a particular contract and a set of protocols as defined by the binding configuration. For each service, one or more endpoints may be exposed if multiple contracts are present or if multiple protocols are desired to access service functionality. Figure 1-20 illustrates how the ServiceHost instance exposes endpoints to clients and how the proxy invokes service operations at a particular endpoint.

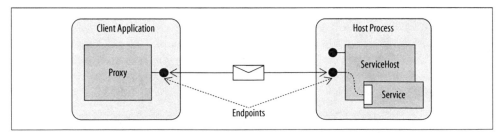

Figure 1-20. ServiceHost exposes endpoints and client proxies target a specific endpoint

As the lab illustrates, to create a service endpoint you provide an address, a binding, and a contract.

Addresses

The address can be a complete URI or a relative address like that used in the lab. The following shows you how to initialize an endpoint with a complete URI without supplying a base address to the ServiceHost:

```
using (ServiceHost host = new ServiceHost(typeof(HelloIndigo.HelloIndigoService)))
{
   host.AddServiceEndpoint(typeof(HelloIndigo.IHelloIndigoService),
new BasicHttpBinding( ), "http://localhost:8000/HelloIndigo/HelloIndigoService");
   // other code
}
```

If you supply a relative address it is concatenated with the ServiceHost base address for the matching protocol. The following illustrates providing an HTTP base address to the ServiceHost constructor and providing a relative address to AddServiceEndpoint( ):

```
using (ServiceHost host = new ServiceHost(typeof(HelloIndigo.HelloIndigoService),
new Uri("http://localhost:8000/HelloIndigo")))
{
   host.AddServiceEndpoint(typeof(HelloIndigo.IHelloIndigoService),
new BasicHttpBinding( ), "HelloIndigoService");
   // other code
}

// Resulting endpoint address
http://localhost:8000/HelloIndigo/HelloIndigoService
```

In practice, a base address should be supplied for each transport protocol over which the service can be accessed—for example, HTTP, TCP, named pipes, or MSMQ. In the event an endpoint address includes a complete URI, the base address will be ignored.

 Using relative endpoint addressing makes it possible to modify the base URI to move all associated relative endpoints to a new domain or port. This can simplify the deployment process.

Bindings

The binding provided to an endpoint can be any of the standard bindings supplied by the service model. In this example, a new instance of the standard BasicHttpBinding is used to initialize the endpoint:

```
host.AddServiceEndpoint(typeof(HelloIndigo.IHelloIndigoService),
   new BasicHttpBinding( ), "HelloIndigoService");
```

The choice of binding defines the communication channel. For an endpoint, BasicHttpBinding, for example, supports requests over HTTP protocol sent in text format without any additional protocols for addressing, reliable messaging, security, or transactions.

 In this chapter, you will employ other standard bindings, but you should look to Chapter 3 for an in-depth discussion of bindings, channels, and overall service model architecture.

Contracts

Each endpoint is associated with a particular service contract that determines the operations available at the endpoint. Only one service contract exists in this lab, but a service with multiple contracts could expose a different endpoint for each contract it wants to make accessible to clients.

Creating a Client Proxy

Clients use a proxy to consume a service endpoint. A proxy can be created manually using a channel factory, or it can be generated using tools. This lab explores the former and shows you the bare necessities required to communicate with a service:

- The address of the service endpoint
- The protocols required to communicate with the service endpoint, or the binding
- The service contract metadata as described by the service contract associated with the endpoint

Essentially, the client proxy requires information about the service endpoint it wishes to consume. In this lab, you learned how to manually create the proxy using ChannelFactory<T>, as shown here:

```
EndpointAddress ep = new
EndpointAddress("http://localhost:8000/HelloIndigo/HelloIndigoService");

IHelloIndigoService proxy = ChannelFactory<IHelloIndigoService>.
CreateChannel(new BasicHttpBinding( ), ep);
```

ChannelFactory<T> is a service model type that can generate the client proxy and underlying channel stack. You provide the address, binding, and service contract type and call CreateChannel( ) to generate the channel stack discussed earlier. In this lab, you made a copy of the service contract (not the implementation) in the client application in order to supply it as the generic parameter type to ChannelFactory<T>. The address and binding supplied matched those of the service. The result is that the client proxy knows where to send messages, what protocols to use, and which operations it can call.

In order for communication between client and service to succeed, the binding must be equivalent to the binding specified for the service endpoint. *Equivalence* means that the transport protocol is the same, the message-encoding format is the same, and any additional messaging protocols used at the service to serialize messages are also used at the client. This lab achieves this by applying the same standard binding, `BasicHttpBinding`, at the client and service—thus, they are equivalent. Another requirement for successful communication is that the service contract used to initialize the proxy has equivalent operation signatures and namespace definitions. This is achieved in this lab by making an exact copy of the service contract at the client.

 You may be wondering: how can the client discover the correct address, binding, and contract associated with a service endpoint? In the next lab, you'll learn how to generate client proxies and configuration to consume a service without having access to the service code base.

Generating a Service and Client Proxy

In the previous lab, you created a service and client from scratch without leveraging the tools available to WCF developers. Although this helps you to understand the raw requirements for sending messages between clients and services, in reality, developers need tools to be productive. This time around, I'll show you how to use several such tools that help you to generate services, access metadata, create configuration settings, and generate proxies. Specifically, you'll use the following:

- Visual Studio service templates
- Service Configuration Editor
- ServiceModel Metadata Utility (SvcUtil)

The primary goal of the lab in this section will be to improve your productivity for building clients and services, but several other concepts will be discussed in the process. To begin with, you'll use declarative configuration settings instead of code to configure the service host and client. To enable proxy generation, you'll access service metadata, which involves enabling a service behavior. In addition, you'll learn more about service configuration settings for base addresses, endpoints, bindings and behaviors.

After you complete the lab, I'll spend some time discussing these concepts.

Lab: Using Tools to Generate Clients and Services

In this lab, you will generate service code using two approaches: by adding a service to an existing host and by generating a new service library, both using Visual Studio templates. To configure service endpoint for the host, this time you'll use the Service Configuration Editor. To generate client proxies and related configuration you'll use the ServiceModel Metadata Utility (SvcUtil). Both of these tools are available through Visual Studio.

Visual Studio 2008 includes productivity tools for WCF that are available only in CTP format for Visual Studio 2005.

Using the WCF Service template

In this first section of the lab, you'll create a new service using the *WCF Service* template and add it to an existing project. This template will add a sample service contract and service type to the project, along with the required service model assembly references.

1. Start by opening an existing Visual Studio solution that contains two projects: a shell console client and host. The solution is located at <*YourLearningWCFPath*>\ *Labs\Chapter1\HelloIndigo\HelloIndigo.sln*.

2. First, you will add a new service to the host project. From Solution Explorer, right-click on the Host project node and select Add → New Item. Select the WCF Service template and name the file *HelloIndigoService.cs*. Two files are generated: *HelloIndigoService.cs* and *IHelloIndigoService.cs*.

3. Open *IHelloIndigoService.cs* in the code window and add a namespace qualifier for the service contract, then modify the service operation name and signature to match the following code in bold:

```
[ServiceContract(Namespace="http://www.thatindigogirl.com/samples/2006/06")]
public interface IHelloIndigoService
{
  [OperationContract]
  string HelloIndigo();
}
```

4. Open *HelloIndigoService.cs* and modify the service implementation to implement the correct operation signature. This is how the resulting service type should look:

```
public class HelloIndigoService : IHelloIndigoService
{
  public string HelloIndigo()
  {
    return "Hello Indigo";
  }
}
```

5. Open *Program.cs* and add code to the new Main() entry point so that it looks as follows:

```
using System.ServiceModel;

static void Main(string[] args)
{
  using (ServiceHost host = new ServiceHost(typeof(HelloIndigoService)))
  {
    host.Open();
```

```
        Console.WriteLine("Press <ENTER> to terminate the host application");
        Console.ReadLine();
      {
    }
  }
}
```

6. Compile the Host project.

At this point, you have defined a service inside the Host project and added code to host the service, but the implementation is incomplete. The ServiceHost requires at least one endpoint before clients can invoke the service.

Configuring service endpoints using the Service Configuration Editor

In this section, you will provide an endpoint for the ServiceHost—this time using the Service Configuration Editor. Unlike in the previous lab, endpoints will be configured using an external application configuration file. As such, you'll open the application configuration file for the Host application using the tool to configure ServiceHost endpoints in that file.

1. From Solution Explorer, go to the Host project and open the *app.config* file. A sample configuration has been created by the WCF Service template added in the previous section—but you will create a similar configuration from scratch. Delete this configuration so that the configuration file contains only the following:

   ```
   <?xml version="1.0" encoding="utf-8" ?>
   <configuration>
   </configuration>
   ```

2. From Solution Explorer, right-click on the *app.config* file. Select Edit WCF Configuration. You'll see the Service Configuration Editor interface shown in Figure 1-21.

 If the context menu Edit WCF Configuration does not appear you may have to open the Service Configuration Editor once from the main menu. Select Tools → WCF Service Configuration Editor to launch the editor, close the dialog and retry the context menu.

Go to the Tasks pane and click "Create a New Service"; the New Service Element Wizard will be displayed.

Follow these instructions as you go through each page in the wizard:

   a. On the first page, you are asked to provide the service type. Browse to *<YourLearningWCFPath>\Labs\Chapter1\HelloIndigo\Host\Bin\Debug* and select *Host.exe*. The Type Browser dialog (shown in Figure 1-22) will list Host.HelloIndigoService as the only service available in the assembly. Select it from the list and click Open. Click Next to continue.

   b. Now you will be asked to specify a service contract. There is only one service contract implemented by HelloIndigoService, so the selected service contract should be Host.IHelloIndigoService. Click Next to continue.

c. Select HTTP as your service communication mode and click Next.

d. Select Basic Web Services interoperability as your interoperability method and click Next.

e. Now you'll be asked to provide an endpoint address. Here you can provide a relative address by clearing the current text and typing "HelloIndigoService." Click Next.

f. Review the configuration you have chosen for the service, then click Finish.

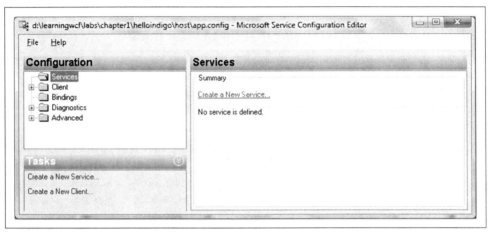

Figure 1-21. Service Configuration Editor for WCF

3. Go to the Configuration pane in the Service Configuration Editor interface and expand the Endpoints folder beneath Host.HelloIndigoService. Select the only endpoint labeled (Empty Name).

Go to the Service Endpoint pane, and in the General tab, provide the name basicHttp as shown in Figure 1-23. At this point, you have created a single, relative service endpoint.

4. In this lab, the client will generate a proxy using SvcUtil. To support this, you'll enable the metadata exchange behavior by adding a behavior to the service configuration.

Go to the Configuration section and expand the Advanced folder. Select Service Behaviors and go to the Tasks pane to select New Service Behavior Configuration.

Go to the Behavior pane and set the configuration name to serviceBehavior. Click the Add button to add a behavior element and select serviceMetadata from the list provided.

Go to the Configuration pane and you'll now see a new serviceMetadata node beneath serviceBehavior. Select the node and review the default settings in the General tab.

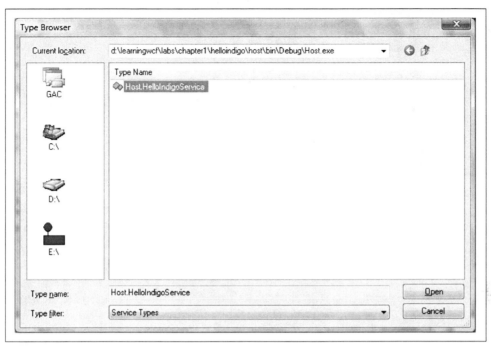

Figure 1-22. The service type browser lists all service types in a particular assembly

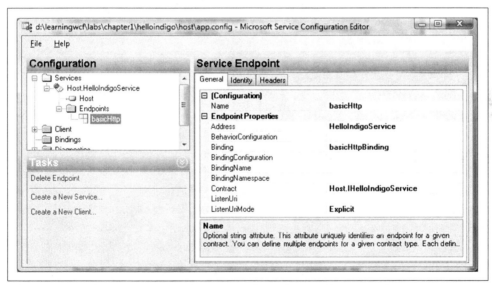

Figure 1-23. Configuring a service endpoint using the Service Configuration Editor

5. The behavior must be explicitly associated to the service. Go to the Configuration pane and select the service node, Host.HelloIndigoService. Go to the Service pane and set the BehaviorConfiguration property to serviceBehavior (you can select it from the dropdown list).

6. Enabling the metadata behavior is a good start, but a new endpoint is also required to support metadata exchange. Go to the Configuration pane, right-click on the Endpoints folder, and select New Service Endpoint.

   Go to the Service Endpoint pane and set the name to mex. In the Endpoint Properties section, set the Binding to mexHttpBinding. For the Contract property type, IMetadataExchange.

7. In order to support metadata exchange, the host must have a base address for the metadata exchange protocol being used. In addition, since you supplied a relative address for the service endpoint, it also requires a base address matching the binding protocol. In this case, an HTTP base address will be used.

   Go to the Configuration pane and select the Host node beneath Host. HelloIndigoService. Go to the Host pane and select New to create a new base address. From the Base Address Editor, supply the following base address: *http:// localhost:8000/HelloIndigo*.

8. Save the configuration settings you just generated. Select File → Save followed by File → Exit. Return to Visual Studio and open the *app.config* for the Host project. You will see a <system.serviceModel> section like the one shown in Example 1-5.

9. Compile the Host project and then run it without debugging. Leave the host running for the next step.

 In Visual Studio 2008, you cannot add a service reference to a client application while the service is running in debug mode within the same Visual Studio instance. If you run the host project without debugging you will be able to add a service reference.

Example 1-5. Service model configuration generated by Service Configuration Editor

```
<system.serviceModel>
  <behaviors>
    <serviceBehaviors>
      <behavior name="serviceBehavior">
        <serviceMetadata />
      </behavior>
    </serviceBehaviors>
  </behaviors>
  <services>
    <service behaviorConfiguration="serviceBehavior"
name="Host.HelloIndigoService" >
      <endpoint address="HelloIndigoService" binding="basicHttpBinding"
name="basicHttp" contract="Host.IHelloIndigoService" />
      <endpoint binding="mexHttpBinding" name="mex" contract="IMetadataExchange" />
      <host>
        <baseAddresses>
```

```
              <add baseAddress="http://localhost:8000/HelloIndigo" />
          </baseAddresses>
        </host>
      </service>
    </services>
  </system.serviceModel>
```

You just created a declarative configuration for the ServiceHost, instead of program-matically initializing its base addresses and service endpoints. In addition, you enabled the service metadata behavior and created a metadata exchange endpoint so that clients can generate a proxy using SvcUtil. That's the next step.

Generating a proxy with Add Service Reference

It's time to generate code for the client to consume the service, starting by generating a client proxy. To achieve this you will use the *Add Service Reference* functionality exposed by Visual Studio, which uses the *ServiceModel Metadata Utility* (SvcUtil) to generate a proxy and configuration settings for that proxy.

1. Go to the Client project and from Solution Explorer, right-click on the Client project node and select Add Service Reference. The dialog presented requires you to provide a valid base address to the service. Supply the base address *http://localhost:8000/HelloIndigo* and set the namespace to localhost. When you click OK to close this dialog, a service proxy and configuration file will be generated for the client application.

   To see the proxy, go to the Client project and expand the Service References folder. Beneath it you will see *Reference.svcmap*, and beneath that *Reference.cs*—the latter of which contains the proxy.

   A new configuration file, *app.config*, was also added to the project. This contains the service model configuration for the proxy. Later I'll talk about how these things come together.

2. Add code to the client application to invoke the service using the generated proxy. Go to the Client project and open *Program.cs*. Add code to the Main( ) entry point as shown in bold in Example 1-6.

   Compile the solution and run the Client project. The client's console output should show the result of invoking the service's HelloIndigo operation. After testing, stop debugging the Client project and close the Host console.

 Most labs and sample code from this book use the same port numbers for HTTP and TCP respectively. Thus, if you forget to close down a host that is using a particular port number, and try to run a different host that uses the same, you will see an error since the port is already in use.

Example 1-6. Using a generated proxy to invoke a service

```
static void Main(string[] args)
{
  localhost.HelloIndigoServiceClient proxy = new
Client.localhost.HelloIndigoServiceClient( ) ;
  string s = proxy.HelloIndigo( );
  Console.WriteLine(s);

  Console.WriteLine("Press <ENTER> to terminate Client.");
  Console.ReadLine( );
}
```

This concludes one technique for generating a service, ServiceHost configuration, and a client proxy.

Creating a WCF Service Library

In this section, you will generate a service using another technique: adding a new class library that includes a WCF service. The *WCF Service Library* template is a quick and easy way to generate a new class library with a sample service contract, service type, and the appropriate assembly references.

1. Go to the Solution Explorer and right-click on the solution node. Select Add → New Project and select the WCF Service Library template. Name the project HelloIndigo.

2. Rename *Service1.cs* and *HelloIndigoService.cs* and *Service1.cs* to *IHelloIndigoService.cs* and *HelloIndigoService.cs*, respectively.

3. Modify the service contract that is supplied by the project template. Open *IHelloIndigoService.cs* in the code window and provide a namespace for the ServiceContractAttribute and change the interface definition to look as follows:

   ```
   [ServiceContract(Namespace="http://www.thatindigogirl.com/samples/2006/06")]
   public interface IHelloIndigoService
   {
     [OperationContract]
     string HelloIndigo( );
   }
   ```

4. Now, modify the service implementation so that it implements the new contract. Open *HelloIndigoService.cs*, rename the service to HelloIndigoService and implement IHelloIndigoService as shown here:

   ```
   public class HelloIndigoService: IHelloIndigoService
   {
     public string HelloIndigo( )
     {
       return "Hello Indigo";
     }
   }
   ```

   Compile the HelloIndigo project.

The default data contract created when you used the WCF Service template, the CompositeType class, is not necessary for this lab.

5. Delete the *app.config* file created for the HelloIndigo project, and then compile the project.

 The release of Visual Studio 2008 and .NET Framework 3.5 introduced a WCF Service Host and a WCF Test Client to simplify testing WCF services. When you create a new WCF Service Library the *app. config* file is used to configure the WCF test host. I'll briefly discuss these test tools in a later section.

6. Now you will modify the existing host project so that it hosts this new service. From Solution Explorer, go to the Host project and select the files *IHelloIndigoService.cs* and *HelloIndigoService.cs*. Right-click on the selection and select Exclude From Project to avoid collision with the HelloIndigo library you're about to reference.

7. Add a reference to the HelloIndigo class library project. Right-click on the Host node and select Add Reference. From the Projects tab, select the HelloIndigo project.

8. The ServiceHost must be modified to refer to the service type from this project. In the *Program.cs* file, modify the ServiceHost constructor to use the fully qualified name of the service, HelloIndigo.HelloIndigoService, as shown here:

```
host = new ServiceHost(typeof(HelloIndigo.HelloIndigoService))
```

9. You'll also have to edit the service model section of the configuration file to use the correct service and contract types. Go to the Host project and open the *app. config* file. Change the service type and contract type for the <service> configuration section as shown here in bold:

```
<service behaviorConfiguration="serviceBehavior" name="HelloIndigo.
HelloIndigoService">
  <endpoint address="HelloIndigoService" binding="basicHttpBinding"
name="basicHttp" contract="HelloIndigo.IHelloIndigoService" />

  <!-- other settings -->

</service>
```

10. Test the solution again by compiling and running the Host and then the Client.

Now you have learned how to create a new class library with a sample WCF service and seen the changes required to the service model configuration and ServiceHost to reference a different service type.

Generating a proxy using the Service Model Metadata Utility

In this section, you will generate a client proxy using the SvcUtil directly instead of using Add Service Reference. The purpose of this exercise is to show you how to exercise greater control over the generation of proxies and configuration settings.

1. First, run the Host project without debugging so that the endpoint is available to generate a proxy.

   From the Windows Start menu, find the Microsoft Visual Studio 2008 program group and launch the *Visual Studio 2008 Command Prompt* beneath the Visual Studio Tools folder in the program group. Run the following command to generate a new proxy for the client application and replace the application configuration settings generated previously:

   ```
   svcutil /d:<YourLearningWCFPath>\Labs\Chapter1\HelloIndigo\Client /o:
   serviceproxy.cs /config:app.config http://localhost:8000/HelloIndigo
   ```

   The output should look similar to Figure 1-24.

   The /d: option for SvcUtil allows you to provide a path where output files will be generated. In the Preface, I explained that I would be using the term *<YourLearningWCFPath>* to refer to your base path—where you unzipped the file provided with the book. Thus, if your base path is *c:\LearningWCF*, then your SvcUtil command in this example would be:

   ```
   svcutil /d:c:\LearningWCF\Labs\Chapter1\HelloIndigo\Client
   /o:serviceproxy.cs/config:app.config http://localhost:8000/
   HelloIndigo
   ```

   If your path includes spaces, such as *c:\Learning WCF*, then you will have to provide quotes to the path, as shown here:

   ```
   svcutil /d:"c\Learning WCF\Labs\Chapter1\HelloIndigo\Client"
   /o:serviceproxy.cs/config:app.config http://locahost:8000/
   HelloIndigo
   ```

2. To use this proxy you'll have to modify the client application. Go to the Client project. If you select the "Show all files" icon in Solution Explorer, you'll see a new file beneath the project node. Right-click *serviceproxy.cs* and select "Include in Project." Right-click *localhostreference.svcmap* beneath Service References\localhost and select "Exclude from Project."

   Now open *Program.cs* and modify the code that constructs the service proxy. The proxy that was generated does not belong to a namespace, so you must remove the fully qualified name for HelloIndigoServiceClient. The resulting code is:

   ```
   using (HelloIndigoServiceClient proxy = new HelloIndigoServiceClient())
   ```

3. Compile and run the Client and test the solution once again.

Now let's examine some of the ideas introduced in this lab in greater detail.

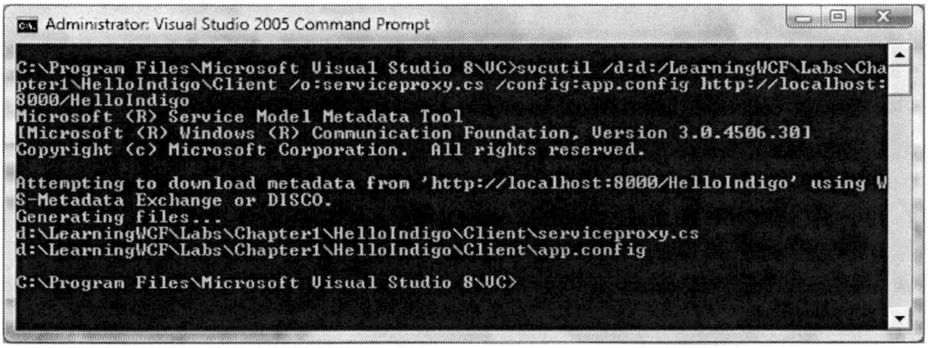

Figure 1-24. Output generated when SvcUtil generates a service proxy and configuration settings for the client

Service Templates

This lab introduces several Visual Studio templates for generating service code. In an existing project—no matter whether it is a class library, console application, Windows application, or web site—you can add a new *WCF Service*. This template generates a sample service contract and service type to get you started and adds the necessary service model assembly references. It also includes a sample data contract (to be discussed in Chapter 2). When you want to create a separate class library for your services, to isolate it from the host project (my personal preference) you can either create a Class Library project and add a WCF Service, or create a *WCF Service Library* project. The latter template creates a new class library, including a sample service contract and service type, in addition to adding the service model assembly references. The WCF Service Library template also makes use of the new WCF Service Host and WCF Test Client tools introduced with Visual Studio 2008 (to be discussed). To host services belonging to a class library project you can either use the WCF Service Host create a separate host project for the service. Although the WCF Service Host is convenient for simple tests, this lab illustrates the latter which gives you greater control over ServiceHost initialization—a practical necessity in most development environments.

Service templates for web sites are slightly different from other projects because the hosting environment is slightly different. The overall result is the same—sample code is generated and assembly references are added. The difference is that an additional file is generated with a *.svc* extension for web hosting. You'll see this in the next lab.

Service Testing Tools

Visual Studio 2008 introduced two tools for testing WCF services:

- WCF Service Host (WcfSvcHost.exe)
- WCF Test Client (Wcf TestClient.exe)

The WCF Service Host executable provides a host process for the WCF services in a specific assembly, using the configuration settings provided by a specific application configuration file. One example of the command line to launch the test host is:

```
wcfsvchost /service:pathtoserviceassembly /config:pathtoserviceconfig
```

When you create a new project using the WCF Service Library template, the project is configured so that you can launch the resulting class library in debug mode (F5) and host all services in the assembly, using the configuration supplied by the app. config file created in the project. In addition, the project settings launch the WCF Test Client so that you can also test the services in the project without creating a test client application.

The WCF Test Client executable provides a dynamically generated user interface to test services described by a specific metadata endpoint. Thus, the command line instruction to do this is:

```
wcftestclient metadataexchangeaddress
```

These tools are useful for very simple and rapid testing scenarios however in most development environments it is necessary to generate richer test scenarios that include configurations for both client and service host that will be applicable in production. In fact, I recommend you create your WCF service libraries using the standard Class Library template rather than the WCF Service Library template to avoid cluttering your projects with configuration files and project settings that will not be useful in production.

 For more information about the test tools visit the following links: *http://msdn.microsoft.com/en-us/library/bb552363.aspx* and *http:// msdn.microsoft.com/en-us/library/bb552364.aspx*.

ServiceModel Metadata Utility

The ServiceModel Metadata Utility is a command-line tool that is installed with the Windows SDK for .NET 3.0—an executable file named *svcutil.exe*. This tool can be used for two key purposes:

- To generate code and configuration settings from metadata
- To generate metadata from code and configuration

With SvcUtil you can export and import metadata, validate services, and manipulate how types are generated and shared between services and clients. Add Service Reference uses SvcUtil to generate proxies and configuration, but from the command line, you can exercise greater control over this process.

This lab illustrates a very simple command-line instruction for generating a proxy and configuration file from a metadata exchange endpoint as follows:

```
svcutil /d:<YourLearningWCFPath>\Labs\Chapter1\HelloIndigo\Client /o:serviceproxy.cs
/config:app.config http://localhost:8000/HelloIndigo
```

You can also suppress the generation of configuration output with the following instruction:

```
svcutil /d:<YourLearningWCFPath>\Labs\Chapter1\HelloIndigo\Client /o:serviceproxy.cs
/config:noconfig http://localhost:8000/HelloIndigo
```

To see all the options for SvcUtil, from the command line you can type:

```
svcutil /?
```

Using Add Service Reference to generate the client configuration and proxy will work for many cases. As of Visual Studio 2008 the Add Service Reference dialog supplies advanced options to control things such as how arrays are serialized, generating a proxy that can make asynchronous calls, and generating a proxy that shares assembly types with the service. Using the command line utility directly is still useful for automating how proxies and service contracts generated, and for things such as controlling the choice of WCF serializer the proxy should use. I'll explore other uses for SvcUtil throughout this book.

Service Configuration Editor

The *Service Configuration Editor* is another tool that is available through Visual Studio 2008—an executable file named *svcconfigeditor.exe*. This tool is a wizard that helps you configure service model settings for WCF clients and services. You can launch the Service Configuration Editor directly from Solution Explorer to edit the <system.serviceModel> section for any client or host application configuration file (as the lab illustrates). The wizard guides you through steps to configure services, bindings, behaviors, and more, which is particularly useful when you are new to WCF since you may not be familiar with each section of the configuration file.

The service model configuration for clients and service are both encapsulated within the <system.serviceModel> configuration section so you can use this tool to edit both sides. When starting from scratch, you can use the tool to add new services or client endpoints, to attach behaviors to services or endpoints, to supply base addresses for the host, to supply metadata exchange endpoints, and even to customize binding configurations (something I'll talk about in Chapter 3). For existing applications, you may just use the tool to view settings and make minor changes.

As I show you configuration settings throughout this book, I'll talk about many settings in the <system.serviceModel> section—all of which can be configured using the Service Configuration Editor. But you'll find that as you gain more experience with <system.serviceModel> settings, it is much more productive to edit the configuration file directly, relying on Intellisense.

ServiceModel Configuration

This lab illustrates the use of declarative configuration settings to configure the ServiceHost and the client proxy—although, in the latter case, you generated the configuration. Both ServiceHost and proxy types rely on programmatic or declarative configuration to initialize endpoints and configure behaviors. The latter technique provides greater deployment flexibility while programmatic settings enable you to enforce certain settings. In this section I'll focus on the service model configuration settings.

All configuration settings related to the service model are contained within the <system.serviceModel> section new to WCF. Any application configuration file can contain this section, which means *app.config* for executables, and *web.config* for web sites. The service model is vast and there are many configuration options, most of which will be explored throughout the book. However, the core elements of this configuration you will repeatedly use are: <services>, <client>, <bindings>, <behaviors>. Table 1-1 provides a brief explanation of each section.

Table 1-1. Summary of core <system.ServiceModel> sections

Section	Description
<services>	This element contains one or more <service> definitions. Each <service> section is associated with a particular service type and includes any base addresses and endpoints to be exposed for that type.
<client>	This element contains one or more <endpoint> definitions for each service endpoint the client may consume. Each individual <endpoint> includes an address, binding, and contract matching a service endpoint. Client proxies select an endpoint to configure the client communication channel.
<bindings>	This element contains one or more binding configuration sections. This makes it possible to customize a binding instead of using the defaults provided by a standard binding, such as BasicHttpBinding. I'll explore bindings in Chapter 3.
<behaviors>	This element contains <serviceBehaviors> and <endpointBehaviors>. At the host, the <service> configuration section may reference an element from the <serviceBehaviors> section to apply local behavioral settings to all endpoints for the service. Service endpoints can reference <endpointBehaviors> that apply only to that specific endpoint for the service. At the client, endpoints defined in the <client> section may reference an element from the <endpointBehaviors> section to apply local behavioral settings to the client communication channel.

Service model configuration settings can also be set at runtime through the proxy or ServiceHost; however, declarative configuration is often preferred to hardcoding settings in code. You can modify configuration files without impacting the compiled service or client code and this supports more flexible deployment scenarios.

Throughout this book, you will see examples that configure the service model in code where there are practical applications for it.

ServiceHost Initialization

The first lab illustrates how to configure the ServiceHost programmatically. This lab illustrates how to configure the ServiceHost declaratively using the service model configuration section. But how does the ServiceHost know which configuration section to use? When the ServiceHost is opened, it reads the <services> section looking for a <service> element that matches its service type. From the lab, consider this ServiceHost constructor:

```
ServiceHost myServiceHost = new ServiceHost(typeof(HelloIndigo.HelloIndigoService));
```

The ServiceHost will look for a <service> section using the name HelloIndigo. HelloIndigoService, as shown here:

```
<service behaviorConfiguration="serviceBehavior"
name="HelloIndigo.HelloIndigoService" >
  <host>...</host>
  <endpoint... />
  <endpoint... />
</service>
```

The <service> element can include base addresses and service endpoints, as shown previously in Example 1-5. You can supply a base address for any protocol so that you can expose relative service endpoints over that protocol. The following illustrates the <host> section with base addresses for HTTP, TCP, and named pipe protocols:

```
<host>
  <baseAddresses>
    <add baseAddress="http://localhost:8000/HelloIndigo" />
    <add baseAddress="net.tcp://localhost:9000/HelloIndigo" />
    <add baseAddress="net.pipe://localhost/HelloIndigo" />
  </baseAddresses>
</host>
```

One or more <endpoint> sections may also be provided. As discussed previously, an endpoint is defined by an address, contract, and binding. If address is omitted altogether, the base address for the related binding protocol is used (and required). If the address omits the full URI, it is appended to the base address matching the binding protocol. However, you can specify a complete address that ignores the base address. The following illustrates these three choices for an endpoint configuration:

```
<endpoint binding="basicHttpBinding" name="basicHttp" contract="Host.
IHelloIndigoService" />
<endpoint address="HelloIndigoService" binding="basicHttpBinding" name="basicHttp"
contract="Host.IHelloIndigoService" />
<endpoint address="http://localhost:8001/HelloIndigo/HelloIndigoService"
binding="basicHttpBinding" name="basicHttp" contract="Host.IHelloIndigoService" />
```

Endpoints have to be unique for a particular service. When multiple endpoints are exposed by a service, they must differ in address, contract, or transport protocol.

There are several reasons why a service may expose multiple endpoints, including the following:

- The service implements multiple contracts, each requiring its own endpoint
- The same or different service contracts must be accessible over multiple protocols
- The same or different service contracts must be accessible by clients with different binding requirements, possibly related to security, reliable messaging, message size, or transactions

These topics will be explored throughout the book.

Enabling Metadata Exchange

A *metadata exchange* endpoint is required to support the dynamic generation of proxy and configuration for client applications. You must explicitly enable metadata exchange by adding the endpoint and enabling the metadata exchange behavior.

A metadata exchange (*mex*) endpoint is just like any other service endpoint in that it requires an address, contract, and binding. The address for a metadata exchange endpoint requires a base address for the selected binding protocol. The contract must be IMetadataExchange, a predefined service contract belonging to the System.ServiceModel.Description namespace (see Example 1-7).

Example 1-7. IMetadataExchange contract as defined by the service model

```
[ServiceContract(ConfigurationName="IMetadataExchange", Name="IMetadataExchange",
Namespace="http://schemas.microsoft.com/2006/04/mex")]

public interface IMetadataExchange
{
  [OperationContract(Action="http://schemas.xmlsoap.org/ws/2004/09/transfer/Get",
ReplyAction="http://schemas.xmlsoap.org/ws/2004/09/transfer/GetResponse",
AsyncPattern=true)]
IAsyncResult BeginGet(Message request, AsyncCallback callback, object state);

  Message EndGet(IAsyncResult result);

  [OperationContract(Action="http://schemas.xmlsoap.org/ws/2004/09/transfer/Get",
ReplyAction="http://schemas.xmlsoap.org/ws/2004/09/transfer/GetResponse")]
  Message Get(Message request);
}
```

As for the binding, there are several predefined mex bindings, including MexHttpBinding, MexHttpsBinding, MexTcpBinding, and MexNamedPipeBinding. That means you can expose a mex endpoint over HTTP, HTTPS, TCP, or named pipes and have SvcUtil consume those endpoints.

Like any other endpoint, metadata exchange endpoints can also be consumed at runtime by clients. Applications can call mex endpoints to dynamically generate proxies or just to request information about the associated service.

The following illustrates a service exposing two TCP endpoints: one for the service, another for metadata exchange:

```
<service behaviorConfiguration="serviceBehavior"
name="HelloIndigo.HelloIndigoService">
  <endpoint address="HelloIndigoService" binding="netTcpBinding" name="netTcp"
contract="HelloIndigo.IHelloIndigoService" />
  <endpoint binding="mexTcpBinding" name="mex" contract="IMetadataExchange" />
  <host>
    <baseAddresses>
      <add baseAddress="net.tcp://localhost:9000/HelloIndigo" />
    </baseAddresses>
  </host>
</service>
```

Supplying the endpoint is not sufficient on its own. The service metadata behavior must also be enabled. Example 1-5 shows you how to enable the behavior by associating a service behavior to the service and including the <serviceMetadata> element. Once the behavior is enabled, you can use SvcUtil for proxy generation against any mex endpoint. For example, to generate a service proxy and configuration using the TCP endpoint with SvcUtil, you can type this instruction at the command line:

```
svcutil /d:<YourLearningWCFPath>\Labs\Chapter1\HelloIndigo\Client /o:serviceproxy.cs
/config:app.config net.tcp://localhost:9000/HelloIndigo/mex
```

It might seem a little annoying at first that you have to enable metadata exchange before you can generate a client proxy. This opt-in behavior is actually a good thing in the long run. You don't want your services exposing endpoints of which you aren't aware or that you don't want to support.

Working with Behaviors

As you've seen, the ServiceHost is initialized by the <service> configuration section associated with its service type. At least one endpoint must be configured for the service to be useful to clients. In this lab, a single service endpoint and a metadata exchange endpoint are exposed—both over HTTP. While endpoints describe where to reach the service, which operations are available at the specified address, and what protocols are required—behaviors affect the service model locally at the client or service. What that means is that behaviors are not exposed as part of metadata, and they are not shared between clients and services. Instead, they locally affect how the service model processes messages.

Behaviors can be defined in configuration or in code. Different behaviors are available to clients and services, since the local affect on the service model also differs. There are two types of behaviors: service behaviors and endpoint behaviors. Service behaviors apply only to services, while endpoint behaviors can be associated with service endpoints or client endpoints.

Service behaviors

Service behaviors are types that implement IServiceBehavior from the System. ServiceModel.Description namespace. There are service behaviors to control debugging, metadata, security features, serialization, and throttling. When enabled, each behavior interacts with the service model to achieve its goal. For example, when the metadata behavior is enabled, the service model will allow requests to a metadata exchange endpoint. Otherwise, it will not.

Service behaviors are configured in the <serviceBehaviors> section. The following example illustrates enabling service debug and service metadata behaviors:

```
<behaviors>
    <serviceBehaviors>
      <behavior name="serviceBehavior">
        <serviceDebug includeExceptionDetailInFaults="true"/>
        <serviceMetadata />
      </behavior>
    </serviceBehaviors>
</behaviors>
```

To associate a set of behaviors with a service use the behaviorConfiguration attribute of the <service> section (see Example 1-8).

Example 1-8. Associating a service behavior to a service

```
<system.serviceModel>
  <behaviors>
    <serviceBehaviors>
      <behavior name="serviceBehavior">
        <serviceMetadata />
      </behavior>
    </serviceBehaviors>
  </behaviors>
  <services>
    <service behaviorConfiguration="serviceBehavior"
name="Host.HelloIndigoService" >
    ...
    </service>
  </services>
</system.serviceModel>
```

You may forget to make the association between the service and behavior at least a few times. Don't forget to double-check your configuration when you aren't seeing the expected results at runtime!

You can also programmatically configure service behaviors through the ServiceHost instance. The Description property of the ServiceHost has a Behaviors collection. You can see if a behavior exists by calling the Find<T>( ) method on the collection. You can add new behaviors by calling Add( ) on the collection. Example 1-9 shows an example that looks to see if the ServiceMetadataBehavior exists, and if not adds it to the collection and enables browsing.

Example 1-9. Adding the metadata service behavior programmatically

```
ServiceHost host = new ServiceHost(typeof(HelloIndigo.HelloIndigoService));

ServiceMetadataBehavior mexBehavior =
host.Description.Behaviors.Find<ServiceMetadataBehavior>( );

if (mexBehavior == null)
{
  mexBehavior = new ServiceMetadataBehavior( );
  mexBehavior.HttpGetEnabled = true;
  host.Description.Behaviors.Add(mexBehavior);
}

host.Open( );
```

Endpoint behaviors

Endpoint behaviors implement IEndpointBehavior, also from the System.ServiceModel.Description namespace. To configure proxies, for example, there are endpoint behaviors to control debugging, security, serialization, timeouts, and routing. These endpoint behaviors interact with the service model at the client and are configured in the <endpointBehaviors> section. The following example enables exception debugging for callbacks:

```
<behaviors>
  <endpointBehaviors>
    <behavior>
      <callbackDebug includeExceptionDetailInFaults="true"/>
    </behavior>
  </endpointBehaviors>
</behaviors>
```

Endpoint behaviors are associated with client endpoints using the behaviorConfiguration attribute of the <endpoint> section (see Example 1-10).

Example 1-10. Associating an endpoint behavior to a client endpoint

```
<system.serviceModel>
  <behaviors>
    <endpointBehaviors>
      <behavior name="clientBehavior">
        ...
      </behavior>
    </endpointBehaviors>
  </behaviors>
```

Example 1-10. Associating an endpoint behavior to a client endpoint (continued)

```
  <client>
    <endpoint address="net.tcp://localhost:9000/" binding="netTcpBinding"
contract="Client.localhost.IHelloIndigoService"
behaviorConfiguration="clientBehavior">
    </endpoint>
  </client>
</system.serviceModel>
```

To programmatically configure endpoint behaviors at the client, you can use the object model of the client proxy. The `Endpoint` property of the client proxy has a `Behaviors` collection through which you can search for existing behaviors and add behaviors—similar to the way you would for the `ServiceHost`. Example 1-11 shows an example that looks to see if the `ServiceDebugBehavior` exists, and if not adds it to the collection.

Example 1-11. Adding the debug service behavior programmatically

```
HelloIndigoServiceClient proxy = new HelloIndigoServiceClient();

ServiceDebugBehavior debugBehavior =
proxy.Endpoint.Behaviors.Find<ServiceDebugBehavior>();

if (debugBehavior == null)
{
  debugBehavior = new ServiceDebugBehavior();
  debugBehavior.IncludeExceptionDetailInFaults = true;
  proxy.Endpoint.Behaviors.Add(debugBehavior);
}
```

 I will explore other behaviors for the client and service throughout this book as I review features related to each behavior. At this point, I want you to understand how services and client endpoints are related to behaviors.

Proxy Initialization

For a client to invoke service operations, it must open a communication channel to a particular service endpoint. This channel is bound to a particular endpoint—its address, binding, and contract. This is done by creating a proxy.

In the first lab, a proxy is created directly by using the channel factory:

```
IHelloIndigoService proxy =
ChannelFactory<IHelloIndigoService>.CreateChannel(new BasicHttpBinding(), new
EndpointAddress("http://localhost:8000/HelloIndigo/HelloIndigoService"));
```

This approach assumes that:

- You have prior knowledge of the endpoint address.
- A copy of the service contract definition is locally available.

- You have prior knowledge of the required protocols or binding configuration.

If you own both sides (client and service), it is feasible to share an assembly that contains service metadata and to separately communicate the address and binding requirements. When you don't own both sides, generating the proxy is a more effective way to import the metadata necessary to construct the client channel. In this lab, the proxy is generated with SvcUtil. This proxy includes a generated copy of the service contract and a channel wrapper to simplify the client code necessary to consume the service. SvcUtil also generates the service model configuration necessary to initialize the proxy.

The service contract generated by SvcUtil looks similar to the contract at the service with the exception of additional details specified in the ServiceContractAttribute and OperationContractAttribute, shown in Example 1-12.

Example 1-12. Service contract generated by SvcUtil

```
[System.ServiceModel.ServiceContractAttribute(Namespace=
"http://www.thatindigogirl.com/samples/2006/06",
ConfigurationName="Client.localhost.IHelloIndigoService")]
public interface IHelloIndigoService
{
  [System.ServiceModel.OperationContractAttribute(Action=
"http://www.thatindigogirl.com/samples/2006/06/IHelloIndigoService/HelloIndigo",
ReplyAction=
"http://www.thatindigogirl.com/samples/2006/06
/IHelloIndigoService/HelloIndigoResponse")]
  string HelloIndigo();
}
```

The namespace specified by the ServiceContractAttribute is the same as at the service. This is critical to compatible message serialization.

The SvcUtil that generated the client-side service contract also generated a proxy type. The proxy type is a partial class that inherits ClientBase<T> from the System.ServiceModel namespace (T is the service contract type). As shown in bold in Example 1-13, the proxy exposes service contract operations and internally uses its reference to the client communication channel to invoke each service operation. In fact, this inner channel reference is like the one you previously created with the channel factory.

Example 1-13. Proxy type generated by SvcUtil

```
public partial class HelloIndigoServiceClient :
System.ServiceModel.ClientBase<Client.localhost.IHelloIndigoService>,
Client.localhost.IHelloIndigoService
{
  ...overloaded constructors

  public string HelloIndigo()
  {
    return base.Channel.HelloIndigo();
```

Example 1-13. Proxy type generated by SvcUtil (continued)

```
  }
}
```

When the first operation is invoked on this proxy, the inner channel is created based on the endpoint configuration for the proxy. Since in this lab only one endpoint is available, the construction of the proxy looks something like this:

```
HelloIndigoServiceClient proxy = new HelloIndigoServiceClient();
```

If there are several endpoints to choose from in the <client> configuration section, you are required to provide an endpoint configuration name to the proxy constructor:

```
// Proxy construction
HelloIndigoServiceClient proxy = new HelloIndigoServiceClient("basicHttp");

// Endpoint configuration
<endpoint address="http://localhost:8001/HelloIndigo/HelloIndigoService"
binding="basicHttpBinding" name="basicHttp" contract="Host.IHelloIndigoService" />
```

Once the client channel has been used (by invoking an operation), the proxy is bound to the endpoint configuration that initialized it. The same proxy instance cannot be used to invoke another service endpoint and no changes to protocols or behaviors are allowed. A new proxy (channel) must be constructed if such changes are required.

Hosting a Service in IIS

How messages reach a service endpoint is a matter of protocols and hosting. IIS can host services over HTTP protocol, the Windows Activation Service (WAS) can support others such as TCP and named pipes, and self-hosting can support many protocols and includes several deployment options such as console or Windows Forms applications and Windows services. Selecting a hosting environment has nothing to do with service implementation, but everything to do with service deployment and overall system design.

This lab will show you how to host an existing service type as part of a web site hosted in IIS. In the process, I'll also be illustrating other extended concepts such as:

- The WCF Service web site template
- Message-based activation
- Additional metadata behavior settings
- Exporting service descriptions
- Consuming service description documents to generate client code

As always, after the lab I'll describe some of these features in greater detail.

Lab: Creating an IIS Host and Browsing Metadata

For this lab, you will work with an existing solution that contains a completed service library and shell client application. Using Visual Studio templates, you'll create a new IIS web site project that contains a service and modify it to host a preexisting service. To consume the service, you'll generate a client proxy from static service documentation exported using SvcUtil.

Creating a WCF Service web site

The first thing to do is create a WCF-enabled web site using the WCF Service template, which is new to WCF. When services are added to a web site, the supplied sample service is accompanied by a *.svc* file, the web server endpoint.

1. Open the startup solution for the lab, located at *<YourLearningWCFPath>\Labs\ Chapter1\IISHostedService\IISHostedService.sln*. This solution contains a copy of the HelloIndigo project from earlier labs and a shell client application.

2. You are going to create a new web site to host the service. Go to Solution Explorer, right-click the solution node and select Add → New Web Site. Select the WCF Service template and make sure the location type for the new web site is HTTP (see Figure 1-25). Set the location value to *http://localhost/IISHostedService*.

    When Visual Studio creates a new HTTP web site, a virtual application is created in IIS pointing to a directory beneath *c:\inetpub\ wwwroot* (or wherever your Default Web Site is pointing). In Figure 1-25, the path to the IISHostedService project might be *c:\ inetpub\wwwroot\IISHostedService*.

3. The WCF Service template generates a new web site with a default service implementation. You can delete the service implementation since you will be hosting an existing service. Go to Solution Explorer and expand the *App_Code* folder for the web site (see Figure 1-26). There you'll see the files *IService.cs* and *Service.cs*. Delete them from the project.

4. Go to the web site project and add a reference to the HelloIndigo project, which contains the service you're about to host.

5. You now can modify the web endpoint for the service so that it is associated with the correct service type. Open *Service.svc* in the code window and modify the @ServiceHost directive to associate the web endpoint with the service type HelloIndigo.HelloIndigoService. Remove the other attributes so that the end result looks as shown here:

   ```
   <%@ ServiceHost Service="HelloIndigo.HelloIndigoService" %>
   ```

Now, when a request arrives to *Service.svc*, the service model will activate a new ServiceHost instance associated with the HelloIndigoService type.

6. The WCF Service template also generated configuration settings for the host, but these settings are based on the service supplied by the template. You must modify these settings to reflect the correct service contract and service type.

   Open the *web.config* file and find the <service> section. Change the name attribute of the <service> section to HelloIndigo.HelloIndigoService and change the contract attribute of the <endpoint> section to HelloIndigo.IHelloIndigoService. While you're at it, change the binding to basicHttpBinding instead of wsHttpBinding, remove the identity settings for the endpoint, and remove the metadata endpoint. The <service> section should look as shown here when you are done:

   ```
   <service name="HelloIndigo.HelloIndigoService"
   behaviorConfiguration="ServiceBehavior">
     <endpoint address="" binding="basicHttpBinding"
   contract="HelloIndigo.IHelloIndigoService"
   />
   </service>
   ```

Modify the service behavior to remove metadata exchange support for now. The behavior should look as follows when you are done:

```
<behaviors>
  <serviceBehaviors>
    <behavior name="ServiceBehavior">
      <serviceDebug includeExceptionDetailInFaults="false" />
    </behavior>
  </serviceBehaviors>
</behaviors>
```

You now have a web site that will expose an endpoint to reach HelloIndigoService. Before generating the client proxy, I'll show you some useful metadata features.

Browsing service metadata

In this part of the lab, you'll make changes to the configuration file so that metadata can be viewed in a browser. In order to understand more about metadata you will manually configure some of the configuration settings removed in the previous section.

1. Before making any changes, test the web endpoint in a browser. Go to Solution Explorer and right-click on the web site project node; select "Set as Startup Project." Run the web site from within Visual Studio (F5). This launches the service endpoint located at *http://localhost/IISHostedService/Service.svc* in a browser. What you should see is a web page indicating that metadata publishing has been disabled for the service.

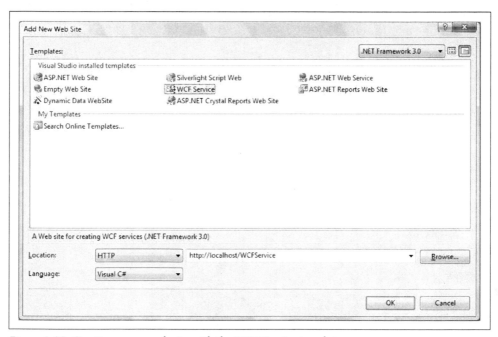

Figure 1-25. Creating a new web site with the WCF Service template

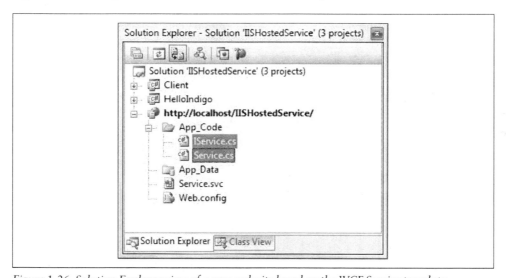

Figure 1-26. Solution Explorer view of a new web site based on the WCF Service template

2. Add metadata support to the service model configuration for the web site. Open the *web.config* file and modify the previously generated service behavior to add the <serviceMetadata> behavior. You will also add a metadata exchange endpoint for the service. The changes are shown in bold in Example 1-14.

Example 1-14. Adding metadata browsing support to the web host

```
<system.serviceModel>
  <services>
    <service name="HelloIndigo.HelloIndigoService"
behaviorConfiguration="ServiceBehavior">
      <endpoint contract="HelloIndigo.IHelloIndigoService"
binding="basicHttpBinding"/>
      <endpoint contract="IMetadataExchange" binding="mexHttpBinding" address="mex"
/>
    </service>
  </services>
  <behaviors>
    <serviceBehaviors>
      <behavior name="ServiceBehavior">
        <serviceDebug includeExceptionDetailInFaults="false"/>
        <serviceMetadata/>
      </behavior>
    </serviceBehaviors>
  </behaviors>
</system.serviceModel>
```

3. Run the web site again (F5). This time you should see the service help page in the browser, providing some instructions for SvcUtil. Leave the browser running and return to Visual Studio.

4. Without restarting the host, you're going to make a change that enables HTTP GET access to the service metadata. Open the *web.config* file and set httpGetEnabled to true for the <serviceMetadata> behavior:

```
<behavior name="returnFaults">
  <serviceDebug includeExceptionDetailInFaults="false"/>
  <serviceMetadata httpGetEnabled="true"/>
</behavior>
```

Save this change and return to the browser instance showing the service help page.

5. Refresh the browser (F5) to see what has changed. This time, you should observe the SvcUtil instruction has an active link with a *?wsdl* suffix after the service endpoint (see Figure 1-27). Click the link, and you'll be taken to the WSDL document for the service (see Figure 1-28).

Exporting metadata for proxy generation

In this part of the lab, you will export the service metadata to a set of files that can later be distributed and used to generate a proxy, offline. The files exported will be WSDL documents.

1. Launch the Visual Studio 2008 Command Prompt. Run the following command to instruct SvcUtil to export the service metadata and its associated schemas for the HelloIndigoService:

```
svcutil /d:<YourLearningWCFPath>\Labs\Chapter1\IISHostedService /t:metadata http:
//localhost/IISHostedService/service.svc
```

This will generate two *.wsdl* files and two *.xsd* files in the solution directory.

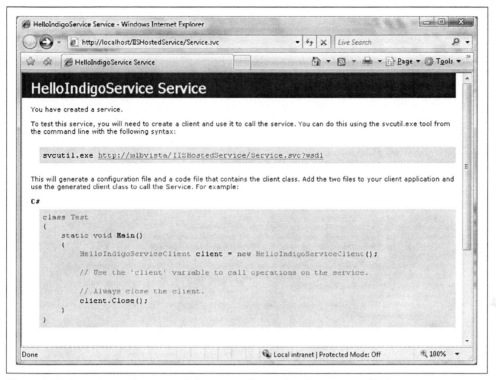

Figure 1-27. Browsing to the service help page with metadata browsing enabled

2. Use these files to generate the application configuration and proxy required for clients to consume the service. In the same command window, execute the following command:

```
svcutil /d:<YourLearningWCFPath>\Labs\Chapter1\IISHostedService\Client /o:
serviceproxy.cs /config:app.config <YourLearningWCFPath>\Labs\Chapter1\
IISHostedService\*.wsdl <YourLearningWCFPath>\Labs\Chapter1\IISHostedService\*.
xsd
```

The result of this command will be *serviceproxy.cs* and *app.config* files generated for the client application.

3. Add the two files just generated to the client project. The proxy and configuration will be used to invoke the service hosted in IIS. Go to the Client project and refresh the file list in Solution Explorer. You should see the two new files appear; include them in the project.

4. Invoke the service using the generated proxy. Open *Program.cs* in the code window and modify the Main( ) entry point adding code to create a proxy and invoke the HelloIndigo( ) operation. The resulting additions are shown in bold in Example 1-15.

5. Compile and run the Client project. The output should be similar to that in earlier labs.

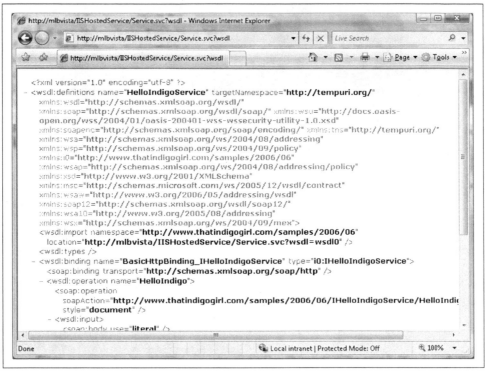

Figure 1-28. Browsing to the dynamically generated WSDL document

Example 1-15. Invoking a service hosted in IIS through its proxy

```
static void Main(string[] args)
{
  HelloIndigoServiceClient proxy = new HelloIndigoServiceClient( );
  string s = proxy.HelloIndigo( );
  Console.WriteLine(s);
  Console.WriteLine("Press <ENTER> to terminate Client.");
  Console.ReadLine( );
}
```

Web Site Templates

Many web site templates exist for creating new ASP.NET applications, so it shouldn't surprise you that there is a template to get you started with WCF. The new *WCF Service* template can be used to create a new web site that is file-based or hosted in IIS. This lab illustrates how to create an IIS-hosted site—the preferred way to test your services if you want an accurate depiction of security-related behavior. Regardless, if you create an IIS- or file-based web site, the files generated are the same:

- A sample service contract and implementation
- A *.svc* endpoint for the sample service

- A *web.config* file with service model configuration settings for the sample service

@ServiceHost Declarations

IIS hosting requires a file-based endpoint with a *.svc* extension. That's because it relies on file-extension mappings to determine how incoming requests should be delegated. The *.svc* extension is a new extension specific to WCF, and IIS knows to pass those requests to the service model for processing (via ASP.NET). In this hosting environment, each unique service must have a *.svc* endpoint. Chapter 4 discusses hosting in detail.

The *.svc* endpoint has one job to do—help the service model find the correct service type to host. The @ServiceHost directive is the link between the incoming request and the service model. In theory this directive can point to a service type declared with inline code based on a source file or belonging to a compiled assembly.

Similar to inline ASMX web services, *.svc* files can contain the actual source code for the service contract and type. This makes it possible to deploy just the *.svc* file without any accompanying source, as shown in Example 1-16. In this case, the Service attribute refers to the inline service type, and you can even enable inline debugging by setting the Debug attribute to true. Although ASP.NET 2.0 introduced the possibility of compiling this inline code into an application assembly to protect the source, I still consider this a tight coupling of the service implementation to the hosting environment—and that doesn't promote reuse or deployment flexibility.

Example 1-16. Inline service code

```
<%@ ServiceHost Language="C#" Debug="true" Service="MyService" %>

using System;
using System.ServiceModel;

[ServiceContract()]
public interface IMyService
{
  [OperationContract]
  string SomeOperation(string myValue);
}

public class MyService: IMyService
{
  public string SomeOperation(string myValue)
  {
    return "Hello: " + myValue;
  }
}
```

Another approach is to associate the *.svc* file with a code file in the web site as the original sample service did in this lab. For ASP.NET 2.0 web sites this means placing the source in the *\App_Code* directory. In this case, the Service attribute still refers to the service type, but the CodeBehind attribute is present to indicate the location of its source file:

```
<% @ServiceHost Language=C# Debug="false" Service="MyService"
CodeBehind="~/App_Code/MyService.cs" %>
```

This approach still couples the source to the host and lacks autonomous version control over services apart from their host.

Ultimately, the preferred way to associate a service type with its *.svc* endpoint is to add an assembly reference to the project and specify the fully qualified service type in the Service attribute:

```
<% @ServiceHost Service="MyNamespace.MyService" %>
```

This approach gives you the desired autonomy and reuse for the service.

Message-Based Activation

One of the benefits of using a fully featured host such as IIS or WAS is that it handles service activation on your behalf as messages arrive to the service. In the first and second labs in this chapter, you hosted a service in a console application. In all such self-hosting environments, you must explicitly run the host process before clients can invoke the service. The ServiceHost instance is constructed and opened explicitly, and its lifetime is tied to the lifetime of the host process.

IIS and WAS, on the other hand, are system services that are equipped to process incoming messages even if the ServiceHost has not yet been constructed. For example, when a request arrives for a particular *.svc* endpoint, the request is ultimately forwarded to the service model. The service model looks at the @ServiceHost declaration to find the associated service type. It then instantiates the ServiceHost instance for that type on your behalf, within an ASP.NET worker process. The *web.config* settings are used to initialize the ServiceHost and then Open( ) is called—at which point the first request is forwarded to the appropriate channel listener. Once the ServiceHost has been constructed and opened, subsequent requests for the same service are directed to it. Simply put, with IIS or WAS hosting, you needn't manually create the ServiceHost instance—this is handled for you by the host process. This is called *message-based activation*. The details of hosting are discussed in Chapter 4.

Another convenience of IIS and WAS hosting is that you can modify *web.config* settings for a service and the changes are reflected in subsequent calls without restarting IIS or WAS. That's because changes to configuration files are detected, and if necessary, a new application domain is constructed to service requests. For example, if changes to the service model configuration require that a new ServiceHost instance be constructed to reflect the changes. In a self-hosting environment, new settings are not known to the host process and thus are not reflected until you restart. You could optionally build logic into the host to detect changes and recycle any ServiceHost instances. With IIS and WAS, configuration changes are detected and a new ServiceHost is created to handle subsequent requests.

Browsing and Exporting Metadata

To consume a service, clients require access to service metadata, including the service contract, any custom data types, and binding requirements. Earlier in this chapter, you learned how to enable the service metadata behavior and how to expose a metadata exchange endpoint to support proxy generation using SvcUtil. This lab illustrates how to view metadata in the browser and how to export that metadata to files for offline consumption. This capability is useful for a few reasons:

- For debugging purposes, it can be helpful to view the WSDL document, for example when trying to solve interoperability issues between platforms.

- Allowing client developers to eat up web server resources by browsing to dynamically created metadata is suboptimal. Instead, once the contract is stable, you should export it and allow developers to browse static files.

- It may be helpful to send developers the WSDL document via some other delivery mechanism such as email. This way they can generate proxies while offline.

Browsing metadata

Services may expose one or more endpoints, all of which are included in the service metadata. When a WSDL document is generated, for example, this document describes the contracts exposed across all endpoints. In other words, the WSDL document is one-to-one with the service. You can browse to any service if they have an HTTP base address. In the case of self hosting environments, the <host> section of the service configuration can supply the base address.

For services hosted in IIS, the base address is the application directory in IIS with the *.svc* endpoint. For example, in this lab you would browse to *http://localhost/IISHostedService/Service.svc*.

When you browse to a service's base address you are presented with the service help page. The service model dynamically generates this for you. If you haven't enabled the metadata behavior, the help page will still be presented with instructions on how to do this. If you have enabled the metadata behavior but have forgotten to enable browsing, you'll receive the same instructions. In configuration, if you set httpGetEnabled to true, the help page will produce a link to the WSDL document (Figures 1-27 and 1-28):

```
<behavior name="serviceBehavior">
  <serviceMetadata httpGetEnabled="true" />
</behavior>
```

The service metadata behavior is required if you expose a metadata exchange endpoint for generating proxies, but you may want to explicitly disable both the help page and metadata browsing by adding the service debug behavior with httpHelpPageEnabled set to false and by setting httpGetEnabled to false:

```
<behavior name="serviceBehavior">
  <serviceDebug httpHelpPageEnabled="false" />
  <serviceMetadata httpGetEnabled="false" />
</behavior>
```

The WSDL document is dynamically generated each time metadata is accessed. During development this is a useful feature to have, but once you publish your service to production, it may be desirable to suppress dynamic generation to reduce overhead on the web server. But what if you want to provide a link to static metadata? An alternative is to leave metadata browsing enabled and provide a static file where the WSDL document can be retrieved. This is achieved by providing a value for the externalMetadataLocation attribute:

```
<behavior name="serviceBehavior">
  <serviceDebug httpHelpPageEnabled="false" />
  <serviceMetadata httpGetEnabled="true" externalMetadataLocation="http://localhost/
IISHostedService/www.thatindigogirl.com.samples.2006.06.wsdl"/>
</behavior>
```

Exporting metadata

To produce a static WSDL document, you can export service metadata using SvcUtil, as illustrated in this lab. SvcUtil uses the mex endpoint to retrieve service metadata and save it to a WSDL document that can be stored on the filesystem.

The command switch for SvcUtil to export metadata is /t:metadata. This command dumps the service metadata to several *.wsdl* and *.xsd* files in the specified directory:

```
svcutil /d:<YourLearningWCFPath>\Labs\Chapter1\IISHostedService /t:metadata http://
localhost/IISHostedService/service.svc
```

The service model spreads the service description across multiple files. These files have a hierarchical relationship where a root *.wsdl* imports child *.wsdl* and *.xsd* files. In reality they are all one service description if you denormalize the output. With this output, you can still use SvcUtil to generate code for client applications as this lab illustrates.

Exposing Multiple Service Endpoints

So far in this chapter, I have shown you different ways to create services, how to expose a service endpoint and metadata exchange endpoint, how to generate client proxies, how to work with metadata, and how to configure service behaviors. In this section, I'll place the emphasis on endpoints, binding configuration, and allocation of assemblies for a more complex solution.

WCF includes a number of standard bindings that allow you to quickly configure a service for a particular set of protocols. Clients must use compatible protocols when they communicate with each endpoint. Services can expose multiple endpoints for the same service contract in order to expose functionality over different protocols. For example, a service may be called by internal clients over TCP, but by external clients over HTTP. In addition to supporting different protocols, internal and external clients may not have access to the same service contracts. Some operations may be allowed only by clients within the domain, while others are publicly available to remote clients on the Internet.

In this lab you will configure multiple endpoints for a service to support different endpoint and binding configurations. In the process you'll explore the following concepts:

- Hosting multiple services
- Configuring multiple endpoints for a service
- Accessing a service from a Windows client application
- Initializing proxies from multiple endpoint and binding configurations
- Comparing proxy generation to sharing types between services and clients

Lab: Hosting Multiple Services and Sharing Types

In this lab, you'll modify an existing solution to implement a service contract and an administrative contract on two distinct services. You'll then host each service in the same host process, a console application. An internal client presumed to be behind the firewall will consume each service using network protocols such as TCP and named pipes. This client will have access to service operations exposed by the service contract and administrative contract. An external client, presumed to be accessing the service over the Internet will have access only to operations exposed by the service contract over HTTP. The internal client will share class libraries to access service contracts, while the external client will use traditional methods for generating service proxies.

Implementing multiple contracts on a service

In this section, you're going to implement the predefined service contracts on two distinct services. Each service will expose two contracts: one for business functionality core to the service, the other for administrative functionality. Both services will implement the same administrative contract. This illustrates an example of contract factoring for reuse.

1. Start by opening the solution *<YourLearningWCFPath>\Labs\Chapter1\ MultiContractService\MultiContractService.sln*. This solution contains several shell projects, including a service library, a host, and two Windows client applications as follows:

BusinessServiceContracts
A class library containing three contracts: IAdmin, IServiceA, and IServiceB. IAdmin defines administrative operations. IServiceA and IServiceB respectively describe functionality to be exposed by ServiceA and ServiceB.

BusinessServices
A class library that will contain two services: ServiceA and ServiceB.

Host
A console application that will host ServiceA and ServiceB.

InternalClient
A windows client application that will access services behind the firewall.

ExternalClient
A windows client application that will access services over the Internet.

 Putting service contracts into a separate class library facilitates sharing metadata with client applications when you own both sides of the development effort.

2. The first thing you'll do is provide an implementation for ServiceA, which is located in the BusinessServices class library. First, take a look at the contracts you will implement. Go to the BusinessServiceContracts project and open *IServiceA.cs*; you'll see a contract with two operations. Now open *IAdmin.cs* and you'll see another contract with two different operations.

To implement these contracts, go to the BusinessServices project. First, add a reference to the BusinessServiceContracts project so you can access the contracts it defines. Then open *ServiceA.cs* and add a using statement for the BusinessServiceContracts namespace, as shown here:

```
using BusinessServiceContracts;
```

Modify the definition of ServiceA so that it derives from IServiceA and IAdmin as follows:

```
public class ServiceA : IServiceA, IAdmin
```

Implement both contracts implicitly. You can use a shortcut by hovering your mouse over IServiceA and using the *smart tag* to select "Implement interface IServiceA," as shown in Figure 1-29.

```
public class ServiceA: IServiceA, IAdmin
{



}
```
Implement interface 'IServiceA'
Explicitly implement interface 'IServiceA'

Figure 1-29. Using smart tags to implement an interface

Complete the implementation by adding the code shown in Example 1-17.

Example 1-17. Implementation for ServiceA

```
public class ServiceA : IServiceA, IAdmin
{
  public string Operation1( )
  {
    return "IServiceA.Operation1( ) invoked.";
  }
  public string Operation2( )
  {
    return "IServiceA.Operation2( ) invoked.";
  }
  public string AdminOperation1( )
  {
    return "IAdmin.AdminOperation1 invoked.";
  }
  public string AdminOperation2( )
  {
    return "IAdmin.AdminOperation2 invoked.";
  }
}
```

3. Follow a similar set of steps to implement ServiceB. Open *ServiceB.cs* and derive the class from IServiceB and IAdmin. Implement both interfaces implicitly so that the result looks like the code in Example 1-18. Don't forget to add the using statement for the BusinessServiceContracts namespace.

Example 1-18. Implementation for ServiceB

```
using BusinessServiceContracts;

public class ServiceB:  IServiceB, IAdmin
{
  public string Operation3( )
  {
    return "IServiceB.Operation3( ) invoked.";
  }
  public string AdminOperation1( )
  {
    return "IAdmin.AdminOperation1 invoked.";
  }
  public string AdminOperation2( )
  {
    return "IAdmin.AdminOperation2 invoked.";
  }
}
```

4. Verify that the BusinessServices project compiles without error.

Hosting two services with multiple contracts

Now you will host both services in a single console application. This will require you to create two ServiceHost instances and provide two <service> configuration sections, one for each service type.

1. First, make sure the Host project can access the service contracts and service types. Go to the Host project and add assembly references to two projects: BusinessServiceContracts and BusinessServices.

2. In the application configuration file provided for the Host, provide configuration settings for both services. Open the *app.config* file and add the <system. serviceModel> section shown in Example 1-19. This section belongs inside the <configuration> section of the file.

   The configuration section for ServiceA exposes two endpoints for the service contract IServiceA: one for Internet access over HTTP, another for TCP access behind the firewall. ServiceB also exposes two endpoints for the service contract IServiceB: one for Internet access and another for named pipe access restricting communications to the same machine.

   Both services expose the IAdmin contract over TCP and named pipes, respectively, allowing callers on the same machine, or on remote machines behind the firewall.

   Each service configuration also provides the appropriate base addresses for the protocols they support across all endpoints.

Example 1-19. Service model configuration for ServiceA and ServiceB

```
<system.serviceModel>
  <services>
    <service name="BusinessServices.ServiceA"
behaviorConfiguration="serviceBehavior">
      <host>
        <baseAddresses>
          <add baseAddress="http://localhost:8000"/>
          <add baseAddress="net.tcp://localhost:9000"/>
        </baseAddresses>
      </host>
      <endpoint address="Admin" contract="BusinessServiceContracts.IAdmin"
binding="netTcpBinding" />
      <endpoint address="ServiceA" contract="BusinessServiceContracts.IServiceA"
binding="basicHttpBinding"  />
      <endpoint address="ServiceA" contract="BusinessServiceContracts.IServiceA"
binding="netTcpBinding"  />
    </service>
    <service name="BusinessServices.ServiceB"
behaviorConfiguration="serviceBehavior">
      <host>
        <baseAddresses>
          <add baseAddress="http://localhost:8001"/>
```

```
        <add baseAddress="net.pipe://localhost"/>
      </baseAddresses>
    </host>
    <endpoint address="Admin" contract="BusinessServiceContracts.IAdmin"
binding="netNamedPipeBinding" />
    <endpoint address="ServiceB" contract="BusinessServiceContracts.IServiceB"
binding="basicHttpBinding"  />
    <endpoint address="ServiceB" contract="BusinessServiceContracts.IServiceB"
binding="netNamedPipeBinding"  />
  </service>
 </services>
 <behaviors>
   <serviceBehaviors>
     <behavior name="serviceBehavior">
       <serviceMetadata httpGetEnabled="true"/>
     </behavior>
   </serviceBehaviors>
 </behaviors>
</system.serviceModel>
```

Each <service> section holds configuration settings for its own base
addresses and endpoints. Recall that the configuration for a particular
service is used to initialize a ServiceHost instance for that service type.
Be mindful that base addresses across all sections must have unique
ports since a port can be opened only once per machine.

3. Now that service model configuration has been provided for each service, you
   will write code to initialize and open a ServiceHost instance for both. Go to the
   Host project and open *Program.cs*. Modify the Main( ) entry point so that it
   includes the code shown in Example 1-20. You will also need to add a using
   statement for System.ServiceModel.

   This code creates two distinct ServiceHost instances, one for each service. They
   are both constructed and opened within a try...finally block to ensure that
   Close( ) is called for each when the host shuts down or if a fatal exception
   occurs. In addition, the code calls Abort() if the ServiceHost instance is in a
   faulted state, since Close() would throw an exception in this case.

Example 1-20. Initializing the ServiceHost for ServiceA and ServiceB

```
using System.ServiceModel;

static void Main(string[] args)
{
  ServiceHost hostA = null;
  ServiceHost hostB = null;

  try
  {
    hostA = new ServiceHost(typeof(BusinessServices.ServiceA));
```

```
    hostB = new ServiceHost(typeof(BusinessServices.ServiceB));

    hostA.Open( );
    hostB.Open( );

    Console.WriteLine( );
    Console.WriteLine("Press <ENTER> to terminate Host");
    Console.ReadLine( );
  }
  finally
  {
    if (hostA.State == CommunicationState.Faulted)
      hostA.Abort( );
    else
      hostA.Close( );

    if (hostB.State == CommunicationState.Faulted)
      hostB.Abort( );
    else
      hostB.Close( );
  }
}
```

    4. Compile and run the Host project once to verify that no errors occur.

Because metadata browsing is enabled in the configuration section for each service type, you can browse to the WSDL document for each service by providing the HTTP base address for each service. Note that each service has its own distinct WSDL document, but for each individual service, all endpoints for the service are included in its WSDL document.

Consuming internal services using shared contracts

In this part of the lab, you will implement the internal client application and invoke service operations over TCP and named pipe protocols. The purpose of this exercise is to illustrate how you might share service metadata when you own both sides of the development effort for intranet clients. Sharing contract libraries ensures both sides are compiling against the latest contract versions throughout the development cycle. In addition, this exercise will illustrate the use of different standard bindings for TCP and named pipes.

    1. First, go to the InternalClient project and add a reference to the BusinessServiceContracts project. This will give the client application direct access to the service contract necessary to invoke the service.

    2. The client application requires prior knowledge of the service endpoints it can reach before it can configure a proxy. Under the assumption that you own both sides, client developers will manually configure client endpoints to reach each service endpoint. In this case, you'll consume ServiceA over TCP and ServiceB over named pipes.

Open the *app.config* file and add the `<system.serviceModel>` section shown in Example 1-21. This includes two endpoints for each service: one for the main service contract, the other for the administrative contract. The binding for each endpoint matches the binding configuration for the same endpoint at the service. In this case, TCP endpoints use `netTcpBinding`, and named pipe endpoints use `netNamedPipeBinding`.

Example 1-21. Service model configuration for the InternalClient

```
<system.serviceModel>
  <client>
    <endpoint address="net.tcp://localhost:9000/ServiceA"
contract="BusinessServiceContracts.IServiceA" binding="netTcpBinding"  />
    <endpoint address="net.tcp://localhost:9000/Admin"
contract="BusinessServiceContracts.IAdmin" binding="netTcpBinding"
name="TCP_IAdmin" />
    <endpoint address="net.pipe://localhost/ServiceB"
contract="BusinessServiceContracts.IServiceB" binding="netNamedPipeBinding"  />
    <endpoint address="net.pipe://localhost/Admin"
contract="BusinessServiceContracts.IAdmin" binding="netNamedPipeBinding"
name="IPC_IAdmin"/>
  </client>
</system.serviceModel>
```

> Remember that when you select a binding, you are selecting a transport protocol, a message encoding format, and possibly other messaging protocols for security and reliability, for example. The details of what goes into a binding will be discussed in Chapter 3. The important thing is that if you use the defaults on both sides, the communication channel at each end will be compatible.

3. Now you will write some code to invoke each service endpoint on both services. To do this, you will need four proxy references: one for each service and contract.

   Open *Form1.cs* and add a using statement for `BusinessServiceContracts`. In addition, declare a proxy for each contract, scoped to the lifetime of the application, adding the following definitions as members of `Form1`:

   ```
   using BusinessServiceContracts;

   public partial class Form1 : Form
   {
     IServiceA m_proxyA;
     IAdmin m_adminProxyA;

     IServiceB m_proxyB;
     IAdmin m_adminProxyB;

     // more code
   }
   ```

4. In the form constructor, initialize each proxy using ChannelFactory<T>. The proxies for IServiceA and IServiceB can use the default client endpoint for each contract. Because there is only one endpoint for each contract type, you don't have to specify which <endpoint> section will initialize the proxy.

Since IAdmin has two endpoints defined, one for TCP and another for named pipes, you must specify which endpoint will initialize the proxy when you construct ChannelFactory<T>. Do this by passing the appropriate endpoint name from Example 1-21.

You'll see the resulting code for the form constructor in Example 1-22. You must also add a reference to System.ServiceModel, as shown.

Example 1-22. Code to initialize ServiceA and ServiceB proxies

```
using System.ServiceModel;

public Form1( )
{
  InitializeComponent( );

  ChannelFactory<IServiceA> factoryA = new
ChannelFactory<IServiceA>("");
  m_proxyA = factoryA.CreateChannel( );

  ChannelFactory<IAdmin> adminFactoryA = new
ChannelFactory<IAdmin>("TCP_IAdmin");
  m_adminProxyA = adminFactoryA.CreateChannel( );

  ChannelFactory<IServiceB> factoryB = new
ChannelFactory<IServiceB>("");
  m_proxyB = factoryB.CreateChannel( );

  ChannelFactory<IAdmin> adminFactoryB = new
ChannelFactory<IAdmin>("IPC_IAdmin");
  m_adminProxyB = adminFactoryB.CreateChannel( );
}
```

5. The user interface for the client has already been created. If you look at *Form1.cs* in design view, you'll see a button to test each service and administrative operation. Now you'll add code to invoke each operation using the appropriate proxy. For each button on the form, add a handler for the Click event; you can do this by double-clicking each button from design view. Inside each Click event handler, add code to invoke the appropriate operation and show the result in a message box. The resulting code for each of these handlers is shown in Example 1-23.

Just adding the code from Example 1-23 will not be sufficient to hook up the event handlers. When you double-click each button in design view, this generates designer code to hook up each event handler to its Button control.

Example 1-23. Code to invoke all service operations

```
private void button1_Click(object sender, EventArgs e)
{
  string s = m_adminProxyA.AdminOperation1( );
  MessageBox.Show(s);
}
private void button2_Click(object sender, EventArgs e)
{
  string s = m_adminProxyA.AdminOperation2( );
  MessageBox.Show(s);
}
private void button3_Click(object sender, EventArgs e)
{
  string s = m_adminProxyB.AdminOperation1( );
  MessageBox.Show(s);
}
private void button4_Click(object sender, EventArgs e)
{
  string s = m_adminProxyB.AdminOperation2( );
  MessageBox.Show(s);
}
private void button5_Click(object sender, EventArgs e)
{
  string s = m_proxyA.Operation1( );
  MessageBox.Show(s);
}
private void button6_Click(object sender, EventArgs e)
{
  string s = m_proxyA.Operation2( );
  MessageBox.Show(s);
}
private void button7_Click(object sender, EventArgs e)
{
  string s = m_proxyB.Operation3( );
  MessageBox.Show(s);
}
```

6. It is always good practice to release resources when you are finished with them. To make sure that each of the channels are properly disposed of when the application exits, add code to explicitly close each proxy. First, add a new private function named CloseProxy( ) that will cast each proxy to ICommunicationObject and invoke its Abort( ) operation if the proxy is in the faulted state, and call the Close( ) operation otherwise. Then, add an event handler for the FormClosing event of Form1 and add code to call CloseProxy( ) for each proxy. The code to add is shown in Example 1-24.

Example 1-24. Code to close each proxy

```
private void CloseProxy(ICommunicationObject proxy)
  {
    if (proxy != null)
    {
```

Example 1-24. Code to close each proxy (continued)

```
    if (proxy.State == CommunicationState.Faulted)
      proxy.Abort();
    else
        proxy.Close();
  }
}

private void Form1_FormClosing(object sender, FormClosingEventArgs e)
{
  CloseProxy(m_proxyA as ICommunicationObject);
  CloseProxy(m_proxyB as ICommunicationObject);
  CloseProxy(m_adminProxyA as ICommunicationObject);
  CloseProxy(m_adminProxyB as ICommunicationObject);
}
```

7. Compile the solution and test the internal client. Run the Host project first, and then run InternalClient. Click each button to invoke operations exposed by ServiceA and ServiceB.

Consuming external services with a generated proxy

Now you will implement the external client application and invoke service operations over HTTP. In this case, the client will rely on the WSDL document to generate a proxy and related configuration to call the service. This exercise will illustrate how the proxy generation process handles multiple contracts and endpoints.

1. Start by running the Host project without debugging so that you can generate proxies for each service.

2. Go to the ExternalClient project in Solution Explorer and add a service reference for ServiceA. Provide the base address *http://localhost:8000* and provide the namespace ServiceA. This will generate a proxy for each contract exposed by ServiceA and create an application configuration file with client endpoints.

3. Now add a service reference for ServiceB. This time, provide the base address *http://localhost:8001* and provide the namespace ServiceB. This will generate a proxy for each contract exposed by ServiceB, adding new client endpoints to the application configuration file.

 The application configuration file is not overwritten when you add new service references. A merge is performed to add to configuration settings. SvcUtil also supports merge through command-line options.

4. This application will invoke each service using the proxies generated by SvcUtil. Like with the InternalClient application, you'll create a proxy reference for each service contract, initialize them in the form constructor, and then close them in the FormClosing event. The code will be simplified somewhat since the generated

---

proxy hides some of the complexity of creating the communication channel, and directly exposes close functionality. The resulting code is shown in Example 1-25.

Example 1-25. Code to initialize and close generated proxies for ServiceA and ServiceB

```
public partial class Form1 : Form
{
  ServiceA.ServiceAClient m_proxyA;
  ServiceB.ServiceBClient m_proxyB;

  public Form1( )
  {
    InitializeComponent( );

    m_proxyA = new ExternalClient.ServiceA.ServiceAClient("BasicHttpBinding_IServiceA");
    m_proxyB = new ExternalClient.ServiceB.ServiceBClient("BasicHttpBinding_IServiceB");
  }
  private void Form1_FormClosing(object sender, FormClosingEventArgs e)
  {
    if (this.m_proxyA.State == CommunicationState.Faulted)
     this.m_proxyA.Abort();
    else
    this.m_proxyA.Close( );

    if (this.m_proxyB.State == CommunicationState.Faulted)
      this.m_proxyB.Abort();
    else
      this.m_proxyB.Close( );

  }
}
```

You'll notice that each proxy is initialized by passing the name of a particular endpoint from the application configuration file. Each service exposes multiple endpoints, but because this is an Internet client, the assumption is that the client won't have permissions to call the TCP nor be able to invoke services over named pipes (named pipes require same-machine calls). Still, add service reference generated configuration for all endpoints because the WSDL document includes all endpoints for a service.

5. Now you can add code to invoke each operation. If you look at the form in design view, you'll see that only three buttons are present to invoke the collective operations of both service contracts. Create Click event handlers for each button and add code to invoke each operation through the appropriate proxy. Example 1-26 shows the resulting code.

Example 1-26. Code to invoke each service operation

```
private void button1_Click(object sender, EventArgs e)
{
  string s = m_proxyA.Operation1( );
  MessageBox.Show(s);
```

Example 1-26. Code to invoke each service operation (continued)

```
}
private void button2_Click(object sender, EventArgs e)
{
  string s = m_proxyA.Operation2();
  MessageBox.Show(s);
}
private void button3_Click(object sender, EventArgs e)
{
  string s = m_proxyB.Operation3();
  MessageBox.Show(s);
}
```

6. Compile and test the external client application. First run the Host, and then run ExternalClient. Click each button to invoke the service operations exposed by ServiceA and ServiceB.

Let's look at the new concepts and tools introduced in this lab.

Implementing Multiple Contracts

Designing service contracts is not as simple as just exposing existing business components as services. In all likelihood, services will aggregate calls to many logically related business components. This requires forethought into the use cases through each service. Irrespective of this aggregation and design effort, it is still possible that the functionality exposed by a single service should not be lumped into one big service contract. Here are some cases in which multiple contracts could exist on a single service:

- To separate logically related operations for different features
- To separate queued operations from non-queued operations
- To provide a different entry point for external and internal consumers of the service

If your service contracts are implemented on CLR interfaces (as I've recommended) then implementing multiple contracts on a service is as simple as implementing multiple interfaces. In this lab, each service implements a main service contract (IServiceA and IServiceB, respectively) and an administrative contract (IAdmin).

Contracts can facilitate the logical separation of functionality exposed by a service. For example, in the lab the main service contract for each service holds core business operations for the service. The administrative contract provides a consistent set of administrative functions that any service can expose. Both services implement the same administrative contract, which means both services expose a consistent set of operations, although the internal implementation may be quite different. Because of the presumed sensitivity of administrative operations, the lab exposes these operations over TCP or named pipes, which implies access behind the firewall. To enable internal applications and business partners to access the core service functionality, the main service contracts are exposed over two endpoints: one for TCP or named pipes, the other for Internet access over HTTP.

Hosting Multiple Services

A ServiceHost instance is required for each service type in order to expose endpoints to calling clients. When you host in IIS or WAS, a *.svc* endpoint is supplied for each service type, with a @ServiceHost directive that links the *.svc* endpoint to the actual service type. Thus, if you have multiple services to host in IIS, you provide a *.svc* for each to support message-based activation and configure the service model section as you would for any service type.

In self-hosting environments, you are responsible for initializing each ServiceHost instance. You can initialize a ServiceHost for each service type as shown here (the complete code listing is shown in Example 1-20):

```
ServiceHost hostA = new ServiceHost(typeof(BusinessServices.ServiceA));
ServiceHost hostB = new ServiceHost(typeof(BusinessServices.ServiceB));

hostA.Open();
hostB.Open();
```

Each ServiceHost is initialized with its own base addresses and service endpoints according to the <service> section with the matching type (see Example 1-19). Each ServiceHost can also be programmatically initialized using the techniques illustrated earlier in this chapter.

Proxy Generation for Multiple Contracts and Endpoints

Adding a service reference generates the proxy and configuration settings necessary to access a particular service. If the service implements multiple contracts, a proxy type is generated for each contract. For example, in this lab when you add a service reference to ServiceA in the ExternalClient project, the following proxies are generated—one for IServiceA, another for IAdmin:

```
public partial class ServiceAClient :
System.ServiceModel.ClientBase<ExternalClient.ServiceA.IServiceA>,
ExternalClient.ServiceA.IServiceA

public partial class AdminClient :
System.ServiceModel.ClientBase<ExternalClient.ServiceA.IAdmin>,
ExternalClient.ServiceA.IAdmin
```

Likewise, when you add a service reference to ServiceB a proxy is generated for both contracts: IServiceB and IAdmin.

 In theory, because the IAdmin service contract is the same for both services, they could share a proxy, but SvcUtil generates proxy types for all contracts and has no knowledge of the code you have already generated.

In addition to generating proxies, SvcUtil generates the configuration necessary for each endpoint exposed by each service. SvcUtil always provides a name for each <endpoint> element, so you can specify the correct endpoint to use by name when constructing each proxy. Example 1-27 shows the client endpoints generated for ServiceA and ServiceB; the endpoints used in the lab for the ExternalClient are shown in bold.

Example 1-27. Client endpoints generated for ServiceA and ServiceB

```
<client>
  <endpoint address="net.tcp://localhost:9000/Admin" binding="netTcpBinding"
bindingConfiguration="NetTcpBinding_IAdmin"
contract="ExternalClient.ServiceA.IAdmin"
name="NetTcpBinding_IAdmin" />
  <endpoint address="http://localhost:8000/ServiceA" binding="basicHttpBinding"
bindingConfiguration="BasicHttpBinding_IServiceA"
contract="ExternalClient.ServiceA.IServiceA"
name="BasicHttpBinding_IServiceA" />
  <endpoint address="net.tcp://localhost:9000/ServiceA" binding="netTcpBinding"
bindingConfiguration="NetTcpBinding_IServiceA"
contract="ExternalClient.ServiceA.IServiceA"
name="NetTcpBinding_IServiceA" />
  <endpoint address="net.pipe://localhost/Admin" binding="netNamedPipeBinding"
bindingConfiguration="NetNamedPipeBinding_IAdmin"
contract="ExternalClient.ServiceB.IAdmin"
name="NetNamedPipeBinding_IAdmin" />
  <endpoint address="http://localhost:8001/ServiceB" binding="basicHttpBinding"
bindingConfiguration="BasicHttpBinding_IServiceB"
contract="ExternalClient.ServiceB.IServiceB"
name="BasicHttpBinding_IServiceB" />
  <endpoint address="net.pipe://localhost/ServiceB" binding="netNamedPipeBinding"
bindingConfiguration="NetNamedPipeBinding_IServiceB"
contract="ExternalClient.ServiceB.IServiceB"
name="NetNamedPipeBinding_IServiceB" />
</client>
```

Although the client may not have network rights to invoke the TCP or named pipe endpoints, these endpoints are still part of the service description (WSDL) and therefore are visible to the client.

Recall that a WSDL document is created for each service type. Thus, to prevent remote clients from seeing internal endpoints that they should not access, you can create different service types for internal and external use—funneling them to the same implementation code. On external service types, you can expose endpoints only for supported contracts over HTTP. For internal service types, you can expose internal contracts and TCP and named pipes endpoints. To modify the lab in support of this scenario, you might see the following service types:

```
public class ServiceA : IServiceA {...}
public class InternalServiceA : IServiceA, IAdmin {...}
public class ServiceB : IServiceB {...}
public class InternalServiceB : IServiceB, IAdmin {...}
```

In the host configuration, each service type would be defined in a separate <service> element, exposing only the required endpoints. A compressed view of the required <service> elements is shown here:

```
<service name="BusinessServices.ServiceA" ...>
<service name="BusinessServices.InternalServiceA" ...>
<service name="BusinessServices.ServiceB" ...>
<service name="BusinessServices.InternalServiceB" ...>
```

 The following sample illustrates this scenario: *<YourLearningWCFPath>\ Samples\ServiceContracts\MultiContractServices_UniqueServiceTypes*.

Proxy Initialization and Lifetime

Each client proxy opens a communication channel to invoke a service endpoint. The proxy can be programmatically initialized in code or declaratively initialized per the client's service model configuration. If there is only one endpoint configured for a particular service contract, there is no need to specify an endpoint configuration name to the constructor of the channel factory or proxy.

When you use `ChannelFactory<T>` to create the channel from the default endpoint, you pass empty quotes to the constructor. This example expects that only one endpoint is configured for `IServiceA`:

```
ChannelFactory<IServiceA> factoryA = new
ChannelFactory<IServiceA>("");
m_proxyA = factoryA.CreateChannel();
```

Generated proxies provide a default constructor to achieve the same result:

```
m_proxyA = new ExternalClient.ServiceA.ServiceAClient();
```

On the other hand, when multiple endpoints exist for the same contract, you must provide a configuration name as shown here for `ChannelFactory<T>` and for a generated proxy:

```
ChannelFactory<BusinessServiceContracts.IServiceA> factoryA = new
ChannelFactory<BusinessServiceContracts.IServiceA>("BasicHttpBinding_IServiceA");
proxyA = factoryA.CreateChannel();

m_proxyA = new
ExternalClient.ServiceA.ServiceAClient("BasicHttpBinding_IServiceA");
```

In either case, the lifetime of the communication channel is controlled by the proxy reference. If the client application intends to invoke the service endpoint repeatedly, it is better not to recreate the proxy each time an operation is invoked. Instead, the proxy should be scoped to the lifetime of the application.

When the application is shutting down, you should close the proxy to speed up the release of resources. When you are working with a channel factory to create the proxy reference, you must cast to `ICommunicationObject` in order to call its `Close()` method (see Example 1-24). The equivalent inline steps would be as follows:

```
ICommunicationObject proxyACommunication = m_proxyA as ICommunicationObject;
...
proxyACommunication.Close();
```

This step is required because the channel factory returns a reference to the service contract, which doesn't expose a Close() method. Still, the underlying object is a CommunicationObject that implements ICommunicationObject.

Proxies generated with SvcUtil include code to wrap the inner communication channel. In addition, each generated proxy type implements ICommunicationObject directly, and thus provides a Close() method.

 Be aware that the channel stack beneath the proxy reference can be put into a faulted or invalid state. For example, if the service is no longer available, or if the service throws an exception, or if a timeout occurs at either end. In this case Close() will throw an exception and Abort()should be called to clean up channel resources. In Chapter 8, I'll discuss exception handling.

Another point to note is that the lifetime of the communication channel should not be confused with the lifetime of the service instance instantiated by the host to handle a request. In fact, a different service instance may be allocated for every call even if the client uses the same channel. This behavior is controlled by the service. Service instancing and throttling behaviors are covered in Chapter 5.

Sharing Service Contracts

This lab illustrates an alternate approach for sharing metadata with the client. Instead of generating a proxy using SvcUtil, a class library containing only service contracts is shared by the service library and the internal client application. This approach is useful in an environment where you own both sides: client and service. This approach can simplify steps in development, help you avoid the internal complexity of types generated by SvcUtil, and even allow you to exercise more control over service contract versioning on both ends.

Realistically, remote clients such as Internet clients may not be owned, which is why the more traditional approach of sharing contracts via add service reference is used.

Duplicating Operations

This lab illustrates exposing two different contracts on each service. These contracts each have unique operations: a set for the business functionality exposed by the service, and a set for administrative functions. You may also want to expose a subset of business operations for external clients while exposing the complete set of business functionality to internal clients.

To achieve this, you could create internal and external interfaces for the service contract, for example: IServiceA and IInternalServiceA. The external interface, IServiceA, would in this case contain a subset of the functionality exposed by IInternalServiceA (see Example 1-28).

Example 1-28. Internal and external service contracts with duplicate operations

```
[ServiceContract(Namespace = "http://www.thatindigogirl.com/samples/2006/06")]
public interface IServiceA
{
  [OperationContract]
  string Operation1();
  [OperationContract]
  string Operation2();
}

[ServiceContract(Namespace = "http://www.thatindigogirl.com/samples/2006/06")]
public interface IInternalServiceA
{
  [OperationContract]
  string Operation1();
  [OperationContract]
  string Operation2();
  [OperationContract]
  string Operation3();
}
```

If you expose each of these contracts on their own service types (ServiceA and InternalServiceA, respectively), external clients will never see the functionality exposed to internal clients because they work from a different WSDL document. However, the implementation can still be the same for each service implementation.

The following sample illustrates the scenario: <*YourLearningWCFPath*>\ *Samples\ServiceContracts\InternalExternalServiceTypes.sln*.

Summary

This chapter covered a lot of ground, beginning with a look at the purpose of WCF, the problems it solves and its alignment with SOA, through discussion of the fundamentals developers should know before they begin working with WCF. I also touched on the overall architecture of WCF, though this is covered in greater detail in Chapter 3. Through hands-on practice and discussion you should be comfortable now with the following concepts:

- Defining service contracts and services
- Hosting services in a console application or in IIS
- Exposing endpoints for a service using various standard bindings
- Working with Visual Studio templates and WCF tools to improve productivity
- Working with service metadata and configuring related service behaviors
- Generating proxies to invoke services

Of course, the next step is to start diving into the details of service contracts, bindings, and hosting. In addition, you'll need to learn more about service behaviors and messaging protocols that handle instancing, throttling, reliability, security and exception handling.

Since service contracts are central to defining the messages exchanged between clients and services, the next chapter will focus on this subject. In Chapter 2, I'll explain how to approach service contract design, how to work with complex types and how to control serialization on many levels. In the process of reading Chapter 2, you'll further solidify your knowledge of the fundamental concepts touched on in this chapter.

CHAPTER 2

Contracts

In Chapter 1, you were introduced to fundamental WCF concepts, including how to create and consume a service, how to host a service and expose endpoints where it can be reached by clients, how to support metadata exchange so that clients can generate service contracts, and how to work with client proxies to invoke service operations. In Chapter 1, you also learned the importance of service metadata, which is shared with clients through a WSDL document. Service metadata includes all of the necessary information for a client to invoke service operations, including:

- The address where messages should be sent
- The protocols supported by the service, including transport protocol, message encoding format, and other messaging protocols
- A list of service operations and the required information to be passed to or returned from those operations

The service contract is the hub of this metadata—defining a set of operations, parameters, and return values. Each service contract represents a group of logically related operations that are exposed through endpoints. Endpoints describe the address where messages can be sent to reach those operations and the other required protocols to process those messages. Services may implement one or more service contracts, and thus may have different logical groupings of operations, but all of this is still ultimately included in the WSDL document.

As discussed in Chapter 1, clients communicate with services by exchanging messages that are serialized on the wire and deserialized into CLR types at each end. In the simplest scenario, client and service developers work only with objects, and all the serialization magic happens somewhere down below in the plumbing. WCF provides this plumbing. WSDL describes the protocols required to reach the service, clients use proxies to communicate with the service, and messages just happen. There are times, however, when developers must exercise more control over service contract design over message serialization and over the choice of protocols. For these scenarios, it helps to understand the options available.

This chapter is all about contracts and serialization. I'll be describing in detail how to design service contracts, how to work with complex types using data contracts and other serializable types, and how to gain more control over the entire message structure using message contracts. Toward the end of the chapter, I'll also be discussing ways you can interact with raw messages. Before I dive into these core concepts, I'll provide you with a brief overview of the messaging protocols supported by WCF, since those are what define the message format. I'll also provide you with more details on the WSDL document that guides serialization between clients and services.

Messaging Protocols

Regardless of the transport protocol (TCP, named pipes, MSMQ, or HTTP), messages are represented by the runtime in the same way, as a `Message` type from the `System.ServiceModel.Channels` namespace. The `Message` type is essentially a runtime representation of a SOAP message. When serialized, the wire format of the message complies with SOAP 1.1 or 1.2 depending on the binding configuration for the endpoint.

The `Message` type also holds addressing headers, consistent with the WS-Addressing standard. These are serialized with the message if the binding supports addressing. When the service model processes messages, other standards may also come into play to add features such as security and reliability. The service model supplies channels for many of the emerging protocols, usually referred to as WS* (pronounced WS-Star). Through bindings (discussed in Chapter 3), you can enable features that use these protocols. In short, WCF relies on standards to serialize messages; here I'll provide you with an overview in this chapter of the core standards that will be elaborated on throughout this book.

 Keep in mind that you will rarely need to worry about the details of messaging protocols because WCF implements them in the plumbing of the service model.

SOAP

SOAP was introduced in 1999—a short specification that finally made it possible to standardize how messages are exchanged on the wire, using XML at its core to support interoperability. A SOAP message contains message headers and a message body. The basic XML structure for a SOAP message contains a root `Envelope` element with two child elements: an optional `Header` element and a required `Body` element as follows:

```
<Envelope>
  <Header>
    <!-- message headers -->
  </Header>
```

```
<Body>
  <!-- message body elements -->
</Body>
</Envelope>
```

The *message body* is required. It contains data custom to an application. For example, when a client invokes a service operation, a *request message* is sent containing the data required by the operation. For each parameter, a separate XML element is provided within the message body. These elements are ultimately deserialized into the appropriate associated CLR types. If the operation returns a value, or if there are any out parameters, a *response message* is sent containing these values, each wrapped in an XML element. These are deserialized at the client into the appropriate CLR type.

A *message header* contains information that supports communication but is not usually directly tied to the business functionality of the specific service operation. Message headers are a useful way to pass addressing and routing instructions, credentials, message identifiers, and other details that support communications. Many specifications exist that provide standardized headers to accomplish these types of goals.

Message headers are usually handled by the underlying plumbing, while the message body is defined by the application. The serialized format of the SOAP message depends on the version of the SOAP specification being used: SOAP 1.1 or 1.2. SOAP 1.1 is the original specification supported by earlier web service platforms, and SOAP 1.2 is the more commonly used standard today. Consider this service contract with a single operation:

```
[ServiceContract(Namespace = "http://www.thatindigogirl.com/samples/2006/06")]
public interface IRequestReply
{
  [OperationContract]
  bool RequestReply(string param1, int param2, DateTime param3);
}
```

Without adding any fancy protocols for security or reliability, the request message would look like Example 2-1.

Example 2-1. SOAP request message

```
<s:Envelope xmlns:s="http://schemas.xmlsoap.org/soap/envelope/">
  <s:Header>
    <To s:mustUnderstand="1"
xmlns="http://schemas.microsoft.com/ws/2005/05/addressing/none">
http://localhost:8000/Soap11</To>
    <Action s:mustUnderstand="1"
xmlns="http://schemas.microsoft.com/ws/2005/05/addressing/none">
http://www.thatindigogirl.com/samples/2006/06/IRequestReply/RequestReply</Action>
  </s:Header>
  <s:Body>
    <RequestReply xmlns="http://www.thatindigogirl.com/samples/2006/06">
```

Example 2-1. SOAP request message (continued)

```
        <param1>string value</param1>
        <param2>10</param2>
        <param3>2007-02-17T12:13:35.0903315-08:00</param3>
      </RequestReply>
    </s:Body>
</s:Envelope>
```

In the request message, you'll notice the following characteristics:

- The To header indicates the URI of the service endpoint.
- The Action header indicates the URI for the operation being invoked.
- The message body includes a wrapper element named for the operation, RequestReply, which has a child element for each parameter.
- The message body wrapper uses the namespace of the service contract.

The message response for the same operation would look as shown in Example 2-2. In this case, no headers are present, and the message body contains a wrapper named for the operation with the suffix "Response." Inside the wrapper is a child containing the actual return value named for the operation with the suffix "Result."

Example 2-2. SOAP response message

```
<s:Envelope xmlns:s="http://schemas.xmlsoap.org/soap/envelope/">
  <s:Body>
    <RequestReplyResponse xmlns="http://www.thatindigogirl.com/samples/2006/06">
      <RequestReplyResult>true</RequestReplyResult>
    </RequestReplyResponse>
  </s:Body>
</s:Envelope>
```

My point is not to inspect each aspect of the SOAP message format here, but to raise awareness to the contents of a SOAP message so that when I discuss features of WCF that control how messages are serialized, you'll know which aspect of the message I'm referring to.

WS*

SOAP describes a general format for messages. The actual contents of the message header and body are not controlled by the SOAP specification. An application can fully customize what headers it expects and what data the body should include to do meaningful work. Certain common needs are shared, however, across most business implementations of SOAP—the need to communicate securely and reliably at the forefront. That's where *WS** comes in.

WS* is a growing set of standard protocols developed with wide industry backing to handle common messaging needs between applications. The list of WS* protocols is long, but there are a set of standards that are quite well-adopted today across platforms, and a few more that are well on their way. Here are some of the key protocols that I'll be touching on in this book:

WS-Addressing
> Describes a standard set of message headers that describe which operation the message is targeting (To), where the operation should reply to (ReplyTo), which application the message is from (From), and other information that can impact the routing of the message. I'll touch on various addressing headers throughout the book.

WS-MetadataExchange
> Is a protocol for discovering the messaging requirements and policy for a particular service endpoint. SvcUtil uses this protocol to generate WSDL documents from a service description.

WS-Policy
> Is a protocol for describing information about WS* protocol requirements inside the WSDL document or in WS-MetadataExchange operations.

MTOM
> Is an encoding format that is useful for sending large messages over HTTP. I'll discuss this in Chapter 3.

WS-Security, WS-Trust, and WS-SecureConversation
> Are standard protocols for securing message exchanges. I'll discuss these in detail in Chapter 7.

WS-ReliableMessaging
> Is a protocol for improving reliable transfer of messages by providing delivery guarantees. This is discussed in Chapter 6.

WS-AtomicTransaction
> Is a protocol for distributing transactions over HTTP. I'll also discuss this in Chapter 6.

I want to emphasize that each of these sets of protocols are described in quite lengthy documents at the W3C (*www.w3c.org*) or at OASIS (*www.oasis-open.org*). The beauty of WCF is that it hides the plumbing related to these standards so that developers do not have to learn the details. It helps to have a high-level understanding of each protocol, and I will provide this as I touch on each throughout this book.

Service Description

While messaging protocols are responsible for message serialization formats, there must be a way to capture the protocols required to communicate between clients and services. In Chapter 1, you worked with WSDL documents, which describe the requirements of a service, including the operations associated with each endpoint and the protocols used by each endpoint. In this section, I'll discuss the relationship between the service description, message exchange patterns, and WSDL.

ServiceDescription

Services may implement one or more endpoints, each possibly supporting a different set of operations, messaging protocols, message encoding formats, and transport protocols. Collectively, this information about a service is part of the service metadata, as I discussed in Chapter 1. This can also be referred to as the *service description*. In fact, WCF represents this information at runtime as a `ServiceDescription` type from the `System.ServiceModel` namespace.

The `ServiceDescription` type is a runtime representation of all service endpoints and their associated service contracts, the binding configuration that describes protocol support, and local behaviors that affect how the service model processes messages. It is the `ServiceDescription` type that is used to generate the WSDL document, and it also supports dynamic metadata exchange so that clients can discover at runtime what protocols are required to invoke service operations. Recall from Chapter 1 that SvcUtil is used to generate proxies for clients by consuming a WSDL document or using dynamic metadata exchange, which is based on *WS-MetadataExchange* protocol (see Figure 2-1).

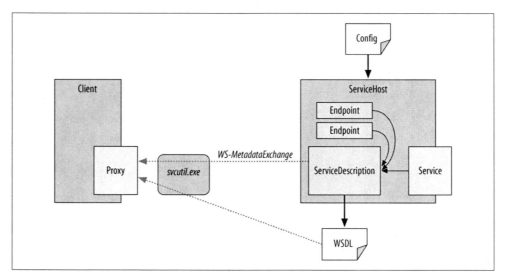

Figure 2-1. SvcUtil can generate proxies from a WSDL document or by using dynamic metadata exchange

WSDL

SOAP protocol defines the basic requirements to allow platforms to process SOAP messages, extracting headers and body elements to perform work. Obviously, to understand the header and body elements, the platform also needs to know the format of those elements. That's where WSDL comes in.

WSDL describes the core messaging requirements for communicating with a service. As you learned in Chapter 1, an XML document describes a service, its available endpoints and associated addresses, the protocols supported by each endpoint, and the list of operations and messages associated with each endpoint. It includes XSD schema describing each message and the contents of the message. While the message is framed in SOAP, WSDL describes the application-specific schema for each header and each body element. In this chapter, I'll be discussing how service contracts and data contracts contribute to the WSDL document.

WSDL is enough to describe application messaging requirements; however, it is not enough to describe other protocol support related to WS*, for example. That's where WS-Policy comes in.

WS-Policy

WS-Policy is an interoperable standard for describing extended protocol requirements, or *policy*, for a particular endpoint. The WS-Policy specification describes how to include policy in the WSDL document either directly or as an attachment (actually, that specification is called *WS-PolicyAttachment*).

While policy does not have an effect on the business messages exchanged between clients and services, it does affect how the plumbing provided by the service model builds and serializes messages. WS-Policy extensions exist for security, transactions, reliable messaging, sessions, and other features that are defined by attributes applied to the service contract or through binding configuration. Most aspects of the binding configuration are shared with clients through the policy section of the WSDL document, enabling clients to build an equivalent channel stack to call services.

 Throughout this book as I discuss bindings (Chapter 3) and other features related to security and reliability, I'll discuss policy-related features.

WS-MetadataExchange

WS-MetadataExchange is a standard protocol that defines how to retrieve some or all of the service description at runtime. This includes retrieving the contents of the entire WSDL document or possibly retrieving specific policy requirements related to security, for example. SvcUtil uses this protocol to generate proxies.

WCF Contracts and Serialization

So far I've talked about the standards behind it all, but in fact WCF hides most of this from the developer by providing a programming interface for designing service contracts and controlling the message format. Application messaging requirements are described by *contracts* in WCF. There are three types of formal contracts that clients and services rely on to control messaging. The *service contract* describes the operations exposed by a particular service endpoint. Each operation, through parameters and return types, defines the format of request and response messages. A *data contract* describes how a complex type is serialized as part of a message. Data contracts are the preferred way to include complex types in a service contract. A *message contract* provides control over the format of the entire SOAP message, including support for custom message headers and individual body elements that can be described by data contracts.

By default, message serialization is handled by the DataContractSerializer. This is a new serializer introduced with WCF that requires all types to opt-in their exact requirements for serialization—in compliance with SOA tenets. The DataContractSerializer can serialize data contracts, message contracts, and other serializable types such as those marked with the SerializableAttribute or those that inherit IXmlSerializable (see Figure 2-2). It is also possible to tell WCF to use the XmlSerializer that ASP.NET web services use (useful only in rare cases). The XmlSerializer provides much less control over serialization in that all public members are serialized. I'll discuss these and other serialization concepts later in this chapter.

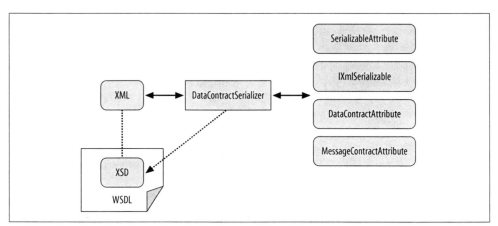

Figure 2-2. The DataContractSerializer can serialize message contracts, data contracts, and other serializable types

As you complete the labs in this chapter, you will practice working with service contracts, data contracts, message contracts, other serializable types, and raw messages. Throughout, I'll provide you with practical design tips, discuss approaches in contract versioning, and teach you how to override default serialization behaviors.

Service Contracts

A *service contract* describes the operations supported by a service, the message exchange pattern they use, and the format of each message. The service contract is also the main driver for generating a service description. A valid WCF service implements at least one service contract. The following attributes play an important role in defining service contracts: ServiceContractAttribute, OperationContractAttribute, and MessageParameterAttribute. Collectively, these attributes provide control over the way messages are formatted.

In this section, the first thing you'll do is complete a lab that exercises each of these attributes. Following the lab, I'll summarize the features of each of these attributes and their roles in service contract design. In the process, I'll also cover other related concepts such as:

- How service contracts map to WSDL elements
- Service contract design
- Operations signatures and messages
- Versioning scenarios

Lab: Designing a Service Contract

In this lab, you will begin with an existing solution that includes three projects: a service, a host, and a client. The solution includes a working implementation of a very simple service contract, and you will edit this implementation to exercise more control over the service contract to control the resulting service description. In the process, you'll also test service contract version tolerance.

Exploring service contract compatibility

In the first part of this lab, you'll modify an existing service contract to use an explicit contract name and namespace while testing compatibility between proxy and service as changes are made.

1. Start by opening the solution for this lab: *<YourLearningWCFPath>\Labs\ Chapter2\ServiceContracts\ServiceContracts.sln*.

2. Test the solution first to see that it works. Compile the solution and run the Host project followed by the WinClient project. From the WinClient application interface, click each button to test the two operations exposed by the service contract: Operation1( ) and Operation2( ).

3. Review how the service you just tested is implemented. Go to the BusinessServices project and open *IServiceA.cs*. Example 2-3 shows the service contract, which defines two operations.

Example 2-3. IServiceA service contract

```
[ServiceContract]
public interface IServiceA
{
  [OperationContract]
  string Operation1();
  [OperationContract]
  string Operation2();
}
```

Now open *ServiceA.cs* in the code window to view the implementation of this contract.

4. Modify the service contract by providing a friendly name for the contract and a namespace to reduce ambiguity. Open *IServiceA.cs* once again and set the Name and Namespace properties of the ServiceContractAttribute, as shown in bold here:

```
[ServiceContract(Name="ServiceAContract",
Namespace = "http://www.thatindigogirl.com/samples/2006/06")]
public interface IServiceA
```

5. Try to test the solution again. This time when you select either button in the WinClient interface, an ActionNotSupportedException is thrown. The error message should look similar to the following:

```
The message with Action 'http://tempuri.org/IServiceA/Operation1' cannot be
processed at the receiver, due to a ContractFilter mismatch at the
EndpointDispatcher. This may be because of either a contract mismatch (mismatched
Actions between sender and receiver) or a binding/security mismatch between the
sender and the receiver.  Check that sender and receiver have the same contract
and the same binding (including security requirements, e.g. Message, Transport,
None).
```

The SOAP action property of a message indicates the operation being invoked at the destination. Changing the namespace at the service causes the service to expect a different SOAP action for each operation. Since the client proxy is still using a service contract with a different namespace, messages from the client are now incompatible with the service.

6. Changing the namespace of the service contract also changes the expected format of messages to the service. To fix this, update the client proxy so that it reflects the namespace change. Go to the WinClient project node and expand the Service References folder. Drill down from *localhost.cs* to *Reference.cs* and open it in the code window.

Modify the definition of IServiceA so that the ServiceContractAttribute uses the name and namespace of the service contract. Add the changes shown in bold here:

```
[System.ServiceModel.ServiceContractAttribute(
Namespace="http://www.thatindigogirl.com/samples/2006/06",
Name="ServiceAContract", ConfigurationName="WinClient.localhost.IServiceA")]
public interface IServiceA
```

You must also update the Action and ReplyAction properties of the OperationContractAttribute for each operation, as shown here:

```
[System.ServiceModel.OperationContractAttribute(
Action="http://www.thatindigogirl.com/samples/2006/06/
ServiceAContract/Operation1",
ReplyAction="http://www.thatindigogirl.com/samples/2006/06/
ServiceAContract/Operation1Response")]
string Operation1( );

[System.ServiceModel.OperationContractAttribute(
Action="http://www.thatindigogirl.com/samples/2006/06/
ServiceAContract/Operation2",
ReplyAction="http://www.thatindigogirl.com/samples/2006/06/
ServiceAContract/Operation2Response")]
string Operation2( );
```

7. Compile and run the solution again and test each operation. This time, no exception is thrown since the messages are once again compatible.

8. Synchronize the client proxy with the service by regenerating the proxy. First, go to the WinClient project and delete the service reference, *localhost*. Now run the Host without debugging and generate a new proxy for WinClient. Go to the WinClient project and add a service reference providing the URI *http://localhost: 8000* and setting the namespace to localhost.

You can also right-click *localhost* and select Update Service Reference, but this operation fails at times depending on the nature of the changes you have made to the service.

9. Close the Host console and try to recompile the solution. This will fail because the proxy type name, formerly ServiceAClient, has changed to reflect the new service contract name, ServiceAContractClient. Open *Form1.cs* in the code window and modify the statement that instantiates the proxy to reflect the changes shown in bold here:

```
localhost.ServiceAContractClient m_proxy = new
WinClient.localhost.ServiceAContractClient( );
```

Verify that you can recompile the solution.

Customizing message parameters

In this section of the lab, you'll modify the service contract operations to control how parameters and return values are serialized using the MessageParameterAttribute. You'll also test the effect on communications between proxy and service when you add and remove operations at the service.

1. Add a new method to the service contract. Open *IServiceA.cs* and add this method signature:

```
[OperationContract]
string NewOperation(string string);
```

2. Implement this new operation on the service type. Open *ServiceA.cs* and add this method to the class:

```
public class ServiceA : IServiceA
{
  // other methods

  public string NewOperation(string s)
  {
    return string.Format("IServiceA.NewOperation( ) invoked with {0}", s);
  }
}
```

3. Try to compile the solution. It won't compile because string is a type and cannot be used as a parameter name.

4. Use the MessageParameterAttribute to control the serialized name of the string parameter. Modify the method signature so that the string parameter name is "s" and supply the name "string" to the MessageParameterAttribute for the parameter:

```
[OperationContract]
string NewOperation([MessageParameter(Name = "string")]string s);
```

5. Try to compile the solution—this time, it works. Run the solution and test Operation1( ) to verify that the addition of a new operation hasn't affected the client.

Modifying service operations and dealing with version tolerance

This part of the lab explores how communication between client and service are affected when the service contract is changed.

1. Let's see what happens when you make a change to an existing operation signature. Open *IServiceA.cs* in the code window and change the signature of Operation1( ) to the following:

```
[OperationContract]
string Operation1(DateTime dt);
```

   Open *ServiceA.cs* and change the implementation as well:

```
string IServiceA.Operation1(DateTime dt)
{
   return string.Format("IServiceA.Operation1( ) invoked at {0}.",
dt);
}
```

2. Compile and run the solution, and test Operation1( ) once again. Surprisingly, there will not be an exception even though the client proxy doesn't share the same signature for Operation1( ). Instead, the DateTime parameter is initialized to its default when the service operation is invoked.

3. Now, remove Operation2( ) from the service contract. Do this by commenting the following lines for the definition of IServiceA:

```
//[OperationContract]
//string Operation2( );
```

4. Test this result by recompiling and running the solution again. From the client, test Operation2( ). This time, an ActionNotSupportedException is thrown since there are no operations on the service contract matching the action header specified by the message.

Now let's look more closely at what you've done in working through this lab.

Mapping Services to WSDL

When a service is hosted, the service model generates a runtime service description that can ultimately be viewed as a WSDL document. For the most part it isn't necessary for you to understand WSDL in depth, but it can be helpful to have a general understanding of the way service contracts, operations, and other service characteristics are mapped to WSDL elements.

The WSDL output in Example 2-4 is representative of the initial sample provided for this lab. Table 2-1 explains how each of the high-level WSDL elements used in this listing is derived from service characteristics.

Example 2-4. Partial view of the WSDL document generated for the initial lab solution

```
1  <?xml version="1.0" encoding="utf-8" ?>
2    <wsdl:definitions name="ServiceA" targetNamespace="http://tempuri.org/"
3  xmlns:tns="http://tempuri.org/" ...>
4    <wsdl:types>
5      <xsd:schema targetNamespace="http://tempuri.org/Imports">
6        <xsd:import schemaLocation="http://localhost:8000/?xsd=xsd0"
7  namespace="http://tempuri.org/" />
```

Example 2-4. Partial view of the WSDL document generated for the initial lab solution

```
 8          <xsd:import schemaLocation="http://localhost:8000/?xsd=xsd1"
 9  namespace="http://schemas.microsoft.com/2003/10/Serialization/" />
10      </xsd:schema>
11    </wsdl:types>
12    <wsdl:message name="IServiceA_Operation1_InputMessage">
13      <wsdl:part name="parameters" element="tns:Operation1" />
14    </wsdl:message>
15    <wsdl:message name="IServiceA_Operation1_OutputMessage">
16      <wsdl:part name="parameters" element="tns:Operation1Response" />
17    </wsdl:message>
18  + <wsdl:message name="IServiceA_Operation2_InputMessage">
19  + <wsdl:message name="IServiceA_Operation2_OutputMessage">
20    <wsdl:portType name="IServiceA">
21      <wsdl:operation name="Operation1">
22        <wsdl:input wsaw:Action="http://tempuri.org/IServiceA/Operation1"
23  message="tns:IServiceA_Operation1_InputMessage" />
24        <wsdl:output wsaw:Action="http://tempuri.org/IServiceA/Operation1Response"
25  message="tns:IServiceA_Operation1_OutputMessage" />
26      </wsdl:operation>
27  +   <wsdl:operation name="Operation2">
28    </wsdl:portType>
29    <wsdl:binding name="BasicHttpBinding_IServiceA" type="tns:IServiceA">
30      <soap:binding transport="http://schemas.xmlsoap.org/soap/http" />
31      <wsdl:operation name="Operation1">
32        <soap:operation soapAction="http://tempuri.org/IServiceA/Operation1"
33  style="document" />
34  +     <wsdl:input>
35  +     <wsdl:output>
36      </wsdl:operation>
37  +   <wsdl:operation name="Operation2">
38    </wsdl:binding>
39    <wsdl:service name="ServiceA">
40      <wsdl:port name="BasicHttpBinding_IServiceA"
41  binding="tns:BasicHttpBinding_IServiceA">
42        <soap:address location="http://localhost:8000/ServiceA" />
43      </wsdl:port>
44    </wsdl:service>
45  </wsdl:definitions>
46
```

Table 2-1. A look at how service characteristics map to high-level WSDL elements

WSDL element	Service characteristic
`<wsdl:definitions>` (at line 2)	Describes the target namespace for the contract, which ultimately is the target namespace for each message.
`<wsdl:service>` (at line 39)	Maps to the service type, ServiceA. Includes nested `<wsdl:port>` elements for each endpoint.
`<wsdl:port>` (at lines 40, 41)	Maps to the service endpoint at the specified address. Also refers to the WSDL binding section.
`<wsdl:binding>` (at line 29)	Describes the transport protocol to reach the endpoint. Also includes a `<wsdl:operation>` element for each operation on the endpoint (based on the service contract).

Table 2-1. A look at how service characteristics map to high-level WSDL elements (continued)

WSDL element	Service characteristic
`<wsdl:portType>` (at line 20)	Describes the messages for each operation in the service contract within a `<wsdl:operation>` element. For request/reply messages, a `<wsdl:input>` and `<wsdl:output>` message will be listed.
`<wsdl:operation>` (at lines 21, 27, 31, 37)	Describes each operation in the service contract. Each operation can have a `<wsdl:input>`, `<wsdl:output>` or `<wsdl:fault>` associated with it. These elements lead to a schema describing the message format for input, output and declared faults. The information to support this schema is derived from operation signatures on the service contract.
`<wsdl:message>` (at lines 12, 15, 18, 19)	Indicates which type describes each message. Types are found in the `<wsdl:types>` section.
`<wsdl:types>` (at line 4)	Either contains or imports the XSD schemas describing each operation message and any other complex types those messages rely on. You'll notice that the `schemaLocation` attribute defines the namespace to which the import refers.

Each service type has an associated service description, thus WSDL. Remember that WSDL documents and their associated XSD schema can be used by SvcUtil to generate client proxies and related configuration. Thus, every piece of information necessary for clients to communicate with a service is contained in the WSDL. The location of each endpoint, the protocols supported by that endpoint, the list of operations for that endpoint, and the messages associated with each operation are all described here.

Every message has an associated schema, so when something does not go as expected you can compare what was sent on the wire with what is expected by the WSDL document. Messages for each operation are described in an imported schema file referred to at line 6 as *http://localhost:8000/?xsd=xsd0*. Consider this operation signature that has no parameters and returns a string:

```
string Operation1();
```

If you navigate to this URI in the browser, you'll see something like the listing shown in Example 2-5.

Example 2-5. Partial view of the XSD schema describing messages for IServiceA

```
<?xml version="1.0" encoding="utf-8" ?>
<xs:schema elementFormDefault="qualified" targetNamespace="http://tempuri.org/"
xmlns:xs="http://www.w3.org/2001/XMLSchema" xmlns:tns="http://tempuri.org/">
  <xs:element name="Operation1">
    <xs:complexType>
      <xs:sequence />
    </xs:complexType>
  </xs:element>
  <xs:element name="Operation1Response">
    <xs:complexType>
      <xs:sequence>
        <xs:element minOccurs="0" name="Operation1Result" nillable="true"
type="xs:string" />
      </xs:sequence>
    </xs:complexType>
```

```
    </xs:element>
+ <xs:element name="Operation2">
</xs:schema>
```

It can also help to look at the WSDL document produced by your services in order to consider naming conventions for the service, its operations and complex types. After all, this is a document that your business partners will consume, so some level of consistency with naming conventions is appropriate.

Designing Service Contracts

By now you already know that the ServiceContractAttribute and OperationContractAttribute are used to define service contracts. Service contracts are any interface or type with the ServiceContractAttribute applied. Operations inside the contract are determined by those methods with the OperationContractAttribute applied. These attributes have several properties that can be used to control how the service description is generated and how messages should be formatted. In this section, I'll provide you with an overview of the capabilities of these attributes and of the MessageParameterAttribute of which this lab makes use.

ServiceContractAttribute

The ServiceContractAttribute is part of the System.ServiceModel namespace primarily used for describing a set of related operations and setting the target namespace for messages. This attribute also has other features that influence message exchange patterns, message security, and whether the service supports sessions. Here is a list of the properties the ServiceContractAttribute exposes:

Name
> Specifies a different name for the contract, instead of using the interface or class type name.

Namespace
> Specifies a target namespace for messages. The default namespace is *http://tempuri.org*.

CallbackContract
> Associates another service contract as a callback contract. This allows clients to receive asynchronous messages from the service. Chapter 3 will discuss asynchronous messages and callbacks.

ProtectionLevel
> Allows you to control how messages to all operations in the contract are protected on the wire—if they are signed and encrypted. This is explored in Chapter 7.

SessionMode
> Determines if sessions are supported by the endpoint exposing this service contract. Sessions are discussed in Chapter 5.

At a minimum, you should always provide a Namespace to disambiguate messages on the wire. In the initial code sample for this lab, a namespace was not provided for the ServiceContractAttribute. Instead, the default namespace, *http://tempuri.org*, is used to serialize messages (indicated by the targetNamespace in Example 2-4). The result is that request and response messages use this namespace as illustrated in Example 2-6.

Example 2-6. Message body for Operation1() request and response

```
// Request message body
<s:Body>
  <Operation1 xmlns="http://tempuri.org/"></Operation1>
</s:Body>

// Response message body
<s:Body>
  <Operation1Response xmlns="http://tempuri.org/">
    <Operation1Result>IServiceA.Operation1() invoked.</Operation1Result>
  </Operation1Response>
</s:Body>
```

The namespace can be any unique name, usually in the form of an URI or URN, but web services usually lean toward a corporate or base application URI, followed by the year, month, and any other service or application naming conventions. For example, I use the following namespace for samples in this book:

```
[ServiceContract(Namespace = "http://www.thatindigogirl.com/samples/2006/06")]
public interface IServiceA
```

You can also provide a friendly name for the service contract. This is more of a "nice to have" feature; the important thing is to be consistent across all service contracts. If you don't customize service contract names, CLR interface names will be used in the WSDL contract as shown by this portType from Example 2-4:

```
<wsdl:portType name="IServiceA">
```

Being explicit in the contract does have merit. It makes it clear to developers which name is published in the service description and prevents developers from accidentally causing a breaking change to the service description if they refactor CLR types. This lab uses ServiceAContract as the contract name:

```
[ServiceContract(Name="ServiceAContract"
Namespace="http://www.thatindigogirl.com/samples/2006/06")]
public interface IServiceA
```

As the lab illustrates, when you change the contract name, it affects the name of client proxies generated by SvcUtil. If the contract name is IServiceA, the client proxy type is named ServiceAClient. SvcUtil drops the "I" prefix for you on the client side (other platform tools may not do this). If the contract is renamed to ServiceAContract, the proxy type becomes ServiceAContractClient.

OperationContractAttribute

The OperationContractAttribute, also part of System.ServiceModel, is used to promote methods to service operations so that they can be included in the service description. Simply applying this attribute to a method is good enough to opt-in to the contract; however, there are other features of the attribute that influence how messages are exchanged and which features are supported by the operation.

Name
> Specifies a different name for the operation, instead of using the method name.

Action
> Controls the action header for messages to this operation.

ReplyAction
> Controls the action header for response messages from this operation.

IsOneWay
> Indicates whether the operation is one-way and has no reply. When operations are one-way, ReplyAction is not supported.

ProtectionLevel
> Allows you to control how messages to this particular operation are protected on the wire. Setting this property per operation overrides the service contract setting for ProtectionLevel.

IsInitiating
> Indicates whether the operation can be used to initiate a session. Sessions are discussed in Chapter 4.

IsTerminating
> Indicates whether the operation terminates a session.

Setting the Name property for an operation is not required, but like with the ServiceContractAttribute, it does make it clear to developers which name is published in the service description. If you follow my recommendation in Chapter 1 that service contracts are not coupled to business interfaces, there is less need to consciously separate what names are used in the service description versus which names are used in code. You can adopt an approach that service contracts are immutable and developers can never change them, and provide operation names appropriate for the service description from the start.

As for Action and ReplyAction, these are properties that derive from the service contract namespace and the operation name—you need not specify an explicit value. Of course, when SvcUtil generates the client proxy, it populates these properties explicitly, based on the service description:

```
[System.ServiceModel.OperationContractAttribute(Action=
"http://www.thatindigogirl.com/samples/2006/06/ServiceAContract/Operation1",
ReplyAction="http://www.thatindigogirl.com/samples/2006/06/
ServiceAContract/Operation1Response")]
string Operation1();
```

Action is generated by concatenating the service contract namespace with the service contract friendly name and the operation name. The ReplyAction appends "Response" to this. If you set your target namespace appropriately, and use consistent naming conventions for the service contract and each operation, the generated value should suffice. Sometimes, you need to explicitly set these values when you are building a service contract based on a predefined specification. In this case, there may be a WSDL document that specifies the action header required for incoming and outgoing messages. Example 2-7 shows the request and response message for Operation1( ), with the action header shown in bold.

Example 2-7. Request and response messages for Operation1()

```
// Request message
<s:Envelope xmlns:s="http://schemas.xmlsoap.org/soap/envelope/">
  <s:Header>
    <To s:mustUnderstand="1"
xmlns="http://schemas.microsoft.com/ws/2005/05/addressing/none">
http://localhost:8000/ServiceA</To>
    <Action s:mustUnderstand="1"
xmlns="http://schemas.microsoft.com/ws/2005/05/addressing/none">
http://www.thatindigogirl.com/samples/2006/06/ServiceAContract/Operation1</Action>
  </s:Header>
  <s:Body>
    <Operation1 xmlns="http://www.thatindigogirl.com/samples/2006/06"></Operation1>
  </s:Body>
</s:Envelope>

// Response message
<s:Envelope xmlns:s="http://schemas.xmlsoap.org/soap/envelope/">
  <s:Header>
    <Action s:mustUnderstand="1"
xmlns="http://schemas.microsoft.com/ws/2005/05/addressing/none">
http://www.thatindigogirl.com/samples/2006/06/ServiceAContract/Operation1Response
    </Action>
  </s:Header>
  <s:Body>
    <Operation1Response xmlns="http://www.thatindigogirl.com/samples/2006/06">
      <Operation1Result>IServiceA.Operation1( ) invoked.</Operation1Result>
    </Operation1Response>
  </s:Body>
</s:Envelope>
```

When the action header for incoming messages does not match any operation descriptions at the endpoint, the channel listener at the service cannot process the request. That's because by default, the service model expects the action header to exactly match an operation in the contract.

 Services have an address filtering behavior that determines how action headers are evaluated when messages arrive to client and service channels. Later in this chapter, I'll show you how to control the address filter mode for an advanced scenario.

MessageParameterAttribute

The MessageParameterAttribute, part of System.ServiceModel, is used to control the name of parameter and return values in the service description. This attribute has only one property, the Name property. In the operation signature, parameters become part of the request message body. Each parameter is serialized to an element named for the parameter name. The response is serialized to an element named for the operation name with "Response" appended. Consider this operation signature:

```
[OperationContract]
string NewOperation(string s);
```

Example 2-8 shows what the resulting message body looks like for the request and response message.

Example 2-8. Message body for NewOperation() request and response

```
// Request message body
<s:Body>
  <NewOperation xmlns="http://www.thatindigogirl.com/samples/2006/06">
    <s>hello</s>
  </NewOperation>
</s:Body>

// Response message body
<s:Body>
  <NewOperationResponse xmlns="http://www.thatindigogirl.com/samples/2006/06">
    <NewOperationResult>IServiceA.NewOperation() invoked with </NewOperationResult>
  </NewOperationResponse>
</s:Body>
```

You can apply the MessageParameterAttribute to control serialization. The following code applies this attribute to parameters and return values:

```
// Operation signature
[OperationContract]
[return: MessageParameter(Name = "responseString")]
string NewOperation([MessageParameter(Name = "string")]string s);
```

This attribute can be particularly useful when you want to use a keyword or type name in the resulting XSD schema that describes an incoming message. Likewise, you can control the XML element name for the return value in a response message. Example 2-9 shows what the resulting messages look like for NewOperation() after applying the attribute.

Example 2-9. Request and response messages after applying the MessageParameterAttribute

```
//Request SOAP body
<s:Body>
  <NewOperation xmlns="http://www.thatindigogirl.com/samples/2006/06">
    <string>hello</string>
  </NewOperation>
</s:Body>
```

```
//Reply SOAP body
<s:Body>
  <NewOperationResponse xmlns="http://www.thatindigogirl.com/samples/2006/06">
    <responseString>IServiceA.NewOperation( ) invoked with hello</responseString>
  </NewOperationResponse>
</s:Body>
```

As with keywords and type names, you may also find `MessageParameterAttribute` useful for standardizing on XML element naming conventions separate from CLR naming conventions. For example, you may use camel case for parameter names and prefer Pascal case for XML.

Versioning Service Contracts

The previous section described how to design service contracts using attributes to control the resulting service description. If any changes are made to the service contract after the first version has been published, it is important that those changes don't impact existing clients. This lab illustrates that the service contracts are version tolerant by default. Table 2-2 summarizes some possible changes to a service contract and the affect it has on existing clients, if any.

Table 2-2. Service contract changes and their impact on existing clients

Service contract changes	Impact on existing clients
Adding new parameters to an operation signature	Client unaffected. New parameters are initialized to default values at the service.
Removing parameters from an operation signature	Client unaffected. Superfluous parameters passed by clients are ignored, and the data is lost at the service.
Modifying parameter types	An exception will occur if the incoming type from the client cannot be converted to the parameter data type.
Modifying return value types	An exception will occur if the return value from the service cannot be converted to the expected data type in the client version of the operation signature.
Adding new operations	Client unaffected. The client will not invoke operations about which it knows nothing.
Removing operations	An exception will occur. Messages sent by the client to the service are considered to be using an unknown action header.

The bulk of these changes have no direct affect on clients, although the results may be undesirable. The forgiving nature of the service model can be a blessing or a curse depending on how you look at it. The upside is that developers can make changes without impacting existing clients. For example, you can add new operations, add new parameters, decide you no longer care about certain parameters—and preexisting clients can still call the service successfully. Here are some downsides:

- You can unwittingly lose information passed by the client.
- Missing data from the client may not be detected.
- Type conversions may work, yet the data is semantically invalid.

You can remove the risks of these unexpected results by using data contracts as message parameters and return types. I'll discuss data contracts in the next section.

Of course, you are entitled to come up with your own strategy for version tolerance, but I recommend that if the implementation semantics of the service contract have changed or if new clients are to be given additional features via extended parameters or new operations, you should version the service contract, rather than accepting version tolerance.

To properly version a service contract you should provide a new contract and modify the namespace specified in the `ServiceContractAttribute`. To version the namespace, you can supply a new value for the year and month if you follow the naming conventions I've recommended. In the next two sections, I'll compare two versioning approaches.

Versioning with contract inheritance

One likely scenario is that you will add new operations without changing the existing service contract. You may want to support these new operations at the same endpoint, though. You can achieve this by creating a new contract that inherits the old contract, adding new operations to the new one. Consider the contract shown in Example 2-10 as the first published version of the service contract.

Example 2-10. Version 1 of the contract, IServiceA

```
[ServiceContract(Name="ServiceAContract",
Namespace = "http://www.thatindigogirl.com/samples/2006/06")]
public interface IServiceA
{
  [OperationContract]
  string Operation1();
  [OperationContract]
  string Operation2();
}
```

The endpoint configuration for the service implementing the contract might look like:

```
<endpoint address="ServiceA" contract="BusinessServiceContracts.IServiceA"
binding="basicHttpBinding" />
```

When new operations are added to the service to extend its features, you may want to expose the same endpoint to old and new clients while still somehow tracking the contract version related to new features. If you extend the original service contract, you can add operations under a new namespace, as shown in Example 2-11.

Example 2-11. Version 2 of the contract, IServiceA2

```
[ServiceContract(Name="ServiceAContract",
Namespace = "http://www.thatindigogirl.com/samples/2006/08")]
public interface IServiceA2:IServiceA
{
  [OperationContract]
```

Example 2-11. Version 2 of the contract, IServiceA2 (continued)

```
  string Operation3( );
}
```

Note the service contract name is the same, but the namespace has changed. The service type can implement IServiceA2 and it will be able to expose the original operations with their original namespace, while exposing the new operation with the versioned namespace. As such, original clients can hit the same endpoint without impact, while new clients who download the metadata when version 2 is available, can access all operations.

This scenario does not address the following:

- You can't modify existing operations with contract inheritance. Only new operations are added.

- You can't differentiate old clients from new clients because they hit the same endpoint.

The next section will discuss an alternative that addresses these issues.

 A sample illustrating this versioning scenario can be found at *<YourLearningWCFPath>\Samples\ServiceContracts\ ServiceContractVersioning_Inheritance.*

Versioning with separate contracts

A stricter approach to versioning would be to version the entire contract and expose a new endpoint for new clients. In this case, version 2 of the contract might look like Example 2-12.

Example 2-12. Version 2 of the contract, IServiceA2

```
[ServiceContract(Name="ServiceAContract",
Namespace = "http://www.thatindigogirl.com/samples/2006/08")]
public interface IServiceA2
{
  [OperationContract]
  string Operation1( );
  [OperationContract]
  string Operation2( );
  [OperationContract]
  string Operation3( );
}
```

In this case, all operations are defined even if they are not changed. This way, they all gain the new namespace to distinguish calls to version 1 endpoints. In order to provide a unique WSDL containing only one or the other contract, a unique service type must be created to implement the new contract. Both versions of the service can still share implementation behind the scenes.

With this implementation the following restrictions apply:

- You can differentiate old and new clients by service entry point.
- You can modify existing operations in the new interface (not recommended; you should really provide new operation names).
- New clients cannot send messages to the original endpoint.
- Old clients cannot send messages to the new endpoint.

 A sample illustrating this versioning scenario can be found at *<YourLearningWCFPath>\Samples\ServiceContracts\ ServiceContractVersioning_NoInheritance.*

Strict versus non-strict versioning

To summarize the discussion of service contract versioning, Figures 2-3 and 2-4 illustrate the decision flow for non-strict and strict versioning policy, respectively.

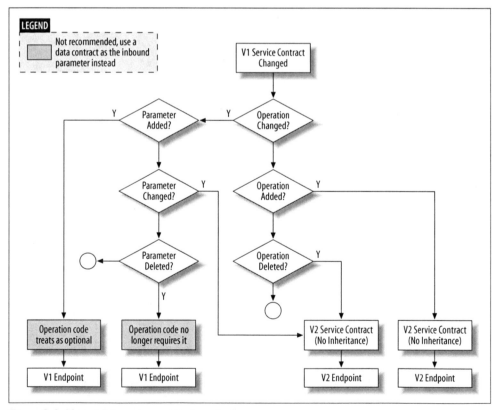

Figure 2-3. Non-strict service contract versioning

Non-strict versioning allows changes to service contracts that do not break existing clients. This means you can add or remove parameters without versioning the service

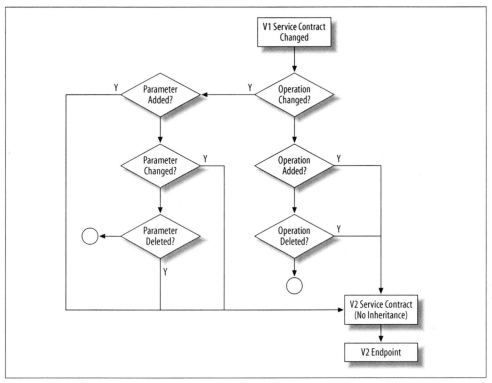

Figure 2-4. Strict service contract versioning

contract. The implementation code may need to accommodate how to handle version 1 and version 2 clients. Though possible, the idea of operation signature changes can be very difficult to track, for example adding and removing parameters.

 Using a data contract as the service operation parameter at least allows for explicitly required and nonrequired parameters (discussed in the upcoming "Data Contracts" section).

With strict service contract versioning, any change to an operation leads to a new service contract. A new endpoint is always provided to ensure version 2 clients can be differentiated from version 1 clients.

Data Contracts

A *data contract* describes how CLR types map to XSD schema definitions. Data contracts are the preferred way to enable serialization of complex types included in operation signatures as parameters or return values. You create a data contract by applying the DataContractAttribute to a type. To include members in serialization, you decorate them with the DataMemberAttribute; this is an opt-in process that has nothing to do with visibility of members (public, protected, private). By default, serialization is handled by the DataContractSerializer, a new serializer for WCF that succeeds the XmlSerializer used for earlier technologies such as ASMX.

In this section, you will become acquainted with the key features of data contracts and common serialization practices, including the following:

- How to apply data contract attributes to exercise control over type serialization
- Version tolerance and data contract versioning techniques
- Implementing IExtensibleDataObject to support version tolerance
- How to work with polymorphic types in the service contract
- How enumerations, arrays, and collections are serialized

First you'll complete a lab that illustrates many of these scenarios, and then I'll explain the related attributes and features in greater detail.

Lab: Working with Data Contracts

For this lab you will modify a preexisting type, turning it into a data contract so that it can be included in the service contract. Using the DataContractAttribute and the DataMemberAttribute, you will control type serialization through the DataContractSerializer. You'll also test data contract version tolerance and implement the IExtensibleData interface in support of versioning.

Creating a data contract

In this part of the lab, you'll turn a complex type into a data contract so that it can be included in a service contract, and then take a look at the XSD schema produced for the type in the WSDL document.

1. Open the startup solution for this lab: *<YourLearningWCFPath>\Labs\Chapter2\ DataContracts\DataContracts.sln*. This solution includes the following projects:

ContentTypes
> A class library that contains a LinkItem type used by the service. LinkItem is a custom type that holds a title, description, URL and other details that can be associated with events, articles, photos, files, and so forth. In this example, LinkItem is used to hold information about a gig (or event) for a band.

GigManager
> A class library containing the service contract and service type. The service contract exposes operations to save a LinkItem, and retrieve the saved LinkItem. This example uses session to save the item. See Chapter 5 for more on sessions.

Host
> A console application for hosting the service.

`GigEntry`

A Windows client application that presents an interface for users to create and save a gig entry and retrieve the saved entry.

2. Try to run the solution at first. From Visual Studio, press F5 to run the `Host` and the `GigEntry` client application.

An `InvalidDataContractException` will be thrown when the `ServiceHost` attempts to initialize. The error message indicates that the type `ContentTypes.LinkItem` cannot be serialized.

3. Review the service contract for the solution. Go to the `GigManager` project and open *GigManagerService.cs*. The service contract is shown in Example 2-13.

The `ContentTypes.LinkItem` type is included in both operation signatures.

Example 2-13. IGigManagerService service contract

```
[ServiceContract(Name = "GigManagerServiceContract",
Namespace = "http://www.thatindigogirl.com/samples/2006/06",
SessionMode = SessionMode.Required)]
public interface IGigManagerService
{
  [OperationContract]
  void SaveGig(LinkItem item);

  [OperationContract]
  LinkItem GetGig();
}
```

4. You are going to modify the `LinkItem` type to make it a valid data contract that can be included in the service contract. Go to the `ContentTypes` project and add a reference to the `System.Runtime.Serialization` assembly. Next, open *LinkItem.cs* and apply the `DataContractAttribute` to the class definition, and apply the `DataMemberAttribute` to each private field so that they are included in the serialized type definition. Add a using statement for `System.Runtime.Serialization` as well. The resulting type should appear as shown in Example 2-14.

Example 2-14. LinkItem as a data contract

```
using System.Runtime.Serialization;

[DataContract]
public class LinkItem
{
  [DataMember]
  private long m_id;
  [DataMember]
  private string m_title;
  [DataMember]
  private string m_description;
  [DataMember]
  private DateTime m_dateStart;
```

Example 2-14. LinkItem as a data contract (continued)

```
[DataMember]
private DateTime m_dateEnd;
[DataMember]
private string m_url;

// properties
}
```

5. Compile the solution and attempt to run the host once again. This time you won't see an exception because LinkItem is now a data contract.

6. View the service description in the browser; you want to see the XSD schema representation of the LinkItem data contract. Browse to the following address: *http://localhost:8000* and click the *?wsdl* link to navigate to the service description. This will generate the service description so that you can browse to the following address: *http://localhost:8000/?xsd=xsd2*. You should see a schema like the one shown in Example 2-15.

Example 2-15. Schema generated for the LinkItem data contract

```
<?xml version="1.0" encoding="utf-8" ?>
<xs:schema elementFormDefault="qualified"
targetNamespace="http://schemas.datacontract.org/2004/07/ContentTypes"
xmlns:xs="http://www.w3.org/2001/XMLSchema"
xmlns:tns="http://schemas.datacontract.org/2004/07/ContentTypes">
  <xs:complexType name="LinkItem">
    <xs:sequence>
      <xs:element minOccurs="0" name="m_dateEnd" type="xs:dateTime" />
      <xs:element minOccurs="0" name="m_dateStart" type="xs:dateTime" />
      <xs:element minOccurs="0" name="m_description" nillable="true"
type="xs:string" />
      <xs:element minOccurs="0" name="m_id" type="xs:long" />
      <xs:element minOccurs="0" name="m_title" nillable="true" type="xs:string" />
      <xs:element minOccurs="0" name="m_url" nillable="true" type="xs:string" />
    </xs:sequence>
  </xs:complexType>
  <xs:element name="LinkItem" nillable="true" type="tns:LinkItem" />
</xs:schema>
```

Notice that the naming convention for each data member matches the field name in the type definition. In addition, the order of each element in the schema sequence is alphabetical, as opposed to the order of appearance in the type definition. Another thing to note is that the namespace for the type does not match the service contract target namespace; instead, it uses the domain *shemas.datacontract.org*.

> Other .NET serialization techniques are dependent on the reflection order of types. This can introduce problems when developers inadvertently reorder the class definition, not realizing it can cause incompatibilities.

Customizing data contract serialization

Now the LinkItem type is a valid data contract but you may want to provide a namespace consistent with the namespace in your service contract, indicating that this type belongs to your application. Furthermore, you may want to provide more formal names for each of the data members. Another thing you may want to control is the order in which members appear in the schema—recall that the default behavior is to present them in alphabetical order. In this section, you'll customize the data contract to address these issues.

1. Modify the LinkItem type definition to provide a proper namespace, friendly names for each data member, and appropriate order for data members in the schema. Start by supplying a Namespace value for the DataContractAttribute. Also provide values for the following DataMemberAttribute properties: Name, IsRequired, and Order. Example 2-16 provides you with the values to use for each attribute. Pay attention to the IsRequired property for each. It will be significant later in the lab.

Example 2-16. Customizing serialization with DataContractAttribute and DataMemberAttribute

```
[DataContract(Namespace="http://schemas.thatindigogirl.com/samples/2006/06")]
public class LinkItem
{
  [DataMember(Name = "Id", IsRequired = false, Order = 0)]
  private long m_id;
  [DataMember(Name = "Title", IsRequired = true, Order = 1)]
  private string m_title;
  [DataMember(Name = "Description", IsRequired = true, Order = 2)]
  private string m_description;
  [DataMember(Name = "DateStart", IsRequired = true, Order = 3)]
  private DateTime m_dateStart;
  [DataMember(Name = "DateEnd", IsRequired = false, Order = 4)]
  private DateTime m_dateEnd;
  [DataMember(Name = "Url", IsRequired = false, Order = 5)]
  private string m_url;

  // Properties
}
```

2. Compile the host and run it without debugging. Return to the browser and review the new LinkItem schema by browsing to *http://localhost:8000/?xsd=xsd2* (be sure to refresh). The schema should now look like the one shown in Example 2-17.

Example 2-17. Schema generated for the modified LinkItem data contract

```
<?xml version="1.0" encoding="utf-8" ?>
  <xs:schema elementFormDefault="qualified"
targetNamespace="http://schemas.thatindigogirl.com/samples/2006/06"
xmlns:xs="http://www.w3.org/2001/XMLSchema"
xmlns:tns="http://schemas.thatindigogirl.com/samples/2006/06">
```

```
<xs:complexType name="LinkItem">
  <xs:sequence>
    <xs:element minOccurs="0" name="Id" type="xs:long" />
    <xs:element name="Title" nillable="true" type="xs:string" />
    <xs:element name="Description" nillable="true" type="xs:string" />
    <xs:element name="DateStart" type="xs:dateTime" />
    <xs:element minOccurs="0" name="DateEnd" type="xs:dateTime" />
    <xs:element minOccurs="0" name="Url" nillable="true" type="xs:string" />
  </xs:sequence>
</xs:complexType>
<xs:element name="LinkItem" nillable="true" type="tns:LinkItem" />
</xs:schema>
```

Now the elements in the schema use the formal property name and are pre-sented in the order specified by each DataMemberAttribute. Required and optional members also have an affect on the minOccurs schema attribute; required elements use the implicit value for minOccurs, which is 1.

Leave the host running as you move to the next step in the lab.

Consuming data contracts at the client

Now it's time to add some code to the client application to save and retrieve gig information using the LinkItem type. In this section of the lab, you'll see how SvcUtil generates data contracts for complex types exposed at the service.

1. Start by generating a proxy for the client. Go to the GigEntry project and add a service reference supplying the base address for the GigManagerService: *http://localhost:8000*. Use the namespace localhost.

2. Open *GigInfoForm.cs* in the code window and add the following code beneath the GigInfoForm definition to construct the proxy:

   ```
   public partial class GigInfoForm : Form
   {
      localhost.GigManagerServiceContractClient m_proxy = new
      GigEntry.localhost.GigManagerServiceContractClient( );

      // other code
   }
   ```

   Find the cmdSave_Click( ) event and add code to create a LinkItem instance that will hold gig information input by the user. Example 2-18 shows the code to initialize the LinkItem. You must also add the using statement for GigEntry.localhost.

Example 2-18. Code to save a LinkItem

```
using GigEntry.localhost;

private void cmdSave_Click(object sender, EventArgs e)
{
  LinkItem item = new LinkItem( );
```

Example 2-18. Code to save a LinkItem (continued)

```
    item.Id = int.Parse(this.txtId.Text);
    item.Title = this.txtTitle.Text;
    item.Description = this.txtDescription.Text;
    item.DateStart= this.dtpStart.Value;
    item.DateEnd= this.dtpEnd.Value;
    item.Url= this.txtUrl.Text;

    m_proxy.SaveGig(item);
}
```

3. Now add code to the cmdGet_Click( ) event handler to retrieve the saved LinkItem storing gig information. This code is shown in Example 2-19.

Example 2-19. Code to retrieve a previously saved LinkItem

```
private void cmdGet_Click(object sender, EventArgs e)
{
  LinkItem item = m_proxy.GetGig( );
  if (item != null)
  {
    this.txtId.Text = item.Id.ToString( );
    this.txtTitle.Text = item.Title;
    this.txtDescription.Text = item.Description;

    if (item.DateStart != DateTime.MinValue)
      this.dtpStart.Value = item.DateStart;
    if (item.DateEnd != DateTime.MinValue)
      this.dtpEnd.Value = item.DateEnd;

    this.txtUrl.Text = item.Url;
  }
}
```

4. Now you are ready to test the solution. Compile the solution and run both the Host and GigEntry client application. The GigEntry client application is prepopulated with some default values in the user interface (see Figure 2-5).

   Select Save to populate a LinkItem with gig information and pass it to the SaveGig( ) service operation. Clear some text from the description and select Get to retrieve the LinkItem you previously saved.

At this point, you have turned the LinkItem complex type into a data contract, exposed this type as part of the service description, and generated a client proxy to consume operations that rely on the LinkItem type. To developers, the client code works directly with the LinkItem. In fact, the service model relies on a client-side version of the data contract to handle serialization. If you open the proxy, you'll see a copy of the LinkItem data contract. I'll discuss this further after you complete the lab.

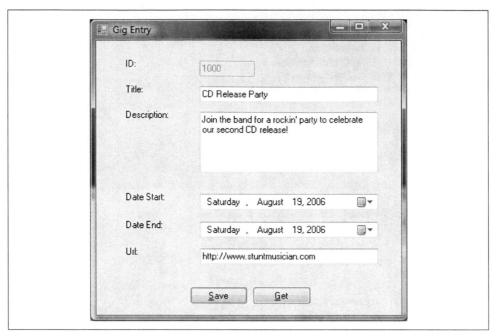

Figure 2-5. GigEntry client user interface

Exploring version tolerance

In this section, of the lab you'll play with some data contract versioning scenarios. You'll add and remove items from the contract, and you'll see what the limitations are on adding new parameters.

1. To begin with, remove one of the data members from the LinkItem data contract. Open *LinkItem.cs* and comment the DataMemberAttribute for m_url:

   ```
   //[DataMember(Name = "Url", IsRequired = false, Order = 5)]
   private string m_url;
   ```

   Compile and run the solution again and test the impact of this change. In the GigEntry interface select Save, then select Get. The URL textbox will be cleared because the value was lost at the service.

2. Change the LinkItem type so that it preserves unknown data elements provided by the client. Modify the LinkItem class definition to inherit IExtensibleDataObject. Implement the interface by adding the new ExtensionData member and property accessor shown in Example 2-20.

Example 2-20. Implementing IExtensibleDataObject

```
public class LinkItem: IExtensibleDataObject
{
  private ExtensionDataObject m_extensionDataObject;
```

Example 2-20. Implementing IExtensibleDataObject (continued)

```
  public ExtensionDataObject ExtensionData
  {
    get {return m_extensionDataObject; }
    set { m_extensionDataObject = value; }
  }
}
```

Test the result of this change by compiling and running the solution once again. From the GigEntry interface select Save. Clear the URL textbox and select Get. This time, the URL you originally saved is returned.

3. Now add a new enum field to the data contract. Open *LinkItem.cs* and add the enumeration defined in Example 2-21 to the ContentTypes namespace.

Example 2-21. Definition for LinkItemCategories

```
[DataContract(Namespace="http://schemas.thatindigogirl.com/samples/2006/06")]
public enum LinkItemCategories
{
  [EnumMember]
  Gig,
  [EnumMember]
  MP3,
  [EnumMember]
  Photo
}
```

Add the following required data member named LinkItemCategories to the LinkItem definition:

```
[DataMember(Name = "Category", IsRequired = true, Order = 6)]
public LinkItemCategories m_category;
```

Compile and run the solution again. From the GigEntry interface, select Save; this time a FaultException is thrown indicating an error while deserializing the message. The error indicates that a different element was expected, which essentially means an expected field is missing or out of order.

4. Change the definition so that the LinkItemCategories data member is no longer required:

```
[DataMember(Name = "Category", IsRequired = false, Order = 6)]
public LinkItemCategories m_category;
```

Compile and run the solution, executing the same test. This time there won't be an exception because the new data member, unknown to the client proxy, is no longer required.

Let's take a closer look at the attributes and features used in this lab.

Mapping Data Contracts to XSD Schema

Data contracts included in service contracts become part of the service description and thus the WSDL document. For each data contract included a schema is generated, and this schema is referenced by the operation messages that rely on the type. In an operation signature that has multiple parameters and a return value, each may be a distinct data contract represented as individual schema.

Example 2-22 illustrates a schema generated for the LinkItem type (repeated from the lab). This schema describes the following:

- The target namespace of the serialized type. Messages that include a serialized LinkItem will use this namespace to disambiguate from other LinkItem types if they exist.

- The definition of the type. In the case of the LinkItem, the outer element name is <LinkItem> and it contains a sequence of child elements.

- The expected name for each child element.

- The data type of each child element. Examples of schema types used in this schema are string, long, and dateTime.

- If the element is required or not as indicated by the minOccurs attribute. If minOccurs is omitted, the implied value is 1. If minOccurs is 0, the element may be omitted and the serialized type will still be valid against the schema.

- If the element can be empty or not as indicated by the nillable attribute. If nillable is set to false, the element cannot be passed without contents.

- The layout order of each child element.

Example 2-22. LinkItem schema

```
<?xml version="1.0" encoding="utf-8" ?>
  <xs:schema elementFormDefault="qualified"
targetNamespace="http://schemas.thatindigogirl.com/samples/2006/06"
xmlns:xs="http://www.w3.org/2001/XMLSchema"
xmlns:tns="http://schemas.thatindigogirl.com/samples/2006/06">
  <xs:complexType name="LinkItem">
    <xs:sequence>
      <xs:element minOccurs="0" name="Id" type="xs:long" />
      <xs:element name="Title" nillable="true" type="xs:string" />
      <xs:element name="Description" nillable="true" type="xs:string" />
      <xs:element name="DateStart" type="xs:dateTime" />
      <xs:element minOccurs="0" name="DateEnd" type="xs:dateTime" />
      <xs:element minOccurs="0" name="Url" nillable="true" type="xs:string" />
    </xs:sequence>
  </xs:complexType>
  <xs:element name="LinkItem" nillable="true" type="tns:LinkItem" />
</xs:schema>
```

Schema can also represent hierarchical relationships in the event a data contract inherits other base data contracts. Each data contract would still have its own schema, but the inheritance hierarchy is preserved. Collections, dictionaries, and arrays are all represented in schema as arrays.

The WSDL document thus carries not only all the information about endpoints, protocols, and operations, it also includes schema for each complex type used by each operation. That's how SvcUtil is able to reconstruct data contracts during proxy generation. Although the resulting types may not look exactly like those at the service, the reverse-engineered types will successfully be serialized into a format that the service can deserialize to reconstruct appropriate CLR types.

In some cases, you may be presented with a preexisting schema that should be used in your service contracts. You can use SvcUtil to generate data contracts for this schema in the same way you use SvcUtil to generate a proxy for the client.

Designing Data Contracts

As the lab illustrates, to create a data contract you apply DataContractAttribute to your custom types and apply the DataMemberAttribute to each field or property you want to include in serialization. This opt-in approach forces developers to consider what information should be transferred between clients and services. The service model uses the DataContractSerializer to convert between data contracts and schema. Any data contracts included in service operations are included in the service description. Thus, proxy generation can generate copies of those types for client use.

DataContractAttribute and DataMemberAttribute each have properties that help you control the schema generated for a complex type. There are also other attributes that support enumerations and collections, specifically. They are the EnumMemberAttribute and the CollectionDataContractAttribute, respectively. In this section I'll talk about each of these attributes and their relevance to serialization.

DataContractAttribute

The DataContractAttribute is part of the System.Runtime.Serialization namespace. As discussed earlier, it is used to turn complex types into data contracts to support service model serialization. This attribute has only two properties:

Name

> Controls the complex type name generated for the schema. By default the CLR type name is used.

Namespace

> Sets the target namespace for the schema. This defaults to *http://schemas.datacontract.org/2004/07/[CLR namespace]*. The CLR namespace is the namespace in which the complex type is defined.

Setting each of these properties can be important since the desired schema conventions may not align with CLR naming conventions developers use.

At a minimum, you should provide a value for Namespace. By default, the namespace used for data contracts uses the prefix *http://schemas.datacontract.org/2004/07*. Like with the target namespace for the service, complex types described in schema should have a namespace that relates the type to your specific company or application. This can also help to resolve ambiguities if other types are used with the same name. A common convention in web service specifications is to take the target namespace for the service and replace "www" (for example) with "schemas." The lab illustrates this pattern:

```
[DataContract(Namespace="http://schemas.thatindigogirl.com/samples/2006/06")]
```

DataMemberAttribute

The DataMemberAttribute is also part of the System.Runtime.Serialization namespace. This attribute is used to opt-in the field or properties to be included in serialization. This attribute provides several properties for controlling the resulting schema generated for a complex type:

Name

Controls the schema element name generated for the field or property. The default behavior is to use the field or property name as defined in the CLR type.

IsRequired

Controls the minOccurs attribute for the schema element. By default, all elements are optional (minOccurs=0).

Order

Controls the order of each element in the schema. By default, nonordered data members appear alphabetically, followed by any ordered elements.

EmitDefaultValue

Controls if default values will be included in serialization. By default, all data members are serialized. If this property is set to false, any member that is set to the default value for its type (null reference types, for example) will not be serialized. This can cause problems if IsRequired is set to true.

By default all data members are ordered alphabetically, they carry the name of the associated field or property, and they become nonrequired schema elements. In this section, I'll explain how to control these characteristics.

You can apply the DataMemberAttribute to a field or property definition regardless of visibility (public, protected, private). Applying the DataMemberAttribute to properties enables you to serialize values that may not have field storage (they may be dynamically calculated at runtime). In either case, this attribute explicitly includes the field or property in the data contract. It can be confusing if you mix the application of this attribute among fields and properties, so I recommend that you generate property accessors for all fields (public, protected, private) so that you can apply the attribute to properties instead of fields. If you name your properties in such a way that they also fit naming conventions for the schema, you needn't set the Name property of this attribute.

 If you apply the DataMemberAttribute to both property and its associated field, you'll end up with duplicate members in the schema.

By default, data members are not required. That means if the client fails to supply a value, the complex type will be initialized with defaults for those members. If you require certain fields to operate, you should set the IsRequired property to true. IsRequired affects the minOccurs attribute for the associated element in the schema. If messages arrive with missing required elements the service model throws an exception, something this lab illustrates. If you introduce new required fields to a complex type after version 1 of the contract has been published, existing clients will not be compatible. To support backward compatibility, you should not make new data members required. I'll talk more about versioning practices shortly.

The nillable schema attribute cannot be controlled by a DataMemberAttribute property. The default behavior is that reference types have nillable set to true, while value types (structures) have nillable set to false. This is illustrated in Example 2-17; string elements are nillable, dateTime elements are not. You can modify this behavior by using the nullable type in .NET. The following code shows you how to declare a nullable type using shorthand ("?" suffix) or the more formal notation with Nullable<T>:

```
[DataMember(Name = "DateEnd", IsRequired = false, Order = 4)]
private DateTime? m_dateEnd;

public Nullable<DateTime> DateEnd
{
  get { return m_dateEnd; }
  set { m_dateEnd = value; }
}
```

The resulting schema will now support empty values for the DateEnd element:

```
<xs:element minOccurs="0" name="DateEnd" nillable="true" type="xs:dateTime" />
```

 A sample illustrating Nullable<T> can be found at <YourLearningWCF Path>\Samples\DataContracts\NullableTypes.

You can also control the order that elements appear in the schema. By default, the DataContractSerializer generates a schema for each data contract with data member order based on the following rules:

- Starting from the topmost class in the hierarchy and working down through the inheritance tree.

- Within each individual data contract, data members are ordered alphabetically.

- Any data members with a specified order will be ordered alphabetically within the order grouping. For example, ordered elements can be grouped within a type such that all members with `Order=1` are alphabetical, followed all members with `Order=2`, and so on.

To simplify matters, developers should apply an explicit order to each data member, within a type. After all, how does it look to business partners that consume your services if the `Id` field is in the middle of the elements in the schema instead of at the top? What happens when there are 100 elements in a complex type and there is no sense to its organization?

 If you need greater control over the resulting schema for a complex type or hierarchy of types, you should consider using the `IXmlSerializable` approach. I'll discuss this later in this chapter.

The important thing to consider is that naming conventions and element order for data contracts should be consistent and professional.

 Here are several samples related to `DataContractAttribute` and `DataMemberAttribute`:

- *<YourLearningWCFPath>\Samples\DataContracts\ DataContracts_FieldMembers*

- *<YourLearningWCFPath>\Samples\DataContracts\ DataContracts_PropertyMembers*

EnumMemberAttribute

Enumerations are implicitly data contracts, which means you don't have to decorate them with the `DataContractAttribute` in order to expose them in a service contract. By default, all members are included in the schema for the enumeration, and the default namespace will use the prefix *http://schemas.datacontract.org/2004/07*. To be consistent with your other data contracts, you should probably provide a namespace for your enumerations, as shown in Example 2-21 from this lab. But, once you decorate enumerations with `DataContractAttribute` you are obligated to opt-in each member you want to include in the enumeration. There is a catch to this: you must use the `EnumMemberAttribute` instead of the `DataMemberAttribute`.

 Using the `DataMemberAttribute` will result in an empty schema definition for the enumeration.

The resulting schema definition for the `LinkItemCategories` enumeration in this lab is shown in Example 2-23.

Example 2-23. Schema generated for LinkItemCategories

```
<xs:simpleType name="LinkItemCategories">
  <xs:restriction base="xs:string">
    <xs:enumeration value="Gig" />
    <xs:enumeration value="MP3" />
    <xs:enumeration value="Photo" />
  </xs:restriction>
</xs:simpleType>
```

The `EnumMemberAttribute` has a single property, `Value`. You can use this property to control how enum members are named in the schema:

```
[EnumMember(Value="Event"]
Gig,
[EnumMember(Value="Music"]
MP3,
[EnumMember(Value="Pics"]
Photo
```

CollectionDataContractAttribute

You may need to create a custom collection at some point, and expose it as part of a service contract. The `CollectionDataContractAttribute` is a special attribute specifically for this purpose. This attribute has the following members:

Name
> Controls the collection type name generated for the schema. By default, the CLR type name is used.

Namespace
> Sets the target namespace for the schema with default behavior like the `DataContractAttribute`.

ItemName
> Controls the name for each element in the collection.

KeyName
> Controls the key name for dictionary collections only. This is invalid if the collection type is not a dictionary.

ValueName
> Controls the value name for dictionary collections only. This is invalid if the collection type is not a dictionary.

You apply the `CollectionDataContractAttribute` to the custom collection like this:

```
[CollectionDataContract(Namespace=
"http://schemas.thatindigogirl.com/samples/2006/06",ItemName="Item")]
public class LinkItemCollection: List<LinkItem>
{
}
```

A sample illustrating `CollectionDataContractAttribute` can be found at *<YourLearningWCFPath>\Samples\DataContracts\ CollectionDataContract.*

Mapping CLR Namespace to Schema Namespace

Service contracts and data contracts (including complex types, enumerations, and collections) all belong to a target namespace in the WSDL document. By default, the service contract and data contracts are granted different default target namespaces in schema; however, you can control the namespace explicitly via the attributes discussed in this section.

You can also use the `ContactNamespaceAttribute` to automatically map CLR namespaces to a particular schema namespace. Example 2-24 shows how to do this.

Example 2-24. Applying the ContractNamespaceAttribute

```
[assembly: ContractNamespace("http://schemas.thatindigogirl.com/samples/2006/06",
ClrNamespace="ContentTypes")]

namespace ContentTypes
{
  [DataContract]
  public class LinkItem
  {...}
}
```

The `ContractNamespaceAttribute` should be used with care. If service contracts and types happen to share the same CLR namespace, this attribute will map services and types to the same target namespace. This reduces developer awareness of the namespaces used and may inadvertently lead to changes in code that cause compatibility issues with existing clients.

 A sample illustrating `ContractNamespaceAttribute` can be found at *<YourLearningWCFPath>\Samples\DataContracts\ CLRNamespaceMapping.*

Configuring Known Types

The service description will only include data contracts that are known to the `DataContractSerializer`. By default, that means only data contracts explicitly included in at least one operation signature. When operations use a base type, an interface, or an `object` in their signature, other types that inherit those base types and interfaces are not known during serialization. You need a way to tell the `DataContractSerializer` about the other polymorphic types that may be included in calls to such operations. This is achieved with *known types*. Consider the three classes shown in Example 2-25 that inherit `LinkItem`—the type used in this lab.

Example 2-25. Classes that derive from LinkItem

```
[DataContract(Namespace = "http://schemas.thatindigogirl.com/samples/2006/06")]
class GigInfo: LinkItem
{
  public GigInfo( )
  {
    this.Category = LinkItemCategories.Gig;
  }
}


[DataContract(Namespace = "http://schemas.thatindigogirl.com/samples/2006/06")]
class MP3Link: LinkItem
{
  public MP3Link( )
  {
    this.Category = LinkItemCategories.MP3;
  }
}


[DataContract(Namespace = "http://schemas.thatindigogirl.com/samples/2006/06")]
class PhotoLink: LinkItem
{
  public PhotoLink( )
  {
    this.Category = LinkItemCategories.Photo;
  }
}
```

Despite the relationship between types, the following operations will not support anything besides a LinkItem type:

```
[OperationContract]
void SaveGig(LinkItem item);

[OperationContract]
LinkItem GetGig( );
```

You can change this by specifying one or more known types to the service contract. There are a few ways to achieve this:

- Apply one or more KnownTypeAttribute to a type indicating the polymorphic types with which it is compatible
- Apply the ServiceKnownTypeAttribute to the service contract or to a particular operation indicating any polymorphic types that should be supported
- Configure known types globally for the DataContractSerializer

Regardless of how you configure known types, the result is that the service description will include these types. In terms of the WSDL document, this means that schema definitions for known types are included, and any hierarchical relationship with other types is preserved. The behavior of the service model when known types are present is also important to understand. When a message is sent that includes one of the known types, for example GigInfo, the DataContractSerializer knows how to construct it into a CLR type because it has access to the schema definition. Thus, even if the service operation is expecting a LinkItem, a GigInfo type is initialized and passed to the LinkItem parameter. This behavior works at the client as well, when the service returns polymorphic types.

KnownTypeAttribute

Base types can supply a list of known types by applying one or more KnownTypeAttribute indicating related polymorphic types. The following example shows how to associate several known types to a common base type:

```
[DataContract(Namespace = "http://schemas.thatindigogirl.com/samples/2006/06")]
[KnownType(typeof(GigInfo))]
[KnownType(typeof(PhotoLink))]
[KnownType(typeof(MP3Link))]
public class LinkItem
```

These known types will be included in the service description for any service contract that employs the base type, LinkItem, in its operation signature. The benefits of this are that the base data contract always carries with it a list of compatible types, and any service contract will automatically know about those types. The downside of this is that you may not want to support all of the polymorphic types in every service contract. The ServiceKnownTypeAttribute lets you control known types at the service contract.

ServiceKnownTypeAttribute

Another way to support known types is to apply the ServiceKnownTypeAttribute. This attribute can be applied to the entire service contract to associate known types with all operations, or to individual operations in order to control which types are associated with each. Example 2-26 shows an example where each operation supports a different polymorphic type. Example 2-27 shows how to support all types for all operations in the service contract.

Example 2-26. Applying the ServiceKnownTypeAttribute to individual operations

```
[OperationContract]
[ServiceKnownType(typeof(ContentTypes.GigInfo))]
void SaveGig(LinkItem item);

[OperationContract]
[ServiceKnownType(typeof(ContentTypes.PhotoLink))]
void SavePhoto(LinkItem item);

[OperationContract]
[ServiceKnownType(typeof(ContentTypes.MP3Link))]
void SaveMP3(LinkItem item);
```

Example 2-27. Applying the ServiceKnownTypeAttribute at the service contract

```
[ServiceContract]
[ServiceKnownType(typeof(ContentTypes.GigInfo))]
[ServiceKnownType(typeof(ContentTypes.PhotoLink))]
[ServiceKnownType(typeof(ContentTypes.MP3Link))]
public interface IContentManagerService
{
  [OperationContract]
  void SaveItem(LinkItem item);

  [OperationContract]
  LinkItem GetItem( );
}
```

Declarative known types

In some cases you may not know all of the known types when you build the service and related data contracts. It is also possible that you will add new polymorphic types after you publish the service. To add known type support without recompiling assemblies that contain service contracts or data contracts, you can configure them declaratively in the `<system.runtime.serialization>` section of your application configuration file. Example 2-28 shows you how to initialize the `DataContractSerializer` with a list of known types for the `LinkItem` type.

Example 2-28. Declaratively supplying the DataContractSerializer with known types

```
<configuration>
  <system.serviceModel>...</system.serviceModel>
  <system.runtime.serialization>
    <dataContractSerializer>
      <declaredTypes>
        <add type="ContentTypes.LinkItem, ContentTypes, Version=1.0.0.0,
Culture=neutral, PublicKeyToken=null">
          <knownType type="ContentTypes.GigInfo, ContentTypes, Version=1.0.0.0,
Culture=neutral, PublicKeyToken=null" />
          <knownType type="ContentTypes.MP3Link, ContentTypes, Version=1.0.0.0,
Culture=neutral, PublicKeyToken=null" />
          <knownType type="ContentTypes.PhotoLink, ContentTypes, Version=1.0.0.0,
Culture=neutral, PublicKeyToken=null" />
        </add>
      </declaredTypes>
    </dataContractSerializer>
  </system.runtime.serialization>
</configuration>
```

With this configuration, clients can successfully pass a `GigInfo` type instead of a `LinkItem` type for any operation that uses `LinkItem` in the signature:

```
GigInfo item = new GigInfo( );
// Initialize item

m_proxy.SaveGig(item);
```

Here are some samples illustrating known types:

- *<YourLearningWCFPath>\Samples\DataContracts\ KnownTypesDataContract*
- *<YourLearningWCFPath>\Samples\DataContracts\ KnownTypesServiceContract*
- *<YourLearningWCFPath>\Samples\DataContracts\ KnownTypesDeclarative*
- *<YourLearningWCFPath>\Samples\DataContracts\ KnownTypesCallback*

Versioning Data Contracts

As with service contracts, it is important to make sure that the changes made to data contracts do not affect existing clients using the originally published service contract. Changes to data contracts impact the service contract since they are associated with service operations. This lab illustrates only a few versioning scenarios for data contracts. Table 2-3 summarizes possible changes to a data contract and the affect it has on existing clients, if any.

Table 2-3. Data contract changes and their affect on existing clients

Data contract changes	Impact on existing clients
Add new nonrequired members	Client unaffected. Missing values are initialized to defaults.
Add new required members	An exception is thrown for missing values.
Remove nonrequired members	Data is lost at the service. The service may be unable to return the information back to the client, for example. No exceptions are thrown.
Remove required members	An exception is thrown when the client receives responses from the service with missing values.
Modify existing member data types	If the types are compatible, no exception is thrown, but the client may receive unexpected results.

Making changes to data contracts once they have been published is a delicate matter. Even if no exception is thrown for the change, the data may lack integrity once it is deserialized on either end. To avoid this, a few general guidelines should be followed if you are not creating a new data contract version:

- Require data members on which the business depends.
- Do not remove or change data types for members, ever.
- If adding new members, make sure they are not required so that version 1 clients don't break. Remember that missing fields will be initialized to default values, so you must be sure these defaults are acceptable or perform some low-level message modifications to provide meaningful defaults prior to deserialization.
- You may consider supporting IExtensibleDataObject so that extra data sent by clients or returned by services is preserved for round trips. This, however, can have some negative impact, which I'll discuss next.

IExtensibleDataObject

As the lab illustrates, implementing this interface allows you to preserve unknown members included in the serialized type. The result is that the `DataContractSerializer` populates the `ExtensionDataObject` dictionary on deserialization and uses the same dictionary to serialize additional elements in serialized messages. This is useful in a few scenarios: when clients send additional unknown data to the service that should be returned intact, and when a version 2 client sends data to a version 1 service, in which case you may want to preserve unknown data for version tolerance. Predicting future versioning issues is difficult, so providing this property bag for unknown members can ease versioning pain.

If you implement this interface on your data contracts and later decide that it is not a required or desirable feature, you can tell the `DataContractSerializer` to ignore the `IExtensibleDataObject` implementation. This is done by enabling the data contract serializer behavior, which you can do declaratively by adding the `<dataContractSerializer>` behavior element and setting `ignoreExtensionDataObject` to true:

```
<behavior name="serviceBehavior">
  <dataContractSerializer ignoreExtensionDataObject ="true"/>
</behavior>
```

This behavior can also be set declaratively on the service type:

```
[ServiceBehavior(IgnoreExtensionDataObject=true)]
```

When this behavior is enabled, any data contracts implementing `IExtensibleDataObject` are ignored. Disabling support for `IExtensibleDataObject` can have a negative impact when client and service versions are out of sync, but it is a useful tool for preventing unwanted data from being processed at the service.

 You should use `IExtensibleDataObject` with caution because it opens the service, in particular to denial-of-service attacks where malicious clients send large amounts of unwanted data to be deserialized at the service. Both the deserialization effort and memory usage can have negative effects on performance and scalability.

At the client, SvcUtil generates data contracts that implement `IExtensibleDataObject`. This ensures that extra data sent to clients by the service will not be lost in a round trip—something you want in the event that version 1 clients call version 2 services.

Explicit versioning

To properly version a data contract, you should create a new type and supply it with a new data contract namespace using the `DataContractAttribute`. Since it is a new type, you are free to remove, add, or change any member, but remember that if the semantics of the type are significantly different it is probably not even related to any existing types.

When you change a data contract that is included in a service operation, you are also affecting the service contract that exposes the type. In fact, the minute you decide to version a data contract, you must also version any service contract that uses it.

In summary, existing clients must always be able to access an endpoint that exposes the original contract. The only way this is possible is if the original contract does not change!

Versioning flow diagrams

Figures 2-6 and 2-7 illustrate the decision flow for data contract versioning based on non-strict and strict approaches, respectively.

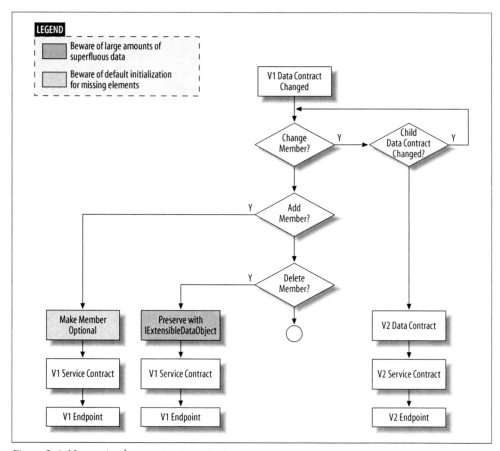

Figure 2-6. Non-strict data contract versioning.

With non-strict versioning, you can add optional members and ignore (yet preserve) superfluous members that may result from future versions of the contract. Ignoring optional members requires you to be aware of the default initialization of members that are missing, if you want to differentiate between version 1 and version 2 clients.

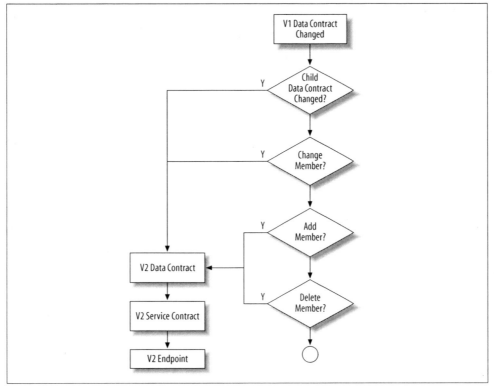

Figure 2-7. Strict data contract versioning.

Allowing superfluous members to be ignored solves the problem of newer version clients pushing data to an older version of the data contract, but this carries risks if clients send an inordinate amount of extra data. You should still consider IExtensibleDataObject for your own versioning needs, but perhaps monitor the message size to prevent possible denial-of-service attacks.

With strict data contract versioning, all changes lead to a new data contract. That means that any service contract that exposes this new data contract must also be versioned per the rules of strict service contract versioning.

Data Contracts As Operation Messages

Earlier in this chapter, I explained that service contracts allow signature changes such as adding or removing parameters without impacting existing clients. This means that you can't require specific parameters be passed to an operation. The client can omit them, and the service model will simply initialize them to their default values.

You can use data contracts to describe the request and response message to an operation. Specifically for the request parameter, this enables you to enforce that certain values are passed. Consider this operation:

```
[OperationContract]
string Operation1(string param1, string param2);
```

If either parameter is omitted, it will be initialized to an empty string. Using data contracts, the same operation might look like this:

```
[OperationContract]
Operation1Response Operation1(Operation1Request requestMessage);
```

Operation1Request and Operation1Response are data contracts, as seen in Example 2-29. Notice that each parameter is a required data member of Operation1Request. If you add new nonrequired members, you can still have the effect of forgiving new parameters passed in the message.

Example 2-29. Data contracts describing request and response messages

```
[DataContract(Namespace = "http://schemas.thatindigogirl.com/samples/2006/06")]
public class Operation1Request
{
  [DataMember(IsRequired = true, Order = 1)]
  public string param1;
  [DataMember(IsRequired = true, Order = 2)]
  public string param2;
}

[DataContract(Namespace = "http://schemas.thatindigogirl.com/samples/2006/06")]
public class Operation1Response
{
  [DataMember(IsRequired = true, Order = 1)]
  public string responseString;
}
```

This technique is also helpful in describing response messages in the event several complex types should be returned from the operation.

Message Contracts

When you define a service contract, you traditionally describe a set of operations that may include a parameter list and a return value. Each operation is ultimately linked to a request, a response message, or both in the service description, depending on the message exchange pattern for the operation. A *message contract* is a more formal way to describe operation messages. It gives you more granular control over the actual structure of the message (the SOAP envelope), which can be important for the web service savvy. You can use message contracts as the only parameter and as the return type for any operation, in lieu of a parameter list or return value-comprising data contracts or serializable types.

Data contracts are still very important to the message contract. In fact, message contracts internally describe what would have been a parameter list or return value. The value added by message contracts is in their ability to exercise greater control over how message headers and message body elements are serialized. The following attributes will be introduced in this section as I show you how to work with message contracts: `MessageContractAttribute`, `MessageHeaderAttribute`, and `MessageBodyMemberAttribute`.

Lab: Controlling Message Serialization with Message Contracts

In this lab, you will modify an existing service contract that uses traditional operation signatures and replace that approach with message contracts. A new message contract type will be created for each message. Each message contract will encapsulate the parameters or return values applicable to the message. In addition, you'll learn how to create a custom message header.

Creating message contracts

1. Open the startup solution for this lab, located in *<YourLearningWCFPath>\ Labs\ Chapter2\ MessageContracts\MessageContracts.sln.*

2. Take a look at the existing service contract first. Go to the `GigManager` project and open *GigManagerService.cs*. The operations in the service contract look like this:

   ```
   [OperationContract]
   void SaveGig(LinkItem item);

   [OperationContract]
   LinkItem GetGig();
   ```

3. The first thing you'll do is create two message contracts for the `SaveGig()` operation: one for the request, another for the response. Start by adding a new class to the `GigManager` project. Name the class file *Messages.cs*.

   Add two new message contract classes to this file: `SaveGigRequest` and `SaveGigResponse`. Apply the `MessageContractAttribute` to each class and apply the `MessageBodyMemberAttribute` to the `LinkItem` property. Add using statements for `ContentTypes` and `System.ServiceModel`. The resulting file should match the code in Example 2-30.

Example 2-30. SaveGig() message contracts

```
using System.ServiceModel;
using ContentTypes;

namespace GigManager
{
  [MessageContract]
  public class SaveGigRequest
  {
    private LinkItem m_linkItem;

    [MessageBodyMember]
    public LinkItem Item
```

Example 2-30. SaveGig() message contracts (continued)

```
    {
      get { return m_linkItem; }
      set { m_linkItem = value; }
    }
  }

  [MessageContract]
  public class SaveGigResponse
  {
  }
}
```

> With message contracts, body elements are equivalent to operation parameters. You can specify order, and you must use data contracts or serializable types.

4. In the same file, create two more message contracts, this time for GetGig( ). The type names for these new message contracts will be: GetGigRequest and GetGigResponse. The request message will also include a custom message header, LicenseKey. You'll use the MessageHeaderAttribute to mark the LicenseKey property as a header. The final result should match the code in Example 2-31.

Example 2-31. GetGig() message contracts

```
[MessageContract]
public class GetGigRequest
{
  private string m_licenseKey;

  [MessageHeader]
  public string LicenseKey
  {
    get { return m_licenseKey; }
    set { m_licenseKey = value; }
  }
}

[MessageContract]
public class GetGigResponse
{
  private LinkItem m_linkItem;

  public GetGigResponse( )
  {
  }

  public GetGigResponse(LinkItem item)
  {
    this.m_linkItem = item;
  }
```

Example 2-31. GetGig() message contracts (continued)

```
[MessageBodyMember]
public LinkItem LinkItem
{
  get { return m_linkItem; }
  set { m_linkItem = value; }
}
}
```

 Header elements must also be valid data contracts or serializable types.

At this point, you have defined four message contracts that will be applied to the service contract in the next step. The point thus far is to give you an idea what goes into creating a message contract, exposing properties that will be either headers or body elements.

Implementing message contracts in a service

Now you will use the new message contracts in the service contract for this solution. You'll change the signatures of SaveGig( ) and GetGig( ) so that instead of using parameters and return types, they rely on message contracts for both.

1. Go to the GigManager project and open *GigManagerService.cs*. Modify the service contract, IGigManagerService, so that the operations reflect the changes shown in bold here:

   ```
   [OperationContract]
   SaveGigResponse SaveGig(SaveGigRequest requestMessage);

   [OperationContract]
   GetGigResponse GetGig(GetGigRequest requestMessage);
   ```

2. After changing the service contract, you'll have to update the service implementation to use the message contracts as well. First, edit the signature of SaveGig( ) in the GigManagerService type. Modify the code to use message contracts to access the LinkItem parameter and to generate the empty return value. The result should match Example 2-32.

Example 2-32. SaveGig() implementation using message contracts

```
public SaveGigResponse SaveGig(SaveGigRequest requestMessage)
{
  m_linkItem = requestMessage.Item;
  return new SaveGigResponse( );
}
```

3. Follow similar steps to update the GetGig( ) implementation to match its new operation signature. This implementation will also inspect the LicenseKey

message header to verify it matches a particular string. If the license key is invalid, you'll throw a FaultException. If it is valid, you'll return the LinkItem instance. Example 2-33 has the complete implementation.

Example 2-33. GetGig() implementation using message contracts

```
public GetGigResponse GetGig(GetGigRequest requestMessage)
{
  if (requestMessage.LicenseKey != "XXX")
    throw new FaultException("Invalid license key.");
  return new GetGigResponse(m_linkItem);
}
```

 FaultException is an exception type representative of a SOAP fault. There are many ways to generate and handle SOAP faults. This is discussed at length in Chapter 8.

4. Verify that the solution compiles.

Using proxies and message contracts

Now that you've updated the service to use the message contracts, you will create a proxy for the client to consume the service.

1. Start by running the host project so that the metadata exchange endpoint (already configured) can be reached to generate a proxy for the client. Go to the GigEntry project and add a service reference supplying the address *http://localhost:8000* and leaving the namespace as localhost.

2. Add code to the client that will invoke the service. Open *GigInfoForm.cs* and create a proxy reference scoped to the form, as shown here:

```
public partial class GigInfoForm : Form
{
    localhost.GigManagerServiceContractClient m_proxy = new
GigEntry.localhost.GigManagerServiceContractClient();

    // Other code
}
```

3. Use this new proxy reference to invoke SaveGig(). Find the Click event handler for the Save button, cmdSave_Click(), and add the code shown in Example 2-34 to create a LinkItem type and call SaveGig(). You will also need to add a using statement for GigEntry.localhost.

Example 2-34. Client code to invoke SaveGig()

```
using GigEntry.localhost;

private void cmdSave_Click(object sender, EventArgs e)
{
  LinkItem item = new LinkItem();
```

Example 2-34. Client code to invoke SaveGig() (continued)

```
item.Id = int.Parse(this.txtId.Text);
item.Title = this.txtTitle.Text;
item.Description = this.txtDescription.Text;
item.DateStart = this.dtpStart.Value;
item.DateEnd = this.dtpEnd.Value;
item.Url = this.txtUrl.Text;

m_proxy.SaveGig(item);
}
```

 Notice that the client code knows nothing about any message contracts—it simply passes the required LinkItem parameter to the proxy.

4. Do the same for GetGig( ). Find the cmdGet_Click( ) handler and add the code
   shown in Example 2-35. This time, you'll notice that an extra parameter has
   been added to the operation to support the custom message header.

Example 2-35. Client code to invoke GetGig()

```
private void cmdGet_Click(object sender, EventArgs e)
{
  LinkItem item = m_proxy.GetGig("XXX");
  if (item != null)
  {
    this.txtId.Text = item.Id.ToString();
    this.txtTitle.Text = item.Title;
    this.txtDescription.Text = item.Description;

    if (item.DateStart != DateTime.MinValue)
      this.dtpStart.Value = item.DateStart;
    if (item.DateEnd != DateTime.MinValue)
      this.dtpEnd.Value = item.DateEnd;

    this.txtUrl.Text = item.Url;
  }
}
```

5. Compile and run the solution, running the Host project first, followed by the
   GigEntry client. From the client, select Save to invoke SaveGig( ). Clear one of
   the input fields and select Get to invoke GetGig( ) to restore the interface to the
   values you saved.

6. Test what happens when the LicenseKey header is invalid. Modify the call to
   GetGig( ) so that you pass an invalid header value. Change the code as shown in
   bold here:

   ```
   LinkItem item = m_proxy.GetGig("abc");
   ```

7. Compile and run the solution again, running the same tests. This time, you will
   see the FaultException thrown by the service.

Message Contracts and SOAP

Service operations are defined by method signatures in the service contract, usually as part of an interface definition. Each service operation describes the parameters clients should pass and the return value they will receive (if any). When represented in XML, however, parameters and return values are actually wrapped in the body of a SOAP message. When you use a message contract as the operation parameter and return value, you are essentially taking control over the entire SOAP envelope with the ability to define custom message headers and individual body elements.

By default, without message contracts, messages are serialized so that the body element contains a child wrapper element matching the operation name. This element in turn wraps any parameters or return values, and it may even be empty if there are no parameters or if the return type is void. Example 2-36 shows the request and response message for SaveGig( ) (from the lab) before applying message contracts.

Example 2-36. Request and response message for SaveGig( )

```
// SaveGig( ) request
<s:Envelope ...>
  <s:Header>
    <!-- Standard headers -->
  </s:Header>
  <s:Body>
    <SaveGig xmlns="http://www.thatindigogirl.com/samples/2006/06">
      <item xmlns:b="http://schemas.thatindigogirl.com/samples/2006/06"
xmlns:i="http://www.w3.org/2001/XMLSchema-instance">
        <!-- Contents of Item -->
      </item>
    </SaveGig>
  </s:Body>
</s:Envelope>

// SaveGig( ) response
<s:Envelope ...>
  <s:Header>
    <!-- Standard headers -->
  </s:Header>
  <s:Body>
    <SaveGigResponse
xmlns="http://www.thatindigogirl.com/samples/2006/06"></SaveGigResponse>
  </s:Body>
</s:Envelope>
```

The presence of this wrapper and its naming convention is of no importance if the client proxy can serialize messages according to the same format. Refactoring operations to use message contracts introduces some minor naming changes. Specifically, the default wrapper element for request and response message will match the name of the message contract type. Consider this signature for SaveGig( ) using message contracts:

```
[OperationContract]
SaveGigResponse SaveGig(SaveGigRequest requestMessage);
```

The resulting message body for the request and response will look as shown in Example 2-37.

Example 2-37. Request and response body element for SaveGig() when message contracts are employed

```
// SaveGig( ) request body
<s:Body>
  <SaveGigRequest xmlns="http://www.thatindigogirl.com/samples/2006/06">
    <Item xmlns:b="http://schemas.thatindigogirl.com/samples/2006/06"
xmlns:i="http://www.w3.org/2001/XMLSchema-instance">
      <!-- Contents of Item -->
    </Item>
  </SaveGigRequest>
</s:Body>

// SaveGig( ) response body
<s:Body>
  <SaveGigResponse xmlns="http://www.thatindigogirl.com/samples/2006/06">
  </SaveGigResponse>
</s:Body>
```

Without message contracts, the request message wrapper will contain any parameters to the operation. The response wrapper contains the return type. With message contracts, the request and response wrapper both contain any body elements from their respective message contracts defined with the `MessageBodyMemberAttribute`.

You can also add one or more header elements to a message contract using the `MessageHeaderAttribute`. Each header is then added to the header section of serialized messages, as shown here:

```
<s:Envelope ...>
  <s:Header>
    <!-- Standard headers -->
    <h:LicenseKey
xmlns:h="http://www.thatindigogirl.com/samples/2006/06">XXX</h:LicenseKey>
  </s:Header>
  <s:Body>...</s:Body>
</s:Envelope>
```

The subtleties of how messages are formed with and without message contracts matter mostly when interoperability between platforms is at stake. In the next sections, I'll talk about how you can apply features of the `MessageContractAttribute`, `MessageHeaderAttribute`, and `MessageBodyMemberAttribute` to exercise greater control over message serialization.

Designing Message Contracts

Message contracts are types decorated with the `MessageContractAttribute`. You can supply these in lieu of data contracts in any service operation signature. A single message contract type takes the place of multiple parameters and instead supplies those parameters as body elements marked with the MessageBodyMemberAttribute.

There are several reasons why you might want to move to message contracts, including:

- To control how the message body is wrapped
- To supply custom headers
- To control message protection requirements on specific message elements

In the following sections, I'll describe how to apply attributes related to message contracts, including MessageContractAttribute, MessageBodyMemberAttribute, and MessageHeaderAttribute.

MessageContractAttribute

The MessageContractAttribute provides you with ways to control whether the message body is wrapped or unwrapped—something that is important in some interoperability scenarios because of the way different platforms serialize the message body. You can also control whether and how messages are signed and encrypted. The following are the properties of the MessageContractAttribute and their usage:

IsWrapped
>If true, the message body includes a wrapper element named for the message contract type or the WrapperName if specified. If false, the message body is unwrapped, and body elements appear directly beneath it.

ProtectionLevel
>Allows you to control how message header and body elements inside the contract are protected on the wire—if they are signed and encrypted. ProtectionLevel settings are covered in Chapter 7.

WrapperName
>Supplies a custom name for the body wrapper element.

WrapperNamespace
>Supplies a namespace for the body wrapper element.

Typically, you will leave the defaults for body wrapping, and the namespace will derive from your service contract namespace by default. So, this would be an acceptable message contract declaration:

```
[MessageContract]
public class SaveGigRequest
```

You can suppress wrapping as shown here:

```
[MessageContract(IsWrapped=false)]
public class SaveGigRequest
```

The resulting message body might look as shown in Example 2-38 for the SaveGig( ) operation.

Example 2-38. Unwrapped body elements the SaveGig() operation

```
// Request message body
<s:Body>
  <Item xmlns="http://www.thatindigogirl.com/samples/2006/06"
xmlns:b="http://schemas.thatindigogirl.com/samples/2006/06"
xmlns:i="http://www.w3.org/2001/XMLSchema-instance">
    <!-- Contents of Item -->
  </Item>
</s:Body>

// Response message body
<s:Body></s:Body>
```

When you apply message contracts to a service operation, the message contract must be the only parameter and of course the only return type.

MessageBodyMemberAttribute

Body elements in a message contract are the equivalent of parameters or return values for an operation. Like any parameter, they must be data contracts to be included in the service contract. Using the `MessageBodyMemberAttribute`, you can opt-in message contract fields or properties to become part of the message body, and you can control other aspects such as order, message protection, and naming conventions. The `MessageBodyMemberAttribute` has only one property, `Order`. This property allows you to control the order that message body elements appear; the default behavior is to serialize them alphabetically.

In fact, the `MessageBodyMemberAttribute` inherits `MessageContractMemberAttribute`—a base type also used by the `MessageHeaderAttribute` (to be discussed later). `MessageContractMemberAttribute` supplies these common properties:

Name
  Controls the name of the serialized body or header element.

Namespace
  Supplies a namespace for the body or header element and its children unless otherwise overridden at the type level.

ProtectionLevel
  Allows you to control how body or header element is protected—if they are signed and encrypted.

Typically, you will name the body element the way it should appear in the serialized message so that specifying a custom name is not required. The namespace will inherit the service contract namespace, and this is usually OK as well. At a minimum, as with data contracts, you should supply order for each body element to ensure predictability in the resulting message schema.

MessageHeaderAttribute

The `MessageHeaderAttribute` is the easiest way to add custom headers to your service contract messages. To add a custom header to a message contract, you apply the `MessageHeaderAttribute` to fields or properties that should be included in header serialization. Similar to the `MessageBodyMemberAttribute`, you can control naming conventions and protection level by setting properties on the common base type `MessageContractMemberAttribute` (discussed in the previous section). You can also control other features specific to message headers such as `Actor`, `MustUnderstand`, and `Relay` settings. The properties of the `MessageHeaderAttribute` are listed here:

Actor
> URI value indicating for whom the header is intended. By default, the receiving application is assumed.

MustUnderstand
> Indicates whether the recipient of the header (`Actor`) is required to process this header. If this is set to `true` and the actor doesn't understand the header, the actor should fault.

Relay
> Indicates whether this header should be forwarded to the next recipient of the message in the event the message is not being processed by the actor.

 You can find more information about SOAP header attributes in the *SOAP 1.2 specification: http://www.w3.org/TR/soap12-part0*.

Headers decorated with the `MessageHeaderAttribute` must be a data contract or a serializable type to be included in the service contract. Typically, you'll try to name headers in message contract according to the name that should be defined in the schema.

The `MustUnderstand` property can be useful when the header is required to successfully process messages. Clients can specify that a header must be understood and the expectation is that if the receiving service cannot process the header, it will throw an exception. From the lab, for example, you can modify the client's version of the `SaveGigRequest` message contract to add this requirement:

```
[System.ServiceModel.MessageHeaderAttribute(MustUnderstand=true,
Namespace="http://www.thatindigogirl.com/samples/2006/06")]
public string LicenseKey;
```

This causes the `MustUnderstand` attribute to be set in the serialized header:

```
<h:LicenseKey s:mustUnderstand="1" xmlns:h="http://www.thatindigogirl.com/samples/
2006/06">XXX</h:LicenseKey>
```

If the service operation does not require the header (you can simulate this by commenting the `MessageHeaderAttribute`), you'll see the exception.

Client Message Contracts

When message contracts are used to define service operations, the client proxy appears to be unaffected at the surface. Your client code still creates a proxy instance and invokes operations as usual—passing parameters in, receiving results back. One change noticeable in this lab is the additional parameters inserted when message headers are included in the message contract.

Internally, the proxy uses message contracts to issue requests and to retrieve responses from service operations. You'll notice that the generated proxy code includes types for each message contract at the client, almost identical to those at the service. Normally, you won't care about this unless you want to interact with the message headers directly and supply MustUnderstand or Actor settings. In this case, you'll have to modify the client-side message contract as discussed in the previous section.

Versioning Message Contracts

Message contracts are used in the service contract; thus, any changes made to a message contract affect the service contract. This can potentially cause versioning issues with clients, as I've discussed in earlier sections. Table 2-4 summarizes the effect of changes to the message contract on existing clients, if any.

Table 2-4. Message contract changes and their impact on existing clients

Message contract changes	Impact on existing clients
Add new message body members	Client unaffected. Missing body elements are initialized to their default value.
Remove message body members	Data lost at the service. The service is unable to return superfluous information back to the client. No exceptions are thrown.
Add new message headers	Client unaffected. Missing header elements are initialized to their default value.
Remove message headers	Superfluous headers ignored at the service. An exception will be thrown if the client has enabled the MustUnderstand property of the header at their end.

As I've discussed with service contracts and data contracts, message contracts are quite forgiving of missing or superfluous data—in both directions. Unfortunately, that also means that you can't explicitly require a message body or header member unless you write code to verify if the value has been initialized to something other than its default. For complex types, you can check for null values. For other types, it may be more difficult. How do you know whether the intended value was the default as initialized?

A more important concern is support for backward compatibility with earlier clients. Whether the service model is forgiving or not, you should not remove features from a contract once it's published. If you want to add new headers or body elements, only new clients (or those that refresh their proxies) will know about them. If that is acceptable, feel free to add features so long as you don't impact earlier clients.

To properly version the message contract in the event of significant change, you should create new service operations, possibly even a new service contract.

Approaches to Serialization

At this point in the chapter, you have learned how to create a service contract, expose complex types as data contracts, and create message contracts for greater control over message format. These are the serialization staples for WCF services. In a perfect situation, when you go about designing your services, you can create data contracts representative of the types used by service operations; you'll let the service description be generated from the service contract and these data contract types; and you won't ever have to look at XML. But things aren't always that simple.

Despite the fact that data contracts are the preferred format for exposing complex types in the service contract, there are times when other approaches to serialization may be necessary. Here are some scenarios you may need to consider:

- Exposing preexisting types that implement the SerializableAttribute and ISerializable
- Conforming messages to a specific XSD schema
- Mapping incoming messages to existing types that are not serializable or that don't match a predefined schema

In this section, I'll discuss other serialization concepts and explain practical approaches to these scenarios.

Types Supporting Serialization

Although the focus has been on data contracts thus far, the following types can all be serialized through the DataContractSerializer:

- Data contracts are complex types decorated with the DataContractAttribute or the CollectionDataContractAttribute.
- Serializable types are types decorated with the SerializableAttribute that optionally implement the ISerializable interface for custom serialization, and types that implement IXmlSerializable.
- Message contracts are complex types decorated with the MessageContractAttribute and containing only data contracts or serializable types as header and body members.

Any of these types can be included in a service contract, but your choice of serializer may affect the resulting message format.

Serialization Format

By default, the `DataContractSerializer` is what the service model uses to handle all message serialization for clients and services. It supports data contracts, serializable types, and message contracts. WCF also supports the `XmlSerializer` for backward compatibility with ASMX web services, and in some rare cases to provide additional control over the mapping between XSD schema and CLR types. Table 2-5 summarizes how these two serializers handle different types for serialization.

Table 2-5. Comparing DataContractSerializer and XmlSerializer

Serialization type	DataContractSerializer	XmlSerializer
Data contracts	Opt-in data members of any visibility are serialized using CLR type to XSD schema type mapping.	Ignored. Public fields and properties are serialized. Default CLR type to XSD schema type mapping is used unless XML serialization attributes are applied.
SerializableAttribute	All fields (any visibility) are serialized using CLR type to XSD schema type mapping.	Ignored. Public fields and properties are serialized. Default CLR type to XSD schema type mapping is used unless XML serialization attributes are applied.
IXmlSerializable	You provide schema and control serialization.	You provide schema and control serialization.
Message contracts	Opt-in header and body members are serialized according to their type (data contract or serializable type).	Ignored. Public fields and properties are serialized. Default CLR type to XSD schema type mapping is used unless XML serialization attributes are applied.

Generally, it is best to stick with the `DataContractSerializer` (the default), since it provides opt-in control over which members are serialized, simplifies schema constructs to promote interoperability, and supports data contracts, serializable types, and message contracts.

If you require the `XmlSerializer` for backward compatibility with ASMX or for more granular control over XSD schema mapping, you can apply the `XmlSerializerFormatAttribute` to the service contract, or to individual operations. I'll talk about this shortly.

Message Encoding

The original SOAP specification supported RPC message encoding (section 5 of the specification) and encoded parameters (section 7). Very early web service platforms and toolkits used to default to RPC with encoded parameters. Document/literal format has been the standard since SOAP version 1.2. This implies that SOAP messages conform to schema rather than using self-describing (encoded) types. A detailed discussion of RPC versus document/literal encoding is not within the scope of this book, but I can simplify it this way:

- You will almost always use the default, document/literal encoding.
- The only reason to change from the default is to communicate with a legacy SOAP platform.

Both the `DataContractSerializer` and the `XmlSerializer` default to document/literal format but can be instructed to use RPC encoding using the `OperationFormatStyle` enumeration in the event you need it. Each serializer has a `Style` property based on this enumeration and can be set to one of its two elements: `Document` and `Rpc`. I'll show this setting in the next sections.

DataContractFormatAttribute

The service model uses the `DataContractSerializer` by default. If you want to change the `Style` property of the serializer, you can apply the `DataContractFormatAttribute` to the service contract or to any individual operation.

```
[ServiceContract(Name="ServiceAContract",
Namespace = "http://www.thatindigogirl.com/samples/2006/06")]
[DataContractFormat(Style=OperationFormatStyle.Rpc)]
public interface IServiceA
```

There is no other style to set, so this is about the only reason you would explicitly apply the attribute. This attribute can also be applied to service operations to override the setting on the service contract.

XmlSerializerFormatAttribute

To enable the `XmlSerializer`, you can apply the `XmlSerializerFormatAttribute` to the service contract or to individual operations. This causes all types to be treated as discussed for the `XmlSerializer` in Table 2-5. You can also set the `Style` property of the formatter, and an additional property exists for parameter encoding. The `Use` property is based on the `OperationFormatUse` enumeration and has two elements: `Encoded` and `Literal`. Once again, you will rarely need these settings, but if you are familiar with RPC or encoded SOAP formats, these attributes may be useful to you at some point in time. Here's an example of how to set them:

```
[ServiceContract(Name="ServiceAContract",
Namespace = "http://www.thatindigogirl.com/samples/2006/06")]
[XmlSerializerFormat(Style=OperationFormatStyle.Rpc,
Use=OperationFormatUse.Encoded)]
public interface IServiceA
```

Applying the XmlSerializer

To interoperate with ASMX web services as you migrate to WCF, you may need to apply the `XmlSerializer`. As I mentioned earlier, when types are passed through the `DataContractSerializer`, those marked with the `SerializableAttribute` will by default be serialized similar to the old SOAP formatter—all fields regardless of visibility are included. This is also known as "wrapping the wire."

The *SOAP formatter* serializes types to XML in alignment with the SOAP specification—type information is wrapped in a SOAP envelope and body. In the version 1.x of the .NET Framework, the SOAP formatter was used to serialize object graphs across application domains in *.NET Remoting* scenarios. In version 2.0 and beyond, this formatter is not recommended since it cannot support improved serialization support for versioning and generics. The *binary formatter* is still useful for cross-application domain calls within the same process, which is for the most part the only place where .NET Remoting might still be recommended over WCF.

When the XmlSerializer is employed, types are serialized as they were with ASMX web services—all public fields are included. Fortunately, you can apply XML serialization attributes to control the outcome of serialization in this case.

Controlling serialization

You can control the outcome of type serialization through the XmlSerializer with XML serialization attributes just like you would use with ASMX web services. XmlElementAttribute, XmlAttributeAttribute, XmlIgnoreAttribute, XmlTypeAttribute, and XmlRootAttribute are all examples of these attributes that control serialization of types, their public members, naming conventions, data formats, and position in the schema. For example, by applying the XmlAttributeAttribute to a public field or property, you can serialize it as an XML attribute instead of as an XML element (the default behavior).

These XML attributes share many common properties, for example they can all control the naming convention of the resulting schema construct. To provide an example, the following are the key properties of the XmlElementAttribute:

DataType
> Makes it possible to change the schema data type mapping from the CLR type. For example, by default DateTime types map to the dateTime schema type. You can optionally map the DateTime type to date or time schema types as well.

ElementName
> Controls the formal name for the public field or property. The default behavior is to use the name from the type definition.

Form
> Controls the schema form. Options include XmlSchemaForm.None, XmlSchemaForm.Qualified, and XmlSchemaForm.Unqualified. This attribute basically controls whether or not XML elements must be qualified by a namespace prefix.

IsNullable
> Indicates if the type can be nillable when serialized to schema. This cannot be used for value types.

Namespace
> The namespace associated with the element.

Order
> The order that the element appears in the schema. By default the XmlSerializer uses reflection order.

Type
> An alternate (yet compatible) CLR type to map to the schema.

 A sample illustrating the XmlSerializer and some of these attributes can be found at *<YourLearningWCFPath>\Samples\AdvancedSerialization\XmlSerializer*.

Proxy generation and the XmlSerializer

By default, SvcUtil generates a proxy that uses the DataContractSerializer. In fact, the DataContractSerializer is quite capable of serializing messages based on the service description, regardless of whether it was generated by the XmlSerializer at the other end. If the schema elements in the WSDL document use XSD schema features that the DataContractSerializer is unable to handle, it may be necessary to use the XmlSerializer at the client.

 Clients generally should not care if the service uses the DataContractFormatter or the XmlSerializer so long as the client proxy can adequately serialize according to the WSDL document.

SvcUtil supplies a */serializer* switch to generate code that uses the XmlSerializer. Here's an example of the command line instruction to generate a proxy that uses the XmlSerializer:

```
Svcutil.exe /o:serviceproxy.cs /config:app.config /serializer:XmlSerializer
http://localhost:8000
```

The resulting service contract (part of the proxy) will apply the XmlSerializerAttribute.

There is also some built-in intelligence to SvcUtil that tries to detect when a WSDL document uses schema elements that require the XmlSerializer, but the switch is useful for explicitly requesting it. You will rarely, if ever, use this feature.

Applying IXmlSerializable Types

Relying on data contracts and serializable types to generate the service description and allowing the service model to handle mapping between CLR types and XSD schema is an extremely productive way to build and consume services. There are a few situations, however, where this approach will not be appropriate. For example, what happens if you're given a monstrous XSD schema by a standards body in your industry, and you have to receive messages that conform to that schema at your

---

service operations? The schema could be a nasty mess of hierarchical relationships that won't map well to data contracts or serializable types. In another situation, you may be using an *Object-Relational Mapper* (O/RM) or other business entities that are neither data contracts nor serializable types. Furthermore, these types may not be exactly what you want to expose in your service contract. You could create new data contracts to generate the service description and let the runtime interact with those types during serialization—but then you are creating overhead at the service by creating intermediate types that are ultimately thrown away as you map them to underlying business entities.

What you really want is to be able to process the incoming message and map it to your internal types without creating other throwaway types in the process. In this situation, IXmlSerializable types provide the best of all worlds:

- You can control XSD schema and object mapping.
- You can hook the serialization stages for individual types.
- You can generate meaningful WSDL documents and service metadata using predefined XSD schema.

Implementing IXmlSerializable

IXmlSerializable types have a few responsibilities: supply a schema representative of the type for the service description, control how XML is generated from CLR types, and control how XML is used to construct CLR types. The following are members of the IXmlSerializable interface:

GetSchema
> Invoked by the service model when the service description is generated. This function should return an XSD schema representative of the type.

ReadXml
> Invoked by the service model during deserialization. Provides an opportunity to create business entities from XML.

WriteXml
> Invoked by the service model during serialization. Provides an opportunity to write business entities to XML.

ReadXml( ) supplies an XmlReader for direct access to the XML representation of the type. You can validate the content against a schema or simply read the XML content and validate as you convert to CLR types. WriteXml( ) provides an XmlWriter where you can write your CLR types to XML. The result should conform to the schema you provided if you want types to be understood by calling clients. Example 2-39 illustrates a shell implementation of this interface.

Example 2-39. Shell implementation of IXmlSerializable

```
public class LinkItem : IXmlSerializable
{
  // Properties and fields

  void IXmlSerializable.WriteXml(System.Xml.XmlWriter writer)
  {
    // code to write XML from business entities
  }

  System.Xml.Schema.XmlSchema IXmlSerializable.GetSchema()
  {
    // code to provide the schema for the service description
  }

  void IXmlSerializable.ReadXml(System.Xml.XmlReader xmlReader)
  {
    // code to read XML and geneate business entities
  }
}
```

The downside of working with IXmlSerializable types is that it requires you to have more intimate knowledge of XSD schema and XML.

Supplying a schema

When you design a service contract and supply operations with parameter and return types, the DataContractSerializer generates a schema for those types and includes it in the service description. The whole point of using IXmlSerializable types is to control what the schema looks like for a particular type, while also controlling the actual mapping process between schema and CLR type. As such, GetSchema() is called when the service model is generating the service description and your job is to supply the right schema.

There is one drawback to the GetSchema() method of IXmlSerializable. It requires the runtime to create an instance of the type in order to request the schema. It would be better if a static method could be used, and fortunately there is an attribute you can apply to the type to supply such a method.

The XmlSchemaProviderAttribute allows you to specify a static method responsible for returning the schema. Example 2-40 shows the implementation of this attribute on an IXmlSerializable type.

Example 2-40. XmlSchemaProviderAttribute implementation

```
[XmlSchemaProvider("GetSchema")]
public class LinkItemWrapper: IXmlSerializable
{

  static string ns = "http://www.thatindigogirl.com/samples/2006/06";
```

Example 2-40. XmlSchemaProviderAttribute implementation (continued)

```
  public static XmlQualifiedName GetSchema(XmlSchemaSet schemaSet)
  {
      string schemaString = String.Format("<xs:schema xmlns:tns='{0}'
xmlns:xs='http://www.w3.org/2001/XMLSchema' targetNamespace='{0}'
elementFormDefault='qualified' attributeFormDefault='unqualified'><xs:complexType
name='LinkItem'><xs:sequence><xs:element name='Id' type='xs:string'
nillable='false'/><xs:element name='Title' type='xs:string'
nillable='false'/><xs:element name='Description' type='xs:string'
nillable='false'/><xs:element name='DateStart' type='xs:dateTime'
nillable='false'/><xs:element name='DateEnd' type='xs:dateTime' nillable='true'
minOccurs='0'/><xs:element name='Url' type='xs:string' nillable='false'
minOccurs='0'/></xs:sequence></xs:complexType></xs:schema>", ns);

      XmlSchema schema = XmlSchema.Read(new StringReader(schemaString), null);
      schemaSet.XmlResolver = new XmlUrlResolver();
      schemaSet.Add(schema);

      return new XmlQualifiedName("LinkItem", ns);
  }

  System.Xml.Schema.XmlSchema IXmlSerializable.GetSchema()
  {
    // should never be called!
    throw new NotImplementedException("IXmlSerializable.GetSchema() is not
      implemented. Use static GetSchema() instead.");
  }

  // More properties and methods
}
```

You'll notice that the GetSchema() implementation for the IXmlSerializable interface throws an exception. It will never be called by the service model once the XmlSchemaProviderAttribute is in place.

 A sample illustrating this IXmlSerializable implementation can be found at *<YourLearningWCFPath>\Samples\AdvancedSerialization\ IXmlSerializable*.

The Message Type

There are a number of scenarios where you may need to get your hands on raw messages that pass between client and service. The service model provides you with a Message type with direct access to message headers, message body elements, and other properties associated with a SOAP message. *Untyped messages* like this make it possible to develop generic service operations that do not do the work of serialization and deserialization; instead, they act as a pass-through for messages. Web service intermediaries and content-based routers are examples of service endpoints that can accept any message while still inspecting appropriate message headers or content and forwarding to the rightful recipient.

In this section, I'll introduce you to several advanced concepts related to the use of untyped messages including:

- Defining a service contract that works with untyped messages
- Using the Message type to create and process messages
- Encapsulating functionality by inheriting Message
- Working with the MessageHeader type

Lab: Working with Raw Messages

For this lab, you will convert an existing service to work with raw messages. In the process you'll learn how to create messages from scratch, how to process incoming untyped messages, and how to work with the serialization process between messages and CLR types. The purpose of this lab is to illustrate several aspects of raw message serialization, using the Message type. Later in this section of the chapter, I'll discuss some more practical uses for working with raw messages as well.

Using untyped messages in the service contract

In the first part of this lab you'll open a preexisting solution that uses message contracts and data contracts at the client and service. You're going to change the service to expose operations that use untyped messages.

1. First, open the startup solution for this lab located in *<YourLearningWCFPath>\ Labs\Chapter2\RawMessages\RawMessages.sln*.

2. Test the solution before making any changes. Compile and run the solution, running the Host and GigEntry client projects. From the GigEntry interface, select Save, then clear one of the fields and select Get to restore the information.

3. You're going to modify the service so that it processes incoming messages using the raw Message type, instead of a strongly typed message. Go to the GigManager project and open *GigManagerService.cs*. Find the service contract, IGigManagerService, and modify the SaveGig( ) operation to look as shown here:

   ```
   [OperationContract]
   void SaveGig(Message requestMessage);
   ```

   You will also need to add the following using statement to the file:

   ```
   using System.ServiceModel.Channels;
   ```

 Operations that work with raw messages are defined using the abstract Message type for parameter and return value. This base type gives you direct access to header, body, and other message properties. You can optionally create a subclass to encapsulate how you process the message. The subclass, however, cannot be exposed as part of the operation signature.

4. You'll have to make some changes to SaveGig( ) to reflect its new signature and to update the implementation to work with the Message type. Since the runtime won't be deserializing to the LinkItem type, the new implementation will read the body of the message directly and build a LinkItem from it.

Replace the existing SaveGig( ) implementation with the one shown in Example 2-41. Don't forget to add the using statement for System.Xml.

What this code does is access the XmlDictionaryReader for the message body contents and reads the message body directly. A LinkItemHelper type has been provided to do the work of parsing the XML and populating the LinkItem type.

5. Compile and run the solution again to test this new functionality. Repeat the same test and verify that no errors occur.

Example 2-41. Updated SaveGig() implementation

```
using System.Xml;

public void SaveGig(Message requestMessage)
{
  XmlDictionaryReader xmlReader = requestMessage.GetReaderAtBodyContents( );
  xmlReader.MoveToContent( );
  xmlReader.Read( );
  xmlReader.MoveToContent( );
  xmlReader.Read( );

  this.m_linkItem = LinkItemHelper.ReadLinkItem(xmlReader);

  xmlReader.Close( );
}
```

Accessing message headers

Next you're going to modify the other service operation, GetGig( ), so that you can not only work with the raw message body, but also interact with message headers. This code will be similar to the message contracts lab you completed earlier where the client sent a LicenseKey header. If the LicenseKey is valid, the code will serialize a response message that includes the LinkItem.

1. First, modify the GetGig( ) operation to work with raw messages. Go to the GigManager project and open *GigManagerService.cs*. Change the signature of GetGig( ) to look as shown here:

   ```
   [OperationContract]
   Message GetGig(Message requestMessage);
   ```

2. In the current implementation, a LicenseKey header is passed to GetGig( ) and deserialized by the service model. If this header is accurate, a response is generated to return the LinkItem. You're going to modify the code so that it accesses this via the Message type. You'll then generate the response message using a custom Message type, GetGigResponse. Example 2-42 shows the new implementation of GetGig( ).

Example 2-42. Updated GetGig() implementation

```
public Message GetGig(Message requestMessage)
{
  string licenseKey = requestMessage.Headers.GetHeader<string>("LicenseKey",
"http://www.thatindigogirl.com/samples/2006/06");

  if (licenseKey != "XXX")
    throw new FaultException("Invalid license key.");

  return new GetGigResponse(this.m_linkItem, requestMessage.Version);
}
```

The implementation of GetGig( ) is not complete yet; you'll need to create a custom type that inherits Message to override serialization of the message body when the response is generated. You'll create this custom type in the next step.

Extending the message type

Now you will create a new type that inherits Message. The purpose of this exercise is to show you how you would interact with the serialization process when working with raw messages. When you return a Message instance from a service operation, the service model hangs on to that custom message type and at the appropriate moment, during serialization, invokes serialization methods such as OnWriteBodyContents( ). You'll explore this now.

1. To support the new implementation of GetGig( ) you'll create a new GetGigResponse type. Go to the GigManager project and open *Messages.cs*. This file currently contains message contract definitions from the original service contract when you began the lab. You can now delete all of the types in this file since they are no longer in use.

2. Add the type definition for GetGigResponse shown in Example 2-43, adding the using statements for System.ServiceModel.Channels and System.Xml.

   The type inherits Message and provides some overloaded constructors to build the LinkItem type from existing messages, XML streams, or objects. It also overrides OnWriteBodyContents( ) to interact with the serialization process and uses an internal Message object to supply information to Version, Properties, and Headers property overrides.

    This implementation is quite detailed, but it will give you a realistic picture of the work necessary to implement a custom Message type for this purpose. You may want to copy the implementation from the completed lab to save yourself some typing. Just make sure you review it well.

3. Compile and run the solution, executing the same test as before. You should see the same results.

Example 2-43. GetGigResponse implementation

```
using System.ServiceModel.Channels;
using System.Xml;

public class GetGigResponse : Message
{

  private const string Action =
"http://www.thatindigogirl.com/samples/2006/06/GigManagerServiceContract/GetGigResp
onse";
  private const string ns = "http://www.thatindigogirl.com/samples/2006/06";

  private Message m_innerMessage;

  private LinkItem m_linkItem = new LinkItem( );
  public LinkItem Item
  {
    get { return m_linkItem; }
    set { m_linkItem = value; }
  }

  public GetGigResponse( )
  {
  }

  public GetGigResponse(Message message)
  {
    this.m_innerMessage = message;

    XmlDictionaryReader reader = message.GetReaderAtBodyContents( );
    this.m_linkItem = LinkItemHelper.ReadLinkItem(reader);
  }

  public GetGigResponse(LinkItem linkItem, MessageVersion version)
  {
    m_innerMessage = Message.CreateMessage(version, Action);

    this.m_linkItem = linkItem;
  }

  public GetGigResponse(XmlReader xmlReader, MessageVersion version)
  {
    m_innerMessage = Message.CreateMessage(version, Action);

    XmlDictionaryReader reader =
XmlDictionaryReader.CreateDictionaryReader(xmlReader);
    this.m_linkItem = LinkItemHelper.ReadLinkItem(reader);
  }

  public override MessageHeaders Headers
  {
    get
    {
      if (m_innerMessage == null)
```

Example 2-43. GetGigResponse implementation (continued)

```
      {
        throw new FaultException("Invalid operation.
Inner message has not been set.");
      }
      else
        return this.m_innerMessage.Headers;
    }
  }

  protected override void OnWriteBodyContents(System.Xml.XmlDictionaryWriter
xmlWriter)
  {
    xmlWriter.WriteStartElement("GetGigResponse", ns);
    xmlWriter.WriteStartElement("Item", ns);

    LinkItemHelper.WriteLinkItem(this.m_linkItem, xmlWriter);

    xmlWriter.WriteEndElement( ); //Item
    xmlWriter.WriteEndElement( ); //GetGigResponse

  }

  public override MessageProperties Properties
  {
    get
    {
      if (m_innerMessage == null)
      {
        throw new FaultException("Invalid operation.
Inner message has not been set.");
      }
      else
        return this.m_innerMessage.Properties;
    }
  }

  public override MessageVersion Version
  {
    get
    {
      if (m_innerMessage == null)
      {
        throw new FaultException("Invalid operation.
Inner message has not been set.");
      }
      else
        return m_innerMessage.Version;
    }
  }
}
```

Let's look more closely at the concepts introduced in this lab.

Untyped Messages and WSDL

When a service operation uses the Message type for the incoming parameter or return type, there isn't any useful type metadata associated with the operation. In fact, the XSD schema type for Message is a complex type that includes the any schema type. That means that the service description and resulting WSDL document will not have meaningful type descriptions for request and response messages.

The point is that it is unlikely you'll design a service contract with operations that receive or return the Message type in this way unless you are creating a pass-through service that receives and forwards messages, perhaps after performing some sort of auditing or logging activity. Services such as these can interact with any message, regardless of the message headers and body elements present, using the Message type, which provides an object model for accessing the message headers, message body elements, and other properties of the message including the SOAP version. I'll show you an example of a pass-through message router shortly.

Working with the Message Type

Message is an abstract type from the System.ServiceModel.Channels namespace. It provides functionality for working with messages in the following ways:

- It provides static methods for creating new messages, including fault messages.
- It has overridable methods that subclasses can use to interact with serialization of a message, useful for writing headers, body elements, and other message properties.
- It provides methods for accessing message headers and message body elements.

Creating messages

You can use the Message type to create a new message. The Message type exposes the following key properties:

Version
> This refers to the SOAP and WS-Addressing protocol versions on which the message is based. The MessageVersion enumeration provides options from which to select. I discuss this in Chapter 3 when I review web service bindings.

Headers
> This provides access to predefined addressing headers and custom message headers through the MessageHeaders type.

State
> This describes the current state of a message based on the MessageState enumeration using the following elements: Created, Read, Written, Copied, and Closed. A Message traverses these states as it is processed by the runtime or by your code. For example, when a request arrives for a particular service operation, the service model creates a Message object to represent it. During deserialization, the

service model reads the message. Once the service model has finished processing the request, the Message is closed and no longer accessible. You will interact with these states only in advanced scenarios.

You can use one of the overloaded CreateMessage( ), methods to construct a new message. When you construct a new message, you must always supply a version, since this is a read-only property once the message is constructed. Likewise, you can provide the action header during construction as shown here:

```
System.ServiceModel.Channels.Message requestMessage =
System.ServiceModel.Channels.Message.CreateMessage(
MessageVersion.Soap12WSAddressing10,
"http://www.thatindigogirl.com/samples/2006/06/
GigManagerServiceContract/GetGig");
```

Once constructed, you can set common addressing header values directly through the MessageHeaders type. This type exposes properties for the following addressing headers: Action, FaultTo, From, MessageId, RelatesTo, and To. For example:

```
requestMessage.Headers.Action =
"http://www.thatindigogirl.com/samples/2006/06/GigManagerServiceContract/GetGig";
```

Of course, initializing a Message with the correct version and addressing headers isn't very useful on its own. You can also add other custom headers to the heads collection through the Headers property of the Message. More importantly, you should supply information for the message body by passing an XML reader or writer to one of the overloaded CreateMessage( ) functions. Presumably, if you are creating a message using CreateMessage( ), you already have some XML you'd like to serialize within the body element. You can also create a custom type that derives from Message and override key members to produce a message, as the lab illustrates. For example, in the lab, the service returns a message by constructing a custom Message type and providing an override for OnWriteBodyContents( ) to inject the correct XML into the message body element.

Accessing message headers

You can access headers using the Headers property of the Message type. As I mentioned, this property is a MessageHeaders type that supplies methods for finding headers by index, type, or name; supplies strongly typed methods for deserializing headers into their CLR format; provides direct access to common addressing headers; and has additional functionality for programmatically interacting with the headers collection of a message.

One reason why you might need access to the header collection is if an operation accepts raw messages (using the Message type as a parameter) and performs some action based on header values. For example, before forwarding the message to a strongly typed service, the intermediate service looks for a particular header to determine the correct destination. You can use the overloaded GetHeader<T>( ) method to retrieve specific headers for this purpose. The lab illustrates retrieving the LicenseKey header as shown here:

```
string licenseKey = requestMessage.Headers.GetHeader<string>(
    "LicenseKey","http://www.thatindigogirl.com/samples/2006/06");
```

You can also create a custom header type by inheriting the base type MessageHeader. This gives you access to the serialization process for the header if it is a complex type. Example 2-44 shows an implementation of a custom MessageHeader called LicenseKeyHeader, which overrides the Name, Namespace, and OnWriteHeaderContents( ) members.

Example 2-44. LicenseKeyHeader implementation

```
public class LicenseKeyHeader : MessageHeader
{
  private const string ns = "http://www.thatindigogirl.com/samples/2006/06";

  public override string Name
  {
    get { return "LicenseKey"; }
  }
  public override string Namespace
  {
    get { return ns; }
  }
  public LicenseKeyHeader(string licenseKey)
  {
    this.m_licenseKey = licenseKey;
  }

  private string m_licenseKey;
  public string LicenseKey
  {
    get { return m_licenseKey; }
    set { m_licenseKey = value; }
  }

  protected override void OnWriteHeaderContents(XmlDictionaryWriter writer,
MessageVersion version)
  {
    writer.WriteString(this.m_licenseKey);
  }
}
```

If you add an instance of this header to the Headers collection of a new message, the service model will invoke OnWriteHeaderContents( ) during serialization. Here is an example of the code to construct a message and initialize the message header:

```
System.ServiceModel.Channels.Message requestMessage =
System.ServiceModel.Channels.Message.CreateMessage(
MessageVersion.Soap12WSAddressing10,
"http://www.thatindigogirl.com/samples/2006/06/GigManagerServiceContract/GetGig");

requestMessage.Headers.Action =
"http://www.thatindigogirl.com/samples/2006/06/GigManagerServiceContract/GetGig";
```

```
LicenseKeyHeader licenseKeyHeader = new LicenseKeyHeader("XXX");
requestMessage.Headers.Add(licenseKeyHeader);
```

 A sample illustrating the use of custom headers can be found at
<YourLearningWCFPath>\Samples\AdvancedSerialization
RawMessagesClient.

Filtering Messages

Using the Message type in an operation signature doesn't by definition mean that any
message can be processed by the service. By default, the action header in a message is
used to target a particular operation. The service model inspects incoming messages
and looks for an operation on the endpoint that has a matching action header. If it
can't find a match, the request is rejected. The service contract lab in this chapter
illustrates the scenario of mismatched action headers.

When would action headers not match the operation being invoked? One possibility
is when an intermediary or routing service is placed between the client and the application service. In this scenario, the client application doesn't know of the presence of
the intermediate service and the action header targets the application service.

Recall from earlier discussions that the service contract usually generates the
required action headers based on the target namespace, the contract name, and the
operation name. Client proxies usually explicitly state request and reply action headers, as shown here:

```
[System.ServiceModel.OperationContractAttribute(
Action="http://www.thatindigogirl.com/samples/2006/06/GigManagerServiceContract/
SaveGig", ReplyAction="http://www.thatindigogirl.com/samples/2006/06/
GigManagerServiceContract/SaveGigResponse")]
GigEntry.localhost.SaveGigResponse SaveGig(GigEntry.localhost.SaveGigRequest
request);

[System.ServiceModel.OperationContractAttribute(
Action="http://www.thatindigogirl.com/samples/2006/06/GigManagerServiceContract/
GetGig", ReplyAction="http://www.thatindigogirl.com/samples/2006/06/
GigManagerServiceContract/GetGigResponse")]
GigEntry.localhost.GetGigResponse GetGig(GigEntry.localhost.GetGigRequest request);
```

For an intermediate service to intercept "any" message, it must not have explicit
action header requirements. To achieve this, you can specify an Action and
ReplyAction with "*", as shown here:

```
[ServiceContract(Name = "IntermediaryServiceContract", Namespace =
"http://www.thatindigogirl.com/samples/2006/06")]
public interface IIntermediaryService
{
  [OperationContract(Action = "*", ReplyAction = "*")]
  Message ProcessMessage(Message requestMessage);
}
```

Services also have an addressing filter that by default requires strict matching of action headers from incoming messages to the operation contract. You can set the address-filtering mode for the service by applying the following `ServiceBehaviorAttribute` to the service type:

```
[ServiceBehavior(AddressFilterMode=AddressFilterMode.Any)]
public class IntermediaryService : IIntermediaryService
```

The `ServiceBehaviorAttribute` will be discussed in detail in later chapters. It is essentially a declarative way to control local behaviors of the service, something I discussed in Chapter 1. One such behavior is address filtering, for which there are three options specified by the `AddressFilterMode` enumeration as follows:

Exact

This is the default mode, which means action headers in the message must exactly match the action or reply action specified in the service contract.

Prefix

This setting requires only a prefix match, such as the domain of the action header.

Any

This setting indicates that any action header is supported, useful for intermediate services.

 An example illustrating the intermediary concept can be found at *<YourLearningWCFPath>\Samples\AdvancedSerialization\ MessagingIntermediary*.

Summary

This chapter focused on contracts and serialization to provide you with the tools you need to design service contracts and where applicable, exercise greater control over serialization. You learned about classic code-first approaches to building a service description, which means relying on service contracts, data contracts, message contracts and other serializable types to produce WSDL. You also learned some techniques that can be applied to contract-first scenarios, where the WSDL or XSD schema is provided up front and your service must conform. Namely, using `IXmlSerializable` you can respect preexisting XSD schema while still building a service contract to frame the operations available at an endpoint.

Things you should take away from this chapter include the following recommendations:

- Where possible, try to use code-first approaches, which will improve your productivity in designing services.
- Develop a consistent set of naming conventions that you apply across all of your services, including those for the target namespace, the schema namespace, and operation and parameter names.

- Decide whether you will use strict or non-strict approaches to versioning and follow the guidelines I have provided for achieving those results.
- Use message contracts if you need custom headers.
- Consider IXmlSerializable for situations where the XSD schema has been provided in advance, for example by standards organizations in your industry.

Now that you have learned almost all there is to know about contracts, it's time to dive in and discuss the various bindings provided by the service model to control how the communication channel is built. The next chapter will focus on how to work with the standard bindings and how to customize those bindings to meet the needs of some typical application scenarios. You'll learn how to build intranet services, Internet web services, and control message-encoding formats, and how to configure callbacks. You'll also learn how to build custom bindings when the standard bindings aren't meeting the needs of your scenario.

CHAPTER 3

Bindings

So far in this book, you have learned how to create and consume services; how to design and implement service contracts; how to host services and configure service endpoints; and learned various ways to generate proxies for clients to invoke service operations. In the process, you have worked with a few of the standard bindings such as `NetTcpBinding` and `BasicHttpBinding` to establish communication channels between clients and services. Although I've shown you how to select a binding for a service endpoint, and I've discussed how bindings determine the protocols used to communicate, I haven't begun to show you scope of what bindings can do. In this chapter, I'll focus on bindings, explaining how to choose from the different standard bindings, how to customize them to meet your deployment needs, and how to create custom bindings to address special situations where the standard bindings don't satisfy your requirements. In the process, you'll learn how to work with web service bindings and connection-oriented bindings, how to implement two-way communication scenarios, and how to handle large messages.

How Bindings Work

Every service endpoint is associated with a particular binding. A *binding* is a runtime type that derives from the common base type `Binding`. Bindings describe the transport protocol, message-encoding format and other messaging protocols for the communication channel. In this section, I'm going to introduce you to each of the standard bindings, explain the features provided by the service model for bindings, and explain how binding configuration builds the communication channel.

Standard Bindings

In Chapter 1, I showed you how to configure an endpoint and its associated binding in two ways:

- Declaratively, using service model configuration settings
- Programmatically, by adding endpoints to the `ServiceHost`

Declaratively, you set the binding property for each service or client <endpoint> by referring to it by its configuration name, as shown here:

```
// service endpoint
<endpoint address="HelloIndigoService" binding="basicHttpBinding"
contract="Host.IHelloIndigoService" />

// client endpoint
<endpoint address="http://localhost:8000/HelloIndigo/HelloIndigoService"
binding="basicHttpBinding" contract="Client.localhost.IHelloIndigoService" />
```

Programmatically, you construct a binding instance and associate it with endpoints added to the ServiceHost or client proxy. In either case, you create an instance of the desired binding by its CLR type, for example:

```
BasicHttpBinding basicBinding = new BasicHttpBinding();
NetTcpBinding tcpBinding = new NetTcpBinding();
```

Each binding is represented at runtime by its CLR type, but when you set the binding property for declarative configuration you refer to the binding by its configuration name.

 I'm making the distinction between the CLR type name and configuration name so that you can relate them as you read this book. In the book, I will usually refer to bindings in a discussion by the proper CLR type name, even while describing a declarative example that uses the configuration name.

Table 3-1 shows a complete list of the standard bindings that come with WCF. The table shows the CLR type name, the configuration name, and provides a brief description of the purpose of each binding.

Table 3-1. A summary of the standard bindings

Binding type	Configuration name	Description
BasicHttpBinding	basicHttpBinding	A web service binding used for compatibility with earlier web service stacks such as ASP.NET web services (ASMX).
WSHttpBinding	wsHttpBinding	A web service binding that supports the latest in interoperable web service standards (WS*) and is compatible with more recent web service stacks.
WSDualHttpBinding	wsDualHttpBinding	A web service binding supporting WS* and two-way communication.
WSFederationHttpBinding	wsFederationHttp Binding	A web service binding that supports WS* as it relates to federated and single sign-on security scenarios. This binding is discussed in Chapter 7.
NetNamedPipeBinding	netNamedPipeBinding	A connection-oriented binding for communications on the same machine over named pipes.
NetTcpBinding	netTcpBinding	A connection-oriented binding for communications across process and machine boundaries over TCP.

Table 3-1. A summary of the standard bindings (continued)

Binding type	Configuration name	Description
NetPeerTcpBinding	netPeerTcpBinding	Supports peer-to-peer and broadcast communications. NetPeerTcpBinding is not covered in this book.
NetMsmqBinding	netMsmqBinding	Supports durable reliable messaging over MSMQ. This binding is discussed in Chapter 6.
MsmqIntegrationBinding	msmqIntegration Binding	Supports integration with legacy MSMQ components. This binding is discussed in Chapter 6.

When you choose one of the standard bindings you're getting a default set of features for the communication channel. Each binding supplies a set of default features according to its typical usage. You can also modify the feature selection through properties exposed by the binding: declaratively or programmatically. In the next section, I'll discuss the features that you can choose from when you configure the communication channel for an endpoint.

Binding Features

At a minimum, every binding configuration must supply a transport protocol, a message-encoding format, and a relevant message version, but there are additional features for security, duplex communication, reliable messaging, and transactions that may also be enabled. The following is a list of binding features and their purposes.

Transport protocols

This is used to transfer messages on the wire. This can be HTTP, HTTPS, TCP, named pipes, or MSMQ. For advanced scenarios you can also add support for other transport protocols.

Message encoding

This describes how messages are formatted on the wire. You can choose from the following: Binary, Text, or Mtom. Mtom is a new encoding format useful for optimizing how large blocks of binary data are transferred over HTTP, described in detail later in this chapter. For advanced scenarios, you can also create custom message-encoding formats.

Message version

Regardless of the message-encoding format, messages are represented on the wire as either SOAP 1.1 or SOAP 1.2. In addition, the message version indicates if WS-Addressing protocol is supported (recall from Chapter 2) and more specifically, which version of the specification. You'll care about this only when you expose endpoints using web service bindings for interoperability. I'll discuss this later in this chapter.

Transport security

Transport security refers to the ability to transfer credentials and sign and encrypt messages on the wire. SSL is generally used when this feature is enabled. Security is covered in Chapter 7.

Message security

Message security refers to the ability to transfer credentials and sign and encrypt messages independent of the transport layer. There are a number of interoperable specifications to support this, discussed in Chapter 7.

Duplex

Two-way communication is inherently supported by TCP and named pipes. HTTP protocol doesn't support two-way communication normally, but there are binding features that enable this to be discussed in this chapter.

Reliable messaging

Some transport protocols are inherently reliable, such as TCP. There is also an interoperable standard for reliable messaging that is available on some bindings. This is discussed in Chapter 6.

Transactions

Supporting distributed transactions across service boundaries is critical for enterprise systems. This feature enables transaction flow and determines the protocol supported. This is discussed in Chapter 6.

Features such as these are enabled by setting binding properties, also called *binding elements*. Not all features are supported by all bindings. Essentially, each standard binding exposes an object model for initializing features that it supports. You can also configure these features declaratively.

Binding Elements

All bindings have a collection of binding elements that are used to initialize the communication channel. This collection holds at least one transport binding element, a message-encoding element, and possibly other binding elements if other features are supported. Internally, each of the standard bindings initializes its own `BindingElementsCollection` with a set of default binding elements. Binding elements derive from the common `BindingElement` base type.

Common binding elements are as follows:

`TransportBindingElement`

Each binding has a transport-binding element that defines the transport protocol for the binding. It can be one of these types:

```
NetNamedPipeTransportBindingElement
NetTcpTransportBindingElement
HttpTransportBindingElement
HttpsTransportBindingElement
MsmqTransportBindingElement
MsmqIntegrationTransportBindingElement
NetPeerTransportBindingElement
```

MessageEncodingBindingElement

Each binding has a message encoder that controls the wire format of each message. It can be one of these types:

BinaryMessageEncodingBindingElement
TextMessageEncodingBindingElement
MtomMessageEncodingBindingElement

SecurityBindingElement

Describes the security protocols for a binding, discussed in Chapter 7.

CompositeDuplexBindingElement, OneWayBindingElement

These binding elements enable composite duplex communication.

ReliableSessionBindingElement

Configures reliable messaging protocols for a binding, discussed in Chapter 6.

TransactionFlowBindingElement

Configures transaction protocols for the binding, discussed in Chapter 6.

With standard bindings, you'll usually work with binding elements indirectly through properties of the binding. You can set properties of any of the standard bindings declaratively by associating its endpoint with a customized binding section. In Example 3-1, the endpoint is configured to use WSHttpBinding. The endpoint's bindingConfiguration name maps to a customized <wsHttpBinding> section that enables transaction flow and reliable messaging, and modifies security settings to use transport security instead of message security.

Example 3-1. Setting binding properties declaratively

```
<system.serviceModel>
  <services>
    <service name="HelloIndigo.HelloIndigoService">
      <endpoint contract="HelloIndigo.IHelloIndigoService" binding="wsHttpBinding"
      bindingConfiguration="wsHttpSecureAndReliable"/>
    </service>
  </services>
  <bindings>
    <wsHttpBinding>
      <binding name="wsHttpSecureAndReliable" maxReceivedMessageSize="100000"
transactionFlow="true"  >
        <reliableSession enabled="true" />
        <security mode="Transport"/>
      </binding>
    </wsHttpBinding>
  </bindings>
</system.serviceModel>
```

To do the same programmatically, you set properties on the binding CLR type, which is WSHttpBinding in this case. Example 3-2 shows an example of this.

Example 3-2. Setting binding properties in code

```
WSHttpBinding binding = new WSHttpBinding( );
binding.Security.Mode = SecurityMode.Transport;
binding.ReliableSession.Enabled=true;
binding.TransactionFlow=true;
```

The point is that binding elements have runtime abstractions that are set through binding declarations or binding properties. In most cases, you'll initialize bindings declaratively.

Later sections in this chapter will elaborate on some typical modifications you can make to standard binding configurations to control these binding elements and their associated features.

Building the Channel Stack

Bindings provide the necessary elements to build the communication channels for clients and services to communicate. In fact, each binding element ultimately maps to a channel—thus the terms *binding element* and *channel* are interchangeable. On the service side, a binding is used to build a layered channel stack that begins with the transport channel and message encoder, and follows with each of the protocol channels specified through the binding configuration. Essentially, binding elements configure the channel stack. The client side is handled in a similar fashion—bindings are used to build a channel stack accessible through the client proxy. This time, the order of the channel stack is reversed. Figure 3-1 illustrates the flow of messages between clients and services through their respective channels.

At the client, bindings are used to initialize a ChannelFactory that is in turn used to create the channel stack for the client. When you invoke a method on the proxy, the message flows through each channel allowing it to interact with the message before forwarding to the next channel. Ultimately, the transport channel and message encoder write the message to the wire. At the service, the transport channel and message encoder touch the message first to build a runtime representation, and the message then traverses each protocol channel until finally the dispatcher invokes the service operation, passing any input parameters.

On reply messages, the reverse takes place. Protocol channels at the service are responsible for preparing the message for delivery to the client. Ultimately, the transport channel and message encoder write the message to the wire, which is received by the client's transport channel and message encoder before passing the response message through the protocol channels to the proxy.

Both channel stacks have to be equivalent for messages to be processed successfully between client and service. This is made possible through WSDL and WS-Policy (discussed in Chapter 2).

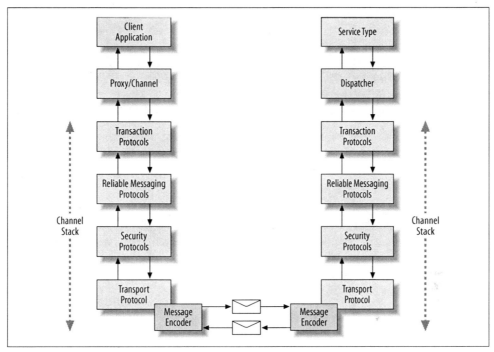

Figure 3-1. Message flow through the channel stack for clients and services

Web Service Protocols

Chapter 2 provides you with an overview of the messaging protocols that WCF supports—namely SOAP and the collective WS*. While most standard bindings default to using SOAP 1.2 and WS-Addressing, other WS* standards are employed only as you opt-in binding features. Although WS* standards for things such as security, reliable messaging, and transactions are interoperable protocols that are particularly useful when exposing web service endpoints, many of these protocols can still be employed over TCP, named pipes, and MSMQ. That's because the service model provides plumbing to handle binding features in the same way, regardless of the transport protocol or message-encoding format.

The messaging protocols discussed in Chapter 2 are either ratified standards or in the process of becoming so, under the following organizations:

W3C
World Wide Web Consortium (*www.w3.org*)

OASIS
Organization for the Advancement of Structured Information Standards (*www. oasis-open.org*)

The collective standards between these organizations are vast, and so another organization known as the Web Services Interoperability Organization or *WS-I* (*http://www.ws-i.org*) has the mission of helping vendor platforms like WCF implement standards in a consistent manner to handle common scenarios. There are two key profiles defined by WS-I that I will make reference to when I describe binding support for protocols in this book:

WS-I Basic Profile

A specification that provides guidance on the base web service specifications such as SOAP 1.1, WSDL 1.0 and related bindings such as HTTP. The goal of Basic Profile is to constrain use of the base web service specifications to an agreed upon set of core scenarios.

WS-I Basic Security Profile

A specification that provides guidance on a core set of OASIS WS-Security standards, specifically, the SOAP Message Security specification and related token profiles for UsernameToken and X.509 credentials. The goal of Basic Security Profile is to constrain use of these security standards to an agreed-upon set of core scenarios.

In this chapter, as I discuss each binding, I'll provide you with a list of binding features and related standards supported by each, also commenting on any support for Basic Profile or Basic Security Profile.

Bindings and Metadata

Clients typically rely on proxy generation to create the client proxy and related configuration. Recall from Chapter 2 that the service description comprises information about each endpoint and its protocol support according to the binding configuration. The resulting WSDL document and related WS-Policy sections included within it describe the transport protocol, message-encoding format, and other protocols supported for each endpoint.

In order for clients to build an equivalent binding configuration, there must be sufficient information described by the WSDL document to infer the correct choice of binding elements. WS-Policy extensions exist for security, transactions, reliable messaging, sessions, and other features that are described as part of the service contract or binding configuration. Features of the binding configuration that are not considered local to the service are described in the policy section of the WSDL document, enabling clients to build an equivalent communication stack to call services.

Constraints on Binding Selection

Service contract design can and should be approached independently of the expected deployment model, but that doesn't mean that there isn't a possible coupling between a service contract and its binding. There are attributes for your service contracts and services that may require a particular type of binding. For example, if you require sessions (discussed in Chapter 5), you can only use a binding that supports sessions.

In addition, you have to consider that a binding applies to a particular endpoint, and thus applies to all operations on a particular contract. The semantics of certain operations in a service contract may by definition require a separate binding configuration, which may mean separating those operations to a separate contract, although they are still implemented on the same service type. Here are some examples:

- Operations that support large message transfers or streaming should be placed in a separate service contract so that they can be assigned an appropriate binding configuration that supports larger messages and protocols for that purpose.
- Service contracts that support callback operations should be placed in a separate service contract that can be assigned a binding that supports two-way calls.
- One-way operations that require durable reliability should be placed in a separate contract that supports MSMQ bindings.

I'll discuss these types of constraints as we encounter related scenarios in this chapter and in subsequent chapters.

Web Service Bindings

Web services make it easy to expose system functionality to remote clients. For one, web services are typically exposed over HTTP or HTTPS through ports that administrators allow to be open. More importantly, web services provide an interoperable way to communicate using standards such as SOAP, WSDL, and XML, making them the ideal conduit for communication between trading partners, independent systems, and heterogeneous environments.

Several of the standard WCF bindings can be used to expose web services, including `BasicHttpBinding`, `WSHttpBinding`, `WSDualHttpBinding`, and `WSFederationHttpBinding`. `BasicHttpBinding` supports SOAP 1.1 by default, whereas the other three bindings default to SOAP 1.2 with support for WS-Addressing among other protocols.

This section will focus on the fundamental web service bindings, `BasicHttpBindng` and `WSHttpBinding`. The first thing you'll do is complete a lab that exercises each binding. After the lab, I'll explain the following concepts:

- Binding features and their applicability to these bindings
- Scenarios in which each binding is appropriate
- `MessageVersion` settings
- Serialization differences for SOAP 1.1 and SOAP 1.2
- Alternatives for exposing a single service over two bindings

Lab: Exposing Web Services with BasicHttpBinding and WSHttpBinding

In this lab, you'll exposed web service endpoints for a service that lets users upload photos and save a record of each upload to a database. You'll provide endpoints for SOAP 1.1 and SOAP 1.2 with WS-Addressing in order to support clients using web service platforms with different capabilities.

Exposing multiple web service endpoints

The first thing you will do in this lab is open an existing solution and expose endpoints for an existing service using `BasicHttpBinding` and `WSHttpBinding`. You'll see how to configure multiple *.svc* endpoints in a web host.

1. Open the startup solution for this lab at *<YourLearningWCFPath>\Labs\ Chapter3\WebServiceBindings\WebServiceBindings.sln*. This solution contains several projects:

   ContentTypes
   > Contains several data contracts including one for the `PhotoLink` type used in this lab.

   FileManager
   > A class library with file access functionality.

   LinkItems.Dalc
   > A class library containing the data access layer for the database in this sample.

   PhotoManager
   > A class library providing functionality to upload photos. It coordinates saving the file and database record.

   PhotoManagerService
   > A class library for the service contracts and implementation.

   PhotoApplication
   > A web site to host the `PhotoManagerService`.

   PhotoUploadClient
   > A client application using SOAP 1.2 with WS-Addressing to access services.

   LegacyPhotoUploadClient
   > A client application using SOAP 1.1 to access services.

2. This lab requires you to install the database script *<YourLearningWCFPath>\ SupportingFiles\DatabaseScripts\Photos_CreateDB.sql*. You must also check the connection string located in the *web.config* file of the `PhotoApplication` web site to be sure it is configured according to your database environment. See the "Database Setup" section in Appendix A for detailed instructions.

3. Go to the `PhotoManagerService` project. In this project, you'll find a service contract, `IPhotoUpload`, with a single operation:

```
[ServiceContract(Name="PhotoUploadContract",
Namespace="http://www.thatindigogirl.com/samples/2006/06")]
public interface IPhotoUpload
{
  [OperationContract]
  void UploadPhoto(PhotoLink fileInfo, byte[] fileData);
}
```

This contract has already been implemented on the `PhotoManagerService` type. The `UploadPhoto( )` operation calls down into the `PhotoManager` business component to save an uploaded file and record the associated database record.

4. Since the service is already implemented, your first step is to host the service in the web site provided. Go to the `PhotoApplication` web site and add a new WCF Service, name it *PhotoManagerService.svc*. You will associate this *.svc* endpoint with the `PhotoManagerService`. First, add reference to the `PhotoManagerService` project. Then, open *PhotoManagerService.svc* and modify the `@ServiceHost` declaration to point at the correct service implementation, as shown here:

```
<%@ ServiceHost Service="PhotoManagerService.PhotoManagerService" %>
```

5. Now, configure the new service endpoint. Open the *web.config* file and add the `<system.serviceModel>` section shown in Example 3-3. This configuration exposes the `PhotoManagerService` over SOAP 1.1 (`BasicHttpBinding`) and enables metadata exchange for proxy generation.

Example 3-3. Service model configuration for PhotoManagerService.svc

```
<system.serviceModel>
  <services>
    <service name="PhotoManagerService.PhotoManagerService"
behaviorConfiguration="serviceBehavior">
    <endpoint contract="PhotoManagerService.IPhotoUpload"
binding="basicHttpBinding"/>
    <endpoint contract="IMetadataExchange" binding="mexHttpBinding" address="mex"/>
    </service>
  </services>
  <behaviors>
    <serviceBehaviors>
      <behavior name="serviceBehavior">
        <serviceMetadata httpGetEnabled="true"/>
      </behavior>
    </serviceBehaviors>
  </behaviors>
</system.serviceModel>
```

6. Check the connection string settings in the *web.config* file to make sure it is correct for your database environment. See the section "Database Setup" in Appendix A for additional instructions.

7. Compile the web site and test this endpoint by browsing to the *.svc* endpoint. You can right-click the `PhotoApplication` project node and select "View in Browser." From the directory listing, click the link for *PhotoManagerService.svc*, and you'll see the service help page.

8. Now add a second endpoint to the service configuration in *web.config*. This endpoint will make the service available over SOAP 1.2 with WS-Addressing support using `WSHttpBinding`. The new endpoint is shown in bold here:

```
<service name="PhotoManagerService.PhotoManagerService" ... >
  <endpoint contract="PhotoManagerService.IPhotoUpload"
  binding="wsHttpBinding"/>
  <!-- other endpoints -->
</service>
```

Differences between `BasicHttpBinding` and `WSHttpBinding` run deeper than the format of the SOAP message. This will be discussed after the lab.

9. Save the changes to the *web.config* and refresh the *PhotoManagerService.svc* endpoint in the browser. This time, you will see an `InvalidOperationException` indicating that two endpoints can't share the same URI unless they share the same binding configuration. The same error would occur if you were self-hosting and exposed two HTTP endpoints with the same address, contract, and binding.

   You can solve this problem by providing a unique address for each endpoint. You can achieve this by providing a relative address for each endpoint.

10. Go to the *web.config* file and add a relative address for each endpoint configuration. For the `BasicHttpBinding` endpoint, use "Soap11." For the `WSHttpBinding` endpoint use "Soap12." The resulting change to the *web.config* is shown in bold here:

```
<endpoint address="Soap11" contract="PhotoManagerService.IPhotoUpload"
binding="basicHttpBinding"/>
<endpoint address="Soap12" contract="PhotoManagerService.IPhotoUpload"
binding="wsHttpBinding"/>
```

   Save the changes again and refresh the browser. This time you should see the service help page.

11. One more configuration setting must be verified for the service. The `FileManager` project depends on an application setting for the path to save uploaded files. In the *web.config,* verify the path for the `fileUploadDir` application setting and replace *<YourLearningWCFPath>* accordingly. The subdirectory should already exist:

```
<appSettings>
  <add key="fileUploadDir" value="<YourLearningWCFPath>\Labs\UploadedPhotos"/>
</appSettings>
```

Adding a web reference for the legacy client

Web reference is a term used to describe a client proxy for a web service. Prior to .NET 3.0, this was the mechanism used to generate proxies for ASMX web services. As with adding a service reference, adding a web reference generates a proxy for the target web service, including any types necessary for parameters and return values. It does this by calling *wsdl.exe*, passing the WSDL document generated for the target web service. In this part of the lab, you'll add a web reference for the SOAP 1.1 client to illustrate interoperability with earlier platforms.

1. For the purpose of this lab, you can assume that LegacyPhotoUploadClient can consume only SOAP 1.1 endpoints and does not have access to .NET 3.0 at the client.

   Go to the LegacyPhotoUploadClient project and add a web reference to the BasicHttpBinding service endpoint. To do this, right-click the project node and select Add Service Reference. From the Add Service Reference dialog click the Advanced button and then click the Add Web Reference button. In the dialog provided (shown in Figure 3-2), include the URI *http://localhost:3107/PhotoApplication/ PhotoManagerService.svc*. Use the default reference name localhost.

 Since this solution uses a file-based web site instead of IIS, a unique port is supplied. Your port may be a different value, be sure to check this when you browse to the service endpoint.

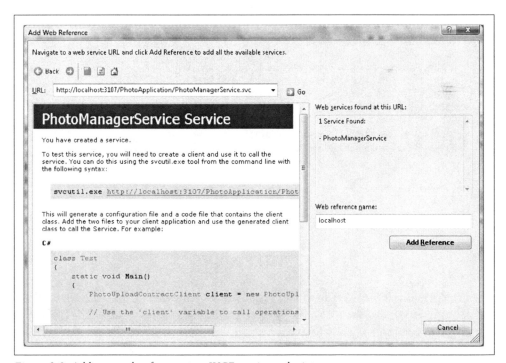

Figure 3-2. Adding a web reference to a WCF service endpoint

This generates a proxy for the client application to consume the service and a configuration setting specifying the endpoint as shown here:

```
http://localhost:3107/PhotoApplication/PhotoManagerService.svc/Soap11
```

2. In the same project, add code to *Form1.cs* to create an instance of the new PhotoManagerService proxy for the BasicHttpBinding endpoint. You'll also add code to the Click event handler for the Save button, cmdSave_Click( ), to create a PhotoLink item and pass it with the image data to the UploadPhoto( ) operation. Example 3-4 shows the changes you'll make to *Form1.cs* in bold.

Example 3-4. Code to invoke UploadPhoto( ) using the web reference

```csharp
using LegacyPhotoUploadClient.localhost;

public partial class Form1 : Form
{
  PhotoManagerService m_proxy = new PhotoManagerService( );

  private void cmdSave_Click(object sender, EventArgs e)
  {
    try
    {
      PhotoLink fileInfo = new PhotoLink( );

      fileInfo.Title = this.txtTitle.Text;
      fileInfo.Description = this.txtDescription.Text;
      fileInfo.DateStart = this.dtpStart.Value;
      fileInfo.Url = this.txtUrl.Text;
      fileInfo.Category="General";

      MemoryStream stm = new MemoryStream( );
      this.pic.Image.Save(stm, this.pic.Image.RawFormat);
      byte[] fileData = new byte[stm.Length];
      fileData = stm.ToArray( );

      m_proxy.UploadPhoto(fileInfo, fileData);
      MessageBox.Show("File uploaded!");

    }
    catch (Exception ex)
    {
      string s = String.Format("{0}\r\nERROR:{1}", ex.GetType( ), ex.Message);
      MessageBox.Show(s);
    }
  }
}
```

3. Compile and test the LegacyPhotoUploadClient application. From the client interface, click the browse ("...") button, select the image *<YourLearningWCFPath>\ SupportingFiles\SampleImages\theband.jpg* and click Upload Photo. You should see a message box indicating the file was uploaded.

By default, the size of the message payload is restricted, so it is important you choose a small file (under 16K) like the one I suggest. I'll discuss how to handle large messages later in this chapter.

Adding a service reference for the non-legacy client

Now you'll generate a proxy for the SOAP 1.2 client. You can assume that this client can use .NET 3.0, and therefore use the add service reference technique.

1. Go to the `PhotoUploadClient` project and add a service reference supplying the same URI and namespace as in the previous section.

   Open *Form1.cs* and add code to invoke the `WSHttpBinding` endpoint of the service. In fact, you will add the same code as shown in Example 3-4 with the exception of the using statement and proxy constructor. These differences are shown here:

   ```
   using PhotoUploadClient.localhost;

   PhotoUploadContractClient m_proxy = new
   PhotoUploadContractClient("WSHttpBinding_PhotoUploadContract");
   ```

2. Compile and test the `PhotoUploadClient` application. Repeat the same steps as before to upload a photo, and you should see the same message box after the file is successfully uploaded.

In this lab, you configured two web service endpoints using the default settings for `BasicHttpBinding` and `WSHttpBinding`. You created a .NET 2.0 proxy for the former and a WCF proxy for the latter—the .NET 2.0 web service stack and the service model respectively handling serialization. In the sections to follow, I'll elaborate on the features of each binding and other possible configurations.

Choosing a Web Service Binding

Your choice of web service binding influences the protocols used for communication between clients and services. As I mentioned earlier, the standard bindings that are intended for web service style communications are `BasicHttpBinding`, `WSHttpBinding`, `WSDualHttpBinding`, and `WSFederationHttpBinding`. Although each of these standard bindings can be customized to meet different needs, they each provide their own set of default values and properties for customization that make sense for certain scenarios.

You know you need a web service binding if you require interoperability with other platforms, if you want to provide access to services over the Internet or if you require HTTP communication through firewalls. Having established this requirement, the key drivers for selecting each of the standard web service bindings are summarized here:

- Use `BasicHttpBinding` to expose or consume services consistent with earlier web service stacks requiring SOAP 1.1 or for compliance with WS-I Basic Profile and Basic Security Profile.

- Use `WSHttpBinding` to expose or consume services leveraging SOAP 1.2 and more recent WS* standards for addressing, security, reliable messaging, transactions, and more.
- Use `WSDualHttpBinding` to support two-way communications with support for SOAP 1.2 and WS*. This binding is discussed later in this chapter.
- Use `WSFederationHttpBinding` to support federated security scenarios with support for SOAP 1.2, WS*, and additional security standards. This binding is discussed in Chapter 7.

In the next sections I'll discuss `BasicHttpBinding` and `WSHttpBinding` in greater depth, explaining the differences between them including their influence on message serialization.

BasicHttpBinding Features

`BasicHttpBinding` supports Basic Profile and Basic Security Profile. Very simply put that means:

- Messages are serialized using SOAP 1.1.
- Message security is supported based on the earlier WS-Security specifications.

A few common reasons to use `BasicHttpBinding` are to expose services that can interoperate with clients relying on earlier SOAP 1.1 platforms, to replace existing ASMX services without impact to existing clients, and to consume services based on SOAP 1.1 and early security standards. Table 3-2 provides a summary of core binding features and their applicability to `BasicHttpBinding`.

Table 3-2. Summary of BasicHttpBinding features

Binding feature	BasicHttpBinding support
Transport Protocols	HTTP, HTTPS
Message Encoding	Text, MTOM
Message Version	SOAP 1.1, no addressing headers
Transport Security	SSL with Basic, Digest, Ntlm, Windows, or Certificate credentials
Message Security	SOAP Message Security
Duplex	No
Reliable Messaging	No
Transactions	No

BasicHttpBinding defaults

You can apply `BasicHttpBinding` to an endpoint without any customization as follows:

```
<endpoint address="Soap11" contract="PhotoManagerService.IPhotoUpload"
binding="basicHttpBinding"/>
```

Example 3-5 shows an expanded BasicHttpBinding configuration representative of the default values. This expanded view should also give you a hint as to what settings you can control when you employ this binding.

Example 3-5. Default settings for BasicHttpBinding

```
<basicHttpBinding>
  <binding name="basicHttpBindingDefaults" allowCookies="false"
bypassProxyOnLocal="false" hostNameComparisonMode="StrongWildcard"
maxBufferPoolSize="524288" maxBufferSize="65536" maxReceivedMessageSize="65536"
messageEncoding="Text" proxyAddress="" textEncoding="utf-8" transferMode="Buffered"
useDefaultWebProxy="true" closeTimeout="00:01:00" openTimeout="00:01:00"
receiveTimeout="00:10:00" sendTimeout="00:01:00" >
    <readerQuotas maxArrayLength="16384" maxBytesPerRead="4096" maxDepth="32"
maxNameTableCharCount="16384" maxStringContentLength="8192" />
    <security mode="None">
      <transport clientCredentialType="None" proxyCredentialType="None" realm=""/>
      <message algorithmSuite="Basic256" clientCredentialType="UserName" />
    </security>
  </binding>
</basicHttpBinding>
```

Highlighted in bold are default settings that are often inadequate. For example, by default the security mode is set to "None," so transport and message security are both disabled. Another issue that you'll frequently encounter is size limitations for messages, strings, and arrays. Messages will be rejected if they exceed any of these defaults. You can easily address this by customizing the binding configuration.

Customizing BasicHttpBinding

You can customize BasicHttpBinding declaratively by providing an expanded <basicHttpBinding> section with overriding values. Example 3-6 shows a modified binding typical of web services. Transport security (SSL) is enabled for transfer security, and a username and password are required to authenticate users. The binding also increases message sizes and array lengths to accommodate up to 100KB of data. This setting is not intended for extremely large message payloads, but it does leave some breathing room for general messaging to increase beyond the 64K default.

Example 3-6 shows this customized BasicHttpBinding.

Example 3-6. Customizing BasicHttpBinding defaults declaratively

```
<basicHttpBinding>
  <binding name="basicHttpSecure" maxBufferSize="100000"
maxReceivedMessageSize="100000">
    <readerQuotas maxArrayLength="100000" maxStringContentLength="100000"/>
    <security mode="TransportWithMessageCredential" />
  </binding>
</basicHttpBinding>
```

There are many ways to secure services exposed over `BasicHttpBinding` and `WSHttpBinding`. Chapter 7 will discuss how to approach authentication, authorization, and message protection in more detail.

To achieve the same results at runtime, construct an instance of the `BasicHttpBinding` type and override the same settings. Example 3-7 illustrates how a client application would create an equivalent binding to invoke a service.

Example 3-7. Overriding BasicHttpBinding default in code

```
BasicHttpBinding binding = new
BasicHttpBinding(BasicHttpSecurityMode.TransportWithMessageCredential);
binding.MaxBufferSize=100000;
binding.MaxReceivedMessageSize=100000;
binding.ReaderQuotas.MaxArrayLength=100000;
binding.ReaderQuotas.MaxStringContentLength=100000;

EndpointAddress address = new
EndpointAddress("https://localhost/BasicHttpBinding_Secure_WebHost/Service.svc");

HelloIndigoServiceClient proxy = new HelloIndigoServiceClient(binding, address);
```

 A sample illustrating this custom `BasicHttpBinding` configuration can be found at *<YourLearningWCFPath>\Samples\Bindings\BasicHttpBinding_ Secure*.

WSHttpBinding Features

`WSHttpBinding` supports SOAP 1.2 and other advanced web service standards that provide addressing, security, reliable messaging, and transaction support. As web service platforms evolve, they also strive to implement these standards to provide a richer communication experience over HTTP. `WSHttpBinding` makes it easy for you to configure interoperable web service endpoints with these features.

`WSHttpBinding` support for core binding features is shown in Table 3-3.

Table 3-3. Summary of WSHttpBinding features

Binding feature	WSHttpBinding support
Transport Protocols	HTTP, HTTPS
Message Encoding	Text, Mtom
Message Version	SOAP 1.2, WS-Addressing
Transport Security	SSL with Basic, Digest, Ntlm, Windows, or Certificate credentials
Message Security	SOAP Message Security, WS-Security, WS-Trust, WS-SecureConversation
Duplex	No
Reliable Messaging	Yes
Transactions	Yes

`WSHttpBinding` provides a much richer set of standards, making it possible to have distributed transactions and reliable messaging over HTTP. The security scenarios supported by this binding are also far superior to `BasicHttpBinding`. You should prefer `WSHttpBinding` so that you can provide endpoints with improved security and reliability. You can use `BasicHttpBinding` to support communication with very early web service platforms.

WSHttpBinding defaults

You can apply `WSHttpBinding` to an endpoint without any customization as follows:

```
<endpoint address="Soap12" contract="PhotoManagerService.IPhotoUpload"
binding="wsHttpBinding"/>
```

Unlike `BasicHttpBinding`, `WSHttpBinding` is secure by default, as illustrated by the expanded view of default settings in Example 3-8.

Example 3-8. Default settings for WSHttpBinding

```
<wsHttpBinding>
  <binding name="wsHttpDefaults" allowCookies -="false" bypassProxyOnLocal="false"
closeTimeout="00:01:00" hostNameComparisonMode="StrongWildcard"
maxBufferPoolSize="524288" maxReceivedMessageSize="65536" messageEncoding="Text"
openTimeout="00:01:00" receiveTimeout="00:10:00" proxyAddress=""
sendTimeout="00:01:00" textEncoding="utf-8" transactionFlow="false"
useDefaultWebProxy="true" >
    <readerQuotas maxArrayLength="16384" maxBytesPerRead="4096" maxDepth="32"
maxNameTableCharCount="16384" maxStringContentLength="8192" />
    <reliableSession enabled="false" ordered="true" inactivityTimeout="00:10:00"/>
    <security mode="Message">
      <message algorithmSuite="Basic256" clientCredentialType="Windows"
establishSecurityContext="true" negotiateServiceCredential="true"/>
      <transport clientCredentialType="Windows" proxyCredentialType="None"
realm=""/>
    </security>
  </binding>
</wsHttpBinding>
```

Again, I've highlighted in bold the settings that you typically need to consider changing for this binding.

Here are some considerations for deploying web services over `WSHttpBinding`:

- Will you use transport or message security?
- Will callers be part of a Windows domain, or will they provide alternate credentials such as username and password or Certificate?
- Can callers support advanced features such as reliable messaging, transactions, credential negotiation, and secure sessions?
- What message size are you expecting for this particular endpoint?

When you expose WSHttpBinding endpoints, your choices of features to enable should be considered alongside expectations of client platforms. You should enable only features that they can also support. For this reason, it is usually important to provide alternate endpoints for clients that don't support more recent WS* protocols.

Customizing WSHttpBinding

To customize the defaults for WSHttpBinding declaratively, provide an expanded binding section for <wsHttpBinding> with appropriate overrides. Ideally, when you expose WSHttpBinding endpoints, you are servicing callers that support the latest and greatest web service standards. As such, you may want to take advantage of reliable messaging and transaction capabilities. In addition, you'll have to select security settings fitting for the environment and adjust your message sizes accordingly. Example 3-9 shows how to declaratively customize WSHttpBinding to modify these settings.

Example 3-9. Customized settings for WSHttpBinding

```
<system.serviceModel>
  <services>
    <service name="HelloIndigo.HelloIndigoService"
behaviorConfiguration="serviceBehavior">
      <endpoint contract="HelloIndigo.IHelloIndigoService" binding="wsHttpBinding"
      bindingConfiguration="wsHttpSecureAndReliable"/>

      // more settings
    </service>
  </services>
  <bindings>
    <wsHttpBinding>
      <binding name="wsHttpSecureAndReliable" maxReceivedMessageSize="100000"
transactionFlow="true"  >
        <readerQuotas maxArrayLength="100000" maxStringContentLength="100000" />
        <reliableSession enabled="true" />
        <security mode="Message">
          <message clientCredentialType="UserName" negotiateServiceCredential="false"/>
        </security>
      </binding>
    </wsHttpBinding>
  </bindings>
  <behaviors>
    <behavior name="serviceBehavior">
      <serviceCredentials>
        <serviceCertificate findValue="RPKey" storeLocation="LocalMachine"
storeName="My" x509FindType="FindBySubjectName"/>
      </serviceCredentials>
    </behavior>
  </behaviors>
</system.serviceModel>
```

A sample illustrating this custom WSHttpBinding configuration can be found at *<YourLearningWCFPath>\Samples\Bindings\WSHttpBinding_ SecureAndReliable*.

This configuration is representative of a service endpoint exposed over the Internet that protects messages with a service certificate (provided in the <serviceCertificate> section) instead of relying on SSL. By default, user credentials are authenticated against a Windows domain. A more common scenario for Internet communications would be to authenticate users against a custom database, which means configuring a different membership provider. This and other security scenarios are discussed in Chapter 7.

As for settings related to reliable messaging and transactions, these topics are discussed in Chapter 6.

MessageVersion

One of the key differences between BasicHttpBinding and WSHttpBinding is their support for message version. Every standard binding has a MessageVersion property that is initialized to a default value representative of the binding. The options are:

- Soap11
- Soap11WSAddressing10
- Soap11WSAddressingAugust2004
- Soap12
- Soap12WSAddressing10
- Soap12WSAddressingAugust2004

MessageVersion comprises two key parts: EnvelopeVersion and AddressingVersion. EnvelopeVersion can be either Soap11 or Soap12. AddressingVersion can be based on the original (nonratified) WS-Addressing specification or the more recent submission to the W3C—WSAddressingAugust2004 and WSAddressing10, respectively.

Example 3-10 shows an example of a request and response message serialized for SOAP 1.1, while Example 3-11 shows the same set of messages serialized for SOAP 1.2.

Example 3-10. SOAP 1.1 request and response messages

```
// request message

<soap:Envelope xmlns:soap="http://schemas.xmlsoap.org/soap/envelope/" >
  <soap:Body>
    <UploadPhoto xmlns="http://www.thatindigogirl.com/samples/2006/06">
      <fileInfo xmlns:a="http://schemas.thatindigogirl.com/samples/2006/06"
xmlns:i="http://www.w3.org/2001/XMLSchema-instance">
        <a:Id>0</a:Id>
```

Example 3-10. SOAP 1.1 request and response messages (continued)

```
        <a:Title>The Band</a:Title>
        <a:Description>Photo of the band</a:Description>
        <a:DateStart>2006-01-11T00:00:00</a:DateStart>
        <a:DateEnd>0001-01-01T00:00:00</a:DateEnd>
        <a:Url>theband.jpg</a:Url>
        <a:Category>General</a:Category>
      </fileInfo>
      <fileData>(base64 encoded data)</fileData>
    </UploadPhoto>
  </soap:Body>
</soap:Envelope>

// response message

<s:Envelope xmlns:s="http://schemas.xmlsoap.org/soap/envelope/">
  <s:Body>
    <UploadPhotoResponse xmlns="http://www.thatindigogirl.com/samples/2006/06">
    </UploadPhotoResponse>
  </s:Body>
</s:Envelope>
```

Example 3-11. SOAP 1.2 request and response messages

```
// request message

<s:Envelope xmlns:a="http://www.w3.org/2005/08/addressing"
xmlns:s="http://www.w3.org/2003/05/soap-envelope">
  <s:Header>
    <a:Action s:mustUnderstand="1" u:Id="_2" xmlns:u="http://docs.oasis-
open.org/wss/2004/01/oasis-200401-wss-wssecurity-utility-1.0.xsd">
http://www.thatindigogirl.com/samples/2006/06/PhotoUploadContract/UploadPhoto
</a:Action>
    <a:MessageID u:Id="_3" xmlns:u="http://docs.oasis-open.org/wss/2004/01/oasis-
200401-wss-wssecurity-utility-1.0.xsd">
urn:uuid:940d5687-fcb2-44b5-a696-cc7eba22524b</a:MessageID>
    <a:ReplyTo u:Id="_4" xmlns:u="http://docs.oasis-open.org/wss/2004/01/oasis-
200401-wss-wssecurity-utility-1.0.xsd">
      <a:Address>http://www.w3.org/2005/08/addressing/anonymous</a:Address>
    </a:ReplyTo>
    <a:To s:mustUnderstand="1" u:Id="_5" xmlns:u="http://docs.oasis-
open.org/wss/2004/01/oasis-200401-wss-wssecurity-utiliy-1.0.xsd">
http://localhost:3045/PhotoApplication/PhotoManagerService.svc/Soap12</a:To>
    <o:Security .../>
  </s:Header>
  <s:Body u:Id="_0" xmlns:u="http://docs.oasis-open.org/wss/2004/01/oasis-200401-
wss-wssecurity-utility-1.0.xsd">
    <UploadPhoto xmlns="http://www.thatindigogirl.com/samples/2006/06">
      <fileInfo xmlns:a="http://schemas.thatindigogirl.com/samples/2006/06"
xmlns:i="http://www.w3.org/2001/XMLSchema-instance">
        <a:Id>0</a:Id>
        <a:Title>The Band</a:Title>
        <a:Description>Photo of the band</a:Description>
```

Example 3-11. SOAP 1.2 request and response messages (continued)

```
        <a:DateStart>2006-01-11T00:00:00</a:DateStart>
        <a:DateEnd>0001-01-01T00:00:00</a:DateEnd>
        <a:Url>theband.jpg</a:Url>
        <a:Category>General</a:Category>
      </fileInfo>
      <fileData>(base64 encoded data)</fileData>
    </UploadPhoto>
  </s:Body>
</s:Envelope>

// response message

<s:Envelope xmlns:s="http://www.w3.org/2003/05/soap-envelope"
xmlns:a="http://www.w3.org/2005/08/addressing" >
  <s:Header>
    <a:Action s:mustUnderstand="1" u:Id="_2">
http://www.thatindigogirl.com/samples/2006/06/PhotoUploadContract/
UploadPhotoResponse</a:Action>
    <a:RelatesTo u:Id="_3">
urn:uuid:940d5687-fcb2-44b5-a696-cc7eba22524b</a:RelatesTo>
    <o:Security .../>
  </s:Header>
  <s:Body>
    <UploadPhotoResponse
xmlns="http://www.thatindigogirl.com/samples/2006/06"></UploadPhotoResponse>
  </s:Body>
</s:Envelope>
```

Only BasicHttpBinding defaults to Soap11 without support for addressing. All of the other standard bindings default to Soap12Addressing10, regardless of the transport protocols they support. Understanding the message version support for each binding is important for interoperability. For example, many platforms don't support the latest addressing specification, which means you may need to customize the binding.

 Standard bindings do not allow you to set the MessageVersion property directly. To control MessageVersion for a binding, you have to create a custom binding, discussed later in this chapter.

Isolating SOAP 1.1 and SOAP 1.2 Endpoints

This lab illustrates how to allow clients to access a web service over two different protocols: SOAP 1.1 and SOAP 1.2. In Figure 3-3, you can see that a single *.svc* file is exposed over two endpoints, each addressed uniquely.

Recall the two configured endpoints for BasicHttpBinding and WSHttpBinding:

```
<endpoint address="Soap11" contract="PhotoManagerService.IPhotoUpload"
binding="basicHttpBinding"/>
<endpoint address="Soap12" contract="PhotoManagerService.IPhotoUpload"
binding="wsHttpBinding"/>
```

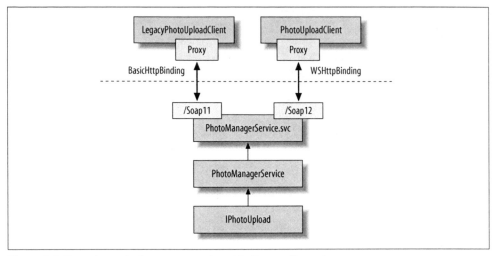

Figure 3-3. Exposing a single .svc over unique binding configurations

Clients address a specific endpoint by providing the */Soap11* and */Soap12* relative address as a suffix to the *.svc* address as follows:

```
http://localhost/PhotoApplication/PhotoManagerService.svc/Soap11
http://localhost/PhotoApplication/PhotoManagerService.svc/Soap12
```

In some cases, you may want to expose these two endpoints through unique *.svc* files to provide each client with a single binding option when they generate their proxy. This could be for simplicity, or to prevent clients from knowing all of the binding configurations they may not be entitled to for reasons of security, for example. I discussed this concept briefly in Chapter 1.

Connection-Oriented Bindings

Connection-oriented transports such as named pipes and TCP are ideal for crossing process and machine boundaries, and yield greater performance and reliability than HTTP transport. *Named pipes* support reliable and sequential data transfer (FIFO) via memory-mapped files. Communications may be handled over one-way pipes (caller writes, receiver reads), or half-duplex (both caller and receiver read and write to the pipe—just not at once). *TCP sockets*, on the other hand, provide endpoints through which caller and receiver communicate, as a full-duplex implementation (two-way).

WCF provides standard bindings for both of these protocols. NetNamedPipeBinding wraps communication over named pipes, and limits that communication to the same machine for security reasons (you can be certain your named pipe endpoints cannot be called remotely). NetTcpBinding enables TCP socket communication for RPC and streaming scenarios. In this section, I'll show you how to work with

`NetNamedPipeBinding` and `NetTcpBindng` endpoints and discuss scenarios in which each binding is most applicable. You'll complete a lab first to put them to use, and then I'll dig into the details.

 `NetPeerTcpBinding` is also based on the TCP protocol, offering peer-to-peer communications. This binding has implications beyond WCF and is too broad to cover in this book.

Lab: Distributing Calls with NetNamedPipeBinding and NetTcpBinding

In this lab, you will turn a two-tier web application into an n-tier, service-oriented application by wrapping business functionality into a WCF service and consuming it from the application. At first, you'll invoke the service using named pipes, and then simulate distributing the same functionality across machines with TCP sockets. To achieve this, you'll use `NetNamedPipeBinding` and `NetTcpBinding`.

Setting up the lab

In this section, you'll do some preliminary work before starting the lab. You'll examine the state of the application as it currently exists, and you'll verify that the application can communicate properly with the database.

1. Open the startup solution for this lab, located in *<YourLearningWCFPath>\Labs\ Chapter3\ConnectionOrientedBindings\ConnectionOrientedBindings.sln*. This solution contains several projects in common with the previous lab. Specifically `ContentTypes`, `FileManager`, `LinkItems.Dalc`, `PhotoManager`, and `PhotoManagerService` serve the same function as described earlier. The following projects are new to this lab:

   Host
   > The host process for the `PhotoManagerService`. This is a console application.

   PhotoApplication
   > A web application with functionality to view and upload photos.

   To begin with, the web application is directly invoking class libraries to communicate with the database.

2. This lab requires you to install the database script *<YourLearningWCFPath>\ SupportingFiles\DatabaseScripts\Photos_CreateDB.sql*. You must also check the connection string located in the *web.config* file of the `PhotoApplication` web site to be sure it is configured according to your database environment. See the "Database Setup" section of Appendix A for detailed instructions. If you have already installed the database for an earlier lab, clear all existing records by running the following database script: *<YourLearningWCFPath>\SupportingFiles\ DatabaseScripts\Photos_DeleteAll.sql*.

3. Before testing the current state of the solution, configure the PhotoApplication web site to read and write photos to the correct directory on your machine. Open the *web.config* and modify the fileUploadDir application setting to reflect your path as follows:

```
<add key="fileUploadDir" value="<YourLearningWCFPath>\Labs\Chapter3\
ConnectionOrientedBindings\PhotoApplication\UploadedPhotos"/>
```

4. Now, run the web application to test it. Follow these steps to upload a photo and then view the uploaded photo details:

    a. Click the Upload Photos menu item. From the Upload Photos page, click the Browse button and select the sample image at *<YourLearningWCFPath>\ SupportingFiles\SampleImages\theband.jpg*. Type in some information about the band (see Figure 3-4 for an example) and click Upload Photo to save the photo and database record.

    b. Click the Home menu item to return to the main page. The uploaded photo should appear in the list.

    c. Click the photo. This takes you to the details page showing the information you saved about the photo.

    Stop debugging when you're finished with this test.

After completing this test, you can be sure that the application functionality works properly. Next you'll change the code to leverage services on the back end.

Moving from components to services

SOA implies designing services to wrap major chunks of business functionality behind the firewall, possibly exposing this functionality to remote clients, or leveraging it internally to distribute functionality behind the web application tier. In this next part of the lab, you'll change the PhotoApplication web site to consume services instead of directly calling business components, to simulate this architecture.

1. Take a look at the service contracts and their implementation in the PhotoManagerService project. You'll notice that the PhotoManagerService type implements two contracts as shown here:

```
public class PhotoManagerService: IPhotoUpload, IPhotoManagerService
```

IPhotoUpload has a single operation, UploadPhoto( ), also used in the previous lab. UploadPhoto( ) will be called from *UploadPhotos.aspx*. IPhotoManagerService has three operations: GetPhotos( ), GetPhoto( ), and GetCategories( ). The first two will be used by *Default.aspx* and *DisplayPhoto.aspx*, respectively, and the latter from *UploadPhotos.aspx* to provide a category list.

The code behind each web page should not include any core business logic, but in a two-tier design, pages will often consume business assemblies that run in the same ASP.NET worker process. Changing this functionality to invoke services across a process or machine boundary introduces fault tolerance and a security boundary that can prevent hackers from gaining control over protected resources.

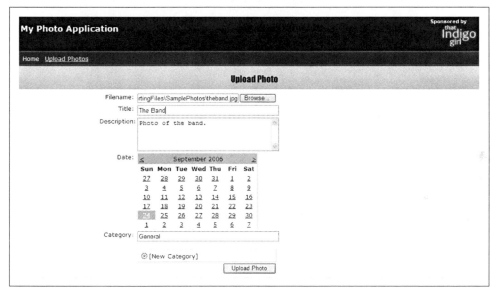

Figure 3-4. Uploading a photo from the PhotoApplication

2. To invoke the `PhotoManagerService` from the web application, you'll create a façade layer. This facade will use service proxies to invoke each service endpoint and will expose public methods that can be called by each page directly or using an `ObjectDataSource` control.

   Add a new class to the `PhotoApplication` beneath the *App_Code* directory, and name the file *PhotoManagerFacade.cs*. In this file, implement the `PhotoManagerFacade` as shown in Example 3-12, including the necessary using statements. This class provides an implementation for `GetPhotos( )`, `GetPhoto( )`, `GetCategories( )`, and `UploadPhoto( )`. Each method creates an instance of either the `PhotoManagerServiceClient` or `PhotoUploadClient` proxy to invoke its matching operation.

The proxies used by this façade were pre-created using SvcUtil with the following command:

```
svcutil /noconfig /o:serviceproxy.cs /r:ContentTypes.dll /ct:
System.Collections.Generic.List`1 http://localhost:8000/
PhotoManagerService
```

This command instructs the utility to generate proxies that use the types from *ContentTypes.dll* and to import arrays as collection type List<T>. With Visual Studio 2008, Add Service Reference also supports this using Advanced options.

Example 3-12. PhotoManagerFacade implementation

```
using System;
using ContentTypes;
using System.Collections.Generic;
using System.ServiceModel;

public class PhotoManagerFacade
{
  public List<PhotoLink> GetPhotos()
  {
    List<PhotoLink> photos = null;
    using (PhotoManagerContractClient proxy = new PhotoManagerContractClient())
    {
      photos = proxy.GetPhotos();
    }
    return photos;
  }
  public PhotoLink GetPhoto(int id)
  {
    PhotoLink photo = null;
    using (PhotoManagerContractClient proxy = new PhotoManagerContractClient())
    {
      photo = proxy.GetPhoto(id);
    }
    return photo;
  }
  public void UploadPhoto(PhotoLink fileInfo, byte[] fileData)
  {
    using (PhotoUploadContractClient proxy = new PhotoUploadContractClient())
    {
      proxy.UploadPhoto(fileInfo, fileData);
    }
  }
  public List<string> GetCategories()
  {
    List<string> categories = null;
    using (PhotoManagerContractClient proxy = new PhotoManagerContractClient())
    {
      categories = proxy.GetCategories();
    }
```

Example 3-12. PhotoManagerFacade implementation (continued)

```
    return categories;
  }
}
```

3. Although the service proxies already exist, you still need to provide service model configuration for each endpoint. Open the *web.config* and inside the existing <system.serviceModel> section add a new <client> section with the two NetNamedPipeBinding endpoints shown in Example 3-13.

Example 3-13. Adding endpoints for the client proxy

```
<system.serviceModel>
  <!-- other settings -->

  <client>
    <endpoint address="net.pipe://localhost/PhotoManagerService"
binding="netNamedPipeBinding" contract="PhotoManagerContract" />
    <endpoint address="net.pipe://localhost/PhotoManagerService"
binding="netNamedPipeBinding" contract="PhotoUploadContract"  />
  </client>
</system.serviceModel>
```

4. Now you're ready to change the actual page code to use the façade layer to access each service endpoint, instead of directly calling business logic. Open *Default.aspx* in HTML view and edit the declaration for ObjectDataSource1 so that its SelectMethod calls the GetPhotos() method on the PhotoManagerFacade type. The changes are shown in bold here:

```
<asp:ObjectDataSource ID="ObjectDataSource1" runat="server"
SelectMethod="GetPhotos" TypeName="PhotoManagerFacade"></asp:ObjectDataSource>
```

5. Open *DisplayPhoto.aspx* and modify its declaration for ObjectDataSource1 as well. In this case, the SelectMethod should call GetPhoto() of the PhotoManagerFacade type. The changes are shown here in bold:

```
<asp:ObjectDataSource ID="ObjectDataSource1" runat="server"
SelectMethod="GetPhoto"
TypeName="PhotoManagerFacade">
  <SelectParameters>
    <asp:QueryStringParameter Name="id" QueryStringField="id" Type="Int32" />
  </SelectParameters>
</asp:ObjectDataSource>
```

6. For the *UploadPhotos.aspx* page located in the *Admin* folder, you'll be modifying page declarations and page code. First, edit the declaration for ObjectDataSource1 so that it calls the GetCategories() method of the façade, then edit ObjectDataSource2 to call the UploadPhoto() method of the façade. The changes are shown in bold here:

```
<asp:ObjectDataSource ID="ObjectDataSource2" runat="server"
SelectMethod="GetCategories" TypeName="PhotoManagerFacade"></asp:
ObjectDataSource>
```

```
<asp:ObjectDataSource ID="ObjectDataSource1" runat="server"
InsertMethod="UploadPhoto" TypeName="PhotoManagerFacade"
OldValuesParameterFormatString="original_{0}" SelectMethod="GetPhotos">
  <!-- parameters -->
</asp:ObjectDataSource>
```

Now open the code for the page, *UploadPhotos.aspx.cs*, and edit the `cmdUploadPhoto_Click()` handler so that the code to invoke business logic through the `PhotoUploadUtil` component is commented and new code to use the `PhotoManagerFacade` is added, as shown here:

```
//PhotoManager.PhotoUploadUtil photoUploadUtil = new
//PhotoManager.PhotoUploadUtil();
//photoUploadUtil.SavePhoto(fileInfo, fileData);

PhotoManagerFacade facade = new PhotoManagerFacade();
facade.UploadPhoto(fileInfo, fileData);
```

At this point, you have updated all aspects of the `PhotoApplication` so that it uses services instead of direct calls to business logic.

7. The `Host` project has already been configured to expose each service contract implemented by `PhotoManagerService` over `NetNamedPipeBinding`. What it is missing is the configuration settings necessary for the business components to function. Because the `FileManager` and `LinkItems.Dalc` components were previously loaded into the `PhotoApplication` process, the *web.config* held its settings. You'll need to copy those settings to the `Host` project's *app.config* file, as shown in Example 3-14.

Example 3-14. Configuration settings required by FileManager and LinkItems.Dalc

```
<appSettings>
  <add key="fileUploadDir"
value="<YourLearningWCFPath>\Labs\Chapter3\ConnectionOrientedBindings\
PhotoApplication\UploadedPhotos"/>
</appSettings>
<connectionStrings>
  <add name="LinkItemsConnectionString" connectionString="Data
Source=localhost;Initial Catalog=Photos;Integrated Security=True"
providerName="System.Data.SqlClient"/>
</connectionStrings>
```

8. At last you are ready to test the changes. Compile the solution and run the `Host` project first so that the services can be reached. Next, launch the `PhotoApplication` in a browser, repeating the same tests as before.

Crossing machine boundaries

Now that you've tested `NetNamedPipeBinding`, try `NetTcpBinding` to simulate crossing a machine boundary from the web application tier.

1. Edit the *app.config* of the `Host` project to add a `NetTcpBinding` base address and one endpoint for each of the service contracts, as shown in bold in Example 3-15.

Example 3-15. Adding NetTcpBinding endpoints for PhotoManagerService

```
<service name="PhotoManagerService.PhotoManagerService"
behaviorConfiguration="serviceBehavior">
  <endpoint contract="PhotoManagerService.IPhotoUpload"
binding="netNamedPipeBinding"/>
  <endpoint contract="PhotoManagerService.IPhotoUpload" binding="netTcpBinding"/>
  <endpoint contract="PhotoManagerService.IPhotoManagerService"
binding="netNamedPipeBinding"/>
  <endpoint contract="PhotoManagerService.IPhotoManagerService"
binding="netTcpBinding"/>
  <host>
    <baseAddresses>
      <add baseAddress="net.tcp://localhost:9000/PhotoManagerService"/>
      <add baseAddress="net.pipe://localhost/PhotoManagerService"/>
      <add baseAddress="http://localhost:8000/PhotoManagerService "/>
    </baseAddresses>
  </host>
</service>
```

2. Edit the `PhotoApplication` to use the TCP endpoints instead of named pipes. Open the *web.config* and replace the two `NetNamedPipeBinding` endpoints with `NetTcpBinding` endpoints. The resulting changes to the `<client>` section are shown in bold here:

```
<client>
  <endpoint address="net.tcp://localhost:9000/PhotoManagerService"
binding="netTcpBinding" contract="PhotoManagerContract" />
  <endpoint address="net.tcp://localhost:9000/PhotoManagerService"
binding="netTcpBinding" contract="PhotoUploadContract" />
</client>
```

3. Test the solution again by running the `Host` first, then launching the `PhotoApplication` in a browser. Repeat the same tests to verify that everything works as expected.

Now let's look more closely at what you've done in this lab.

Choosing a Connection-Oriented Binding

Connection-oriented protocols such as named pipes and TCP make it possible to communicate with services in-process, out-of-process, and across machines boundaries. `NetNamedPipeBinding` and `NetTcpBinding` are the two standard bindings for this type of communication. Unlike the web service bindings discussed in the previous section, selecting between these connection-oriented bindings is not a matter of interoperable protocol support. Your selection of `NetNamedPipeBinding` or `NetTcpBinding` is largely related to the location of your services. The key drivers for choosing between the two bindings are:

`NetNamedPipeBinding`

Use to expose or consume services in-process, across application domains, or out-of-process on the same machine only. Security requirements may limit the usefulness of this binding, for example if you need to forward credential types not supported by the binding.

NetTcpBinding

Use to expose or consume services out-of-process on the same machine or across machine boundaries.

In both cases, the assumption is WCF-to-WCF communication since these bindings are typically only applicable to situations where interoperability or messaging through firewalls is not required. Both of these bindings use binary message encoding, but the serialized message is still based on SOAP protocol.

In the next sections, I'll discuss the details of these bindings.

NetNamedPipeBinding Features

Named pipes provide a mechanism for interprocess communication (IPC) ideal for crossing process boundaries on the same machine. It can also be used as an alternative to .NET Remoting for in-process calls within the same application domain or that traverse application domains.

A *named pipe* enables interprocess communication both locally and remotely. The pipe is a file that can be accessed by the pipe server (the process that created the pipe) and the pipe client (the process communicating with the pipe server). The underlying path to a named pipe is a UNC path that specifies the machine name only if the pipe is remote:

```
\\<MachineName>\Pipe\<PipeName>
\\.\Pipe\<PipeName>
```

NetNamedPipeBinding only supports named pipes on the local machine. This is an added security feature provided by WCF so that you can be sure services exposed over named pipes can only be accessed by clients on the same machine.

Primary scenarios where this binding is employed include:

- Services running on the client machine as part of the client application deployment.
- Services running in-process as part of a server application that may later be deployed in a separate process or on another machine for distribution.
- Services running on a server that should never be invoked from another machine, where rich message-level security scenarios are not required.

With NetNamedPipeBinding, messages are binary-encoded over named pipes. It is the only binding that restricts communication to the same machine, and for services that live on the same machine as the caller, NetNamedPipeBinding can yield slightly better performance over NetTcpBinding.

Table 3-4 provides a summary of core binding features and their applicability to NetNamedPipeBinding.

Table 3-4. Summary of NetNamedPipeBinding features

Binding feature	NetNamedPipeBinding support
Transport Protocols	Named pipes
Message Encoding	Binary
Message Version	SOAP 1.2, WS-Addressing 1.0
Transport Security	SSL
Message Security	No
Duplex	Yes
Reliable Messaging	No
Transactions	Yes

NetNamedPipeBinding defaults

The default settings for NetNamedPipeBinding are shown in Example 3-16.

Example 3-16. Default settings for NetNamedPipeBinding

```
<netNamedPipeBinding>
  <binding name="netPipeDefaults" closeTimeout="00:01:00"
hostNameComparisonMode="StrongWildcard" maxBufferPoolSize="524288"
maxBufferSize="65536" maxConnections="10" maxReceivedMessageSize="65536"
openTimeout="00:01:00" receiveTimeout="00:10:00" sendTimeout="00:01:00"
transactionFlow="false" transactionProtocol="OleTransactions"
transferMode="Buffered">
    <readerQuotas maxArrayLength="16384" maxBytesPerRead="4096" maxDepth="32"
maxNameTableCharCount="16384" maxStringContentLength="8192" />
    <security mode="Transport"/>
  </binding>
</netNamedPipeBinding>
```

NetNamedPipeBinding does not support message level security, but messages are indeed secure by default—relying on transport security to authenticate, sign, and encrypt messages. As with any binding, you'll want to consider message size requirements and transaction support.

 You can also control MaxConnections directly in the binding configuration, but this is a throttling behavior that I'll discuss in Chapter 5.

Customizing NetNamedPipeBinding

Example 3-17 shows a customized NetNamedPipeBinding implementation.

Example 3-17. Customized settings for NetNamedPipeBinding

```
<netNamedPipeBinding>
  <binding name="netNamedPipeBindingDefaults" maxReceivedMessageSize="100000"
transactionFlow="true" maxBufferSize="100000">
    <readerQuotas maxArrayLength="100000" maxStringContentLength="100000"/>
```

Example 3-17. Customized settings for NetNamedPipeBinding (continued)

```
  </binding>
</netNamedPipeBinding>
```

The most common changes you'll consider will be to increase message buffers and to enable transaction flow (to be discussed in Chapter 6). You can also stream messages over named pipes by setting the TransferMode property. I'll talk about streaming later in this chapter.

NetTcpBinding Features

TCP protocol is a reliable communication protocol useful for calls that cross processes and machines. In fact, when interoperability is not a concern, you should try to use NetTcpBinding for the performance gains it offers; TCP protocol and binary serialization is the fastest binding configuration, particularly across machine boundaries. Similar to named pipes, TCP sockets also support streaming.

TCP sockets enable two-way (full duplex) interprocess communication both locally and remotely. There are two modes for sockets. Stream sockets guarantee delivery in sequence of data without record boundaries. Datagram sockets send data with record boundaries, but are not guaranteed delivery, nor in order, nor unduplicated. NetTcpBinding supports both datagram and streamed sockets.

Typical uses for this binding include:

- Intranet applications with traditional client-server application deployment
- Services running behind the firewall that are invoked within the intranet for internal applications
- Large enterprise systems that distribute business functionality across machines for load balancing, to enforce security boundaries, and to offload work from web servers for scalability

Table 3-5 provides a summary of core binding features and their applicability to NetTcpBinding.

Table 3-5. Summary of NetTcpBinding features

Binding feature	NetTcpBinding support
Transport Protocols	TCP
Message Encoding	Binary
Message Version	SOAP 1.2, WS-Addressing 1.0
Transport Security	SSL with Windows or Certificate credentials
Message Security	SOAP Message Security, WS-Trust, WS-SecureConversation
Duplex	Yes
Reliable Messaging	Yes
Transactions	Yes

NetTcpBinding defaults

The default settings for `NetTcpBinding` are shown in Example 3-18.

Example 3-18. Default settings for NetTcpBinding

```
<netTcpBinding>
  <binding name="netTcpDefaults" closeTimeout="00:01:00"
hostNameComparisonMode="StrongWildcard" maxBufferPoolSize="524288"
maxBufferSize="65536" maxConnections="10" maxReceivedMessageSize="65536"
openTimeout="00:01:00" portSharingEnabled="false" receiveTimeout="00:10:00"
sendTimeout="00:01:00" transactionFlow="false"
transactionProtocol="OleTransactions" transferMode="Buffered" >
    <readerQuotas maxArrayLength="16384" maxBytesPerRead="4096" maxDepth="32"
maxNameTableCharCount="16384" maxStringContentLength="8192" />
    <reliableSession enabled="false" ordered="true" inactivityTimeout="00:10:00"/>
    <security mode="Transport">
      <transport clientCredentialType="Windows" />
      <message clientCredentialType="Windows" algorithmSuite="Basic256" />
    </security>
  </binding>
</netTcpBinding>
```

`NetTcpBinding` has many features beyond `NetNamedPipeBinding`, specifically for security and reliable messaging. In addition, you can enable TCP port sharing and control `MaxConnections` from the binding.

Customizing NetTcpBinding

Example 3-19 shows one example of a customized `NetTcpBinding` implementation.

Example 3-19. Customized settings for NetTcpBinding

```
<netTcpBinding>
  <binding name="netTcpTrans" maxReceivedMessageSize="1000000"
transactionFlow="true" >
  <readerQuotas maxArrayLength="1000000" maxStringContentLength="100000" />
  <reliableSession enabled="true" />
</binding>
```

Again, increasing message buffers and enabling transaction flow are common considerations, but there are other considerations that require additional thought, such as:

- Do you want to stream data such as large documents, media files, or video?
- Do you require message level reliability beyond what TCP already provides point-to-point?
- What type of transfer and credential security is required for the deployment scenario?

Streaming will be discussed later in this chapter. Reliability and security features will be discussed in later chapters.

Calling Services In-Process

I mentioned previously that NetNamedPipeBinding can be useful for in-process service calls. This might be useful for client applications that have been designed with service-orientation in mind. Perhaps they call local services when offline and connect to remote services when online. Another scenario could be for enterprise services that are hosted in IIS for remote clients but are also leveraged for same machine calls behind the firewall.

Whatever the scenario, the client instantiates both the ServiceHost and proxy, managing both of their lifetimes. Your client application can create and open the ServiceHost instance when the application starts as follows:

```
// ServiceHost instance scoped to the application domain
public static ServiceHost s_serviceHost;

// During intialization...code to instantiate the ServiceHost
s_serviceHost = new ServiceHost(typeof(HelloIndigo.HelloIndigoService));
s_serviceHost.AddServiceEndpoint(typeof(HelloIndigo.IHelloIndigoService), new
NetNamedPipeBinding(), "net.pipe://localhost/HelloIndigoService");

// During shutdown...code to close the ServiceHost
S_serviceHost.MyHost.Close();
```

You can hardcode the configuration given that the application owns both sides. To call the service, you can use the same service contract as for the host and initialize the proxy with the same binding configuration as the host:

```
// Channel proxy reference
private IHelloIndigoService m_proxy;

// Code to create the channel proxy
ChannelFactory<IHelloIndigoService> factory = new
ChannelFactory<IHelloIndigoService>(new NetNamedPipeBinding(), new
EndpointAddress("net.pipe://localhost/HelloIndigoService"));
m_proxy = factory.CreateChannel();

// Code to call the in-process service
string s = this.MyProxy.HelloIndigo(String.Format("Hello from client process: {0}",
Process.GetCurrentProcess().Id));
```

 A sample illustrating this in-process scenario can be found at *<YourLearningWCFPath>\Samples\Bindings\InProcessCalls*.

You can also create a new application domain for the service host, to provide a level of fault tolerance between it and the application process. Providing a separate application domain can also be useful for recycling the ServiceHost, providing a way to unload the assembly (with the application domain) when configuration changes have been deployed in a self-hosting environment.

Distribution of Services

This lab demonstrates a scenario in which a web application that initially makes direct calls to an assembly is modified to consume services—first using named pipes, then TCP sockets. Wrapping business functionality in a service makes it possible to distribute that functionality across process and machine boundaries without affecting the code base.

In the initial application for this lab, `ObjectDataSource` controls communicate directly with the `PhotoManager` assembly to save and retrieve photo records. Figure 3-5 illustrates this architecture.

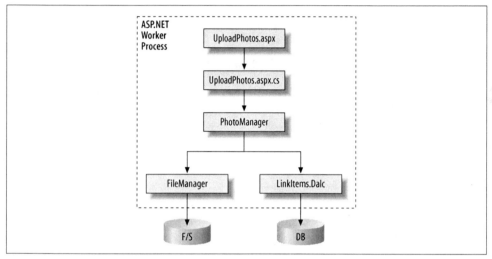

Figure 3-5. ASP.NET application with in-process assemblies

After introducing a service-oriented application design, `ObjectDataSource` controls communicate with a new façade layer that is introduced to wrap calls to the service proxy, which invokes each service endpoint. This same architecture (see Figure 3-6) is used whether the service is called on the same machine over named pipes or on a different machine over TCP sockets.

There are many reasons to consider distributing functionality across process and machine boundaries behind a web application, including security and scalability:

- When a *Demilitarized Zone* (DMZ) is put in place, you'll be required to cross machine boundaries that are protected by a second firewall.
- Services can provide a security boundary that makes it more difficult for hackers to access protected resources. For example, if the ASP.NET worker process is compromised, the malicious caller would still need to authenticate to the service boundary to access resources it controls.

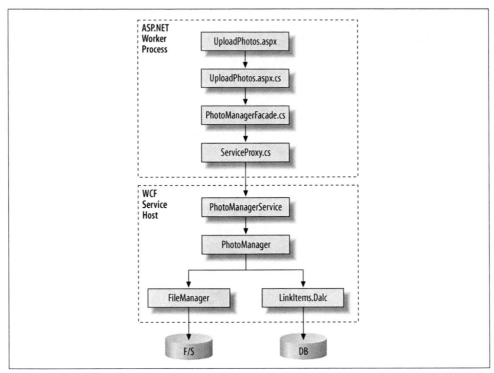

Figure 3-6. ASP.NET application with out-of-process services

- When you have business functionality that consumes resources such as the file-system or large amounts of memory, distributing those horizontally across load-balanced machines can actually improve overall throughput regardless of the introduction of serialization overhead and network latency.

One-Way and Duplex Communication

A *message exchange pattern* describes the way messages are sent between applications. There are three classic message exchange patterns: request-reply, one-way, and duplex (callbacks). Figure 3-7 illustrates these patterns. So far in this book, I have focused on examples that use the classic *request-reply* pattern, that is, service operations that receive parameters and return values synchronously while clients wait for the response. There are cases where clients want to send messages and do not need a response—that is, the operation performs a function that can succeed or fail and the client either does not care, or does not care right away. In other cases, communication may be initiated at the other end of a communication channel—for example, a service sending unsolicited messages to a client application. This type of communication implies two-way communication between client and service, and it requires the support of a binding that can support duplex communications.

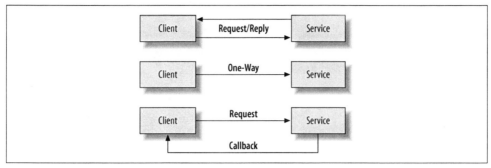

Figure 3-7. Message exchange patterns

One-way operations are useful because once the message reaches the receiving end, the client connection is released so that the client can continue doing other work. Furthermore, they won't be affected if a problem occurs at the other end, since no exceptions are reported. One-way messages are also known as *asynchronous messages*.

Duplex or *two-way* operations play a key role in applications that send notifications, issue events, or implement some form of publish-subscribe pattern.

In this section, I'll explain how to implement one-way operations and duplex patterns while also discussing the following concepts:

- How to implement message exchange patterns with WCF
- Scenarios for one-way operations and duplex communications
- WSDualHttpBinding features
- Supporting callbacks
- Concurrency issues for the service and client

Before you do a lab that shows you how to work with one-way and duplex communications, I'll spend some time explaining message exchange patterns and callback contracts. After you complete the lab, I'll talk about WSDualHttpBinding in greater detail and discuss related duplex communication topics.

Message Exchange Patterns

You can implement all three message exchange patterns, request-reply, one-way and duplex, using service contracts. Service contracts expose these messaging patterns as follows:

- Request-reply is the default behavior for service operations that are not labeled as one-way operations.
- One-way operations are labeled using the OperationContractAttribute.
- Duplex communication is possible when a callback contract is supplied to the service contract, and a binding that supports duplex is selected.

Request-reply

By default, all service operations use the request-reply pattern—even if they don't explicitly return a result (returning void). The following two operation signatures are valid examples of request-reply operations:

```
[OperationContract]
string HelloIndigo(string message);
[OperationContract]
void HelloIndigo(string message);
```

With this pattern, clients will block until they receive a reply or time out. At the service, the dispatcher waits for the operation to complete before sending a reply. If an exception occurs at any point during processing at the service, a SOAP fault (see Chapter 8) is included in the reply.

One-way

The `OperationContractAttribute` has an `IsOneWay` property that defaults to `false`. You can set it to `true` for operations that return void, as shown here:

```
[OperationContract(IsOneWay=true)]
void HelloIndigo(string message);
```

This setting turns a request-reply operation into a one-way operation. With one-way operations, the service model releases the client connection once the message arrives to the channel and before invoking the operation. That means the client doesn't block; the call is asynchronous. That also means that clients do not receive any notification of exceptions that occur.

 Although exceptions are not propagated to the client, an uncaught exception at the service will cause the server channel to fault. When sessions are involved, subsequent calls to the service will fail and the client channel is rendered useless. Sessions are discussed in Chapter 5.

One-way operations are useful in many scenarios, including:

Fire-and-forget
Operations that need not report success or failure, such as logging or auditing activities or event publishing.

Polling
Long running operations where clients can find out the results of the operation through another request.

Duplex
One-way operations should be used for callbacks and publish-subscribe scenarios where the service may need to call the client independent of a particular request.

Duplex

Duplex communication refers to bi-directional flow between a client and service. To implement this pattern, service contracts provide a callback contract. A callback contract looks just like a service contract; it is an interface that has methods marked with the OperationContractAttribute as shown here:

```
public interface IHelloIndigoServiceCallback
{
  [OperationContract]
  void HelloIndigoCallback(string message);
}
```

Notice that the ServiceContractAttribute is missing. That's because it is implied by the usage of this contract. Alone, the contract is not a callback contract. It becomes one when it is associated to a service contract implemented by a service type. The ServiceContractAttribute has a CallbackContract property that can be associated with an interface that contains service operations. This example associates IHelloIndigoServiceCallback as the callback contract for the IHelloIndigoService service contract:

```
[ServiceContract(Namespace="http://www.thatindigogirl.com/samples/2006/06",
CallbackContract=typeof(IHelloIndigoServiceCallback))]
public interface IHelloIndigoService
```

Operations defined in a callback contract are not required to be one-way; however, they should be one-way to avoid contention, as shown here:

```
public interface IHelloIndigoServiceCallback
{
  [OperationContract(IsOneWay=true)]
  void HelloIndigoCallback(string message);
}
```

Likewise, for service contracts that implement a callback contract, any operation that will call back to the client should be designed as a one-way operation. I'll talk about this after the lab.

Both TCP protocol and named pipes support bidirectional flow. TCP protocol supports full-duplex messaging, while named pipes are half-duplex—meaning messages can move in both directions, but not simultaneously. For both of these protocols, the network connection can support calls initiated by the service to the client. Consequently, NetNamedPipeBinding and NetTcpBinding support callback contracts.

HTTP protocol does not support duplex communication—responses are valid only for each request. This prevents HTTP-based bindings such as BasicHttpBinding and WSHttpBinding from supporting duplex. To address this limitation, WCF provides WSDualHttpBinding. This binding uses composite duplex communication, which means two communication channels are created to support calls in both directions. I'll more talk about this binding shortly.

Working with Callbacks

To define a *callback contract,* you create an interface that implements one or more operations decorated with the OperationContractAttribute. Though not required, these operations should be one-way to reduce the potential for deadlocks. This shouldn't have any impact since the service shouldn't generally care if an exception takes place at the client during a callback. Callbacks are customarily fire-and-forget operations.

Once associated with a service contract, the callback contract is emitted as part of the WSDL document for the service so that clients can generate an equivalent callback contract during proxy generation.

 Recall from Chapter 2 that WSDL describes each operation with <input>, <output>, and <fault> elements. Callback contracts add operations to the WSDL document that have no <input>, one <output>, and may include <fault> elements.

Duplex proxies

Proxy generation produces slightly different results for duplex scenarios:

- Configuration settings for each endpoint are generated as expected.
- A client-side version of the service contract and the callback contract are created.
- The proxy inherits DuplexClientBase<T> instead of ClientBase<T>.

DuplexClientBase<T> provides a special constructor that requires a reference to the callback contract implementation, wrapped in an InstanceContext, as shown here:

```
public partial class HelloIndigoContractClient :
System.ServiceModel.DuplexClientBase<Client.localhost.HelloIndigoContract>,
Client.localhost.HelloIndigoContract
{...}
```

DuplexChannelFactory<T>

You can also create the duplex channel proxy at the client directly, using DuplexChannelFactory<T> instead of ChannelFactory<T>. As with DuplexClientBase<T>, the constructor of the factory requires you to pass the callback instance, as shown here:

```
CallbackType cb = new CallbackType();
InstanceContext context = new InstanceContext(cb);

WSDualHttpBinding binding = new WSDualHttpBinding();
binding.ClientBaseAddress=new Uri("http://localhost:8100");

DuplexChannelFactory<IHelloIndigoService> factory = new
DuplexChannelFactory<IHelloIndigoService>(context, binding, new
EndpointAddress("http://localhost:8000/wsDual"));
IHelloIndigoService proxy = factory.CreateChannel();
```

A sample that uses `DuplexChannelFactory<T>` to construct the duplex channel can be found here: *<YourLearningWCFPath>\Samples\ Bindings\DuplexChannelFactory*.

Callback instance

Clients must provide an implementation for the callback contract. You can implement the callback contract on any type. After you construct an instance of this type, you wrap it in a `InstanceContext` for the proxy to reference. Ultimately, this creates a client endpoint where the service can send messages.

```
CallbackType cb = new CallbackType( );
InstanceContext context = new InstanceContext(cb);
```

The lifetime of the client endpoint is critical to two-way communication with the service. By default, its lifetime will match the lifetime of the proxy. So, if you keep the proxy alive for the duration of the application, the service will be able to issue it callbacks for the same duration (assuming no other problems fault the client channel). When the proxy is closed or disposed through garbage collection, the client endpoint is destroyed along with it.

Services have no control over the way clients manage the callback instance lifetime. Thus services should catch any exceptions when issuing callbacks and verify that the callback channel has not faulted after every call. Channel state is discussed in Chapter 5.

Client endpoint

Duplex proxies generate an endpoint for services to call over the established communication channel. Duplex protocols such as named pipes or TCP implicitly support callbacks. It isn't necessary to indicate an explicit endpoint for the service to issue callbacks to the client over these protocols. For HTTP, however, callbacks can work only if the client explicitly creates an endpoint (like a service endpoint) to receive messages. In other words, another communication channel must be created for calls in the opposite direction.

`DuplexClientBase<T>` handles creating the client endpoint, and `WSDualHttpBinding` provides a property to configure the base address for this endpoint. When this base address isn't specified, one is generated on your behalf using port 80 and with a temporary address that includes a unique GUID:

```
http://localhost:80/Temporary_Listen_Addresses/7e7e9b66-2112-473d-8401-a8404fde6a8d/
```

This is a problematic for machines with IIS installed and running on port 80, and in general it can be a problem since other applications may also consume specific ports. To provide a base address declaratively, you use the configuration setting shown here:

```
<wsDualHttpBinding>
  <binding name="WSDualHttpBinding_HelloIndigoContract" clientBaseAddress="http://
```

```
localhost:8100" />
</wsDualHttpBinding>
```

You can also set this property dynamically in code:

```
WSDualHttpBinding binding = m_proxy.Endpoint.Binding as WSDualHttpBinding;
binding.ClientBaseAddress = new Uri("http://localhost:8100");
```

Practically speaking, declarative configuration offers more flexibility. You should avoid hardcoding ports in the client code. You could also do interesting things such as dynamically finding an open port within a particular range to support the client endpoint.

In this lab, you will explore duplex communication over NetTpcBinding and WSDualHttpBinding. First, you will design a callback contract; associate it to a service contract; and implement the service contract and related code inside the service to issue callbacks. You'll host this service in a console application and consume it from two clients—a console application and a Windows application—to compare results. In the process, you'll test the differences between using request-reply and one-way where callbacks are concerned and compare the functionality of the two bindings.

Designing the callback contract

The first thing you'll do is create a new callback contract. You'll create an interface with service operations representing the callback operation.

1. Open the startup solution for this lab, located in *<YourLearningWCFPath>\Labs\Chapter3\Duplex\Duplex.sln*. This solution contains a partially completed service project, service host, console client, and Windows Forms client.

2. First, implement the service starting with the callback contract. Go to the HelloIndigo project and open *HelloIndigoService.cs*. Add the following callback contract definition:

   ```
   public interface IHelloIndigoServiceCallback
   {
     [OperationContract]
     void HelloIndigoCallback(string message);
   }
   ```

Callback contracts do not require a ServiceContractAttribute, but it would not cause any problems if the attribute were present. The problem is that this could become confusing if you set the Name, and Namespace attributes for the attribute on the callback contract since they are ignored when the contract is used as a callback contract. The callback contract inherits those settings from the service contract to which it is associated.

Operations must still be decorated with the OperationContractAttribute to be included in the WSDL document.

---

3. Associate this callback contract with the service contract so that its metadata will be included in the service description and WSDL document. Do this by setting the CallbackContract property of the ServiceContractAttribute, as shown here:

```
[ServiceContract(Name="HelloIndigoContract",
Namespace="http://www.thatindigogirl.com/samples/2006/06",
CallbackContract=typeof(IHelloIndigoServiceCallback))]
public interface IHelloIndigoService
```

Now you have a callback contract, and have associated it with the service contract. The next step is to write code in the service to issue callbacks.

Issuing callbacks

The service type has already been created, but the HelloIndigo( ) operation has not yet been implemented. Now you'll add code to the method that issues callbacks to clients.

1. When clients create a proxy for a service contract that supports callbacks, they are required to implement the callback contract and supply a channel to receive callbacks. The client proxy will send information about the callback endpoint with each call to the service. You can access this through the OperationContext GetCallbackChannel<T>( ) method. This returns a strongly typed reference to a proxy that can be used to invoke any callback operation at the client.

   The code to add to HelloIndigo( ) is shown here in bold:

```
public void HelloIndigo(string message)
{
    IHelloIndigoServiceCallback callback =
OperationContext.Current.GetCallbackChannel<IHelloIndigoServiceCallback>();
    callback.HelloIndigoCallback(message);
}
```

 Each operation that supports callbacks will have similar code. Services can also save a reference to the callback endpoint and invoke callbacks outside the context of a call from the client—for example, in publish-subscribe scenarios (I'll discuss this after the lab).

2. Build the HelloIndigo service project to verify it compiles.

Choosing a duplex-compatible binding

Now you will host the service using the Host console application. In fact, the project already contains the necessary code to host the service and has a single endpoint configuration over WSHttpBinding.

1. Test this implementation by running the Host project. During ServiceHost initialization, an InvalidOperationException is thrown indicating that the service contract requires a duplex binding, and WSHttpBinding is unable to support this.

2. Configure the endpoint to support duplex communication. Go to the Host project and open the *app.config* file. Edit the endpoint so that it uses NetTcpBinding, as shown here in bold:

```
<endpoint address="HelloIndigoService" binding="netTcpBinding"
contract="HelloIndigo.IHelloIndigoService" />
```

3. Run the Host project again to verify there are no exceptions. Leave it running for the next section of the lab.

Implementing the callback contract

Now you are going to implement the callback contract. Recall that the WSDL document for the service will publish enough information to describe the callback contract for the service. That means that SvcUtil will be able to generate an equivalent callback contract at the client and create a special type of proxy that supports duplex communication. You'll test this by adding a service reference to both clients.

1. Go to the Client project and add a service reference using the path *http://localhost:8000* for the service URI and localhost as the namespace. Do the same for WinClient.

2. Both clients now have proxies and configuration necessary to call the service. In addition, they both have a copy of the service metadata associated with the callback—the callback contract. You will implement the callback contract for both clients in order to provide an endpoint for the service to invoke.

   Go to the Client project first and add a new class to the project. Name the file *CallbackType.cs*. Open the file and modify the class definition so that it implements the callback contract, as shown in Example 3-20. When the callback is invoked, this code will write the current thread identifier to the console. For this code to work, you must add a using statement for System.Threading.

Example 3-20. Implementing the callback contract on a separate type

```
using System.Threading;

class CallbackType: localhost.HelloIndigoContractCallback
{
  public void HelloIndigoCallback(string message)
  {
    Console.WriteLine("HelloIndigoCallback on thread {0}",
Thread.CurrentThread.GetHashCode());
  }
}
```

3. Construct the callback type in the Main() entry point, then construct the proxy and invoke HelloIndigo(). In duplex scenarios, the proxy constructor requires you to provide the callback instance wrapped in an InstanceContext type. Example 3-21 shows the code to add to *Program.cs* to achieve this.

The proxy generated for duplex contracts derives from a different base type, DuplexClientBase<T>. This type takes the callback instance and ultimately turns it into a client endpoint that the service can reach.

Example 3-21. Code to construct the callback type and construct the proxy

```
using Client.localhost;

static void Main(string[] args)
{

  Console.WriteLine("Client running on thread {0}",
Thread.CurrentThread.GetHashCode( ));
  Console.WriteLine( );

  CallbackType cb = new CallbackType( );
  InstanceContext context = new InstanceContext(cb);

  using (HelloIndigoContractClient proxy = new HelloIndigoContractClient(context))
  {
    Console.WriteLine("Calling HelloIndigo( )");
    proxy.HelloIndigo("Hello from Client.");
    Console.WriteLine("Returned from HelloIndigo( )");

    Console.ReadLine( );
  }
}
```

4. Compile the solution and test this by running the Host and then the Client. You'll receive an InvalidOperationException at the service stating that the operation will deadlock. That's because the service is not reentrant or multithreaded. If the service operation calls another service, it will not be able to return.

 I'll be talking about concurrency issues in Chapter 5, but I'll broach the subject after the lab as it relates to the duplex discussion.

5. To fix this issue, add a ServiceBehaviorAttribute to the service type in *HelloIndigoService.cs* and set the ConcurrencyMode property to Reentrant, as shown here:

```
[ServiceBehavior(ConcurrencyMode=ConcurrencyMode.Reentrant)]
public class HelloIndigoService : IHelloIndigoService
```

6. Compile the solution and test the Host and Client again, this time it will work. Notice that the callback operation is executed on a separate thread from the initial application thread, and that the callback is received before the call to HelloIndigo( ) returns from the service.

7. Now add some code to complete the `WinClient` application. This time, you'll implement the callback contract directly on Form1. Open *Form1.cs* and add the code shown in Example 3-22. Don't forget the using statement for the proxy namespace.

Example 3-22. Implementing the callback contract on an existing type

```
using WinClient.localhost;

public partial class Form1 : Form, HelloIndigoContractCallback
{
  // other code

  public void HelloIndigoCallback(string message)
  {
    MessageBox.Show(string.Format("Received callback on thread {0}. {1}",
System.Threading.Thread.CurrentThread.GetHashCode(), message));
  }
}
```

8. The code to invoke the service will be similar to the code for the `Client` application, but the scope of the proxy will be for the lifetime of the Windows application. Inside Form1 type, add a proxy reference scoped to the lifetime of the form. In the form constructor, create the `InstanceContext` type to wrap Form1 as the callback instance, and instantiate the proxy. Lastly, add code to the `cmdInvoke_Click()` event handler to call `HelloIndigo()`. The resulting additions to *Form1.cs* are shown in bold in Example 3-23.

Example 3-23. Scoping the proxy and callback instance

```
public partial class Form1 : Form, HelloIndigoContractCallback
{
  private HelloIndigoContractClient m_proxy = null;

  public Form1()
  {
    InitializeComponent();

    InstanceContext context = new InstanceContext(this);
    m_proxy = new HelloIndigoContractClient(context);
  }

  private void cmdInvoke_Click(object sender, EventArgs e)
  {
    m_proxy.HelloIndigo("Hello from WinClient");
  }

  // other code
}
```

9. Compile the solution and test this by running the Host and then the WinClient application. Click the Invoke Service button to test the callback. The UI will become locked, and eventually you'll receive a TimeoutException. That's because the client UI thread is blocking while the client calls in to the service, but the service is attempting to reach the client on the same thread.

> With a Windows client, the callback implementation will synchronize with the UI thread by default. That means the callback executes on the same thread as the primary thread for the application. This is problematic if the calls to the service and callbacks are not one-way operations.

10. You can fix the deadlock problem by instructing the callback endpoint to run on a separate thread from the UI thread. Open *Form1.cs* and apply the CallbackBehaviorAttribute to the callback type, setting its UseSynchronizationContext to false, as shown here:

```
[CallbackBehavior(UseSynchronizationContext=false)]
public partial class Form1 : Form, HelloIndigoContractCallback
```

11. Compile the solution and run the same test as before. This time you'll receive the callback on another thread without any contention.

Issuing callbacks over WSDualHttpBinding

In this section, you will use WSDualHttpBinding to support callbacks and learn some of the required configuration settings to support it.

1. Now switch the binding from NetTcpBinding to WSDualHttpBinding. Go to the Host project, open *app.config* and modify the endpoint configuration, as shown here:

```
<endpoint address="HelloIndigoService" binding="wsDualHttpBinding"
contract="HelloIndigo.IHelloIndigoService" />
```

Update the configuration for both clients to reflect this change.

2. The next thing you'll do is set an appropriate base address for the callback on the client. Try to test the Client application first, by running the Host and then the Client. You may receive an AddressAlreadyInUseException because the service model is attempting to register port 80 for the WSDualHttpBinding callback endpoint. That's because an application has already acquired that port, usually IIS.

> If you don't receive this error, port sharing may be enabled on the machine.

To address this, you'll modify the binding configuration and supply a new base address for the callback endpoint. Open the *app.config* for the Client project and edit the <wsDualHttpBinding> section to add the following bold setting for clientBaseAddress:

```
<wsDualHttpBinding>
  <binding name="WSDualHttpBinding_HelloIndigoContract" clientBaseAddress="http:/
/localhost:8100" ... >
    <!-- other settings -->
  </binding>
</wsDualHttpBinding>
```

 ClientBaseAddress is a local setting for the client, so it is not provided through proxy generation. To provide other than the default port 80, you must configure this declaratively or programmatically on the binding.

3. Compile the solution and run the same test. This time it should work as expected.

4. Now, configure the same setting for WinClient programmatically. In the Form1 constructor, set the ClientBaseAddress property for the proxy by adding the following code shown in bold:

```
m_proxy = new HelloIndigoContractClient(context);

WSDualHttpBinding binding = m_proxy.Endpoint.Binding as WSDualHttpBinding;
if (binding!=null)
binding.ClientBaseAddress=new Uri("http://localhost:8101");
```

5. Compile the solution again and test the WinClient application again; it should work as expected.

Callbacks and one-way operations

Now you're going to modify the service and callback contracts so that their operations are one-way and test the results.

1. Open *HelloIndigoService.cs* and edit the two operations, HelloIndigo( ) and HelloIndigoCallback( ), so that they are one-way, by setting IsOneWay to true for both, as shown here:

```
// in the service contract
[OperationContract(IsOneWay=true)]
void HelloIndigo(string message);

// in the callback contract
[OperationContract(IsOneWay=true)]
void HelloIndigoCallback(string message);
```

2. Comment the ServiceBehaviorAttribute applied to the service type so that reentrancy will no longer be enabled:

```
//[ServiceBehavior(ConcurrencyMode=ConcurrencyMode.Reentrant)]
```

3. Before you can test this, you'll have to update the proxies for both clients to reflect the new one-way operations in both contracts. To do this, run the Host and update the service references for Client and WinClient.

   Because this regenerates the *app.config*, you will also have to re-add the clientBaseAddress setting to the Client project's <wsDualHttpBinding> section.

4. Go to *Form1.cs* and comment the CallbackBehaviorAttribute that you applied earlier:

   ```
   //[CallbackBehavior(UseSynchronizationContext=false)]
   ```

5. Compile the solution and test both client applications once again. Both applications will successfully call the service and receive their callbacks.

 A sample that illustrates the use of NetNamedPipeBinding, NetTcpBinding, WSDualHttpBinding and a CustomBinding that supports duplex, can be found at <*YourLearningWCFPath*>*Samples**Bindings**DuplexAllBindings*.

Now for a closer look at the ideas and features at work in this lab.

WSDualHttpBinding Features

HTTP doesn't support duplex communication at the transport level, but WSDualHttpBinding makes this possible by providing two channels for bidirectional communication. This is known as a *composite duplex channel* because it consists of two one-way channels based on WSHttpBinding (although WSDualHttpBinding does not support all of the binding features of WSHttpBinding).

Table 3-6 describes the core features supported by WSDualHttpBinding.

Table 3-6. Summary of WSDualHttpBinding features

Binding feature	WSDualHttpBinding support
Transport Protocols	HTTP
Message Encoding	Text, Mtom
Message Version	SOAP 1.2, WS-Addressing
Transport Security	No
Message Security	SOAP Message Security, WS-Trust
Duplex	Yes
Reliable Messaging	Yes
Transactions	Yes

With WSDualHttpBinding messages are based on SOAP 1.2 protocol. Addressing headers are also required to support reliable messaging (see Chapter 6)—a requirement of this binding. Notable differences with WSHttpBinding include lack of support for HTTPS and any form of transport security. Though most of the features of message security are supported, secure sessions are excluded from this list (these security concepts are covered in Chapter 7).

WSDualHttpBinding defaults

Example 3-24 shows the default settings for WSDualHttpBinding.

Example 3-24. Default settings for WSDualHttpBinding

```
<wsDualHttpBinding>
  <binding name="wsDualDefaults" bypassProxyOnLocal="false" closeTimeout="00:01:00"
hostNameComparisonMode="StrongWildcard"
maxBufferPoolSize="524288" maxReceivedMessageSize="65536" messageEncoding="Text"
openTimeout="00:01:00" receiveTimeout="00:10:00"
sendTimeout="00:01:00" textEncoding="utf-8" transactionFlow="false"
useDefaultWebProxy="true" >
    <readerQuotas maxArrayLength="16384" maxBytesPerRead="4096" maxDepth="32"
maxNameTableCharCount="16384" maxStringContentLength="8192"  />
    <reliableSession ordered="true" inactivityTimeout="00:10:00" />
    <security mode="Message">
      <message algorithmSuite="Basic256" clientCredentialType="Windows"
negotiateServiceCredential="true"/>
    </security>
  </binding>
</wsDualHttpBinding>
```

As with other bindings, before deploying services with WSDualHttpBinding defaults, you should consider message size and security requirements at the very least. You should also notice that reliable messaging is required—it is enabled by default, and there isn't an option to disable it as with other bindings.

Customizing WSDualHttpBinding

You can customize WSDualHttpBinding declaratively as I've shown for other bindings in this chapter by providing an expanded <wsDualHttpBinding> section like the one in Example 3-25.

Example 3-25. Customized settings for WSDualHttpBinding

```
<wsDualHttpBinding>
  <binding name="wsDualCustom" maxReceivedMessageSize="100000"
transactionFlow="true">
    <readerQuotas maxArrayLength="100000" maxStringContentLength="100000" />
    <security>
      <message clientCredentialType="UserName"/>
    </security>
  </binding>
</wsDualHttpBinding>
```

In this example transaction flow is enabled, size constraints adjusted and alternate credentials are supported.

A sample illustrating this customized `WSDualHttpBinding` configuration can be found at *<YourLearningWCFPath>\Samples\Bindings\WSDualUsernameSecurity*.

Services and Callback References

When a callback contract is present, service operations receive a reference to a client callback endpoint with each operation, making it possible to issue callbacks during the operation. In publish-subscribe scenarios, services must retain a list of callback references so they can issue callbacks outside of the scope of an operation. Example 3-26 shows how `Subscribe( )` and `Unsubscribe( )` operations might be implemented to support this.

Example 3-26. Subscribe and unsubscribe operations

```
// dictionary to store callback endpoints
public Dictionary<Guid, IPublisherEvents> m_listCallbacks = new Dictionary<Guid,
IPublisherEvents>( );

// subscribe operation
public void Subscribe(Guid id)
{
  IPublisherEvents callback =
    OperationContext.Current.GetCallbackChannel<IPublisherEvents>( );
  if (!m_listCallbacks.ContainsKey(id))
    m_listCallbacks.Add(id, callback);
}

// unsubscribe operation
public void Unsubscribe(Guid id)
{
  if (m_listCallbacks.ContainsKey(id))
    m_listCallbacks.Remove(id);
}
```

When something triggers the service to publish a notification, it can iterate through the dictionary of endpoints and invoke the appropriate callback operation as follows:

```
foreach (KeyValuePair<Guid, IPublisherEvents> obj in this.m_listCallbacks)
{
  obj.Value.Notify( );
}
```

The complete sample illustrating this publish-subscribe scenario is found at *<YourLearningWCFPath>\Samples\Bindings\DuplexPublishSubscribe*.

Callbacks and Concurrency

Callbacks have the potential for introducing concurrency issues. Figure 3-8 illustrates the flow of messages when operations in service and callback contracts are not one-way.

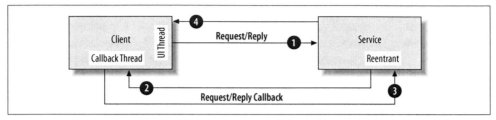

Figure 3-8. Request-reply operations and callbacks

The explanation is as follows:

- The client calls the service and awaits a reply. The client blocks on its calling thread until the call returns.
- The service issues a callback to the client and awaits a reply. This is possible only if the service is reentrant or multithreaded. If it isn't, a deadlock is guaranteed because the return call will not be able to acquire the lock on the service type. Fortunately, an InvalidOperationException notifies you of this potential when the ServiceHost is opened, so you can fix the problem.
- The client receives the callback from the service. This is only possible if the callback instance is on a different thread from the originating client call. The original thread is still blocked waiting for the service response.
- The client callback returns to the service and releases the lock so another call can get in.
- The service operation returns to the client and the UI thread is no longer blocking.

Reentrancy is necessary when services attempt to call other operations that aren't one-way. This applies not only to callbacks issued by the service, but the invocation of other services as well. Reentrancy may also be required on the client callback type if callback implementations call out to other services. This is applied using the CallbackBehaviorAttribute, as follows:

```
[CallbackBehavior(ConcurrencyMode=ConcurrencyMode.Reentrant)]
```

For Windows clients, the client callback type receives requests on the UI thread. This is problematic when service operations that aren't one-way invoke the calling client via callback. To mitigate this risk, the CallbackBehaviorAttribute can be used to indicate the callback type should receive calls on a separate thread, setting the UseSynchronizationContext property to false, as shown here:

```
[CallbackBehavior(UseSynchronizationContext=false)]
```

Code running on any other thread from the UI thread cannot directly interact with forms and controls. This subject is discussed further in Chapter 5.

Figure 3-9 illustrates a different scenario where the service and callback contract define one-way operations instead of request-reply. This removes the requirement for reentrancy and multithreading.

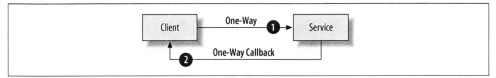

Figure 3-9. One-way operations and callbacks

Here's the explanation:

- The client calls the service. The service model releases the connection before invoking the service operation. The client no longer blocks on its calling thread.
- The service issues a callback to the client. The service model at the client releases the connection before invoking the callback operation. The service no longer blocks on its calling thread.

Service designers can be good citizens by making all callback operations one-way, and all service operations that invoke callbacks one-way.

Large Message Transfers

Transferring large amounts of data between clients and services requires forethought. When messages are text encoded, large binary payloads introduce certain inefficiencies. Binary data is Base64 encoded, which adds overhead to message processing for encoding and decoding efforts. In addition, encoding binary data bloats the size of the data by an added 33 percent (or so), thus impacting the transfer rate. Beyond encoding and transfer rate, there are other considerations relevant to large binary transfers including the need to reduce the overhead of memory usage at the client and service.

 Base64 is a type of transfer encoding that converts binary data to a textual (ASCII) representation used for MIME encoding email attachments or embedding binary data in an XML document.

Dealing with these distinct issues requires consideration for binding configurations, and, in some cases, service design. With WCF, you can reduce the overhead of binary encoding and payload bloat with binary or MTOM message encoding.

To reduce the memory footprint of large transfers, you can turn to streaming transfer modes for binary data. In this section, you'll complete two labs to work with MTOM and streaming. Following the labs, I'll explain these concepts.

Lab: Using MTOM to Handle Large Messages with Binary Data

In this lab, you will upload photos over HTTP using optimized MTOM encoding. You'll modify an existing solution, changing the binding configuration of both client and service to support larger messages and select MTOM message encoding.

1. Open the startup solution for this lab, located in *<YourLearningWCFPath>\Labs\ Chapter3\LargeMessages\LargeMessages.sln*. This solution includes the clients and services from the first two labs in this chapter, including the `PhotoManagerService`, its `PhotoApplication` web host, and a `PhotoUploadClient` application.

2. This lab requires you to install the database script *<YourLearningWCFPath>\ SupportingFiles\DatabaseScripts\Photos_CreateDB.sql*. You must also check the connection string located in the web.config file of the PhotoApplication web site, and in teh app.config file of the Host project, to be sure they are both configured according to your database environment. See the "Database Setup" section in Appendix A for detailed instructions. If you have already installed the database for an earlier lab, clear all existing records by running the following SQL script: *<YourLearningWCFPath>\SupportingFiles\ DatabaseScripts\Photos_ DeleteAll.sql*.

3. Check your file paths for uploading photos. For the `PhotoManagerService` hosted by the web site, `PhotoApplication`, check the `fileUploadDir` setting in the *web.config* and make sure it reflects your path:

   ```
   <add key="fileUploadDir" value="<YourLearningWCFPath>\Labs\Chapter3\
   LargeMessages\PhotoApplication\UploadedPhotos"/>
   ```

   Do the same for the service hosted by the `Host` application—checking the *app.config* setting for `fileUploadDir`.

4. Compile the solution and run it (F5). The `PhotoApplication` will launch in a browser. The `PhotoUploadClient` will also be loaded.

   Try uploading a photo from the `PhotoUploadClient`. Click the Browse button and select the sample image located here: *<YourLearningWCFPath>\ SupportingFiles\ SampleImages\tig.jpg*. Click the Upload File button, and an error message indicating an HTTP 400 exception (bad request) will appear. Though cryptic, the exception happens because that the maximum request length has been exceeded for the binding configuration.

 Chapter 8 explains how to enable debugging behaviors so that more intelligible exception details are reported to clients. Still, the underlying exception is sometimes not presented and you may need to enable diagnostic tracing for this. Chapter 6 illustrates how to enable tracing in the reliable sessions lab.

5. You're now going to modify the client and service configuration so that larger images can be transferred. In addition, you'll enable MTOM message encoding to optimize how binary data is transferred with the message. Open the *web.config* file for the `PhotoApplication` and provide a custom `<wsHttpBinding>` configuration for the `Soap12` endpoint. The binding configuration should increase the `MaxMessageReceived` size to 5MB, and set `MessageEncoding` to `Mtom`. The changes are shown in bold in Example 3-27.

Example 3-27. WSHttpBinding customized to support large messages

```
<system.serviceModel>
  <services>
    <service name="PhotoManagerService.PhotoManagerService" ...>
      <endpoint address="Soap12" contract="PhotoManagerService.IPhotoUpload"
binding="wsHttpBinding" bindingConfiguration="wsHttpLargeMessage"/>
      <!-- other endpoints -->
    </service>
  </services>
  <bindings>
    <wsHttpBinding>
      <binding name="wsHttpLargeMessage" maxReceivedMessageSize="5000000"
messageEncoding="Mtom" />
    </wsHttpBinding>
  </bindings>
  <!-- other settings -->
</system.serviceModel>
```

6. The client application will also have to reflect this change before it will allow large messages to be sent. Open the *app.config* for the `PhotoUploadClient` project and edit the `<wsHttpBinding>` section so that its `MaxReceivedMessageSize` and `MessageEncoding` properties reflect the changes in Example 3-27.

7. Now, compile and run the solution again and try to upload the same photo. This time a `FaultException` is thrown indicating that the maximum array length has been exceeded for the XML reader.

 You may be wondering why you received a better error message this time around. The fact is that a different part of the service model validates reader quotas (to be discussed) and so it happens that a better exception detail is provided in the response.

8. Return to the `PhotoApplication` *web.config* and increase the value of the `MaxArrayLength` reader quota in the custom `<wsHttpBinding>` section. You'll need to expand the binding section to insert a `<readerQuotas>` section. The resulting change is shown in bold here:

```
<wsHttpBinding>
  <binding name="wsHttpLargeMessage" maxReceivedMessageSize="5000000"
messageEncoding="Mtom">
```

```
    <readerQuotas maxArrayLength="5000000"/>
  </binding>
</wsHttpBinding>
```

9. Open the *app.config* for the `PhotoUploadClient` project and edit the `MaxArrayLength` value for the `<wsHttpBinding>` section so that messages will pass validation at the client as well.

10. Compile and run the solution again, repeating the same test. This time, the file should be successfully uploaded. You can verify this by refreshing the browser showing the *Default.aspx* page of the `PhotoApplication`.

In this lab, you learned about restrictions on message and array size, and you configured MTOM protocol for large message transfer. As for the application of MTOM, this was largely invisible to you, but after you complete the streaming lab, I will explain how MTOM works in detail.

 In order to see MTOM encoding, you can use tools like TcpTrace to view the raw HTTP request. To pass messages through TcpTrace you must use some features of the client and service binding to allow messages to pass through an intermediary application. The step-by-step instruction for this is explained in the reliable sessions lab of Chapter 6.

Lab: Enabling Streaming for Large File Transfers

In this lab, you'll stream large media files from the server filesystem directly to the calling client. You'll create a service contract that streams media files and create a binding configuration that enables streaming over TCP.

Streaming from the service

The first part of the lab requires you to enable streaming at the service. To support streaming in any direction, the service operation must support only the `Stream` type for its parameter or return value. In addition, the binding configuration must enable streaming in the appropriate direction.

1. Open the startup solution for this lab, located in *<YourLearningWCFPath>\Labs\Chapter3\Streaming\Streaming.sln*. This solution includes a service library, a host application, and a client application: `MediaManagerService`, `Host`, and `MediaClient`, respectively. The client will attempt to play *.wav* files directly streamed from the service.

2. In the `MediaManagerService` project, two service contracts have already been defined: `IMediaManagerService` and `IMediaStreaming`. The first contract has a single operation, `GetMediaList()`, that has already been implemented on the `MediaManagerService` type as follows:

```
public string[] GetMediaList()
{
  string[] mediaList = new string[3];
  mediaList[0] = "moviestar.wav";
  mediaList[1] = "amsterdam.wav";
  mediaList[2] = "thejimihendrixtheory.wav";
  return mediaList;
}
```

3. Open *MediaManagerService.cs* and implement the second contract. The service type, MediaManagerService, already derives from the contract IMediaStreaming, but the operation is not implemented. The implementation of the operation will receive an input string indicating the file to stream back to the client. When you implement the operation, the code will open the file stream and return it, cleaning up the stream if any exceptions occur along the way. The resulting implementation should look like Example 3-28.

Example 3-28. Returning a file stream

```
public Stream GetMediaStream(string media)
{
  string mediaFile = String.Format("{0}\\{1}",
System.Configuration.ConfigurationManager.AppSettings["mediaPath"], media);

  FileInfo fi = new FileInfo(mediaFile);
  if (!fi.Exists)
    throw new FileNotFoundException("File does not exist: {0}. Check host
configuration for 'mediaPath' setting.", media);

  FileStream fs = null;
  try
  {
    fs = new FileStream(mediaFile, FileMode.Open, FileAccess.Read, FileShare.Read);
  }
  catch
  {
    if (fs != null)
      fs.Close();
  }

  return fs;
}
```

4. Configure the host to support a streaming endpoint for the IMediaStreaming contract. If you open the *app.config* for the Host application, you'll see there is already a NetTcpBinding endpoint exposed for this contract. To customize the binding to support streaming, you'll provide a custom <netTcpBinding> section and reference it from the endpoint's bindingConfiguration setting. The customized binding will set the TransferMode property to StreamedResponse. The changes are shown in bold in Example 3-29.

Example 3-29. Enabling streaming on NetTcpBinding

```
<services>
  <service name="MediaManagerService.MediaManagerService"
behaviorConfiguration="serviceBehavior">
    <endpoint address="MediaManager"
contract="MediaManagerService.IMediaManagerService" binding="basicHttpBinding" />
    <endpoint address="MediaStream" contract="MediaManagerService.IMediaStreaming"
binding="netTcpBinding" bindingConfiguration="netTcpStreaming"/>
    <!-- other settings -->
  </service>
</services>
<bindings>
  <netTcpBinding>
    <binding name="netTcpStreaming" transferMode="StreamedResponse" />
  </netTcpBinding>
</bindings>
```

 There is no need to increase the message size at the service since the service will be streaming the response.

5. Before you test the Host, check the mediaPath application setting in the *app. config* file and make sure it reflects your path:

    ```
    <add key="mediaPath" value="<YourLearningWCFPath>\SupportingFiles\SampleMedia"/>
    ```

6. Compile and run the Host project to verify that there are no exceptions. Leave the Host running for the next section of the lab.

Streaming from the client

Now you can configure the MediaClient application to receive streamed response from the service.

1. Go to the MediaClient project and add a service reference to the MediaManagerService. Provide the URI *http://localhost:8000* and leave the namespace as localhost.

2. Open the *app.config* file and modify the binding configuration associated with the IMediaStreaming endpoint so that it supports streaming and large messages. Find the <netTcpBinding> section and set the maxReceivedMessageSize and transferMode attributes to the following values:

    ```
    transferMode="Streamed"
    maxReceivedMessageSize="40000000"
    ```

3. Add functionality to the client application so that it loads the play list from the IMediaManagerService endpoint into the ListBox control. Open *Form1.cs* in code view and create an instance of the MediaManagerContractClient proxy as a member of Form1, then add code to the cmdGetMedia_Click() handler that invokes GetMediaList(), as shown in Example 3-30.

Example 3-30. Code to retrieve the playlist

```
localhost.MediaManagerContractClient m_mediaManagerProxy = new
MediaClient.localhost.MediaManagerContractClient();

private void cmdGetMedia_Click(object sender, EventArgs e)
{
  this.listBox1.DataSource=m_mediaManagerProxy.GetMediaList();
}
```

4. Now add code to read the stream from the service through its IMediaStreaming end-point. Create an instance of the MediaStreamingContractClient as a member of Form1, and add code to the cmdPlay_Click() handler that invokes GetMediaStream() and plays the stream using the SoundPlayer instance, m_mediaPlayer. The code is shown in Example 3-31.

Example 3-31. Code to retrieve the media stream

```
localhost.MediaStreamingContractClient m_mediaStreamingProxy = new
localhost.MediaStreamingContractClient();

private void cmdPlay_Click(object sender, EventArgs e)
{
  string media = this.listBox1.SelectedItem as string;
  if (!String.IsNullOrEmpty(media))
  {
    Stream serverStream = m_mediaStreamingProxy.GetMediaStream(media);
    this.m_mediaPlayer.Stream=serverStream;
    this.m_mediaPlayer.Play();
  }
}
```

 If streaming is working, the call to GetMediaStream() will return immediately and the stream will be read during the call to Play().

5. Compile and test the solution. Run the Host first, followed by the MediaClient. Click Get Media to retrieve a list of media files, and select one to play. Press play and the selected file will stream from the service.

Streaming only works if the service operation uses the Stream type and the binding configuration supports streaming in the appropriate direction. The message size is important only to the stream reader, to support buffering as the stream is read. In the next sections, I'll explain the problem statement related to large messages and discuss the alternatives: MTOM protocol and streaming.

Handling Large Messages

Large messages can result from scenarios such as transferring large files or including binary attachments as part of a message. Messages can also become quite large when large numbers of records are passed between clients and services. The labs in this section illustrate how to increase quotas to support large images and streamed media, but there is more to consider than simply accommodating size requirements. When dealing with large messages, you should control the payload size on the wire to reduce bandwidth usage, reduce processing overhead, and throttle memory consumption for both client and service.

Controlling payload size

Message size is influenced by your choice of message encoder: `BinaryMessageEncoder`, `TextMessageEncoder`, or `MtomMessageEncoder`. As I discussed earlier, the web service bindings default to `Text` encoding, but web service bindings also support `Mtom` encoding. Non-HTTP bindings default to `Binary` encoding and don't provide an alternate encoding. Here are some details on each message encoder:

`BinaryMessageEncoder`

> Serializes messages in a compact binary format, which yields the smallest footprint of the three encoders. The SOAP 1.2 message is still preserved, but the serialization format is not interoperable.

`TextMessageEncoder`

> Serializes messages in text format as SOAP 1.1 or SOAP 1.2. This format is interoperable but message sizes are much larger than with binary encoding. Furthermore, any binary data such as byte arrays are base64 encoded to be represented in XML. This bloats messages up to 33 percent more.

`MtomMessageEncoder`

> Serializes messages in text format as SOAP 1.1 or SOAP 1.2, but moves any binary data to MIME encoded attachments that are referenced from their original location in the message. This is an interoperable way to reduce the bloat of text encoding, based on XOP and MTOM specifications.

Binary serialization is already compact, but any time you expect to move large amounts of binary data over HTTP, you should consider enabling MTOM encoding on the binding. This will yield optimizations in cases where messages contain large binary elements that can be optimized with MTOM. If not, the message is sent without optimization.

Beyond the choice of encoding format you can resort to compression to further reduce the overall message payload transferred between clients and services.

Reducing memory consumption

By default, messages are buffered by the service model as they are sent and received. This can put significant pressure on server memory when multiple concurrent requests are in progress. At the client, this can also be crippling when very large files are transferred and buffered.

One option to reduce memory usage is to stream messages as illustrated in the streaming lab. This prevents the service model from reading the entire message into

---

memory, and allows the stream recipient (client or service) to control how the stream is read. For large files, this could mean directly writing the stream to disk or streaming media to an application that can begin to play the stream while it buffers the remainder.

Message Size Quotas

There are several settings that influence how the service model processes messages. Some are specific settings that limit the size of strings, array lengths, object graphs, XML nesting and overall message size. Other settings control how buffering is handled and act as a throttle for memory usage and garbage collection overhead. The following are the different binding properties and behaviors that control these settings. I've broken them down into three categories:

The following properties are binding quotas—a direct property of the binding:

MaxBufferPoolSize
> Preallocates the buffer to process incoming requests instead of allocating from the heap. You can tune this to reduce pressure on the garbage collector.

MaxBufferSize
> Limits the buffer size of incoming messages. When messages are buffered, this must match MaxReceivedMessageSize, and for streaming, this should be less to reduce buffering.

MaxReceivedMessageSize
> Limits the overall serialized message size received by services and clients. This has nothing to do with memory usage—deserialized messages may consume additional memory.

The following properties are reader quotas—part of the ReaderQuotas binding property that affects how XML readers process messages:

MaxArrayLength
> Limits the length of strings and other arrays including byte arrays for large binary transfers.

MaxBytesPerRead
> Limits the number of bytes per read operation.

MaxDepth
> Limits the nesting depth of XML elements. Data contracts with nested objects will generate nested XML, for example.

MaxNameTableCharCount
> Limits the size of the reader nametable, which includes prefixes and namespaces in the XML stream.

MaxStringContentLength
> Limits the length of string elements.

The last behavior is a data contract serializer quota. This quota is provided through a behavior, as opposed to a binding property:

MaxItemsInObjectGraph
> Limits the number of objects that can be present in an object graph during serialization. If you are passing around objects with many nested reference types, you may exceed this limit.

The defaults for each of these settings are shown in Example 3-32. The important thing to note, however, is that they are local settings. That means they are not included in the service description, and thus won't be known to the client. Clients can throttle quotas to accommodate their own needs. In fact, the client's proxy validates messages against client quotas so that outbound messages exceeding quotas will not burden the service.

Example 3-32. Sample service configuration with default quotas

```
<system.serviceModel>
  <services>
    <service name="HelloIndigo.HelloIndigoService"
behaviorConfiguration="serviceBehavior">
      <endpoint address="net.tcp://localhost:9000/HelloIndigoService"
contract="HelloIndigoService.IHelloIndigoService" binding="netTcpBinding" />
    </service>
  </services>
  <bindings>
    <netTcpBinding>
      <binding name="defaults" maxBufferPoolSize="524288" maxBufferSize="65536"
maxReceivedMessageSize="65536">
        <readerQuotas maxArrayLength="16384" maxBytesPerRead="4096" maxDepth="32"
maxNameTableCharCount="32" maxStringContentLength="8192" />
      </binding>
    </netTcpBinding>
  </bindings>
  <behaviors>
    <serviceBehaviors>
      <behavior name="serviceBehavior">
        <dataContractSerializer maxItemsInObjectGraph="32" />
      </behavior>
    </serviceBehaviors>
  </behaviors>
</system.serviceModel>
```

While you may need to loosen quota constraints to accommodate expectations of large message payloads, strings, arrays, and more, each of these constraints provides protection against possible denial-of-service (DoS) attacks and should be carefully considered. Furthermore, it is best to design service contracts such that messages requiring loosened quotas are separate from general messaging.

MTOM Encoding

Text message encoding is important for interoperability, but it causes messages to be bloated when binary data is included in the XML payload. That's because binary data must be base64 encoded for XML parsers to work with it effectively. Beyond the bloat of the message payload, there is an additional performance hit because XML parsers don't handle large blocks of opaque data efficiently. MTOM makes it possible to solve this problem in an interoperable way.

Message Transmission Optimization Mechanism (MTOM) is an XML messaging standard that enables you to send binary data more efficiently with a SOAP message. MTOM has been a W3C Recommendation since January 2005, inspired by earlier specifications that tried to solve similar problems: SOAP with Attachments (SwA) and Direct Internet Message Encapsulation (DIME).

Together with the XML-binary Optimized Packaging (XOP) standard, MTOM describes how to send a SOAP envelope and any large binary elements within it, in separate MIME-encoded parts of the message transmission.

Enabling MTOM is as simple as setting the `MessageEncoding` property on a binding. Bindings that support HTTP protocol all default to `Text` encoding but also support `Mtom` encoding, as shown here:

```
<basicHttpBinding>
  <binding name="basicHttpStreaming" messageEncoding="Mtom" />
</basicHttpBinding>
```

When you enable MTOM encoding, the content type of the message becomes multi-part/related. The first message part is the SOAP envelope, and if any optimizations are made to the SOAP message, to extract large binary content, those are inserted into message parts that follow. MIME encoding is the foundation of this, but MTOM builds on this by making it possible to reference the extracted binary content from the SOAP envelope so that the message receiver can reconstitute the XML infoset—or put another way, so that the binary data can be properly included in its associated parameter or return type.

If the SOAP envelope doesn't contain any large binary content, only one MIME part is sent: the SOAP envelope. Example 3-33 shows an MTOM message without any optimizations. In this case, the binary data inside the `<fileData>` element is base64 encoded.

A Lesson in MIME

Multipurpose Internet Mail Extensions, or MIME, specifies a standard format for encapsulating multiple pieces of data into a single Internet message. *Multipart/related* content indicates that the message includes one or more different parts separated by a unique string boundary. A multipart message stream consists first of headers, followed by a carriage return and linefeed <CRLF>, and the content enclosed in an opening and closing boundary. The *boundary* is indicated in the Content-Type header. This boundary must appear prefixed with two hyphens (--) at the beginning of the entire message content and between each message part in the content. A closing boundary must appear at the end of the message to indicate the final message part has been read. This closing boundary includes a double hyphen prefix and suffix. Here's a simple view of how that looks:

```
Content-Type: multipart/related; boundary=mime_boundary1

--mime_boundary1

Content-Type: text/plain; charset=us-ascii
Content-Transfer-Encoding: 7bit

[text part]
--mime_boundary1

Content-Type: application/octet-stream
Content-Disposition: attachment; filename="data.zip"
Content-Transfer-Encoding: base64

[binary part]
--mime_boundary1--
```

This illustrates sending a multipart/related message that contains two parts: the plaintext message and a zipped file attachment. The boundary string is "mime_boundary1" in this example, but can be any unique string value. Headers are placed within each message part following the separation boundary, to specify things such as content type and transfer encoding for each message part.

Example 3-33. MTOM request without optimizations

```
POST /PhotoApplication/PhotoManagerService.svc/Soap12NoSecurity HTTP/1.1
MIME-Version: 1.0
Content-Type: multipart/related; type="application/xop+xml";
start="<http://tempuri.org/0>";boundary="uuid:3f2c77b2-933f-4b20-9a3c-
f60ae3534129+id=2";start-info="application/soap+xml"
Host: localhost:8080
Content-Length: 1376
Expect: 100-continue
Connection: Keep-Alive
```

Example 3-33. MTOM request without optimizations (continued)

```
--uuid:3f2c77b2-933f-4b20-9a3c-f60ae3534129+id=2
Content-ID: <http://tempuri.org/0>
Content-Transfer-Encoding: 8bit
Content-Type: application/xop+xml;charset=utf-8;type="application/soap+xml"

<s:Envelope xmlns:s="http://www.w3.org/2003/05/soap-envelope"
xmlns:a="http://www.w3.org/2005/08/addressing"><s:Header><a:Action
s:mustUnderstand="1">http://www.thatindigogirl.com/samples/2006/06/PhotoUploadContr
act/UploadPhoto</a:Action><a:MessageID>urn:uuid:e69e4058-52ed-4a2f-971e-
2945e1b84ae1</a:MessageID><a:ReplyTo><a:Address>http://www.w3.org/2005/08/addressin
g/anonymous</a:Address></a:ReplyTo><a:To
s:mustUnderstand="1">http://localhost:8080/PhotoApplication/PhotoManagerService.svc
/Soap12NoSecurity</a:To></s:Header><s:Body><UploadPhoto
xmlns="http://www.thatindigogirl.com/samples/2006/06"><fileInfo
xmlns:b="http://schemas.thatindigogirl.com/samples/2006/06"
xmlns:i="http://www.w3.org/2001/XMLSchema-instance"><b:Id>0</b:Id><b:Title>The
Band</b:Title><b:Description>Photo of the band</b:Description><b:DateStart>2006-01-
11T00:00:00</b:DateStart><b:DateEnd>0001-01-
01T00:00:00</b:DateEnd><b:Url>reallytinyimage.bmp</b:Url><b:Category>General</b:Cat
egory></fileInfo><fileData>Qk1CAAAAAAAAD4AAAAoAAAAAQAAAAEAAAABAAEAAAAAAAAAAAAADEDgAA
xA4AAAIAAAACAAAAAAA//////8AAAAA</fileData></UploadPhoto></s:Body></s:Envelope>
--uuid:3f2c77b2-933f-4b20-9a3c-f60ae3534129+id=2--
```

When a larger block of binary data is passed, MTOM optimizes by moving it to another MIME part and referencing it from the envelope with a unique identifier. This identifier is also referenced in the MIME header, Content-ID. Example 3-34 shows a message with MTOM optimizations.

 You can use a tool such as TcpTrace to view messages on the wire to see the format of MTOM encoded messages.

Example 3-34. MTOM request with optimizations

```
POST /PhotoApplication/PhotoManagerService.svc/Soap12NoSecurity HTTP/1.1
MIME-Version: 1.0
Content-Type: multipart/related;
type="application/xop+xml";start="<http://tempuri.org/0>";boundary="uuid:3f2c77b2-
933f-4b20-9a3c-f60ae3534129+id=3";start-info="application/soap+xml"
Host: localhost:8080
Content-Length: 2360935
Expect: 100-continue
Connection: Keep-Alive


--uuid:3f2c77b2-933f-4b20-9a3c-f60ae3534129+id=3
Content-ID: <http://tempuri.org/0>
Content-Transfer-Encoding: 8bit
Content-Type: application/xop+xml;charset=utf-8;type="application/soap+xml"

<s:Envelope xmlns:s="http://www.w3.org/2003/05/soap-envelope"
```

Example 3-34. MTOM request with optimizations (continued)

```
xmlns:a="http://www.w3.org/2005/08/addressing"><s:Header><a:Action
s:mustUnderstand="1">http://www.thatindigogirl.com/samples/2006/06/PhotoUploadContr
act/UploadPhoto</a:Action><a:MessageID>urn:uuid:e2484b1e-db6d-428f-9a47-
eb0065fb8f2d</a:MessageID><a:ReplyTo><a:Address>http://www.w3.org/2005/08/addressin
g/anonymous</a:Address></a:ReplyTo><a:To
s:mustUnderstand="1">http://localhost:8080/PhotoApplication/PhotoManagerService.svc
/Soap12NoSecurity</a:To></s:Header><s:Body><UploadPhoto
xmlns="http://www.thatindigogirl.com/samples/2006/06"><fileInfo
xmlns:b="http://schemas.thatindigogirl.com/samples/2006/06"
xmlns:i="http://www.w3.org/2001/XMLSchema-instance"><b:Id>0</b:Id><b:Title>The
Band</b:Title><b:Description>Photo of the band</b:Description><b:DateStart>2006-01-
11T00:00:00</b:DateStart><b:DateEnd>0001-01-
01T00:00:00</b:DateEnd><b:Url>tig.bmp</b:Url><b:Category>General</b:Category></file
Info><fileData><xop:Include
href="cid:http%3A%2F%2Ftempuri.org%2F1%2F632949795039248526"
xmlns:xop="http://www.w3.org/2004/08/xop/include"/></fileData></UploadPhoto></s:Bod
y></s:Envelope>
--uuid:3f2c77b2-933f-4b20-9a3c-f60ae3534129+id=3
Content-ID: <http://tempuri.org/1/632949795039248526>
Content-Transfer-Encoding: binary
Content-Type: application/octet-stream

[binary data]
--uuid:3f2c77b2-933f-4b20-9a3c-f60ae3534129+id=3--
```

The `<xop:Include>` element refers to the MIME part identified by the matching Content-ID.

The MTOM encoder decides when to optimize based on an internal threshold of approximately 200 bytes. The rule of thumb is if the addition of the MIME encoded boundaries will add more to the message payload than what would have been saved by removing the base64 encoded data, don't optimize.

Streaming

Streaming is useful for large file transfers. Instead of buffering messages in memory on send and receive, streaming makes it possible for the sender to provide a stream object that is read by the receiver incrementally. This reduces memory usage, in particular if file streams are employed, making it possible for a file at the server, for example, to be directly streamed to a file at the client. For servers, this is highly advantageous since it prevents the server from loading individual instances of a file in memory for concurrent requests, something that could quickly lead to memory exceptions, preventing any requests from being serviced. At the client, this is helpful when files are very large since they may not have enough memory to buffer the entire file.

To properly support streaming there are a few basic requirements:

- The operation receives or returns a single Stream type.
- The binding protocol for the service contract must support streaming.
- You must enable streaming on the binding.

Designing a service contract for streaming

Streaming has implications on service contract design. For an operation to stream content, it must have a single input or output value that is a Stream type. For request streaming, a single Stream parameter should be present. For response streaming, a single out parameter or return value of type Stream should be present. These are all valid signatures that will result in streaming the request, response, or in both directions:

```
void StreamIn(Stream inputStream);
Stream StreamOut();
Stream StreamInAndOut(Stream inputStream);
void StreamInAndOutUsingParam(Stream inputStream, out Stream outputStream);
void StreamOutUsingParam(out Stream outputStream);
```

Even if you enable streaming on the binding, if you attempt to stream a request or reply that has additional parameters or return values (besides the Stream type), the service model will revert to buffering. In that sense, you can enable streaming for a contract that has some operations that use streaming, others that don't. But in reality, you probably have very different requirements for the streaming operations than for other service operations. For that reason, you should separate the streaming operations to a separate contract to support a different binding configuration.

Enabling streaming

You can enable streaming on these bindings: NetNamedPipeBinding, NetTcpBinding, and BasicHttpBinding. This is done by setting the TransferMode property of the binding. The options for this property are as follows:

Buffered
> This is the default setting. No streaming.

Streamed
> Enables streaming on request and reply for the binding.

StreamedRequest
> Enables streaming on request only.

StreamedResponse
> Enables streaming on reply only.

TransferMode is a local setting on the binding. That means that it may not propagate to the client when you generate a proxy from the service description—except in the case of NetNamedPipeBinding and NetTcpBinding. A custom WS-Policy extension is provided for bindings that use named pipes or TCP protocol, and this makes it possible for WCF clients to be aware that the service endpoint is streaming. As a result,

SvcUtil respects this policy extension and enables streaming when it generates the client configuration for the binding. The policy assertion, `<msf:Streamed>`, is shown in bold in Example 3-35.

 If you create a `CustomBinding` that streams over TCP or named pipes protocols, the same policy extension is generated in the resulting WSDL description.

Example 3-35. WS-Policy extension for streaming

```
<wsp:Policy wsu:Id="NetTcpBinding_MediaStreamingContract_policy">
  <wsp:ExactlyOne>
    <wsp:All>
      <msb:BinaryEncoding .../>
      <sp:TransportBinding .../>
      <msf:Streamed
xmlns:msf="http://schemas.microsoft.com/ws/2006/05/framing/policy" />
      <wsaw:UsingAddressing />
    </wsp:All>
  </wsp:ExactlyOne>
</wsp:Policy>
```

Who closes the stream?

Streaming is a local activity in that the service is responsible for its own stream, and the client is responsible for its own stream. That said, there are a few participants in the streaming process. Consider the lab in this section, which streams from service to client:

- The service operation is responsible for creating the `Stream` object, for example, initializing the `FileStream` to a particular file. The operation then returns this stream to the service model.

- The service model holds a reference to the stream. If streaming is enabled on the binding, instead of buffering the file to create the message, it waits for the client to read the stream.

- At the client, the service model constructs a stream reference for the client to read the remote stream. After this point, closing the proxy at the client makes no difference since the client will be pulling the stream directly from the server stream, facilitated by the service model.

- After the client performs its last read, the service model at the service will close its stream. In other words, the service model is responsible for closing the stream at the server.

- The client is responsible for closing its own stream reference at the client, which can escalate closing the stream at the service.

When the client is sending a stream to the service, the roles are reversed in that the client side service model closes the stream when the server has completed its last read.

Alternatives to streaming

While streaming enables you to reduce memory consumption, it is only as reliable as the transport protocol. HTTP is not as reliable as named pipes or TCP, so an alternative to streaming could be to use a custom chunking channel that sends the file in chunks over a binding that has reliable messaging enabled (see Chapter 6). In this way, you can keep a memory usage log (by chunk) and yet ensure all packets arrive in order to their destination, with resiliency to transient network interruptions. This approach can also be helpful when the file being transferred must be sent along with other data, something not possible when a single Stream parameter or return value is involved.

 A sample that traces streaming activities at the service can be found at *<YourLearningWCFPath>\Samples\Bindings\Streaming_WithTrace.*

Custom Bindings

Standard bindings were designed to simplify how developers configure services, providing a predefined set of binding elements with the ability to customize settings for the most common features. Standard bindings will satisfy the most common cases, but at times you need more control over the channel stack, for example:

- When none of the standard bindings provide the combination of features required
- When you want to use features not exposed by standard bindings

For these situations you must create a CustomBinding and select the binding elements and related settings you require. The key is to configure the binding elements in the correct order and with settings that don't conflict with one another. The possible combinations with a CustomBinding may seem overwhelming, a problem that standard bindings solve by providing a reduced set of features with which to work.

In this section, I'll take you on a tour through the binding elements available to a CustomBinding and provide some examples. In later chapters, you'll see more uses of CustomBinding as I explore some specific scenarios that require it.

CustomBinding Features

When you work with a CustomBinding, you have access to all of the same binding elements each of the standard bindings support and more. There are some extended settings for each binding element that are not available from the standard bindings for simplicity's sake, and there are additional binding elements that are not available unless you create a CustomBinding because they represent advanced features that are not common.

In the beginning of this chapter, I discussed binding elements as they relate to specific features exposed by most of the standard bindings. I also mentioned that binding elements form the channel stack; in fact, each binding element is used to add a channel to the channel stack. Table 3-7 summarizes an extended list of binding elements available to you when you build a CustomBinding. Some of these overlap with binding elements and features discussed so far, while others are only readily accessible through custom bindings.

Table 3-7. Summary of binding elements available to a CustomBinding

Binding element	Description
UseManagedPresentation	Optional. Setting related to Windows CardSpace. Used by security token services to indicate support for managed information cards.
PrivacyNoticeAt	Optional. Publishes a privacy notice Url and version in the WSDL document. Used by Windows CardSpace.
UnrecognizedPolicyAssertions	Optional. Includes support for unrecognized policy assertions in the WSDL.
TransactionFlow	Optional. Transaction protocol settings beyond the standard bindings.
ReliableSession	Optional. Reliable messaging protocol settings beyond the standard bindings.
Security	Optional. Many security settings beyond the standard bindings.
CompositeDuplex	Optional. Adds two-way messaging support to the channel. Required for callback support with nonduplex transports such as HTTP.
OneWay	Optional. Additional settings for one-way calls.
SslStreamSecurity, WindowsStreamSecurity	Optional. Choose one of these security settings for SSL or Windows transport security on top of the transport protocol.
BinaryMessageEncoding, MtomMessageEncoding, TextMessageEncoding	One required. This configures the wire format of messages.
TcpTransport, HttpTransport, HttpsTransport, PeerTransport, MsmqTransport, MsmqIntegration, NamedPipeTransport	One required. This configures the transport protocol for the channel stack.

The order of appearance in this table is an example of a legal ordering for these binding elements in the BindingElementsCollection. At the very least, you must provide a transport binding element and a message encoder with the transport-binding element at the bottom. The message encoder is typically above the transport-binding element, although this is not a rigid requirement.

Creating a CustomBinding

As with standard bindings, you can create a CustomBinding declaratively or in code. The order of each binding element is controlled in declarative configuration by the order in which binding elements are placed in the configuration. Example 3-36 shows an example of a CustomBinding configuration with transactions, reliable messaging, text encoding, and HTTP protocol.

You'll notice that the binding element name in configuration matches the programmatic binding element listed in Table 3-7, but in camel case form. Similar to naming conventions for standard bindings, binding elements are represented as CLR types in camel case, but in configuration use Pascal case XML element names.

Example 3-36. CustomBinding constructed declaratively

```
<customBinding>
  <binding name="customHttp">
    <transactionFlow transactionProtocol="WSAtomicTransactionOctober2004"/>
    <reliableSession ordered="true" />
    <textMessageEncoding messageVersion="Soap12WSAddressing10"
writeEncoding="utf-8"/>
    <httpTransport />
  </binding>
</customBinding>
```

When you create a `CustomBinding` programmatically, binding element order is controlled as you add binding elements to the `BindingElementCollection`. This is shown in Example 3-37.

Example 3-37. CustomBinding constructed in code

```
using (ServiceHost host = new ServiceHost(typeof(HelloIndigo.HelloIndigoService),
new Uri("http://localhost:8000")))
{
  BindingElementCollection elements = new BindingElementCollection( );
  elements.Add(new TransactionFlowBindingElement(
TransactionProtocol.WSAtomicTransactionOctober2004));
  elements.Add(new ReliableSessionBindingElement(true));
  elements.Add(new TextMessageEncodingBindingElement(
MessageVersion.Soap12WSAddressing10, Encoding.UTF8));
  elements.Add(new HttpTransportBindingElement( ));

  CustomBinding binding = new CustomBinding(elements);

  host.AddServiceEndpoint(typeof(HelloIndigo.IHelloIndigoService), binding,
"HelloIndigoService");
  host.Open( );
}
```

Samples illustrating `CustomBinding` configuration using configuration settings and code can be found here:

- *<YourLearningWCFPath>\Samples\Bindings\ CustomBindingConfig*
- *<YourLearningWCFPath>\Samples\Bindings\ CustomBindingInCode*

Now I'll show you two simple examples that require the creation of a `CustomBinding` to overcome limitations of the standard bindings.

Binary encoding over HTTP

By default, the standard bindings that support HTTP protocol only support Text or Mtom encoding. There are cases where you are exposing services as part of your internal network and don't require interoperability, yet you must use HTTP protocol to traverse firewalls through port 80. For performance reasons, you still want to use binary encoding since interoperability is not a requirement. You can achieve this by creating a CustomBinding like the one shown in Example 3-38.

Example 3-38. CustomBinding configuration for binary encoding over HTTP

```
<customBinding>
  <binding name="binaryOverHttp">
    <transactionFlow transactionProtocol="WSAtomicTransactionOctober2004"/>
    <reliableSession ordered="true"/>
    <binaryMessageEncoding />
    <httpTransport />
  </binding>
</customBinding>
```

This binding configuration not only uses binary encoding, it also adds reliable messaging and transaction support over HTTP.

 A sample illustrating binary encoding over HTTP can be found at *<YourLearningWCFPath>\Samples\Bindings\BinaryOverHttp*.

SOAP 1.2 without addressing headers

Each standard binding exposes a MessageVersion property (discussed earlier), which controls the format of the SOAP envelope and the presence and format of addressing headers. BasicHttpBinding defaults to SOAP 1.1 without addressing headers, while the rest of the standard bindings default to SOAP 1.2 with WS-Addressing protocol version 1.0. To control MessageVersion explicitly, you have to create a CustomBinding.

If you need to expose SOAP 1.2 protocol without addressing headers, you can create a custom binding like the one shown in Example 3-39.

Example 3-39. CustomBinding for SOAP 1.2 without addressing headers

```
<customBinding>
  <binding name="soap12noaddressing">
    <textMessageEncoding messageVersion="Soap12"/>
    <httpTransport />
  </binding>
</customBinding>
```

 A sample illustrating SOAP 1.2 without WS-Addressing can be found at *<YourLearningWCFPath>\Samples\Bindings\Soap12NoAddressing*.

Another reason to control `MessageVersion` is to interoperate with earlier web service stacks that still support the original WS-Addressing specification. Example 3-40 shows a custom binding for this case.

Example 3-40. CustomBinding to support WS-Addressing from August 2004

```
<customBinding>
  <binding name="wseaddressing">
    <textMessageEncoding messageVersion="Soap12WSAddressingAugust2004"/>
    <httpTransport />
  </binding>
</customBinding>
```

Summary

This chapter started with an overview of how bindings work. I discussed each of the available standard bindings; listed the binding features that you may require in your applications; and explained how bindings build the channel stack. This chapter also explores core standard bindings by scenario: Internet scenarios for web service bindings; intranet scenarios for connection-oriented bindings; two-way communications and large message transfers; and custom bindings. From all of this discussion you should take away the following guidance:

- Prefer `WSHttpBinding` for web service endpoints and use `BasicHttpBinding` in for backward compatibility with older web service stacks only. The configuration for `WSHttpBinding` will vary according to protocol support for sessions, reliable messaging, transactions, and security. These topics will be discussed in later chapters.

- Use `NetNamedPipeBinding` for communications on the same machine, and `NetTcpBinding` to support calls across machine boundaries. You may also choose `NetTcpBinding` for same machine communications if you require support for non-Windows credentials. Chapter 7 will discuss this further.

- Use `WSDualHttpBinding` if you need to support callbacks over HTTP.

- Be mindful of expected message payload size and set binding configuration accordingly. Use MTOM protocol for large binary payloads over HTTP and Streaming to reduce memory overhead if you are working with file transfers.

- Apply custom bindings only when the standard bindings do not support a particular combination of features you wish to apply.

At this point, you have the complete foundation for designing contracts and configuring service endpoints. You should also have a clear picture for how to access binding features, though there are still many features to explore such as reliable sessions, transactions and security. Before I get to those topics, however, you should have a better foundation for hosting services. In the next chapter, I will show you how to choose between hosting services in console or Windows applications, IIS 6, or the new WAS hosting environment for IIS 7.

CHAPTER 4

Hosting

For a service to be accessible at runtime, it must be hosted in a managed process. WCF services can be hosted with Internet Information Services (IIS) 6.0; with the new Windows Activation Service (WAS) installed with IIS 7.0; or with any other managed application process, including console, Windows Forms, Windows Presentation Foundation (WPF), or Windows service applications. Selecting the right hosting environment for services is a choice driven by the application deployment scenario, including the requirements for transport protocol and operating platform. There are also other features available to each hosting environment that can further influence deployment decisions and thus the choice of host.

In this chapter, I'll first describe the desired features of a hosting environment and the fundamentals of WCF service hosting. After that I'll drill deeper into hosting semantics and features of Windows applications, Windows services, IIS, and WAS. In the process, you'll learn practical implementations for each hosting environment, gain insight into their specific features and benefits, learn how to select the right host for your service, and complete several hands-on labs to solidify your understanding of each environment.

Hosting Features

There are three types of hosting environments for WCF services. You can host services in IIS 6.0 over HTTP protocol; with the WAS over any protocol; or by self-hosting. The term *self-hosting* refers to any application that provides its own code to initialize the hosting environment, like you have seen in earlier chapters with console and Windows host applications. Self-hosting can also include Windows Presentation Foundation (WPF) and managed Windows service applications.

Each hosting environment enables you to expose services to client applications. Through the service model, they facilitate request processing to service operations, but some hosts can also play a critical role in the availability and scalability of your services. Here are some important features that a great hosting environment should provide:

Executable process/application domain
Any managed process can host WCF services, which implies the existence of an *application domain*. All .NET code is run inside an application domain, which is a .NET construct that acts as a security boundary and provides fault isolation. A process can load one or more application domains, each with different code access security settings. If an unexpected problem propagates an exception up to the runtime, the application domain is torn down, but the process can remain alive if the main application domain is still present.

Configuration
Hosts should provide a way to configure services, supporting a flexible and manageable deployment model. All managed applications provide an application configuration file for this purpose (*app.config* or *web.config*).

Activation
Services must be running to process incoming requests. Some hosts will initialize services when the application starts, and some have the ability to activate services on demand when messages arrive.

Idle-time management
To conserve server resources during idle time, some hosts can stop inactive services based on a configurable timeout. This implies that the host also supports message-based activation to restart services on demand.

Health monitoring
To ensure availability, a host process must always be running to handle requests. Some hosting environments can proactively monitor the health of their running processes to ensure a new host process is started when existing processes are unable to handle requests.

Process recycling
To avoid problems associated with memory leaks or faulty code, some hosting environments support configurable process recycling to "freshen up" running host processes.

Management tools
Sophisticated hosting environments also provide tools for configuring hosting features for greater control and manageability. This toolset sometimes contains tools for monitoring the health and status of running host processes.

Unfortunately, not all hosting environments support all of these features. Table 4-1 provides a summary of the three hosting environments and the features they support.

Table 4-1. A summary of hosting options and supported features

Feature	Self-hosting	IIS hosting	WAS hosting
Executable process/app domain	Yes	Yes	Yes
Configuration	*app.config*	*web.config*	web.config
Activation	Manual	Message-based	Message-based
Idle-time management	No	Yes	Yes
Health monitoring	No	Yes	Yes
Process recycling	No	Yes	Yes
Management tools	No	Yes	Yes

At a minimum, all WCF hosts must provide an executable process and app domain in which services are loaded, in addition to configuration support. The remaining hosting features discussed here are built-in to IIS and WAS, but not provided by self-hosting environments. Throughout this chapter I'll be discussing each of these hosting environments and their appropriate usage.

ServiceHost

Regardless of the hosting environment, the service model provides a consistent run-time experience for host initialization, operation calls, and message processing. The ServiceHost type, part of the System.ServiceModel namespace, is the centerpiece of this hosting story. All WCF services must be associated with a ServiceHost instance to be accessible at runtime. Figure 4-1 illustrates the allocation of ServiceHost and associated service types for Windows service and IIS hosting.

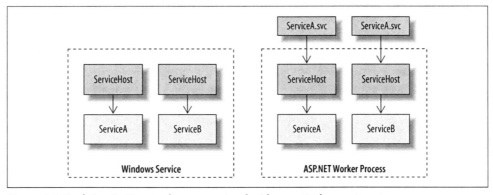

Figure 4-1. Each ServiceHost is always associated with a particular service type

Each ServiceHost instance is initialized with information about the service type, one or more service endpoints, optional base addresses, and behaviors that govern how the service model processes requests to the service. In this section, I'll explain the mechanics of the ServiceHost.

Initializing the ServiceHost

Example 4-1 illustrates a simple example of a console host application initializing the ServiceHost programmatically. In fact, this is the entire listing for the host application. When the application is launched, the ServiceHost is constructed with the service type, HelloIndigo.HelloIndigoService. A single endpoint is created, exposing its operations from the HelloIndigo.IHelloIndigoService service contract over NetTcpBinding. Recall from the introduction to these concepts in Chapter 1 that when a complete URI is provided for the endpoint address, you needn't provide any base addresses to the ServiceHost constructor.

Example 4-1. Initializing the ServiceHost programmatically

```
static void Main(string[] args)
{
  using (ServiceHost host = new
ServiceHost(typeof(HelloIndigo.HelloIndigoService)))
  {
    host.AddServiceEndpoint(typeof(HelloIndigo.IHelloIndigoService)
, new NetTcpBinding(), "net.tcp://localhost:9000/HelloIndigo");
    host.Open();

    Console.WriteLine("Press <Enter> to terminate the Host
application.");
    Console.WriteLine();
    Console.ReadLine();
  }
}
```

The Open() method initializes the ServiceHost instance and begins listening for messages at each configured endpoint. Even though the Console.ReadLine() statement blocks the console application to keep the process alive, incoming requests are processed on their own threads taken from the thread pool. When the console is closed, the using statement shown in Example 4-1 disposes of the ServiceHost instance calling its Close() method.

 In this example, only one service is exposed by the host application. To expose multiple services, multiple ServiceHost instances can be opened within the same host process as illustrated by the sample in the directory *<YourLearningWCFPath>\Samples\Hosting\MultipleServiceHost.*

Declarative Configuration

The ServiceHost will normally be initialized declaratively via application configuration. The <system.serviceModel> section may have one or more services described in the <services> section. Here is an example of declarative service configuration:

```
<service name="HelloIndigo.HelloIndigoService"
behaviorConfiguration="serviceBehavior">
  <endpoint address=
```

```
        "net.tcp://localhost:9000/HelloIndigoService" binding="netTcpBinding"
        contract="HelloIndigo.IHelloIndigoService" />
    </service>
```

As with programmatic initialization, you must specify the service type and one or more endpoints (explained in Chapter 1). This example illustrates how to configure a single endpoint similar to the code in Example 4-1.

When the ServiceHost instance is constructed, it looks for a <service> section matching its service type, and initializes itself from those settings. Initializing the ServiceHost declaratively removes hardcoded base addresses and endpoints from the code, as shown in Example 4-2.

Example 4-2. Initializing the ServiceHost declaratively

```
using (ServiceHost host = new ServiceHost(typeof(HelloIndigo.HelloIndigoService)))
{
    host.Open( );

    Console.WriteLine("Press <Enter> to terminate the Host application.");
    Console.WriteLine( );
    Console.ReadLine( );
}
```

 Managing deployments to staging, test, and production servers throughout the development cycle is much easier when you use declarative configuration. Deployment scripts can be used to modify endpoint addresses and port assignments to automate the process. The downside can be that any text editor may be used to modify configuration settings, which makes it difficult to prevent unwanted changes.

Base Addresses

If you specify a fully qualified URI for each service endpoint, a base address is not required to initialize the ServiceHost. If you provide base addresses to the ServiceHost constructor, you can optionally provide a relative URI to the endpoint address, as shown in Example 4-3.

Example 4-3. Initializing the ServiceHost with a base address and relative endpoint

```
using (ServiceHost host = new ServiceHost(typeof(HelloIndigo.HelloIndigoService),
new Uri("net.tcp://localhost:9000")))
{
    host.AddServiceEndpoint(typeof(HelloIndigo.IHelloIndigoService),
new NetTcpBinding( ), "HelloIndigo");
    host.Open( );

    Console.WriteLine("Press <Enter> to terminate the Host application.");
    Console.WriteLine( );
    Console.ReadLine( );
}
```

Base addresses and relative endpoints can also be provided declaratively in the <host> section of the service configuration, as shown in Example 4-4.

Example 4-4. Declarative configuration of base addresses and relative endpoints

```
<service name="HelloIndigo.HelloIndigoService"
behaviorConfiguration="serviceBehavior">
  <host>
    <baseAddresses>
      <add baseAddress="http://localhost:8000"/>
      <add baseAddress="net.tcp://localhost:9000"/>
    </baseAddresses>
  </host>
  <endpoint binding="netTcpBinding" contract="HelloIndigo.IHelloIndigoService" />
  <endpoint  address="mex" binding="mexHttpBinding" contract="IMetadataExchange"/>
</service>
```

Endpoints without a complete URI will be addressed relative to the base address matching their binding protocol. For example, the NetTcpBinding endpoint shown in Example 4-4 uses the *net.tcp* base address, while the metadata exchange endpoint relies on the *http* base address. If you omit the address altogether from the <endpoint> configuration, the base address for the endpoint's protocol is assumed to be the endpoint address.

 You should use base addresses and relative endpoints whenever possible so that only the base address need be modified when services are deployed to multiple machines.

ServiceHost and ServiceDescription

Chapter 2 explains the concept of a service description, which incorporates information about the service, its endpoints, and any behaviors that are attached to the service. The service description is represented by the ServiceDescription type, which is ultimately used to generate the WSDL document for the service and to support interactive metadata exchange (discussed in Chapters 1 and 2).

The ServiceHost is responsible for generating this service description for its service. ServiceHost has a Description property that can be used to access the ServiceDescription instance. The instance is generated when the Open() method is called, at which time the description is generated by using reflection on the service type, its contracts, and relevant service behaviors.

Under most circumstances, you will not interact directly with the process of generating the ServiceDescription. For advanced scenarios, however, you can control how this ServiceDescription is generated by overriding the CreateDescription() method in a class that extends the ServiceHost.

Closing the ServiceHost

Once you have initialized and opened the ServiceHost instance, channel listeners are created for each endpoint to process requests to each endpoint (discussed in Chapter 2). If the host process is shut down, each of its ServiceHost instances will be closed either explicitly with a call to its Close( ) or Dispose( ) method, or implicitly by the service model when the type is disposed. While the ServiceHost is closing, new requests to that particular ServiceHost instance are rejected, but any requests that are already in queue will be completed. Although a rare occurence, it is possible for the ServiceHost to be put into a faulted state. For example, if there are errors in the service model configuration. If the ServiceHost State property is set to CommunicationState.Faulted, when Close( ) is called an exception will be thrown. For this reason, it is best to check the State property of the ServiceHost instance and call Abort( ) if it is in a faulted state. This technique was illustrated in Chapter 1.

Communication Events

ServiceHost inherits ServiceHostBase, which inherits CommunicationObject. CommunicationObject is a common base type for many objects participating in the communication channel, providing a consistent state machine. This type exposes events including Opening, Opened, Closing, Closed, and Faulted. To be notified of state changes in the channel stack for each hosted service, you can hook these communication events.

Closing and Faulted can be particularly useful for writing event logs or notifying administrators when the communication channel for your service is closing or has encountered a problem. Just add these event handlers to the ServiceHost instance before you open the communication channel, as shown here:

```
using (ServiceHost host = new ServiceHost(typeof(HelloIndigo.HelloIndigoService)))
{
  host.Closed += new EventHandler(host_Closed);
  host.Closing += new EventHandler(host_Closing);
  host.Faulted += new EventHandler(host_Faulted);
  host.Open( );

  // other code
}
```

The ServiceHost also has a State property based on the CommunicationState enumeration. You can use this property to detect the following states: Created, Opening, Opened, Closing, Closed, or Faulted.

 Client-side proxies also inherit CommunicationObject. After each call, clients should check the proxy's state to ensure that the communication channel has not faulted.

Self-Hosting

Self-hosting is the simplest way to host your services, but it is also the approach that yields the least number of hosting features. As the label implies, self-hosting requires you to write the code necessary to initialize the ServiceHost and manage its lifetime. At a minimum, you provide a managed process, instantiate a ServiceHost for each service, and then initialize them with endpoints and binding configurations that define the communication channel for each endpoint for incoming messages.

Typically, you'll keep ServiceHost instances alive for the lifetime of the application in which they are hosted. The ServiceHost is normally constructed on the application thread, but the service model allocates worker threads for incoming requests to its service endpoints. Your job is to keep that application thread and the ServiceHost alive as long as you want to process requests. Any managed process will suffice for this purpose including console, Windows Forms, WPF, and Windows services, as I discussed earlier.

Console Applications

Console applications are a popular hosting environment for developing and testing services. As I discussed earlier, you need only create and open the ServiceHost instance and keep the console process alive to receive and process requests. Example 4-2 illustrates how a typical console application achieves this, using Console.ReadLine( ) to keep the thread alive.

Console applications are ultimately impractical for deploying production services for a two reasons:

1. They require a user be logged in to the machine to start the process.
2. The console can be easily closed, taking the communication channel along with it.

Still, you can expect to use console hosts to verify basic service functionality in unit tests and in early prototypes.

Windows Applications

Both Windows Forms and WPF applications can be useful for hosting WCF services associated with a user interface (UI). In this case, the UI thread keeps the application alive, thus any ServiceHost instances can receive requests for the duration of the application lifetime, unless it is explicitly closed.

Here are a few possible scenarios for Windows application hosts:

- Chat applications that participate in a peer mesh will expose services to receive broadcast messages and likely provide a UI.
- Windows client applications may host services in-process to consume local services without crossing a process boundary. For example, a smart client application may

use local services when operating offline, and remote services while online. Another example could be when two applications on the client must share functionality hosted in another process.

- Services deployed to client (less likely on server machines) may have an associated UI if the service presents an activity log or provides some administrative controls for service activation and deactivation.

Hosting services inside a Windows application does, however, have some drawbacks. For one, they require a user to be logged in to start the application, which limits their usefulness in server deployments since server machines are generally unattended. More importantly, when UI threads are involved, you must understand which thread the service will be hosted on, and deal with possible concurrency implications. Hosting on the UI thread will be explored shortly.

Windows Services

Unlike console and Windows applications, Windows services do not require a user to be logged in to the machine to start the service. In fact, Windows services are traditionally configured to start automatically on unattended server machines and do not require user interaction.

As with console and Windows applications, any ServiceHost instances must be kept alive for the lifetime of the Windows service. Due to the server-side nature of this hosting environment, concurrency is still a concern, though it may not specifically be related to a UI thread since most Windows services do not have an associated interface (and should not on a server machine). Windows services will usually allow multiple concurrent requests to increase throughput, making it necessary to protect any other shared resources used by hosted services.

Later in this chapter, I'll explain how to host services in a managed Windows service.

Hosting on the UI Thread

Windows applications provide functionality by responding to messages. Each Windows application has a message queue and a window procedure that contains a *message loop*. The message loop retrieves messages from the message queue, one by one, and processes them, usually by forwarding the message to the appropriate target window. All controls on a form, for example, are also windows that have a unique window handle (HWND) and functionality to respond to particular windows messages.

Windows applications usually include some form of user interface that runs on a *UI thread*, meaning that messages are processed through the message loop. When WCF services are hosted inside a Windows application, operations can execute on thread pool threads or on the UI thread—as determined by design choices of both the service and its host. This brings to light some interesting considerations:

- When services are hosted in a Windows application and hosted on the UI thread, the UI thread acts as a throttle for message processing—that is, messages are processed one at a time in the order received. To achieve additional throughput (process many requests concurrently) you may want to avoid hosting on the UI thread.

- If you are concerned about hosting on the UI thread, you must also consider the location where you construct the ServiceHost. ServiceOperationBehavior settings can be used to control whether services allow messages to be processed on the UI thread.

- When you are hosting a service on the UI thread, that usually implies some level of coupling between the service and the user interface. As such, your choice to host on the UI thread, or not, may also influence your decisions about assembly allocation for services, hosts, and related UI components.

When you create the ServiceHost on the UI thread, all requests are processed through the message loop. In a service that supports multithreading (to be discussed in Chapter 5), this throttles how many messages can be processed concurrently since the message loop processes one message at a time. One of the benefits of this is that requests can freely interact with form and control properties, since they are all running on the same thread (concurrency issues are also discussed in Chapter 5).

There are ways for both the host and service to control if the service runs on the UI thread. Hosts have control over which thread constructs the ServiceHost. Services can reject the UI thread using the UseSynchronizationContext property of the ServiceBehaviorAttribute. These are all considerations that I will elaborate on in this section. You'll also complete a lab to gain some experience with each option.

Windows Applications and UI Threads

Both Windows Forms and WPF can be used to create Windows applications. Although each provides a distinct approach to UI design and internal application architecture, both types of applications usually create a main window running on the UI thread. The safest and simplest way to host services in a Windows application is for requests to be processed on this UI thread because it removes concerns over concurrency and complexities associated with multiple threads and communication with UI components. In fact, the default behavior for services hosted in a Windows application is to process requests on the UI thread if you construct the ServiceHost instance while running on that UI thread. Example 4-5 illustrates constructing the ServiceHost in the form constructor for a Windows Forms application.

Example 4-5. Constructing a ServiceHost instance in the Form constructor

```
public partial class Form1 : Form
{
  ServiceHost m_serviceHost;
```

```
public Form1( )
{
  InitializeComponent( );

  m_serviceHost = new ServiceHost(typeof(Messaging.MessagingService));
}

// other code
}
```

You can verify that the service is running on the UI thread by checking the `Application.MessageLoop` property as the operation executes. The following code, when placed inside any service operation, will throw an exception while debugging if the service is not running on the UI thread:

```
Debug.Assert(Application.MessageLoop);
```

When requests are processed through the message loop, service operations (including downstream code) can freely interact with the user interface, setting form and control properties for example. The only downside, as I have mentioned, is that the message loop acts as a throttle for request processing, even if the service were configured to allow multiple concurrent requests.

From the same Windows Form application, if you construct the `ServiceHost` instance before the UI thread is started, the host instance will run on its own thread. That means messages are processed by worker threads allocated from the thread pool, instead of passing through the message loop. This enables services to process multiple concurrent requests but introduces the need to provide multithreading protection when communicating with controls and forms and other shared application resources (concurrency is discussed in Chapter 5).

Processing requests on the UI thread is not practical for services that require decent throughput. By definition this usually rules out server deployments. In fact, most services requiring any level of throughput on the server will not be associated with a user interface. However, assuming some service operations do interact with the UI thread, while others do not and require throughput, services can request to be run on a separate thread to ensure this throughput using the `ServiceBehaviorAttribute`.

Synchronization Context

As I have mentioned, you can control which thread the `ServiceHost` is constructed on either at the host or service implementation. If you create the `ServiceHost` on the UI thread, messages are processed by that thread. If you create the `ServiceHost` before the UI thread is created, by default the `ServiceHost` creates a new thread when the `ServiceHost` is initialized. It is said that in the former case, the service joins the synchronization context of the UI, where in the latter case the service creates a new synchronization context. The *synchronization context* refers to the thread in which code is executing.

Example 4-6 shows how to construct the ServiceHost before Application.Run( ), which means the service executes in a new synchronization context.

Example 4-6. Initializing the ServiceHost before Application.Run()

```
static class Program
{
  public static ServiceHost MessageServiceHost;

  [STAThread]
  static void Main( )
  {
    Program.MessageServiceHost = new
ServiceHost(typeof(Messaging.MessagingService));
    Program.MessageServiceHost.Open( );

    Application.EnableVisualStyles( );
    Application.SetCompatibleTextRenderingDefault(false);
    Application.Run(new Form1( ));
  }
}
```

If you want to initialize the ServiceHost on a separate thread, after the UI thread has been created, you can use the technique shown in Example 4-7. In this example, to avoid synchronization with the UI thread a new thread is run to create and open the ServiceHost.

 The following code sample illustrates this scenario: *<YourLearningWCF Path>\Samples\Hosting\ ServiceHostNewThread*.

Example 4-7. Constructing the ServiceHost on a new thread

```
// procedure to run on a new thread
private void StartService( )
{
  m_serviceHost = new ServiceHost(typeof(Messaging.MessagingService));
  m_serviceHost.Open( );
}

// starting the thread
Thread t;
t = new Thread(StartService);
t.IsBackground = true;
t.Start( );
```

The point is that a new synchronization context is created for the ServiceHost if the current synchronization context is not the UI thread. As I have stated, this means that messages are processed on threads from the thread pool instead of through the message loop. To synchronize with the UI thread, the host can construct each

ServiceHost instance after the UI thread has been created. This is particularly valuable when the service operation will interact with the UI.

Services can also prevent synchronization with the UI thread using the UseSynchronizationContext property of the ServiceBehaviorAttribute. This property defaults to true, which is why services will join the UI thread if one exists. By setting it to false, even if the host constructs the ServiceHost on the UI thread, it will use a new thread. You apply this attribute to a service type as follows:

```
[ServiceBehavior(UseSynchronizationContext=false)]
public class MessagingService : IMessagingService
```

Table 4-2 summarizes the resulting synchronization context for a ServiceHost instance based on the thread on which it is constructed, and the UseSynchronizationContext setting.

Table 4-2. ServiceHost synchronization context options

UI thread created	UseSynchronizationContext	Synchronization context
Non-UI thread	True or false	New thread
UI thread	True (default)	UI thread
UI thread	False	New thread

ServiceHost Lifetime

By default, the lifetime of a ServiceHost instance is that of its thread. Typically, that means the lifetime of the application unless you explicitly call the Close( ) method of the ServiceHost. If you allow the application to be shut down without closing the ServiceHost and its associated channel listeners first, messages may continue to flow in while the application is about to dispose of all channels. To avoid this race condition between the time that the host application is shut down and incoming client requests, it is best to explicitly close each ServiceHost instance.

When the ServiceHost lifetime is tied to a particular form, you can hook the FormClosing event as shown in Example 4-8.

Example 4-8. Cleaning up the ServiceHost in the FormClosing event handler

```
private void Form1_FormClosing(object sender, FormClosingEventArgs e)
{
  DialogResult result = MessageBox.Show("Are you sure you want to close the
service?", "Service Controller", MessageBoxButtons.YesNo, MessageBoxIcon.Question,
MessageBoxDefaultButton.Button2);

  if (result == DialogResult.Yes)
  {
    if (m_serviceHost!=null)
    {
      m_serviceHost.Close( );
```

```
      m_serviceHost =null;
    }
  }
  else
    e.Cancel=true;
}
```

If the `ServiceHost` instance is tied to the application lifetime, as opposed to a particular form, you can hook the `Application` object's `Exit` event. This is shown later in Example 4-11.

You can also call `Open( )` and `Close( )` methods of the `ServiceHost` while the host is running, to start and stop the service when it is running on the UI thread. When the `ServiceHost` is not running on the UI thread, `Close( )` ends the thread on which it initialized. This cleans up the `ServiceHost` instance and renders any references you have useless. In this case, your application must recreate and open the `ServiceHost` in order to receive subsequent requests.

Lab: Working with a Windows Forms Host

In this lab, you will host an existing service inside a Windows Forms application. During the lab, you'll experiment with the effects of constructing the `ServiceHost` from different locations. You'll also use the `ServiceBehaviorAttribute` to control whether services can be hosted on the UI thread.

Configuring the ServiceHost

To get started, the first thing you'll do is set up the host.

1. Open the startup solution for this lab at *<YourLearningWCFPath>\Labs\ Chapter4\WindowsApplicationHost\WindowsApplicationHost.sln*. This solution contains a completed service and a shell service host and client application.

2. Modify the `WindowsHost` project to host the `MessagingService` type from the `Messaging` assembly. Start by adding a reference to the `Messaging` project so that you'll have access to the service.

3. Now, add a `<system.serviceModel>` section to the *app.config* for the `WindowsHost` project. Add a `<service>` section for the `Messaging.MessagingService` type with a `NetTcpBinding` endpoint, a metadata exchange endpoint, and a base address for TCP and HTTP protocols. The resulting configuration is shown in Example 4-9.

Example 4-9. WindowsHost configuration for MessagingService

```
<system.serviceModel>
  <services>
    <service name="Messaging.MessagingService"
```

Example 4-9. WindowsHost configuration for MessagingService (continued)

```
behaviorConfiguration="serviceBehavior">
      <endpoint contract="Messaging.IMessagingService" binding="netTcpBinding" />
      <endpoint contract="IMetadataExchange" binding="mexHttpBinding" />
      <host>
        <baseAddresses>
          <add baseAddress="net.tcp://localhost:9000"/>
          <add baseAddress="http://localhost:8000"/>
        </baseAddresses>
      </host>
    </service>
  </services>
  <behaviors>
    <serviceBehaviors>
      <behavior name="serviceBehavior">
        <serviceMetadata/>
      </behavior>
    </serviceBehaviors>
  </behaviors>
</system.serviceModel>
```

At this point, you have configured a Windows application to host a service, which looks a lot like what you have seen in earlier chapters for console hosts. What will be different is the location where you will initialize the ServiceHost.

Opening and closing the ServiceHost

As with all of the self-hosting examples shown in this book so far, you have to construct a ServiceHost to host a service. In this step, you're going to construct and open the ServiceHost before creating the UI thread and provide code to close the ServiceHost gracefully on application exit.

1. Go to the WindowsHost project and add a reference to the System.ServiceModel assembly.

2. Next, open *Program.cs* and add code to construct a static reference to the ServiceHost instance, scoped to the application domain. Initialize the ServiceHost instance before the Application.Run( ) command, which creates the UI thread. Example 4-10 shows the changes you'll make to *Program.cs*.

Example 4-10. Creating the ServiceHost instance before the UI thread

```
static class Program
{
  public static ServiceHost MessageServiceHost;

  [STAThread]
  static void Main( )
  {
    Program.MessageServiceHost = new
ServiceHost(typeof(Messaging.MessagingService));
    Program.MessageServiceHost.Open( );
```

Example 4-10. Creating the ServiceHost instance before the UI thread (continued)

```
    Application.EnableVisualStyles();
    Application.SetCompatibleTextRenderingDefault(false);
    Application.Run(new Form1());
  }
}
```

3. With the code just added, the ServiceHost lifetime is for the duration of the application. Once the application is closed, its application domain and the ServiceHost instance will be destroyed along with it. As a matter of good practice, the ServiceHost should be closed immediately when the application is exiting to prevent new requests from being processed. In the *Program.cs* file where the ServiceHost is created, add some code to hook the ApplicationExit event and call the Close() method of the ServiceHost to speed up this process.

   Add the code shown in bold in Example 4-11 to achieve this.

Example 4-11. Hooking the ApplicationExit event to close the ServiceHost

```
static void Main()
{
  Application.ApplicationExit += new EventHandler(Application_ApplicationExit);
  Program.MessageServiceHost = new ServiceHost(typeof(Messaging.MessagingService));
  Program.MessageServiceHost.Open();

  // other code
}

static void Application_ApplicationExit(object sender, EventArgs e)
{
  if (Program.MessageServiceHost != null)
  {
    Program.MessageServiceHost.Close();
    Program.MessageServiceHost = null;
  }
}
```

4. Compile and run the WindowsHost project to verify that there are no exceptions. Leave the host running for the next section of the lab.

Now you have created a Windows host for your services. Next, you will configure the client application to call the service.

Calling services on a non-UI thread

In this part of the lab, you will add code to the client application to invoke service operations.

1. Go to the Client project and add a service reference to the MessagingService providing the base address *http://localhost:8000* and using localhost as the namespace.

2. Open *Form1.cs* and create a Click event handler for the Call Service button. Add code to the event handler to construct the proxy and call its SendMessage( ) function, as shown here:

```
private void button1_Click(object sender, EventArgs e)
{
  localhost.MessagingServiceClient proxy = new
localhost.MessagingServiceClient( );
  proxy.SendMessage(string.Format("Hello from {0}", this.Text));
}
```

3. Compile and run the WindowsHost and the Client application. Click the Call Service button to invoke the MessagingService and a message box will display with the following information:

```
Message 'Hello' from Client: Process [processId]' received on thread [threadId]:
MessageLoop = False
```

The value for threadId represents the server thread processing the call to SendMessage( ). You should note that this thread is different from the UI thread indicated in the Service Controller UI shown in Figure 4-2.

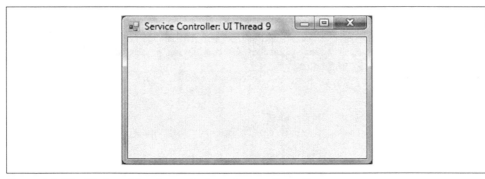

Figure 4-2. The UI thread for the service host, Service Controller

Calling services on the UI thread

Now you'll switch gears and see what happens when you create the ServiceHost instance on the UI thread.

1. Go to the WindowsHost project and open *Program.cs* and remove the code that you just wrote so that the file is left with only the code shown in Example 4-12.

Example 4-12. Program.cs after removing ServiceHost code

```
using System;
using System.Collections.Generic;
using System.Windows.Forms;

namespace WindowsHost
{
  static class Program
```

Example 4-12. Program.cs after removing ServiceHost code (continued)

```
  {
    [STAThread]
    static void Main( )
    {
      Application.EnableVisualStyles( );
      Application.SetCompatibleTextRenderingDefault(false);
      Application.Run(new Form1( ));
    }
  }
}
```

2. Open *Form1.cs* in design view and add two Button controls. Set their Text properties to Start Service and Stop Service, respectively, as shown in Figure 4-3.

Figure 4-3. The Service Controller UI after adding two Button controls

3. Add code to the form to create and initialize the ServiceHost instance; to clean up the instance when the form is closed; and to start and stop the service through the command buttons. Add Click event handlers for each button and then open *Form1.cs* in code view. Add code to each of the handlers as shown in bold in Example 4-13.

   You'll notice that the code is similar to what was removed from *Program.cs*, with the exception that you're now scoping the ServiceHost instance to the form's lifetime, allowing the user to start and stop the service, and cleaning up the ServiceHost immediately when the user confirms exiting the application.

Example 4-13. Creating the ServiceHost instance on the UI thread

```
public partial class Form1 : Form
{
  ServiceHost m_serviceHost;

  public Form1( )
  {
    InitializeComponent( );
    this.button2.Enabled=false;
```

```
    m_serviceHost = new ServiceHost(typeof(Messaging.MessagingService));
}

private void button1_Click(object sender, EventArgs e)
{
  this.button1.Enabled = false;
  this.button2.Enabled = true;
  m_serviceHost.Open();
}

private void button2_Click(object sender, EventArgs e)
{
  this.button1.Enabled = true;
  this.button2.Enabled = false;
  m_serviceHost.Close();
}

private void Form1_FormClosing(object sender, FormClosingEventArgs e)
{
    DialogResult result = MessageBox.Show("Are you sure you want to close the
service?", "Service Controller", MessageBoxButtons.YesNo, MessageBoxIcon.Question,
MessageBoxDefaultButton.Button2);

    if (result == DialogResult.Yes)
    {
      if (m_serviceHost != null)
      {
        m_serviceHost.Close();
        m_serviceHost = null;
      }
    }
    else
      e.Cancel=true;
}
}
```

4. Compile and run the WindowsHost and Client projects. This time, you'll have to click Start Service in the Service Controller UI before you can invoke the service from the client. Once the service is started, click Call Service from the client and observe the message box text. This time, you'll notice that the host's UI thread matches that of the request thread and that the request thread is running on the message loop.

Preventing services from joining the UI thread

In this part of the lab, you'll edit the MessagingService so that it explicitly prevents the service from running on the UI thread, using the OperationBehaviorAttribute.

1. Go to the Messaging project and open *MessagingService.cs*. Add the ServiceBehaviorAttribute to the MessagingService type and set the synchronization context to false, as shown here:

```
[ServiceBehavior(UseSynchronizationContext=false)]
public class MessagingService : IMessagingService
```

2. Compile and run the WindowsHost and Client projects again. Run the same tests as before. This time, observe that calls to the service operation are executed on a thread other than the UI thread.

In the following sections I'll discuss the concepts introduced in this lab in more detail.

Callbacks and the UI Thread

In Chapter 3, I explained how to work with callbacks and duplex communication. In the section "One-Way and Duplex Communication," you completed a lab that illustrates the use of one-way operations, callbacks, and duplex bindings. I also briefly touched on synchronization context for callbacks. In this section, I'll give a quick review and discuss the similarities between how services and client callback types behave in relation to the UI thread.

Recall that when services support callbacks, the client exposes an endpoint to receive messages from the service. At the service, the service contract includes a callback contract as Example 4-14 illustrates. In this example, the service operation is one-way, as is the callback operation.

Example 4-14. Adding a callback contract to the MessagingService

```
[ServiceContract(Namespace = "http://www.thatindigogirl.com/samples/2006/06",
CallbackContract=typeof(IMessagingServiceCallback))]
public interface IMessagingService
{
  [OperationContract(IsOneWay - true)]
  void SendMessage(string message);
}

public interface IMessagingServiceCallback
{
  [OperationContract(IsOneWay = true)]
  void MessageNotification(string message);
}
```

Clients implement the callback contract as shown in Example 4-15 and pass the callback instance to the proxy. For Windows clients, the default behavior is for callback operations to execute on the UI thread. If the service operation is one-way, this is a nonissue. If the service operation is not one-way, the UI thread will be blocking on the outgoing call and be unable to receive a callback on the UI thread.

Example 4-15. Implementation of IMessagingServiceCallback

```
class MessagingServiceCallback:IMessagingServiceCallback
{
  public void MessageNotification(string message)
  {
```

Example 4-15. Implementation of IMessagingServiceCallback (continued)

```
    MessageBox.Show(String.Format("Message '{0}' received on thread {1} :
MessageLoop = {2}", message, Thread.CurrentThread.GetHashCode(),
Application.MessageLoop), "IMessagingServiceCallback.MessageNotification()");
  }
}

// initializing the MessagingService proxy
MessagingServiceCallback callbackType = new MessagingServiceCallback();
InstanceContext context = new InstanceContext(callbackType);
m_proxy = new localhost.MessagingServiceClient(context);
```

In general practice, because clients can't control when the service will invoke the callback, they should have callback operations execute on a new thread for non-one-way calls. This is achieved by applying the CallbackBehaviorAttribute to the callback type and setting UseSynchronizationContext to false. By default, UseSynchronizationContext is set to true, as with the ServiceBehaviorAttribute discussed earlier. Here is an example where the CallbackBehaviorAttribute is applied:

```
[CallbackBehavior(UseSynchronizationContext=false)]
class MessagingServiceCallback:IMessagingServiceCallback
```

> See the following code samples for an implementation of callbacks with and without UI thread synchronization:
>
> - *<YourLearningWCFPath>\Samples\Hosting\Callbacks_Synchronized*
> - *<YourLearningWCFPath>\Samples\Hosting\Callbacks_NoSynchronization*

UI Hosting Scenarios

Now that you have more information about the process of hosting in a Windows application, I'll discuss some implementation patterns. The truth is that you will rarely, if ever, host services on a UI thread when they are deployed to server machines. So, most of what I have discussed in this section relates to client-side service deployment. Assuming that the service you are creating is associated with a user interface, and does not run on an unattended server machine, one of the following implementation techniques apply:

- The service may be coupled to the host user interface such that as operations are invoked, the user interface is immediately updated. This means that the service operations must know something about the host UI to interact with it.

- The service may provide information to its own user interface that can be shown or hidden at the discretion of the host application. In this case, the service knows about its own UI but exposes static operations for the host to show or hide that UI.

- The service may not concern itself with a user interface, but host applications may choose to present information related to service execution. In this case, the service is independent of UI, but it may expose static properties or push data to a common data store that the host can access.

In this section, I'll discuss how to handle each approach.

Coupling services to the host user interface

If the user interface exposed by the host is directly related to service functionality, it is likely that the service will not be exposed by another hosting environment. This removes the need to decouple service code from the host; in fact, it will probably reduce confusion if the service is part of the host assembly, as illustrated in Figure 4-4.

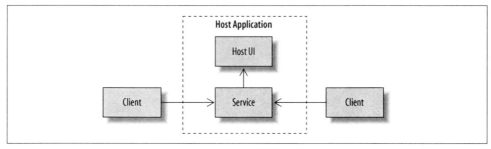

Figure 4-4. Coupling service and host

In this scenario, the following settings apply:

- `UseSynchronizationContext` is set to `true` (the default).
- The UI thread initializes the `ServiceHost`.
- Services can safely communicate directly with forms and controls.

Since the service and host are coupled, to communicate with controls, the service can use the `OpenForms` collection for the application. For example, the following code assumes that the first form in the `OpenForms` collection is the `MessagingForm`:

```
MessagingForm f = Application.OpenForms[0] as MessagingForm;
f.AddMessage(s);
```

In this case, the `MessagingForm` exposes a public `AddMessage()` method that the service calls to add information to a `ListBox` control:

```
void IMessagingForm.AddMessage(string message)
{
  this.lstMessages.Items.Add(message);
}
```

To achieve some measure of decoupling, and to support the case where the service is indeed hosted elsewhere, the service could look for a particular interface to be implemented on the form. Consider this interface, for example:

```
public interface IMessagingForm
{
  void AddMessage(string message);
}
```

If the form implements this interface, the service code changes to this:

```
IMessagingForm messagingForm = null;
foreach (Form f in Application.OpenForms)
{
  messagingForm = f as IMessagingForm;
  if (messagingForm != null) break;
}
if (messagingForm!=null)
  messagingForm.AddMessage(s);
```

 See the following code samples illustrating service and host UI coupling:

- *<YourLearningWCFPath>\Samples\Hosting\CouplingServiceAndHostUI*
- *<YourLearningWCFPath>\Samples\Hosting\CouplingServiceAndHostUI_InterfaceBased*

Exposing a reusable service user interface

In some cases, it may make more sense to couple the service with its own user interface and provide methods that a host can call to show the interface on demand. This makes it possible to provide multiple hosts for the service and share a common UI for functionality directly associated with the service. It also makes it possible for hosts to determine if and when it is appropriate to show the UI. The assembly allocation is illustrated in Figure 4-5.

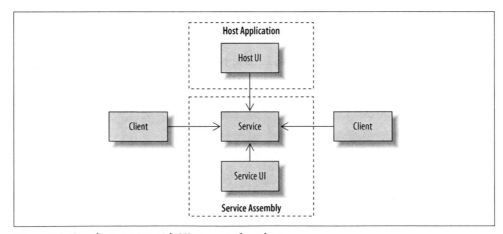

Figure 4-5. Coupling service with UI separate from host

In this scenario, the following settings apply:

- `UseSynchronizationContext` is set to `true` if all service operations communicate with the UI, and `false` if some operations require more throughput than that provided through the message loop.
- The UI thread may or may not initialize the `ServiceHost`—this is host dependent.
- Services may not be running on the UI thread, so the service UI should handle the possibility of communication from a non-UI thread.

In this case, the service could provide a static method so that the host application can show or hide the service UI. The service can directly access its UI through a static member, in this case sending messages to the UI only if the form is visible:

```
public class MessagingService : IMessagingService
{
  private static ServiceForm m_form;

  public void SendMessage(string message)
  {
    if (m_form != null && m_form.Visible)
      m_form.AddMessage(message);
  }

  // other code
}
```

Since the service is not guaranteed to run on the UI thread, the service form should encapsulate a check to see if calls should be explicitly invoked on the UI thread:

```
public void AddMessage(string message)
{
  if (this.InvokeRequired)
  {
    MethodInvoker del = delegate
      {
        this.listBox1.Items.Add(message);
      };
    this.Invoke(del);
  }
  else
    this.listBox1.Items.Add(message);
}
```

 `InvokeRequired` is a property of forms and controls indicating if the calling thread is not the same as the thread where the form or control was constructed (usually the UI thread). If this property is set to `true`, the `Invoke()` method of the form or control must be used to interact with its methods and properties that interact with UI elements.

Code like this must be written for all communication with form and control members if service operations aren't guaranteed to run on the UI thread.

The following code sample illustrates a service that owns its own UI: *<YourLearningWCFPath>\Samples\Hosting\ ServiceWithThreadSafeUI.*

Decoupling services from user interfaces

More than likely, services and UI are not coupled, but they may share a common data store. A user interface may be used to present this data to users, and it could be owned by the host, as illustrated in Figure 4-6.

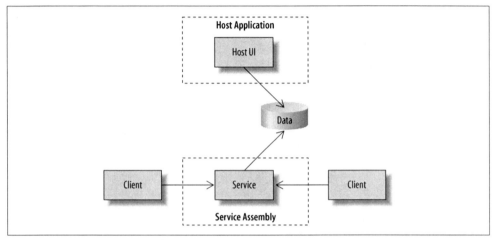

Figure 4-6. Decoupling service from UI

In this case the following settings apply:

- `UseSynchronizationContext` should be set to `false` so that the service can optionally have increased throughput via multithreading.
- The service host may have a UI thread but it will be completely independent of the service code.
- Services push data to a cache or data store.
- Hosts present data from that same cache or data store without communicating with the service type.

Hosting in a Windows Service

Windows services are the most useful of the self-hosting environments for WCF services. In fact, for services deployed in a production server system, the Windows service is the only practical self-hosting choice for a few reasons:

- Windows services can be configured to start when the system starts without requiring a user to log in to the machine.

- The Service Control Manager can be used to manage service startup, restarts, and other run behaviors—no custom user interface required.
- The service can be configured to restart when it encounters a failure, increasing overall availability.

Windows services are a self-hosting environment for WCF services, thus you write the same code as with console and Windows hosts to initialize the ServiceHost. The main difference for Windows services is in the location where initialization and cleanup take place. In this section I'll walk you through creating and deploying a Windows service and using it to host a WCF service.

I'll provide you with a brief review of Windows services, followed by an explanation for how this relates to WCF. Then you will complete a lab that walks you through creating and testing a Windows service host. After that, I'll discuss some scenarios for applying Windows services.

What Are Windows Services?

Windows services are applications whose lifetime is controlled through the *Service Control Manager* (SCM). The SCM is automatically started when a Windows machine boots, allowing local or remote control over the machine's Windows services. You can access the SCM through the Control Panel under Administrative Tools → Services. Through the SCM you can: start, stop, pause, and continue services, and edit configuration settings for a service.

Controlling service startup

Windows services are normally installed as part of an automated deployment script, rather than directly through the SCM interface. Configuration settings for the service can also be scripted, but are also editable through property dialogs provided by the SCM. Figure 4-7 shows general properties for a Windows service. Aside from descriptive information, such as the service name, display name, and description, you can also control the service startup type and explicitly start, stop, pause, or resume the service from here.

Startup type is an important setting since this determines whether the service is enabled or not, and whether the service should be automatically started when the machine boots. The options are:

Disabled
    The service is disabled.

Manual
    The service must be manually started using the SCM.

Automatic
    The service should start when the machine is booted.

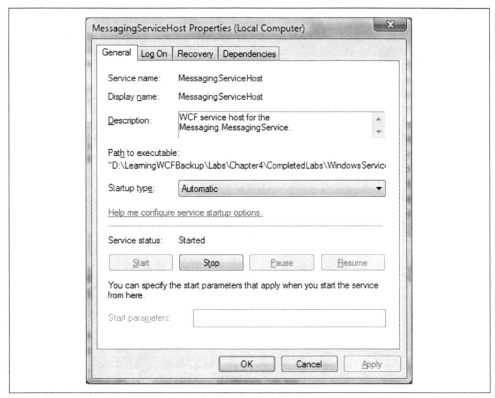

Figure 4-7. General Windows Service configuration options

Automatic (delayed start)
> The service should start after other nondelayed (higher-priority) services have started.

Runtime identities

You can control the identity under which the service runs from the Log On tab of the service properties dialog (see Figure 4-8). This account identity is important because it governs the Windows resources that the service will have access to at runtime, along with the credentials that will be passed if the service calls out to another process.

Options for identity are as follows:

Local Service
> This is a special identity that presents anonymous credentials for outgoing calls.

Local System
> This represents a risky, very high-privileged account.

Network Service
> This represents a safer, lower-privileged account, which also means that the service will have reduced access to Windows resources.

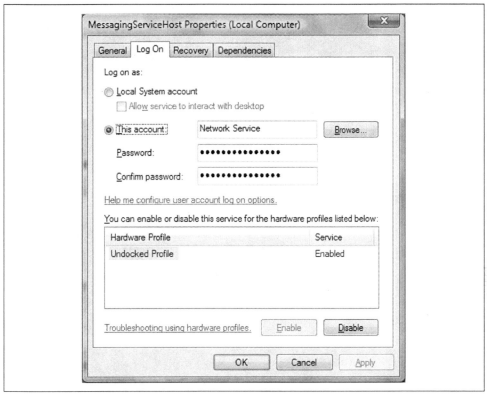

Figure 4-8. Identity configuration for a Windows service

Specific User
    This represents a particular user and requires a password be provided, prefera-bly one that won't expire.

Services can have a user interface only if they run as the local system account.

Recovery

Another feature of Windows services is their recovery options. For example, in the event of failure, the service can be configured to restart. As Figure 4-9 illustrates, you can set the recovery action for the first and second failures, and all subsequent fail-ures. In addition, you can control the delay before restarting the service and reset the failure count after some duration.

Options for recovery are as follows:

• Take no action.
• Run a program.
• Restart the service.
• Restart the computer.

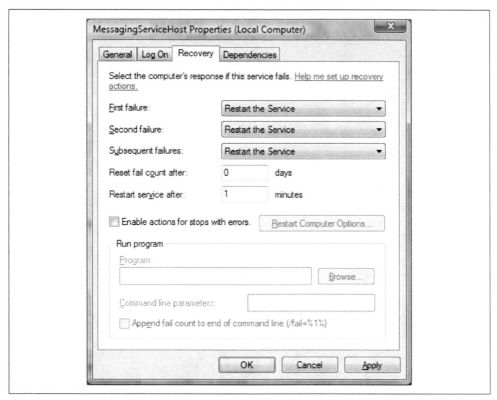

Figure 4-9. Recovery configuration for a Windows service

Creating and Installing Windows Services

You can use the Windows Service template provided with Visual Studio to generate a Windows application that contains a Windows service—a type that extends ServiceBase from the System.ServiceProcess namespace. In fact, you can create more than one Windows service type in a single executable process. To implement a Windows service, your job is to set properties and override the appropriate methods on ServiceBase and optionally provide an installer to streamline the installation process.

Extending ServiceBase

You will typically override the OnStart( ) and OnStop( ) methods in a Windows service to provide functionality appropriate for service startup and shutdown. When a service is started, through the SCM or when the machine boots if configured to do so, the OnStart( ) override is called, giving you a chance to initialize. Likewise, when the service is stopped, through the SCM or when the machine is shut down, the OnStop( ) override is called so that you can respond and clean up any allocated resources.

Optionally, services can also support pause and continue behavior, suspend behavior when the machine is operating on low battery power, and respond specifically to machine shutdown. Your service must explicitly subscribe to these lifecycle events by enabling the appropriate property, as shown in bold in Example 4-16. By enabling CanHandlePowerEvent, CanPauseAndContinue, and CanShutdown properties, your respective overrides for OnPowerEvent( ), OnPause( ), OnContinue( ), and OnShutdown( ) will be invoked at the appropriate times.

Example 4-16. Responding to pause, continue, shutdown, and power events

```
public partial class TraceWindowsService : ServiceBase
{
  public TraceWindowsService( )
  {
    InitializeComponent( );
    this.ServiceName = "TraceWindowsService";

    this.CanHandlePowerEvent = true;
    this.CanPauseAndContinue = true;
    this.CanShutdown = true;
  }

  protected override bool OnPowerEvent(PowerBroadcastStatus powerStatus)
  {...}

  protected override void OnPause( )
  {...}

  protected override void OnContinue( )
  {...}

  protected override void OnShutdown( )
  {...}

  // other code
}
```

 The following code sample illustrates a Windows service that traces each of these events: *<YourLearningWCFPath>\Samples\Hosting\ TraceWindowsService.*

Event log access

The AutoLog property of ServiceBase is enabled by default. That means all start, stop, pause, and continue events will be recorded in the application event log. ServiceBase also provides a direct reference to the event log through its EventLog property. Using this reference, you can write application-specific details directly to the event log, as shown here:

```
    this.EventLog.WriteEntry("This is an information log entry.",
```

```
EventLogEntryType.Information);

this.EventLog.WriteEntry("This is an error log entry.", EventLogEntryType.Error);

this.EventLog.WriteEntry("This is a warning log entry.",
EventLogEntryType.Warning);
```

The EventLogEntryType enumeration has the following options:

Information
> To trace non-critical information useful to administrators

Warning
> To indicate a problem that does not necessarily prevent the service from functioning yet

Error
> To log exceptions or internal errors

SuccessAudit
> To audit successful attempts to access a resource

FailureAudit
> To audit failed attempts to access a resource

Registering the Windows service

When you generate a new Windows service application using the Windows Service template, the following code is added to the Main( ) entry point of the application:

```
ServiceBase[] ServicesToRun;
ServicesToRun = new ServiceBase[] { new MessagingServiceHost() };
ServiceBase.Run(ServicesToRun);
```

ServiceBase.Run( ) asks the SCM to add one or more Windows services to the database of installed services located in the Windows registry. You can add additional service types to this list if you have more than one Windows service in the application.

When the service is registered, the location of the executable process containing the service is recorded. Thus, the application configuration file—where service model configuration is placed for the executable—should be located in the same directory as the service, like you would expect with any self-hosting environment.

Providing an installer

The *Installer Tool* (*installutil.exe*) is a command-line utility used to execute the installer components in a specified assembly. This tool is commonly used to install database scripts and Windows services, but can be used to run any installer component that implements the RunInstallerAttribute and inherits the Installer base type.

In the lab, you will create an installer component, similar to the implementation shown in Example 4-17, with the exception of the user account settings. When the installer tool is run with the Windows service assembly, the installer type (MessagingServiceHostInstaller) is constructed which initializes the settings for MessagingServiceHost with the SCM. These settings can be altered during installation with a proper setup program or directly through the SCM interface discussed earlier.

Example 4-17. Providing a specific user account for a Windows service

```
[RunInstaller(true)]
public class MessagingServiceHostInstaller : Installer
{
  public MessagingServiceHostInstaller()
  {
    ServiceProcessInstaller processInstaller = new ServiceProcessInstaller();
    ServiceInstaller serviceInstaller = new ServiceInstaller();

    processInstaller.Account = ServiceAccount.User;
    processInstaller.Username = "WindowsServiceUser";
    processInstaller.Password = "p@ssw0rd";

    serviceInstaller.DisplayName = "MessagingServiceHost_EventLog";
    serviceInstaller.Description = "WCF service host for the
Messaging.MessagingService.";
    serviceInstaller.ServiceName = "MessagingServiceHost_EventLog";
    serviceInstaller.StartType = ServiceStartMode.Automatic;

    Installers.Add(processInstaller);
    Installers.Add(serviceInstaller);
  }
}
```

Lab: Creating a Windows Service Host

In this lab, you will create and install a new Windows service and use it to host an existing WCF service. During the lab you'll use the Windows Service project template to create the host, create an installer class to help with installation settings, and install and run the Windows service. Once the service is running, you'll complete the client application to consume the service.

Creating a new Windows Service

The first step is to create the service from the Windows Service project template.

1. First, open the startup solution for this lab at *<YourLearningWCFPath>\Labs\ Chapter4\WindowsServiceHost\WindowsServiceHost.sln*. So far, this solution contains a completed service and a shell client application.

2. Let's start by adding a new Windows Service project to the solution. From the Add New Project dialog, select the *Windows Service* template from the list of Windows templates (see Figure 4-10). Name the project MessagingServiceHost.

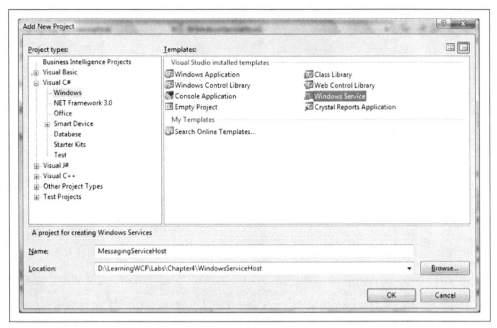

Figure 4-10. Selecting the Windows Service project template

3. The newly generated project files include a service file, *Service1.cs*. From Solution Explorer, rename this file to *MessagingServiceHost.cs*; this will also rename the underlying Windows service class. Open the file in the code window to verify that the class and constructor were renamed to MessagingServiceHost, as shown in Example 4-18.

Example 4-18. The renamed Windows Service type

```
public partial class MessagingServiceHost : ServiceBase
{
  public MessagingServiceHost( )
  {
    InitializeComponent( );
  }

  // other code
}
```

4. MessagingServiceHost inherits ServiceBase. Recall that this is the base type for all Windows service components, supplying some basic properties including a ServiceName property that identifies the service in the SCM. In the constructor of the Windows service, set the ServiceName to MessagingServiceHost, as shown here:

```
public MessagingServiceHost( )
{
  InitializeComponent( );
  this.ServiceName = "MessagingServiceHost";
}
```

Handling start and stop events

In this part of the lab, you'll introduce code related to hosting the WCF service in a Windows service application.

1. You'll need a configuration file to provide service model settings. Add a new application configuration file to the project (*app.config*) and create a <system. serviceModel> section inside the <configuration> section. Configure the service to be accessed over TCP protocol, and provide a metadata exchange endpoint over TCP as well. The completed configuration is shown in Example 4-19.

Example 4-19. Host configuration settings for MessagingService

```
<system.serviceModel>
  <services>
    <service name="Messaging.MessagingService"
behaviorConfiguration="serviceBehavior" >
      <endpoint address="MessagingService" contract="Messaging.IMessagingService"
binding="netTcpBinding" />
      <endpoint address="mex" contract="IMetadataExchange" binding="mexTcpBinding" />
      <host>
        <baseAddresses>
          <add baseAddress="net.tcp://localhost:9100"/>
        </baseAddresses>
      </host>
    </service>
  </services>
  <behaviors>
    <serviceBehaviors>
      <behavior name="serviceBehavior" >
        <serviceMetadata />
      </behavior>
    </serviceBehaviors>
  </behaviors>
</system.serviceModel>
```

2. Now add the code to initialize the MessagingService when the Windows service is started. Go to the MessagingServiceHost project and add an assembly reference to System.ServiceModel and a project reference to the Messaging project that holds the WCF service.

   Open *MessagingServiceHost.cs* and add a using statement for System.ServiceModel, as shown here:

   ```
   using System.ServiceModel;
   ```

3. Inside the MessagingServiceHost type, create a ServiceHost member named m_serviceHost. In addition, add code to the OnStart() method override to construct the ServiceHost instance, as shown here:

   ```
   ServiceHost m_serviceHost;

   protected override void OnStart(string[] args)
   {
     m_serviceHost = new ServiceHost(typeof(Messaging.MessagingService));
   ```

```
m_serviceHost.Open( );
}
```

 ServiceBase provides a number of virtual methods where you can interact with Windows service events such as start, stop, pause, continue, and shutdown. Typically, you'll at least handle start and stop events.

4. When the Windows service is stopped, you should clean up the ServiceHost instance and free the TCP port. Do this by adding code to the OnStop( ) method override, as shown here:

```
protected override void OnStop( )
{
  if (m_serviceHost != null)
    m_serviceHost.Close( );
  m_serviceHost = null;
}
```

At this point the implementation of your Windows service host is complete. Now, you will create an installer for it.

Creating a Windows service installer

Windows services typically provide an installer component to support the installation process, so in this part of the lab, I'll walk you through creating one for this Windows service. This is not necessary to hosting services in the Windows service— it is merely a convenience for installation that you may find useful.

1. Go to the WindowsServiceHost project and add a reference to the System. Configuration.Install assembly so that the installer component will have access to it. Then add a new class to the project, naming the file *MessagingServiceHostInstaller.cs*.

2. Edit the MessagingServiceHostInstaller class so that it inherits the Installer type from the System.Configuration.Install namespace, and make the type public. Also add a using statement for the namespace. Apply the RunInstallerAttribute to the MessagingServiceHostInstaller class and add a using statement for the System.ComponentModel namespace. The changes are shown here in bold:

```
using System.Configuration.Install;
using System.ComponentModel;

namespace MessagingServiceHost
{
  [RunInstaller(true)]
  public class MessagingServiceHostInstaller: Installer
  {
  }
}
```

3. Run the client application to test the service. Click the Call Service button to verify that no exceptions occur.

Considerations for WCF Services

When hosting WCF services in a Windows service application, at a minimum, you will initialize the ServiceHost in the OnStart() override and close the ServiceHost in the OnStop() override, as illustrated in the lab.

 Failure to properly close the ServiceHost instance can result in problematic delays freeing ports used by the service.

Example 4-21 shows the same MessagingServiceHost as you completed in the lab with the following added functionality:

- A handler is provided for the Faulted event of the ServiceHost to add an error entry to the event log for administrators.
- An information entry is written to the event log entry to inform administrators of the base addresses and ports that the ServiceHost is listening on once opened.
- Another information entry is written when the ServiceHost is closed.

Example 4-21. MessagingServiceHost with additional functionality

```
public partial class MessagingServiceHost : ServiceBase
{
  ServiceHost m_serviceHost;
  public MessagingServiceHost()
  {
    InitializeComponent();
    this.ServiceName = "MessagingServiceHost";
  }

  protected override void OnStart(string[] args)
  {
    m_serviceHost = new ServiceHost(typeof(Messaging.MessagingService));
    m_serviceHost.Open();
    m_serviceHost.Faulted += new EventHandler(m_serviceHost_Faulted);

    string baseAddresses = "";
    foreach (Uri address in m_serviceHost.BaseAddresses)
    {
      baseAddresses += " " + address.AbsoluteUri;
    }
    string s = String.Format("{0} listening at {1}", this.ServiceName,
baseAddresses);
    this.EventLog.WriteEntry(s, EventLogEntryType.Information);
  }
```

Example 4-21. MessagingServiceHost with additional functionality (continued)

```
  void m_serviceHost_Faulted(object sender, EventArgs e)
  {
    string s = String.Format("{0} has faulted, notify administrators of this
problem", this.ServiceName);
    this.EventLog.WriteEntry(s, EventLogEntryType.Error);
  }

  protected override void OnStop()
  {
    if (m_serviceHost != null)
    {
      m_serviceHost.Close();
      string s = String.Format("{0} stopped", this.ServiceName);
      this.EventLog.WriteEntry(s, EventLogEntryType.Information);
    }

    m_serviceHost = null;
  }
}
```

In theory, the service shouldn't stop unless something goes wrong, or an administrator explicitly stops it through the SCM. Fortunately, in the former case, the service can also be configured in the SCM to restart on failure as discussed earlier—a necessary feature for an unattended server machine.

Though the hosting code is much the same as in other self-host environments I've discussed, there are some special considerations for hosting WCF services in a Windows service:

- For a Windows service, OnStart() must execute within 30 seconds by default, or it will fail to start the service. If the startup code will take longer to execute, you can implement a timer to delegate longer-running initialization after startup is complete. Initializing your ServiceHost instances should fall within the 30-second timeframe.

- OnStart() will record exceptions in the event log. In the event a service will not start, you should look to the event log for information indicating the cause. Figure 4-12 shows the properties of an event log entry when a port conflict caused a problem opening the ServiceHost during the OnStart() method.

- Uncaught exceptions after OnStart() may not be recorded unless you explicitly catch the exception and record it. For example, if you delegate ServiceHost initialization using a timer, be sure to catch exceptions thrown by the Open() function and log them for administrators to see.

- As with any hosting environment, the identity under which the Windows service runs will govern the Windows resources it has access to at runtime. You might not want to run your WCF services under the NETWORKSERVICE account, which means your deployment scripts will have to customize the account under which the service is configured to avoid hardcoding account information into the Windows service installer.

Figure 4-12. Event log results after opening the ServiceHost during OnStart() fails

Windows Service Hosting Scenarios

You can use Windows services to host WCF services on client and server machines. It is more common to host on server machines, simply because the extra deployment effort of installing a Windows service at the client may be undesirable. For server deployments, Windows services provide the most reliable way to host services over non-HTTP protocols when IIS 7.0 and the WAS are unavailable. Specifically, since Windows Server 2003 machines do not support WAS, the Windows service is the best choice for hosting services over named pipes, TCP, or MSMQ protocols. In particular, this would apply to scenarios such as intranet applications, or distributed services behind the firewall. Here are some scenarios that might warrant employing Windows services:

- In a classic client-server deployment in which clients are part of a Windows domain and communicate with services on remote servers using TCP.
- ASP.NET web applications typically do not store business functionality in page code. Business tier assemblies provide functionality that is consumed by each page according to functionality. In a service-oriented system, the page consumes business services, not business assemblies, which would mean calling across process and possibly machine boundaries for distribution or security reasons (more on security boundaries in Chapter 7). Figure 4-13 illustrates this scenario.

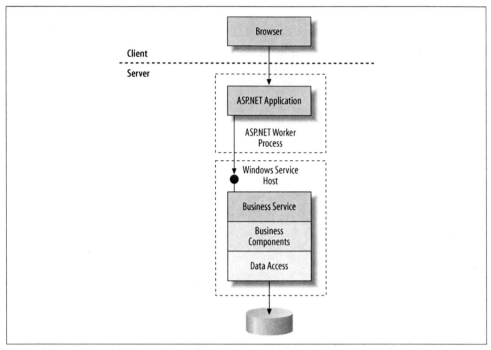

Figure 4-13. An ASP.NET application leveraging WCF services for business functionality

- WCF services exposed over HTTP protocol are usually hosted in the ASP.NET worker process through IIS on Windows Server 2003 machines. The ASP.NET worker process usually doesn't have rights to talk to protected Windows resources such as databases, thus another tier of services may be necessary to create a trusted subsystem model. Figure 4-14 illustrates this scenario.

- In general, any Windows 2003 server exposing WCF services over non-HTTP protocols will find Windows services the only viable option to ensure automatic startup and restarts on failure.

Server machines for these deployments are typically unattended, and Windows services would be configured to start on machine boot and restart on the first two failures (after the third failure you might notify administrators). In addition, Windows services will run with an identity that is granted access to the server resources it uses. For communication to services on the same machine, named pipes protocol would be used, while TCP protocol is used for cross-machine calls. MSMQ may also be employed for one-way reliable messaging.

Hosting in IIS 6.0

When you expose WCF services over the Internet using HTTP protocol on a Windows Server 2003 machine, IIS 6.0 provides a much richer hosting environment than self-hosting. Unlike self-hosting, no code is required to instantiate

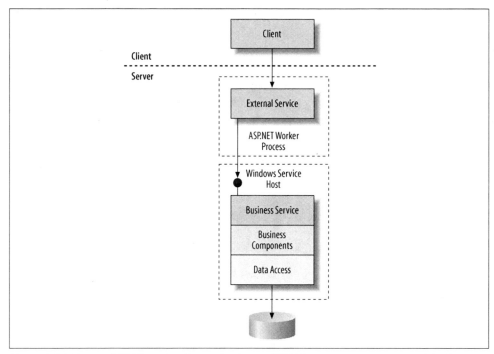

Figure 4-14. External WCF services leveraging internal WCF services to create a trusted subsystem model

ServiceHost instances, but you can still use declarative configuration in the application's *web.config* file. More importantly, IIS 6.0 provides other much-needed hosting features for idle-time management, health monitoring, process recycling, and management tools for configuring application pools.

In the first three chapters of this book, you have created ASP.NET web sites to host WCF services, completed labs that used the various WCF service templates to help get you started, and experienced some of the differences between self-hosting and IIS hosting. In this section, I'll review how IIS hosting works in general terms, discuss its distinct behaviors and added value, and provide you with an architectural overview of the IIS 6.0 hosting environment. In addition, I'll discuss ASP.NET compatibility mode, which allows you to host WCF services through the ASP.NET pipeline to assist with migration of ASP.NET web services.

IIS Service Endpoints

When you host your services with any version of IIS, you must provide at a minimum the following:

- An addressable web site or virtual directory for your service endpoints
- A file with the extension *.svc* that will help activate the ServiceHost instance
- A service type that is linked to the *.svc* file for activation

As illustrated in labs from earlier chapters, you can use the WCF Service project template when you create a new web site project using Visual Studio. This template generates a project with a *.svc* endpoint, a sample service implementation, and a *web.config* with the appropriate <service> element to initialize the ServiceHost.

The *.svc* endpoint is the file that clients will address in their target URI to reach the service. It contains a @ServiceHost directive that indicates the service type, and if applicable, the source code in the *App_Code* directory where the service code can be found:

```
<% @ServiceHost Language=C# Debug="true" Service="MyService" CodeBehind="~/App_Code/
Service.cs" %>
```

In reality, your services will be compiled into separate assemblies, so your web site project must reference those assemblies, and the *.svc* endpoint will reference the type only through the Service property of the @ServiceHost directive. For example, this *Service.svc* endpoint references the service type HelloIndigo.HelloIndigoService:

```
<% @ServiceHost Service="HelloIndigo.HelloIndigoService" %>
```

As I explained in earlier chapters, the service type specified in the @ServiceHost directive also tells the service model which <service> section to use from the *web.config* to initialize the ServiceHost instance.

One of the distinctions between self-hosting and IIS hosting is that the base address is provided by the web site or virtual directory for the application. The <service> section needn't provide an address for each endpoint, since the *.svc* file is the endpoint:

```
<service name="HelloIndigo.HelloIndigoService" >
  <endpoint contract="HelloIndigo.IHelloIndigoService" binding="wsHttpBinding"/>
</service>
```

Clients address the service using the *.svc* endpoint, for example:

```
<client>
  <endpoint address="http://localhost/IISHost/Service.svc" binding="wsHttpBinding"
contract="Client.localhost.HelloIndigoContract" />
</client>
```

In cases where you might want to expose multiple endpoints for the same *.svc* endpoint, you can use relative addressing. This example illustrates a case where a single IIS endpoint, *Service.svc*, can be accessed using BasicHttpBinding or WSHttpBinding to support different web service protocols. The <endpoint> configuration for the service uses relative addressing, appending "/Soap11" and "/Soap12" to the endpoint address:

```
<service name="HelloIndigo.HelloIndigoService" >
  <endpoint address="Soap11" contract="HelloIndigo.IHelloIndigoService"
binding="basicHttpBinding"/>
  <endpoint address="Soap12" contract="HelloIndigo.IHelloIndigoService"
binding="wsHttpBinding"/>
</service>
```

 The web service lab from Chapter 3 shows you how to implement multiple WCF endpoints for a single IIS service endpoint.

Clients address these service endpoints in this way:

```
http://localhost/IISHost/Service.svc/Soap11
http://localhost/IISHost/Service.svc/Soap12
```

For file-based web sites, the *ASP.NET Development Web Server* is used instead of IIS, which can be useful for testing only. Endpoints function in the same way as with HTTP-based web sites hosted in IIS, with the exception that a dynamically generated port assignment will exist in the endpoint address; for example, *http://localhost:1260/FileBasedHost/Service.svc*. This port is saved in the project settings so that the same port is used on subsequent tests.

 At times this port assignment can change, and if so will invalidate hardcoded client endpoints. If you see unexpected behavior, don't forget to check that the client and service are using the same port.

IIS 6.0 Hosting Architecture

One of the most important features IIS provides your WCF services is *message-based activation*, something I touched on in Chapter 1. ServiceHost instances need not be open prior to processing requests for a given endpoint. Instead, the *World Wide Web Publishing Service* ("WWW Service") is responsible for ensuring that a worker process is present to handle requests. Then, when requests for a particular *.svc* endpoint are forwarded to the worker process, the service model initializes the corresponding ServiceHost (if necessary) before the request is dispatched.

This message-based activation process allows IIS to balance the number of worker processes required to service the request load, releasing unused resources where appropriate. IIS also monitors the health of each worker process and will launch a new, healthy worker process for requests as needed. In addition, IIS can be configured to periodically recycle worker processes to reduce the risk of resource and memory leaks. These features improve the overall reliability and availability of your WCF services.

There are a few key participants in this activation process:

- The *HTTP Protocol Stack* (*http.sys*) was introduced with IIS 6.0. It is a kernel-mode message processing service that can receive messages even while worker processes are not yet running. All requests arrive and return through this service.

- The *WWW Service* is responsible for launching worker processes on demand to handle requests. It also determines the correct request queue (application pool) for messages to be sent from *http.sys* for processing. WWW is a Windows service that must be running for *http.sys* to successfully forward requests.

- Requests for *.svc* endpoints are forwarded to an ASP.NET worker process because IIS is configured to forward requests to *.svc* extensions to the *ASP.NET ISAPI Extension* (*aspnet_isapi.dll*). The ASP.NET processing pipeline then relies on HTTP modules and handlers to process the request. An *HTTP module* is a component that can interact with any part of the request lifecycle by handling application events that are fired at specific points during request processing. An *HTTP handler* is the component responible for processing the incoming request stream and writing an appropriate response to the response stream. The service model provides implementations of these components to intercept and handle service requests, ensuring (as appropriate) that they are processed by the service model rather than the traditional ASP.NET pipeline.

Figure 4-15 illustrates how IIS 6.0 processes requests to WCF services. In fact, up to the point that the request reaches the worker process, it behaves much like any other request that is handled by *aspnet_isapi.dll*. The difference is in what happens after the ASP.NET pipeline gets hold of the request. For all requests, configured HTTP modules have an opportunity to interact with request processing at specific points in the lifecycle of the request by handling specific application events.

At some point during request processing, the pipeline also looks for an HTTP handler type that should be constructed to process the request according to file extension. Ultimately, the HTTP handler is responsible for processing requests, but this usually happens after the pipeline has had a chance to authenticate the call, verify that the request was not previously cached, reestablish the session if applicable, and process any other code injected by HTTP modules early in the request lifecycle. After the handler executes, HTTP modules then have another opportunity to interact with the response as it flows back through IIS to the client. Since service operations should be handled by the WCF processing model, not ASP.NET, the service model alters this pocessing lifecycle.

The service model provides its own `HttpModule` and `HttpHandler` types, located in the `System.ServiceModel.Activation` namespace. Both of these components interact with requests directed to a *.svc* endpoint using traditional ASP.NET configuration settings. As far as ASP.NET is concerned, the `HttpHandler` type is the target for request processing, but that would mean the request would pass through the usual ASP.NET pipeline with all of the configured modules for forms authentication, caching, and session, for example. By default, the service model bypasses this by pipeline, by hijacking requests targeting *.svc* endpoints and forwarding them to the service model for processing.

The service model `HttpModule` gets engaged very early in the lifecycle, handling the `PostAuthenticateRequest` event and, by default, forwarding the request to the service model. In fact, the service model allocates a thread from the WCF thread pool (to be discussed in Chapter 5) and releases the ASP.NET thread so that another incoming request can use it. This behavior ensures that all requests to WCF services are processed in a consistent manner, regardless of whether they are self-hosted or hosted in IIS. The service model handler is never invoked unless ASP.NET compatibility mode is enabled—something I'll talk about shortly.

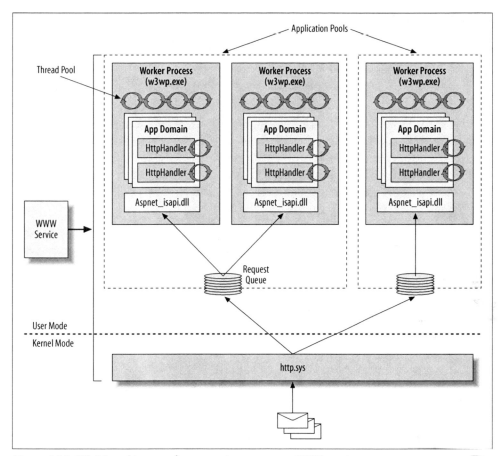

Figure 4-15. IIS 6.0 architecture for processing requests to WCF services

ASP.NET Compatibility Mode

Once the ServiceHost is activated, hosting a WCF service with IIS operates much the same as self-hosted services. That is, the service model has a consistent way of processing requests. By default, the ASP.NET processing model is only involved until the service model's HTTP module forwards requests to a WCF thread, allowing the initial ASP.NET thread to be returned to the ASP.NET thread pool.

In fact, the service model has two modes for hosting WCF services:

Mixed Transports Mode

This is the default hosting mode. In this mode, service requests are not processed by the ASP.NET pipeline. This makes it possible for endpoints to be exposed for multiple transports in a consistent manner.

ASP.NET Compatibility Mode

> This hosting mode restricts an application to exposing only HTTP services. When this is enabled, the features supplied by HTTP modules, such as file and URL authorization, session state, caching, and profile, are available to the service. In addition, HttpContext.Current is initialized to provide access to ASP.NET specific context.

In most cases, access to ASP.NET features and the HttpContext should not be necessary. The service model provides a much richer set of authentication and authorization features that are more appropriate for SOA. A global OperationContext is also supplied with access to contextual information for the request, including the security context, the request message and related headers, and information about the hosting environment.

If you are porting existing ASP.NET web services (ASMX) you may have existing code that relies on the HttpContext or other ASP.NET features. For example, you may want to access the ASP.NET Session, Cache, or Profile objects to provide a consistent runtime experience as you would have with ASMX. In this case, ASP.NET compatibility mode may be appropriate. You can enable ASP.NET compatibility by setting the aspNetCompatibilityEnabled property to true in the <serviceHostingEnvironment> section:

```
<system.serviceModel>
  <serviceHostingEnvironment aspNetCompatibilityEnabled="true"/>
<system.serviceModel>
```

This makes it possible for your service code, or its downstream objects, to interact with these aforementioned ASP.NET features. For example, you can write code that relies on the ASP.NET Profile. Consider this <profile> section in the *web.config*:

```
<profile enabled="true" automaticSaveEnabled="true">
  <properties>
    <add name="Culture" allowAnonymous="true" defaultValue=""/>
  </properties>
</profile>
```

This profile creates a single property, Culture. Your service code could access the profile for the current user as follows, using the current HttpContext:

```
// set the culture preference
string culture = HttpContext.Current.Profile["Culture"];

// get the culture preference
HttpContext.Current.Profile["Culture"] = culture;
```

If a service plans to use these features, because it was migrated from an ASMX web service perhaps, it should require that they are deployed to a hosting environment that supports ASP.NET compatibility by applying the AspNetCompatibilityRequirementsAttribute from the System.ServiceModel.Activation namespace, as follows:

```
[AspNetCompatibilityRequirements(
RequirementsMode=AspNetCompatibilityRequirementsMode.Required)]
public class ProfileService : IProfileService
```

Other than porting ASMX services, you will most likely avoid using this feature in order to provide a consistent hosting model for your services over multiple protocols.

 The following code sample illustrates ASP.NET compatibility: *<YourLearningWCFPath>\Samples\Hosting\ASPNETCompatibility*.

IIS 7.0 and Windows Activation Service

On Windows Vista and Windows Server 2008 machines you can host your WCF services with *Windows Activation Service* (WAS). WAS is a process activation service installed with IIS 7.0 that decouples the activation architecture from IIS in order to support non-HTTP protocols such as named pipes, TCP, and MSMQ. Like IIS 6.0, WAS also provides features for idle-time management, health monitoring, process recycling, and management tools for configuring application pools among other things. Although supported by Windows Vista, hosting in the WAS is not incredibly useful for client deployments.

In this section, I'll explain how WAS hosting works, show you how the hosting architecture compares to IIS 6.0 hosting, and provide you with some tips for getting started with the WAS.

WAS Hosting Architecture

IIS 7.0 introduces some architectural changes necessary to expand support for named pipes, TCP, and MSMQ protocols. The new architecture relies on protocol listeners, listener adapters and protocol handlers to process requests.

Protocol listeners
> A protocol listener is responsible for receiving requests for a particular protocol. There is a protocol listener provided for HTTP, named pipes, TCP, and MSMQ. For HTTP, the listener is *http.sys* (same as IIS 6.0). Listeners for other protocols are provided by their respective listener adapter service.

Listener adapters
> A listener adapter is responsible for bridging requests between the WAS and the ASP.NET worker process for a particular protocol. There is a listener adapter for HTTP, named pipes, TCP, and MSMQ. The HTTP listener adapter is provided by the WWW service (*w3svc*). Each of the other protocols has a Windows service that supplies a protocol listener and listener adapter pair.

Protocol handlers

A protocol handler channels requests through the service model for a particular protocol. WCF provides managed protocol handlers for HTTP, named pipes, TCP, and MSMQ.

Figure 4-16 illustrates how protocol listeners, listener adapters, and protocol handlers participate in request processing. As each protocol listener receives requests, the WAS checks for the existence of a worker process to handle the request (according to application pool configuration). The listener adapter's job is then to pull requests from the application pool's queue and forward to the appropriate protocol handler for processing.

To support this new architecture there are two core services:

Windows Activation Service (WAS)

This service handles configuration, application pooling, and process activation for all protocols.

WWW Service

This service provides the listener adapter for the HTTP listener, *http.sys*.

These and other services supporting the architecture in Figure 4-16 are listed in Table 4-3. Ultimately, it's the protocol handler provided by WCF that ensures the ServiceHost instance has been created before requests can be processed.

Regardless of protocol, the service model handles all requests in a consistent manner, but WAS provides a message-based activation mechanism like IIS 6.0 to increase the overall reliability and scalability for requests over any protocol.

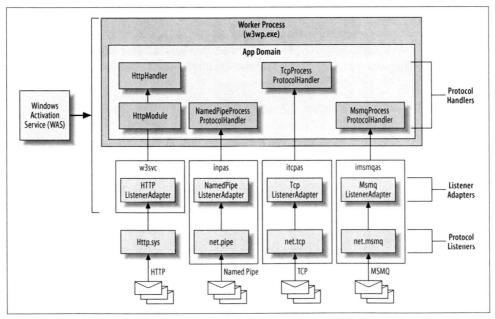

Figure 4-16. IIS 7.0 and WAS architecture for processing requests to WCF services

Table 4-3. Services supporting WCF hosting with the WAS

Process	Service	Description
smsvchost.exe	Net.Tcp Port Sharing Service (itcppss)	Enables multiple listeners on the same port.
smsvchost.exe	Net.Tcp Listener Adapter Service (itcpas)	Processes TCP requests.
smsvchost.exe	Net.Pipe Listener Adapter Service (inpas)	Processes named pipes requests.
smsvchost.exe	Net.Msmq Listener Adapter Service (imsmqas)	Processes MSMQ requests.
	HTTP Listener (*http.sys*)	Forwards HTTP requests to the WAS.
svchost.exe	WWW Service (w3svc), includes the HTTP Listener Adapter	Processes HTTP requests.
svchost.exe	Windows Activation Service (WAS)	Provides configuration for protocol listeners and listener adapters, handles process activation for requests, provides health monitoring and other hosting features.

Installing IIS 7.0, WAS, and WCF Communications

Before you can successfully host WCF services on a Windows Vista or Windows Server 2008 machine, you must enable IIS 7.0, WAS, and WCF communications. On a Windows Vista machine, you can do this through the Control Panel. From classic view, select "Programs and Features," and from the task pane select "Turn Windows features on or off." In the Windows Features dialog, you should do the following:

- Enable IIS, including the management tools checked in Figure 4-17. Installing IIS 6 compatibility is optional, but it can be helpful if you have existing *.vbs* scripts.
- Enable WWW Services, accepting the defaults in addition to the common HTTP features checked in Figure 4-18. In particular, you should make sure ASP.NET is enabled.
- Enable WAS, labeled Windows Process Activation Service in Figure 4-19. In this case, enable all features.
- Enable WCF communication protocols for .NET 3.0 as shown in Figure 4-20. You should enable both HTTP and non-HTTP support if you plan to host services over all protocols in WAS.

Configuring IIS 7.0 and WAS

Once IIS 7.0, WAS, and WCF communication features are installed, you can configure activation over named pipes, TCP, and MSMQ; by default, HTTP protocol is supported. IIS provides a new command-line utility to configure IIS applications, *appcmd.exe*, located in the *C:\Windows\System32\inetsrv* directory. With this utility, you can enable support for named pipes, TCP, or MSMQ for any web site or application directory.

Figure 4-17. Enabling IIS features

Figure 4-18. Enabling WWW features

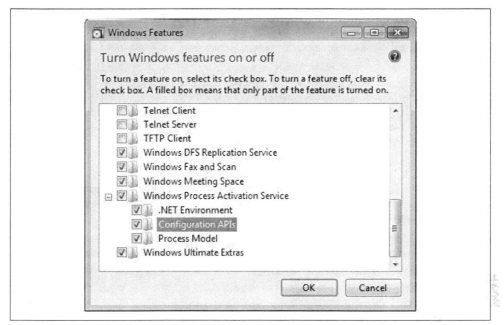

Figure 4-19. Enabling WAS

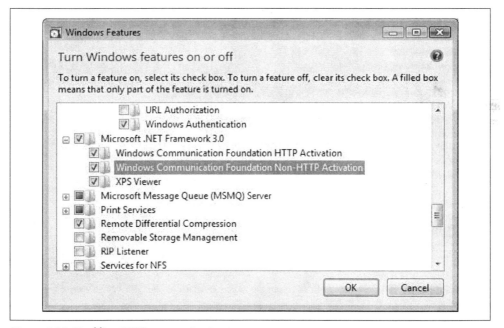

Figure 4-20. Enabling WCF communication

In order to support non-HTTP protocols for any of your applications, you must first enable that protocol support for the web site it belongs to. The following set of commands shows how to enable named pipes and TCP support for the default web site:

```
%windir%\system32\inetsrv\appcmd.exe set site "Default Web Site" -
+bindings.[protocol='net.pipe',bindingInformation='*']

%windir%\system32\inetsrv\appcmd.exe set site "Default Web Site" -
+bindings.[protocol='net.tcp',bindingInformation='9200:*']
```

 A batch file named *enablewasnonhttp.bat* is located in the *<YourLearningWCFPath>\Samples\Hosting\WASHosting* directory with these commands. Execute this batch file to enable non-HTTP support for the default web site on your machine.

IIS 7.0 configuration is stored in the *applicationHost.config* file, located in the *c:\ Windows\System32\inetsrv\config* directory (or, your equivalent System32 path). After executing these commands the configuration file is updated with new <binding> entries for the default web site. Site configuration is nested inside the <system.applicationHost> section, as shown in Example 4-22.

Example 4-22. Supported binding protocols for the default web site

```
<system.applicationHost>
  <sites>
    <site name="Default Web Site" id="1">
      <!-- other settings -->
      <bindings>
        <binding protocol="http" bindingInformation="*:80:" />
        <binding protocol="net.pipe" bindingInformation="*" />
        <binding protocol="net.tcp" bindingInformation="9200:*" />
      </bindings>
    </site>
  </sites>
</system.applicationHost>
```

 When you enable support for the TCP protocol, you must specify a port number as part of the bindingInformation setting. For the WAS hosting samples provided with this book, port 9200 is used for WAS hosting.

This section of the *applicationHost.config* file governs what protocols the web site can support, as well as WCF services hosted within that web site. Once the web site supports a protocol, individual applications can be configured to support that protocol. In fact, you must specifically enable non-HTTP protocols for each application on the machine, once again using the *appcmd.exe* utility. Service endpoints can use only bindings that match the supported protocols for the application.

To enable support for HTTP, TCP, and named pipes for a particular application you can issue a command like the following:

```
%windir%\system32\inetsrv\appcmd.exe set app "Default Web Site/[application
directory]" /enabledProtocols:http,net.tcp,net.pipe
```

The placeholder application directory should be replaced with the name of the specific application to be configured. This IIS setting is not inheritable, so you must repeat this for each application that requires additional protocol support.

This command also updates configuration settings for the application directory in the *applicationHost.config* file. The <site> section contains a list of application directories in individual <application> sections as shown in Example 4-23. Each application has a comma-delimited list of enabled protocols. This is the setting modified by the previous command.

Example 4-23. Supported protocols for a particular application directory in IIS

```
<sites>
  <site name="Default Web Site" id="1" serverAutoStart="true">
    <application path="/WASHost" enabledProtocols="http,net.tcp,net.pipe,net.msmq">
      <virtualDirectory path="/" physicalPath="C:\inetpub\wwwroot\WASHost" />
    </application>

    <!-- more applications -->

    <bindings>...</bindings>
  </site>
</sites>
```

Once you've enabled the appropriate protocol support in IIS, you can begin hosting WCF services over those protocols using WAS.

Hosting WCF Services with WAS

On machines where IIS 7.0 and WAS are enabled, you can host WCF service endpoints over any protocol without self-hosting in a Windows service. From a development perspective, you still create an ASP.NET web site project, optionally using the WCF Service template. The only restriction is that the web site can't be file-based—it must be an IIS application.

The following steps summarize how you would go about creating a new web site with WCF services that can be hosted over HTTP, named pipes, and TCP. MSMQ is covered in Chapter 6.

1. Create a new ASP.NET HTTP-based web site using the WCF Service template.

2. Use the *appcmd.exe* utility to enable named pipes and TCP support as discussed in the previous section. For example, if the web site is located at *http://localhost/WASHost*, you would execute the following command:

```
%windir%\system32\inetsrv\appcmd.exe set app "Default Web Site/WASHost" /
enabledProtocols:http,net.tcp,net.pipe
```

You can verify that the correct protocols are supported for the application in the IIS administrative console (see Figure 4-21).

3. Now you can configure the ServiceHost as you would for any IIS-hosted application, with the exception that you can now specify endpoints that support HTTP, named pipes, or TCP protocol (see Example 4-24). Like with other IIS-hosted applications, a base address is not required for each protocol—this is provided by the application.

4. To generate a proxy for your WAS-hosted services, you must enable metadata exchange as with any other IIS or self-hosted service. The *.svc* endpoint is the address provided for metadata exchange.

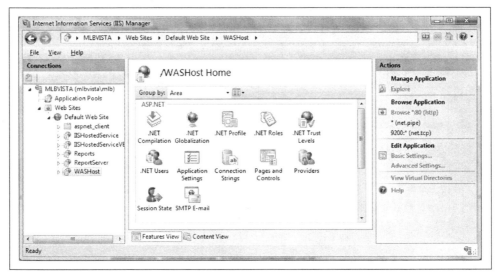

Figure 4-21. Protocol support is indicated for an application directory under Browse Application actions

 See the following code sample for a complete implementation of a WAS-hosted service: *<YourLearningWCFPath>\Samples\Hosting\WASHosting*.

Example 4-24. ServiceHost configuration for a WAS-hosted service

```
<service name="HelloIndigo.HelloIndigoService" >
  <endpoint address="netPipe" contract="HelloIndigo.IHelloIndigoService"
binding="netNamedPipeBinding"/>
  <endpoint address="netTcp" contract="HelloIndigo.IHelloIndigoService"
binding="netTcpBinding"/>
  <endpoint address="basicHttp" contract="HelloIndigo.IHelloIndigoService"
binding="basicHttpBinding"/>
  <endpoint address="wsHttp" contract="HelloIndigo.IHelloIndigoService"
```

```
binding="wsHttpBinding"/>
</service>
```

Choosing the Right Hosting Environment

As I mentioned at the beginning of this chapter, choosing a hosting environment for your services is something that is largely driven by your operating platform and choice of protocol. Now that you've had a chance to explore the different hosting environments, you can probably guess that the best possible hosting environment would be the WAS for its rich set of features and protocol support. Unfortunately, WAS is available only on Windows Vista or Windows Server 2008 machines.

Table 4-4 summarizes the hosting options available to you on each operating platform, including client and server platforms. Based on this summary, here are the likely choices you'll make for your production services on each server platform:

- For Windows Server 2003 machines, you'll use IIS 6.0 for HTTP and Windows Services for other protocols.
- For Windows Server 2008 machines, you'll use IIS 7.0/WAS.

Table 4-4. A summary of hosting options based on operating platform and communication protocol

Operating platform	Protocol	Hosting options
Windows XP/SP2	HTTP	IIS 5.1 or self-host
	Named pipes, TCP, MSMQ	Self-host
Windows Vista	HTTP, named pipes, TCP, MSMQ	IIS 7.0/WAS or self-host
Windows Server 2003	HTTP	IIS 6.0
	Named pipes, TCP, MSMQ	Self-host
Windows Server 2008	HTTP, named pipes, TCP, MSMQ	IIS 7.0/WAS or self-host

For client systems, the choice is a little bit more complex. In-process services introduce the least configuration overhead for clients; thus, you'll be using Windows Forms or WPF clients as your self-hosting environment. If the system is a complex, distributed system where you have significant control over setup, you may install Windows services to provide services for Windows XP machines. For Windows Vista machines, your choice of self-hosting with Windows services or enabling WAS may be governed by client preferences.

Summary

This chapter focused solely on the various hosting options for your WCF services. I started by providing you with an overview of desirable hosting features, with a summary of which features are supported by each environment. I then went on to explain in greater detail how self-hosting in console, Windows, and Windows services compares to IIS and WAS hosting. You learned some of the specific challenges associated with hosting in a Windows application, you learned how to create and deploy a Windows service host, you learned how IIS and WAS hosting architecture handles message-based activation, and you learned how to host services with ASP.NET compatibility mode. In all cases, I provided you with example architectures for deploying each type of host.

Now, it is time to dive into some of the extended features of WCF, namely sessions and throttling, reliability, security, and exception handling. In the next chapter, I'll explain service instancing modes and how to support sessions and create singleton services. I'll also talk about how to handle multiple concurrent calls and how to throttle sessions and calls.

CHAPTER 5

Instancing and Concurrency

The first four chapters of this book have focused on how to create, host, and configure services and clients. You've learned how to design service contracts, how to work with most of the standard bindings, and how to select an appropriate hosting environment for your production services. In Chapter 4, I provided more detail about the ServiceHost type, which is at the heart of hosting WCF services. What haven't been discussed yet are the features that control the lifetime of individual service instances allocated as messages are processed, and the features that support opposing needs for throughput and request throttling.

As I have mentioned before, WCF represents the unification of several server technologies: .NET Remoting, Enterprise Services, and ASMX. That means that WCF can support the following invocation scenarios:

- Calls that cross application domains
- Classic client-server calls where clients hold a reference to remote, state-aware objects and have some control over its lifetime
- Distributed application calls that conserve resources by releasing remote objects while not in use
- Singletons whose state is shared by multiple clients
- Classic state-unaware web service calls

These scenarios imply that the lifetime of a service might be only for the duration of an operation, for the duration of a client session, or forever, in the case of the singleton. The choice of service lifetime varies by application—the expected calling pattern of clients, requirements for state-awareness, and the expected throughput necessary to serve requests.

Scalability and throughput requirements of services hosted on a client machine, versus on those deployed to server environments, are not equivalent. Services hosted in-process are initialized and invoked on demand, and those hosted on client machines at best may be consumed by multiple client threads, rarely from other machines.

When services are deployed to server machines—either web servers exposed to the Internet or servers behind the firewall that satisfy intranet clients—they can expect to serve a significantly higher number of concurrent requests. The number of requests may be predictable if the number of clients is controlled, or may increase in exponential proportions due to a much wider client-base with potential for continued growth.

Ideally, your services will always be ready to process incoming requests and juggle the expected load, while not maxing out host machine resources and crippling the application. WCF provides the following features to control instancing, throughput, and throttling in support of this need:

Instancing mode
> This feature controls the lifetime of each service instance, letting you allocate an instance per call or per session, or a single instance for all clients.

Concurrency mode
> This feature determines how and if each service instance allows concurrent calls, which can affect throughput.

Throttling behavior
> This feature allows you to control load on each service, restricting the number of concurrent calls and session and service instances.

This chapter will explore each of these features in detail and provide guidance on their use based on the deployment scenario.

OperationContext

OperationContext is a type from the System.ServiceModel namespace that provides access to the execution context for a service request. OperationContext.Current provides access to this context for the lifetime of a request. You used the OperationContext in Chapter 3 to access the callback channel for duplex communications, but there are other properties that will be useful in this chapter and in subsequent chapters. Here are a few of the key properties exposed by the OperationContext:

Host
> Provides access to the ServiceHost instance associated with the service type. Through this reference, you can access information about service endpoints, the service description, and service behaviors associated with the request channel.

Channel
> Provides access to the callback channel if applicable. In this case, the channel reference is returned as an IContextChannel reference. When you invoke GetCallbackChannel<T>( ), a method exposed by OperationContext, the strongly typed channel is returned (see Chapter 3).

SessionId

Provides access to the session identifier if the request is part of a session. This will be put to use in this chapter.

ServiceSecurityContext

Provides access to the security context for the request, which means you can access information about the authenticated caller among other security details to be discussed in Chapter 7.

Instancing

Instancing modes in WCF control the way that service objects are allocated to requests. Once the ServiceHost has been constructed and channel listeners have been created for each endpoint, requests to each endpoint are processed by the appropriate service object based on the instancing mode for the service type. Instancing modes are based on the InstanceContextMode enumeration from the System.ServiceModel namespace:

PerCall

A new service object is created for each call to the service.

PerSession

A new service object is created for each client. This is the default behavior.

Single

A single service object is created and used for all calls from all clients.

You can use the ServiceBehaviorAttribute to set the InstanceContextMode for each service type. For example, the following shows how to configure the service type as a singleton:

```
[ServiceBehavior(InstanceContextMode=InstanceContextMode.Single)]
public class SingletonService:ISingletonService
```

This setting essentially controls the lifetime of each service object. The ServiceHost constructs the service instance immediately for singletons, or when the first request arrives for the service type. Subsequent requests are directed to the same instance if appropriate, and when the lifetime of the instance has expired, it is disposed of. In fact, if you implement IDisposable on the service type, you can intercept the Dispose() call and potentially clean up allocated resources. Example 5-1 illustrates a service type that shows a message when the service object is constructed and implements IDisposable to show a message when the service object is disposed.

Example 5-1. Implementing IDisposable on a service type

```
public class MyService: IMyService, IDisposable
{
  public MyService()
  {
```

Example 5-1. Implementing IDisposable on a service type (continued)

```
    MessageBox.Show("Constructing MyService");
  }

  #region IMyService Members
  ...
  #endregion

  #region IDisposable Members

  void IDisposable.Dispose()
  {
    MessageBox.Show("Disposing MyService");
  }
  #endregion
}
```

 It is not likely that you'll allocate resources that require explicit disposal, but if you do, be careful not to use the service OperationContext during disposal, as it may not always be available.

In the next few sections, I'll discuss each instancing mode in detail including the appropriate use for each instancing mode, and issues related to sessions, including operation order, session timeout, and exception handling. You'll also complete a lab to practice working with these features.

PerCall Services

In a typical web service scenario, when clients invoke a service, they expect only to call a single operation without maintaining state between calls. This is also true of any remote calls in high throughput environments. To achieve this with WCF, services are configured for PerCall instancing mode by applying the following service behavior to the service implementation:

```
[ServiceBehavior(InstanceContextMode=InstanceContextMode.PerCall)]
public class PerCallService:IPerCallService
```

The lifecycle of a PerCall request is as follows:

- Clients create a proxy to invoke the service.
- Calls to each service operation dispatch messages to the service channel.
- A new instance of the service type is constructed for each call, even if the same client channel issues the calls.
- The service model disposes the service type when the call has completed.

When an uncaught exception is thrown by the service during a call the server channel is put into a faulted state. That's because when the service model at the service receives an uncaught exception, it assumes that the channel may have been compromised in some way and thus faults the channel. If the call is not one-way, the client receives the exception in the form of a SOAP fault (to be discussed in Chapter 8). With `PerCall` services, the client channel is not faulted since there isn't a session. That means the proxy can be used for subsequent calls, a new service instance allocated for each call. For one-way calls, clients are not notified of the exception at all.

The allocation of service objects for `PerCall` services is illustrated in Figure 5-1. Despite the potential for multiple service objects being created for multiple concurrent calls, this instancing mode yields the best overall throughput for a few reasons:

- Since state is not maintained between calls, service types aren't likely to have a heavy constructor initializing other objects.

- By freeing unused service objects and resources consumed by the service for a single operation, overall memory consumption at the server is reduced. Other instancing modes retain service objects and other state-related objects even while clients are inactive for some period.

- Since a new object is allocated for each call, concurrency issues are not a concern at the service layer. Other objects or resources shared by each service object still require protection for concurrent access, however.

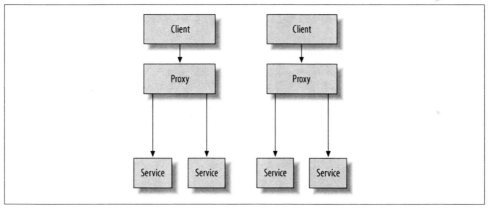

Figure 5-1. PerCall services allocate a service object for every call

Operations still construct the necessary business and data access objects to complete their work. These objects, like the service object, usually do not maintain state between calls and are released with the completion of each service operation, as illustrated in Figure 5-2.

Although this is a typical scenario, this doesn't preclude you from sharing business objects or cached data across service instances, as illustrated respectively in Figures 5-3 and 5-4. These scenarios also introduce the possibility of concurrency issues, something I'll discuss later in this chapter.

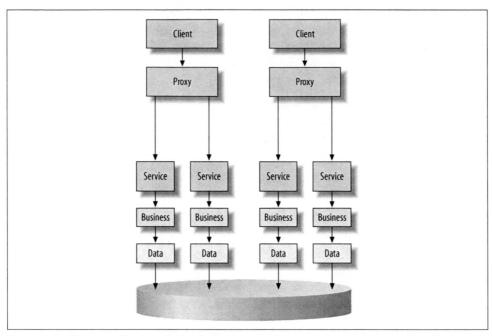

Figure 5-2. Allocation of objects for each service operation

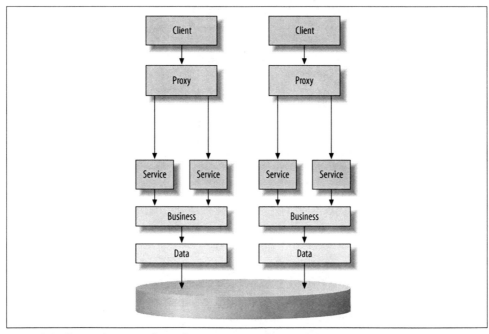

Figure 5-3. Sharing business objects between service objects

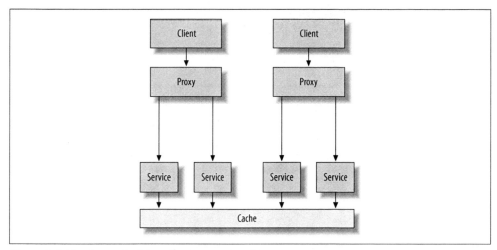

Figure 5-4. Sharing cached data between service objects

PerSession Services

There are four types of sessions supported by WCF services: application sessions, transport sessions, reliable sessions, and secure sessions. An *application session* refers to a session in the classic sense of client-server communications. In WCF terms, this means that service objects are kept alive for subsequent calls by the same client proxy until a timeout period has elapsed. A *transport session* can be a named pipes session or a TCP session. A *reliable session* provides delivery guarantees and message correlation so that calls from the same client proxy can survive transient network interruptions and so that those calls can be optionally delivered to the service object in the order they were sent. Unlike application sessions, reliable sessions do not send requests to the same service object—the session is maintained in the underlying channel layer. Reliable sessions are discussed in Chapter 6. A *secure session* makes it possible for a client proxy to call service operations without re-authenticating each time. In this case, the channel layer relies on a security context token to reconstruct the security context with the identity of the caller. Once again, secure sessions do not require the same service object to handle requests. Secure sessions are discussed in Chapter 8.

 In this chapter, unless otherwise specified, the term *session* refers only to an application session. Where appropriate, in this chapter I will also discuss the impact of reliable sessions and secure sessions on instancing, concurrency and throttling.

Figure 5-5 illustrates that service objects are kept alive to handle requests from the same client proxy for the duration of a session. To enable sessions for a service type, you apply the ServiceBehaviorAttribute and configure its instancing mode to PerSession, as shown here:

```
[ServiceBehavior(InstanceContextMode=InstanceContextMode.PerSession)]
public class PerSessionService:IPerSessionService
```

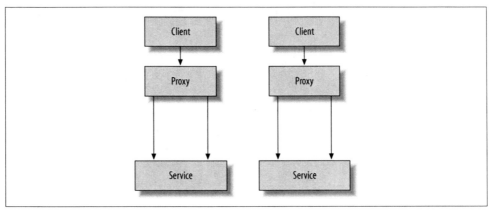

Figure 5-5. PerSession services allocate a service object for each client

This is the default behavior, which means that by default service objects are kept alive for the duration of a client session when endpoints are exposed over a binding that supports sessions. NetNamePipeBinding and NetTcpBinding support sessions inherently at the transport layer. WSHttpBinding and WSFederationHttpBinding support sessions only when reliable sessions or secure sessions are enabled—and secure sessions are enabled by default. If you disable both reliable sessions and secure sessions on these two bindings, application sessions cannot be supported. WSDualHttpBinding always supports reliable sessions.

The lifecycle of a PerSession request is as follows:

- Clients create a proxy to invoke the service.
- Calls to each service operation dispatch messages to the service.
- A new instance of the service type is constructed for the first call from the client proxy, and kept alive for subsequent calls from the same client proxy.
- If the client is inactive for some duration beyond the session timeout, which defaults to 10 minutes, the service instance is disposed.

Since each client gets the same service object for the duration of its session, the service object can hold references to state-aware business objects that live for the duration of the session as shown in Figure 5-6. Another alternative could be to maintain tangential state information in the service object, while allowing each request to construct its own business objects for operation calls as shown in Figure 5-7. The main distinction between these two approaches is in which objects require protection against concurrent access within a session, and in how much memory is consumed while sessions are alive.

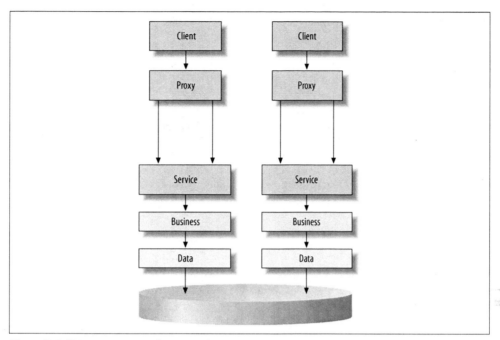

Figure 5-6. Using state-aware business objects per session

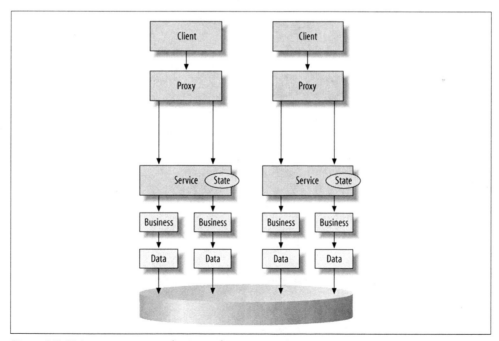

Figure 5-7. Using state-unaware business objects per session

Requiring sessions

To require that service endpoints are exposed over session-capable bindings, you can set the SessionMode property of the ServiceContractAttribute to Required:

```
[ServiceContract(Namespace="http://www.thatindigogirl.com/samples/2006/06",
SessionMode=SessionMode.Required)]
public interface IPerSessionService
```

Session mode options are supplied by the SessionMode enumeration in the System. ServiceModel namespace. The options are:

Allowed

> This is the default setting, which means that a session will be created if the service instancing mode and binding support it. Otherwise, the services behave as PerCall services.

NotAllowed

> This setting prevents an endpoint from using a binding that has a transport session, reliable session, or secure session. In this case, NetNamedPipes, NetTcpBinding, WSDualHttpBinding, and WSFederationHttpBinding are never supported because they always have some form of session. WSHttpBinding can be used if reliable sessions and secure sessions are disabled.

Required

> This setting requires an endpoint to be session-capable, which means that BasicHttpBinding is not supported, and other HTTP protocol bindings must enable reliable sessions or secure sessions.

Session identifier

Application sessions, transport sessions, reliable sessions, and secure sessions all result in a session-aware channel being created at the server. A unique session identifier is always created for a session-aware channel. Where HTTP sessions are concerned, this identifier acts as the glue between the client proxy and the server channel, since there is no transport session to help with message correlation at each end.

At the service, you can access the session identifier through the SessionId property of the OperationContext as follows:

```
OperationContext.Current.SessionId
```

From the client, the session identifier is accessible through the client channel. If you use the proxy generated by SvcUtil, which inherits ClientBase<T>, use the InnerChannel property to access SessionId, as shown here:

```
// creating the client proxy
SessionServiceClient m_proxy = new SessionServiceClient();

// retrieving the session identifier
string s = m_proxy.InnerChannel.SessionId
```

If you create the client channel using ChannelFactory<T>, you are returned a reference to a strongly typed service contract. The underlying object is a transparent proxy for the channel, thus you have access to all properties of the channel if you cast to the correct interface. You can cast the channel to IContextChannel from the System.ServiceModel namespace to access the SessionId property, as shown here:

```
// creating the client proxy
ChannelFactory<ISessionService> factory = new ChannelFactory<ISessionService>( );
ISessionService proxy = factory.CreateChannel( );

// retrieving the session identifier
IContextChannel obj = proxy as IContextChannel;
string s = obj.SessionId;
```

The session identifier at the client and service are not always the same. For transport sessions present with NetNamedPipeBinding and NetTcpBinding, the session identifier is created when the channel is created on either side. These are distinct identifiers that respectively remain the same for the lifetime of the proxy and server channel. It is the transport session in this case that correlates messages, not the session identifiers. For WSHttpBinding and other HTTP bindings that support sessions, however, a session identifier is established through a series of messages exchanged between client and service—thus both sides share the same identifier. Over HTTP, application sessions can be established only when reliable sessions or secure sessions are enabled.

WSHttpBinding supports secure sessions by default. This binding feature can be controlled declaratively by the establishSecurityContext setting, as shown in Example 5-2.

Example 5-2. Secure sessions enabled on WSHttpBinding

```
<wsHttpBinding>
  <binding name="wsHttpSecureSession">
    <security>
      <message establishSecurityContext="true"/>
    </security>
  </binding>
</wsHttpBinding>
```

In the case of secure sessions, you cannot access SessionId until after the first call has been made to the service. During this first call, a Request Security Token message (RST) is issued to retrieve a security context token for secure message exchange. A Request Security Token Response (RSTR) is returned with the security token and a token identifier, which is used as the session identifier. Example 5-3 shows the identifier returned as part of the <SecurityContextToken> element. Security concepts are discussed at length in Chapter 7.

Example 5-3. Session identifier created for a secure session

```
<s:Envelope>
  <s:Header>...</s:Header>
  <s:Body>
```

Example 5-3. Session identifier created for a secure session (continued)

```
    <t:RequestSecurityTokenResponse
xmlns:t="http://schemas.xmlsoap.org/ws/2005/02/trust"
xmlns:u="http://docs.oasis-open.org/wss/2004/01/oasis-200401-wss-wssecurity-
utility-1.0.xsd">
      <t:TokenType>http://schemas.xmlsoap.org/ws/2005/02/sc/sct</t:TokenType>
      <t:RequestedSecurityToken>
        <c:SecurityContextToken u:Id="uuid-0600d9f8-3807-4330-8014-ed03dabe2896-2"
xmlns:c="http://schemas.xmlsoap.org/ws/2005/02/sc">
          <c:Identifier>
urn:uuid:d277f69e-c9c3-4436-b1fd-449b8e5a5af1</c:Identifier>
        </c:SecurityContextToken>
      </t:RequestedSecurityToken>
      <!-- other elements -->
    </t:RequestSecurityTokenResponse>
  </s:Body>
</s:Envelope>
```

That same identifier is passed in the <SecurityContextToken> element with each request to the service in a message header for the duration of the session, as shown in Example 5-4. This identifier allows the client and service to correlate messages as part of a session.

Example 5-4. Passing the secure session identifier for a secure session

```
<s:Envelope>
  <s:Header>
    <o:Security s:mustUnderstand="1" xmlns:o="http://docs.oasis-
open.org/wss/2004/01/oasis-200401-wss-wssecurity-secext-1.0.xsd">
      <c:SecurityContextToken u:Id="uuid-0600d9f8-3807-4330-8014-ed03dabe2896-2"
xmlns:c="http://schemas.xmlsoap.org/ws/2005/02/sc">
        <c:Identifier>urn:uuid:d277f69e-c9c3-4436-b1fd-449b8e5a5af1</c:Identifier>
      </c:SecurityContextToken>
      <!-- other elements -->
    </o:Security>
  </s:Header>
  <s:Body>...</s:Body>
</s:Envelope>
```

Reliable sessions are enabled by default on WSDualHttpBinding, and can be enabled on WSHttpBinding or WSFederationHttpBinding. In this case, a Create Sequence request is sent to the service to establish a session identifier. This session identifier is returned in the Create Sequence Response shown in Example 5-5.

Example 5-5. Session identifier created for reliable sessions

```
<s:Envelope>
  <s:Header>...</s:Header>
  <s:Body>
    <CreateSequenceResponse xmlns="http://schemas.xmlsoap.org/ws/2005/02/rm">
      <Identifier>urn:uuid:4030917f-0000-4879-b961-32cec764c4c5</Identifier>
      <!-- other elements -->
```

```
        </CreateSequenceResponse>
    </s:Body>
</s:Envelope>
```

Reliable sessions are typically established on a secure channel, thus the security context token is also issued for the session. In this case, the reliable session identifier is the overarching session identifier used to correlate messages, shown in the <Sequence> header in Example 5-6.

Example 5-6. Passing the reliable session identifier for a reliable session

```
<s:Envelope>
    <s:Header>
        <r:Sequence s:mustUnderstand="1" u:Id="_2" xmlns:u="http://docs.oasis-
open.org/wss/2004/01/oasis-200401-wss-wssecurity-utility-1.0.xsd"
xmlns:r="http://schemas.xmlsoap.org/ws/2005/02/rm">
            <r:Identifier>urn:uuid:4030917f-0000-4879-b961-32cec764c4c5</r:Identifier>
            <r:MessageNumber>1</r:MessageNumber>
        </r:Sequence>
        <o:Security s:mustUnderstand="1" xmlns:o="http://docs.oasis-
open.org/wss/2004/01/oasis-200401-wss-wssecurity-secext-1.0.xsd">
            <c:SecurityContextToken u:Id="uuid-0600d9f8-3807-4330-8014-ed03dabe2896-16"
xmlns:c="http://schemas.xmlsoap.org/ws/2005/02/sc" xmlns:u="http://docs.oasis-
open.org/wss/2004/01/oasis-200401-wss-wssecurity-utility-1.0.xsd">
                <c:Identifier>urn:uuid:a628dd31-a47d-4318-91b6-25b3a40f5831</c:Identifier>
            </c:SecurityContextToken>
            <!-- other elements -->
        </o:Security>
        <!-- other headers -->
    </s:Header>
    <s:Body>...</s:Body>
</s:Envelope>
```

Other aspects of reliable sessions and secure sessions are discussed in Chapters 6 and 7, respectively. For this discussion, just realize the role they play in creating an application session identifier when a binding that supports HTTP protocol is employed, and that this session identifier is what correlates messages between client and service channels.

Session lifetime

Once constructed, an application session lasts until it either times out or is explicitly terminated. Session timeout is controlled by the receive timeout setting at the service. Each standard binding configuration has a receiveTimeout property, shown here for NetTcpBinding:

```
<netTcpBinding>
    <binding name="netTcp" receiveTimeout="00:10:00" />
</netTcpBinding>
```

This property can also be set programmatically:

```
NetTcpBinding binding = new NetTcpBinding( );
binding.ReceiveTimeout = new TimeSpan(0, 10, 0);
```

In the preceding examples, the timeout is set for 10 minutes, which is the default setting. This timeout operates on a sliding scale, which means that it begins from the last request during the session. Timeout affects the duration of the application session, transport session, reliable session or secure session.

> Reliable sessions and secure sessions also have timeout properties but they do not control the timeout of the overall session. These properties are described in later chapters.

When the client channel is destroyed, this also terminates the session at the service. This is handled by the transport for named pipes and TCP sessions, and via a session cancellation message for reliable sessions and secure sessions.

> A sample that illustrates session expiry can be found at *<YourLearningWCFPath>\Samples\Instancing\SessionExpiry*.

Service operations can also be configured to control the lifetime of an application session. When a PerSession service is called for the first time by a particular client, a session is created. The same session is kept alive until the client explicitly closes the proxy and terminates the session, or until the session times out at the server. By default, any operation on a service contract can be called to create the session, and no operations on the service contract will terminate the session explicitly. That's because the IsInitiating and IsTerminating properties of the OperationContractAttribute default to the following:

```
[OperationContract(IsInitiating = true, IsTerminating = false)]
void MyOperation( );
```

These properties have the following effect as calls arrive to a particular operation, assuming application sessions have been enabled for the service:

IsInitiating
> If true, if a session has not yet been created for the client, a session is created. If false, if a session has been created, the call can execute, but if a session has not been created, an InvalidOperationException is thrown.

IsTerminating
> If true, if a session exists, it will be terminated when the call completes. If false, if a session exists, it will not be automatically terminated.

Using these properties you can design a service contract that requires operations be completed in a particular order. Example 5-7 shows an example of a service contract that requires StartSession( ) to be called prior to all other operations, in order to initialize a session. When StopSession( ) is called, the session is explicitly terminated.

Example 5-7. Initializing and terminating sessions

```
[ServiceContract(Namespace = "http://www.thatindigogirl.com/samples/2006/06",
SessionMode = SessionMode.Required)]
public interface ISessionService
{
  [OperationContract(IsInitiating = true, IsTerminating = false)]
  void StartSession( );
  [OperationContract(IsInitiating = false, IsTerminating = false)]
  void IncrementCounter( );
  [OperationContract(IsInitiating = false, IsTerminating = false)]
  int GetCounter( );
  [OperationContract(IsInitiating = false, IsTerminating = false)]
  string GetSessionId( );
  [OperationContract(IsInitiating = false, IsTerminating = true)]
  void StopSession( );
}
```

 The following sample illustrates initiating and terminating operations: *<YourLearningWCFPath>\Samples\Instancing\SessionLifetime.*

Exception handling

When you're working with sessions, you must pay special attention to exception handling at both the client and service. If an exception is thrown at the service, it faults the server channel, taking any form of existing session along with it. Assuming the operation that threw the exception is not one-way, the exception will be propagated to the client—putting the client channel into a faulted state as well. This renders the proxy useless for future calls to the service, and a new channel must be created by constructing a new proxy. Clients must check the state of the channel after each call to the service, particularly when sessions are enabled. If the channel is faulted, the client may choose to create a new proxy instance before proceeding, or may choose to notify the user of the problem to let them decide. This decision should be based on the application's requirements, possibly depending on the type of exception that faulted the channel.

Consider the service contract and implementation in Example 5-8.

Example 5-8. Throwing exceptions and faults

```
[ServiceContract(Namespace="http://www.thatindigogirl.com/samples/2006/06",
SessionMode=SessionMode.Required)]
public interface ICounterServiceSession
{
  [OperationContract]
  int IncrementCounter( );
```

Example 5-8. Throwing exceptions and faults (continued)

```
    [OperationContract]
    void ThrowException( );
    [OperationContract]
    void ThrowFault( );
}

[ServiceBehavior(InstanceContextMode=InstanceContextMode.PerSession)]
public class CounterServiceSession:ICounterServiceSession
{
    private int m_counter;

    int ICounterServiceSession.IncrementCounter( )
    {
        return m_counter++;
    }

    public void ThrowException( )
    {
        throw new NotImplementedException("The method or operation is not
implemented.");
    }

    public void ThrowFault( )
    {
        throw new FaultException("The method or operation is not
implemented.");
    }
}
```

Creating a new client proxy will start a session, and calls to `IncrementCounter( )` will increment the same `m_counter` instance. Within the context of this session, if `ThrowException( )` is called, an exception is propagated to the client. At this point the client channel's communication state is `Faulted`, as indicated by the `State` property of the proxy reference shown here:

```
    CounterServiceSessionClient proxy = new CounterServiceSessionClient( );
    proxy.IncrementCounter( );
    proxy.IncrementCounter( );

    proxy.ThrowException( );
    // after catching the exception
    Debug.Assert(proxy.State == CommunicationState.Faulted);
```

While in this faulted state, subsequent attempts to use the proxy will result in a `CommunicationObjectFaultedException`.

If the service explicitly throws a `FaultException` instead of allowing an uncaught exception to be processed by the server channel, the channel and its session will not be faulted. Faults can be generated in several ways. Example 5-8 shows an undeclared `FaultException` being generated by the `ThrowFault( )` operation:

```
    throw new FaultException("The method or operation is not
    implemented.");
```

You can also declare faults in the service contract, and throw a strongly typed FaultException, as shown here:

```
// fault declaration
[OperationContract]
[FaultContract(typeof(InvalidOperationException))]
void ThrowFault();

// throwing a declared fault
throw new FaultException<NotImplementedException>(new
NotImplementedException("Not implemented."), "Not implemented.");
```

In either case, because a FaultException is raised to the server channel instead of a standard Exception type, the service channel is not faulted. Thus, the client can continue to call the service. The detailed semantics of declaring and throwing faults are discussed in Chapter 8.

For one-way operations, exceptions are not propagated to the client, but uncaught exceptions at the service will still fault the server channel, rendering the client proxy useless. This means that even for one-way calls that don't throw an exception, it is possible that the client channel may be put into a faulted state on the next call. Once again, clients are forced to check the state of the channel after each call and determine the best course of action.

Consider the case where the ThrowException() operation from Example 5-8 is one-way:

```
[OperationContract(IsOneWay=true)]
void ThrowException();
```

There is no need to catch an exception thrown by the service when one-way operations are involved. After the exception is thrown, although the server channel has faulted, the client proxy is not immediately faulted. When the client issues another call to the service, this puts the client channel into a faulted state:

```
CounterServiceSessionClient proxy = new CounterServiceSessionClient();
proxy.IncrementCounter();
proxy.IncrementCounter();

// one-way exception
proxy.ThrowException();
Debug.Assert(proxy.State != CommunicationState.Faulted);

// another call after the exception
proxy.IncrementCounter();
// after catching the exception
Debug.Assert(proxy.State == CommunicationState.Faulted);
```

When an application session, transport session, or reliable session exists, and the client invokes an operation on a faulted server channel, a CommunicationException is received at the client indicating the problem. If a secure session is in place, a MessageSecurityException is received at the client. In any case, the exception indicates the reason for the faulted server channel and puts the client channel into a faulted state. Future calls would yield a CommunicationObjectFaultedException.

For duplex communication (discussed in Chapter 3), there is always a session present to correlate callback messages. In this case, if the client callback throws an uncaught exception, it will also fault the channel. Clients should take care to throw an appropriate FaultException to report problems to avoid disrupting communications.

 You should check the state of the client proxy, in particular where sessions of any kind are involved, and take appropriate action after failure. What action depends on your application. For example, if the fact that the session was terminated abruptly means the user will have to re-enter data for the session, he should be informed of this before a new session is constructed. If the user won't notice the difference, perhaps you can just construct a new proxy and let him continue working. A few samples that illustrate how clients respond to exceptions and faults for request/reply and one-way operations can be found here:

- *<YourLearningWCFPath>\Samples\Instancing\ InstancingExceptions*
- *<YourLearningWCFPath>\Samples\Instancing\ InstancingExceptionsOneWay*

Singleton Services

When a WCF service is configured to be a singleton, the same service instance is used to handle all requests from all clients. The instancing mode in this case is set to Single, as shown here:

```
[ServiceBehavior(InstanceContextMode=InstanceContextMode.Single)]
public class SingletonService:ISingletonService
```

In this case, the service instance is created when the ServiceHost is constructed and lives until the ServiceHost is closed or until the application domain is unloaded when the host process is shut down. For singleton services, it is also possible to pre-construct the service instance and pass it to the ServiceHost constructor before opening the channel, which is useful in cases where significant initialization is required:

```
Singleton.SingletonService serviceInstance = new Singleton.SingletonService( );
// initialize singleton properties
ServiceHost host = new ServiceHost(serviceInstance);
host.Open( );
```

Since a singleton service object is shared across all client requests, it is really up to the singleton to determine how its state is managed across those requests. By definition, any references to business objects held by the singleton will be shared by all requests, as shown in Figure 5-8.

If the binding supports sessions and the SessionMode is set to Allowed or Required, a session is created for each client. The same singleton object handles each request, but a session identifier is assigned for each client to distinguish them from one another. It is up to you to use this session identifier to allocate state to each client. Example 5-9 shows an example that stores a different counter for each client. Figure 5-9 illustrates the potential allocation of business objects based on this scenario.

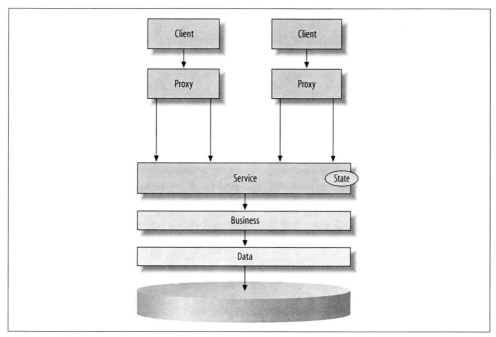

Figure 5-8. Business objects shared by all requests

Example 5-9. Tracking sessions in a singleton service

```
[ServiceBehavior(InstanceContextMode = InstanceContextMode.Single)]
public class SingletonService : ISingletonService
{
  Dictionary<string, int> m_counters = new Dictionary<string, int>();

  public void IncrementCounter()
  {
    if (!m_counters.ContainsKey(OperationContext.Current.SessionId))
      m_counters.Add(OperationContext.Current.SessionId, 0);

    m_counters[OperationContext.Current.SessionId]++;

    MessageBox.Show(String.Format("Incrementing counter to {0} on session {1}.",
m_counters[OperationContext.Current.SessionId],
OperationContext.Current.SessionId));
  }
}
```

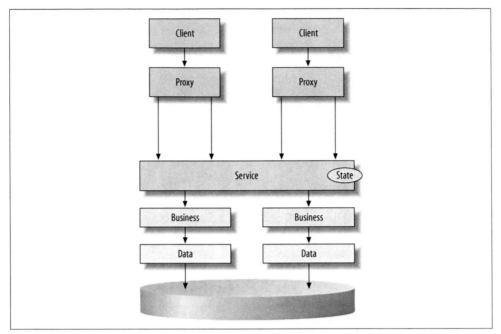

Figure 5-9. Allocating business objects per session in a singleton

If the singleton chooses not to track sessions, requests will all funnel through the singleton while each operation constructs its own business objects, as shown in Figure 5-10. In some respects, this removes the value of having a singleton in the first place, so it is an unlikely scenario. Singletons are usually chosen because there is a need to share some state between clients.

By design, singletons handle all requests from all clients, which is a very real scalability concern for server deployments. Even if you configure a singleton to allow multiple concurrent requests, any shared resources must be protected from concurrent access. If resource locks are poorly implemented, the same scalability concerns exist as if the singleton allows only one request to process at a given time. For this reason, singletons are more likely to be useful in client deployments with limited concurrent users. I'll talk about concurrency later in this chapter.

 The following samples illustrate singleton scenarios discussed in this section:

- *<YourLearningWCFPath>\Samples\Instancing\ SingletonConstructor*
- *<YourLearningWCFPath>\Samples\Instancing\ SingletonLifetime*
- *<YourLearningWCFPath>\Samples\Instancing\SingletonSession*

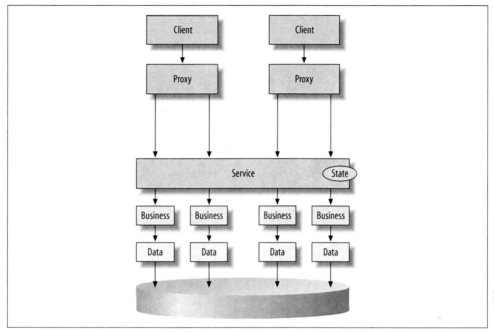

Figure 5-10. Ignoring state in a singleton

Lab: Controlling Service Instancing

This lab will show you how to work with PerCall, PerSession, and Single instancing modes, while also illustrating the relevance of session identifiers and the impact of exceptions and faults. You'll start by opening an existing solution that is configured PerCall and then modifying the service to test PerSession and Single configuration.

Working with PerCall services

In this section, you'll test how PerCall services behave with and without the presence of a session, and how the client proxy reacts to exceptions and faults.

1. Open the startup solution for this lab at *<YourLearningWCFPath>\Labs\Chapter5\Instancing\Instancing.sln*. This solution contains an implementation of a service, a console host, and a client application. The service is a simple counter service that will illustrate instancing results.

2. Before testing the service, review its current implementation. The service contract includes three operations, which in the service implementation increment a counter value, throw an InvalidOperationException, and throw a FaultException, respectively. The contract and implementation are shown in Example 5-10.

Example 5-10. Initial CounterService implementation

```
[ServiceContract(Namespace="http://www.thatindigogirl.com/samples/2006/06")]
public interface ICounterService
{
  [OperationContract]
  int IncrementCounter();
  [OperationContract]
  void ThrowException();
  [OperationContract]
  void ThrowFault();
}

[ServiceBehavior(InstanceContextMode=InstanceContextMode.PerCall)]
public class CounterService:ICounterService
{
  private int m_counter;

  int ICounterService.IncrementCounter()
  {
    m_counter++;
    MessageBox.Show(String.Format("Incrementing counter to {0}.\r\nSession Id:
{1}", m_counter, OperationContext.Current.SessionId));
    return m_counter;
  }

  public void ThrowException()
  {
    throw new NotImplementedException("This is an Exception.");
  }

  public void ThrowFault()
  {
    throw new FaultException("This is a FaultException.");
  }
}
```

The service exposes endpoints for NetNamedPipeBinding, NetTcpBinding, BasicHttpBinding, WSHttpBinding without session, WSHttpBinding with secure sessions enabled, and WSHttpBinding with reliable sessions enabled. The client (shown in Figure 5-11) is already coded to exercise each of these endpoints.

3. Start by testing the service's instancing behavior. First, run the Host project without debugging, and then run the WinClient application. From the WinClient interface, select BasicHttpBinding and select No Exception. This creates a new proxy for the selected endpoint and calls IncrementCounter() twice:

```
CounterServiceClient proxy = GetProxy();
proxy.IncrementCounter();
proxy.IncrementCounter();
```

4. You'll notice in each message box presented that the session identifier is not set because there is no session for PerCall services. Also notice that repeated calls to IncrementCounter() result in a new service instance because a new service instance is allocated; thus, the counter is reinitialized each time.

Figure 5-11. WinClient application interface

5. Try the same test for each binding and you will see that the session identifier is not set for WSHttpBinding without session, but for the remaining bindings that support some form of session, the identifier is set.

6. Now test how the client responds to exceptions. Select BasicHttpBinding again, and select Exception. This creates a new proxy and calls IncrementCounter( ), ThrowException( ), and then IncrementCounter( ):

```
CounterServiceClient proxy = GetProxy( );
proxy.IncrementCounter( );
proxy.ThrowException( );

// exception handling

proxy.IncrementCounter( );
```

You'll notice that the client receives a FaultException and after catching the error is able to continue using the proxy.

Try the same test for each binding—the behavior is not consistent across all bindings. WSHttpBinding without session behaves similar to BasicHttpBinding. For all other bindings, which, coincidently, have some type of session, a CommunicationObjectFaulted exception is thrown when the proxy is used after the FaultException.

7. Now test how each binding responds to faults. Select each binding and select the Fault button. This creates a new proxy and calls IncrementCounter( ), ThrowFault( ), and then IncrementCounter( ):

```
CounterServiceClient proxy = GetProxy( );
proxy.IncrementCounter( );
proxy.ThrowFault( );

// exception handling
proxy.IncrementCounter( );
```

This time, in all cases the proxy is functional after the FaultException is handled. That's because the service explicitly threw a FaultException instead of allowing an uncaught exception to trickle up the channel stack.

Working with sessions

In this section, you'll modify the service to support application sessions and then test the resulting instancing behavior when sessions are disallowed or required. You'll also see how the client proxy reacts to exceptions and faults when sessions are enabled.

1. Modify the service to support sessions. Go to the Counters project and open *CounterService.cs*. Change the service behavior to use PerSession instancing mode, as shown here:

   ```
   [ServiceBehavior(InstanceContextMode=InstanceContextMode.PerSession)]
   public class CounterService:ICounterService, IDisposable
   ```

    Although this is the default behavior, it helps to be explicit in your service implementation so that the expected behavior of the service is clear to all developers.

2. Test the instancing behavior of the service once again. Run the Host and WinClient project as before, and select each binding and the No Exception button. The counter will increment to two for those bindings that support sessions, indicating that the same service instance is being called for the lifetime of the proxy. Notice that the session identifier is also only present for those bindings that support sessions, as before.

3. Now test the behavior of the proxy with exceptions and faults. For each binding, once again select the Exception button and then the Fault button. The results should be the same as with the PerCall service where sessions were involved—the proxy is not usable after an uncaught exception is thrown by the service, but when a FaultException is thrown, the service instance and its associated client session are not faulted.

4. Modify the service to disallow sessions. Open *CounterService.cs* and edit the ServiceContractAttribute to provide a SessionMode setting NotAllowed:

   ```
   [ServiceContract(Namespace="http://www.thatindigogirl.com/samples/2006/06",
   SessionMode=SessionMode.NotAllowed)]
   ```

   Try to run the Host project and you'll receive an InvalidOperationException indicating that the service cannot be exposed over any bindings that require session support, specifically NetNamedPipeBinding and NetTcpBinding.

   Open the *app.config* for the Host project and comment the two endpoints that use these bindings, as shown here:

   ```
   <service name="Counters.CounterService" behaviorConfiguration="serviceBehavior">
     <host>...</host>
     <!--<endpoint address="netPipe" binding="netNamedPipeBinding"
   ```

```
contract="Counters.ICounterService" />
   <endpoint address="netTcp" binding="netTcpBinding"
contract="Counters.ICounterService" /> -->
   <!-- other endpoints -->
</service>
```

Run the Host without debugging, and it will initialize without a problem. Now run the WinClient and test each of the other endpoints. You'll notice that a session identifier is not present for any of the HTTP bindings—even those that support secure and reliable sessions. You'll also notice that an application session doesn't exist for any of the bindings; thus, the counter is reinitialized as in a PerCall service configuration.

 This last result may be a little misleading. The fact that sessions are disallowed refers only to application sessions. Reliable sessions and secure sessions are still present if configured on the binding, but since application sessions are disallowed, the session identifier is not populated with the underlying session identifier.

5. Now modify the service to require sessions. Open the *app.config* for the Host project and restore the commented NetNamedPipeBinding and NetTcpBinding endpoints. Open *CounterService.cs* and edit the ServiceContractAttribute to provide a SessionMode setting Required:

   ```
   [ServiceContract(Namespace="http://www.thatindigogirl.com/samples/2006/06",
   SessionMode=SessionMode.Required)]
   ```

   Try to run the Host project and you'll receive an InvalidOperationException indicating that the service cannot be exposed over any bindings that do not support sessions. This affects both the BasicHttpBinding endpoint and the WSHttpBinding endpoint that has secure sessions disabled. Comment these endpoints and run the Host project without debugging.

   ```
   <!--<endpoint address="CounterServiceBasicHttp" binding="basicHttpBinding"
   contract="Counters.ICounterService" />
   <endpoint address="wsHttpNoSession" binding="wsHttpBinding" contract="Counters.
   ICounterService" bindingConfiguration="wsHttpNoSession"/>-->
   ```

   Run the WinClient project and test all bindings, selecting the No Exception button. This time a session identifier is present and the counter is incremented indicating the same service object servicing requests per proxy.

Working with singletons

In this section, you'll turn the service into a singleton and test configuration and behavior related to instancing, sessions, and faults.

1. Change the service to a singleton. Open *CounterService.cs* and set the service behavior to use Single instancing mode, as shown here:

   ```
   [ServiceBehavior(InstanceContextMode=InstanceContextMode.Single)]
   public class CounterService:ICounterService, IDisposable
   ```

2. Test the instancing behavior of the singleton. Start by running the Host and WinClient project. The current configuration still requires sessions, so test only the bindings that support sessions, and select the No Exception button for each. You'll notice that a unique session identifier is used for each proxy instance—maintained for the two calls to IncrementCounter( )—however, the counter is incremented across all calls since the same service instance handles all requests. Exceptions and faults behave in the same way as with application sessions—exceptions fault the channel, rendering the proxy useless, and faults preserve the channel.

3. Modify the service contract so that sessions are Allowed instead of Required, as shown here:

```
[ServiceContract(Namespace="http://www.thatindigogirl.com/samples/2006/06",
SessionMode=SessionMode.Allowed)]
```

In addition, restore the commented BasicHttpBinding and WSHttpBinding endpoints for the Host. Run the solution again and test all endpoints. You'll notice that a session identifier is only present for those bindings that support session, but all requests are still sent to the same service instance. As with PerCall services, for those bindings without session support, exceptions do not fault the channel.

 For a sample that tests all instancing modes, see the following: *<YourLearningWCFPath>\Samples\Instancing\Instancing*. See the samples mentioned earlier that also illustrate exceptions.

Concurrency

Concurrency issues arise when multiple threads attempt to access the same resources at runtime. When requests arrive to a service, the service model dispatches the message on a thread from the thread pool. Certainly, if multiple clients call the same service, multiple concurrent requests can arrive at the service. The particular service object handling each request is based on the instancing mode for the service. For PerCall services, a new service object is granted for each request. For PerSession services, the same service object receives requests from the same client. For Single instancing mode, all client requests are sent to the same singleton service object. Based on this alone, PerSession services are at risk of concurrent access when the client is multithreaded, and Single services are perpetually at risk.

By default, only one request thread is granted access to any service object, regardless of the instancing mode. The concurrency setting for a service is controlled by the ConcurrencyMode property of the ServiceBehaviorAttribute. The default setting is Single, as shown here:

```
[ServiceBehavior(ConcurrencyMode=ConcurrencyMode.Single)]
public class MessagingService : IMessagingService
```

This property can be set to any of the following ConcurrencyMode enumeration values:

Single

A single request thread has access to the service object at a given time.

Reentrant

A single request thread has access to the service object, but the thread can exit the service and reenter without deadlock.

Multiple

Multiple request threads have access to the service object and shared resources must be manually protected from concurrent access.

In the following sections, I'll discuss the implications of each setting and their appropriate use.

Single Concurrency Mode

When the service is configured for Single concurrency mode, a lock is acquired for the service object while a request is being processed by that object. Other calls to the same object are queued in order of receipt at the service—subject to the client's send timeout, or the service's session timeout if applicable. When the request that owns the lock has completed, and thus released the lock, the next request in queue can acquire the lock and begin processing. This configuration reduces the potential throughput at the service, when sessions or singletons are involved, but it also yields the least risk for concurrency issues.

Restricting concurrent access using Single concurrency mode is often a trade-off for throughput. For PerCall services, this is not the case since a new service is allocated for each request, as shown in Figure 5-12. For PerSession services, Single concurrency disallows multiple concurrent calls from same client while not impacting throughput of multiple clients (see Figure 5-13). For Single instancing mode, only one request can be processed across all clients, as shown in Figure 5-14.

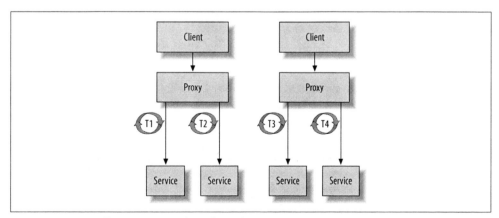

Figure 5-12. PerCall instancing mode with Single concurrency

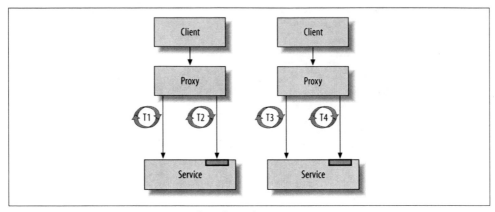

Figure 5-13. PerSession instancing mode with Single concurrency

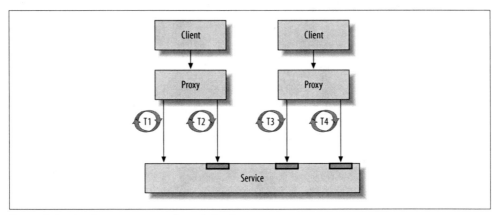

Figure 5-14. Single instancing mode with Single concurrency

Although Single concurrency mode is the safest and simplest way to protect shared resources from multithreaded clients in session and from all clients for singleton services, reentrancy and increased throughput is sometimes necessary, introducing the need for more advanced multithreading techniques.

Reentrant Concurrency Mode

Reentrant mode is necessary when a service issues callbacks to clients, unless the callback is a one-way operation (discussed in Chapter 3). That's because the outgoing call from service to client would not be able to return to the service instance without causing a deadlock. The service model detects this situation on the outgoing call and an InvalidOperationException is thrown indicating that the operation would deadlock. Services configured for Reentrant concurrency mode behave similar to Single mode in that concurrent calls are not supported from clients; however, if an outgoing call is made to a downstream service or to a client callback, the lock on the service instance is released so that another call is allowed to acquire it. When the outgoing call returns, it is queued to acquire the lock to complete its work.

Figure 5-15 illustrates how PerCall services would behave with and without reentrancy for non-one-way callbacks. In this case, the only thread that might need to reenter the service is the outgoing callback. In Single mode, deadlock is guaranteed, whereas in Rentrant mode, the callback return simply reacquires the lock.

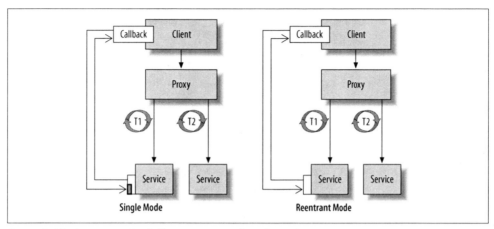

Figure 5-15. Comparing PerCall instancing mode with Single or Reentrant concurrency on non-one-way calls

Reentrant PerSession services may actually achieve greater throughput from a multithreaded client because while the callback is in progress, another call from the client can acquire the service instance lock. Figure 5-16 illustrates that a second thread (T2) can acquire the lock, as the first thread (T1) releases it to issue a callback. T1 blocks on return, waiting for T2 to complete its work.

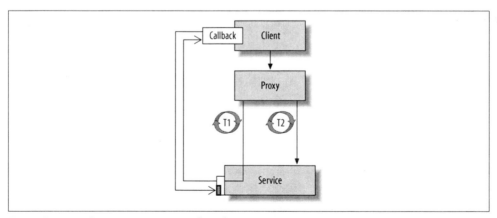

Figure 5-16. PerSession instancing mode with Reentrant concurrency

For singleton services, reentrancy means that the next queued request thread from any client can enter the service while an outgoing call is being executed. Figure 5-17 illustrates that T3 has acquired the lock while T1 is queued to reenter from its callback.

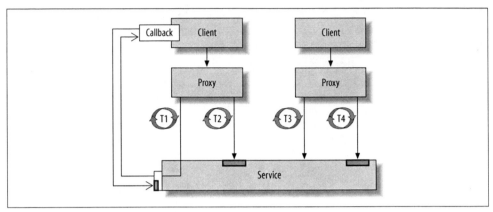

Figure 5-17. Single instancing mode with Reentrant concurrency

Reentrancy has the potential to affect the integrity of the state of the object when PerSession and Single instancing mode is configured. A new request thread may use the same service instance, while another thread has not yet completed its work. Pay special attention to the information persisted in the state of the service to ensure that outgoing calls have either completed work on this state, that threads allocate custom locks on resources that should not be touched by concurrent threads, or that a thread's state is always persisted safely with a resource manager such as a database before releasing the lock. This same state could be retrieved upon the callback's return if applicable.

Multiple Concurrency Mode

To increase throughput for PerSession and Single instancing mode, multiple threads are allowed entry to a shared service instance. In this case, no locks are acquired on the service instance, and all shared state and resources must be protected with manual synchronization techniques. In the case of PerSession and Single instancing, state is contained by the service instance. If the state references threadsafe objects that encapsulate their own concurrency protection, the first thread to access the object will acquire the lock for that object. If not, the service code should implement synchronization locks before accessing those resources.

When UI hosting is involved, as discussed in Chapter 4, it makes more sense for services to use Single concurrency mode (Reentrant only if necessary) so that the UI thread is not burdened with throttling requests.

Although a new service instance is allocated for each request with PerCall services, Multiple concurrency mode is still useful in the case where there is a session to increase throughput for multithreaded clients. That's because the lock acquired when the first request is received from a particular client proxy is actually on the context, not on the service object. When a session is present, this lock prevents more than one thread from entering the same session—which means the TCP socket, the named pipe, or the reliable or secure session.

Custom Synchronization

`PerCall` services aren't immune to synchronization woes. As Figure 5-18 illustrates, shared resources aren't always the result of shared state in the service instance. Downstream calls can also share resources, such as a global object, a shared cache, or a database. Databases of course rely on resource managers and transactions to manage concurrent access and consistency—something I'll discuss in Chapter 6. Other resources require an approach to synchronization that protects concurrent threads from accessing the object while a particular thread or call has not yet finished its work.

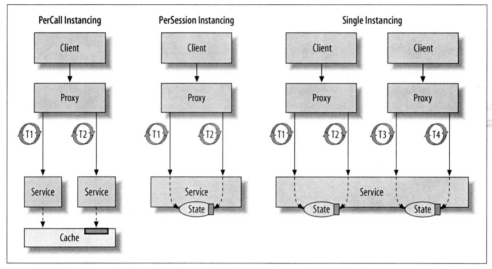

Figure 5-18. Applying custom synchronization to shared resources

In the case of `PerCall` services, individual service instances may access a shared resource, like a cache. Figure 5-18 illustrates that if a lock is applied to the cache, T1 will acquire it and T2 will queue if it tries to access the same object. `PerSession` services may also share downstream objects but are also likely to have shared state. If a multithreaded client attempts to access that state, and T1 has acquired a lock on it, T2 will queue if it tries to access the same state. Singletons most definitely have shared state; otherwise why would they be singletons? They can protect that state by associating a lock with it to block calls that attempt to access the same state.

In fact, in all of these scenarios, it is entirely possible that multiple types of shared state exist, and to increase throughput, different locks should be acquired for related types of state as shown in the `Single` instancing example of Figure 5-18. This way, both T1 and T3 can complete processing concurrently since they don't share state, and T2 and T4 queue waiting for their respective resource locks to free.

The following samples illustrate the use of custom synchronization mechanisms at the service tier:

- *<YourLearningWCFPath>\Samples\Concurrency\GlobalLocks*
- *<YourLearningWCFPath>\Samples\Concurrency\StaticLock*
- *<YourLearningWCFPath>\Samples\Concurrency\Mutex*

.NET Synchronization Techniques

There are a number of ways to implement custom synchronization, including `Monitor`, `Mutex`, `Semaphore`, `ReadWriterLock`, and `Interlocked` operations. There are also .NET attributes that can be used to synchronize access to a type. This section will provide you with a brief overview of the multithreading techniques that will be used in the upcoming lab to provide you with some background.

Using `Monitor` you can acquire a global lock on an object instance using `Enter()` and `Exit()` as follows:

```
try
{
  Monitor.Enter(this);
  // access shared members
}
finally
{
  Monitor.Exit(this);
}
```

In fact, the `lock()` statement compiles to the same result:

```
lock(this)
{
  // access shared members
}
```

Static resources can also be protected using either syntax; in this case, the type is specified instead of a particular instance:

```
// locking a static type
lock(typeof(MessagingService))
{
  // access static members
}
```

`Mutex` are more granular, allowing you to associate a lock with any critical section of code. Construct the `Mutex` and when a critical section associated with the particular `Mutex` instance is reached, call `WaitOne()` to acquire the lock. This code will block if another thread has already acquired the lock. You must call `ReleaseMutex()` for each call to `WaitOne()`, so the use of a `try...finally` clause is recommended:

```
Mutex m_mutex = new Mutex(false);
// some time later
```

```
try
{
  m_mutex.WaitOne( );
  // access protected resources of any kind
}
finally
{
  m_mutex.ReleaseMutex( );
}
```

 For additional information on .NET multithreading techniques, I recommend *Programming .NET Components* by Juval Löwy (O'Reilly).

Asynchronous Proxies

In addition to manual synchronization techniques, the next lab will also show you how to improve perceived performance for client applications. Clients can optionally generate an *asynchronous proxy* to invoke services, using the /*async* option for SvcUtil. This generates a proxy that includes synchronous and asynchronous operation signatures so that you can make calls to the service using a thread from the thread pool. Consider the following operation:

```
public void SendMessage(string message)
{
  base.Channel.SendMessage(message);
}
```

When an asynchronous proxy is generated, these additional methods are added to the proxy:

```
public System.IAsyncResult BeginSendMessage(string
message, System.AsyncCallback callback, object asyncState)
{
  return base.Channel.BeginSendMessage(message, callback, asyncState);
}

public void EndSendMessage(System.IAsyncResult result)
{
  base.Channel.EndSendMessage(result);
}
```

This is similar to the asynchronous design pattern used for delegates, whereby the call is split into two parts:

Begin*OperationName*
> Expects you to pass the parameters required of the operation, plus two additional parameters—an AsyncCallback delegate with the method to call when the operation is complete, and any state object you want to pass to the call. Begin*OperationName* returns an IAsyncResult reference, which you can save and later use to poll for status or retrieve results from the call.

End*OperationName*

>Expects you to pass the IAsyncResult reference returned from the begin operation, to retrieve the results of the call. When you call End*OperationName*, the return type matches that of the service operation. You will also pass any out parameters to retrieve those returned by the service.

To invoke asynchronous operations without receiving a callback notification from the client channel, you can call the begin operation as follows:

```
proxy.BeginSendMessage("Message", null, null);
```

To receive a callback, and provide some state information for the callback, do this:

```
AppState stateObject = new AppState();
// set state object properties
proxy.BeginSendMessage("Message", OnCallback, stateObject);
```

The callback can use the IAsyncResult parameter to access the state information and to retrieve any return values from the operation (if applicable):

```
private void OnCallback(IAsyncResult asyncResult)
{
  proxy.EndSendMessage(asyncResult);
  AppState stateObject = asyncResult.AsyncState as AppState;
  Debug.Assert(stateObject!=null);
}
```

You will practice working with asynchronous proxies in the following lab.

Lab: Protecting Shared Resources from Concurrent Access

In this lab, you will create an asynchronous client proxy and write code to issue concurrent requests to a singleton service. You'll then test different concurrency modes for the service, review the implications of concurrent access to a shared resource, and implement custom synchronization techniques.

Generating an asynchronous proxy

In this section, you'll review the existing service implementation and generate a proxy that is capable of making asynchronous calls to the service.

1. Open the startup solution for this lab at *<YourLearningWCFPath>\Labs\Chapter5\Concurrency\Concurrency.sln*. This solution contains an implementation of a service and console host, along with a shell client application without a proxy.

2. Review the existing implementation of the Messaging project before generating the client proxy. Open *MessagingService.cs* and you'll see that the service contract includes three operations: SendMessage1(), SendMessage2() and SendMessage3(). This contract is implemented on a singleton service shown in Example 5-11. This service maintains a counter and a dictionary of messages shared by all calls. Each operation increments the counter and adds an item to the dictionary.

Example 5-11. Singleton service implementation

```csharp
[ServiceContract(Namespace = "http://www.thatindigogirl.com/samples/2006/06")]
public interface IMessagingService
{
  [OperationContract(IsOneWay=true)]
  void SendMessage1(string message);

  [OperationContract(IsOneWay=true)]
  void SendMessage2(string message);

  [OperationContract(IsOneWay=true)]
  void SendMessage3(string message);
}

[ServiceBehavior(InstanceContextMode=InstanceContextMode.Single,
ConcurrencyMode=ConcurrencyMode.Single, UseSynchronizationContext=false)]
public class MessagingService : IMessagingService
{
  int m_messageCounter;
  Dictionary<int, string> m_messages = new Dictionary<int, string>();

  public void SendMessage1(string message)
  {
    m_messages.Add(m_messageCounter, message);
    Trace.WriteLine(string.Format("Message {0}: {1}", m_messageCounter, message));
    m_messageCounter++;
  }

  public void SendMessage2(string message)
  {
    m_messages.Add(m_messageCounter, message);
    Trace.WriteLine(string.Format("Message {0}: {1}", m_messageCounter, message));
    m_messageCounter++;
  }

  public void SendMessage3(string message)
  {
    m_messages.Add(m_messageCounter, message);
    Trace.WriteLine(string.Format("Message {0}: {1}", m_messageCounter, message));
    m_messageCounter++;
  }
}
```

3. The client code to invoke the service is not yet implemented. You will start by generating an asynchronous proxy for the client application. First, run the Host project, and then open the Visual Studio 2008 Command Prompt and type the following:

```
svcutil /a /d:"<YourLearningWCFPath>\Labs\Chapter5\Concurrency\Client"
/o:proxy.cs /config:app.config http://localhost:8000
```

This will produce two new files in the Client project directory: *proxy.cs* and *app.config*. Stop debugging and include these two files in the Client project.

You must also add a reference to the System.ServiceModel assembly so that the proxy can be compiled. After adding the reference, compile the project.

4. Add code to the client application to invoke each service operation asynchronously. Go to the Client project and open *Form1.cs*. Add a MessagingServiceClient proxy reference to the form and close the proxy in the Form1_FormClosed( ) event handler. Click event handlers for each button have already been created, but they have no code. Add code to each event handler to loop 200 times and invoke the corresponding operation asynchronously. Pass null to the callback and state parameters.

These additions to *Form1.cs* are shown in bold in Example 5-12.

Example 5-12. Client code to invoke each operation asynchronously

```csharp
public partial class Form1 : Form
{
  public Form1( )
  {
    InitializeComponent( );
    this.Text += ": Process " + Process.GetCurrentProcess().Id.ToString( );
  }


  MessagingServiceClient proxy = new MessagingServiceClient( );

  private void button1_Click(object sender, EventArgs e)
  {
    for (int i = 0; i < 200; i++)
    {
      proxy.BeginSendMessage1("SendMessage1( )", null, null);
      Application.DoEvents( );
    }

  }

  private void button2_Click(object sender, EventArgs e)
  {
    for (int i = 0; i < 200; i++)
    {
      proxy.BeginSendMessage2("SendMessage2( )", null, null);
      Application.DoEvents( );
    }
  }

  private void button3_Click(object sender, EventArgs e)
  {
    for (int i = 0; i < 200; i++)
    {
      proxy.BeginSendMessage3("SendMessage3( )", null, null);
      Application.DoEvents( );
    }
  }
```

Example 5-12. Client code to invoke each operation asynchronously (continued)

```
private void Form1_FormClosed(object sender, FormClosedEventArgs e)
{
  proxy.Close();
}
}
```

5. Run the solution and test its current implementation. From the Client user interface, click each button rapidly. You'll see trace statements emitted to the Output window. Since the service is configured for Single concurrency mode, concurrent thread access to the singleton service state is protected.

Allowing concurrent access to the singleton

Now you'll test what happens when the singleton allows concurrent access to operations and thus to its state.

1. Modify the service implementation to allow concurrent access to operations. Go to the Messaging project and open *MessagingService.cs*. Change the ConcurrencyMode setting for the service to Multiple, as shown in bold here:

```
[ServiceBehavior(InstanceContextMode=InstanceContextMode.Single,
ConcurrencyMode=ConcurrencyMode.Multiple, UseSynchronizationContext=false)]
public class MessagingService : IMessagingService
```

2. Test the results of this change by running the solution once again, and selecting all three buttons from the Client interface. At some point, you should receive an ArgumentException indicating that an attempt has been made to add a duplicate key to the dictionary. The reason for this error is that between the following two lines of code, two threads have concurrently entered:

```
m_messages.Add(m_messageCounter, message);
m_messageCounter++;
```

Before the m_messageCounter variable can be incremented by the first thread, another thread attempts to add an entry with the same counter value. The solution to this is to add manual synchronization to prevent threads from accessing the Add() method until the current thread has completed both the Add() and counter increment step.

Adding manual synchronization with global locks

When the service is configured for Multiple to allow concurrent access, you have to acquire your own lock to protect access to shared resources. In this section, you will acquire a global lock on the service type when a thread is accessing shared resources.

1. Acquire a global lock on the service object when SendMessage1() is invoked, using Monitor. Open *MessagingService.cs* and change the code for SendMessage1(), adding the code shown in bold here:

```
public void SendMessage1(string message)
{
```

```
try
{
  Monitor.Enter(this);
  m_messages.Add(m_messageCounter, message);
  Trace.WriteLine(string.Format("Message {0}: {1}", m_messageCounter,
message));
  m_messageCounter++;
}
finally
{
  Monitor.Exit(this);
}
}
```

When a thread enters this operation, the entire singleton instance will be locked, preventing other threads from accessing any and all operations until the lock is released.

2. You will also place a lock on other operations that access shared resources. For SendMessage2( ), use the shortcut for acquiring a global lock on the service object by applying the lock statement shown in bold here:

```
public void SendMessage2(string message)
{
  lock(this)
  {
    m_messages.Add(m_messageCounter, message);
    Trace.WriteLine(string.Format("Message {0}: {1}", m_messageCounter,
message));
    m_messageCounter++;
  }
}
```

Again, the service instance is protected from concurrent access until the lock is released.

3. For SendMessage3( ), use a declarative alternative to acquire a global lock. Apply the MethodImplAttribute to the operation passing the Synchronized element of the MethodImplOption enumeration. The changes are shown in bold here:

```
[MethodImpl(MethodImplOptions.Synchronized)]
public void SendMessage3(string message)
{
  m_messages.Add(m_messageCounter, message);
  Trace.WriteLine(string.Format("Message {0}: {1}", m_messageCounter, message));
  m_messageCounter++;
}
```

Now the singleton is protected from concurrent access using a different technique to lock the service type when a request thread successfully reaches an operation.

4. Test these changes to ensure that the concurrency issue has been resolved. Compile and run the solution once more, clicking each of the buttons in the Client interface. This time, no exceptions are thrown as the dictionary is populated.

Acquiring global locks when all operations are called is not much better than configuring the service for Single concurrency mode. It can yeild some performance benefit, however, if some operations do not access shared resources while others do. That means that multiple concurrent calls would be allowed to methods that do not acquire locks until a lock as been acquired.

Adding more granular synchronization for increased throughput

Instead of acquiring global locks when requests arrive to each operation that accesses shared resources, you can apply a more granular locking mechanism to protect related types of shared resources. In this section, you'll add a second dictionary and apply two separate Mutex instances to protect access to each.

1. Start by adding a new dictionary and message counter to the MessagingService definition in addition to creating two separate Mutex instances to protect each set. Open *MessagingService.cs* and beneath the definition for m_messageCounter and m_messages, construct a Mutex instance named m_mutex. In addition, add a new message counter and dictionary named m_messageCounter2 and m_messages2—and a Mutex instance to protect them named m_mutex2. The changes are shown in bold here:

```
int m_messageCounter;
Dictionary<int, string> m_messages = new Dictionary<int, string>();
Mutex m_mutex = new Mutex(false);

int m_messageCounter2;
Dictionary<int, string> m_messages2 = new Dictionary<int, string>();
Mutex m_mutex2 = new Mutex(false);
```

2. Modify SendMessage1() so that instead of using a global lock, you use the Mutex to acquire a more granular lock that protects access to the original dictionary and counter. The resulting code should look as follows:

```
public void SendMessage1(string message)
{
  try
  {
    m_mutex.WaitOne();

    m_messages.Add(m_messageCounter, message);
    Trace.WriteLine(string.Format("Message {0}: {1}", m_messageCounter,
message));
    m_messageCounter++;
  }
  finally
  {
    m_mutex.ReleaseMutex();
  }
}
```

3. Modify SendMessage2( ) to use the same lock, protecting access to the original dictionary and counter. Here's the resulting code for the operation:

```
public void SendMessage2(string message)
{
  try
  {
    m_mutex.WaitOne( );

    m_messages.Add(m_messageCounter, message);
    Trace.WriteLine(string.Format("Message {0}: {1}", m_messageCounter,
message));
    m_messageCounter++;
  }
  finally
  {
    m_mutex.ReleaseMutex( );
  }
}
```

Passing false to the Mutex constructor indicates that the Mutex is initially unowned. The first thread to call WaitOne( ) will acquire the lock (own the Mutex) until the same thread calls ReleaseMutex( ).

4. Lastly, modify the SendMessage3( ) operation so that the new counter and dictionary are accessed instead of the original. In addition, use the second lock, m_mutex2, to protect access to both resources. The resulting implementation is shown here:

```
public void SendMessage3(string message)
{
  try
  {
    m_mutex2.WaitOne( );

    m_messages2.Add(m_messageCounter2, message);
    Trace.WriteLine(string.Format("Message {0}: {1}", m_messageCounter2,
message));
    m_messageCounter2++;
  }
  finally
  {
    m_mutex2.ReleaseMutex( );
  }
}
```

By supplying different locks for different groups of resources, concurrent requests will be allowed into the service so long as they don't access the same resources. This increases overall throughput, as opposed to locking the entire object when any resources are being accessed.

5. Test the results by running the solution once again and selecting all buttons in the Client interface. No exceptions will be thrown.

Instance Throttling

In order to increase throughput at the service, multiple concurrent calls must be allowed to process. PerCall services are capable of multiple concurrent calls by default since each call is allocated its own service instance. PerSession services also allow throughput from unique clients, but allow only requests from the same client session one at a time. Single instancing mode allows only one request to be processed at a time by default, regardless of the client, which can impact throughput. To increase throughput for multithreaded sessions and singleton services, you can set the concurrency mode to Multiple and provide more granular synchronization mechanisms, as discussed in the previous section.

Regardless of the concurrency mode, server resources are not generally capable of servicing an unlimited number of concurrent requests. Each request may require a certain amount of processing, memory allocation, hard disk and network access, and other overhead. Sessions also require the allocation of resources that usually outlive an individual request, as do singletons. WCF provides a throttling behavior to manage server load and resource consumption with the following properties:

MaxConcurrentCalls
> Limits the number of concurrent requests that can be processed by all service instances. The default value is 16.

MaxConcurrentInstances
> Limits the number of service instances that can be allocated at a given time. For PerCall services, this setting matches the number of concurrent calls. For PerSession services, this setting matches the number of active session instances. This setting doesn't matter for Single instancing mode, since only one instance is ever created. The default value for this setting is 2,147,483,647.

MaxConcurrentSessions
> Limits the number of active sessions allowed for the service. This includes application sessions, transport sessions, reliable sessions, and secure sessions. The default value is 10.

Each of these settings are applied to a particular ServiceHost instance, and associated with all its service endpoints. To set these values declaratively, you associate a service behavior and add the <serviceThrottling> section. Example 5-13 shows a service behavior with the default throttling values.

Example 5-13. Default service throttling values

```
<system.serviceModel>
  <services>
    <service name="Counters.CounterService"
```

Example 5-13. Default service throttling values (continued)

```
behaviorConfiguration="serviceBehavior">
      <endpoint address="CounterService" binding="basicHttpBinding"
contract="Counters.ICounterService" />
    </service>
  </services>
  <behaviors>
    <serviceBehaviors>
      <behavior name="serviceBehavior">
        <serviceThrottling maxConcurrentCalls="16"
maxConcurrentInstances="2147483647" maxConcurrentSessions="10" />
      </behavior>
    </serviceBehaviors>
  </behaviors>
</system.serviceModel>
```

To configure this behavior programmatically, you can add a ServiceThrottle behavior to the service description at runtime. Keep in mind that if settings have already been provided, the behavior will already exist. The following example adds the ServiceThrottle behavior if it does not exist, to override the defaults:

```
ServiceHost host = new ServiceHost(typeof(Counters.CounterService));

ServiceThrottle throttle = hostA.Description.Behaviors.Find<ServiceThrottle>();
if (throttle != null)
{
  throttle.MaxConcurrentCalls = 30;
  throttle.MaxConcurrentInstances = 30;
  throttle.MaxConcurrentSessions = 100;
}

host.Open();
```

The appropriate settings for throttling behavior depend on a number of factors including the instancing mode for the service, the number of services exposed by the application, and the desired outcome of throttling. Binding configurations may also play a role in the desired throttling values. In the next sections, I'll discuss throttling in the context of these different factors.

Throttling PerCall Services

PerCall services allow for increased scalability and throughput since they release associated resources after each call and allow multiple concurrent calls to be processed by unique service instances. The throttle for MaxConcurrentCalls affects the number of concurrent service instances, thus the number of requests that can be concurrently processed at the service. A crude calculation can be made to see what your throughput would be. Let's assume you are hosting a single service type (ServiceHost instance) in a host process. If you set MaxConcurrentCalls to 30, and each request takes approximately .5 seconds to process, your host will be able to process approximately 60 requests per second for that particular service type. If requests take a fraction of a second on average, you may be able to process up to 300 requests per second.

MaxConcurrentInstances should be set equal or greater than MaxConcurrentCalls for PerCall services. The smaller of the two values will be used to throttle concurrent requests.

MaxConcurrentSessions has no affect on application sessions for PerCall services; however, it does affect transport sessions over named pipes or TCP and reliable or secure sessions over HTTP. In fact, services exposed over bindings that support sessions behave quite differently than the expected nature of PerCall services. Introducing sessions implies the allocation of resources at the server to maintain session state and a timeout setting to destroy inactive sessions and conserve resources. Throttling choices for PerCall services exposed over bindings that involve nonapplication sessions should still be evaluated in the same way as for application sessions. I'll discuss throttling for sessions in the next section.

Assuming pure PerCall services without any form of session, which means BasicHttpBinding and WSHttpBinding without reliable sessions or secure sessions—you could start with this throttling configuration:

```
<serviceThrottling maxConcurrentCalls="30" maxConcurrentInstances="30" />
```

The two throttles should be kept in sync since the lower of the two will affect throughput, as I mentioned. The setting for sessions is omitted here since it is ignored on this type of endpoint.

Throttling Sessions

As I have discussed earlier in this chapter, session can be present in the form of a transport session, a reliable session, a secure session, or an application session. Regardless of concurrency mode or the type of session, the throttle for MaxConcurrentCalls should be treated in a similar fashion. The goal is to allow a decent number of requests per second to get through, independent of the number of sessions.

MaxConcurrentInstances should meet or exceed the throttle for MaxConcurrentSessions where application sessions are involved. That's because the value actually limits the number of concurrent service instances that can be kept active to support application sessions.

As for MaxConcurrentSessions, some creativity may be involved in setting the correct throttle value. That's because sessions live longer than requests, yet they consume more resources, so they have conflicting requirements. On the one hand, a session lives longer than a request, thus you don't want to prevent users from connecting to the system if you can afford to accommodate them. On the other hand, if the nature of the session is allocating a large amount of memory (or other resources) the server may only be able to accommodate so many. The number of active application sessions is traditionally low compared to the number of users in the system, but if you have one million users, at 5 percent online, that still means 50,000 sessions might be requested at a given time.

As I discussed in the previous section, for BasicHttpBinding and WSHttpBinding without reliable sessions or secure sessions, this is a nonissue. Even for downstream services behind the firewall that support these outward-facing PerCall services, although you'll likely use NetNamedPipeBinding or NetTcpBinding, those calls will be short-lived and immediately close the transport session as in PerCall to free resources.

In the case of outward-facing PerCall services that also support reliable sessions or secure sessions (via WSHttpBinding), the overhead of the session is minimal compared to application sessions that maintain significant state. These sessions default to a 10 minute expiry, and if your service receives close to 300 requests per second, that could mean up to 180,000 requests in 10 minutes—some percentage of which are in the same session. Even at 5 percent, that's 9,000 concurrent sessions that might need to be supported to allow unique clients to get in the door. The bottom line is that you must be well aware of the usage patterns of your clients and make sure that you have the right balance to prevent request timeouts (waiting for a new session)—while also preventing excessive use of server resources.

For application sessions or transport sessions used in a traditional client-server scenario, the number of active sessions allowed should be weighed against the amount of resources consumed by each session. Ultimately, the purpose of the throttle in this case is to prevent the server from maxing out its memory usage or that of other limited resources consumed by each service instance. Similarly, services exposed over NetNamedPipeBinding or NetTcpBinding require a transport session, which is another resource that has configurable limits on Windows systems.

In any case, for a large-scale enterprise system, you might start with the following settings and adjust according to usage patterns and server capabilities:

```
<serviceThrottling maxConcurrentCalls="30" maxConcurrentInstances="1000"
maxConcurrentSessions="1000" />
```

Be sure to track performance counters for connection timeouts so that you can monitor the need to scale these values up or scale out the number of servers available to handle requests.

Throttling Singletons

For singleton services, MaxConcurrentCalls should follow the guidance provided for PerCall and PerSession services. MaxConcurrentInstances is irrelevant since only one instance of the singleton is ever created. MaxConcurrentSessions should be treated as described in the previous section, considering the distinction between reliable sessions and secure sessions versus application sessions or transport sessions. Again, for large-scale systems you might consider these settings as a starting point:

```
<serviceThrottling maxConcurrentCalls="30" maxConcurrentInstances="1"
maxConcurrentSessions="1000" />
```

Load Balancing and Failover

A very important consideration for scalable enterprise services is distribution, load-balancing, and session failover across multiple server machines. A single host process is not likely to handle more than 350 to 500 requests per second on average, thus the need for multiple processes and eventually multiple server machines to support the load. In a simple case where sessions are not involved (BasicHttpBinding or WSHttpBinding without reliable session or secure session), the distribution of work across server machines can be handled with *load balancing* techniques using hardware-level routing or Windows Network Load Balancing (NLB), for example.

Without sessions, it doesn't matter which server machine processes each request; the load can be distributed based on round-robin system, or more intelligent algorithms that detect the most available server. Figure 5-19 illustrates the same proxy making subsequent calls across multiple server machines.

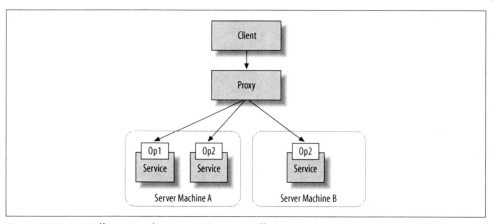

Figure 5-19. PerCall services do not require server affinity

The minute that sessions are introduced, it is important that requests are forwarded to the server maintaining the session. This requirement applies to any type of session, including application sessions, transport sessions, reliable sessions, and secure sessions. In the case of application sessions, the same service object must be allocated, as shown in Figure 5-20. In fact, application sessions in WCF rely on transport sessions, reliable sessions, or secure sessions—and these sessions are also tied to a particular machine.

Even if PerCall services are configured and a unique service object is allocated to each request, calls require server affinity when the underlying channel relies on non-application sessions. For example, endpoints exposed over NetTcpBinding rely on a

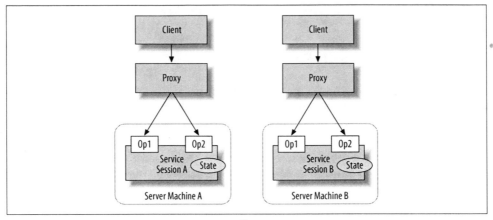

Figure 5-20. PerSession services require server affinity

socket connection, as shown in Figure 5-21. When reliable sessions or secure sessions are enabled, the channel manages session state at the client and service, as shown in Figure 5-22.

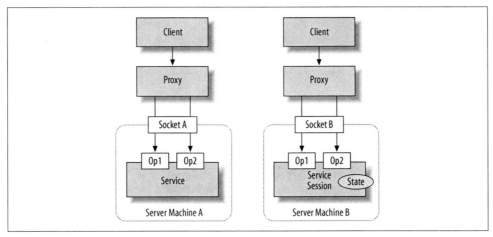

Figure 5-21. TCP sessions require server affinity

In the current release of WCF, session failover is not supported. That means that if a particular server machine goes down, the session cannot be picked up by another server machine that receives subsequent requests. To address this, you must enable *sticky sessions* in the hardware router or in NLB. This ensures that requests for the same session are always directed to the same server.

If a particular server goes down, the sessions on that server are lost. There isn't any way to avoid this problem for transport, reliable, or secure sessions. To prevent the loss of application sessions, you can manually save the contents of the session in a durable resource manager such as a database. With this configuration, you can use PerCall services and reload session data for each call.

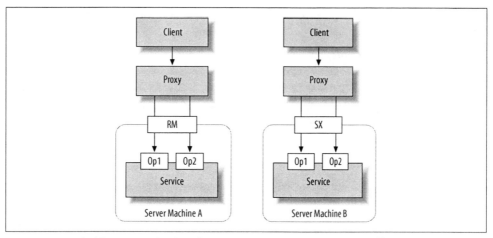

Figure 5-22. Reliable sessions (RM) and secure sessions (SX) require server affinity

 The release of the .NET Framework 3.5 includes a new feature for WCF—Durable Services. This feature makes it possible to have an application session for a WCF service persist to a database between calls and be restored on subsequent calls. This feature relies on the Windows Workflow Foundation persistence services. This feature does not preserve transport sessions, so the client must still recreate the proxy if a particular machine is no longer available, or if the session is terminated for some other reason.

Summary

In this chapter, you learned about instancing modes, concurrency modes and synchronization, as well as throttling behaviors for WCF services. You learned how to apply PerCall, PerSession, and Single instancing modes and the resulting effect on service object allocation; the implications of application sessions, transport sessions, reliable sessions, and secure sessions where exceptions and faults are concerned; how to throttle access for concurrent requests, service instances, and session allocation; and the impact of sessions on load balancing and failover scenarios. Some general recommendations you can take away from this chapter are:

- Use PerCall services whenever possible.
- Avoid PerSession concurrency mode for large-scale deployments.
- When PerSession services are required, try to use Single concurrency mode for synchronization. Require session-capable bindings in the service contract.
- Avoid Single concurrency mode for large-scale server deployments.
- When Single concurrency mode is required and clients are multithreaded, apply custom synchronization only if necessary to increase throughput.

- Always check the proxy state to ensure the server channel has not faulted.
- Try to throw `FaultException` derivatives from services to avoid unnecessarily faulting the server channel.
- Set throttling behaviors to yield as close to 300 requests per second for a single host process as possible and to ensure callers are able to acquire new sessions.
- Pay close attention to performance counters watching for timeouts due to session and request throttling. Adjust throttling and scale out the number of servers when necessary.
- Configure sticky sessions for services that support any form of session.

In the next chapter, I'll talk about reliability including reliable sessions, transactions, and queued services.

CHAPTER 6

Reliability

Distributed, service-oriented systems can be subject to intermittent network failures that can play havoc on the system's overall integrity. Systems must provide sufficient resiliency to failure, and they must be able to recover from failure in a controlled and predictable manner. WCF provides three key features to improve overall reliability and predictability of communications between clients and services: reliable sessions, support for transactions, and queued messaging.

Reliable sessions make it possible to overcome transient network interruptions over TCP, named pipes, or HTTP. When reliable sessions are enabled, clients will attempt to resend messages to a service if it is unavailable. One of the benefits of this is that it is interoperable, and thus can be used to improve the reliability of HTTP messaging.

Transactional programming techniques allow developers to guarantee operations are completed as a single atomic transaction. Performing transactions over process, machine and system boundaries are critical to the overall consistency of an enterprise application. With WCF, you can apply transactions across service boundaries over any protocol including HTTP with interoperable support for other platforms.

Queued messaging, when combined with transactions, provides a foundation for durable, reliable, and one-way messaging that can survive lengthy network outages and machine restarts. WCF uses Microsoft Message Queue (MSMQ) to provide this type of reliability.

In this chapter, I will elaborate on each of these features and explain how to apply them, and you will complete several labs to learn the features hands-on.

Reliable Sessions

When you send messages to a remote service, ideally you'd like to be sure they get there. If the message doesn't arrive, you probably want to resend it and try again. At a minimum, you want to know if the message has never arrived so that you can take corrective action. These delivery assurances are provided by some transport protocols such as TCP and named pipes, but not by the likes of HTTP. Even so, with TCP and named pipes, these assurances can be guaranteed only from point-to-point. If an intermediary, such as a proxy server or message router, exists between the sending and receiving applications, there are no guarantees beyond the assurance that the message reached the first network node in transit.

Reliable sessions improve application reliability in the following manner:

- Messages can be guaranteed to be delivered exactly once and in order, withstanding transient hiccups in network connectivity.
- These delivery assurances are not tied to a particular protocol, thus reliability is possible for HTTP protocol, for example.
- End-to-end reliability is supported so that message delivery is reliable over multiple hops.
- Reliability is based on the entire SOAP message, not just on individual IP packets.
- Reliable sessions are based on interoperable protocols, so delivery can be guaranteed between disparate operating and development platforms.

There is no question that reliability is necessary, but the decision to use reliable sessions is usually driven by the need to add reliability beyond what is already provided by the transport protocol. Given these drivers, you might optionally consider increasing the reliability of your TCP endpoints, but you most definitely should strive for reliable sessions for HTTP endpoints, which have no built-in delivery assurances. Across the board, reliable sessions are a great way to improve guarantees of one-way message delivery since they do not provide an explicit response indicating success or failure.

In the sections that follow, I'll explain how you can add support for reliable sessions to your WCF services. I'll talk about the configuration settings required and how to customize them for specific scenarios, explain the supporting architecture, and discuss the interoperable protocols that make reliable sessions possible across platform boundaries over HTTP.

Configuring Reliable Sessions

Reliable sessions are a binding feature. There are several configurable options for reliable sessions, some which can be directly edited on the standard binding configuration, and others that require a custom binding to control the defaults. The following options are available for reliable sessions:

Acknowledgement Interval
> This is a TimeSpan property indicating how long the receiver should wait before sending acknowledgements of messages received. The default value is 00:00:00.

2000000 (or 0.2 seconds). This property influences only bindings that support duplex communication because request-reply collects acknowledgements and returns them with the next available HTTP response.

Flow Control

This `boolean` property is enabled by default. When enabled, the sender will hold off on sending messages while the receiver transfer window buffer is full. This reduces the number of retry attempts necessary when the receiver buffer is full and thus unable to process an incoming message.

Inactivity Timeout

This is a `TimeSpan` property that controls the duration of the reliable session including channel layer activity. If no messages, including infrastructure messages such as reliable session acknowledgements, are transmitted during this elapsed time, the session is faulted. The default value is 00:10:00 (or 10 minutes).

Max pending Channels

This `int` property controls the number of concurrent requests for new reliable sessions that can queue before rejecting new requests. The default value is 4.

Max Retry Count

This `int` property controls the number of retry attempts from the sender when a message has not been acknowledged. The default value is 8, but this can be configured up to 20. After the number of retries is exhausted for a message, the session is faulted.

Max Transfer Size Window

This `int` property controls the number of messages held in the buffer at the sender or receiver. At the sender, messages are buffered to await acknowledgement. At the receiver, messages are buffered for delivery, optionally to ensure order. The default setting is 8.

Ordered

This `boolean` property is enabled by default, which means that if reliable sessions are enabled, messages are delivered in order.

In most cases, the default values for each of these options should be sufficient. The most common change, however, is to increase the inactivity timeout to better align with your policies on session expiry. For debugging purposes, you might also want to increase the retry count. Adjusting other features such as pending channels and transfer size window should only be considered when performance counters indicate sessions or messages are being rejected at the receiver, indicating a potential bottleneck.

Reliable sessions are supported on many of the standard bindings, and can also be configured with a custom binding. In addition, it is possible to require bindings to support ordered delivery. In the following sections, I'll elaborate on binding configurations and requirements.

Standard bindings

Several standard bindings support reliable sessions, specifically NetTcpBinding, WSHttpBinding, WSFederationHttpBinding, and WSDualHttpBinding. In the latter case, reliable sessions are always enabled and you can't turn it off. The other three bindings can be configured for reliable sessions declaratively by adding a <reliableSession> section to the binding configuration, as shown here:

```
<wsHttpBinding>
  <binding name="wsHttpRM">
    <reliableSession enabled="true" ordered="true" inactivityTimeout="00:10:00"/>
  </binding>
</wsHttpBinding>
```

You can achieve the same result by constructing the binding in code. Each binding that supports reliable sessions exposes a ReliableSession property as follows:

```
WSHttpBinding wsHttpSecure = new WSHttpBinding();
wsHttp.ReliableSession.Enabled=true;
wsHttp.ReliableSession.InactivityTimeout=new TimeSpan(0, 10, 0);
wsHttp.ReliableSession.Ordered=true;
```

Optionally, you can initialize the ReliableSession by using one of the overloaded constructors to enable reliable sessions—if you mean to use the defaults for reliable sessions:

```
WSHttpBinding wsHttp = new WSHttpBinding(SecurityMode.Message, true);
```

Using the standard bindings, you can only enable or disable reliable sessions, control the timeout, and control ordered delivery.

Custom bindings

To override the defaults for any of the other reliable session options, you must construct a custom binding. The following example illustrates how to create a reliable HTTP session. In this case, the <reliableSession> element allows you to configure all options:

```
<customBinding>
  <binding name="wsHttpCustomRM">
    <reliableSession acknowledgementInterval="00:00:00.2000000"
flowControlEnabled="true" inactivityTimeout="00:10:00" maxPendingChannels="4"
maxRetryCount="8" maxTransferWindowSize="8" ordered="true"/>
    <textMessageEncoding />
    <httpTransport/>
  </binding>
</customBinding>
```

To achieve the same results in code, you construct a CustomBinding instance, passing in each binding element:

```
CustomBinding wsHttpCustom = new CustomBinding(new ReliableSessionBindingElement(),
  new TextMessageEncodingBindingElement(), new HttpTransportBindingElement());
```

At least one transport and message encoding binding must be provided when constructing a custom binding. Other features are optional. This and other details about bindings are discussed in detail in Chapter 3.

You may need to use a custom binding at the service to increment the transfer window size or the pending channels buffer due to increased system load. Another reason might be to add reliable sessions to a named pipe channel. At the client, you may need to use a custom binding while debugging to increase the number of retry attempts.

Requiring ordered delivery

You can require service endpoints to have ordered reliable sessions by applying the `DeliveryRequirementsAttribute`, which has two properties: `RequireOrderedDelivery` and `QueuedDeliveryRequirements`. The former is related to reliable sessions. You can apply this attribute to a particular contract so that all services implementing the contract support ordered message delivery as follows:

```
[ServiceContract(Namespace = "http://www.thatindigogirl.com/samples/2006/06")]
[DeliveryRequirements(RequireOrderedDelivery = true)]
public interface IMessagingService
```

This makes sense when the semantics of the contract require that individual operations are processed in a particular order, or when calls to the same operation must be processed in order. If the contract does not require this behavior, you can also configure this at the service implementation and specify which contract this requirement applies to:

```
[DeliveryRequirements(RequireOrderedDelivery=true,
TargetContract=typeof(Messaging.IMessagingService))]
public class MessagingService : IMessagingService
```

If multiple contracts should be ordered, you can stack these attributes—one for each contract. Alternatively, you could apply the attribute to all contracts implemented by the service, but this is too coarse an action:

```
[DeliveryRequirements(RequireOrderedDelivery = true)]
public class MessagingService : IMessagingService
```

I'll discuss `QueuedDeliveryRequirements` later in this chapter with queued services.

In any case, when this attribute is applied, all endpoints for the affected service contracts are validated to ensure ordered delivery is supported by the binding. The following binding configurations will meet this requirement:

acknowledgements for each from the service at the receiving end. As messages arrive, the receiving channel sends acknowledgements after the configured acknowledgement interval, sometimes batching a range of acknowledgements in a single message. If ordered messaging is enabled, messages are buffered at the service up to the configured size of the transfer window. If messages are received in order, they are forwarded to the service immediately. If messages arrive out of order, the channel waits for messages that complete a sequence before forwarding them in order to the service.

Figure 6-1 illustrates the high-level architecture and the flow of messages as clients invoke operations, sending messages to the service. Each outgoing message awaits an acknowledgement, and in this case the Msg2 is acknowledged out of order. At the service, Msg1 would have been forwarded to the service immediately, while Msg2, Msg3, and Msg4 are not forwarded until Msg1 is received and acknowledged.

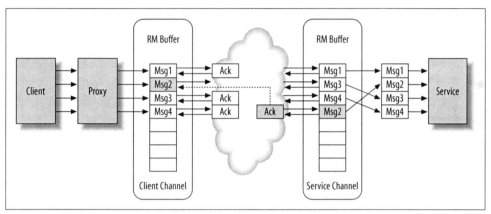

Figure 6-1. A high-level view of WCF's reliable session architecture

This can be reversed for services sending messages back to clients. In that case, the client buffer sends acknowledgements to the service and guarantees ordered delivery, if applicable, back to the client application. In fact, because reliable communication goes in both directions, it is more accurate to talk of the participants as initial sender or *initiator* and the ultimate receiver as *receiver*.

Session identifier

Each reliable session has a unique identifier that is used to correlate messages between client and service channels. As I discussed in Chapter 5, the session identifier is established when the initiator makes its first call to the receiver. This is done through a series of messages between initiator and sender, handled at the channel layer. The resulting session identifier can be accessed after the first call is made. If the initiator is the client proxy, it is available through the SessionId property as follows:

```
SessionServiceClient m_proxy = new SessionServiceClient();
string s = m_proxy.InnerChannel.SessionId
```

When reliable sessions are enabled, the session identifier at the client and the service are the same. Thus, accessing the `SessionId` property of the `OperationContext` yields the same value for the duration of the session:

```
OperationContext.Current.SessionId
```

 In Chapter 5, I discuss session identifiers and other behaviors related to various types of sessions, including the fact the HTTP bindings often rely on reliable sessions in order to establish an application session over HTTP. The following sample illustrates how to access reliable session identifiers: *<YourLearningWCFPath>\ Samples\ReliableSessions\ DuplexReliability*.

Session lifetime

The lifetime of a reliable session is tied to the lifetime of both the initiating and receiving channels. For example, when a client proxy is used to invoke a service, the client channel is constructed when the first call is made to the service. Likewise, on the first call, the service channel is constructed and a reliable session is established. The reliable session ends when any of the following occurs:

- The initiator disposes of its channel—for example, the client disposes of the proxy.
- The receiving channel reaches the configured timeout.
- The initiating or receiving channel is put into a faulted state.

When the initiator disposes of the channel, a series of messages are sent to the receiver to officially terminate the reliable session. I'll talk about the exact messaging shortly. In short, this is the most graceful way to terminate a reliable session since both sides are well informed and can shut down with ease, clearing any remaining buffered messages.

Any form of session timeout is typically controlled by the receive timeout setting of a binding, discussed in Chapter 5. This value is passed in to the reliable channel when it is constructed, so the following configuration would cause the reliable session to time out after 5 seconds instead of the default of 10 minutes:

```
<wsHttpBinding>
<binding name="wsHttpRM" receiveTimeout="00:00:05">
<reliableSession enabled="true" ordered="true" />
</binding>
</wsHttpBinding>
```

You can also explicitly set the inactivity timeout for the reliable session feature of a binding, as I discussed earlier. In that case, the shorter of the two timeout configurations will be respected. For example, the following configuration results in a 5-second timeout for the reliable session:

```
<wsHttpBinding>
    <binding name="wsHttpRM" receiveTimeout="00:00:05">
```

```
          <reliableSession enabled="true" ordered="true" inactivityTimeout="00:10:00"/>
      </binding>
  </wsHttpBinding>
```

The reverse is not always true, however. For example, if a service is configured to support sessions, then setting the activity timeout for reliable sessions to be less than the application session will not have effect. The receive timeout rules where application sessions are involved.

It simplifies matters greatly if you use the receive timeout setting to control session lifetime.

When the reliable session times out at the receiver, the initiator doesn't know of it until the next call—at which point an exception is propagated from the receiver indicating that the reliable session identifier is no longer known.

In Chapter 5, I discussed the effects of exceptions and faults on all types of session, including reliable sessions.

In the case where the receiver channel is put into a faulted state, a similar result occurs. In this case, the next call results in an exception indicating that the reliable session cannot continue since the channel has been aborted abruptly.

The following samples illustrate reliable session expiry due to timeout or faults:

- *<YourLearningWCFPath>\Samples\ReliableSessions\ ReliableSessionTimeout*
- *<YourLearningWCFPath>\Samples\ReliableSessions\ ReliableSessionFaults*
- *<YourLearningWCFPath>\Samples\ReliableSessions\ TimeoutHierarchy*

Retry attempts

Retry attempts are one of the key features of a reliable session. If the network connection is temporarily interrupted, for example, the initiator will attempt to resend each unacknowledged message up to the configured retry limit. This includes retrying attempts to create the reliable session, during the first call. If the retry attempt for a particular message reaches the retry limit, the reliable session is terminated by the initiating channel. As I mentioned earlier, to control the number of retries, a custom binding is required, since the standard bindings do not provide access to this option.

Session throttling

In Chapter 5, I discussed instance-throttling techniques that allow you to control load at the service. In that discussion, I explained how the `MaxConcurrentSessions` property of the `ServiceThrottle` behavior controls the number of concurrent sessions that can be allocated at the service. This property throttles any type of session, including reliable sessions. For example, for a `PerCall` service that enables reliable sessions, the following setting would allow only 1,000 reliable sessions to be active at one time:

```
<serviceThrottling maxConcurrentCalls="30" maxConcurrentInstances="1000"
maxConcurrentSessions="1000" />
```

Chapter 5 explains how to evaluate the right throttling configuration based on your service instancing mode and other factors.

WS-ReliableMessaging Protocol

When reliable sessions are enabled, a lot of work is done at the channel layer to achieve reliability based on the configured options at the client and service. Underneath it all, a sequence of interoperable messages are exchanged based on the *WS-ReliableMessaging* protocol (WS-RM), currently under review with the WS-RX OASIS subcommittee. The specification describes a standards-based protocol that includes a set of messages to be exchanged between parties to establish a reliable session, send messages within that session with receipt acknowledgements, and manage the lifetime of the session with cancellation and termination messages to be used accordingly.

Services publish their support for WS-RM through policy. As I mentioned earlier in this book, WS-Policy is an extensible standard that enables specific protocols to publish metadata. The WS-RM protocol is accompanied by a *WS-ReliableMessaging Policy* (WS-RM Policy) protocol for just this purpose. The protocol describes how to include WS-RM requirements for a service in the WS-Policy section of a WSDL document, or how to supply the same policy information over WS-MetadataExchange (discussed in Chapter 2). If you were to view the WSDL document for an endpoint that enables reliable sessions, you would see a WS-RM Policy assertion such as the following:

```
<wsrm:RMAssertion xmlns:wsrm="http://schemas.xmlsoap.org/ws/2005/02/rm/policy">
  <wsrm:InactivityTimeout Milliseconds="600000" />
  <wsrm:AcknowledgementInterval Milliseconds="200" />
</wsrm:RMAssertion>
```

More information about WS-ReliableMessaging and WS-ReliableMessaging Policy can be found here: *http://www.oasis-open.org/committees/ tc_home.php?wg_abbrev=ws-rx.*

Keep in mind that WCF implements an early version of WS-RM and WS-RM Policy that is not yet ratified by OASIS; thus, when the final version is approved, all platforms, including WCF will eventually update their respective stacks to reflect the latest namespace definitions and messaging formats. For now, many platforms have adopted the same version of the specification as WCF; thus, interoperability can be achieved.

In the sections to follow, I will describe the message exchange involved in establishing a reliable session between client and service to give you some idea how the channel layer achieves reliability.

Message flow

Figure 6-2 illustrates the flow of messages when a client proxy is used to initiate a reliable session with a service. The client constructs the proxy and invokes an operation. This is when the underlying client channel is constructed, and with reliable sessions enabled, it triggers a series of messages between client and service channel to establish the session. Once established, the operation is invoked, passing the sequence identifier, and if all goes well, the service sends a sequence acknowledgement. When the client proxy is closed, the session is terminated with another series of messages. Collectively, each of these messages is defined by the WS-RM specification as follows:

- CreateSequence
- CreateSequenceResponse
- SequenceAcknowledgement
- LastMessage
- TerminateSequence

In the following sections, I'll describe each of these messages and the key elements that make reliable sessions work.

The SOAP messages that I'm about to describe are based on the WS-RM specification implemented by the .NET 3.0 release of WCF. The OASIS specification, which is not yet ratified, has modified some of the namespaces and may also modify the message format before the final version is available. You can use this as an idea of how things work today for interoperability with web service stacks that also implement the same unratified version of WS-RM.

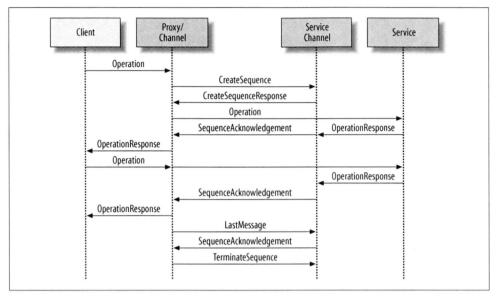

Figure 6-2. WS-RM message flow

CreateSequence

To initialize a reliable session, a CreateSequence message is sent to the service. This message essentially requests a new sequence from the service, awaiting a CreateSequenceResponse with the official sequence identifier. The <CreateSequence> element provides input to the request, as shown in Example 6-1.

Example 6-1. CreateSequence message

```
<s:Envelope xmlns:s="http://www.w3.org/2003/05/soap-envelope"
xmlns:a="http://www.w3.org/2005/08/addressing">
  <s:Header>
    <a:Action s:mustUnderstand="1">
http://schemas.xmlsoap.org/ws/2005/02/rm/CreateSequence</a:Action>
    <a:MessageID>urn:uuid:ede07111-fa4e-4be7-8d83-4400c36bba0a</a:MessageID>
    <a:To s:mustUnderstand="1">
http://localhost:8000/MessagingService/wsHttpRM</a:To>
  </s:Header>
  <s:Body>
    <CreateSequence xmlns="http://schemas.xmlsoap.org/ws/2005/02/rm">
      <AcksTo>
        <a:Address>http://www.w3.org/2005/08/addressing/anonymous</a:Address>
      </AcksTo>
      <Offer>
        <Identifier>urn:uuid:72e24996-f314-417e-8bc4-71eee5bb1dd5</Identifier>
      </Offer>
    </CreateSequence>
  </s:Body>
</s:Envelope>
```

CreateSequenceResponse

The response to the CreateSequence request includes an identifier to be used for sub-sequent communications between the initiator and receiver. This identifier is located in the <Identifier> of the <CreateSequenceResponse> message, shown in bold in Example 6-2.

Example 6-2. CreateSequenceResponse message

```
<s:Envelope xmlns:s="http://www.w3.org/2003/05/soap-envelope"
xmlns:a="http://www.w3.org/2005/08/addressing">
  <s:Header>
    <a:Action s:mustUnderstand="1">
http://schemas.xmlsoap.org/ws/2005/02/rm/CreateSequenceResponse</a:Action>
    <a:RelatesTo>urn:uuid:ede07111-fa4e-4be7-8d83-4400c36bba0a</a:RelatesTo>
  </s:Header>
  <s:Body>
    <CreateSequenceResponse xmlns="http://schemas.xmlsoap.org/ws/2005/02/rm">
      <Identifier>urn:uuid:d7db89c3-e09f-4dde-bfaa-60b90c4882f6</Identifier>
      <Accept>
        <AcksTo>
          <a:Address>http://localhost:8000/MessagingService/wsHttpRM</a:Address>
        </AcksTo>
      </Accept>
    </CreateSequenceResponse>
  </s:Body>
</s:Envelope>
```

SequenceAcknowledgement

All messages sent to the receiver for the duration of the newly created session must include the WS-RM <Sequence> header, which provides the session identifier and message number (for order). Example 6-3 shows this header in bold.

Example 6-3. Sequence header provided with each message

```
<s:Envelope xmlns:s="http://www.w3.org/2003/05/soap-envelope"
xmlns:r="http://schemas.xmlsoap.org/ws/2005/02/rm"
xmlns:a="http://www.w3.org/2005/08/addressing">
  <s:Header>
    <r:Sequence s:mustUnderstand="1">
      <r:Identifier>urn:uuid:d7db89c3-e09f-4dde-bfaa-60b90c4882f6</r:Identifier>
      <r:MessageNumber>1</r:MessageNumber>
    </r:Sequence>
    <!-- other headers -->
  </s:Header>
  <s:Body>...</s:Body>
</s:Envelope>
```

An acknowledgement must be sent for each message that arrives at the receiver channel. The acknowledgment is packaged in a <SequenceAcknowledgement> header that contains the following elements:

Identifier
: This contains the session identifier to correlate sessions.

AcknowledgementRange
: This contains the lower and upper range of acknowledged messages. This tells the client which messages have been acknowledged so that it can remove them from the client buffer.

BufferRemaining
: This indicates the message buffer at the receiver available to queue ordered messages. When flow control is enabled, the initiator will hold messages in its buffer if the service has no available buffer to receive new messages. This prevents the initiator from sending messages that would be rejected by the receiver, thus creating the need for retry attempts.

If the acknowledgement can be piggybacked on to a response message to the client, it will be, as shown in Example 6-4. In the case of one-way messages, or when a duplex-capable transport is employed such as named pipes or TCP, the sequence acknowledgement may be sent explicitly as shown in Example 6-5. The key difference in the latter case is that the action header indicates the SequenceAcknowledgement action (shown in bold) instead of the operation response action header, which indicates that the message may also contain information for the application.

Example 6-4. Sequence acknowledgment attached to response message

```
<s:Envelope xmlns:s="http://www.w3.org/2003/05/soap-envelope"
xmlns:r="http://schemas.xmlsoap.org/ws/2005/02/rm"
xmlns:a="http://www.w3.org/2005/08/addressing">
  <s:Header>
    <r:Sequence s:mustUnderstand="1">
      <r:Identifier>urn:uuid:72e24996-f314-417e-8bc4-71eee5bb1dd5</r:Identifier>
      <r:MessageNumber>1</r:MessageNumber>
    </r:Sequence>
    <r:SequenceAcknowledgement>
      <r:Identifier>urn:uuid:d7db89c3-e09f-4dde-bfaa-60b90c4882f6</r:Identifier>
      <r:AcknowledgementRange Lower="1" Upper="1"></r:AcknowledgementRange>
      <netrm:BufferRemaining
xmlns:netrm="http://schemas.microsoft.com/ws/2006/05/rm">8</netrm:BufferRemaining>
    </r:SequenceAcknowledgement>
    <a:Action s:mustUnderstand="1">
http://www.thatindigogirl.com/samples/2006/06/IMessagingService/SendMessageResponse
</a:Action>
    <!-- other headers -->
  </s:Header>
  <s:Body>...</s:Body>
</s:Envelope>
```

Example 6-5. Sequence acknowledgment message

```
<s:Envelope xmlns:s="http://www.w3.org/2003/05/soap-envelope"
xmlns:r="http://schemas.xmlsoap.org/ws/2005/02/rm"
xmlns:a="http://www.w3.org/2005/08/addressing">
  <s:Header>
    <r:SequenceAcknowledgement>
      <r:Identifier>urn:uuid:2fb53459-2dce-4607-abb0-2e6227b731b5</r:Identifier>
      <r:AcknowledgementRange Lower="1" Upper="3"></r:AcknowledgementRange>
      <netrm:BufferRemaining
xmlns:netrm="http://schemas.microsoft.com/ws/2006/05/rm">8</netrm:BufferRemaining>
    </r:SequenceAcknowledgement>
    <a:Action s:mustUnderstand="1">
http://schemas.xmlsoap.org/ws/2005/02/rm/SequenceAcknowledgement</a:Action>
    <!-- other headers -->
  </s:Header>
  <s:Body></s:Body>
</s:Envelope>
```

LastMessage

When the initiator is ready to terminate the session, it notifies the receiver with a final message—aptly named LastMessage—by the action header shown in Example 6-6. The <Sequence> element also contains a <LastMessage> element.

Example 6-6. LastMessage message

```
<s:Envelope xmlns:s="http://www.w3.org/2003/05/soap-envelope"
xmlns:r="http://schemas.xmlsoap.org/ws/2005/02/rm"
xmlns:a="http://www.w3.org/2005/08/addressing">
  <s:Header>
    <r:Sequence s:mustUnderstand="1">
      <r:Identifier>urn:uuid:72e24996-f314-417e-8bc4-71eee5bb1dd5</r:Identifier>
      <r:MessageNumber>3</r:MessageNumber>
      <r:LastMessage></r:LastMessage>
    </r:Sequence>
    <r:SequenceAcknowledgement>
      <r:Identifier>urn:uuid:d7db89c3-e09f-4dde-bfaa-60b90c4882f6</r:Identifier>
      <r:AcknowledgementRange Lower="1" Upper="3"></r:AcknowledgementRange>
      <netrm:BufferRemaining
xmlns:netrm="http://schemas.microsoft.com/ws/2006/05/rm">8</netrm:BufferRemaining>
    </r:SequenceAcknowledgement>
    <a:Action s:mustUnderstand="1">
http://schemas.xmlsoap.org/ws/2005/02/rm/LastMessage</a:Action>
  </s:Header>
  <s:Body></s:Body>
</s:Envelope>
```

TerminateSequence

A final message is sent by the initiator to notify it of session termination. The action header in this case indicates TerminateSequence, as does the message body, which passes the session identifier in the <TerminateSequence> element, as shown in Example 6-7.

Example 6-7. TerminateSequence message

```
<s:Envelope xmlns:s="http://www.w3.org/2003/05/soap-envelope"
xmlns:r="http://schemas.xmlsoap.org/ws/2005/02/rm"
xmlns:a="http://www.w3.org/2005/08/addressing">
  <s:Header>
    <r:SequenceAcknowledgement>
      <r:Identifier>urn:uuid:d7db89c3-e09f-4dde-bfaa-60b90c4882f6</r:Identifier>
      <r:AcknowledgementRange Lower="1" Upper="3"></r:AcknowledgementRange>
      <netrm:BufferRemaining
xmlns:netrm="http://schemas.microsoft.com/ws/2006/05/rm">8</netrm:BufferRemaining>
    </r:SequenceAcknowledgement>
    <a:Action s:mustUnderstand="1">
http://schemas.xmlsoap.org/ws/2005/02/rm/TerminateSequence</a:Action>
  </s:Header>
  <s:Body>
    <r:TerminateSequence>
      <r:Identifier>urn:uuid:72e24996-f314-417e-8bc4-71eee5bb1dd5</r:Identifier>
    </r:TerminateSequence>
  </s:Body>
</s:Envelope>
```

Lab: Working with Reliable Sessions

In this lab, you will have a chance to test how the reliable sessions feature makes it possible for clients to survive interruptions in network connectivity. To achieve this, you'll use tools such as SvcTraceViewer and TcpTrace.

Tracing reliable sessions messages

The first thing you're going to do is enable WCF tracing to monitor messages sent between the client and service when reliable sessions are enabled.

1. Open the solution for this lab located in *<YourLearningWCFPath>\Labs\Chapter6\ReliableSessions\ReliableSessions.sln*.

2. Before making any changes, run the Host and then the WinClient application (F5 should launch both in that order). From the client interface, click the Send button. As Example 6-8 illustrates, this will create an instance of the service proxy and send two messages. Message boxes will be presented before each message is sent and before the proxy is closed.

Example 6-8. Client code to invoke the MessagingService

```
try
{
  using (MessagingServiceClient proxy = new MessagingServiceClient())
  {
    MessageBox.Show(string.Format("About to send message {0}.", m_counter));
    proxy.SendMessage(string.Format("Message {0}", m_counter++));
```

Example 6-8. Client code to invoke the MessagingService (continued)

```
    MessageBox.Show(string.Format("About to send message {0}.", m_counter));
    proxy.SendMessage(string.Format("Message {0}", m_counter++));

    MessageBox.Show("About to close the proxy.");
  }
}
catch (Exception ex)
{
  MessageBox.Show(ex.ToString( ));
}
```

After verifying that the application works, stop debugging and return to Visual Studio.

3. Review the binding configuration for both client and service in the *app.config* for the Host and WinClient applications, respectively. You'll see that the service endpoint is configured for WSHttpBinding with reliable sessions enabled and security disabled, as shown in Example 6-9. Although you don't currently see the messaging between client and service, the fact that reliable sessions are enabled causes a number of messages to be exchanged to facilitate sessions over HTTP, as I discussed earlier.

Example 6-9. WSHttpBinding with reliable sessions enabled

```
<wsHttpBinding>
  <binding name="wsHttpRM">
    <reliableSession enabled="true" ordered="true" inactivityTimeout="00:10:00"/>
    <security mode="None"/>
  </binding>
</wsHttpBinding>
```

4. Now you will enable WCF tracing so that you can view the reliable session message exchange firsthand. Open the *app.config* file for the WinClient application. In the <system.serviceModel> section, add the <diagnostics> section and <system.diagnostics> sections shown in Example 6-10.

Example 6-10. Diagnostics configuration to enable service model trace

```
<configuration>
  <system.serviceModel>
    <diagnostics>
      <messageLogging logEntireMessage="true" logMessagesAtServiceLevel="true"
logMessagesAtTransportLevel="true"
maxMessagesToLog="100000" />
    </diagnostics>
  </system.serviceModel>
  <system.diagnostics>
    <sharedListeners>
      <add name="sharedListener"
type="System.Diagnostics.XmlWriterTraceListener"
initializeData="<YourLearningWCFPath>\logs\clienttrace.svclog" />
    </sharedListeners>
```

```
    <sources>
      <source name="System.ServiceModel" switchValue="Verbose, ActivityTracing" >
        <listeners>
          <add name="sharedListener" />
        </listeners>
      </source>
      <source name="System.ServiceModel.MessageLogging" switchValue="Verbose">
        <listeners>
          <add name="sharedListener" />
        </listeners>
      </source>
    </sources>
  </system.diagnostics>
</configuration>
```

The <diagnostics> configuration within the <system.serviceModel> element indicates that the entire message should be logged, which enables you to see SOAP message transfers. Tracing at the service level ensures that your application messages are captured, and tracing at the transport level ensures that reliable messages traces (among other messages) are also captured.

The <system.diagnostics> configuration tells WCF to log service model activities and messages and save them to an XmlWriterTraceListener in the specified file. If the file path is invalid, no output is generated.

5. Test the solution once again, clicking the Send button to invoke the service. After completing the test, stop debugging.

6. To view the messages that were traced to the log, you will open the *SvcTraceViewer* utility (*svctraceviewer.exe*) located in your Windows SDK directory, which should be similar to the following:

    C:\Program Files\Microsoft SDKs\Windows\v6.0\Bin\SvcTraceViewer.exe.

   Run SvcTraceViewer and open the log file you just created, *clientrace.svclog*. After clicking on the Message tab in the left pane and in the bottom right pane, the output should look similar to that shown in Figure 6-3. You can click each message in the left pane and view the messages I discussed earlier, related to the WS-ReliableMessaging specification.

Testing reliable session retries

In order to test reliable session retries, you will simulate a situation where the server is unavailable and view the retry attempts made by the reliable channel.

1. To begin with, you'll need to install a tool such as TcpTrace and use it to direct messages through an alternate path to the service. I'll provide you with instructions for TcpTrace.

   First, download TcpTrace from the following Url: *http://www.pocketsoap.com/ tcptrace/tcpTrace081.zip*. Once downloaded, unzip the files.

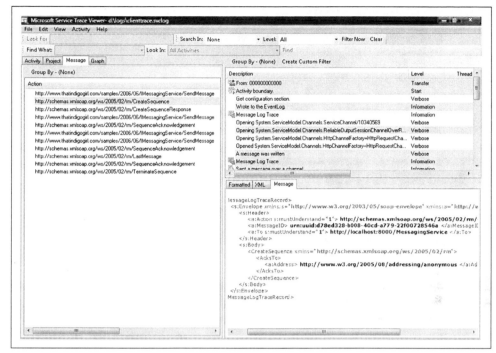

Figure 6-3. SvcTraceViewer output

2. Start a new TcpTrace session by running *TcpTrace.exe*. In the dialog provided (shown in Figure 6-4), enter the settings to listen on port 8080 and forwarded to destination port 8000.

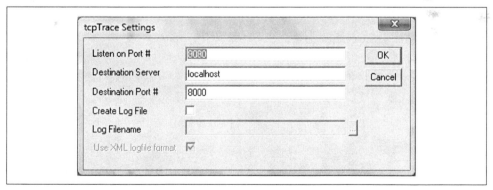

Figure 6-4. TcpTrace settings

3. Return to Visual Studio and modify the client configuration so that messages are sent through port 8080. Open the *app.config* file for the WinClient project and change the port for the client endpoint as shown in bold here:

```
<client>
  <endpoint address="http://localhost:8080/MessagingService"
  binding="wsHttpBinding" bindingConfiguration="wsHttpRM"
  contract="WinClient.localhost.IMessagingService" name="wsHttpRM">
  </endpoint>
</client>
```

4. You'll also have to modify the service to allow messages to arrive via port 8080. Open the *app.config* file for the Host project and change the endpoint address to use port 8080. This will allow the service model to support messages sent to port 8080. In addition, add a listenUri setting to listen on port 8000 so that TcpTrace messages can be forward to this port. The resulting service endpoint should look as shown here:

```
<service name="Messaging.MessagingService" >
  <endpoint address="http://localhost:8080/MessagingService"
  listenUri="http://localhost:8000/MessagingService"
  contract="Messaging.IMessagingService" binding="wsHttpBinding"
  bindingConfiguration="wsHttpRM"/>
</service>
```

5. Now test reliable messaging retries by running the solution again. This time, before you close the dialog to send the second message, stop the TcpTrace session by selecting File → Stop Trace. Once the session is stopped, close the dialog so that the client will attempt to send the second message and immediately return to TcpTrace to start the session once again (with the same settings). The result should be that the message is ultimately sent to the service, which you can confirm by checking the console output.

6. Close the client and service and refresh the view in SvcTraceViewer to see the latest messages sent between client and service. You should notice that after the first session was sent, several attempts are made to send the second message (this may vary based on how long you took to restart the TcpTrace session). Figure 6-5 illustrates this view.

 For more information on *SvcTraceViewer,* see the following resource: *http://msdn2.microsoft.com/en-us/library/ms732023.aspx.*

Transactions

Transactions are a critical feature for system reliability. Transactions are necessary when two or more activities must be coordinated as a single operation, ensuring that the system is always left in a consistent state. The only two viable options are to complete all activities successfully or to leave the system as it was before initiating either activity.

Figure 6-5. SvcTraceViewer output showing reliable session retries

The classic acronym to describe a *transaction* is that it must have ACID properties. *ACID* stands for the following:

Atomic

> A transaction is an all-or-nothing proposition. Suppose a transaction issues an instruction to insert two database records? The two inserts must be completed as a single, atomic operation that either succeeds or fails.

Consistent

> Transactions never leave the system in an inconsistent state. Suppose one of the inserts is completed and another caller sees the inserted record? If the transaction fails and that insert is reversed, the caller will have seen information that inaccurately represents the system state.

Isolated

> Independent transactions operate separately until they complete their work. Suppose a second transaction attempts to insert to one of the same table records while the first transaction is in progress? The second transaction should be locked out until the first has completed, either successfully or not. There are other levels of isolation, but this strict option yields the best possible result in most cases.

Durable

> No transaction should be lost. Suppose a machine goes down while a transaction is in progress? The resource being accessed (usually a database) and the transaction coordinator (usually the DTC) should survive this failure by storing enough information to complete the transaction when the machine is restored.

Transactional programming is a well-known technique for guaranteeing a consistent system state. While .NET 2.0 provides a mechanism for programmatically initiating transactions, WCF makes it possible for services to participate in distributed transactions across process and machine boundaries and to initiate transactions at the service tier. In this section, I will review core concepts of transaction management and explain how you can configure distributed transactions for your WCF clients and services.

Transaction Management

When several activities are included in a transaction, the ACID properties of the transaction can be enforced in a few ways. One approach could be to manually roll back would-be successful activities if even one of the activities in the transaction fails. This is known as a *compensating transaction*. There are a few problems with this approach, such as the following:

Activity coupling
> Each activity must somehow provide a rollback operation that can be called by the coordinator of the transaction—the party responsible for tracking the success or failure of each individual activity.

Coordination challenges
> If many downstream components, operations, and stored procedures are involved in the transaction, how can the coordinator possibly know of the overall success and failure of the transaction? Furthermore, how can the coordinator notify downstream code to roll back?

Although compensating transactions have their place in high-level workflows, fortunately, transaction management techniques exist to automate the plumbing required to coordinate activities across components, processes, machines, and more recently across platform boundaries. Transaction managers and resource managers facilitate this. A *transaction manager* monitors the progress of all participants in a transaction with the help of resource managers. A *resource manager* manages the state of a particular resource involved in a transaction. Resource managers can be associated with durable or volatile (in-memory) data. They cooperate with the transaction manager to commit or roll back based on the outcome of the entire transaction.

In the following sections, I will briefly summarize how transaction managers and resource managers ensure the ACID properties of a transaction and describe the available transaction managers to WCF.

Two-phase commit protocol

Two-phase commit protocol (2PC) is an algorithm that ensures all participating resource managers commit or roll back a transaction with atomicity. The roles in 2PC are that of a coordinator and that of one or more participating resource managers. The root coordinator of the transaction is in charge of starting the 2PC process.

There are two phases in 2PC. In Phase 1, the following activities occur:

- The coordinator asks each resource manager to prepare to commit.
- Each resource manager responds (votes) to commit or abort the transaction.
- The coordinator collects all votes and makes a decision to commit or abort the entire transaction.

In Phase 2:

- The coordinator asks each resource manager to commit or abort based on this decision.
- If the resource manager is asked to commit, it acknowledges completion of the activity. If asked to abort, it rolls back the activity.
- The coordinator waits for acknowledgment from all resource managers that the transaction was successfully committed.

All of this activity is well-encapsulated into the plumbing of transaction managers and resource managers, greatly simplifying the life of developers everywhere, not to mention providing more reliable guarantees of consistency.

Durable versus volatile resource managers

A resource manager can manage durable or volatile data. A *durable resource manager* is able to save information during Phase 1 of 2PC so that if the machine goes down or some other interruption in the transaction occurs, it can reenlist to the coordinator to complete the transaction according to the overall result. All enterprise database platforms, such as Microsoft SQL Server 2005, supply a durable resource manager to cooperate with transaction managers.

A *volatile resource manager* operates on in-memory data but is still able to enlist with the transaction coordinator so that it receives 2PC instructions. The key difference is that volatile resource managers are not able to survive machine failure (for example). The .NET Framework 2.0 introduced the System.Transactions namespace, which enables support for volatile resource managers by providing an enlistment interface and a lightweight transaction manager.

 This MSDN article describes volatile resource managers: *http:// msdn.microsoft.com/msdnmag/issues/05/12/transactions/default.aspx.*

TransactionScope

The System.Transactions namespace introduced with the .NET Framework 2.0 supplies a number of features to facilitate transactional programming. One key feature is the TransactionScope, which allows clients to create a code block that encapsulates activities to be included in a transaction. In Example 6-11, two methods are called as part of a transaction.

Example 6-11. Initiating a transaction with TransactionScope

```
using (TransactionScope scope = new TransactionScope( ))
{
  Operation1( );
  Operation2( );

  scope.Complete( );
}
```

By default, what this block of code does is construct a new transaction, or join an existing transaction if one already exists by an upstream caller. The consistency bit for the TransactionScope defaults to false. At some point before the end of the code block this consistency bit must be set to true to vote to commit the transaction. Any nested TransactionScope allocations, for example in downstream methods, must also set their own consistency bit, to vote on their part in the transaction. Calling the Complete( ) method sets this consistency bit.

Assuming that Operation1( ) or Operation2( ) enlist a resource manager at some point, the transaction manager will handle out-of-band communication with those resource to commit or roll back. None of this is visible to the developer. The choice of transaction manager responsible for coordinating all participating resource managers in the transaction depends on the type of resource managers enlisted, and the distribution requirements. I'll talk about this next.

 The following sample illustrates a simple TransactionScope: *<YourLearningWCFPath>\Samples\Transactions\ SimpleTransactionScope*.

Lightweight Transaction Manager

The .NET Framework 2.0 introduced a new Lightweight Transaction Manager (LTM) to improve performance when the following conditions are met:

- Any number of volatile resource managers can be enlisted.
- Only a single durable resource manager can be enlisted.
- No application domain or process boundaries can be crossed.

Figure 6-6 illustrates a scenario where the transaction root calls components (assemblies) in the same application domain, communicates with multiple volatile resource managers (VRM), and with a single durable resource manager (RM).

When a TransactionScope is first constructed, the LTM is the assigned transaction manager until one of the conditions is no longer met.

Kernel Transaction Manager

Windows Vista introduced the Kernel Transaction Manager (KTM) to manage the resource managers associated with its Transactional Registry (TxR) and its transaction

---

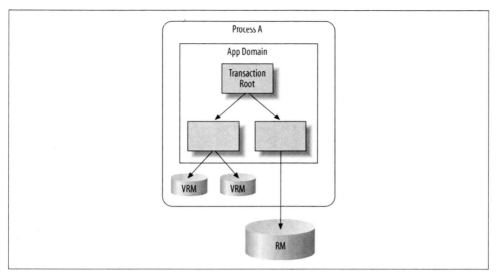

Figure 6-6. An LTM transaction

filesystem, called Transactional NTFS (TxF). When the downstream code within a `TransactionScope` enlists one of these resource managers, the LTM is promoted to KTM automatically. Developers don't see this promotion, but the result is that the new KTM will handle coordination of these new resource managers and still communicate to any enlisted LTM resource managers to make sure that all participants commit or roll back. The KTM is enlisted when the following conditions are met:

- Any number of volatile resource managers can be enlisted.
- Only a single durable or kernel resource manager can be enlisted.
- No application domain or process boundaries can be crossed.

Figure 6-7 illustrates a scenario in which several volatile resource managers and the transactional registry are enlisted in a single transaction.

Distributed Transaction Coordinator

The Microsoft Distributed Transaction Coordinator (DTC) is a transaction manager that is able to coordinate resource managers that span application domain, process, and machine boundaries on the same network. Before the LTM was introduced, the DTC was the only option for transaction coordination with a resource manager, which added overhead to even the simplest transactions. With .NET 2.0, the LTM will first promote to KTM based on the conditions discussed in the previous section but will promote to DTC if any of the following conditions are met:

- An application, process, or machine boundary is crossed.
- More than one durable resource manager is enlisted.

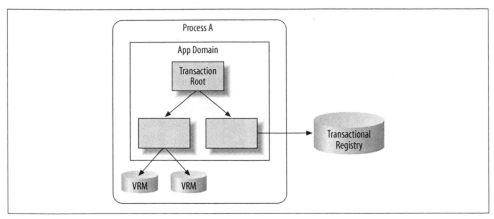

Figure 6-7. A KTM transaction

You can configure local DTC properties using the Component Services MMC Snap-In, shown later in the chapter in Figure 6-12.

The DTC on each machine collects votes for its respective volatile and durable resource managers involved in the transaction. The machine that holds the transaction root also becomes the root DTC, which collects votes from the other machines. Figure 6-8 illustrates this.

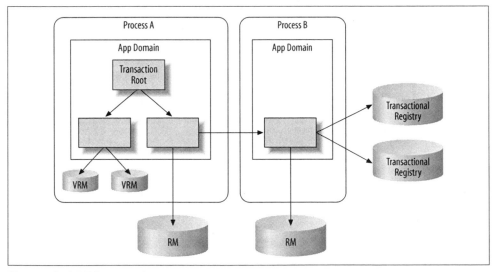

Figure 6-8. A DTC transaction

WS-AtomicTransaction and WS-Coordination protocols

WS-AtomicTransaction (WS-AT) and *WS-Coordination* (WS-COOR) are interoperable protocols that enable message-based distributed transactions over HTTP and across platform boundaries—currently under review with the WS-TX OASIS

subcommittee. Windows platforms support these protocols through the DTC once the WS-AT feature is enabled. In fact, you can think about these two protocols as message-based formats of the messaging that happens today over RPC when the DTC distributes transactions across boundaries and coordinates 2PC activities.

 Unlike WS-RM, the detailed messaging necessary to facilitate interoperable flow of transactions and related coordination activities is too long and complex to discuss here. Based on my earlier discussion of WS-RM, you can imagine that a number of well-defined messages and headers are exchanged, leveraging the distributed transaction identifier assigned by the DTC to correlate those messages. Like with WS-RM, WCF implements an early version of WS-AT and WS-COOR that has not yet been ratified by OASIS; however, there are several platforms that support this early version of the standards in order to support interoperable exchanges. You can read more about the actual protocols involved here: *http://www.oasis-open.org/committees/tc_home.php?wg_abbrev=ws-tx*.

With WS-AT support enabled, the DTC is able to flow transactions and coordinate those transactions regardless of platform and transport protocol. The communication between participants still crosses machine boundaries as shown in Figure 6-9—the key difference is that the same configuration can be achieved over HTTP, as shown in Figure 6-10.

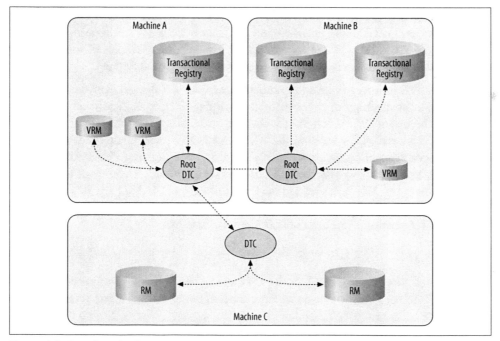

Figure 6-9. Distributed DTC transaction

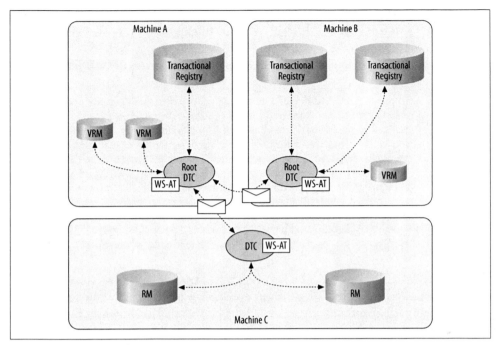

Figure 6-10. Distributed DTC transaction using WS-AT

Promotion to WS-AT is a function of the binding configuration in WCF. When transactions are flowed from client to service, if both sides are configured to support WS-AT, then the DTC will use the necessary WS-AT and WS-COOR messaging at the channel layer. The developer doesn't see these message exchanges.

Even if WS-AT protocol is enabled, and transactions are flowed between machines over HTTP, the messaging involved also includes DTC-specific information that optimizes the use of WS-AT on Windows machines. Thus, the WS-AT interoperable messaging is a conduit for sending the XML required for interoperable transactions, plus some compact information that only the DTC will bother to interpret—so that the DTC doesn't have to parse the XML increasing overhead. If you want to force the DTC to always use WS-AT, you can add the following DWORD registry key to the WS-AT registry configuration section and set it to 0: *HKEY_LOCAL_MACHINE\ SOFTWARE\Microsoft\WSAT\3.0\OleTxUpgradeEnabled*.

Enabling WS-AT

You can configure WS-AT through the DTC using the WS-AT Configuration MMC Snap-In (WsatUI). First, you must add the snap-in using the following command-line instruction:

```
Regasm.exe /codebase wsatui.dll
```

You can find *regasm.exe* in the *\Bin* directory of the Windows SDK. You may need to include the full path in the command-line instruction—for example, *C:\Program Files\Microsoft SDKs\Windows\v6.0\Bin\regasm.exe /codebase wsatui.dll*.

Once this is done, you'll be able to see a WS-AT tab added to the DTC properties dialog (Figure 6-11). This is where you will enable WS-AT support on the machine.

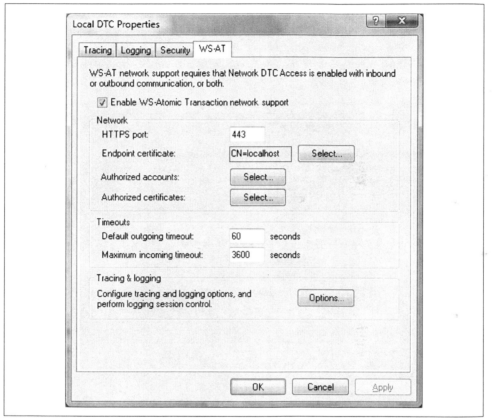

Figure 6-11. WS-AT configuration settings

On Windows XP machines, you must install a hot fix before you can enable WS-AT. The hot fix, with installation instructions, can be found at *http://www.microsoft.com/downloads/details.aspx?familyid=86B93C6D-0174-4E25-9E5D-D949DC92D7E8& displaylang=en*.

Recall from Figure 6-9 that on Windows machines, the DTC on each machine is responsible for coordinating distributed transactions. So for WS-AT and WS-COOR exchanges to work, WS-AT capabilities must be enabled on each machine and configured in a compatible manner. This requires taking a look at the DTC Security settings first. From the Security tab of the DTC (Figure 6-12), you should do the following:

- Enable Network DTC Access.
- Set the Transaction Manager Communication properties so that inbound and outbound are enabled according to the machine's requirements. For example, client machines should be configured to allow outbound transactions to downstream services. Server machines that hold participating resource managers should be configured for inbound transactions and possibly outbound transactions if they will flow to other downstream services distributed to other machines.
- For the most secure results, enable mutual authentication for inbound or outbound communication. For testing purposes, you may disable authentication initially. If authentication is required, certificates must be configured for WS-AT (to be discussed).

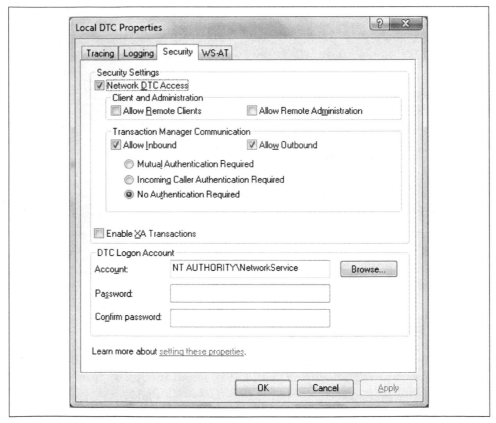

Figure 6-12. Security configuration for the DTC

Then, from the WS-AT tab of the DTC (Figure 6-11):

- Enable WS-AtomicTransaction network support.
- Configure the HTTPS port to be used.

- Select an endpoint certificate and be sure that this certificate matches the machine name.

Once all machines are configured for WS-AT support, your WCF clients and services will be able to distribute transactions over HTTP protocol. Furthermore, if non-Windows systems are participating in the transaction, so long as they have their own transaction manager that supports WS-AT and is configured in a compatible way, you can distribute transactions to those endpoints as well. The root transaction coordinator will be the one that initiated the transaction.

 More detailed instructions for installing the WS-AT can be found here: *http://msdn2.microsoft.com/en-us/library/ms732007.aspx*.

Transactions and System Tiers

A service-oriented enterprise system typically includes many tiers, including clients, services, business components, data access tiers, and of course the actual data store that usually includes stored procedures invoked by the data access tier. Transactions can be initiated at any of these tiers, depending on the application scenario. Stored procedures typically coordinate instructions to multiple database objects as part of a transaction. The data access tier may not need to coordinate calls to multiple stored procedures, and thus can rely on the latter to coordinate the transaction at that level, as shown in Figure 6-13A.

 The following sample illustrates the use of transactions without the presence of a WCF service: *<YourLearningWCFPath>\Samples\Transactions\ TransactionsNoServices*.

When the data access tier coordinates multiple calls to database objects directly or through multiple stored procedures, it may need to wrap that code in a transaction. This ensures that calls to mutually exclusive stored procedures are committed as a single atomic operation, or rolled back. In this case, the data access tier would create a TransactionScope to wrap both calls, and the stored procedures would each join the root transaction. Figure 6-13B illustrates this. Likewise, business tier components may need to include calls to other components as part of a transaction, as shown in Figure 6-13C.

In most cases, each stored procedure or method should care only about the transaction it is coordinating and should either create a new transaction to address its needs or participate in the caller's transaction if one is present. To join an existing transaction, downstream methods must be able to access the caller's transaction, which might mean crossing a service boundary, as shown in Figure 6-13D.

In the next section, I'll describe how you can configure transaction support for your WCF services.

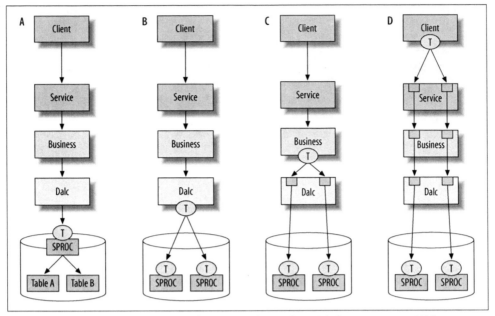

Figure 6-13. Transactions initiated at the (A) stored procedure; (B) data access tier; (C) business tier; (D) client (crossing service boundaries)

Configuring WCF Transactions

Transaction flow between clients and services is a function of the binding configuration, the service contract requirements and the behavior of the service operation being invoked.

- The configured binding must be able to support transaction flow and the feature must be enabled.
- The appropriate transaction protocol must be selected.
- Operations defined in the service contract must specify support for transaction flow.
- Service operations must determine if they require transactions and if they are willing to join a client transaction.

In this section, I'll discuss the implications of each of these settings.

Enabling transaction flow

For a client transaction to flow across a service boundary, the binding must support transaction flow, which immediately limits you to one of these standard bindings: NetNamedPipeBinding, NetTcpBinding, WSHttpBinding, WSDualHttpBinding, and WSFederationHttpBinding. Each binding has a TransactionFlow property that is set to false by default. To enable transaction flow, you can set this property to true using declarative configuration as shown here for WSHttpBinding:

```
<wsHttpBinding>
  <binding name="wsHttpTx" transactionFlow="true" />
</wsHttpBinding>
```

Programmatically, you set the TransactionFlow property like this:

```
WSHttpBinding wsHttp = new WSHttpBinding();
wsHttp.TransactionFlow = true;
```

All the aforementioned bindings can be initialized in a similar fashion. For custom bindings, transaction flow is enabled by adding the <transactionFlow> binding element, as shown here:

```
<customBinding>
  <binding name="wsHttpCustomTx" >
    <transactionFlow transactionProtocol="WSAtomicTransactionOctober2004" />
    <textMessageEncoding />
    <httpTransport/>
  </binding>
</customBinding>
```

In code, you can achieve the same result:

```
CustomBinding wsHttpCustomTx = new CustomBinding();
wsHttpCustomTx.Elements.Add(new
TransactionFlowBindingElement(TransactionProtocol.WSAtomicTransactionOctober2004));
wsHttpCustomTx.Elements.Add(new TextMessageEncodingBindingElement());
wsHttpCustomTx.Elements.Add(new HttpTransportBindingElement());
```

Enabling transaction flow makes it possible for a client transaction to be made available to the service. Otherwise, the client transaction will not be flowed to any of the service calls.

The following samples illustrate how to configure the key standard bindings for transactions:

- *<YourLearningWCFPath>\Samples\Transactions\ TransactionsBindings*
- *<YourLearningWCFPath>\Samples\Transactions\ TransactionsBindings_Code*

Selecting a transaction protocol

As I mentioned earlier, the DTC enables transaction flow across process and machine boundaries using either standard RPC messaging or interoperable messaging based on WS-AT. In some cases, when you enable transaction flow for your service endpoints, you can also control the protocols supported for transaction flow. The TransactionProtocol abstract type has two derivations that define the two options for protocol selection. TransactionProtocol exposes static properties to select the following implementations at runtime:

OleTransactions

This setting indicates that your service endpoint supports standard RPC messaging used by the DTC (OleTx) to coordinate transactions.

`WSAtomicTransactionOctober2004`

This setting indicates support for WS-AT interoperable messaging if the DTC supports it. Currently this is the only version of the specification that is supported by WCF.

For bindings that use HTTP protocol, the `TransactionProtocol` setting is always `WSAtomicTransactionOctober2004`, so you needn't specify it when you configure the binding. Over HTTP, the DTC must use WS-AT to coordinate transactions. For TCP and named pipes, you have the option to choose either setting. By default, `NetTcpBinding` and `NetNamedPipeBinding` support `OleTransactions`. In the event that your services may participate in transactions initiated over HTTP, you should enable WS-AT support. This can be done in the binding configuration as follows:

```
<netTcpBinding>
  <binding name="netTcpTx" transactionFlow="true"
  transactionProtocol="WSAtomicTransactionOctober2004" >
  </binding>
</netTcpBinding>
```

In code, you can achieve the same result by setting the `TransactionProtocol` property explicitly:

```
NetTcpBinding netTcpTx = new NetTcpBinding( );
netTcpTx.TransactionFlow = true;
netTcpTx.TransactionProtocol = TransactionProtocol.WSAtomicTransactionOctober2004;
```

`NetNamedPipeBinding` is configured in the same manner.

OleTx messaging is much faster than WS-AT but communications are the same. In order to enhance performance on Windows, WS-AT protocol as implemented by the DTC also passes OleTx information so that the DTC can optimize processing of those messages, reducing the overhead of parsing WS-AT messages. This has no effect on interoperable endpoints.

Transaction flow options

Enabling transaction flow at the binding makes it possible for a client transaction to flow across service boundaries, but each operation in the service contract ultimately determines its own transaction flow requirements. The `TransactionFlowAttribute` can be applied to each operation in the service contract to explicitly choose one of the following `TransactionFlowOption` enumeration values:

`NotAllowed`

This setting indicates that the service operation will not accept requests that flow a client transaction. If the client does flow a transaction, a `ProtocolException` is thrown at the service. This is the default setting and should be used for service operations that should never participate in a client transaction, such as a one-way operation or an auditing or logging operation.

Mandatory

A client transaction must be flowed to the service or a `ProtocolException` occurs indicating as much. The service model will make the client transaction available for the operation to join. This option is useful only when the service contract includes operations that are always called together and should always be part of a transaction. This should be avoided for the tight coupling it implies on the service contract design.

Allowed

If a client transaction is flowed to the service, the service model will make the transaction available for the service operation to join. This option is the most useful, allowing clients to opt-in to call service operations as part of a transaction.

Example 6-12 shows a service contract in which `TransactionFlowAttribute` is applied to each operation. The choice of `TransactionFlowOption` can be unique to each operation's requirements.

Example 6-12. Setting TransactionFlowOption at the service contract

```
[ServiceContract(Namespace = "http://www.thatindigogirl.com/samples/2006/06")]
public interface ICountersService
{
  [OperationContract]
  [TransactionFlow(TransactionFlowOption.Allowed)]
  void ResetCounters( );

  [OperationContract]
  [TransactionFlow(TransactionFlowOption.Mandatory)]
  void SetCounter1(int counterValue);

  [OperationContract]
  [TransactionFlow(TransactionFlowOption.Mandatory)]
  void SetCounter2(int counterValue);

  [OperationContract]
  [TransactionFlow(TransactionFlowOption.NotAllowed)]
  List<CounterInfo> GetCounters( );
}
```

Clients are able to respect the requirements of the `TransactionFlowOption` for each operation because the service metadata includes this information. When the `TransactionFlowOption` is set to `Allowed`, the WSDL document will include a policy assertion for that operation, indicating that transaction flow is optional as shown here:

```
<wsat:ATAssertion wsp:Optional="true"
xmlns:wsat="http://schemas.xmlsoap.org/ws/2004/10/wsat"
xmlns:wsp="http://schemas.xmlsoap.org/ws/2002/12/policy" />
```

If the operation is configured for `Mandatory` transaction flow, the policy assertion looks like this:

```
<wsat:ATAssertion xmlns:wsat="http://schemas.xmlsoap.org/ws/2004/10/wsat" />
```

For operations that do not use the TransactionFlowAttribute or explicitly indicate it is NotAllowed, there is no policy assertion specified.

 The same information included in the WSDL document is also available at runtime using WS-MetadataExchange.

SvcUtil uses this information to generate the client proxy; so, the client-side version of the service contract reflects the same TransactionFlowOption as was defined at the service.

Service operations and transactions

Although the TransactionFlowOption does influence the presence of a client transaction, it does not guarantee that a service operation will use the transaction. In the implementation of a service contract, each operation must opt-in to support transactions. This is controlled by the TransactionScopeRequired property of the OperationBehaviorAttribute, as shown here:

```
[OperationBehavior(TransactionScopeRequired=true)]
public void ResetCounters( )
{...}
```

This property can be set to true or false with the following results:

- When set to false, which is the default setting, the service will never join a client transaction, nor will it automatically create a new transaction. That means that if the service code requires a transaction, it would have to do so manually using a TransactionScope block.

- When set to true, if a client transaction is flowed to the service, the service operation will join that transaction. If a client transaction is not flowed, a new transaction is created for the service operation to execute in.

An indicator that the service is participating in the client transaction is when the DistributedIdentifier of the current transaction is set:

```
Transaction.Current.TransactionInformation.DistributedIdentifier
```

Another property of the OperationBehaviorAttribute that affects how transactions are handled is the TransactionAutoComplete property. By default, this property is set to true, which means that the consistency bit is set to true automatically if no exceptions are thrown. In rare cases, you may want control over completing the transaction in code. In that case, you can explicitly set TransactionAutoComplete to false and use the SetTransactionComplete( ) method of the OperationContext, as shown here:

```
[OperationBehavior(TransactionScopeRequired=true,TransactionAutoComplete=false)]
public void ResetCounters( )
{
  // do work
  OperationContext.Current.SetTransactionComplete( );
}
```

Controlling IsolationLevel

The `System.Transactions` namespace defines an `IsolationLevel` enumeration that defines the following isolation options: `Chaos`, `ReadCommitted`, `ReadUncommitted`, `RepeatableRead`, `Serializable`, `Snapshot`, and `Unspecified`. The last of these settings, `Unspecified`, is the default, so this configuration is equivalent:

```
[ServiceBehavior(TransactionIsolationLevel=IsolationLevel.Unspecified)]
public class CountersService : ICountersService
```

This setting means that the service will use the isolation level specified by the client in its `TransactionScope`. In the absence of a client transaction, `Serializable` isolation is used.

If the service specifies a specific scope, such as `Serializable`, the client is obligated to flow a transaction using the same scope. Consider this service configuration:

```
[ServiceBehavior(TransactionIsolationLevel=IsolationLevel.Serializable)]
public class CountersService : ICountersService
```

The client must initialize its `TransactionScope` in this way to be compatible:

```
TransactionOptions options = new TransactionOptions();
options.IsolationLevel = IsolationLevel.Serializable;

using (TransactionScope scope = new
TransactionScope(TransactionScopeOption.Required, options))
{
  m_proxy.SetCounter1(int.Parse(this.txtCounter.Text));
  m_proxy.SetCounter2(int.Parse(this.txtCounter.Text));
  scope.Complete();
}
```

If the `IsolationLevel` passed by the client is different from the service, a `ProtocolException` is thrown.

Using `Serializable` isolation is the safest way to maintain a consistent system, but it also yields the least throughput. Here are some general recommendations for choosing an isolation level:

- To enforce consistency, use `Serializable` isolation at the service. Clients will then be forced to also use `Serializable` isolation when they flow transactions.

- For services where consistency is not as critical, and it is acceptable for clients to determine isolation and leave the default `Unspecified`, allowing clients to set the isolation level.

- Any other isolation level should be carefully considered beforehand.

The following sample illustrates how to configure isolation level: *<YourLearningWCFPath>\Samples\Transactions\IsolationLevel*.

Transaction timeout

Transaction timeout settings help you to avoid system deadlocks. By default, the transaction associated with a service operation is set to time out at 60 seconds. This setting is controlled through the `ServiceTimeoutsBehavior`. You can set this declaratively in configuration by adding a `<serviceTimeouts>` behavior section, as follows:

```
<serviceBehaviors>
  <behavior name="serviceBehavior">
    <serviceTimeouts transactionTimeout="00:00:01"/>
  </behavior>
</serviceBehaviors>
```

You can also control the timeout setting from the `ServiceBehaviorAttribute`, as shown here:

```
[ServiceBehavior(TransactionTimeout="00:00:01")]
public class CountersService : ICountersService
```

A `ProtocolException` is thrown when the service operation times out, and this can leave the system in an inconsistent state. The default of 60 seconds should be acceptable for most systems, although it is feasible that a longer running request could take up to 120 seconds while the system still maintains an average of closer to 60 seconds to process each request.

 This sample illustrates transaction timeout: *<YourLearningWCFPath>\ Samples\Transactions\TransactionTimeout.*

Client configuration

For a client to flow transactions to a service, several requirements must be met:

- Transaction flow must be enabled for the binding associated with the client endpoint configuration. When you generate a proxy and configuration using SvcUtil, if the service requires transactions (`TransactionFlowOption.Mandatory`), then the client binding will be configured to enable transaction flow. Otherwise, transaction flow is disabled, allowing the client to opt-in to this feature.

- A transaction must be present in the client thread invoking the service. This is usually accomplished by creating a `TransactionScope` block somewhere in the call chain before executing the proxy.

- The operation being invoked must be configured to allow the client transaction to flow to the service. The client's version of the service contract should reflect this by specifying `TransactionFlowOption.Allowed` or `TransactionFlowOption.Mandatory`. If the former, when a transaction is present it will be flowed to the service, otherwise it is not. If the latter, a client transaction is required or a `ProtocolException` is thrown by the client channel.

Essentially, the only thing the client has to worry about after generating the proxy and configuration file is to decide it wants to invoke the service as part of a transaction, create the TransactionScope, and enable flow if it has not already been enabled.

 You'll practice using these features in the transactions lab shortly.

Transactions and sessions

When sessions are enabled at the service (InstanceContextMode.PerSession, covered in Chapter 5) you expect the same service instance to handle all requests for the lifetime of the client proxy. This way, the service instance can manage the session state that your application requires. When transactions are introduced to this equation, although the same session identifier is maintained for the duration of the proxy, as you would expect, the service instance is released after each operation that participates in a transaction. Consider the following client code that invokes a PerSession service:

```
CountersServiceClient proxy = new CountersServiceClient();

using (TransactionScope scope = new TransactionScope())
{
  proxy.SetCounter1(int.Parse(this.txtCounter.Text));
  proxy.SetCounter2(int.Parse(this.txtCounter.Text));

  scope.Complete();
}
```

When this code block executes, the call to SetCounter1() creates a new service instance and releases it when it commits the transaction. SetCounter2() does the same thing. That's because both operations have the TransactionAutoComplete option turned enabled by default. This option can also be explicitly enabled as follows:

```
[OperationBehavior(TransactionScopeRequired=true,TransactionAutoComplete=true)]
public void SetCounter1(int counterValue)

[OperationBehavior(TransactionScopeRequired=true,TransactionAutoComplete=true)]
public void SetCounter2(int counterValue)
```

It would be better if the service instance didn't release until the transaction was completed, at least. That way, the service instance and any state that is being managed can participate in the transaction. Otherwise, why would you enable sessions? To make this possible you can set the TransactionAutoCompleteOnSessionClose behavior to true:

```
[ServiceBehavior(InstanceContextMode = InstanceContextMode.PerSession,
TransactionAutoCompleteOnSessionClose=true)]
public class CountersService : ICountersService
```

Of course, you must also set the TransactionAutoComplete property of the OperationBehaviorAttribute to false—for those operations requiring a transaction:

```
[OperationBehavior(TransactionScopeRequired=true,TransactionAutoComplete=false)]
public void SetCounter1(int counterValue)

[OperationBehavior(TransactionScopeRequired=true,TransactionAutoComplete=false)]
public void SetCounter2(int counterValue)
```

In fact, for those services that support sessions, this is the only way you can feasibly support transactions. Furthermore, it is best if the service only allows a single request thread at a time, using ConcurrencyMode.Single (discussed in Chapter 5).

 The following sample illustrates sessions and transactions: *<YourLearningWCFPath>\Samples\Transactions\ TransactionsSessions.*

Lab: Configuring WCF Transactions

This lab will walk you through the steps for configuring clients and services to work with transactions. You'll work with the various transaction flow settings, take a look at scenarios where transactions are required by service operations, and test scenarios where transactions are initiated at the client or service.

 Before beginning this lab, configure the DTC to support WS-AT as described in the section "Enabling WS-AT," earlier in this chapter.

Testing service calls without transactions

Before adding support for transactions across service boundaries, it helps to see what happens when transactions are not supported. In this section, you'll open an existing solution and see this result.

1. Start by opening the solution for this lab located in *<YourLearningWCFPath>\ Labs\Chapter6\Transactions\Transactions.sln.* This solution comprises the following projects:

   Counters.Dalc
   > Contains a data access layer to talk to the CountersDemo database.

   Counters
   > Contains the CountersService that coordinates calls to update database counters.

   Host
   > A console application to host the service.

```
CountersClient
```
The client that provides UI to coordinate calls to the `CountersService`.

The purpose of the application is to update two database counters and keep them synchronized.

2. This lab requires you to install the following database script: *<YourLearningWCFPath>\SupportingFiles\DatabaseScripts\CountersDemo.sql*. You must also check the connection string located in the *app.config* file of the Host project to be sure it is configured according to your database environment. See the "Database Setup" section of Appendix A for detailed instructions.

3. Compile and run the solution by running the Host and then CountersClient (F5 should do the trick).

The client interface will display the current values of counters 1 and 2. Select Reset Counters to make sure that both counters are reset to 0. In the Host console, the output should indicate that the reset operation executed within the scope of a transaction. The local transaction identifier is set, while the distributed transaction identifier is not. That's because the transaction is initiated at the service with a `TransactionScope`, but the client did not flow a transaction to the service.

4. Now try changing the values of both counters. Enter the value "2" in the Text-Box provided and select the Set button. You should see the values for the counters updated in the interface, indicating that the operation was successful.

Go to the CountersClient project and open *Form1.cs* in the code window. Find the click event handler for the Set button and you'll see the following code:

```
using (TransactionScope scope = new TransactionScope())
{
  m_proxy.SetCounter1(int.Parse(this.txtCounter.Text));
  m_proxy.SetCounter2(int.Parse(this.txtCounter.Text));

  scope.Complete();
}
```

The client initiates a transaction to ensure that both counters are updated as an atomic transaction. Take a look at the output in the Host console—it will indicate that service operations `SetCounter1()` and `SetCounter2()` were executed without a transaction—despite the positive result.

Select Set again, this time with the value "12". You will receive an exception at the service stating that the counter value exceeds the limit for counter 2. If you continue, this exception will propagate to the client. The user interface will show that the first counter was updated, while the second was not.

Requiring client transactions

In this section, you will add transaction support so that client transactions can flow to the service and ensure consistency.

1. Start by enabling transaction flow for the endpoint. Go to the Host project and open the app.config. Modify the WSHttpBinding configuration by enabling transaction flow as shown here:

```
<wsHttpBinding>
  <binding name="wsHttp" transactionFlow="true" />
</wsHttpBinding>
```

2. Modify the service contract to require transaction flow from the client for SetCounter1( ) and SetCounter2( ). Do this by opening the *CountersService.cs* file and adding the TransactionFlowAttribute to each operation as shown in bold here:

```
[OperationContract]
[TransactionFlow(TransactionFlowOption.Mandatory)]
void SetCounter1(int counterValue);

[OperationContract]
[TransactionFlow(TransactionFlowOption.Mandatory)]
void SetCounter2(int counterValue);
```

Now clients will be required to flow a transaction to the service when these operations are invoked.

3. The previous step will successfully flow a transaction from client to service; however, the service will not participate in that transaction unless the service operation opts in to this. Apply the OperationBehaviorAttribute to the implementations of SetCounter1( ) and SetCounter2( ) on the CountersService type, setting the TransactionScopeRequired property to true like this:

```
[OperationBehavior(TransactionScopeRequired=true)]
public void SetCounter1(int counterValue) {...}

[OperationBehavior(TransactionScopeRequired=true)]
public void SetCounter2(int counterValue) {...}
```

4. Test the solution once again and first reset the counters to 0. Then enter a value under 10 and select the Set button. An exception will occur because the client transaction is not flowed to the service. You must update the client proxy and configuration to facilitate this.

   Stop debugging and go to the CountersClient project. Open the *app.config* file and update the WSHttpBinding configuration to enable transaction flow as shown here:

```
<wsHttpBinding>
  <binding name="wsHttp" transactionFlow="true" />
</wsHttpBinding>
```

When you generate the client proxy and configuration using SvcUtil, transaction flow will be enabled if the service has operations that make transaction flow mandatory. Otherwise, transaction flow is considered optional; thus, the client must explicitly agree to flow them by modifying the binding configuration.

5. Open the client proxy, *localhost.cs*, and add a `TransactionFlowAttribute` to the `SetCounter1()` and `SetCounter2()` operations of the service contract, as shown in bold in Example 6-13.

Example 6-13. ICountersService as defined in the CountersClient proxy

```
[System.ServiceModel.ServiceContractAttribute(
Namespace="http://www.thatindigogirl.com/samples/2006/06",
ConfigurationName="CountersClient.localhost.ICountersService")]
public interface ICountersService
{

    [System.ServiceModel.OperationContractAttribute(
    Action="http://www.thatindigogirl.com/samples/2006/06/
    ICountersService/ResetCounters",ReplyAction="http://www.thatindigogirl.com/
    samples/2006/06/ICountersService/ResetCountersResponse")]
    void ResetCounters();

    [System.ServiceModel.OperationContractAttribute(
    Action="http://www.thatindigogirl.com/samples/2006/06/ICountersService/
    SetCounter1", ReplyAction="http://www.thatindigogirl.com/samples/2006/06/
    ICountersService/SetCounter1Response")]
    [System.ServiceModel.TransactionFlowAttribute(
    System.ServiceModel.TransactionFlowOption.Mandatory)]
    void SetCounter1(int counterValue);

    [System.ServiceModel.OperationContractAttribute(
    Action="http://www.thatindigogirl.com/samples/2006/06/ICountersService/
    SetCounter2", ReplyAction="http://www.thatindigogirl.com/samples/2006/06/
    ICountersService/SetCounter2Response")]
    [System.ServiceModel.TransactionFlowAttribute(
    System.ServiceModel.TransactionFlowOption.Mandatory)]
    void SetCounter2(int counterValue);

    [System.ServiceModel.OperationContractAttribute(
    Action="http://www.thatindigogirl.com/samples/2006/06/
    ICountersService/GetCounters",ReplyAction="http://www.thatindigogirl.com/samples/
    2006/06/ICountersService/GetCountersResponse")]
    System.ComponentModel.BindingList<CountersClient.localhost.CounterInfo>
    GetCounters();
}
```

6. Compile and run the solution once again. Set the counter values to a value under 10 and this time they will be successfully updated. Next, set the counter values to a value between 10 and 20. You will receive the same exception as before; this time counter 1 will not be updated—both counters will remain set to the previous value you entered.

Take a look at the Host console output. Now both SetCounter1() and SetCounter2() participate in the same distributed transaction, the client transaction. Both the local transaction identifier and the distributed transaction identifier are initialized—the latter of which is the DTC transaction that flowed from client to service.

Automating service transactions

Now you will explore how to automatically initialize a transaction at the service boundary, while making client transaction flow optional.

1. Go to the Counters project and open *CountersService.cs*. Modify the CountersService implementation of ResetCounters() by removing the TransactionScope and adding the OperationBehaviorAttribute to require transactions. The changes are shown in bold in Example 6-14.

Example 6-14. Requiring transactions at the service operation

```
[OperationBehavior(TransactionScopeRequired=true)]
public void ResetCounters()
{
  //using (TransactionScope scope = new TransactionScope())
  //{
      TraceTransactionIds("ResetCounters()");

      using (Counters.Dalc.CountersDataAccess countersDataAccess = new
Counters.Dalc.CountersDataAccess())
      {
        countersDataAccess.SetCounter1(0);
        countersDataAccess.SetCounter2(0);
      }
  //    scope.Complete();
  //}
}
```

2. Test the solution by running the Host and CountersClient again. Select Reset Counters and view the Host console output. The local transaction identifier is set as before when manually applying the TransactionScope. The distributed transaction identifier is not set, since the client did not flow a transaction to the service.

3. Stop debugging and add optional support for transaction flow from client to service. Open *CounterService.cs* again and modify the ResetCounters() operation in the ICountersService interface by applying the TransactionFlowAttribute, as shown here:

   ```
   [OperationContract]
   [TransactionFlow(TransactionFlowOption.Allowed)]
   void ResetCounters();
   ```

4. Update the client proxy (shown in Example 6-13) to reflect the same attribute by adding the TransactionFlowAttribute to the operation, as shown in bold here:

   ```
   [System.ServiceModel.OperationContractAttribute(
   Action="http://www.thatindigogirl.com/samples/2006/06/
   ICountersService/ResetCounters",ReplyAction="http://www.thatindigogirl.com/
   samples/2006/06/ICountersService/ResetCountersResponse")]
   [TransactionFlow(TransactionFlowOption.Allowed)]
   void ResetCounters();
   ```

5. Test the solution again. You will not see any change in the Host console output since the client does not flow a transaction to the service. Try wrapping a TransactionScope around the call to ResetCounters( ) and you'll see the distributed transaction identifier will be set. Try throwing an exception at the client after calling ResetCounters( ) and you'll see the reset action is rolled back.

Rejecting client transactions

Services may not want to participate in client transactions. In this section you'll exercise this option.

1. Go to the Counters project and open *CountersService.cs*. Modify the ICountersService contract so that the GetCounters( ) operation does not allow transaction flow. Do this by applying the following TransactionFlowAttribute:

```
[OperationContract]
[TransactionFlow(TransactionFlowOption.NotAllowed)]
void ResetCounters( );
```

2. Modify the client proxy service contract in *localhost.cs* (from Example 6-13) to reflect the same setting:

```
[System.ServiceModel.OperationContractAttribute(
Action="http://www.thatindigogirl.com/samples/2006/06/
ICountersService/GetCounters",ReplyAction="http://www.thatindigogirl.com/samples/
2006/06/ICountersService/GetCountersResponse")]
[TransactionFlow(TransactionFlowOption.NotAllowed)]
System.ComponentModel.BindingList<CountersClient.localhost.CounterInfo>
GetCounters( );
```

You must also add the following using statement:

```
using System.ServiceModel;
```

3. Try to flow a transaction from client to service by adding a TransactionScope to the call to GetCounters( ). Find the GetCounters( ) method in *Form1.cs* and modify it by applying the code shown in bold here:

```
private void GetCounters( )
{
  using (TransactionScope scope = new TransactionScope())
  {
    this.bindingSource1.DataSource = m_proxy.GetCounters( );
    scope.Complete( );
  }
}
```

4. Test the solution once again. When you load the client interface, GetCounters( ) is called without error. That's because the client is not flowing the transaction to the service due to the TransactionScopeAttribute setting of NotAllowed.

5. Modify the client proxy so that it will flow the transaction to the service. Set the TransactionFlowOption for GetCounters( ) to Allowed as shown here:

```
[System.ServiceModel.OperationContractAttribute(
```

```
Action="http://www.thatindigogirl.com/samples/2006/06/
ICountersService/GetCounters",ReplyAction="http://www.thatindigogirl.com/samples/
2006/06/ICountersService/GetCountersResponse")]
[TransactionFlow(TransactionFlowOption.Allowed)]
System.ComponentModel.BindingList<CountersClient.localhost.CounterInfo>
GetCounters( );
```

6. Test the solution again. This time a `ProtocolException` will occur, indicating that the transaction coordination headers were not understood at the service.

 As a point of interest, SOAP headers have a `MustUnderstand` attribute that may be set to true by clients (usually at the plumbing level) to require the target service process the header or throw an exception. This is the case with transaction headers.

Queued Calls

Queued calls are yet another way to achieve reliability in a distributed system. When you send messages using a classic request/reply pattern, the response traditionally indicates if the request was successful, or not. In the case of one-way messages, no response is provided, thus it is difficult to be sure that the message arrived at its destination, and that it was processed successfully. By definition, with one-way calls, you probably care less about the success of the call (given that there isn't a reply), but you do care that the message arrived. Unlike reliable sessions (discussed earlier), queued calls make it possible to not only guarantee arrival of a message, but guarantee that the message will not be lost since it can be stored in a durable message queue. MSMQ is the Windows technology that supports this type of durable and reliable messaging. WCF provides a standard binding for MSMQ protocol so that your services can expose this functionality where appropriate.

MSMQ Overview

Microsoft Message Queue Server (MSMQ) is a durable, reliable messaging technology for the Windows platform. MSMQ 3.0 is an optional Windows component that can be installed on your Windows XP or Windows Server 2003 machines, while MSMQ 4.0 is an optional Windows component for Windows Vista and Windows Server 2008.

You can incorporate MSMQ in your applications to achieve the following:

- Guaranteed message delivery even when the receiver is offline.
- Transactional delivery of messages whereby delivery to the sender queue is rolled back if the client transaction aborts.
- Transactional delivery of messages whereby removal from the target queue is not committed if the server transaction aborts.
- Durable storage of messages until they are picked up by the receiving application.

- Automatic delivery retries and exception management through dead letter queues and poison message queues.

You can create private or public queues using the MSMQ Management Console or through the System.Messaging object model—that latter of which provides additional control over queue features. In the sections that follow, I will provide a brief overview of MSMQ features, and then I'll discuss how you can leverage MSMQ features with WCF.

Private and public queues

MSMQ supports private and public message queues. Private queues can be created on any machine but are available only to applications on the local machine. Public queues must be registered with an Active Directory domain and thus can be accessed by both local and remote applications. The choice of public or private queue is driven by the needs of the application.

For example, for applications that send asynchronous messages on the same machine as part of a logging or auditing activity, a private queue on the local machine will suffice. The use of a local private queue is illustrated in Figure 6-14.

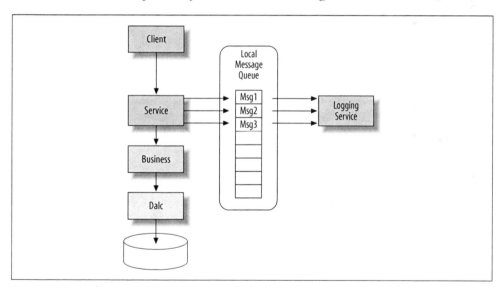

Figure 6-14. Sending messages to a queue on the local machine

For remote applications that send asynchronous messages while the server is offline, to guarantee that the messages reach the server eventually, the server must expose a public queue. In this case, the client must also have MSMQ enabled so that the queue manager on the client machine can create a local queue at the client to store messages for the offline server (Figure 6-15). When the server is back online, the local client queue will send those messages to the server queue (Figure 6-16).

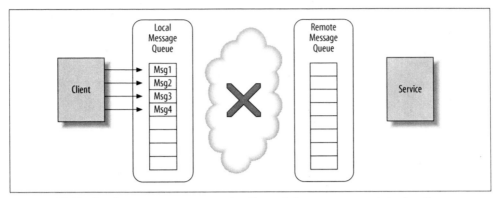

Figure 6-15. The local queue stores messages locally until the remote queue is back online

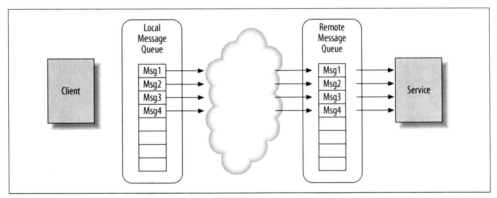

Figure 6-16. The remote queue receives messages and forwards to the service when it is back online

Transactional queues

Both private and public queues can be created as transactional queues. When a queue is transactional, applications can send messages to a queue as part of a transaction. This means that messages are written to the queue only if the entire transaction succeeds. For example, a client application may coordinate a database call with an asynchronous message as part of an atomic transaction. If either fails, the other rolls back.

Remote queues can also participate in this type of transaction, but an interesting thing happens when the server is offline. In this case, the client will send the message to the local queue as part of the transaction. Once the server is brought back online, the local queue will start a new transaction to send the message to the public server queue, only removing the message from the client queue once the transfer is successful. Yet another transaction is initiated at the public queue when the application processes the message. Assuming the application is able to participate in the transaction initiated by the queue, if an exception is thrown during the processing of the message, the message will not be removed from the public queue.

Only transactional queues can guarantee ordered message delivery and support retry attempts in the event of failure.

Delivery failure

Messages that are successfully sent from the client application to MSMQ may not be successfully processed by the server application. For example, when the message is pulled from the queue, the contents of the message may be such that exceptions are generated by the server application. A similar problem is caused when a remote queue never comes back online; thus, messages remain in the client's local queue. Several recovery options are available where transactional queues are involved:

- The queue can be configured to retry message delivery for a specified number of attempts and intervals. A *retry queue* will hold messages until the number of retries expires, at which point the message may be removed from the queue, moved to a poison message or dead-letter queue, or left in the delivery queue awaiting administrative intervention.

- For messages that repeatedly fail processing, the queue may be configured to move those messages to a *poison message queue*, which can be later inspected by administrators to discover the cause.

- Messages can be moved to a *dead letter queue* when they expire, when they are purged from another queue, or when they are directed to a dead letter queue instead of using a poison message queue.

Ideally, what you want to avoid is message loss and blocked transmission of messages, and this can be achieved with the right configuration of these features. In a later section, I'll explain how you can configure queues associated with your WCF services to control these and other features.

Security

MSMQ also provides built-in mutual authentication and message protection security features for queues deployed as part of a Windows domain. Both Windows and certificate credentials are supported for authentication, and you can request that messages are signed to guarantee integrity and encrypted to prevent unauthorized viewing of the message until it reaches its destination. These security concepts are discussed in Chapter 8, but in this chapter I will mention MSMQ specifics as they relate to WCF binding configuration.

MSMQ management console

MSMQ provides an MMC snap-in management console, the MSMQ Management Console. From this console you can manually create new queues, edit a limited set of queue properties, view messages awaiting delivery or retry and so forth. You can reach this console (shown in Figure 6-17) by opening the Computer Management console from Control Panel → Administrative Tools.

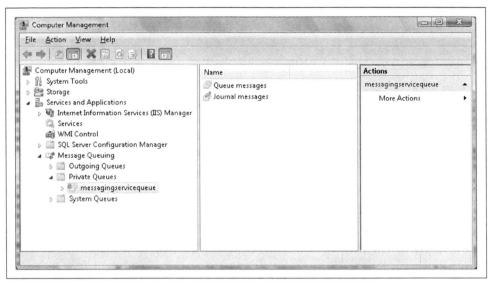

Figure 6-17. MSMQ management console

System.Messaging

The System.Messaging namespace exposes a programming layer to interact with MSMQ. For example, the following code illustrates how to check to see whether a particular local queue exists, creating the queue if it doesn't:

```
using System.Messaging;

string queueName = ".\\private$\\MessagingServiceQueue";
if (!MessageQueue.Exists(queueName))
  MessageQueue.Create(queueName, false);
```

To create a transactional queue, you can pass true to the second parameter of the Create( ) call as follows:

```
string queueName = ".\\private$\\MessagingServiceQueue";
if (!MessageQueue.Exists(queueName))
  MessageQueue.Create(queueName, true);
```

To create or access a private or public queue the following syntax applies:

- *MachineName*\Private$*QueueName*
- *MachineName**QueueName*

Using the MessageQueue object supplied by System.Messaging, you can also do things such as enumerate queues on the machine, send messages to a queue, pull messages from a queue, and control message queue properties including size limitations and storage locations. In this chapter, however, I will focus on how you can interact with message queues using WCF.

NetMsmqBinding Features

WCF supplies two standard bindings to communicate with MSMQ: NetMsmqBinding and MsmqIntegrationBinding—the latter of which is intended to support preexisting MSMQ deployments. I'll focus on NetMsmqBinding in this section and discuss MsmqIntegrationBinding in a later section.

NetMsmqBinding allows WCF clients and services to interact with message queues in scenarios where durable and reliable messaging is required. Like other standard bindings discussed in Chapter 3, NetMsmqBinding provides support for a specific set of protocols as shown in Table 6-1.

Table 6-1. Common binding features applicable to NetMsmqBinding and MsmqIntegrationBinding

Binding feature	NetMsmqBinding support
Transport Protocols	MSMQ
Message Version	SOAP 1.2, WS-Addressing
Reliable Messaging	Yes (provided by MSMQ)
Transactions	Yes
Metadata	WSDL 1.1, WS-Policy, WS-PolicyAttachment, WS-MetadataExchange

As you might expect, NetMsmqBinding also has many unique features that are applicable only to MSMQ, including features that control how reliable delivery is managed and how exceptions are handled. Table 6-2 provides a short description of the specific features available to this binding, many of which also apply to MsmqIntegrationBinding.

Table 6-2. Features specific to NetMsmqBinding

Binding feature	Description
ExactlyOnce	Ensures messages are delivered exactly once. By default, this property is enabled but is only applicable to transactional queues.
Durable	Determines if messages are stored in a persistent or volatile store. By default, this property is enabled. If disabled, messages do not survive restarts of the MSMQ service.
TimeToLive	A TimeSpan value indicating the time after which the message will expire from the queue and be moved to the dead letter queue. The default value is 1.00:00:00 (or 1 day).
QueueTransferProtocol	Indicates the transfer protocol to use for transferring messages: Native, Srmp, or SrmpSecure. The default value is Native, which means that native MSMQ protocols are employed. When Srmp is configured, Soap Reliable Messaging Protocol (SRMP) is employed. When SrmpSecure is configured, SRMP Secure (SRMPS) is employed. SRMP and SRMPS are useful when exposing MSMQ endpoints over the HTTP protocol.
ReceiveRetryCount	Configures the number of times the queue manager should attempt to redeliver a message in a specific retry interval. The default value is 5.
MaxRetryCycles	Configures the number of retry intervals that the queue manager should issue to redeliver a message. The default value is 2.
RetryCycleDelay	A TimeSpan value indicating the delay between retry intervals. The default value is 00:30:00.

Table 6-2. Features specific to NetMsmqBinding (continued)

Binding feature	Description
ReceiveErrorHandling	Specifies how failed messages should be treated based on the following options: Fault, Drop, Reject, or Move.
DeadLetterQueue	Specifies the type of dead letter queue to use: None, System, or Custom. The default value is System.
CustomDeadLetterQueue	The URI for a local custom dead letter queue.
UseMsmqTracing	Configures the use of MSMQ tracing features. By default, this is false.
UseActiveDirectory	Configures the use of Active Directory addressing features. By default, this is false.
UseSourceJournal	Configures the use of MSMQ journaling features. By default, this is false.

 You can find out more about configuring MSMQ for HTTP at *http:// www.microsoft.com/windowsserver2003/techinfo/overview/msmqb2b. mspx.*

In the next sections, I will discuss each of these features as they relate to specific applications of NetMsmqBinding.

Queued Service Contracts

For the most part, you should design and factor your service contracts based on the application's needs without consideration for deployment semantics. There are a few cases in which it is important to allocate operations to separate service contracts based on the need to support callbacks, large message transmissions, and queued calls. In the case of queued calls, it is particularly important since NetMsmqBinding can be used only for service contracts that contain all one-way operations. Example 6-15 shows a simple example of a service contract with a single one-way operation.

Example 6-15. A valid queued contract and implementation

```
[ServiceContract(Namespace = "http://www.thatindigogirl.com/samples/2006/06")]
public interface IMessagingService
{
  [OperationContract(IsOneWay=true)]
  void SendMessage(string message);
}

[ServiceBehavior(InstanceContextMode = InstanceContextMode.PerCall)]
public class MessagingService : IMessagingService
{
  public void SendMessage(string message)
  {
    Console.WriteLine(String.Format("Received message: '{0}'", message));
  }
}
```

This contract can be exposed over NetMsmqBinding. Example 6-16 shows how a local queue is exposed as a WCF endpoint using NetMsmqBinding defaults.

Example 6-16. Exposing an endpoint over NetMsmqBinding

```
<system.serviceModel>
  <services>
    <service name="Messaging.MessagingService" >
      <endpoint
address="net.msmq://localhost/private/MessagingServiceQueue"
contract="Messaging.IMessagingService" binding="netMsmqBinding" />
    </service>
  </services>
</system.serviceModel>
```

If the contract does not consist of all one-way methods, an InvalidOperationException is thrown when the ServiceHost opens the channel.

The client-side configuration to reach this queue targets the same address and of course must use a compatible binding configuration. Many of the NetMsmqBinding options are local settings that apply only to the queue on the machine where the binding is exposed. For example, in the case where the client and server each have queues on different machines, the client configuration controlling retry attempts may be different. Other settings, such as durability and exactly once delivery, must be equivalent for the bindings to be compatible.

 A sample illustrating a simple NetMsmqBinding configuration can be found here:

- *<YourLearningWCFPath>\Samples\QueuedMessages\ SimpleMessageQueue*

You can also require that service endpoints support queued delivery by applying the DeliveryRequirementsAttribute. The QueuedDeliveryRequirements property can be set to any of the following values from the QueuedDeliveryRequirementsMode enumeration:

NotAllowed
> Queued delivery is explicitly not allowed. This usually accompanies ordered messaging.

Allowed
> Queued delivery is allowed but not required of the binding.

Required
> Queued delivery is required of the binding.

When you design a service contract with MSMQ delivery in mind, you should apply this attribute to the service contract so that services that implement the contract are deployed with the appropriate binding configuration:

```
[ServiceContract(Namespace = "http://www.thatindigogirl.com/samples/2006/06")]
[DeliveryRequirements(QueuedDeliveryRequirements =
```

```
QueuedDeliveryRequirementsMode.Required)]
public interface IMessagingService
```

 A sample illustrating how to require queued delivery can be found at
*<YourLearningWCFPath>\Samples\QueuedMessages\
RequiringQueuedDelivery*.

Durable Queues

Durability is a feature that applies to both transactional and nontransactional
queues. By default, `NetMsmqBinding` enables durability. That means that messages
delivered to the queue are persisted in a local store as indicated by storage properties
of MSMQ shown in Figure 6-18. When queues use durable storage, messages are
able to survive restarts of the MSMQ service or of the machine where the queue lives.

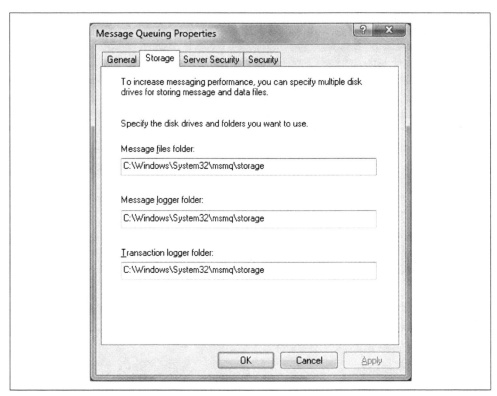

Figure 6-18. Configuring MSMQ storage locations

In some rare cases, you may want to use a nondurable queue, if the reliability of message delivery is a "nice to have" feature. You can disable durability in the binding
configuration as follows:

```
<netMsmqBinding>
  <binding name="netMsmq" durable="false">
    <security mode="None" />
```

```
      </binding>
   </netMsmqBinding>
```

This setting is exposed in the service metadata; thus, clients reflect the same setting when you generate the client configuration.

 Samples illustrating durable and nondurable queues can be found here:

- *<YourLearningWCFPath>\Samples\QueuedMessages\ DurableNonTransactional*
- *<YourLearningWCFPath>\Samples\QueuedMessages\ NonDurableNonTransactional*

Transactional Queues

Queues can be transactional or nontransactional. Transactional queues increase overall system reliability because they support exactly once and in-order delivery, in addition to delivery retries and exception handling. Nontransactional queues do not support such delivery guarantees.

As I discussed earlier, when you incorporate transactional queues into an application, the following transactions may be present:

- Client applications may write to a local or remote queue as part of a transaction. If the transaction fails, the message is not committed to the queue.
- If clients write to a local queue, while the remote queue is unavailable, the queue manager on the local machine will attempt to write to the remote queue in an atomic transaction. The local queue only removes the message after the transaction to the remote queue is successful.
- Message queues associated with a service will attempt to invoke service operations as part of a transaction. If the transaction fails, the message is not removed from the queue. Instead it is handled according to binding features that control reliability.

In this section, I'll talk about the configuration requirements necessary to support each of these transactions in a queued messaging scenario.

Exactly once delivery

By default, NetMsmqBinding enables exactly once delivery, a feature only supported by transactional queues. The following configuration shows how to explicitly set this option:

```
<netMsmqBinding>
  <binding name="netMsmq" exactlyOnce="true"/>
</netMsmqBinding>
```

Endpoints associated with nontransactional queues must disable exactly once delivery since this feature is only supported by transactional queues. The following illustrates how to disable this feature at the binding configuration:

```
<netMsmqBinding>
  <binding name="netMsmq" exactlyOnce="false"/>
</netMsmqBinding>
```

The client configuration will also reflect this setting, since it is exposed in the service metadata.

 If the client were to set exactly once delivery to true, however, an exception is not thrown when the message is sent. Instead, the message is delivered to the nontransactional dead letter queue. I'll discuss dead letter queues in a later section.

Client transactions

Clients initiate a transaction to a transactional queue much like they would initiate any other transaction—using a TransactionScope. Example 6-17 shows a TransactionScope that wraps calls to two queued service operations as part of an atomic transaction. A successful transaction in this case doesn't guarantee that the service operations are actually invoked. It guarantees only that the messages to be delivered to the service operations will be successfully delivered to the target queue. In a distributed situation, if the server is offline, the target queue is the client's local queue. If the server is online, the target queue is the remote queue.

Example 6-17. Sending queued messages as part of a client transaction

```
CountersServiceClient m_proxy = new CountersServiceClient( );

using (TransactionScope scope = new TransactionScope( ))
{
  m_proxy.SetCounter1(int.Parse(this.txtCounter.Text));
  m_proxy.SetCounter2(int.Parse(this.txtCounter.Text));

  scope.Complete( );
}
```

Clients can also coordinate other resource managers inside the TransactionScope. If any resource manager votes to abort the transaction, the message will not be committed to the target queue.

Queue-to-queue transactions

As I mentioned earlier, in the event that a remote public queue is offline, MSMQ will generate a local queue on the client machine to persist messages until the remote queue is reachable. Once the client successfully sends messages to this local transactional queue, as far as the client is concerned, the message is sent. In the meantime, the queue manager will attempt to send the message to the remote queue based on the configured retry settings (I'll discuss these shortly). Transferring messages from the local transactional queue to the remote transactional queue is also treated as an atomic transaction. The message is only removed from the local queue once the remote queue has successfully stored the message. This is all handled by MSMQ.

Queued service transactions

Transactional queues associated with a service endpoint will attempt to send messages to the service once they are received and the ServiceHost is ready to receive messages. The queue will send the message as part of a transaction, but it is ultimately up to the service to participate in this transaction or not. If the service does not participate in the queue transaction, the transaction will be successful so long as it reaches the service operation. Any exceptions thrown by the service operation will not be considered part of the queue transaction, and thus will have no impact on the success of the transaction. This has implications on the reliability of message delivery since after the service fails to process the message, the message is lost.

If the service decides to participate in the transaction, however, any exceptions thrown at the service will cause the transaction to abort, giving the queue a chance to handle the exception according to configuration rules. To participate in the transaction, the service contract must either allow or require transactions as discussed earlier in this chapter. Example 6-18 shows a service contract with three operations, each allowing transactions to be flowed to the service.

Example 6-18. Queued service contract supporting transactions

```
[ServiceContract(Namespace = "http://www.thatindigogirl.com/samples/2006/06")]
public interface ICountersService
{
  [OperationContract(IsOneWay=true)]
  [TransactionFlow(TransactionFlowOption.Allowed)]
  void ResetCounters();

  [OperationContract(IsOneWay = true)]
  [TransactionFlow(TransactionFlowOption.Allowed)]
  void SetCounter1(int counterValue);

  [OperationContract(IsOneWay = true)]
  [TransactionFlow(TransactionFlowOption.Allowed)]
  void SetCounter2(int counterValue);
}
```

In the service implementation, the OperationBehaviorAttribute must be configured so that TransactionScopeRequired is set to true—otherwise the service operation will not participate in the root transaction initiated by the queue. Example 6-19 shows the service implementation from Example 6-18 with this configuration.

Example 6-19. Queued service operations participating in queued transactions

```
public class CountersService : ICountersService
{

    [OperationBehavior(TransactionScopeRequired=true)]
    public void ResetCounters( )
    {...}

    [OperationBehavior(TransactionScopeRequired = true)]
    public void SetCounter1(int counterValue)
    {...}

    [OperationBehavior(TransactionScopeRequired = true)]
    public void SetCounter2(int counterValue)
    {...}
}
```

Essentially, the same configuration necessary to participate in client transactions for nonqueued services still applies to queued services. The difference is that the root of the transaction is the queue manager, not the client application.

The significance of transactions at the service is in the effect this configuration has on other MSMQ features that support reliability.

 A sample illustrating transactional queues can be found at *<YourLearningWCFPath>\Samples\QueuedMessages\ TransactionalQueue.*

Transactions and Delivery Failures

Transactional queues provide delivery assurances according to a number of different configuration settings, including those for retry attempts, exception handling, poison message, and dead letter queue configuration and message expiry. I'll discuss how to configure these features in this section.

Delivery retries

Earlier I summarized several NetMsmqBinding features related to delivery retries, including ReceiveRetryCount, MaxRetryCycles, and RetryCycleDelay. These settings are configured on the binding, as shown here in the following declarative configuration:

```
<netMsmqBinding>
  <binding name="netMsmq" maxRetryCycles="5" receiveRetryCount="3"
retryCycleDelay="00:15:00 "/>
</netMsmqBinding>
```

This particular configuration tells the queue to attempt to deliver the message three times in a single interval, and to repeat this for five intervals with 15 minutes delay between them. If a message expires before all retries have been attempted, the

---

message is moved to the dead letter queue. If a message is not successfully processed by the service after all retry attempts are completed, it is also moved to the dead letter queue unless it is a poison message.

Time-to-live

NetMsmqBinding allows you to configure a time-to-live (TTL) value for messages that indicates when the message should be moved to the dead letter queue if it hasn't been processed yet. You can configure TTL declaratively, as shown here:

```
<netMsmqBinding>
  <binding name="netMsmq" maxRetryCycles="3" receiveErrorHandling="Drop"
retryCycleDelay="00:01:00" receiveRetryCount="2" timeToLive="00:00:30" />
</netMsmqBinding>
```

Once this expiry is reached, the message is moved to the dead letter queue, indicating this reason. TTL takes precedence over retry attempts in moving messages to the dead letter queue.

Poison messages

Despite retry attempts, a message may fail to be processed by the service because the service or network is unavailable for a significant duration. A message may also fail to be processed because the service repeatedly throws exceptions during attempts to process the message—these types of messages are known as *poison messages*. When a poison message is present and retry attempts have been completed, the queue must decide what to do with the message. The ReceiveErrorHandling property of NetMsmqBinding controls this behavior as follows:

Fault
> An exception is sent to the queue where the message originated, and the service will no longer be able to process messages from the queue until it is restarted. This is the default behavior.

Drop
> The message is removed from the queue where it originated unless it has already expired and been moved to the dead letter queue.

Move
> The message is moved to the poison message queue.

Reject
> The originating queue is sent a negative acknowledgement and the message is moved to the dead letter queue.

You can configure this option declaratively using the following binding configuration:

```
<netMsmqBinding>
  <binding name="netMsmq" receiveErrorHandling="Move" maxRetryCycles="3"
retryCycleDelay="00:00:10" receiveRetryCount="2" />
</netMsmqBinding>
```

Fault and Drop are the only options supported by MSMQ 3.0, while MSMQ 4.0 supports all four options.

When set to Fault, the message stays in the originating queue, guaranteeing the order that messages are played but halting other messages from processing. This requires you to restart the service, but further requires that the problem preventing the message from processing must be solved. This may not always be possible, which is why other options are desirable.

When set to Drop, the message is moved to a retry queue, allowing other queued messages to process, while the poison message is retried until it expires and is moved to the dead letter queue or until it exhausts retry attempts. In the latter case, the message is removed from the queue altogether, never to be processed.

Move sends the message to the poison message queue after all retry attempts are exhausted. This is useful if you want to handle poison messages differently from dead letter queue messages that have expired not reached the service. Reject sends the message to the dead letter queue to be processed along with other expired and failed messages that weren't deemed poison.

Poison message queue

MSMQ 4.0 automatically creates a poison message queue as a subqueue of the target message queue, if you set ReceiveErrorHandling to Move. The address of the poison message queue is the same as the target queue with a ";poison" suffix. Consider the following message queue:

    net.msmq://localhost/private/MessagingServiceQueue

The following poison message queue address could be used to process poison messages:

    net.msmq://localhost/private/MessagingServiceQueue;poison

Messages sent to the poison message queue are compatible with the service contract of its parent queue; thus, you can implement a service with the same service contract to pull messages from the poison queue. The goal would be to reliably process poison messages before throwing them away—thus, you might not want to Drop the message; instead Reject it so that it can retry or move to the dead letter queue, as shown in Example 6-20.

Example 6-20. Poison message service configuration

```
<system.serviceModel>
  <services>
    <service name="Messaging.MessagingServicePoison" >
      <endpoint address="net.msmq://localhost/private/MessagingServiceQueue;poison"
contract="Messaging.IMessagingService" binding="netMsmqBinding"
bindingConfiguration="netMsmq"/>
    </service>
  </services>
  <bindings>
    <netMsmqBinding>
```

Example 6-20. Poison message service configuration (continued)

```
      <binding name="netMsmq" maxRetryCycles="3" receiveErrorHandling="Reject"
retryCycleDelay="00:01:00" receiveRetryCount="2" />
    </netMsmqBinding>
  </bindings>
</system.serviceModel>
```

Since messages in the poison message queue target a different service address, you have to configure the poison service implementation so that it doesn't filter based on exact addressing. You can do this by setting the AddressFilterMode on the ServiceBehaviorAttribute, as shown here:

```
[ServiceBehavior(AddressFilterMode=AddressFilterMode.Any)]
public class MessagingServicePoison : IMessagingService
```

Dead letter queues

By default, MSMQ provides two system-wide queues to store failed messages—one for nontransactional dead letter messages and another for transactional dead letter messages (see Figure 6-19). You can programmatically inspect either dead letter queue to take action on failed messages using the following addresses:

```
net.msmq://localhost/system$;DeadXact
net.msmq://localhost/system$;DeadLetter
```

In the same way that you would process poison messages, a WCF service can be configured to process messages from either dead letter queue.

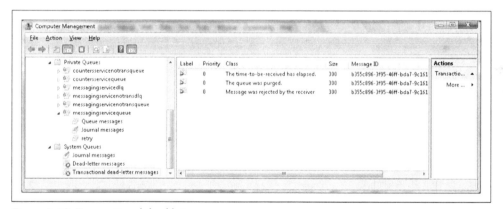

Figure 6-19. Transactional dead letter queue

It can be more convenient to use a custom dead letter queue for your specific application. MSMQ 4.0 supports this concept, so on Windows Vista and Windows Server 2008, you can use WCF to configure a custom dead letter queue to collect application specific messages.

The first step is to create the message queue to be used as the custom dead letter queue. Then you can configure the NetMsmqBinding properties, specifying a DeadLetterQueue type of Custom and providing the custom queue URI for the CustomDeadLetterQueue property. The following shows how to achieve this configuration declaratively:

```
<netMsmqBinding>
  <binding name="netMsmq"
customDeadLetterQueue="net.msmq://localhost/private/MessagingServiceDLQ"
deadLetterQueue="Custom" />
</netMsmqBinding>
```

Security

NetMsmqBinding supports three modes of security: None, Transport, or Message. I'll be discussing security options at length in Chapter 8, but the short description is as follows:

- Transport security uses the transport protocol such as TCP, IPC, MSMQ, or HTTP to handle mutual authentication and message protection.
- Message security uses the SOAP message to handle mutual authentication and message protection independent of the transport.

Message security for NetMsmqBinding works as I describe it in Chapter 8 for other bindings, but transport security settings are different in that MSMQ requires an Active Directory domain to enable transport security and has the following unique settings:

MsmqAuthenticationMode
    None, WindowsDomain, Certificate

MsmqEncryptionAlgorithm
    RC4Stream, Aes

MsmqProtectionLevel
    None, Sign, EncryptAndSign

MsmqSecureHashAlgorithm
    Sha1, MD5, Sha256, Sha512

The default transport security settings for NetMsmqBinding are shown here:

```
<netMsmqBinding>
  <binding name="netMsmq" >
    <security mode="Transport" >
     <transport msmqAuthenticationMode="WindowsDomain" msmqProtectionLevel="Sign"
msmqEncryptionAlgorithm="RC4Stream" msmqSecureHashAlgorithm="Sha1"/>
    </security>
  </binding>
</netMsmqBinding>
```

MsmqIntegrationBinding

MsmqIntegrationBinding and NetMsmqBinding share similar features in terms of configuring retry attempts, error handling, dead letter queues, and transport security settings. MsmqIntegrationBinding is quite different, however, since it is intended to support WCF communications with existing MSMQ investments such as COM+ components. One of the key differences is that MsmqIntegrationBinding does not support message security. Options for the security mode setting for the binding are limited to those defined by the enumeration MsmqIntegrationSecuriteMode: None or Transport.

MsmqIntegrationBinding also provides different serialization options enabling WCF to interact with different types of message serialization formats, including Xml, ActiveX, Stream, ByteArray, and Binary. The default value is Xml, as shown here:

```
<msmqIntegrationBinding>
  <binding name="msmqIntegration" serializationFormat="Stream" >
    <security mode="Transport" />
  </binding>
</msmqIntegrationBinding>
```

As far as contract definition goes, the service contract can only include operations that take a single parameter of type MsmqMessage<T>. For example, to read a stream you can configure the serialization format as Stream and then receive it as MsmqMessage<Stream> as follows:

```
[OperationContract(IsOneWay=true)]
void SendMessage(MsmqMessage<Stream> message);
```

Lab: Creating a Queued Service

In this lab, you will expose an existing service over MSMQ and test various scenarios such as offline reliability and exception handling.

Exposing an MSMQ endpoint

The first thing you will do is modify an existing solution to create a message queue and then to expose an endpoint over NetMsmqBinding.

1. Open the solution for this lab located in *<YourLearningWCFPath>\Labs\ Chapter6\QueuedServices\QueuedServices.sln*. This solution includes a simple messaging service, a console host, and a client application. Currently, the service is exposed over a WSHttpBinding endpoint. Compile and run the solution once to test the current configuration settings. From the client interface, click Send to send a message to the service. The Host console displays each message it receives.

2. Go to the Host project and modify the *app.config* so that the service is exposed over NetMsmqBinding instead of WSHttpBinding. The resulting <service> section should look as shown in Example 6-21. Provide a custom binding configuration to disable security for NetMsmqBinding (security requires a domain). In the same configuration file, add a <netMsmqBinding> section to the <bindings> section. This change is also shown in Example 6-21.

Example 6-21. Adding a NetMsmqBinding endpoint for the MessagingService

```
<system.serviceModel>
  <services>
    <service name="Messaging.MessagingService" >
      <endpoint address="net.msmq://localhost/private/MessagingServiceQueue"
contract="Messaging.IMessagingService" binding="netMsmqBinding"
bindingConfiguration="netMsmq"/>
      <endpoint address="http://localhost:8000/MessagingService"
contract="Messaging.IMessagingService" binding="wsHttpBinding"
bindingConfiguration="wsHttp"/>
    </service>
  </services>
  <bindings>
    <wsHttpBinding>
      <binding name="wsHttp">
        <security>
          <message establishSecurityContext="false" />
        </security>
      </binding>
    </wsHttpBinding>
    <netMsmqBinding>
      <binding name="netMsmq">
        <security mode="None" />
      </binding>
    </netMsmqBinding>
  </bindings>
</system.serviceModel>
```

3. Add code to the Host project to create the private message queue referenced in the binding configuration. First, add a reference to the System.Messaging assembly, and then open *Program.cs* and to add the code shown in bold in Example 6-22. Don't forget to add the using statement for System.Messaging.

Example 6-22. Using System.Messaging to create a queue

```
using System.Messaging;

using (ServiceHost host = new ServiceHost(typeof(Messaging.MessagingService)))
{
  string queueName = ".\\private$\\MessagingServiceQueue";
  if (!MessageQueue.Exists(queueName))
    MessageQueue.Create(queueName, true);

  host.Open( );
```

Example 6-22. Using System.Messaging to create a queue (continued)

```
  // other code
}
```

 In this example, you'll be working with a transactional queue.

4. Change the client application so that it uses the `NetMsmqBinding` binding endpoint instead of the original `WSHttpBinding` endpoint. Go to the `WinClient` project and open *app.config*. In the `<bindings>` section, provide the `<netMsmqBinding>` section shown in Example 6-23. Modify the endpoint in the `<client>` section to use the new MSMQ endpoint. These changes are also shown in bold in Example 6-23.

Example 6-23. Consuming an MSMQ binding from the client

```
<system.serviceModel>
  <bindings>
    <netMsmqBinding>
      <binding name="netMsmq" >
        <security mode="None" />
      </binding>
    </netMsmqBinding>
  </bindings>
  <client>
    <endpoint address="net.msmq://localhost/private/MessagingServiceQueue"
binding="netMsmqBinding" bindingConfiguration="netMsmq"
contract="WinClient.localhost.IMessagingService" name="netMsmq" />
  </client>
</system.serviceModel>
```

5. Test these changes by compiling and running the solution. Run the `Host` and `WinClient` projects, and click the Send button once again. You will see messages written to the Host console. Leave the solution running for the next section.

Requiring MSMQ

In cases where you design service contracts with one-way operations, often you know in advance if message queuing is required for reliability. In this section, you will modify the service contract to require a queued binding.

1. Go to the Messaging project and open *MessagingService.cs*. Apply the `DeliveryRequirementsAttribute` to `IMessagingService`. As shown here, set the `QueuedDeliveryRequirements` property to `Required` mode:

```
[ServiceContract(Namespace = "http://www.thatindigogirl.com/samples/2006/06")]
[DeliveryRequirements(QueuedDeliveryRequirements=
QueuedDeliveryRequirementsMode.Required)]
```

```
public interface IMessagingService
```

2. Now, try to test the solution again. An `InvalidOperationException` will be thrown by the `Host` application, indicating that one of the service endpoints doesn't support queued messaging. That's because the `WSHttpBinding` endpoint is still present.

3. Open the *app.config* file for the `Host` project and remove the `WSHttpBinding` endpoint from the `<services>` section so that the new section looks as follows:

```
<service name="Messaging.MessagingService" >
  <endpoint address="net.msmq://localhost/private/MessagingServiceQueue"
contract="Messaging.IMessagingService" binding="netMsmqBinding"
bindingConfiguration="netMsmq"/>
</service>
```

4. Try to run the solution again. This time the `Host` and `WinClient` will load successfully. Leave them running for the next test.

Testing offline messaging

Now you are going to test how MSMQ provides clients with offline support when the service isn't available.

1. Leave the `WinClient` application running, and close the `Host` console. From the running `WinClient` interface, select the Send button a few times. Notice that you do not receive an exception.

2. Open the Computer Management console from Control Panel and expand Services and Applications → Message Queuing → Private Queues → MessagingServiceQueue → Queue messages. Select Queue messages and you will see the messages awaiting delivery to the `Host`.

3. Go to Visual Studio and start the `Host` console once again. The queued messages will be immediately processed—and the console will display the output.

4. Return to the queue and refresh. The queued messages have been removed from the queue, since the service processed them.

 Remember that the client and service often do not live on the same machine. Thus, the client queue would be sending messages to the queue on the remote machine for delivery to the service (if it is running).

Testing exception handling

In this section, you will explore delivery failure and exception handling by playing with the configuration settings of the service.

1. Go to the `Host` configuration file, *app.config*, and configure exception-handling features of `NetMsmqBinding` for the endpoint. You'll be reducing the number of retry cycles, retry counts, and the retry cycle delay in order to escalate error handling when a message fails processing. You'll also use the default setting for error handling, `Fault`. The resulting configuration is shown here:

```
<netMsmqBinding>
  <binding name="netMsmq" receiveErrorHandling="Fault" maxRetryCycles="2"
receiveRetryCount="2" retryCycleDelay="00:00:05"  >
    <security mode="None" />
  </binding>
</netMsmqBinding>
```

2. Now, modify the service implementation so that SendMessage() throws an exception. Open *MessagingService.cs* and edit the operation so it looks as follows (changes shown in bold):

```
public void SendMessage(string message)
{
  Console.WriteLine(String.Format("Received message: '{0}'", message));
  throw new FaultException("bad message");
}
```

3. Compile and run the solution again. Select the Send button twice, and this time an exception will be thrown for each message. Return to the Computer Management console and refresh the queue. No messages will be there because they were sent to the service already. In addition, you'll notice that the messages that failed are not retried as you may have expected. That's because the service is not enlisting in the queue transaction.

4. Return to the solution and go to the Messaging project. Open the *MessagingService.cs* file and add transaction flow support to the only operation on the service contract as follows:

```
[OperationContract(IsOneWay=true)]
[TransactionFlow(TransactionFlowOption.Allowed)]
void SendMessage(string message);
```

In addition, modify the implementation on the service type to require transactions:

```
[OperationBehavior(TransactionScopeRequired=true)]
public void SendMessage(string message)
```

5. Once again compile and run the solution. Click Send twice. The first message will fail three times and you'll see output in the Host console reflecting this. The second message will not arrive.

Return to the Computer Management console and refresh the message queue. There should be two messages. The first is the failed message, which is blocking other messages from being processed since the NetMsmqBinding is configured to fault when messages fail processing.

6. Close the Host and restart it. The queued messages will fire in parallel to the service so that they can be processed. At the point when a message is deemed poison after completing a retry interval, it will block the queue again. Any new messages you send will continue to queue behind existing items in the queue. Each time you close the host and restart, queued messages will be forwarded again to be processed, but will eventually block new messages since failed messages are always left in the queue.

7. Change this configuration so that error handling will drop failed messages. Go to the Host project and modify the *app.config* so that `receiveErrorHandling` is set to Drop as shown here:

```
<netMsmqBinding>
  <binding name="netMsmq" receiveErrorHandling="Drop" maxRetryCycles="2"
receiveRetryCount="2" retryCycleDelay="00:00:05"  >
    <security mode="None" />
  </binding>
</netMsmqBinding>
```

8. Compile and run the solution once again and you'll see the messages are processed by the service again, for a single interval. If you refresh the message queue, you'll find that the queue has been emptied.

When you configure `NetMsmqBinding` to drop poison messages, this implies that you are ok with losing messages if they repeatedly fail to be processed. This is not ideal if you want to troubleshoot the cause of the problem.

Summary

In this chapter, I explained how you can support reliable sessions, transactions, and queued messaging to your WCF clients and services to improve the overall reliability of your enterprise systems. As with most complex system features, there are many knobs and buttons that control the functionality of each—and the defaults aren't always desirable. I gave you some recommendations on how to decide when to use each feature and some guidance on their usage.

As far as reliable sessions go, you are most likely to apply them today in a situation where you own both sides (client and service). That generally means it is more useful for intranet than Internet. Although WS-ReliableMessaging is an interoperable standard, it is not yet ratified and not all web service platforms support the feature.

To support a wider audience with your Internet services, you may expose an endpoint that does not support reliable sessions, and another that does for callers that can benefit from it. For intranet services that you control, there are still some things to consider before you apply reliable sessions. The key deterrent is the dependency on sticky sessions (discussed in Chapter 5 as well). You must make sure that messages are sent to the same machine where their reliable session lives, since this session cannot (today) be stored in a shared durable resource manager. If you want the reliability, however, you should definitely consider this trade-off a positive one and use the feature for TCP and HTTP communications alike.

No doubt you need a way to flow transactions across process and machine boundaries. In that respect, transactions are a natural replacement for earlier techniques for achieving this such as Enterprise Services. Thus, for the intranet case, it is a no-brainer to enable transactions at the service so that you can maintain a consistent and reliable system state. Like reliable sessions, transactions are interoperable via the WS-AtomicTransaction and WS-Coordination specifications—and the same problems exist in that the standards aren't yet ratified and are not widely implemented. So for Internet services, you must think about exposing endpoints without it to reach a wider audience.

Another issue with Internet services is the risk associated with allowing clients to lock your resources by including your service in a distributed transaction. For this reason, you should apply transactions with care. Once you have decided to go with transaction support, it is best to configure the service contract to allow transactions, not to make them mandatory. In addition, you can achieve better consistency with the default isolation level (serializable); however, for read-heavy systems, you may need to loosen your grip with the advice of your resident DBA.

Queue messaging over MSMQ provides very specific benefits in the case where calls can be asynchronous but must be absolutely durable and reliable. They make an ideal solution for potentially offline callers, guaranteed message delivery, and absolute control over how to handle problem messages (without losing them). It makes the most sense to use transactional queues for these guarantees. On Windows Server 2003 machines, you should fault messages and manually move messages to the poison queue if a message is blocking beyond a comfortable threshold. For Windows Server 2008, other features are available to move messages automatically to either poison or dead letter queues when they fail repeatedly.

CHAPTER 7
Security

Windows Communication Foundation (WCF) is a secure, reliable, and scalable messaging platform. With WCF, SOAP messages can be transmitted over a variety of supported protocols, including named pipes, TCP, HTTP, and MSMQ. Like any distributed messaging platform, you must establish security policies for protecting messages and for authenticating and authorizing calls.

A consistent set of fundamental security concepts apply in any distributed messaging system. Consider a message from sender (the calling application) to receiver (the target service receiving the message for processing):

Authentication
> We typically think about authentication as identifying the message sender. Mutual authentication involves authenticating both the sender and the message receiver to prevent possible man-in-the-middle attacks.

Authorization
> After authenticating the message sender, authorization determines the system features and functionality they are entitled to execute.

Integrity
> Messages should be digitally signed to ensure they have not been altered between sender and receiver.

Confidentiality
> Sensitive messages or specific message parts should be encrypted to ensure they cannot be openly viewed on the wire.

WCF provides a rich and configurable environment for creating security policies and setting runtime behaviors to control security features. A variety of mutual authentication mechanisms are supported using token formats such as Windows tokens, username and password, certificates, and issued tokens (in a federated environment). Authorization can be based on Windows roles, ASP.NET roles, or you can provide custom authorization policies. Message protection (integrity and confidentiality) can be based on symmetric session keys or asymmetric keys for single-hop protection.

Unlike other technologies for distributed communication, such as .NET Remoting and Enterprise Services, WCF also supports interoperable standards for secure messaging at its core. Although WCF makes use of existing security infrastructure to secure communications behind the firewall, you can enable the latest in SOAP message security standards for secure and interoperable messaging with other applications, platforms, and business partners.

In this chapter, I'll start by explaining some of the fundamental security features of WCF to support these security concepts. I'll explain how to configure security settings for bindings and how to apply other relevant security attributes and behaviors. After providing this overview, I'll explain how to apply these and other advanced security features for scenarios involving intranet and Internet applications, mutual certificate authentication, claims-based and federated security, and Windows CardSpace.

WCF Security Overview

Before looking at specific application scenarios, you should understand how to approach securing your WCF services. Both bindings and behaviors influence aspects of security related to authentication, authorization, and message protection (also called *transfer security*). Many of the security settings are exposed as part of a service security policy that can be consumed by clients. The sections to follow will introduce you to security policy and explain the fundamental security features of WCF that influence that policy.

Security Policy

Security requirements for a WCF service must be well-defined so that client applications can respect the policy and provide the required credentials and message protection expected by the service, and so that services can process incoming messages and handle credentials according to consistent requirements. These requirements collectively comprise the *security policy* for a service.

Security policy is defined primarily by the bindings used for each service endpoint. For example, bindings define the type of credentials expected for authentication and authorization and over what protocol those credentials should be provided. Bindings also identify advanced requirements for negotiating service credentials, secure sessions, and signing and encryption algorithms—things I'll be discussing later. Behaviors describe authentication and authorization policies that are followed when processing client credentials.

As you might suspect, not all aspects of the security policy are published to clients. *WS-SecurityPolicy* is an interoperable standard that is used to describe the public aspects of security policy so that clients can generate code to properly interact with a secure service. WS-SecurityPolicy is a concrete implementation of the WS-Policy standard that I discussed in Chapter 2, and thus is exposed as metadata in the policy section of a service's WSDL document. This means that security requirements of each service are exposed in an interoperable way that can be consumed by tools such as SvcUtil to generate proxies and relevant configuration for clients. Thus, when you add a service reference to a secure service, the client-side binding configuration will be influenced by the service security policy, ensuring that it can communicate to the service successfully.

Binding Security

Binding configuration has the most significant impact on security policy. First and foremost, your binding selection will influence the available security configuration options. When you expose a service endpoint, you select a binding that represents the appropriate communication protocol and message-encoding format. For example, for intranet communications or systems behind the firewall, TCP protocol with binary message encoding is usually preferred. For Internet access, HTTP protocol is a typical choice using text or MTOM encoding (depending on the message size).

There are a standard set of bindings that can satisfy these protocol and encoding choices, as I discussed in Chapter 3. For example, NetTcpBinding is the right choice for binary TCP communications that cross machine boundaries, BasicHttpBinding is the right choice for HTTP communications that must support legacy Web service protocols, and either WSHttpBinding or WSFederationHttpBinding is the right choice for web services that can use a richer set of standards, including those for secure communications (the latter is used for federated security scenarios). Each of these bindings has different defaults and options for securing services.

Default security settings

Each binding has a default set of security settings. Consider the following service endpoint that supports NetTcpBinding:

```
<system.serviceModel>
  <services>
    <service name="HelloIndigo.HelloIndigoService" >
      <endpoint contract="HelloIndigo.IHelloIndigoService"
binding="netTcpBinding"/>
    </service>
  </services>
</system.serviceModel>
```

NetTcpBinding is secure by default. Specifically, callers must provide Windows credentials for authentication, and all message packets are signed and encrypted over TCP protocol. I'll explain signing and encryption later in this chapter. Look at the expanded binding configuration illustrating these default settings:

```
<netTcpBinding>
  <binding name="netTcp">
    <security mode="Transport">
```

```
        <transport clientCredentialType="Windows" />
      </security>
    </binding>
  </netTcpBinding>
```

The same default settings are established when you construct the binding in code, as follows:

```
NetTcpBinding tcpBinding = new NetTcpBinding( );
```

You can customize the default security settings for NetTcpBinding by configuring different values for client credentials, for example. You could also change the security mode from Transport to Message security, which means overriding settings specific to message security. Other bindings, such as WSHttpBinding, default to Message security mode and provide defaults for client credential type and additional settings specific to message security such as secure sessions, service credential negotiation, and signing and encryption algorithms.

Each of the standard WCF bindings supports only relevant security options for their typical usage.

Security mode

Across all service bindings there are six possible security modes:

None
> Turns security off. Not recommended.

Transport
> Uses transport security for mutual authentication and message protection.

Message
> Uses message security for mutual authentication and message protection.

Both
> Allows you to supply settings for transport and message level security (only MSMQ supports this).

TransportWithMessageCredential
> Credentials are passed with the message, and message protection and server authentication are provided by the transport layer.

TransportCredentialOnly
> Client credentials are passed with the transport layer, and no message protection is applied.

You can turn off security completely, or allocate authentication and message protection between transport and message security. When transport security is employed, the transport (named pipes, TCP, HTTP, or MSMQ) employs its own mechanism for passing credentials and handling message protection. For example, HTTP relies on HTTP headers to pass security credentials and usually relies on SSL security to sign and encrypt messages. When transport security is employed, messages are protected only from point-to-point, as shown in Figure 7-1.

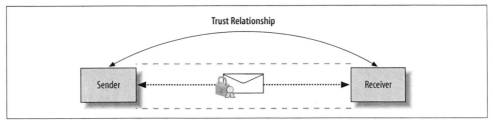

Figure 7-1. Transport security protects messages point-to-point

By comparison, message security uses the SOAP envelope to pass credentials and applies SOAP message security to sign and encrypt message parts. One of the most important aspects of message security is that it uses interoperable standards to apply security. In addition, since message security protects the message independent of transport, it is possible to protect messages all the way through to the ultimate message receiver, providing end-to-end security, as shown in Figure 7-2.

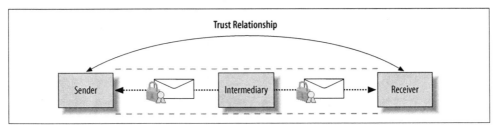

Figure 7-2. Message security protects messages end-to-end

To control the security mode used for a particular binding, you can set the mode property in the binding <security> section. If you set the mode to Transport, TransportWithMessageCredential, TransportCredentialOnly, or Both, you can supply a <transport> section to customize the transport security settings for the binding. If you set the mode to Message or TransportWithMessageCredentials, you can supply a <message> section to customize the message security settings for the binding.

For example, this <basicHttpBinding> configuration section requires Transport security mode, which requires a Windows credential by default:

```
<wsHttpBinding>
  <binding name="basicHttp">
    <security mode="Transport">
      <transport clientCredentialType="Windows" />
    </security>
  </binding>
</wsHttpBinding>
```

You can also control the security mode in code. Each standard binding exposes an object model to control security settings through a Security property. This example illustrates how to initialize a BasicHttpBinding instance to use Transport security defaults:

```
BasicHttpBinding binding = new BasicHttpBinding( );
binding.Security.Mode = BasicHttpSecurityMode.Transport;
```

Not all bindings support all security modes, so what you'll find is that only a subset of the modes described earlier will be available—depending on the binding you are configuring. As I discuss specific security scenarios in this chapter, I'll list the possible security modes for each binding.

Client credential type

Each binding configuration has a clientCredentialType setting that controls the type of client credential expected over transport or message security. When transport security is enabled, the transport provides a way to pass credentials. Across all bindings that support transport security the following client credentials are supported: None, Basic, Digest, NTLM, Windows, and Certificate. Essentially you have a choice between anonymous credentials, some form of Windows credential, or a certificate.

When message security is enabled, credentials are included in the SOAP message and follow interoperable standards. Across all bindings that support message security the following client credentials are supported: None, Windows, UserName, Certificate, and IssuedToken. In this case, the choice is to provide no credentials, Windows credentials (NTLM or Kerberos), username and password, certificate, or a SAML or custom XML token. I'll elaborate on each of these credential types throughout this chapter.

To customize the credential type required for transport or message security, you can provide an alternate setting for clientCredentialType in either the <transport> or <message> section.

The following configuration requires clients to provide a certificate over HTTP transport:

```
<wsHttpBinding>
  <binding name="wsHttp">
    <security mode="Transport">
      <transport clientCredentialType="Certificate"/>
    </security>
  </binding>
</wsHttpBinding>
```

This configuration requires clients to provide a certificate as part of the SOAP message:

```
<wsHttpBinding>
  <binding name="wsHttp">
    <security mode="TransportWithMessageCredential">
      <message clientCredentialType="Certificate"/>
    </security>
  </binding>
</wsHttpBinding>
```

You can accomplish the same in code by setting the binding's security mode and initializing its transport or message security information directly. For transport security mode, you can initialize the binding's transport security settings:

```
WSHttpBinding binding = new WSHttpBinding( );
binding.Security.Mode = SecurityMode.Transport;
binding.Security.Transport.ClientCredentialType = HttpClientCredentialType.
Certificate;
```

For message security, initialize its message security settings:

```
WSHttpBinding binding = new WSHttpBinding( );
binding.Security.Mode = SecurityMode.TransportWithMessageCredential;
binding.Security.Message.ClientCredentialType =
MessageCredentialType.Certificate;
```

Not all transport and message credential types are supported across all bindings. Your choice of client credential type may also affect other configuration settings for the service—for example, UserName credentials require either transport message protection or a service certificate be used to protect the exchange. I will explore credential type support for each binding and the impact of the options throughout this chapter.

Advanced dettings

Security mode and client credential type are security settings that all bindings share. You must always select a security mode and choose the type of credential required to authenticate callers. Some bindings, such as WSHttpBinding and WSFederationHttpBinding, provide additional security settings that can be configured for advanced scenarios. I'll review advanced security settings for each binding later in this chapter.

Supplying Credentials

Both clients and services must provide credentials to support mutual authentication. Clients usually use a proxy to provide credentials matching the requirements of the service security policy. In some cases, it is also useful to provide credentials through a declarative behavior configuration. Likewise, services often rely on behaviors to supply credentials. In the next two sections, I'll describe how clients and services typically supply credentials.

Client credentials

Client credentials are provided by initializing a ClientCredentials type from the System.ServiceModel.Description namespace. This type exposes a number of properties, each associated with a particular type of credential. Each property references a type from the System.ServiceModel.Security namespace that you can initialize if you want to supply those credentials when you communicate with the service. For example, the Windows property references a WindowsClientCredential type, and the

UserName property references a UserNamePasswordClientCredential type. The following list outlines the credential properties and associated types available for a ClientCredentials instance:

Windows *property*, WindowsClientCredential *type*
   Represents a network credential for Digest, NTLM, or Windows security (the latter for transport or message mode).

HttpDigest *property*, HttpDigestClientCredential *type*
   Represents a network credential for Digest transport mode.

UserName *property*, UserNamePasswordClientCredential *type*
   Represents a username and password that can be used for Basic transport mode or UserName message mode.

ClientCertificate *property*, X509CertificateInitiatorClientCredential *type*
   Represents an X.509 certificate for Certificate transport or message security.

ServiceCertificate *property*, X509CertificateRecipientClientCredential *type*
   Represents an X.509 certificate to identify the service when negotiation is disabled (to be discussed later).

IssuedToken *property*, IssuedTokenClientCredential *type*
   Represents a token issued by a security token service (to be discussed later).

Peer *property*, PeerCredential *type*
   Represents credentials used to authenticate a peer node.

The ClientCredentials type is exposed as a property of the proxy and of the channel factory. You will normally initialize the appropriate credentials with code, but for some credentials it is useful to specify properties of the credential declaratively by specifying an endpoint behavior.

Proxies generated by SvcUtil expose a ClientCredentials property, which gives you access to the ClientCredentials instance. By default, this instance is initialized with Windows credentials matching the Windows identity of the client process. The following code illustrates how to explicitly set those Windows credentials with a NetworkCredential instance:

```
m_proxy.ClientCredentials.Windows.ClientCredential = new
NetworkCredential("username", "password", "domain");
```

If the binding requires a UserName credential, you can initialize it this way:

```
m_proxy.ClientCredentials.UserName.UserName = this.m_username;
m_proxy.ClientCredentials.UserName.Password = this.m_password;
```

For the channel factory, the Credentials property represents the ClientCredentials instance. Thus, to initialize Windows or UserName credentials for a channel factory, you would do one of the following:

```
ChannelFactory<IMySecureService> factory = new ChannelFactory<IMySecureService>();

// UserName
```

```
factory.Credentials.UserName.UserName = this.m_username;
factory.Credentials.UserName.Password = this.m_password;

// Windows
factory.Credentials.Windows.ClientCredential = new
NetworkCredential("username", "password", "domain");
```

When a `Certificate` credential is required, it may be desirable to configure the certificate declaratively. In this case, you can provide an endpoint behavior as shown here:

```
<endpointBehaviors>
  <behavior name="clientBehavior">
    <clientCredentials>
      <clientCertificate findValue="SubjectKey" storeLocation="CurrentUser"
storeName="My" x509FindType="FindBySubjectName"/>
    </clientCredentials>
  </behavior>
</endpointBehaviors>
```

In the `<clientCredentials>` section, you can also specify authentication rules for digest and Windows authentication, provide settings for issued tokens and peer credentials, and supply information about the service certificate.

The proxy or channel factory `ClientCredentials` instance will be initialized by its client endpoint.

If you fail to initialize the proxy with credentials necessary to call the service, you'll be notified with an exception indicating the type of credentials needed.

Service credentials

Services also authenticate to clients. When non-Windows credentials are specified as the authentication mechanism, the service must provide a service certificate to satisfy both authentication and message protection needs. This is done by providing a `ServiceCredentials` behavior for the `ServiceHost`.

You can provide this behavior declaratively by adding a `<serviceCredentials>` section as follows:

```
<serviceBehaviors>
  <behavior name="serviceBehavior">
    <serviceCredentials>
      <serviceCertificate findValue="RPKey" storeLocation="LocalMachine"
storeName="My" x509FindType="FindBySubjectName" />
    </serviceCredentials>
  </behavior>
</serviceBehaviors>
```

You can also initialize service credentials in code by setting the `Credentials` property of the `ServiceHost`, as follows:

```
using System.Security.Cryptography.X509Certificates;

// code to initialize the ServiceHost
using (ServiceHost host = new ServiceHost(typeof(HelloIndigo.HelloIndigoService)))
{
  host.Credentials.ServiceCertificate.SetCertificate(StoreLocation.LocalMachine,
StoreName.My, X509FindType.FindBySubjectName, "RPKey");
  host.Open();
}
```

Message Protection

By default, all secure WCF bindings will sign and encrypt messages. Signing protects message integrity and encryption protects message privacy (I'll discuss signing and encryption later in this chapter). You can interact with message protection on several levels:

- You can throttle the level of message protection to use no protection, to sign messages without encryption, or to sign and encrypt.

- You can require that services be deployed with a secure binding that provides the required level of protection.

- You can control the algorithms used to perform signing and encryption activities. This is particularly useful for interoperability scenarios.

Protection level

Protection level settings are controlled by the service contract, operation contract, message contract (see Chapter 2), or fault contract (see Chapter 8). For example, you can specify the protection level for all operations in the service contract using the ServiceContractAttribute. The following example illustrates disabling message protection:

```
[ServiceContract(Name="HelloIndigoContract", Namespace=
"http://www.thatindigogirl.com/samples/2006/06 ",
ProtectionLevel=ProtectionLevel.None)]
public interface IHelloIndigoService
{
  string HelloIndigo(string s);
}
```

The result is that messages to this service will not be signed or encrypted if the binding uses message security. You can also indicate message protection per operation using the OperationContractAttribute:

```
[ServiceContract(Name="HelloIndigoContract",
Namespace=http://www.thatindigogirl.com/samples/2006/06]
public interface IHelloIndigoService
{
  [OperationContract(ProtectionLevel=ProtectionLevel.None)]
  string HelloIndigo(string s);
}
```

The same `ProtectionLevel` property exists on the `FaultContractAttribute`, `MessageContractAttribute`, `MessageBodyMemberAttribute`, and `MessageHeaderAttribute`. You can also set the protection level for transport security in some binding configurations. This can be done programmatically or declaratively, as shown here for `NetTcpBinding`:

```
<netTcpBinding>
  <binding name="netTcp">
    <security mode="Transport">
      <transport protectionLevel="Sign"/>
    </security>
  </binding>
</netTcpBinding>
```

The `ProtectionLevel` enumeration provides the following options: `None`, `Sign`, and `EncryptAndSign`. `None` disables message protection, `EncryptAndSign` provides full message protection, and `Sign` indicates the message should be signed but not encrypted. In truth, there is very little value in reducing the protection level when message security is employed, but it could be useful for transports when an alternate wire-level protection is used such as IPSec.

 Protection level settings have no effect on SSL. SSL will always sign and encrypt messages.

The `ProtectionLevel` property serves a dual role. So far, I've discussed how this property can be used to control the level of message protection. The more useful role of this property is that it specifies the minimum binding requirements for message protection. If the property is not specified, the default behavior is for messages to be signed and encrypted when security is enabled on the binding (security mode is not `None`), but this is not enforced. By specifying a value for the `ProtectionLevel` property at any contract level, if the encompassing service contract is deployed over a binding that does not satisfy the protection level setting, the `ServiceHost` will not be able to initialize because the binding doesn't meet the contract's security requirement.

 Coupling protection level requirements to contracts allows developers to enforce security when sensitive information is being transferred to or from service operations.

Algorithm suite

Your choice of algorithm suite can be particularly important for interoperability. Each binding uses a set of default algorithms for message security. These algorithms effect how messages are signed and encrypted; thus, it is important that algorithms between clients and services agree. You may need to choose alternate signing and encryption algorithms for interoperability with other platforms or to require a preferred set of algorithms.

When you configure message security for a binding, you can select an algorithm from any one of the algorithms specified by the `SecurityAlgorithmSuite` type from the `System.ServiceModel.Security` namespace. You can indicate one of these algorithm suites by setting the `algorithm` attribute for the `<message>` security section. The following illustrates a binding configuration that uses TripleDes instead of Basic256, the default suite:

```
<wsHttpBinding>
  <binding name="wsHttp">
    <security mode="Message">
      <message clientCredentialType="UserName" algorithmSuite="TripleDes" />
    </security>
  </binding>
</wsHttpBinding>
```

The following are valid settings for the algorithmSuite attribute: Basic128, Basic128Rsa15, Basic128Sha256, Basic128Sha256Rsa15, Basic192, Basic192Rsa15, Basic192Sha256, Basic192Sha256Rsa15, Basic256, Basic256Rsa15, Basic256Sha256, Basic256Sha256Rsa15, TripleDes, TripleDesRsa15, TripleDesSha256, and TripleDesSha256Rsa15. Each of these suite names maps to a SecurityAlgorithmSuite instance, which defines algorithms and key lengths for various cryptographic operations.

I'll discuss cryptography and digital signatures in greater detail later in this chapter, but an exhaustive discussion of algorithms is out of the scope of this book.

Authentication, Authorization, and Identities

From the discussion so far, you should gather that messages are secured according to binding configuration. Mutual authentication is performed based on the supplied client and service credentials. Message protection is applied according to transport or message security configuration, which normally means that messages are both signed and encrypted. Token authentication, runtime identities, security principals, and authorization policies also play an important role in the WCF security story.

Access to resources during a service operation is influenced by three key elements:

Process identity
> Service operations are executed under the process identity of the service host. For ASP.NET hosts, this is usually the ASP.NET (on Windows XP) or NET-WORK SERVICE (on Windows Vista and Windows Server 2003) account, and for self-hosting, you may allocate a different account. This process identity is the Windows account that governs what the service code can do at run time when attempting to access Windows resources, such as the database, registry, or filesystem.

Security principal
> If you are familiar with traditional .NET role-based security, you know that there is a security principal attached to each executing thread. That security principal

holds the caller's identity, which may be tied to a Windows account or a custom database credential, and its roles. Roles govern which operations can be executed by the authenticated user when traditional .NET role-based security is applied.

ServiceSecurityContext

This type provides runtime access to other relevant information about the security context for a service operation. The ServiceSecurityContext is a runtime type that includes identities, a set of claims, and authorization policies. This information can be used to apply a more fine-grained security strategy specifically for services.

Figure 7-3 illustrates the relationship between these security elements. While the process identity is constant, each operation is executed on a request thread that contains a unique security principal and security context. In the following sections, I'll elaborate on the authorization process, and the role of these and other security elements.

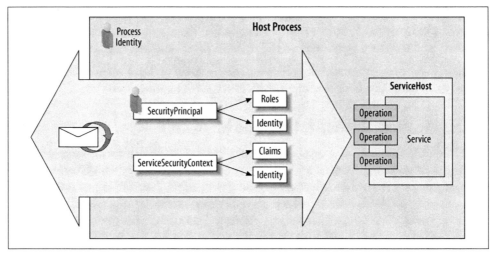

Figure 7-3. The relationship between the ServiceSecurityContext, the thread's security principal, and the host process identity

ServiceSecurityContext

For every message processed by the service model, the ServiceSecurityContext is populated with information about the authenticated caller and the policies used to authenticate that caller. The key properties of the ServiceSecurityContext type are:

PrimaryIdentity

Contains a reference to an IIdentity type such as WindowsIdentity or GenericIdentity, representing the authenticated caller.

WindowsIdentity

Contains a reference to the same identity as the PrimaryIdentity if it is a WindowsIdentity type.

AuthorizationContext

> Contains information about the security token passed in the messages. This information is useful for performing custom authorization, which I'll discuss later in this chapter.

AuthorizationPolicies

> Contains information about the authorization policies used to grant claims, also discussed later.

You can access the ServiceSecurityContext through the current OperationContext, as shown here:

```
ServiceSecurityContext context = OperationContext.Current.ServiceSecurityContext;
```

The ServiceSecurityContext type also supplies a Current property:

```
ServiceSecurityContext context = ServiceSecurityContext.Current;
```

With that reference, you can check the caller's identity using the PrimaryIdentity or WindowsIdentity reference. For example:

```
if (ServiceSecurityContext.Current.PrimaryIdentity.IsAuthenticated)
    userName = ServiceSecurityContext.Current.PrimaryIdentity.Name;
```

The same identity is wrapped in the executing request thread's security principal—an IPrincipal object accessible through the thread's CurrentPrincipal property as shown here:

```
if (Thread.CurrentPrincipal.Identity.IsAuthenticated)
    userName = Thread.CurrentPrincipal.Identity.Name;
```

It is the thread's security principal that is used for role-based security; thus, the ServiceSecurityContext is more useful for implementing custom authorization checks. I'll discuss this later in this chapter.

Security tokens and authentication

To authenticate to a service, client credentials are passed in the security headers of a message and validated against the service security policy. The serialized representation of a credential is often referred to as a *security token*. In fact, for each security token presented in a message, the service model constructs a derivative of the SecurityToken type from the System.IdentityModel.Tokens namespace.

There are a number of security token types that inherit SecurityToken. These types include WindowsSecurityToken, UserNameSecurityToken, X509SecurityToken, and SamlSecurityToken. Each token is authenticated by its own SecurityTokenAuthenticator type. WindowsSecurityTokenAuthenticator or KerberosSecurityTokenAuthenticator, for example, handle Windows credentials, the WindowsUserNameSecurityTokenAuthenticator or CustomUserNameSecurityTokenAuthenticator handles username and password credentials, and the X509SecurityTokenAuthenticator handles certificates.

Windows tokens are authenticated against the Windows domain, UserName tokens are authenticated against either the Windows domain or through a membership provider, and `Certificate` tokens are authenticated against the certificate store. You can provide service behaviors to control authentication parameters for each type of token. For example, you can configure `UserName` token authentication to use the ASP. NET membership provider, and you can control authentication rules for certificates. I'll show you how to customize authentication as I discuss related security scenarios in this chapter.

Regardless of the configuration, successful token authentication results in an identity attached to the security context and a security principal attached to the request thread for role-based authorization.

Role-based authorization

Role-based security features of .NET can also be employed at the service tier to control access to operations. As I have mentioned, after security tokens are authenticated, a security principal is attached to the request thread in the form of an `IPrincipal` type. The type of security principal depends on the type of token authenticated, and the authorization mechanism in place. In cases where a token has not been authenticated, an unauthenticated security principal may be present if the request is not rejected.

The thread's security principal is a wrapper for an identity. The type of identity is directly related to the token type received. For example, it could be a `WindowsIdentity`, `X509Identity`, `GenericIdentity`, or a custom type that implements `IIdentity` from the `System.Security.Principal` namespace.

The actual security principal is a type that implements `IPrincipal` from the `System.Security.Principal` namespace. This interface has two members:

- A read-only `Identity` property that returns a reference to the `IIdentity` instance for the request.
- An `IsInRole()` method that returns a true or false result after checking to see whether the identity is in a particular role.

Your choice of `IPrincipal` type attached to the thread is influenced by your choice of role provider for the service. Options for role provider include:

None
:   A role provider is not used.

Windows
:   Windows roles are used and a `WindowsPrincipal` is added to the security context.

UseAspNetProvider
:   The configured `RoleProvider` type is used, which defaults to the ASP.NET role provider. This adds a `RoleProviderPrincipal` to the security context.

Custom
:   A custom authorization policy is used to add a security principal to the security context. Any `IPrincipal` type is acceptable.

The default role provider is Windows; therefore, a WindowsPrincipal is the default type of security principal. For Windows, UserName, or Certificate credentials (when Certificates are mapped to Windows accounts) this will contain an authenticated WindowsPrincipal, otherwise the principal is unauthenticated and has no runtime use for role-based security.

If you aren't expecting Windows credentials, you can change the role provider by providing a ServiceAuthorization behavior and specifying an alternate role provider. You can do this declaratively by setting the principalPermissionMode for the <serviceAuthorization> behavior. If you are using the ASP.NET credentials database, you can set it to UseAspNetProvider, as shown here:

```
<behavior name="serviceBehavior">
  <serviceAuthorization principalPermissionMode="UseAspNetRoles"/>
</behavior>
```

This causes a RoleProviderPrincipal to be attached to the thread instead of a WindowsPrincipal. This IPrincipal type is new to WCF and holds a reference to the ServiceSecurityContext. The Identity property of this principal actually returns a reference to the PrimaryIdentity of the ServiceSecurityContext (discussed earlier). When IsInRole() is invoked, it uses the configured RoleProvider (in this case, the default ASP.NET role provider) to check whether this identity is in the specified role. You can also customize this behavior with a custom RoleProvider or with a custom authorization policy.

In any case, .NET role-based security relies on the IPrincipal object attached to the thread to perform authorization checks. So even with WCF, you can use the PrincipalPermission type to demand things like:

- Is the user authenticated?
- Is the user is in a particular role?
- Is a particular user calling?

At runtime, this can be done with an imperative permission demand within the WCF operation or any business component. Just create a PrincipalPermission object, initialize the values you want to enforce, and issue the Demand():

```
public string AdminsOnly( )
{
  // unprotected code

  PrincipalPermission p = new PrincipalPermission(null, "Administrators");
  p.Demand( );

  // protected code
}
```

In this example, an exception will be thrown if the user is not in the Administrators group.

You can also place a declarative `PrincipalPermissionAttribute` on any WCF operation or business component method to apply the demand before the operation or method is invoked:

```
[PrincipalPermission(SecurityAction.Demand, Role="Administrators")]
public string AdminsOnly( )
{
    // protected code
}
```

This approach is preferable since it decouples the security requirements from the actual code within the operation.

Ultimately, both of these scenarios use the `PrincipalPermission` type to validate the thread's security principal. This is done by checking the `IsAuthenticated` property of the `IIdentity` type and invoking the `IsInRole( )` method to check membership.

 In this chapter you'll apply role-based security checks at the service tier for `Windows` and `UserName` credentials. I'll also show you how to create a custom claims-based security model using custom attributes and extensibility features of WCF.

Impersonation

With all this talk about authentication and authorization, impersonation is worth discussing. When Windows credentials are used, the service can be configured to impersonate callers so that the request thread operates under the impersonated Windows token. This makes it possible for services to access protected Windows resources under the identity of the caller instead of the process identity of the service—for that request.

Using the `OperationBehaviorAttribute`, you can apply impersonation rules for each operation by setting the `Impersonation` property to one of the following values from the `ImpersonationOption` enumeration:

`NotAllowed`
> The caller will not be impersonated.

`Allowed`
> The caller will be impersonated if a Windows credential is provided and if administrators have enabled impersonation in the `ServiceAuthorizationBehavior` (discussed later).

`Required`
> The caller will be impersonated and a Windows credential *must* be provided to support this.

This example illustrates requiring impersonation at the operation:

```
[OperationBehavior(Impersonation=ImpersonationOption.Required)]
public string DoSomething( )
```

```
{
 ...
}
```

By requiring impersonation, the authenticated Windows token is automatically impersonated for the entire operation. If you want to allow administrators to control impersonation (a strange idea, yet possible) you can set the ImpersonationOption to Allowed:

```
[OperationBehavior(Impersonation=ImpersonationOption.Allowed)]
```

This allows administrators to configure the ServiceAuthorizationBehavior to impersonate callers for all operations, as shown here:

```
<behaviors>
  <serviceBehaviors>
    <behavior name="serviceBehavior">
      <serviceAuthorization impersonateCallerForAllOperations="true"/>
    </behavior>
  </serviceBehaviors>
</behaviors>
```

The ServiceAuthorizationBehavior is also accessible through the Authorization
property of the ServiceHost instance:

```
using (ServiceHost host = new ServiceHost(typeof(HelloIndigo.HelloIndigoService)))
{
  host.Authorization.ImpersonateCallerForAllOperations = true;
  host.Open();
}
```

This behavior cannot be enabled unless you explicitly mark all operations with
ImpersonationOption.Allowed.

 You are not likely to change your policy about impersonation after
deploying a service, since the host identity or impersonated identity
affects the resources that service code has access to at runtime. If your
policy is that services should not impersonate callers because of the
risk associated with promoting services to run with additional privi-
leges, you should programmatically prevent impersonation.

Clients can (and should) also control impersonation, to prevent services from
using their identity to access resources. Windows credentials have an
AllowedImpersonationLevel property that can be set to one of the following values
from the TokenImpersonationLevel enumeration:

- None
- Anonymous
- Identification
- Impersonate
- Delegate

None and Anonymous protect the caller's identity but aren't useful for authentication. Identification is the default and preferred setting since it allows services to identify the caller but disallows impersonation. Impersonate and Delegate will allow impersonation across one machine or delegation with a Kerberos ticket, respectively.

To control this, set the AllowedImpersonationLevel on the proxy, as shown here:

```
HelloIndigoServiceClient proxy = new HelloIndigoServiceClient();
...
proxy.ClientCredentials.Windows.AllowedImpersonationLevel =
TokenImpersonationLevel.Identification;
```

WCF Security Summary

In this section, I explained some of the fundamental features of WCF for creating an overall security policy for your services. Of course binding configuration is at the heart of this, which means when you configure security for a service you are selecting a security mode, client credential type and possibly other security settings, per endpoint. Behaviors also play a role in controlling how client credentials are authenticated and authorized, setting impersonation options, and providing service credentials for mutual authentication. Behaviors are configured per service; thus, when services expose multiple endpoints, although they don't have to share the same binding configuration, they do have to share the same behavior.

I also walked through the lifecycle of a secure request. Clients initialize the channel with the right credentials, as required by the binding, which are then serialized as a security token in the SOAP message. The service deserializes these tokens and authenticates them according to the type of token and related service behaviors, then initializes the security context for role-based security.

The remaining sections of this chapter will take you through intranet, Internet, certificate exchange, claims-based, and federated security scenarios in some detail. I'll expand on the topics already discussed introducing you to details appropriate for each scenario.

Securing Intranet Services

Internal applications that run on an intranet and share the same Windows domain as the services they invoke can usually take advantage of a compact binary protocol like TCP for distributed communications. In a classic client-server scenario involving distributed intranet services, the following security settings may apply:

- The service will be self-hosted in a Windows service or hosted in the Windows Activation Service (WAS) for TCP access.
- Windows credentials are used for mutual authentication.
- Client credentials are authenticated and authorized against the Windows domain using Windows membership and role providers.

- Messages are encrypted and signed at the transport layer.
- The service implements role-based permission demands for protected operations.
- The service applies a trusted subsystem model instead of impersonating Windows accounts.

Figure 7-4 illustrates this scenario.

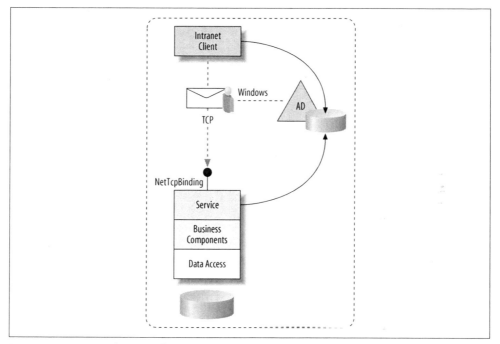

Figure 7-4. Intranet clients on the same Windows domain can rely on TCP protocol and use Windows credentials for mutual authentication and message protection

This section will focus on the intranet application scenario and explain security concepts specific to that scenario. You'll complete a lab implementing many of these concepts, and then I'll discuss the following in greater detail:

- Security features of NetNamedPipeBinding and NetTcpBinding
- Windows role-based security
- Client and server identities
- Impersonation and trusted subsystem models

Lab: Authenticating and Authorizing Windows Credentials

In this lab, you will open an existing solution and test various aspects of Windows authentication and authorization for an intranet scenario. For the service, you'll configure the binding to require Windows credentials and use Windows authentication and authorization, and you'll use role-based security to authorize access to each operation. For the client, you'll allow users to explicitly log in and you'll use this information to initialize the proxy to pass Windows credentials to the service.

Authenticating with Windows credentials

The first thing you will do in this lab is test the application as it currently exists, using two different sets of Windows credentials.

1. Open the solution for this lab located in *<YourLearningWCFPath>\Labs\ Chapter7\RoleBasedServices\ RoleBasedServices.sln.*

2. First, let's review the application functionality. Run the Host and then the WinClient application (F5 should launch both in that order). The client interface will look similar to Figure 7-5, showing your Windows identity and the security principal attached to the thread

 Unless you use the Run As command, executables run with the currently logged in user's identity.

Click each of the buttons to test the three service operations: AdminOperation( ), UserOperation( ), and GuestOperation( ). The Windows identity of the client will be passed to the service for authentication. After authenticating the call, each operation is invoked and returns a string with information about the Windows identity of the service host and the PrimaryIdentity from the ServiceSecurityContext. This string is presented in a message box, and the identities will match your client's Windows identity.

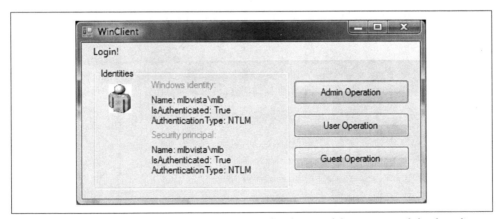

Figure 7-5. WinClient application interface showing the identity of the process and the thread's security principal.

3. Now, log in to the client application with a different Windows account on your machine. Click the Login menu and in the Login Credentials dialog, enter a domain, username, and password to an alternate account on your machine (for the domain, use your machine name to access a local account). After completing this step, the Windows identity and security principal shown in the client interface will be updated to reflect this new user.

 Invoke one of the service operations again. You should notice that the client credentials used to authenticate to the service have not changed. That's because the proxy is sending the same credentials as were sent in the first call. You can create new users with the Computer Management console accessible from Control Panel → Administrative Tools. When you create a new user, it will be added to the Users group, but you can add more groups through the Properties dialog for the user. You may wish to create three test users, one for each of the following built-in Windows groups: Administrators, Users, and Guests.

Initializing the proxy with Windows credentials

Currently, when a new user logs in to the client application, the proxy is not updated to reflect those credentials—thus the same credentials are passed to the service. You're now going to add code to update the client proxy with new credentials when a new user logs in to the application.

1. From Solution Explorer, expand the WinClient project node and open *Form1.cs* in the code window. Find the Login menu click event handler, mnuLogin_Click( ), and add the code shown in bold from Example 7-1 to dispose of the current proxy and create a new proxy.

Example 7-1. Client code to impersonate the logged-in user and update the proxy

```
private void mnuLogin_Click(object sender, EventArgs e)
{
  SecurityUtility.LoginForm f = new SecurityUtility.LoginForm( );
  DialogResult res = f.ShowDialog( );
  if (res == DialogResult.OK)
  {
    try
    {
      ImpersonateUser(f.Username, f.Password, f.Domain);

      m_proxy.Close( );
      m_proxy = new WinClient.localhost.SecureServiceContractClient( );
      UpdateIdentities( );
    }
    catch (Exception ex)
    {
      MessageBox.Show(ex.Message);
    }
  }
}
```

The ImpersonateUser( ) function shown in Example 7-1 belongs to the helper assembly, SecurityUtility. This function uses the credentials provided in the Login Credentials dialog to acquire a Windows token for the user using Win32 functions and subsequently impersonate that account. The result is that the client process identity is updated to reflect the logged-in user. The same code also updates the security principal attached to the client thread, which is why you see the security principal updated in the client interface. While the impersonated identity for the process is used to initialize the proxy and authenticate to the service, the security principal is only used if role-based permission demands are applied in the client code.

2. Test the results of this change by compiling and running the solution (F5). This time invoke the same operations after changing the logged in user, each time observing the identities presented in the message box. The service host identity remains the same, but the security context identity now reflects the credentials of the logged in user at the client.

The client channel is immutable once the proxy makes that first call to the service. To use a new set of credentials, you must construct a new channel at the client.

Applying Windows role-based permission demands

So far, the client is passing Windows credentials and is successfully authenticated at the service. Now it's time to add role-based security checks to protect service operations from unauthorized callers.

1. Go to the RoleBasedServices project and open *SecureService.cs*. Apply a PrincipalPermissionAttribute to each operation and initialize each of them with a permission demand for the built-in Windows groups Administrators, Users, and Guests, respectively. The exact location and syntax for these permission demands is shown in bold in Example 7-2.

    In addition to adding the permission demands, modify each method so that the returned string includes information about the thread's security principal as well as the WindowsIdentity of the security context. The changes to each format string are also shown in bold in Example 7-2.

Example 7-2. Permission demands applied to service operations

```
[PrincipalPermission(SecurityAction.Demand, Role="BUILTIN\\Administrators")]
string ISecureService.AdminOperation( )
{
        string s = String.Format("AdminOperation requested at {0}\r\n Host
identity is {1}\r\n Security context identity is {2}\r\n Security context Windows
identity is {3}\r\n Thread identity is {4}", DateTime.Now,
WindowsIdentity.GetCurrent( ).Name,
ServiceSecurityContext.Current.PrimaryIdentity.Name,
ServiceSecurityContext.Current.WindowsIdentity.Name,
Thread.CurrentPrincipal.Identity.Name);
```

```
  Console.WriteLine(s);
  Console.WriteLine( );
  return s;
}


[PrincipalPermission(SecurityAction.Demand, Role="BUILTIN\\Users")]
string ISecureService.UserOperation( )
{
  string s = String.Format("UserOperation requested at {0}\r\n Host identity is
{1}\r\n Security context identity is {2}\r\n Security context Windows identity is
{3}\r\n Thread identity is {4}", DateTime.Now, WindowsIdentity.GetCurrent( ).Name,
ServiceSecurityContext.Current.PrimaryIdentity.Name,
ServiceSecurityContext.Current.WindowsIdentity.Name,
Thread.CurrentPrincipal.Identity.Name);

  Console.WriteLine(s);
  Console.WriteLine( );
  return s;
}


[PrincipalPermission(SecurityAction.Demand, Role="BUILTIN\\Guests")]
string ISecureService.GuestOperation( )
{
        string s = String.Format("GuestOperation requested at {0}\r\n Host
identity is {1}\r\n Security context identity is {2}\r\n Security context Windows
identity is {3}\r\n Thread identity is {4}", DateTime.Now,
WindowsIdentity.GetCurrent( ).Name,
ServiceSecurityContext.Current.PrimaryIdentity.Name,
ServiceSecurityContext.Current.WindowsIdentity.Name,
Thread.CurrentPrincipal.Identity.Name);

  Console.WriteLine(s);
  Console.WriteLine( );
  return s;
}
```

> The ServiceSecurityContext identities and the identity wrapped by the
> thread's security principal are initialized with the same client creden-
> tial. As I mentioned earlier in this chapter, the thread's security princi-
> pal is the identity used for role-based security.

2. Test these new permission demands by compiling and running the solution once
   again. Invoke the UserOperation( ) first—it should succeed if the logged-in user is
   a member of the Users group. Note that the identities of the thread and security
   context both match the credentials passed from the client application, while the
   host identity matches the account you ussed to log in to the machine. Try accessing GuestOperation( )—it will fail if the user is not a member of the Guests group.

In this lab, you learned how to secure intranet services accessible over TCP protocol.
You applied NetTcpBinding defaults, passed Windows credentials from the client,

authenticated the client against the Windows domain, and performed role-based security checks at each operation.

In the following sections, I'll discuss security features of both intranet bindings, `NetNamedPipeBinding` and `NetTcpBinding`, and elaborate on security concepts specific to intranet security scenarios.

NetNamedPipeBinding Security Features

Named pipes protocol is typically used for in-process calls or inter-process communication on the same machine. WCF services exposed over named pipes are secure by default, although they have limited security options. By default, `NetNamedPipeBinding` provides the following security features:

- Transport security is enabled
- Windows client credentials are required
- Messages are signed and encrypted at the transport layer

`NetNamedPipeBinding` doesn't have much in the way of configurable options. It supports only two security modes: `None` or `Transport`; for transport security settings, only Windows credentials are supported. Table 7-1 summarizes the security options available to `NetNamedPipeBinding`.

Table 7-1. Transport security options for NetNamedPipeBinding

Security feature	Options
Credentials	`Windows`.
Transfer security	SPNego protocol is used to negotiate a session key for signing and encryption.
Protection level	`None`, `Signed`, or `EncryptAndSign` (default).

 Simple and Protected Negotiation (SPNego) protocol is a mechanism for negotiating a security context using Windows credentials. The protocol evaluates client credentials and server authentication capabilities to determine if NTLM or Kerberos will be used to authenticate and to complete an initial handshake that will establish a secure session key for message protection between client and server endpoints. For more information about SPNego, see this link: *http://www.ietf.org/rfc/rfc4559.txt*.

Although not an entirely practical option, you can disable security for the binding by setting the security mode to `None`, as shown here:

```
<netNamedPipeBinding>
  <binding name="netPipe">
    <security mode="None" />
  </binding>
</netNamedPipeBinding>
```

You can also optionally disable or throttle message protection on the wire as shown here:

```
<netNamedPipeBinding>
  <binding name="netPipe">
    <security mode="Transport">
      <transport protectionLevel="Sign"/>
    </security>
  </binding>
</netNamedPipeBinding>
```

Even though named pipes are only used for in-process or same-machine communication, you should still prefer to use the default security settings for the binding. If you need to support a richer set of credentials, you'll likely move to NetTcpBinding, which has more flexible options for credential types in addition to support for message security.

NetTcpBinding Security Features

TCP protocol is typically used for distributed communication across process and machine boundaries on the intranet. NetTcpBinding is secure by default and provides a richer set of options over NetNamedPipeBinding. The default security features of NetTcpBinding are as follows:

- Transport security is enabled.
- Windows client credentials are required.
- Messages are signed and encrypted at the transport layer.

Unlike NetNamedPipeBinding, NetTcpBinding supports several security modes: None, Transport, Message, TransportWithMessageCredential. Table 7-2 summarizes possible security options for NetTcpBinding when transport security is enabled.

Table 7-2. Transport security options for NetTcpBinding

Security feature	Options
Credentials	None, Windows (default), or Certificate.
Transfer security	For Windows credentials, SPNego protocol is used to negotiate a session key for signing and encryption. For Certificate credentials, SSL protocol is used to negotiate a session key.
Protection level	None, Signed, or EncryptAndSign (default).

For classic client-server scenarios, Windows credentials are usually adequate for authentication and authorization. Like with NetNamedPipeBinding, you can throttle the protection level when transport security is used, as shown here:

```
<netTcpBinding>
  <binding name="netTcp">
    <security mode="Transport">
      <transport protectionLevel="Sign"/>
```

```
      </security>
    </binding>
  </netTcpBinding>
```

Certificates can be useful to secure calls across machines behind the firewall, something I'll talk about later in this chapter.

NetTcpBinding also supports message security, which allows you to achieve end-to-end security and pass a richer set of credentials. Table 7-3 summarizes options for message security.

Table 7-3. Message security options for NetTcpBinding

Security feature	Options
Credentials	None, Windows, UserName, Certificate, or IssuedToken.
Transfer security	For Windows credentials, SPNego protocol is tunneled over WS-Trust to negotiate a session key for signing and encryption. For Certificate, UserName, and IssuedToken credentials, TLSNego protocol is tunneled over WS-Trust to negotiate a session key.
Protection level	None, Signed, or EncryptAndSign.
Algorithms	Defaults to Basic256.

 TLSNego protocol is a mechanism for negotiating a security context using over WS-Trust (I will talk about WS-Trust later in this chapter). The protocol completes an initial SSL-like handshake and generates a security context token that can be used to protect messages between client and server endpoints. At the time of this writing, there is no publicly available documentation on TLSNego.

For traditional intranet scenarios, you will most likely choose Windows credentials, even in the event you use message security. The primary driver for using message security in this case is to secure messages end to end instead of point to point, as I discussed earlier in this chapter. Here's an example of NetTcpBinding to illustrate this case:

```
<netTcpBinding>
  <binding name="netTcp">
    <security mode="Message">
      <message clientCredentialType="Windows" />
    </security>
  </binding>
</netTcpBinding>
```

Message security is certainly more heavily used for Internet applications, and I'll be discussing many such scenarios in later sections of this chapter.

Windows Authentication and Authorization

Intranet applications typically rely on Windows credentials, which are authenticated and authorized against the Windows domain. NetNamedPipeBinding and

NetTcpBinding require Windows credentials by default. The ServiceHost has WindowsAuthentication settings that influence authentication for Windows credentials and is also initialized with a ServiceAuthorizationBehavior that defaults to UseWindowsGroups as the PrincipalPermissionMode. Example 7-3 illustrates these default authorization and authentication configuration settings in the <windowsAuthentication> and <serviceAuthorization> sections, respectively.

Example 7-3. Default Windows authentication and authorization settings

```
<serviceBehaviors>
  <behavior name="serviceBehavior">
    <serviceAuthorization impersonateCallerForAllOperations="false"
principalPermissionMode="UseWindowsGroups" />
    <serviceCredentials >
      <windowsAuthentication allowAnonymousLogons="false"
includeWindowsGroups="true" />
    </serviceCredentials>
  </behavior>
</serviceBehaviors>
```

You aren't likely to change these defaults for an intranet scenario. Even if the situation calls for impersonation, you would require that in the contract using the OperationBehaviorAttribute discussed earlier.

Windows Role-Based Security

The setting for PrincipalPermissionMode determines the type of security principal attached to each request thread. When UseWindowsGroups is specified, a WindowsPrincipal is created. This is used for role-based permission demands performed by the PrincipalPermissionAttribute.

For intranet applications, permission demands should be applied to protect any operation that requires particular set of Windows groups, as shown here:

```
[PrincipalPermission(SecurityAction.Demand, Role = "BUILTIN\\Administrators")]
public string AdminOperation()
```

These attributes can also be stacked so that multiple groups can be allowed access to a particular operation:

```
[PrincipalPermission(SecurityAction.Demand, Role = "BUILTIN\\Administrators")]
[PrincipalPermission(SecurityAction.Demand, Role = "BUILTIN\\Users")]
public string AdminOrUserOperation()
```

Windows Client Credentials

In an intranet application, the client-side binding requires Windows credentials. In this situation, when you initialize a proxy, its ClientCredentials property is also initialized with a Windows credential representative of the client process identity—most likely the user logged in to the machine. If this is the credential you want to pass from the client application, your job is done here. If, however, the client application allows different users to log in, a login dialog can be presented to collect credentials. These credentials can be used to authenticate to intranet services, in addition to client-side role-based security.

The ClientCredentials property of the proxy exposes a number of properties for different credential types. The Windows property is a WindowsClientCredential type that holds not only the Windows credential but other rules for authentication, as demonstrated by the following properties:

AllowedImpersonationLevel

> Allows the client application to control the impersonation level as discussed earlier in this chapter. Can be any option from the TokenImpersonationLevel enumeration.

AllowNtlm

> Set to true by default. If set to false, NTLM or workgroup authentication is not permitted.

ClientCredential

> A NetworkCredential type that represents the Windows credential for authentication to the service.

You can specify a new set of Windows credentials by initializing a NetworkCredential and assigning it to this ClientCredential property as shown here:

```
m_proxy.ClientCredentials.Windows.ClientCredential = new
NetworkCredential("username", "password", "domain");
```

ClientCredentials must be initialized before using the proxy. After channel communications have been established (the first operation is called) credentials are immutable. Thus, if you provide a "login as" feature for users, each time a new user logs, in a new proxy must be created representative of their Windows credentials.

NTLM is supported by default, which is useful for testing in a workgroup. You can deny support for workgroup authentication by disabling NTLM support on the WindowsCredential reference, as shown here:

```
m_proxy.ClientCredentials.Windows.AllowNtlm = false;
```

Securing Internet Services

When remote clients are not part of the Windows domain, they use Internet protocols to access services (HTTP or HTTPS). The configuration settings in this case will vary based on many factors, including the type of protocols client applications can support. You'll usually want to expose services so that they can be accessed by earlier web service protocol stacks (Basic Profile) while also supporting emerging web service standards (WS*). I discussed this type of scenario in Chapter 3, without specifically discussing security-related standards. By the same token, you have to consider exposing endpoints with security policies that can be met by your intended client base.

Assuming you want to support interoperability and reach clients using earlier and more recent web service technologies, in addition to clients that support WS*, you'll likely expose several secure service endpoints meeting the following requirements:

- One endpoint can expose a SOAP 1.1 endpoint and comply with Basic Security Profile using SSL/HTTPS for server authentication and message protection or WS-Security.

- Another endpoint can expose a SOAP 1.2 endpoint and use existing and emerging web service security standards such as WS-Security and WS-SecureConversation for server authentication and message protection.

- Both endpoints require UserName credentials for client authentication.

- Authentication and authorization use the built-in ASP.NET membership and role provider.

- Services are hosted in IIS.

Figure 7-6 illustrates this scenario.

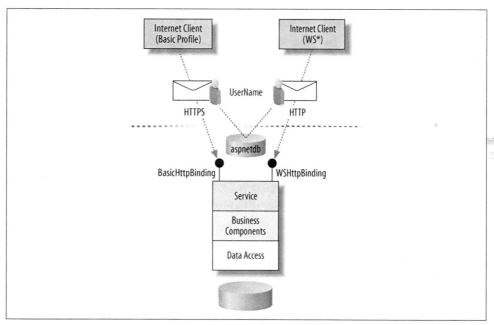

Figure 7-6. A service exposing two endpoints to support BasicHttpBinding and WSHttpBinding; both endpoints require UserName credentials and authenticate using ASP.NET providers

In this section, you'll complete a lab that shows you how to expose secure Internet services using interoperable security protocols. I'll be explaining the following:

- Security features of `BasicHttpBinding` and `WSHttpBinding`
- ASP.NET provider configuration and role-based security
- Authenticating and authorizing `UserName` credentials
- Message security, negotiation, and secure sessions

Lab: Authenticating and Authorizing UserName Credentials

In this lab, you will expose a single service on the Internet through two endpoints. One endpoint will be secured using Basic Security Profile and another will use advanced WS-Security standards. Both service endpoints will be hosted in IIS and share the same service implementation. You'll configure services to authenticate and authorize `UserName` tokens using the ASP.NET provider model.

Creating two service endpoints

In the first portion of the lab, you'll create a new web site to host a service and expose two endpoints for that service.

1. Open the solution for this lab located in *<YourLearningWCFPath>\Labs\ Chapter7\ASPNETAuthentication\ ASPNETAuthentication.sln*.

2. This lab requires you to install two certificates: RPKey and localhost; to give your ASP.NET account access to the private key pair RPKey; to provide an SSL certificate for IIS; and to set up specific users and roles for the ASP.NET Provider Model. Detailed instructions for each of these requirements can be found in Appendix A.

3. Now you'll create a new web site to host a preexisting service. From Solution Explorer, add a new web site using the WCF Service template, set the Location field to HTTP and type in the address *http://localhost/ASPNETAuthenticationWebHost*.

4. This template creates a sample WCF service, but you're going to host the SecureService located in the `RoleBasedServices` project. Go to the web site project and add a reference to the `RoleBasedServices` project. After that, open *service.svc* in the code window and modify the @ServiceHost directive to reflect the settings shown here:

   ```
   <% @ServiceHost Language=C# Service="RoleBasedServices.SecureService" %>
   ```

   You can optionally delete the superfluous *service.cs* file in the `App_Code` directory.

5. Create a service model configuration for this service exposing two endpoints, one for SOAP 1.1, the other for SOAP 1.2. This will include enabling metadata exchange for the service. Open the *web.config* file and modify the `<system.serviceModel>` section to look as shown in Example 7-4.

Example 7-4. Service model configuration for the two service endpoints

```
<services>
  <service name="RoleBasedServices.SecureService" behaviorConfiguration="serviceBehavior">
    <endpoint address="Soap11" contract="RoleBasedServices.ISecureService"
binding="basicHttpBinding" />
    <endpoint address="Soap12" contract="RoleBasedServices.ISecureService"
binding="wsHttpBinding"/>
    <endpoint contract="IMetadataExchange" binding="mexHttpBinding" address="mex"/>
  </service>
</services>
<behaviors>
  <serviceBehaviors>
    <behavior name="serviceBehavior"
      <serviceMetadata httpGetEnabled="true" />
    </behavior>
  </serviceBehaviors>
</behaviors>
```

Intellisense is very helpful while you are directly typing in <system. serviceModel> settings in your *app.config* and *web.config* files. Unfortunately, Intellisense doesn't work properly in the *web.config* unless you delete the namespace declaration shown here:

```
<configuration xmlns="http://schemas.microsoft.com/.
NetConfiguration/v2.0">
```

6. Test the web site in a browser to make sure that the configuration settings are accurate. You should see the test page for the service without errors.

Web sites can only be debugged through Visual Studio if integrated Windows authentication is enabled for the site. See Appendix A for additional details.

Generating the client proxy

Next you'll generate a proxy and configuration settings for the client application.

1. From Solution Explorer add a service reference to the WinClient project using the following address: *http://localhost/ASPNETAuthenticationWebHost/Service.svc*. Leave the service namespace as localhost.

   When you generate configuration settings for the client using SvcUtil, it usually configures the client endpoint address to use the machine name instead of "localhost." For this lab, since the server certificate is named "locahost," you will have to manually edit the proxy to replace your machine name with "localhost."

2. The client already includes the necessary code inside *Form1.cs* to invoke the service. Two proxy references named m_proxySoap11 and m_proxySoap12 are members of the form, and the InitializeProxy( ) method initializes each proxy with the correct client endpoint, as shown in Example 7-5.

Example 7-5. Code to initialize the SOAP 1.1 and SOAP 1.2 endpoint

```
localhost.SecureServiceContractClient m_proxySoap11;
localhost.SecureServiceContractClient m_proxySoap12;

private void InitializeProxy()
{
  m_proxySoap11 = new WinClient.localhost.SecureServiceContractClient(
"BasicHttpBinding_SecureServiceContract");
  m_proxySoap12 = new WinClient.localhost.SecureServiceContractClient(
"WSHttpBinding_SecureServiceContract");

}
```

3. *Form1.cs* also includes the code necessary to invoke each operation of the service: AdminOperation( ), UserOperation( ), and GuestOperation( ). Since the user interface (shown in Figure 7-7) lets you select SOAP 1.1 or 1.2 by a RadioButton selection—a GetProxy( ) method is used to return a reference to the correct proxy based on that selection:

```
private localhost.SecureServiceContractClient GetProxy()
{
  if (radSoap11.Checked)
    return this.m_proxySoap11;
  else
    return this.m_proxySoap12;
}
```

The Click event for each button in the interface (Admin Operation, User Operation, and Guest Operation) first retrieves the correct proxy before invoking the appropriate service operation. For example, the Admin Operation button's click event, cmdAdminOp_Click( ), includes this code:

```
MessageBox.Show(GetProxy().AdminOperation());
```

4. Before adding security features to the solution, test the two endpoints. Compile the solution and run the WinClient project. Test each button using SOAP 1.1 protocol. You'll see a message indicating that the service host is executing under the ASP.NET identity (ASPNET or NETWORK SERVICE) and that the security context is null. That's because BasicHttpBinding has no security by default.

Now test each button using SOAP 1.2 protocol. You'll see a similar message indicating the same identity for the service host. This time the security context is not null since WSHttpBinding requires Windows credentials by default. The message shows the PrimaryIdentity and WindowsIdentity of the ServiceSecurityContext—they both match the client credential passed, as does the thread's identity.

So far, you have only exercised the default security settings for BasicHttpBinding and WSHttpBinding. Next you'll provide more typical security settings for Internet services.

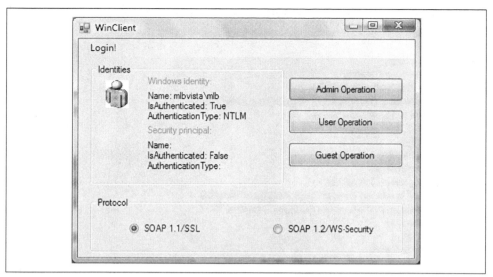

Figure 7-7. The WinClient user interface

Configuring binding security

In this part of the lab, you'll customize the security settings for both endpoints to support UserName credentials and to sign and encrypt messages.

1. Open the *web.config* for the web site and add the <bindings> section, as shown in Example 7-6. This section includes a customized <basicHttpBinding> and <wsHttpBinding> section. The customized <basicHttpBinding> section uses transport security to sign and encrypt messages while requiring that UserName credentials be passed in the SOAP message. The customized <wsHttpBinding> section requires that UserName credentials be passed in the SOAP message but also uses message security to sign and encrypt messages. Disabling negotiation ensures interoperability, something I'll discuss following this lab.

   To associate these customized binding configurations with each endpoint, add a bindingConfiguration attribute to each <endpoint> for the appropriate binding, as shown in bold in Example 7-6.

Example 7-6. Security configuration for BasicHttpBinding and WSHttpBinding

```
<system.serviceModel>
  <services>
    <service name="RoleBasedServices.SecureService"
behaviorConfiguration="serviceBehavior">
      <endpoint address="Soap11" contract="RoleBasedServices.ISecureService"
binding="basicHttpBinding" bindingConfiguration="basicHttp" />
      <endpoint address="Soap12" contract="RoleBasedServices.ISecureService"
binding="wsHttpBinding" bindingConfiguration="wsHttp"/>
      <endpoint contract="IMetadataExchange" binding="mexHttpBinding"
address="mex"/>
    </service>
```

```
    </services>
    <bindings>
      <wsHttpBinding>
        <binding name="wsHttp">
          <security mode="Message">
            <message clientCredentialType="UserName"
negotiateServiceCredential="false" />
          </security>
        </binding>
      </wsHttpBinding>
      <basicHttpBinding>
        <binding name="basicHttp">
          <security mode="TransportWithMessageCredential">
            <message clientCredentialType="UserName"/>
          </security>
        </binding>
      </basicHttpBinding>
    </bindings>
    <!-- other settings -->
</system.serviceModel>
```

2. UserName credentials must be securely passed using transport or message security. The BasicHttpBinding endpoint is configured for transport security, so the site's SSL certificate will be used. The WSHttpBinding endpoint is configured for message security and thus requires a service certificate be provided. To address this, add a <serviceCredentials> section to the service behavior pointing to the RPKey certificate as shown in bold here:

```
<behavior name="serviceBehavior">
  <serviceDebug includeExceptionDetailInFaults="false"/>
  <serviceMetadata httpGetEnabled="true"/>
  <serviceCredentials>
    <serviceCertificate findValue="RPKey" x509FindType="FindBySubjectName"
storeLocation="LocalMachine" storeName="My"/>
  </serviceCredentials>
</behavior>
```

3. Test these changes by launching the *service.svc* endpoint in a browser. Make sure you don't see any errors.

Initializing proxies with UserName credentials

Now you will update the client proxy and configuration to reflect changes at the service, and add code to send a username and password credential to authenticate to the service. You'll set properties of the proxy to accomplish this.

1. Since the service endpoints have been updated, you'll have to update the client proxy and configuration to reflect the new requirements. You can do this by deleting and regenerating the proxy and configuration file.

---

2. To send `UserName` credentials to the service, you'll have to add some code to the `WinClient` application so that users can log in at the client and apply those credentials to the proxy. Part of the work has been completed already.

Open *Form1.cs* in the code window and you'll see two string members, m_ username and m_password (shown in bold in Example 7-7). These members store the username and password entered by users when they select the Login menu. The Click event handler for the Login menu presents the user with a dialog to enter their credentials, and when this dialog is closed, the username and password is stored for later use (also shown in bold in Example 7-7).

Example 7-7. Storing user credentials entered in the Login dialog

```
public partial class Form1 : Form
{
  string m_username;
  string m_password;

  // other code

  private void mnuLogin_Click(object sender, EventArgs e)
  {
    SecurityUtility.LoginForm f = new SecurityUtility.LoginForm();
    f.ShowDomain = false;

    DialogResult res = f.ShowDialog();
    if (res == DialogResult.OK)
    {
      try
      {
        this.m_username = f.Username;
        this.m_password = f.Password;
        InitializeProxy();
        UpdateIdentities();
      }
      catch (Exception ex)
      {
        MessageBox.Show(ex.Message);
      }
    }
  }
}
```

Add these credentials to both proxy references prior to invoking the service. In fact, each time a new user logs in, both proxies must be recreated with the new credentials. In Example 7-7, you can see that `InitializeProxy()` is called each time a user logs in, so you can add code to that method to set the appropriate `ClientCredentials` for each proxy. This code is shown in bold in Example 7-8.

Example 7-8. Initializing UserName credentials on the proxy

```
private void InitializeProxy()
{
  m_proxySoap11 = new WinClient.localhost.SecureServiceContractClient(
"BasicHttpBinding_SecureServiceContract");
  m_proxySoap12 = new WinClient.localhost.SecureServiceContractClient(
"WSHttpBinding_SecureServiceContract");

  if (!(String.IsNullOrEmpty(m_username) || String.IsNullOrEmpty(this.m_password)))
  {
    m_proxySoap11.ClientCredentials.UserName.UserName = this.m_username;
    m_proxySoap11.ClientCredentials.UserName.Password = this.m_password;

    m_proxySoap12.ClientCredentials.UserName.UserName = this.m_username;
    m_proxySoap12.ClientCredentials.UserName.Password = this.m_password;
  }
}
```

3. Run the `WinClient` application to test sending `UserName` credentials. Before calling any of the methods, click the Login menu and supply a valid Windows credential (it can be the same credential as you use to log in to your machine, if you do not have an alternate account with which to test). This will initialize each proxy with the username and password you supplied. Now test, hitting the SOAP 1.1 and SOAP 1.2 endpoints as you did earlier. The result should be that you see a message box indicating the credentials you provided as the `PrimaryIdentity`, `WindowsIdentity`, and thread identity.

In this section, you learned how to pass a username and password to satisfy `UserName` credential requirements of each service endpoint. The username and password is authenticated against the Windows domain by default, which is why you had to supply a Windows credential. Next you'll change this to authenticate against the ASP.NET security database.

Configuring ASP.NET authentication and authorization

In the test you just completed you passed a Windows username and password in the `UserName` credentials provided to the service. Now you're going to modify the service configuration so that these credentials are authenticated and authorized by the ASP.NET membership and role providers.

1. Start by adding the `<serviceAuthorization>` and `<userNameAuthentication>` sections shown in bold in Example 7-9. These sections override the default authentication and authorization modes of `Windows` and `UseWindowsGroups` to `MembershipProvider` and `UseAspNetRoles`, respectively. These new settings tell the service model to use the ASP.NET membership and role providers.

Example 7-9. Specifying service credentials and metadata exchange behaviors

```
<behaviors>
  <serviceBehaviors>
    <behavior name="serviceBehavior">
```

```
        <serviceMetadata httpGetEnabled="true"/>
        <serviceAuthorization principalPermissionMode="UseAspNetRoles"/>
        <serviceCredentials>
          <userNameAuthentication
userNamePasswordValidationMode="MembershipProvider"/>
          <serviceCertificate findValue="RPKey" storeLocation="LocalMachine"
storeName="My" x509FindType="FindBySubjectName"/>
        </serviceCredentials>
      </behavior>
    </serviceBehaviors>
</behaviors>
```

2. Enable role management for the ASP.NET provider model by adding the following `<roleManager>` setting shown in bold to the *web.config* of the web site:

```
        <system.web>
          <roleManager enabled="true"/>
        </system.web>
```

3. Add the following `LocalSqlServer` connection string setting to the *web.config* so that the ASP.NET provider is using the local SQL server database:

```
        <connectionStrings>
          <remove name="LocalSqlServer"/>
          <add name="LocalSqlServer" connectionString="data source=
          localhost;Initial Catalog=aspnetdb;Integrated Security=True;"
          providerName="System.Data.SqlClient" />
        </connectionStrings>
```

4. Launch the web site in a browser at the *service.svc* endpoint to make sure that the configuration settings are OK. You will see an error if there is a problem.

5. Now, run the `WinClient` project to test authentication against the ASP.NET provider database, `aspnetdb`. Select the Login menu and supply the following credentials:

```
        Username: Admin
        Password: p@ssw0rd
```

Call any of the operations and you'll see the `PrincipalIdentity` and thread identity match the username passed from the client. The `WindowsIdentity` will not be set since ASP.NET authorization was used.

Applying custom role-based permission demands

To restrict access to each service operation, you're going to apply role-based permission demands using the roles you created in the ASP.NET database.

1. Open *SecureService.cs* and add `PrincipalPermissionAttribute` declarations, shown in bold in Example 7-10.

Example 7-10. Adding custom role-based permission demands

```
[PrincipalPermission(SecurityAction.Demand, Role = "Administrators")]
string ISecureService.AdminOperation()
```

Example 7-10. Adding custom role-based permission demands (continued)

```
{...}

[PrincipalPermission(SecurityAction.Demand, Role = "Users")]
string ISecureService.UserOperation()
{...}

[PrincipalPermission(SecurityAction.Demand, Role = "Guests")]
string ISecureService.GuestOperation()
{...}
```

2. Compile the solution and launch the web site in a browser (to refresh the ASP. NET cache) and run the client application. Log in as Admin again and test the admin, user, and then guest operations. The first two will succeed, and the guest operation will fail since the Admin account does not belong to the Guests role.

In this lab, you learned how to secure Internet services accessible over HTTP protocol. You exposed a service over two different endpoints to support SOAP 1.1 and 1.2 using BasicHttpBinding and WSHttpBinding, respectively. The former used SSL protocol to protect messages, while the latter relied on web service security standards. In both cases, UserName credentials were passed by the client and authenticated against the ASP.NET membership and role tables, and role-based security was used to authorize access to operations.

In the sections that follow, I'll describe the security features of BasicHttpBinding and WSHttpBinding and then discuss relevant security concepts for exposing Internet services.

BasicHttpBinding Security Features

BasicHttpBinding is typically used to expose services over HTTP protocol to clients that do not support emerging web service standards (WS*). More specifically, it's used to migrate your existing ASMX web services to WCF, to expose endpoints to be consumed by earlier service toolkits, or to expose endpoints that use only the simplest security standards, such as UserName credentials over SSL.

BasicHttpBinding is the only standard binding that is not secure by default, but it does supply several security modes, including None, Transport, Message, TransportWithMessageCredential, and TransportCredentialOnly. Table 7-4 summarizes possible security options for BasicHttpBinding when transport security is enabled.

Table 7-4. Transport security options for BasicHttpBinding

Security feature	Options
Credentials	None, Basic, Digest, Ntlm, Windows (default), Certificate.
Proxy credentials	None (default), Basic, Digest, Ntlm, Windows.
Transfer security	SSL protocol is used to negotiate a session key for signing and encryption.

If the service endpoint is exposed in an intranet setting, transport security may be acceptable. In that case, you'll require one of the Windows credential types or Certificate as your authentication mechanism. In this case, HTTP authentication is used to pass credentials while sitting on an SSL connection. The SSL connection will always both sign and encrypt messages, and there is no protection-level setting to control this. On the other hand, if `TransportCredentialOnly` security mode is used, no message protection is applied.

Internet services often use the security mode `TransportWithMessageCredential`. As it implies, SSL security would be used to sign and encrypt messages while credentials are passed in the SOAP message. In this case, transport credentials are not considered, credential requirements are defined by message security.

Table 7-5 summarizes operations for message security.

Table 7-5. Message security options for BasicHttpBinding

Security feature	Options
Credentials	UserName or Certificate.
Transfer security	For UserName and Certificate credentials, the guidelines established by WS-Security are used for signing and encryption.
Algorithms	Defaults to Basic256.

`BasicHttpBinding` is compliant with message security as described by Basic Security Profile, which describes guidelines for applying *WS-Security* specifications to secure messages. This explains the limited number of credential types supported, as compared to other bindings. In the case of `BasicHttpBinding`, the following OASIS specifications apply:

- SOAP Message Security
- UserName Token Profile
- X.509 Token Profile

 You can find these OASIS Web Services specifications at *http://www. oasis-open.org/committees/tc_home.php?wg_abbrev=wss.*

A few common ways to apply message security with `BasicHttpBinding` are as follows:

- Authenticate with `UserName` credentials, sign messages with the token generated from the credential, and encrypt the messages with the service certificate.
- Authenticate with `Certificate` credentials, sign messages with the client certificate, and encrypt messages with the service certificate.

- Authenticate with `UserName` credentials but supply a client `Certificate` credential as well, sign messages with the client certificate, and encrypt messages with the service certificate.

Certificates play a big part in message security, and I'll be discussing certificates later in a separate section of this chapter.

 `BasicHttpBinding` security is interoperable with WSE 3.0.

WSHttpBinding Security Features

Clients that support emerging web service standards can consume `WSHttpBinding` endpoints. This binding provides additional security features not available to `BasicHttpBinding` such as support for `IssuedToken` client credentials, negotiation, and secure sessions.

The default security features of `WSHttpBinding` are as follows:

- Message security is enabled.
- Windows client credentials are required.
- Messages are signed and encrypted at the message layer.

`WSHttpBinding` supports the following security modes: `None`, `Transport`, `Message`, and `TransportWithMessageCredential`. When transport security is enabled, `WSHttpBinding` behaves just as `BasicHttpBinding`, as described in Table 7-4. The only real difference between the two bindings as far as transport security is concerned is that `WSHttpBinding` doesn't support `TransportCredentialOnly` mode.

Message security is the default and more frequently used security mode for `WSHttpBinding`. Table 7-6 summarizes message security features of the binding.

Table 7-6. Message security options for WSHttpBinding

Security feature	Options
Credentials	None, Windows, UserName, Certificate or IssuedToken
Negotiation	Enabled by default. Has a direct effect on how transfer security is handled.
Transfer security (negotiation enabled)	For Windows credentials, SPNego protocol is tunneled over WS-Trust to negotiate a session key for signing and encryption.
	For Certificate, UserName, and IssuedToken credentials, TLSNego protocol is tunneled over WS-Trust to negotiate a session key.
Transfer security (negotiation disabled)	For Windows credentials a Kerberos domain is required.
	For UserName, Certificate, and IssuedToken credentials the guidelines established by WS-Security are used for signing and encryption.
Secure sessions	Enabled by default. When enabled WS-SecureConversation protocol is used a security context token (SCT) is generated to reduce authentication overhead.

Table 7-6. Message security options for WSHttpBinding (continued)

Security feature	Options
Algorithms	Defaults to Basic256

The following OASIS security specifications are supported by WSHttpBinding:

- SOAP Message Security
- UserName Token Profile
- X.509 Token Profile
- Kerberos Token Profile
- SAML Token Profile
- WS-Trust
- WS-SecureConversation

> You can find reference for these OASIS Web Services specifications at:
>
> - *http://www.oasis-open.org/committees/tc_home.php?wg_abbrev=wss*
> - *http://www.oasis-open.org/committees/tc_home.php?wg_abbrev=security*
> - *http://www.oasis-open.org/committees/tc_home.php?wg_abbrev=ws-sx*

Although the mechanism for signing and encryption varies based on the setting for negotiation, you can still throttle message protection using the protection level options discussed earlier in this chapter. For example, ProtectionLevel.Sign would result in message signing according to the binding configuration without encryption.

A few common ways to apply message security with WSHttpBinding are as follows:

- Authenticate with UserName credentials, enable negotiation, and secure sessions for WCF Clients.
- Authenticate with UserName credentials, disable negotiation, and enable secure sessions for interoperability with SOAP 1.2 clients that support WS-Secure-Conversation.
- Authenticate with UserName credentials, disable negotiation, and disable secure sessions for interoperability with SOAP 1.2 clients that support classic WS-Security.
- If clients use Certificate credentials, the same three combinations for negotiation and secure sessions can be used.

> WSHttpBinding security is also interoperable with WSE 3.0.

Negotiation

Negotiation is a feature of `WSHttpBinding` that allows clients and services to negotiate a secure session key for signing and encryption, using message security. This feature removes the need to provision clients with keys necessary to secure messages because the session key is dynamically negotiated. *WS-Trust* protocol, now part of WS-SX, is used to tunnel SPNego or TLSNego negotiation requests through a series of messages. This generates a security context token (SCT) used for signing and encryption. Developers are largely unaware of this exchange—it happens automatically when the proxy is used to make the first call to an operation.

 WS-Trust is a web service protocol that defines token issuance and related messaging. It is a core specification for interoperable single sign-on (SSO) scenarios. I'll elaborate further on this protocol later in this chapter.

By default, `WSHttpBinding` supports negotiation when message security is used. Although WS-Trust is an interoperable protocol for token issuance, no interoperable guidance exists at the time of this writing for SPNego or TLSNego protocol and WS-Trust. For this reason, it may be desirable to disable negotiation. You can do this by setting the value for `negotiateServiceCredential` to `false` in the `<message>` section for the binding configuration, as Example 7-11 illustrates.

Example 7-11. Disabling negotiation

```
<wsHttpBinding>
  <binding name="wsHttp">
    <security mode="Message">
      <message clientCredentialType="UserName"
negotiateServiceCredential="false" />
    </security>
  </binding>
</wsHttpBinding>
```

When negotiation is disabled for Windows client credentials, a Kerberos domain must exist. For other credential types, the client must have access to the service public key out of band to encrypt messages. I'll talk more about certificates and negotiation in the section "Working with Certificates," later in this chapter.

Secure Sessions

Secure sessions are another feature of message security supported by `WSHttpBinding`. Secure sessions reduce the overhead for repeat communications between clients and services by removing the need to reauthenticate credentials or revalidate certificates supplied by the caller. By default, secure sessions are enabled. This means that a

---

security context token (SCT) is generated through an initial exchange between client and service using *WS-SecureConversation* protocol, now part of WS-SX. This token is used to authorize subsequent message exchanges.

If the caller plans to make several calls to a service, secure sessions are more efficient. For a single call, however, you can disable this feature by setting establishSecurityContext to false (see Example 7-12).

Example 7-12. Disabling secure sessions

```
<wsHttpBinding>
  <binding name="wsHttp">
    <security mode="Message">
      <message clientCredentialType="UserName"
establishSecurityContext="false" />
    </security>
  </binding>
</wsHttpBinding>
```

Although WS-SecureConversation is an interoperable standard, limited platform support exists at the time of this writing. For that reason as well, you may choose to disable secure sessions for Internet services that require a wider-reaching client base.

ASP.NET Authentication and Authorization

When you require UserName credentials for BasicHttpBinding and WSHttpBinding, by default they are authenticated and authorized with the Windows membership and role providers. For Internet applications, however, it makes more sense to authenticate against a custom database store, such as the one provided by ASP.NET. You can influence how UserName credentials are authenticated and authorized by modifying the ServiceHost settings for UserNameAuthentication and for its ServiceAuthorizationBehavior.

Configuring ASP.NET providers

To authenticate UserName credentials against the ASP.NET membership provider, change the userNamePasswordValidationMode from Windows to MembershipProvider. Example 7-13 shows a <userNameAuthentication> section configured this way. To use the ASP.NET roles provider, set principalPermissionMode to UseAspNetProvider. The <serviceAuthorization> section, also shown in Example 7-13, shows this setting.

Example 7-13. Using the ASP.NET membership and role providers

```
<serviceBehaviors>
  <behavior name="serviceBehavior">
    <serviceAuthorization principalPermissionMode="UseAspNetRoles" />
    <serviceCredentials>
      <userNameAuthentication userNamePasswordValidationMode="MembershipProvider"/>
      <serviceCertificate findValue="RPKey" x509FindType="FindBySubjectName"
```

Example 7-13. Using the ASP.NET membership and role providers (continued)

```
storeLocation="LocalMachine" storeName="My"/>
    </serviceCredentials>
  </behavior>
</serviceBehaviors>
```

These settings engage the default ASP.NET membership and role providers, which rely on a specific set of security tables. If you have a custom database schema for security, you can specify an alternate membership and roles provider—which means creating a custom `MembershipProvider` and `RoleProvider` for ASP.NET. For example, the service model configuration shown in Example 7-14 simply points to the named provider configuration shown in the `<web.config>` section.

Example 7-14. Configuring custom ASP.NET membership and role providers

```
<configuration>
  <system.ServiceModel>
    <!-- other settings -->
    <behaviors>
      <serviceBehaviors>
        <behavior name="serviceBehavior">
          <serviceAuthorization principalPermissionMode="UseAspNetRoles"
roleProviderName="CustomRolesProvider" />
          <serviceCredentials>
            <userNameAuthentication
userNamePasswordValidationMode="MembershipProvider"
membershipProviderName="CustomMembershipProvider"/>
            <serviceCertificate findValue="RPKey" x509FindType="FindBySubjectName"
storeLocation="LocalMachine" storeName="My"/>
          </serviceCredentials>
        </behavior>
      </serviceBehaviors>
    </behaviors>
  </system.serviceModel>
  <system.web>
    <membership>
      <providers>
        <add name="CustomMembershipProvider" type="CustomMembershipProvider"/>
      </providers>
    </membership>
    <roleManager enabled="true">
      <providers>
        <add name="CustomRolesProvider" type="CustomRolesProvider" />
      </providers>
    </roleManager>
    <!-- other settings -->
  </web.config>
</configuration>
```

Custom password validators

An alternative to using the ASP.NET provider model is to supply a custom password validator. Create a class that inherits the UserNamePasswordValidator type, an abstract class with a single method: Validate( ). In the validate method, authenticate the username and password against your membership store and throws an exception if it fails. Example 7-15 shows a simple implementation of this type.

Example 7-15. Implementing a custom password validator

```
using System;
using System.IdentityModel.Selectors;
using System.Security;

public class CustomPasswordValidator: UserNamePasswordValidator
{
  public override void Validate(string userName, string password)
  {
    if (!ValidateUser(userName, password))
      throw new SecurityException("Access denied.");
    return;
  }
}
```

To trigger the validator set the customUserNamePasswordValidatorType to this type as shown here in the <userNameAuthentication> section:

```
<userNameAuthentication
customUserNamePasswordValidatorType="PasswordValidator.CustomPasswordValidator,
PasswordValidator" userNamePasswordValidationMode="Custom" />
```

Be sure to set the userNamePasswordValidationMode to Custom so that the custom password validator will be loaded.

The custom validator type cannot be a class deployed to the *\App_ Code* directory of an ASP.NET web site. It must be compiled into a separate assembly and referenced by the web site project.

Configuring the custom password validator allows you to control authentication, and it also initializes the PrimaryIdentity of the ServiceSecurityContext with an authenticated GenericIdentity representing the username. As for the security principal attached to the thread, it will be an unauthenticated WindowsPrincipal unless you set the principalPermissionMode to UseAspNetRoles:

```
<serviceAuthorization principalPermissionMode="UseAspNetRoles" />
```

If you do this, the security principal attached to the thread will be a RoleProviderPrincipal with the authenticated GenericIdentity inside. But, it will not gather roles from the ASP.NET database for the user, so you can't do role-based security with a custom password validator unless you provide a custom authorization policy to do the role lookup. In fact, it doesn't make much sense to configure a custom password validator without providing a custom authorization policy. I'll talk about custom authorization policies in another section of this chapter.

 A sample illustrating a custom password validator can be found at *<YourLearningWCFPath>\Samples\Security\PasswordValidator*.

Custom Role-Based Security

When you use the ASP.NET membership and role providers, users are authenticated and authorized against the ASP.NET security tables. This configuration also results in a RoleProviderPrincipal being attached to the thread instead of a WindowsPrincipal. This security principal holds a GenericIdentity with the authenticated user, and this identity matches the PrincipalIdentity of the ServiceSecurityContext:

```
Debug.Assert(ServiceSecurityContext.Current.PrimaryIdentity.Name ==
Thread.CurrentPrincipal.Identity.Name);
```

The main purpose of a security principal is to facilitate role-based security using PrincipalPermission demands. As with all IPrincipal types, RoleProviderPrincipal has an IsInRole() method that checks to see whether the user identified by the security principal belongs to the specified role. In the case of the RoleProviderPrincipal, which is new to WCF, it checks the PrimaryIdentity.Name against the role provider (the ASP.NET role provider in this case) to verify its roles. For example, the following demand checks that the user is in the "Administrators" role:

```
[PrincipalPermission(SecurityAction.Demand, Role = "Administrators")]
string ISecureService.AdminOperation( )
```

You can stack these attributes to allow access to multiple roles:

```
[PrincipalPermission(SecurityAction.Demand, Role = "Administrators")]
[PrincipalPermission(SecurityAction.Demand, Role = "Users")]
string ISecureService.AdminOrUserOperation( )
```

UserName Client Credentials

Internet client applications often use UserName credentials to authenticate to remote services. Although it is possible to supply a Windows account to the UserName credential, custom accounts are more typical. How this affects client applications is as follows:

- Applications usually provide a login dialog for users to enter their username and password. This information is stored for the duration of the application lifetime or until a new user logs in.

- If the client application also uses role-based security to authorize access to features, the client may initialize the security principal attached to the thread so that it reflects the logged in user and their roles. This may require a log-in step to the server to retrieve those roles.

- The ClientCredentials property of each proxy must be initialized with the username and password of the logged-in user.

To initialize the UserName property of ClientCredentials you explicitly set its two properties, UserName and Password, as shown here:

```
m_proxy.ClientCredentials.UserName.UserName = this.m_username;
m_proxy.ClientCredentials.UserName.Password = this.m_password;
```

Since the client-side binding requires a UserName credential, this will be serialized into a UserName token when service operations are invoked. Since the channel is immutable, once the first call has been executed, no changes can be made to these credentials. A new proxy must be constructed if a different user logs in to the client application.

Working with Certificates

Certificates are necessary part of securing messages. They make it possible to authenticate clients and services, they can be used for authorization, and they are used to protect messages with digital signatures and encryption. There are a few common scenarios that warrant the use of certificates for client credentials:

- Certificates can be used to identify business partners. The service provider may issue the certificates to trusted partners, or they may collect the public keys of trusted partners for authorization. This scenario is shown in Figure 7-8.

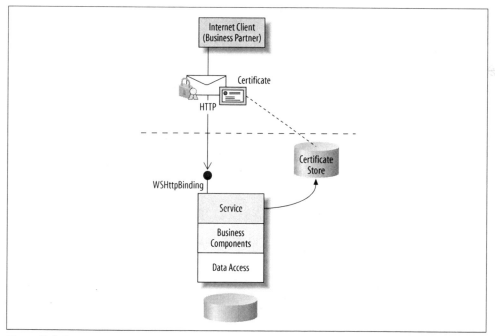

Figure 7-8. Business partner scenario

- Certificates can be useful for authenticating across machine boundaries behind the firewall in a trusted subsystem scenario. In this case, the client may be an application as shown in Figure 7-9 or another service as opposed to an individual or business partner.

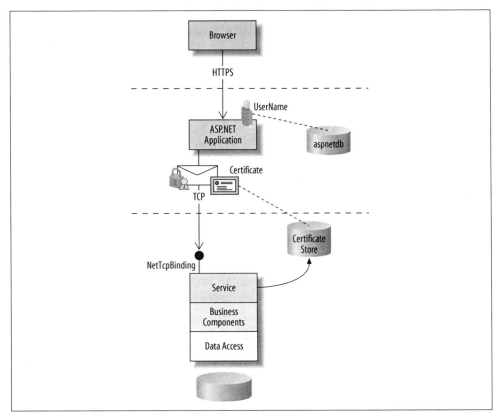

Figure 7-9. Trusted subsystem scenario

In this section, I'll first explain some key terms and concepts related to certificates. After that I'll describe scenarios for using certificates to protect messages and implement mutual authentication scenarios.

Understanding Certificates, Digital Signatures, and Encryption

Public Key Infrastructure (PKI) is a general term that refers to cryptography technologies and related network architecture and software involved in secure communications. Cryptography is a vast subject, but for the purposes of secure messaging, you can boil it down to the need to digitally sign and encrypt messages between parties. Certificates play a key role in this process.

A *certificate* is a block of data that contains information about a subject—which could be a person, application, business, or some other entity—that is digitally signed to guarantee validity. Certificates usually conform to the *X.509* standard. X.509 is an interoperable standard that defines the type of information that can be stored in a certificate, and its storage layout. For example, certificates usually contain the following information:

- They identify the certificate issuer.
- They contain a serial number from the issuer, uniquely identifying the certificate.
- They identify the algorithm used to sign the certificate.
- They contain the subject's name and the public key.
- They may contain the subject's private key.
- They contain a start and end date for validity checks.

A *Certificate Authority* (CA) issues certificates and digitally signs them to vouch for the subject of the certificate and its authenticity. There are a number of trusted CAs, such as VeriSign and Thawte, and Windows Server 2003 has a built-in CA that can be used to issue certificates. A CA represents a trusted third party attesting to the validity of a certificate and the subject it describes. Most software expects the CA's public key to be installed in the Trusted Root Certification Authorities certificate store before it will trust certificates issued by the CA.

Certificates can be validated by checking the *Certificate Revocation List* (CRL) for the CA or by using *Online Certificate Status Protocol* (OCSP) protocol. The latter is the preferred approach for X.509 certificates, providing a way to obtain revocation status in real time with less overhead—something particularly useful when systems are relying on a certificate to establish a trust relationship with other parties. Certificate IDs are added to the revocation list when they have been compromised or intentionally expired.

 You can find a list of specifications related to X.509 on the IETF's Public-Key Infrastructure Charter (X.509) site: *http://www.ietf.org/ html.charters/pkix-charter.html*. RFC 2560 describes OCSP (*http:// tools.ietf.org/html/rfc2560*). RFC 3280 describes X.509 and CRL (*http:// tools.ietf.org/html/rfc3280*).

As I mentioned, certificates can contain a public key and possibly a private key. There is an important distinction between the two. A *public key* is a sequence of numbers that identify a subject; anyone can have access to a public key. Public keys are used to encrypt data sent to the subject and are also used to validate signatures by the subject. A *private key* is a sequence of numbers that are known only to the subject and that have a mathematical relationship to the subject's public key. In fact, private and public keys are stored together as a *key pair*. The private key of the pair can be used to create signatures that can later be validated by a holder of the public key. The public key is often used to encrypt data that can only be decrypted by the private key holder.

Encryption is the process of encoding data so that it cannot be viewed by any party except for the party for which it was destined. This is achieved by applying a *cryptographic algorithm* to the data using a key. The encrypted data can only be deciphered by those that have the right key to decrypt it. There are two forms of encryption: symmetric and asymmetric. *Symmetric encryption* relies on the sender and receiver of the data to share the same key, which requires a key exchange at some point to make sure both parties have the same key. In many cases, symmetric keys are negotiated during an initial handshake instead of using fixed symmetric keys that can be discovered by malicious parties if not protected properly. *Asymmetric encryption* doesn't rely on key exchange in that only one party holds the private key, while anyone can hold the public key. In this way, data encrypted using the public key can only be decrypted by the private key holder. Data encrypted using the private key can be decrypted by anyone holding the public key, so this is used merely as confirmation of who encrypted the data (as in digital signatures), not to protect data.

A *digital signature* produces a small, computed value (or *digest*) of some data using a *hashing algorithm* and then encrypts it using a key that identifies the source of the data. A hashing algorithm is a one-way encryption algorithm (that is, the hash cannot be decrypted) that usually results in a fixed-length output representative of the data being hashed—for example the SHA-256 algorithm produces a 256-byte hash. When data is digitally signed, the signature (the encrypted hash value) along with the original data travels together so that the receiver can verify that the original data was not tampered with. This is done by generating a hash of the original data and comparing that hash with the signature hash. If they match, the data is authentic.

Digital signatures can be useful for:

Authentication
> For example if data is encrypted with the private key, anyone with the public key can decrypt it, and thus verify its origin.

Data Integrity
> The original data can be hashed and compared to the signature to verify integrity.

Non-repudiation
> The origin of the original data cannot be disputed, for example if a private key is used to generate the signature.

Signing and Encrypting Messages

Digital signatures and encryption play an important role in securing communication between parties in a distributed system. As I mentioned earlier in this chapter, all secure bindings automatically sign and encrypt messages, either at the transport layer or using message security. In any case, either symmetric or asymmetric keys are used to accomplish this task.

Symmetric keys are shared secrets by two parties in an exchange, thus the key must either be provisioned in advance (like a password) or negotiated for a secure session. In the case of negotiation, SSL, SPNego, TLSNego, and WS-SecureConversation (discussed in earlier sections) are all mechanisms that support the provisioning of a symmetric key that can be used to sign and encrypt messages for the duration of the session.

When asymmetric keys are used, the keys must be provisioned in advance. Typically this means that the client uses a private key to sign messages and uses the service public key to encrypt. Messages received at the service are decrypted using the service private key and authenticated by verifying the client signature against a list of trusted public keys, and possibly by inspecting other tokens.

Service Certificates and Negotiation

Earlier in this chapter, I discussed how to configure a service certificate declaratively and programmatically—by initializing the `ServiceCertificate` for the host, shown abbreviated here:

```
// declarative setting
<serviceCertificate findValue="RPKey" storeLocation="LocalMachine"
storeName="My" x509FindType="FindBySubjectName" />

// programmatic setting
host.Credentials.ServiceCertificate.SetCertificate(StoreLocation.LocalMachine,
StoreName.My, X509FindType.FindBySubjectName, "RPKey");
```

Service certificates support mutual authentication and message protection. For message protection, a service certificate is required when non-Windows client credentials are specified. If the binding supports negotiation, this certificate can be used to establish a symmetric session key used to sign and encrypt messages. If negotiation is not supported, one-shot security is used, which requires the client to sign messages with a separate key and encrypt messages with the service public key certificate.

When transport security is enabled, the service certificate is used to negotiate an SSL session key to sign and encrypt messages. When message security is enabled, the resulting keys used to sign and encrypt messages are the direct result of the binding's settings for client credential type and negotiation. It can be summarized as follows:

- When negotiation is enabled, the service certificate is used to negotiate an asymmetric session key to sign and encrypt messages.
- When negotiation is disabled, the client must have access to the public key certificate matching the service private key certificate, and the client uses its credential type or a derived token based on that credential to sign messages.

From a configuration perspective, if negotiation is enabled for the binding, clients are not required to have access to the public key ahead of time. Example 7-16 illustrates a service configuration that includes a single `WSHttpBinding` endpoint. The binding configuration requires UserName credentials for client authentication, supports negotiation, and supplies a service certificate for service authentication.

Example 7-16. WSHttpBinding with negotiation enabled

```
<system.serviceModel>
  <services>
    <service name="HelloIndigo.HelloIndigoService"
behaviorConfiguration="serviceBehavior">
      <host>
        <baseAddresses>
          <add baseAddress="http://localhost:8000"/>
        </baseAddresses>
      </host>
      <endpoint contract="HelloIndigo.IHelloIndigoService" binding="wsHttpBinding"
bindingConfiguration="wsHttp"/>
    </service>
  </services>
  <bindings>
    <wsHttpBinding>
      <binding name ="wsHttp">
        <security mode="Message">
          <message clientCredentialType="UserName"
negotiateServiceCredential="true"/>
        </security>
      </binding>
    </wsHttpBinding>
  </bindings>
  <behaviors>
    <serviceBehaviors>
      <behavior name="serviceBehavior">
        <serviceCredentials>
          <serviceCertificate findValue="RPKey" storeLocation="LocalMachine"
storeName="My" x509FindType="FindBySubjectName" />
        </serviceCredentials>
      </behavior>
    </serviceBehaviors>
  </behaviors>
</system.serviceModel>
```

Because negotiation is enabled, the client-side doesn't require access to the service public key certificate, since a symmetric session key will be negotiated for signing and encryption. Example 7-17 shows client configuration when negotiation is enabled.

Example 7-17. Client endpoint configuration when negotiation is enabled

```
<client>
  <endpoint address="http://localhost:8000/" binding="wsHttpBinding"
bindingConfiguration="WSHttpBinding_IHelloIndigoService"
contract="Client.localhost.IHelloIndigoService"
name="WSHttpBinding_IHelloIndigoService">
    <identity>
      <dns value="RPKey" />
    </identity>
```

```
    </endpoint>
</client>
```

The `<identity>` section includes a `<dns>` entry with the subject identifier of the public key, but this is because the example uses a test certificate. If the service certificate matches the domain of the client endpoint, it isn't required.

> A sample illustrating negotiation can be found at *<YourLearningWCF Path>\Samples\Security\UserNameNego*.

When negotiation is enabled for the same `WSHttpBinding`, when you add a service reference, the client configuration includes the base64 encoded public key certificate of the service in the `<identity>` section of the endpoint (see Example 7-18).

Example 7-18. Client endpoint with base64 encoded public key certificate

```
<client>
  <endpoint address="http://localhost:8000/" binding="wsHttpBinding"
bindingConfiguration="WSHttpBinding_IHelloIndigoService"
contract="Client.localhost.IHelloIndigoService"
name="WSHttpBinding_IHelloIndigoService">
    <identity>
      <certificate
encodedValue="AwAAAAEAAAAUAAAAreiGqilku9hngWEQL1g+HolOpWAgAAAAAQAAAO4BAAAwggHqMIIBU
6ADAgECAhDfhrqcaYGUhk2SPYyDX6vrMAOGCSqGSIb3DQEBBAUAMBAxDjAMBgNVBAMTBVJQS2V5MB4XDTA2
MDYxMjIzNDUyM1oXDTM5MTIzMTIzNTk1OVowEDEOMAwGA1UEAxMFUlBLZXkwgZ8wDQYJKoZIhvcNAQEBBQA
DgYOAMIGJAoGBAN98qei7Mc6hJE2VhTk3RZ2u5Yn5COC3b+ZIA3PqmmfWB2l5SExFeOgVbdFaWXkKcP8+ND
JcSURvxofW32cJi1Wrm7VreuoBFwJuIqAir3Ujb4dO7br2jcyPlsZTwjSkxlP83rYjUGJlIr+oifAXAuyJx
5LOv48znNpmvO6sGhAxAgMBAAGjRTBDMEEGA1UdAQQ6MDiAEJlUK+Mc5VUd6vh29RSAOC6hEjAQMQ4wDAYD
VQQDEwVSUEtleYIQ34a6nGmBlIZNkj2Mg1+r6zANBgkqhkiG9wOBAQQFAAOBgQBsOTnPoUSFRx6hc/ZpMWy
eKAZIJod+WENWJ4QWhGy4aRxokuKKps9Pe26DiZgxuOimfiOl2U5qQpljADif900y86i3LmYdorl/bRIIfL
QA+a1ME3MAC3jhinBjWLQhUyxAavWw5jSO/oBdOvDwZaqjy47gOjFV9pFOVHhoVbTtOA==" />
    </identity>
  </endpoint>
</client>
```

Generating a base64 encoded copy of the certificate streamlines the distribution of the service public key, saving clients the trouble of installing it in their local certificate store. You can optionally install the public key to the client machine's certificate store and reference it from the client endpoint. Example 7-19 shows how to accomplish this with an endpoint behavior.

Example 7-19. Client endpoint with endpoint behavior and certificate reference

```
<system.serviceModel>
  <bindings>
    <wsHttpBinding>...</wsHttpBinding>
  </bindings>
```

Example 7-19. Client endpoint with endpoint behavior and certificate reference (continued)

```
    <behaviors>
      <endpointBehaviors>
        <behavior name="clientBehavior">
          <clientCredentials>
            <serviceCertificate>
              <defaultCertificate findValue="RPKey" storeLocation="CurrentUser"
storeName="My" x509FindType="FindBySubjectName"/>
            </serviceCertificate>
          </clientCredentials>
        </behavior>
      </endpointBehaviors>
    </behaviors>
    <client>
      <endpoint address="http://localhost:8000/" binding="wsHttpBinding"
bindingConfiguration="WSHttpBinding_IHelloIndigoService"
contract="Client.localhost.IHelloIndigoService"
name="WSHttpBinding_IHelloIndigoService" behaviorConfiguration="clientBehavior">
        <identity>
          <dns value="RPKey"/>
        </identity>
      </endpoint>
    </client>
  </system.serviceModel>
```

Two samples that illustrate negotiation disabled with base64 encoded certificates and certificate references can be found here:

- *<YourLearningWCFPath>\Samples\Security\ UserNameNoNegoCertRef*
- *<YourLearningWCFPath>\Samples\Security\ UserNameNoNegoEncoded*

Certificate Authentication

In several sections of this chapter, I have discussed client credential requirements for service bindings, and how to initialize proxies to pass the required credentials. *Mutual certificate authentication* is a term used to describe scenarios where both the client and service provide certificates to authenticate one another.

To require clients provide a certificate to authenticate to the service, you can customize the binding and set the clientCredentialType to Certificate. The following illustrates this scenario with WSHttpBinding:

```
    <wsHttpBinding>
      <binding name="wsHttpCert">
        <security mode="Message">
          <message clientCredentialType="Certificate" establishSecurityContext="false"
negotiateServiceCredential="false"/>
        </security>
      </binding>
    </wsHttpBinding>
```

As I discussed earlier, clients can provide a certificate to the proxy using an endpoint behavior, as shown here:

```
<endpointBehaviors>
  <behavior name="clientBehavior">
    <clientCredentials>
      <clientCertificate findValue="SubjectKey" storeLocation="CurrentUser"
storeName="My" x509FindType="FindBySubjectName"/>
    </clientCredentials>
  </behavior>
</endpointBehaviors>
```

This requires the client to have access to the named private key on their local certificate store.

Certificate credentials are authenticated against the certificate store based on authentication rules specified in the ServiceCredentials configuration for the service. Declaratively, these settings are located in the <serviceCredentials> section. The <clientCertificate> section includes an <authentication> section that describes rules for authenticating certificates. Table 7-7 lists the possible settings.

Table 7-7. Declarative settings for certificate authentication

Setting	Description
certificateValidationMode	None, PeerTrust, ChainTrust (default), PeerOrChainTrust, Custom.
trustedStoreLocation	CurrentUser, LocalMachine (default).
customCertificateValidatorType	A type that implements X509CertificateValidator, to be used instead of one of the existing validators. Defaults to null.
includeWindowsGroups	Enabled by default. When disabled, Windows groups are not added to the list of claims in the security context. Relevant only if certificates are mapped to Windows accounts.
mapClientCertificateToWindowsAccount	Disabled by default. When enabled, initializes a WindowsPrincipal for the certificate based on the account it is mapped to in the domain.
revocationMode	NoCheck, Online (default), Offline.

These settings are also programmatically accessible through the ServiceHost configuration. Example 7-20 shows how to set the default values for these settings programmatically.

Example 7-20. Initializing client certificate authentication programmatically

```
ServiceHost host = new ServiceHost(typeof(HelloIndigo.HelloIndigoService));
X509ClientCertificateAuthentication certAuth =
host.Credentials.ClientCertificate.Authentication;

certAuth.CertificateValidationMode = X509CertificateValidationMode.ChainTrust;
certAuth.IncludeWindowsGroups = true;
certAuth.MapClientCertificateToWindowsAccount = false;
```

Example 7-20. Initializing client certificate authentication programmatically (continued)

```
certAuth.RevocationMode = X509RevocationMode.Online;
certAuth.TrustedStoreLocation = StoreLocation.LocalMachine;
```

The default settings are secure, but you may have to change those settings for debugging purposes. Certificate validation defaults to ChainTrust, which means the certificate chain is validated. For test certificates, the chain cannot be validated, but an acceptable alternative that is still secure is to use PeerTrust. PeerTrust requires you to install the certificate in the TrustedPeople certificate store for the CurrentUser or LocalMachine store (depending on which you are using). PeerOrChainTrust means that certificate chains should be validated for those certificates that are not found in the TrustedPeople store. The best overall setting is to install trusted certificates in the TrustedPeople store and use PeerTrust.

The trusted store location defaults to the LocalMachine store, and this is appropriate. Revocation mode defaults to Online, using the protocols discussed earlier in this section. This will not apply to trusted certificates.

Considering these debugging requirements, Example 7-21 shows the appropriate declarative configuration for certificate authentication.

Example 7-21. Initializing client certificate authentication declaratively

```
<serviceBehaviors>
  <behavior name="serviceBehavior">
    <serviceCredentials>
      <clientCertificate>
        <authentication certificateValidationMode="PeerTrust"
trustedStoreLocation="LocalMachine" />
      </clientCertificate>
    </serviceCredentials>
  </behavior>
</serviceBehaviors>
```

A few samples that illustrate mutual certificate authentication can be found here:

- *<YourLearningWCFPath>\Samples\Security\ MutualCertificateAuthentication*
- *<YourLearningWCFPath>\Samples\Security\ MutualCertificateAuthentication_Code*
- *<YourLearningWCFPath>\Samples\Security\ OneShotCertificateOverHttp*

Certificate Authorization

By default, certificates are authorized by placing the corresponding public key of each partner in the TrustedPeople store for the LocalMachine. Simply put, if the caller's public key certificate is not found, it isn't authorized. You can provide a custom authorization policy to override this authorization mechanism, something I'll discuss in the next section.

Building a Claims-Based Security Model

The identity model in WCF supports a rich, claims-based approach to authorization, but so far in this chapter, you haven't seen it in action. That's because discussions so far have centered on Windows, UserName, and Certificate credentials—each of which rely on authentication and authorization features that have nothing to do with claims. As I mentioned earlier, all credentials are ultimately mapped to a set of claims when they are authenticated at the service. In this section, I'll elaborate on this and other important concepts related to building a claims-based security model, including:

- Security tokens and claims
- Working with custom claims
- Custom authorization policies
- Claims-based authorization and related utilities

Security Tokens and Claims

Security tokens are abstractions of credentials that are passed in the security headers of a message and validated against the security policy. When security tokens are validated and processed at the service, claims representative of the token are placed into the security context for the operation being executed. Consider the following examples:

- Windows credential (Windows token) claims include the Windows identity and the groups to which it belongs.
- UserName credential (UserName token) claims include the username.
- Certificate credential (X.509 token) claims include the subject key, thumbprint, public key blob, and other certificate properties.

Each *claim* describes an individual right or action applicable to a particular resource. An identity claim states that the resource is an identity value, such as a username. A possession claim states that the subject possesses a particular right over a resource—for example, you can possess the right to an email address or a birth date. It's like saying you own the claim.

Claims can be represented at runtime as a Claim type from the System.IdentityModel.Claims namespace. This type has three key properties:

ClaimType
> Can be any URI value representing a claim type. A basic set of claims used by WCF can be found in the ClaimTypes static class in the System.IdentityModel.Claims namespace.

Right
> Can be a URI representing an identity claim, or a possession claim. The Rights static class in the System.IdentityModel.Claims namespace contains the correct URI to use.

Resource
> Can be any type but should contain the resource being referred to by the claim. For an email possession claim, this would contain an email address.

To create a claim, construct a Claim instance and provide the constructor with a ClaimType, Resource, and Right as shown here:

```
Claim c = new
Claim("http://schemas.xmlsoap.org/ws/2005/05/identity/claims/emailaddress",
"mlb@idesign.net",
http://schemas.xmlsoap.org/ws/2005/05/identity/right/possessproperty);
```

You can also rely on the ClaimTypes and Rights static classes instead of looking up the correct URI for each:

```
Claim c = new Claim(ClaimTypes.Email, "mlb@idesign.net", Rights.PossessProperty);
```

A *claim set* is a collection of claims granted by a particular issuer. For example, the claims extracted from an X.509 token are vouched for by the certificate authority. The certificate authority is therefore the issuer of the claim set. A claim set can be represented at runtime by the ClaimSet type. The key properties for this type are:

Issuer
> Another ClaimSet describing the issuer

Indexer
> A list of claims common to this issuer

WindowsClaimSet and X509ClaimSet are types that inherit the ClaimSet base type. These are the claim sets generated for Windows and certificate credentials, respectively. You can also create a new claim set by constructing a DefaultClaimSet and providing a list of claims. The following example creates a name claim that contains the URI of an issuer, adds the claim to an array of claims and passes it to the constructor of DefaultClaimSet.

```
Claim c =Claim.CreateNameClaim(
"http://www.thatindigogirl.com/samples/2006/06/issuer");
Claim[] claims = new Claim[1];
claims[0] = c;
ClaimSet issuer = new DefaultClaimSet(claims);
```

AuthorizationContext

Ultimately, claim sets are attached to the `ServiceSecurityContext` during the authentication process. You can access those claim sets through the `AuthorizationContext` property, as shown here:

```
AuthorizationContext authContext =
ServiceSecurityContext.Current.AuthorizationContext;
```

The `AuthorizationContext` is a collection of claim sets that are attached to the security context as security tokens are authenticated during each request. Using the `AuthorizationContext`, you can implement a custom authorization check that is based on claims instead of roles. Example 7-22 shows you how to look for a particular claim set by its type and evaluate individual claims inside the claim set. In this case, it is looking for an `X509CertificateClaimSet` and checking the DNS claim for a particular subject key.

Example 7-22. Performing authorization checks with the AuthorizationContext

```
AuthorizationContext authContext =
ServiceSecurityContext.Current.AuthorizationContext;

X509CertificateClaimSet certClaims = null;
foreach (ClaimSet c in authContext.ClaimSets)
{
  certClaims = c as X509CertificateClaimSet;
  if (certClaims != null)
    break;
}

if (certClaims == null)
  throw new SecurityException("Access is denied. X509CertificateClaimSet is
required.");

if (!certClaims.ContainsClaim(Claim.CreateDnsClaim("RPKey")))
  throw new SecurityException("Access is denied.");
```

Although this technique can help you implement a custom authorization scheme for certificates, it is even more powerful when you apply it to custom claim sets.

 A sample illustrating the use of `X509CertificateClaimSet` can be found at *<YourLearningWCFPath>\Samples\Security\CertificateClaims*.

Custom Claims

The `ClaimTypes` static class has a long list of claim types that are used by WCF, but you can create custom claim types to describe specific features or business entities in your own system. For example, you could create a list of claim types that relate to CRUD operations, such as the claim types listed in Example 7-23.

Example 7-23. Custom claim types

```
public static class ClaimTypes
{
  public const string Create =
"http://schemas.thatindigogirl.com/samples/2006/06/identity/claims/create";
  public const string Read =
"http://schemas.thatindigogirl.com/samples/2006/06/identity/claims/read";
  public const string Update =
"http://schemas.thatindigogirl.com/samples/2006/06/identity/claims/update";
  public const string Delete =
"http://schemas.thatindigogirl.com/samples/2006/06/identity/claims/delete";
}
```

Instead of evaluating `Windows`, `UserName`, and `Certificate` credentials against different authorization policies, you can map each of those credentials to a particular set of custom claims. The issuer of the claims in this case could be your own application. Example 7-24 shows a `MapClaims()` method that is passed an identity to evaluate and returns a `ClaimSet` with the appropriate claims for the identity. In this case, the assumption is that the ASP.NET provider model is used to store users and roles—thus the `Roles.IsUserInRole()` method is called before assigning claims.

Example 7-24. Creating a custom claimset based on roles

```
protected virtual ClaimSet MapClaims(IIdentity identity)
{
  List<Claim> listClaims = new List<Claim>();

  if (Roles.IsUserInRole(identity.Name, "Administrators"))
  {
    listClaims.Add(new Claim(ClaimsAuthorizationPolicy.ClaimTypes.Create,
"http://schemas.thatindigogirl.com/samples/2006/06/identity/resources/application",
Rights.PossessProperty));
    listClaims.Add(new Claim(ClaimsAuthorizationPolicy.ClaimTypes.Delete,
"http://schemas.thatindigogirl.com/samples/2006/06/identity/resources/application",
Rights.PossessProperty));
    listClaims.Add(new Claim(ClaimsAuthorizationPolicy.ClaimTypes.Read,
"http://schemas.thatindigogirl.com/samples/2006/06/identity/resources/application",
Rights.PossessProperty));
    listClaims.Add(new Claim(ClaimsAuthorizationPolicy.ClaimTypes.Update,
"http://schemas.thatindigogirl.com/samples/2006/06/identity/resources/application",
Rights.PossessProperty));
  }
  // other code

  return new DefaultClaimSet(this.Issuer, listClaims);
}
```

The claims created here are all possession claims. To keep it simple, there is no distinction between different resources or features for each CRUD claim. Each claim is a CRUD right to the application as a whole. Meaning, if the user is granted delete rights, it means she possesses the right to delete anything in the application. You can make this more granular by associating claims with particular features of the system.

When the new `DefaultClaimSet` is initialized it is provided with an issuer claim set (like the one already shown) and the list of claims.

If a custom claim set like this is added to the security context, service developers can focus on authorizing a normalized set of claims at each operation, instead of concerning themselves with coarse-grained roles or being impacted by multiple credential type support. If a claim set from a particular issuer is expected for all credential types, developers can write code like that shown in Example 7-25 to authorize calls.

Example 7-25. Authorizing calls based on custom claims

```
string ICrudService.CreateSomething( )
{
  AuthorizationContext authContext =
ServiceSecurityContext.Current.AuthorizationContext;

  ClaimSet issuerClaimSet = null;
  foreach (ClaimSet cs in authContext.ClaimSets)
  {
    Claim issuerClaim = Claim.CreateNameClaim(
"http://www.thatindigogirl.com/samples/2006/06/issuer");

    if (cs.Issuer.ContainsClaim(issuerClaim))
      issuerClaimSet=cs;
  }

  if (issuerClaimSet==null)
    throw new SecurityException("Access is denied. No claims were provided from the
expected issuer.");

  Claim c = new
Claim("http://schemas.thatindigogirl.com/samples/2006/06/identity/claims/create",
"http://schemas.thatindigogirl.com/samples/2006/06/identity/resources/application",
Rights.PossessProperty);
  if (!issuerClaimSet.ContainsClaim(c))
    throw new SecurityException("Access is denied. Required claims not
satisfied.");
}
```

This code traverses the authorization context for a claim set that matches the issuer identified by a single name claim with the URI *http://www.thatindigogirl.com/ samples/2006/06/issuer*. If a claim set from the expected issuer is present, the code proceeds to look for a particular claim. In this case, the `Create( )` operation requires a create claim.

Of course, you probably wouldn't want to litter service operation code with this cumbersome block of code to authorize callers. In the sections that follow, I'll talk about how to create a custom authorization policy to assign the claims to the security context and how to encapsulate claims-based security into a custom `PrincipalPermission` and `PrincipalPermissionAttribute`.

Custom Authorization Policies

A custom authorization policy is a type that implements the IAuthorizationPolicy interface from the System.IdentityModel.Policy namespace. Here are a few useful reasons to create a custom authorization policy:

- When a custom password validator is used, a custom authorization policy must be provided if you want to authorize callers based on information other than the username.

- To replace traditional role-based security with claims-based security, a custom authorization policy can be used to normalize the set of claims received from different tokens into a common set of claims used for claims-based security.

- When the service requires IssuedToken credentials (to be discussed) the security token presented carried claims that are not authorized against any existing role provider. A custom authorization policy can inspect these claims and initialize the security context accordingly.

Authorization policies can inspect the claims that will be attached to the security context. Before operations are called, they can attach new claim sets to the security context, and they are required to create a security principal that will be attached to the request thread before operations are called.

To implement a custom authorization policy, you create a type that implements IAuthorizationPolicy. This interface also inherits IAuthorizationComponent, which means you must also provide implementation for its members. Definitions for the two interfaces are shown in Example 7-26.

Example 7-26. Definitions for IAuthorizationPolicy and IAuthorizationComponent

```
public interface IAuthorizationPolicy : IAuthorizationComponent
{
  ClaimSet Issuer { get; }

  bool Evaluate(EvaluationContext evaluationContext, ref object state);
}

public interface IAuthorizationComponent
{
  string Id { get; }
}
```

The functionality for each member should be implemented as follows:

- Id returns a unique identifier for the authorization policy instance. Can be a GUID.

- Issuer returns a ClaimSet describing the issuer associated with the authorization policy. If claims are generated by this policy, this issuer vouches for the claims.

- The Evaluate( ) method is passed the claim sets evaluated so far by other authorization policies already invoked.

Clearly, Evaluate() is the heart and soul of this implementation. Within the Evaluate() method, a custom authorization policy is responsible for constructing a security principal to be attached to the security context. In addition, the current claim sets (stored in the EvaluationContext reference) should be evaluated and new claim sets applicable to this policy generated for the security context. The method should return false if this authorization policy was not able to complete its authorization. If false, the service model will invoke other authorization policies and then call this one once again, passing the updated claim sets. This gives the authorization policy another chance to complete its work.

Example 7-27 shows an implementation for Evaluate() that creates a security principal for the evaluation context, based on the roles for the authenticated user identity. The EvaluationContext reference has a Properties dictionary, which will include an "Identities" entry if any identities have indeed been authenticated. Recall that the SecurityTokenAuthenticator for each security token provided in a message will run its course to authenticate the token—those identities will be present here.

Example 7-27. Creating a security principal for the evaluation context

```
public bool Evaluate(EvaluationContext evaluationContext, ref object state)
{
  object objIdentities = evaluationContext.Properties["Identities"];
  IList<IIdentity> identities = objIdentities as IList<IIdentity>;

  if (identities != null && identities.Count > 0)
  {
    IIdentity identity = identities[0] as GenericIdentity;
    if (identity != null)
    {
      string[] roles = null;

      if (identity.Name == "Admin")
        roles = new string[] { "Administrators", "Users" };
      else if (identity.Name == "User")
        roles = new string[] { "Users" };
      else
        roles = new string[] { "Guests" };

      evaluationContext.Properties["Principal"] = new GenericPrincipal(identity,
roles);
    }
  }
  return true;
}
```

In this simple example, the roles are hardcoded based on the username to illustrate how a GenericPrincipal is constructed and assigned to the "Principal" entry in the evaluation context Properties dictionary.

If the "Principal" entry is not set by the authorization policies in place, an exception will be thrown by the runtime.

The password validator sample mentioned earlier also illustrates this simple authorization policy: *<YourLearningWCFPath>\Samples\Security\ PasswordValidator*.

GenericPrincipal, like any security principal that implements IPrincipal, only provides an IsInRole() feature for authorization. This has little to no value in a claims-based model. A more complete implementation of the custom authorization policy would not only add a claim set to the evaluation context, it would also create a security principal that can support claims-based authorization for each operation.

In the sections to follow, you will complete a lab that shows you how to build a claims-based model.

Lab: Creating a Custom Authorization Policy

In this lab, you will open an existing solution that includes a service, a web site host, and a client application. The functionality of the solution thus far uses the ASP.NET provider model to authenticate and authorize calls to the service. Create a custom authorization policy that will assign a claim set for each ASP.NET role and then apply claims-based authorization to each service operation. You'll use a preexisting library of claims-based components to streamline the implementation.

Implementing IAuthorizationPolicy

First, you will test the existing solution to make sure it works properly. After this you will implement a custom authorization policy to map ASP.NET users and roles to claims. You'll attach these claims to the authorization context and set the security principal for the thread.

1. Open the solution for this lab located in *<YourLearningWCFPath>\Labs\Chapter7\ ClaimsBasedSecurity\ ClaimsBasedSecurity.sln*.

2. This lab requires you to install the RPKey certificate, to give your ASP.NET account access to the private key pair RPKey, and to set up specific users and roles for the ASP.NET Provider Model. Detailed instructions for each of these requirements can be found in Appendix A.

3. Run the Client and follow the console prompts—you should see the output shown in Figure 7-10. Stop debugging and return to Visual Studio.

4. Now you'll complete a custom authorization policy that has been started for you. Expand ClaimsBasedSecurityComponents and open the *ClaimsAuthorizationPolicy.cs* file in the code window. The current implementation of the authorization policy is shown in Example 7-28.

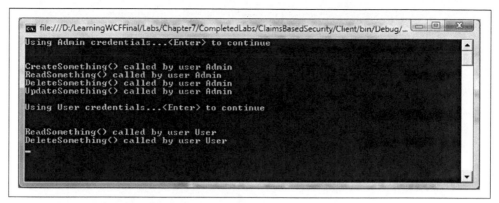

Figure 7-10. Console output for the client application

You'll notice a few nested, static classes: Resources and ClaimTypes. These types define a set of URI to support custom claim generation—consistent with discussions earlier in this section. In addition, the IAuthorizationPolicy and IAuthorizationComponent interfaces have been partially implemented. Specifically, the Id property returns a unique GUID. The Issuer property and Evaluate( ) method have not yet been implemented.

Example 7-28. Initial implementation of ClaimsAuthorizationPolicy

```
public class ClaimsAuthorizationPolicy : IAuthorizationPolicy
{

  public static class Resources
  {
    public const string Application =
"http://schemas.thatindigogirl.com/samples/2006/06/identity/resources/application";
  }

  public static class ClaimTypes
  {
    public const string Create =
"http://schemas.thatindigogirl.com/samples/2006/06/identity/claims/create";
    public const string Read =
"http://schemas.thatindigogirl.com/samples/2006/06/identity/claims/read";
    public const string Update =
"http://schemas.thatindigogirl.com/samples/2006/06/identity/claims/update";
    public const string Delete =
"http://schemas.thatindigogirl.com/samples/2006/06/identity/claims/delete";
  }

  private Guid m_id;

  public ClaimsAuthorizationPolicy( )
  {
    m_id = Guid.NewGuid( );
  }
```

```
public bool Evaluate(EvaluationContext evaluationContext, ref object state)
{
  return true;
}

public ClaimSet Issuer
{
  get { return null;}
}

public string Id
{
  get
  {
    return m_id.ToString( );
  }
}
}
```

5. Start by implementing the Issuer property. Recall that Issuer should contain a ClaimSet that identifies the issuer. In this example, you'll create a new DefaultClaimSet that includes a Name claim and specifies a unique URI for the issuer. Start by adding a ClaimSet reference, m_issuer, to the ClaimsAuthorizationPolicy type and a constant string, IssuerName, that holds the issuer URI shown in Example 7-29. Add code to the constructor to create the issuer ClaimSet and return m_issuer from the Issuer property. All changes are shown in bold in Example 7-29.

Example 7-29. Implementation of Issuer

```
public class ClaimsAuthorizationPolicy : IAuthorizationPolicy
{
  // other code

  private ClaimSet m_issuer;
  public const string IssuerName =
"http://www.thatindigogirl.com/samples/2006/06/issuer";

  public ClaimsAuthorizationPolicy( )
  {
    m_id = Guid.NewGuid( );

    Claim c = Claim.CreateNameClaim(ClaimsAuthorizationPolicy.IssuerName);
    Claim[] claims = new Claim[1];
    claims[0] = c;
    m_issuer = new DefaultClaimSet(claims);
  }
```

Example 7-29. Implementation of Issuer (continued)

```
public ClaimSet Issuer
{
  get { return m_issuer; }
}

// other code
}
```

6. Create a new private method named MapClaims() that will receive an IIdentity type and return a ClaimSet. This method will use the ASP.NET role provider to look up the user and check its roles. Based on the roles, a custom claim set will be generated for the user and returned. The complete implementation of MapClaims() is shown in Example 7-30.

Example 7-30. Implementation of MapClaims()

```
        private ClaimSet MapClaims(IIdentity identity)
        {

            List<Claim> listClaims = new List<Claim>();

            if (!identity.IsAuthenticated)
                throw new NotSupportedException("User not authenticated.");

            if (Roles.IsUserInRole(identity.Name, "Administrators"))
            {
                listClaims.Add(new
Claim(ClaimsAuthorizationPolicy.ClaimTypes.Create,
ClaimsAuthorizationPolicy.Resources.Application, Rights.PossessProperty));
                listClaims.Add(new
Claim(ClaimsAuthorizationPolicy.ClaimTypes.Delete,
ClaimsAuthorizationPolicy.Resources.Application, Rights.PossessProperty));
                listClaims.Add(new Claim(ClaimsAuthorizationPolicy.ClaimTypes.Read,
ClaimsAuthorizationPolicy.Resources.Application, Rights.PossessProperty));
                listClaims.Add(new
Claim(ClaimsAuthorizationPolicy.ClaimTypes.Update,
ClaimsAuthorizationPolicy.Resources.Application, Rights.PossessProperty));
            }
            else if (Roles.IsUserInRole(identity.Name, "Users"))
            {
                listClaims.Add(new Claim(ClaimsAuthorizationPolicy.ClaimTypes.Read,
ClaimsAuthorizationPolicy.Resources.Application, Rights.PossessProperty));
                listClaims.Add(new
Claim(ClaimsAuthorizationPolicy.ClaimTypes.Update,
ClaimsAuthorizationPolicy.Resources.Application, Rights.PossessProperty));
            }
            else
            {
                listClaims.Add(new Claim(ClaimsAuthorizationPolicy.ClaimTypes.Read,
ClaimsAuthorizationPolicy.Resources.Application, Rights.PossessProperty));
            }
```

Example 7-30. Implementation of MapClaims() (continued)

```
        return new DefaultClaimSet(this.m_issuer, listClaims);
    }
```

7. Now it's time to complete the implementation for Evaluate( ). As discussed earlier, you'll check the EvaluationContext for "Identities." You will pass the identity to the new MapClaims( ) method. In the event that no identities are found, you'll return false from Evaluate( ) to give other authorization policies a chance to produce one, before this authorization policy is called again.

    MapClaims( ) will return a new ClaimSet for the identity, which you will add to the EvaluationContext.

    You'll also create an instance of GenericPrincipal and wrap the identity in there without any roles. Since you'll be using claims-based security to authorize calls, the roles don't carry any importance beyond producing a normalized set of claims.

    The final result of these steps is shown in Example 7-31.

Example 7-31. Implementation of Evaluate()

```
        public bool Evaluate(EvaluationContext evaluationContext, ref object state)
        {
            if (evaluationContext.Properties.ContainsKey("Identities"))
            {
                List<IIdentity> identities =
evaluationContext.Properties["Identities"] as List<IIdentity>;
                IIdentity identity = identities[0];

                ClaimSet claims = MapClaims(identity);

            GenericPrincipal newPrincipal = new GenericPrincipal(identity, null);
evaluationContext.Properties["Principal"] = newPrincipal;
                evaluationContext.AddClaimSet(this, claims);
                return true;
            }
            else
                return false;

        }
```

8. To configure the authorization policy, open the *web.config* for the WebHost project. Modify the <serviceAuthorization> section so that the principalPermissionMode is set to Custom. In addition, insert a child <authorizationPolicies> element with configuration for the custom authorization policy (see Example 7-32).

    Add a reference to the ClaimsBasedSecurityComponents project for the WebHost project—so that the assembly containing the authorization policy will be deployed with the web site.

Example 7-32. Configuring a custom authorization policy

```
<serviceBehaviors>
  <behavior name="serviceBehavior">
    <serviceAuthorization principalPermissionMode="Custom" >
      <authorizationPolicies>
        <add policyType="ClaimsBasedSecurityComponents.ClaimsAuthorizationPolicy,
ClaimsBasedSecurityComponents"/>
      </authorizationPolicies>
    </serviceAuthorization>
    <!-- other settings -->
  <behavior>
</serviceBehaviors>
```

At this point, you have completed the IAuthorizationPolicy implementation and configured it so that the service model will pass requests through it. The service can now be designed to authorize against a normalized set of claims and not care about the original user identity.

Authorizing custom claims

In this section, you will add code to authorize callers. You'll do this by inspecting the authorization context for trusted claims by a particular issuer and determining whether the user is allowed access to the operation.

1. To test the new authorization policy, you'll add some code to one of the service operations that will look for a particular claim in the custom claim set. Go to the ClaimsBasedServices project and add a reference to the ClaimsBasedSecurityComponents project. Open the *CrudService.cs* file and add modify the Delete( ) operation, adding code to find the custom claim set issued by your custom authorization policy and verify the presence of the Delete claim. Example 7-33 shows the code to add in bold, including the necessary using statements to add above the namespace declaration.

Example 7-33. Claims-based authorization against custom claims

```
using System.IdentityModel.Policy;
using ClaimsBasedSecurityComponents;

string ICrudService.DeleteSomething( )
{
  AuthorizationContext authContext =
ServiceSecurityContext.Current.AuthorizationContext;

  ClaimSet issuerClaimSet = null;
  foreach (ClaimSet cs in authContext.ClaimSets)
  {
    Claim issuerClaim =
Claim.CreateNameClaim(ClaimsAuthorizationPolicy.IssuerName);

    if (cs.Issuer.ContainsClaim(issuerClaim))
```

```
        issuerClaimSet=cs;
    }

    if (issuerClaimSet==null)
        throw new SecurityException("Access is denied. No claims were provided from the
expected issuer.");

    Claim c = new Claim(ClaimsAuthorizationPolicy.ClaimTypes.Delete,
ClaimsAuthorizationPolicy.Resources.Application, Rights.PossessProperty);
    if (!issuerClaimSet.ContainsClaim(c))
        throw new SecurityException("Access is denied. Required claims not
satisfied.");

    return String.Format("DeleteSomething( ) called by user {0}",
System.Threading.Thread.CurrentPrincipal.Identity.Name);
}
```

2. Compile the solution and test this new functionality. Run the WebHost and Client in that order and follow the client application's console instructions. The Admin account will successfully invoke all CRUD operations, while the User account will be denied access to the Delete( ) operation.

Applying custom security extensions

The code you just introduced into the Delete( ) function is indeed the code you will use to authorize callers against custom claims; however, it isn't practical to introduce this code block into every service operation. I'm going to walk you through applying some custom security extensions to reduce the coding overhead for the same result. Specifically, you'll attach a custom claims-based security principal to the security context and use a custom PrincipalPermission to perform authorization checks against that security principal. After that, you'll apply a custom PrincipalPermissionAttribute to declaratively require claims at each service operation.

1. First, you will modify the authorization policy to add a claims-based security principal to the EvaluationContext. Go to the ClaimsBaseSecurityComponents project and open *ClaimsAuthorizationPolicy.cs*. Modify the Evaluate( ) method so that the GenericPrincipal is replaced with ClaimsPrincipal.

   Remove this line:

   ```
   GenericPrincipal newPrincipal = new GenericPrincipal(identity, null);
   ```

   and replace it with this:

   ```
   ClaimsPrincipal newPrincipal = new ClaimsPrincipal(identity, claims);
   ```

    Note that the ClaimsPrincipal has a constructor that receives an IIdentity and a ClaimSet instead of roles.

2. Now return to `ClaimsBasedServices` and open *CrudService.cs* again. Modify the `Delete()` function again, removing the code you previously added and adding a `ClaimsPrincipalPermission` demand as shown here:

```
string ICrudService.DeleteSomething()
{
    ClaimsPrincipalPermission perm = new ClaimsPrincipalPermission(true,
ClaimsAuthorizationPolicy.IssuerName, ClaimsAuthorizationPolicy.ClaimTypes.
Delete);
    perm.Demand();

    return String.Format("DeleteSomething() called by user {0}",
System.Threading.Thread.CurrentPrincipal.Identity.Name);
}
```

3. Compile the solution again and test the change. Run the same tests as before, and you should receive the same result—the User account will be denied access to the `Delete()` operation.

   Stop debugging and return to Visual Studio.

4. Make one more change to the `Delete()` function. This time you're going to apply a custom attribute to perform claims-based permission demands. Remove the code you previously added and apply the `ClaimsPrincipalPermissionAttribute`, as shown here in bold:

```
[ClaimsPrincipalPermission(SecurityAction.Demand,
IssuerName=ClaimsAuthorizationPolicy.IssuerName,
RequiredClaim=ClaimsAuthorizationPolicy.ClaimTypes.Delete)]
string ICrudService.DeleteSomething()
{
    return String.Format("DeleteSomething() called by user {0}",
System.Threading.Thread.CurrentPrincipal.Identity.Name);
}
```

5. Compile and run the solution again, running the same tests as before. Once again, you should receive the same result—the User account will be denied access to the `Delete()` operation.

This lab took you through a gradual progression from creating a new authorization policy that added custom claims to the authorization context, to leveraging custom components that encapsulate claims-based features into natural constructs developers are accustomed to with .NET. Here is a summary of the components you just used:

ClaimsPrincipal

An implementation of `IPrincipal` that also provides a `HasRequiredClaims()` method that encapsulates checks against the security context for specific claims.

ClaimsPrincipalPermission

An implementation of `IPermission` that retrieves the `IClaimsPrincipal` from the request thread to perform security actions such as permission demands.

`ClaimsPrincipalPermissionAttribute`
> A custom `CodeAccessSecurityAttribute` that provides properties for claims-based checks using the `ClaimsPrincipalPermission`.

The implementation of these components is not specific to WCF, and so exploring all of the details related to implementing `IPrincipal`, `IPermission`, and extending `CodeAccessSecurityAttribute` are out of the scope of this book.

 Additional code samples related to claims-based security can be found here:

- *<YourLearningWCFPath>\Samples\Security\ ClaimsBasedAuthorizationSimple*
- *<YourLearningWCFPath>\Samples\Security\ ClaimsBasedAuthorization*
- *<YourLearningWCFPath>\Samples\Security\ ClaimsBasedAuthorizationClaimsPrincipal*
- *<YourLearningWCFPath>\Samples\Security\ ClaimsBasedAuthorizationPermissionAttribute*
- *<YourLearningWCFPath>\Samples\Security\ ClaimsBasedAuthorizationValidationPolicy*

Exploring Federated Security

A *federated security model* supports the delegation of authentication or authorization activities such that applications and services can authorize calls based on a *federated identity*. This identity, usually represented by a security token, is expected to contain the necessary information to identify the caller or authorize access to features. The key participants in a federated security model are:

Subject
> The calling application, user, or entity that is described by a federated identity.

Relying Party (RP)
> Services that rely on a federated identity to authorize access to features.

Identity Provider (IP)
> A service that authenticates or authorizes calls and issues a federated identity vouching for the subject. This is also called a security token service.

Figure 7-11 illustrates the typical flow of communication between these three parties. The subject authenticates to the identity provider, who then issues a federated security token—which represents proof that the subject has been authenticated. The token is then presented to the relying party for authentication and authorization. For this to work, a trust relationship must exist between the relying party and identity provider, as well as between the subject and the identity provider. Federated security can be useful for the following scenarios:

- Decoupling authentication or authorization from business services.

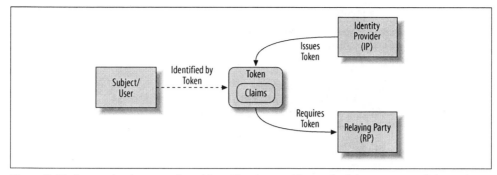

Figure 7-11. Interaction between the subject, identity provider, and relying party in a federated security model

- Supporting multiple authentication mechanisms yet producing a normalized set of claims for each subject.
- Supporting single sign-on (SSO) whereby the federated token can be reused for multiple applications and services.

In this section, I'll explore these and other concepts related to a federated security model; I'll touch on the web service standards that support federated security, including WS-Trust and SAML; and you'll complete a lab that uses WSFederatedHttpBinding to implement federated security—relying on Windows CardSpace to issue the federated token.

Security Token Services

A *security token service* (STS) is another term for an identity provider that issues federated tokens on behalf of a subject in support of a federated security model. An STS is typically interoperable on two levels: it implements the WS-Trust standard for token issuance and issues SAML tokens. In fact, the concept of an STS is derived from the Web Services Trust Model defined in the WS-Trust specification.

WS-Trust is an interoperable protocol for token issuance, renewal, and exchange. At the time of this writing, this standard is included in the OASIS Web Services Secure Exchange (WS-SX) review, along with WS-SecureConversation (discussed earlier). Any platform can implement an interoperable WS-Trust endpoint by following the guidelines of the standard. A complete implementation includes four key operations: Issue( ), Renew( ), Validate( ), and Cancel( ). Example 7-34 shows a service contract including these operations, using the appropriate namespaces for each.

Example 7-34. WS-Trust service contract

```
[ServiceContract(Namespace="http://schemas.xmlsoap.org/ws/2005/02/trust")]
public interface IWSTrustContract
{
  [OperationContract(Name = "Issue", Action =
```

Example 7-34. WS-Trust service contract (continued)

```
"http://schemas.xmlsoap.org/ws/2005/02/trust/RST/Issue", ReplyAction =
"http://schemas.xmlsoap.org/ws/2005/02/trust/RSTR/Issue")]
  Message Issue(Message requestMessage);

  [OperationContract(Name = "Renew", Action =
"http://schemas.xmlsoap.org/ws/2005/02/trust/RST/Renew", ReplyAction =
"http://schemas.xmlsoap.org/ws/2005/02/trust/RSTR/Renew")]
  Message Renew(Message requestMessage);

  [OperationContract(Name = "Validate", Action =
"http://schemas.xmlsoap.org/ws/2005/02/trust/RST/Validate", ReplyAction =
"http://schemas.xmlsoap.org/ws/2005/02/trust/RSTR/Validate")]
  Message Validate(Message requestMessage);

  [OperationContract(Name = "Cancel", Action =
"http://schemas.xmlsoap.org/ws/2005/02/trust/RST/Cancel", ReplyAction =
"http://schemas.xmlsoap.org/ws/2005/02/trust/RSTR/Cancel")]
  Message Cancel(Message requestMessage);
}
```

You can sum up the purpose of each operation in a WS-Trust implementation as follows:

Issue( )

> Receives a request for a security token, authenticates the caller, and if appropriate returns a signed security token.

Renew( )

> Receives a previously issued security token, and if appropriate, returns that token with new expiration.

Validate( )

> Receives a previously issued security token and validates the token. In some cases, returns a new signed security token.

Cancel( )

> Receives reference to the security token to cancel.

Each of these operations receives a message formatted as a *Request Security Token* (RST) message—with a <RequestSecurityToken> wrapper element. The response is always a *Request Security Token Response* (RSTR) with a <RequestSecurityTokenResponse> wrapper element. The contents of the message vary based on the operation being called.

Issue( ) is at the heart of the STS. For the Issue( ) operation, the RST contains information about the type of token being requested and other parameters that influence the resulting token. Example 7-35 shows an example RST. Each RST may vary in the information it provides, but in this case, you can see that the request provides the following information to the STS:

- The relying party that the token applies to is identified in the `<AppliesTo>` element. This allows the STS to verify that it trusts the destination, and it can use the key information provided in the `<Identity>` element to encrypt the token.

- The type of token, in this case SAML 1.1.

- The claims requested for the token, listed in the `<Claims>` element.

- Key material and other information related to the signing and encryption algorithms for the resulting token.

Example 7-35. RST requesting a SAML token

```
<t:RequestSecurityToken xmlns:t="http://schemas.xmlsoap.org/ws/2005/02/trust">
  <t:RequestType>http://schemas.xmlsoap.org/ws/2005/02/trust/Issue</t:RequestType>
  <wsp:AppliesTo xmlns:wsp="http://schemas.xmlsoap.org/ws/2004/09/policy">
    <EndpointReference xmlns="http://www.w3.org/2005/08/addressing">
      <Address>http://localhost:8000/MediaServices/ImagingService</Address>
      <Identity xmlns="http://schemas.xmlsoap.org/ws/2006/02/addressingidentity">
...</Identity>
    </EndpointReference>
  </wsp:AppliesTo>
  <t:Entropy>...</t:Entropy>
  <t:TokenType>http://docs.oasis-open.org/wss/oasis-wss-saml-token-profile-
1.1#SAMLV1.1</t:TokenType>
  <t:KeyType>http://schemas.xmlsoap.org/ws/2005/02/trust/SymmetricKey</t:KeyType>
  <t:KeySize>256</t:KeySize>
  <t:Claims>
    <wsid:ClaimType Uri=
"http://schemas.microsoft.com/ws/2005/05/identity/claims/privatepersonalidentifier"
xmlns:wsid="http://schemas.xmlsoap.org/ws/2005/05/identity"></wsid:ClaimType>
    <wsid:ClaimType Uri=
"http://schemas.thatindigogirl.com/samples/2006/07/identity/claims/create"
Optional="true" ...></wsid:ClaimType>
    <wsid:ClaimType Uri=
"http://schemas.thatindigogirl.com/samples/2006/07/identity/claims/read"
...></wsid:ClaimType>
    <wsid:ClaimType Uri=
"http://schemas.thatindigogirl.com/samples/2006/07/identity/claims/update"
Optional="true" ...></wsid:ClaimType>
    <wsid:ClaimType Uri=
"http://schemas.thatindigogirl.com/samples/2006/07/identity/claims/delete"
Optional="true" ...></wsid:ClaimType>
  </t:Claims>
  <t:CanonicalizationAlgorithm>
http://www.w3.org/2001/10/xml-exc-c14n#</t:CanonicalizationAlgorithm>
  <t:EncryptionAlgorithm>
http://www.w3.org/2001/04/xmlenc#aes256-cbc</t:EncryptionAlgorithm>
  <t:EncryptWith>http://www.w3.org/2001/04/xmlenc#aes256-cbc</t:EncryptWith>
  <t:SignWith>http://www.w3.org/2000/09/xmldsig#hmac-sha1</t:SignWith>
  <t:ComputedKeyAlgorithm>
http://schemas.xmlsoap.org/ws/2005/02/trust/CK/PSHA1</t:ComputedKeyAlgorithm>
</t:RequestSecurityToken>
```

If all goes well, the RSTR contains the signed and encrypted security token. Although the token format is not specified in the WS-Trust specification, SAML is the preferred token format for federated scenarios, as shown in Example 7-36. The heart of this response is the requested token—in this case, a `<saml:assertion>` element.

Example 7-36. RSTR returning a security context token

```
<RequestSecurityTokenResponse xmlns="http://schemas.xmlsoap.org/ws/2005/02/trust">
  <TokenType>http://docs.oasis-open.org/wss/oasis-wss-saml-token-profile-
1.1#SAMLV1.1</TokenType>
  <RequestedSecurityToken>
    <saml:assertion>...</saml:assertion>
  </RequestedSecurityToken>
</RequestSecurityTokenResponse>
```

A complete implementation of an STS will also implement `Renew( )`, `Validate( )`, and `Cancel( )` at the WS-Trust endpoint. WCF provides an internal WS-Trust endpoint for issuing security context tokens when secure sessions are enabled (discussed earlier). Windows CardSpace (to be discussed) also includes a local STS that issues SAML tokens in a federated scenario. In fact, in a later section I'll explain how to use `WSFederationHttpBinding` to trigger the Windows CardSpace STS.

 The roadmap for *Active Directory Federation Services* (ADFS) includes plans for a full-blown STS that can participate in a distributed and interoperable federated identity model. In the meantime, Microsoft has also provided an online STS that you can test with at *http://sts.labs.live.com/*.

SAML Tokens

Security Assertion Markup Language (SAML) is a standard security token format that supports federated and single sign-on (SSO) scenarios. The SAML standard also includes semantics for web-based SSO, but I'll focus on the token format for this discussion. Essentially, a SAML token is an XML format for carrying authentication and authorization statements about a subject. It is also known as a SAML assertion, since the token is wrapped in an `<assertion>` element, as shown in Example 7-37.

Example 7-37. A SAML assertion

```
<saml:Assertion MajorVersion="1" MinorVersion="1" AssertionID="_7a96c90a-6747-
43c0-ac56-1947896cdc1c" Issuer="MySTS" IssueInstant="2006-12-21T17:12:04.003Z"
xmlns:saml="urn:oasis:names:tc:SAML:1.0:assertion">
  <saml:Conditions NotBefore="2006-12-21T17:12:04.003Z" NotOnOrAfter="2006-12-
22T05:12:04.003Z"></saml:Conditions>
  <saml:AttributeStatement>
    <saml:Subject>
      <saml:NameIdentifier>...</saml:NameIdentifier>
      <saml:SubjectConfirmation>
        <saml:ConfirmationMethod>
urn:oasis:names:tc:SAML:1.0:cm:holder-of-key</saml:ConfirmationMethod>
```

Example 7-37. A SAML assertion (continued)

```
        <KeyInfo xmlns="http://www.w3.org/2000/09/xmldsig#">...</KeyInfo>
      </saml:SubjectConfirmation>
    </saml:Subject>
    <saml:Attribute AttributeName="create" AttributeNamespace=
"http://schemas.thatindigogirl.com/samples/2006/07/identity/right">
        <saml:AttributeValue>...</saml:AttributeValue>
    </saml:Attribute>
    <saml:Attribute AttributeName="delete" AttributeNamespace=
"http://schemas.thatindigogirl.com/samples/2006/07/identity/right">
        <saml:AttributeValue>...</saml:AttributeValue>
    </saml:Attribute>
    <saml:Attribute AttributeName="read" AttributeNamespace=
"http://schemas.thatindigogirl.com/samples/2006/07/identity/right">
        <saml:AttributeValue>...</saml:AttributeValue>
    </saml:Attribute>
    <saml:Attribute AttributeName="update" AttributeNamespace=
"http://schemas.thatindigogirl.com/samples/2006/07/identity/right">
        <saml:AttributeValue>...</saml:AttributeValue>
    </saml:Attribute>
  </saml:AttributeStatement>
  <Signature xmlns="http://www.w3.org/2000/09/xmldsig#">...</Signature>
</saml:Assertion>
```

The core elements of the SAML token are as follows:

- The `<saml:conditions>` element indicates the valid timeframe for token usage. This can be renewed at the STS with a call to `Renew( )`. This and other aspects of the token are validated at the STS with a call to `Validate( )`.

- The `<saml:attributeStatement>` element contains a `<saml:subject>` element describing the subject of the token. The method of confirmation employed by the STS to validate the subject is also presented here. In this example, the subject was confirmed by a certificate—as indicated by the holder-of-key confirmation method.

- The `<saml:attributeStatement>` also contains one or more `<saml:attribute>` elements describing the claims presented in the token.

When a SAML token is processed at the service, the `SamlSecurityTokenAuthenticator` validates the token and extracts the attributes. These attributes are mapped to claims and placed into the security context when the token is processed at the relying party.

Windows CardSpace

Windows CardSpace ("CardSpace") is a client technology that is part of the .NET Framework 3.0—used for creating, managing, and sharing digital identities in a secure and reliable manner. You can think of CardSpace as an identity selector that securely stores informational claims about a user, making it easy for that same user to send these claims in a SAML token to a trusted web site for authentication purposes.

An entire book can be written on CardSpace and various usage scenarios, so in this section, I'll just focus on some basics. Some of the core features of CardSpace are as follows:

- You can create *personal cards* that contain a list of common claims, including your name, address, email address, birth date, web site, and more. These cards are securely stored on your computer and can only be accessed through the CardSpace, usually when accessing a web site or service that explicitly demands a set of claims from CardSpace.

- You can install *managed cards* that contain a list of claims issued by a remote STS. When you install a managed card, the actual claims are never stored on the local machine—they are safely stored with the STS. Instead, the card contains information about the remote STS, so that when the card is selected, the remote STS can be engaged to generate the security token with the required claims. The card issuer is entirely responsible for defining what claims their managed cards represent. I won't be discussing managed cards.

- CardSpace has a local STS that can issue SAML tokens. When you select a card in CardSpace to authenticate to an application or service, the local or remote STS (as indicated by the card) generates a SAML token from the claims in the card. You have an opportunity to identify the target application or service before approving sending these claims—a valuable feature that protects users from unknowingly sending personal information to malicious parties. Furthermore, the token is encrypted with the public key of the relying party so that it can only be viewed by that party.

The Windows CardSpace interface is accessible from the Windows CardSpace icon in the Control Panel shown in Figure 7-12. From the interface that is launched (shown in Figure 7-13), you can create and manage your personal and managed cards.

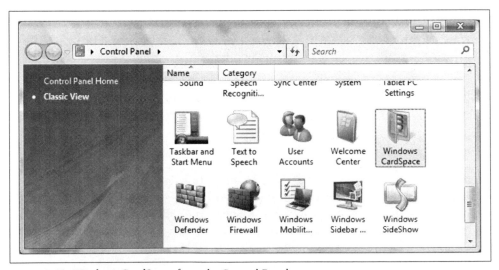

Figure 7-12. Windows CardSpace from the Control Panel

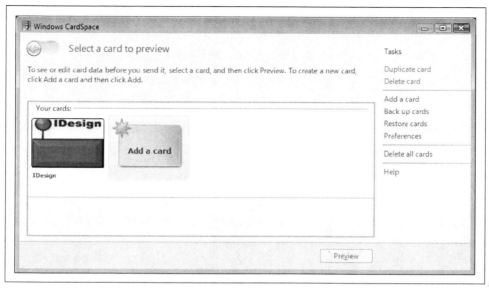

Figure 7-13. The Windows CardSpace interface

You'll notice that when you launch this interface, the rest of the desktop is completely locked down. This is a security measure that prevents other malicious code from interacting with CardSpace as it interacts with the local card store or issues security tokens. The same locked-down interface is presented when you attempt to use an application or service that requires tokens issued through CardSpace.

In the next section, you'll complete a lab that shows you how to use WSFederationHttpBinding to trigger the CardSpace experience for authentication.

> In Appendix B, I have included an article I wrote on CardSpace for *asp.netPRO* magazine. The article focuses on the browser experience, but will provide you with additional detail on the functionality CardSpace provides.

LAB: Working with WSFederationHttpBinding

In a federated security scenario, authentication and sometimes authorization are delegated to an STS. In many cases, the STS is also owned by the same enterprise as the relying party applications and services, and federation is simply a means to have security tokens issued that can be used across multiple applications, sometimes facilitating single sign-on. From a development perspective, this approach allows service developers to focus on claims-based security (assuming a SAML token with claims is provided) while STS developers focus on authenticating different credentials and converting them into security tokens. The client application in this case authenticates to the STS and requests a token for a particular subject (usually a user). The STS returns a signed and encrypted token that can be presented to the relying party and establish a secure session.

For this scenario, a relying party service may have following configuration:

- It must supply a service certificate to identify the service and facilitate token and message transfer security.

- It requires an IssuedToken credential from clients, which implies the use of WSFederationHttpBinding. It also must identify the STS to be trusted for token issuance.

- It should supply a custom authorization policy to authorize claims received in the security token. Since the relying party trusts the token issuer, it need not authenticate beyond verifying that it can decrypt and validate the token.

In this lab, you will use WSFederationHttpBinding to create a federated security scenario. You'll configure WSFederationHttpBinding to require a SAML token issued by CardSpace. When the client application is run, it will launch the CardSpace identity selector, where you will create a new personal card with the required claims and select it to authenticate to the relying party service.

Configuring WSFederationHttpBinding

These first steps will walk you through configuring a WSFederationHttpBinding endpoint. This lab requires you to install two certificates: RPKey and localhost, to give your ASP.NET account access to the private key pair RPKey, and to provide an SSL certificate for IIS and to set up specific users. Detailed instructions for each of these requirements can be found in Appendix A.

1. Open the solution for this lab located in *<YourLearningWCFPath>\Labs\ Chapter7\FederatedSecurity\FederatedSecurity.sln*. This solution includes a service project, a file-based web host, and a console client application.

   If you open the *web.config* for the WebHost, you'll see that it is already configured to expose a single WSFederationHttpBinding endpoint for the SecureService in the ClaimsBasedServices project, as shown here:

   ```
   <service name="ClaimsBasedServices.SecureService"
   behaviorConfiguration="serviceBehavior">
     <endpoint contract="ClaimsBasedServices.ISecureService"
   binding="wsFederationHttpBinding" bindingConfiguration="wsFed"/>
     <endpoint address="mex" contract="IMetadataExchange" binding="mexHttpBinding" /
   >
   </service>
   ```

2. You're going to supply the required configuration settings for the binding in the <wsFederationHttpBinding> section. In the <bindings> section of the *web.config*, insert the settings shown in Example 7-38 to the <wsFederationHttpBinding> section. Disable negotiation for interoperability; specify an IssuedToken format of SAML v1.1, require an email address and date-of-birth claim from callers, and require the token be self-issued by CardSpace.

Example 7-38. Requiring SAML tokens issued by CardSpace

```
<bindings>
  <wsFederationHttpBinding>
    <binding name="wsFed">
      <security mode="Message">
        <message negotiateServiceCredential="false"
issuedTokenType="http://docs.oasis-open.org/wss/oasis-wss-saml-token-profile-
1.1#SAMLV1.1">
          <claimTypeRequirements>
            <add
claimType="http://schemas.xmlsoap.org/ws/2005/05/identity/claims/emailaddress"
isOptional="false"/>
            <add
claimType="http://schemas.xmlsoap.org/ws/2005/05/identity/claims/dateofbirth"
isOptional="false"/>
          </claimTypeRequirements>
          <issuer
address="http://schemas.xmlsoap.org/ws/2005/05/identity/issuer/self" />
        </message>
      </security>
    </binding>
  </wsFederationHttpBinding>
</bindings>
```

3. From the `<serviceBehaviors>` section of the *web.config*, you can see that a service certificate has been configured to facilitate secure message exchanges. In order to support self-signed SAML tokens issued by CardSpace, you'll have to modify the IssuedTokenAuthentication settings and set allowUntrustedRsaIssuers to true as shown in bold in Example 7-39.

Example 7-39. Allowing self-signed SAML tokens

```
<behavior name="serviceBehavior">
  <serviceMetadata httpGetEnabled="true"/>
  <serviceCredentials>
    <issuedTokenAuthentication allowUntrustedRsaIssuers="true" />
    <serviceCertificate findValue="RPKey" storeLocation="LocalMachine"
storeName="My" x509FindType="FindBySubjectName" />
  </serviceCredentials>
</behavior>
```

4. Launch the WebHost application to test the service.svc endpoint in a browser. Do this to verify your configuration settings are accurate. You should see the browser help page for the service. After this test, return to Visual Studio.

5. Now that the WSFederationHttpBinding endpoint has been configured and tested, you can generate the client proxy to access the service. Go to the Client project and add a service reference to the following URL: *http://localhost:64496/WebHost/Service.svc*. As usual, this will generate a client proxy and endpoint configuration setting for the service.

The port number may vary. Be sure to check the port number when you launch the service in the browser.

6. Modify the Main( ) entry point to invoke the SendMessage( ) service operation using the newly generated proxy. The complete listing should look as shown in Example 7-40. Compile the Client project when you're done.

Example 7-40. Code to invoke SendMessage( )

```
static void Main(string[] args)
{
  using (localhost.SecureServiceContractClient proxy = new
Client.localhost.SecureServiceContractClient( ))
  {
    string s = proxy.SendMessage("Hello from Client.");
    Console.WriteLine(s);
  }
  Console.ReadLine( );
}
```

Creating an information card in CardSpace

In this section, I'll walk you through creating and sending a CardSpace personal card to authenticate to the service.

1. Run the Client application and you'll see the CardSpace identity selector presented. When CardSpace is launched, it is passed the list of required claims you specified in the WSFederationHttpBinding from the Client proxy. This information is used to look for existing cards that fulfill those claims. If no cards exist that satisfy the claims, you'll be presented with a dialog like the one shown in Figure 7-14.

   Now you will create a new personal card with claims that can be passed to the SecureService for authentication. Click Add a card from the tasks list to create a new card, and then select "Create a Personal Card." From the Edit a new card dialog, enter values for the Card Name and for required claims Email Address and Date of Birth, as shown in Figure 7-15. Save the card.

2. Select this new card to send to the service. The first time you send the card to the SecureService, you'll be asked to confirm the claims that are being sent. A SAML token will be generated by CardSpace including these claims and sent with the security headers to SendMessage( ).

3. You'll see output to the Client console indicating that the ServiceSecurityContext for the request has an empty PrimaryIdentity, WindowsIdentity. In addition, a security principal will not be attached to the thread.

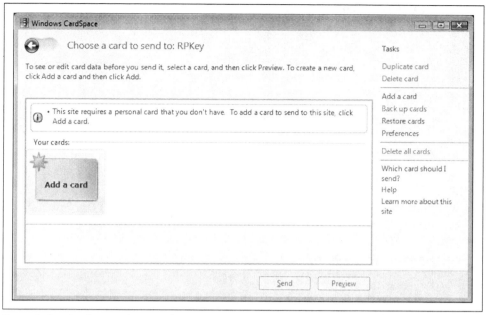

Figure 7-14. CardSpace identity selector requiring a new card to meet the required claims

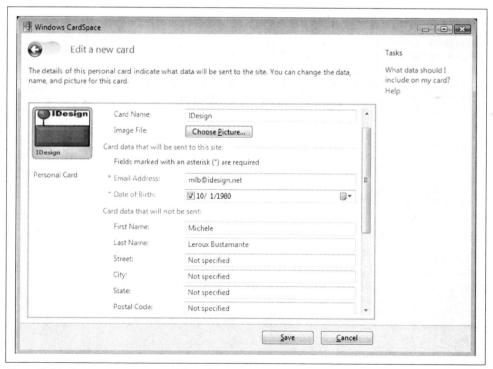

Figure 7-15. Creating a new personal card

Evaluating CardSpace claims

The SAML token generated by CardSpace is validated when it arrives at the service, but the service currently does not process the claims extracted from the token. The following steps will walk you through evaluating the CardSpace claims passed in the SAML token.

1. Go to the ClaimsBasedServices project and open *SecureService.cs*. Modify SendMessage( ) so that it checks the date-of-birth claim, ensuring that callers are at least age 13. Add code to traverse the claim sets passed in the AuthorizationContext. Look for a date-of-birth claim and if one is found, check the age. Throw an exception if a date-of-birth claim is not found or if the age is less than 13. The changes to SendMessage( ) are shown in bold in Example 7-41, including the necessary using statements to place at the top of the file.

Example 7-41. Checking the AuthorizationContext for the date-of-birth claim

```
using System.IdentityModel.Policy;
using System.IdentityModel.Claims;
using System.Security;

string ISecureService.SendMessage(string message)
{

  AuthorizationContext authContext =
ServiceSecurityContext.Current.AuthorizationContext;
  DateTime? birthDate = null;
  foreach (ClaimSet cs in authContext.ClaimSets)
  {
    IEnumerable<Claim> claims = cs.FindClaims(ClaimTypes.DateOfBirth,
Rights.PossessProperty);
    foreach (Claim c in claims)
    {
      birthDate = Convert.ToDateTime(c.Resource);
    }
  }

  if (birthDate == null)
    throw new SecurityException("Missing date of birth claim.");
  if (birthDate.Value.AddYears(13) > DateTime.Now)
    throw new SecurityException("User is too young to access this operation.");

  string s = String.Format("Message '{0}' received. \r\n\r\n\nHost identity is
{1}\r\n Security context PrimaryIdentity is {2}\r\n Security context
WindowsIdentity is {3}\r\n Thread identity is {4}", message,
WindowsIdentity.GetCurrent( ).Name,
ServiceSecurityContext.Current.PrimaryIdentity.Name,
ServiceSecurityContext.Current.WindowsIdentity.Name,
Thread.CurrentPrincipal.Identity.Name);

  return s;
}
```

2. Compile these changes to the ClaimsBasedServices project and then run the WebHost and Client application to test this change. Pass the same card as in the previous test, and if the age is greater than 13, no exceptions will be thrown. Run the test again with a birth date of less than 13 to see the exception.

In this lab, you configured WSFederationHttpBinding to require a specific set of personal claims from CardSpace, issued in a SAML v1.1 token. WSFederationHttpBinding has additional features beyond those exercised in the lab; for example, it can be configured to require tokens from a particular STS. In the next section, I'll discuss other features of the binding.

WSFederationHttpBinding Security Features

WSFederationHttpBinding has roots in WSHttpBinding (discussed in Chapter 3) but adds additional security features that specifically support the federated security model. In fact, the only reason to employ WSFederationHttpBinding is in a federated scenario that relies on IssuedToken credentials.

Table 7-8 summarizes the core binding features of WSFederationHttpBinding. Like WSHttpBinding, the binding uses SOAP 1.2 and WS-Addressing, it can leverage MTOM encoding to optimize large message transfers, and it also supports protocols for reliable messaging and transactions.

Table 7-8. WSFederationHttpBinding features

Binding feature	WSFederationHttpBinding support
Transport protocols	HTTP, HTTPS
Message encoding	Text, MTOM
Message version	SOAP 1.2, WS-Addressing
Reliable messaging	Yes
Transactions	Yes
Metadata	WSDL 1.1, WS-Policy, WS-PolicyAttachment, WS-MetadataExchange

Beyond these core features, WSFederationHttpBinding has additional security features specifically related to federated security scenarios. Table 7-9 summarizes these additional features.

Table 7-9. Extended security features of WSFederationHttpBinding

Security feature	Description
Negotiation	The message security setting includes a NegotiateServiceCredential property that is enabled by default. Disable this for interoperability.
Transfer security (negotiation enabled)	TLSNego protocol is tunneled over WS-Trust to negotiate a session key.

Table 7-9. Extended security features of WSFederationHttpBinding (continued)

Security feature	Description
Transfer security (negotiation disabled)	Guidelines established by WS-Security are used for signing and encryption.
Secure sessions	Always enabled. WS-SecureConversation protocol is always used to generate a security context token (SCT).
Algorithms	Defaults to Basic256.
Privacy notice	The binding's `PrivacyNoticeAt` and `PrivacyNoticeVersion` properties can be initialized to a URI indicating the location of the privacy policy and to an `integer` indicating the version of the policy, respectively.
Issuer configuration	You can specify a particular address and binding for an STS apart from CardSpace and indicate where the STS metadata can be found.

`WSFederationHttpBinding` supports only three security modes: `None`, `TransportWithMessageCredential`, and `Message`, the latter of which is the default setting. Since the binding supports only `IssuedToken` credentials, they must be passed as part of the SOAP message.

An STS must always be indicated as the token issuer. By default, the issuer is assumed to be CardSpace, indicated by the following `<issuer>` element:

```
<issuer address="http://schemas.xmlsoap.org/ws/2005/05/identity/issuer/self" />
```

You can specify an alternate issuer, specify the required claims from that issuer, and describe the binding requirements for communicating with that issuer. Example 7-42 shows a configuration that requires claims issued by a custom STS.

Example 7-42. Configuring an alternate STS as the token issuer

```
<wsFederationHttpBinding>
  <binding name="wsFedBinding" >
    <security mode="Message">
      <message issuedTokenType=
"http://docs.oasis-open.org/wss/oasis-wss-saml-token-profile-1.1#SAMLV1.1" >
        <claimTypeRequirements>
          <add claimType=
"http://schemas.microsoft.com/ws/2005/05/identity/claims/privatepersonalidentifier"
isOptional="false"/>
          <add claimType=
"http://schemas.thatindigogirl.com/samples/2006/07/identity/claims/create"
isOptional="true"/>
          <add claimType=
"http://schemas.thatindigogirl.com/samples/2006/07/identity/claims/read"
isOptional="false" />
          <add claimType=
"http://schemas.thatindigogirl.com/samples/2006/07/identity/claims/update"
isOptional="true"/>
          <add claimType=
"http://schemas.thatindigogirl.com/samples/2006/07/identity/claims/delete"
isOptional="true"/>
```

```
        </claimTypeRequirements>
        <issuer address="http://localhost:2489/TokenIssuer/Service.svc"
binding ="wsHttpBinding"  bindingConfiguration="stsBinding" >
          <identity>
            <certificateReference  findValue="IPKey"
x509FindType="FindBySubjectName" storeLocation="LocalMachine"
storeName="TrustedPeople" />
          </identity>
        </issuer>
      </message>
    </security>
  </binding>
</wsFederationHttpBinding>
```

The <issuer> section can optionally refer to another binding configuration to publish metadata describing how callers can communicate with the STS. In this case, a WSHttpBinding configuration is specified, shown in Example 7-43.

Example 7-43. STS binding requiring certificate credentials

```
<wsHttpBinding>
  <binding name="stsBinding" >
    <security mode="Message">
      <message  clientCredentialType="Certificate"
establishSecurityContext="false" />
    </security>
  </binding>
</wsHttpBinding>
```

 A sample that relies on a custom STS to issue a SAML token can be found at *<YourLearningWCFPath>\Samples\Security\ClaimsBased\ ClaimsBasedAuthorizationWithFederation*.

WSFederationHttpBinding has additional settings available in the binding configuration to specify a privacy notice, shown in bold in Example 7-44. This notice can be presented to callers, for example, through the CardSpace interface.

Example 7-44. Specifying a privacy notice

```
<wsFederationHttpBinding>
  <binding name="wsFed"
privacyNoticeAt="http://localhost:64496/WebHost/PrivacyNotice.txt"
privacyNoticeVersion="1">
    <!-- other settings -->
  </binding>
</wsFederationHttpBinding>
```

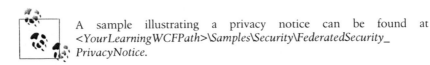

A sample illustrating a privacy notice can be found at *<YourLearningWCFPath>\Samples\Security\FederatedSecurity_PrivacyNotice*.

Summary

In this chapter, I covered a lot of ground related to security features of WCF. I started by explaining how you create a security policy for your services using binding configurations related to authentication, authorization, and message protection. I detailed the possible security settings for each of the core bindings, including NetNamedPipeBinding, NetTcpBinding, BasicHttpBinding, WSHttpBinding, and WSFederationHttpBinding. In addition, I discussed the following security concepts:

- Choices between transport and message security.
- The purpose of message security and extended features provided beyond transport security.
- Runtime identities, security principals, and their relationship to authentication, authorization, and access to operations and resources.
- Credential types supported for various scenarios and how to map to security tokens and claims.
- How to configure credentials for mutual authentication between clients and services.
- How to work with certificates, including a backgrounder on digital signatures and encrypytion.

In an attempt to simplify this otherwise daunting set of features, I then took you through several scenarios for secure communication for intranet, Internet, partner or machine authentication with certificates, and federation. In each section, I provided you with some guidance on how you would configure these scenarios to reduce the noise of features provided by each binding. What you should take away from this chapter are examples for the most common scenarios that can serve as starting templates for your application development efforts in the future. Here is a summary:

- For intranet scenarios, you'll typically rely on Windows credentials for mutual authentication and message protection. You'll also apply traditional role-based security if applicable.
- For Internet scenarios you'll likely supply more than one endpoint configuration to support clients of differing interoperable protocol support. Username and password over SSL will be one common scenario, while you may also expose endpoints that support secure sessions. Again, traditional role-based security can be applied.

- Mutual certificate authentication will be useful for machine-to-machine authentication behind the firewall but can also be used to increase security for public facing services. In the latter case, you'll likely require both a certificate to identify the partner or application and a username and password to identify the actual user.

- There is a fast-growing trend toward claims-based security because it allows service developers to focus on authentication of a single token format while authorizing against a normalized set of claims, instead of handling different credential types. In this case, you'll rely on custom authorization policies or security token services to generate claims for each token format supported by the application. In this chapter, you learned how to create and configure such a custom authorization policy as part of the service implementation, using it to normalize claims. You also employed some utilities I created for claims-based security implementations.

- Last but not least, you may find it useful to employ CardSpace as an identity selector to simplify the user experience for logging in with custom claims (through managed cards) and to increase the security of this exchange.

CHAPTER 8

Exceptions and Faults

Leading up to this final chapter in the book, you have learned how to design service contracts, configure bindings, choose a hosting environment, and select platform features for instancing and concurrency, reliability, and security. Although I have touched on exceptions and faults that may occur in different scenarios, this chapter will focus solely on the exception-handling semantics built-in to WCF.

Component-oriented programming models traditionally rely on exceptions to communicate problems encountered during execution flow. The .NET framework offers structured exception handling for exceptions to be caught, handled, thrown, or otherwise ignored and propagated automatically up the call chain. At some point, if an exception goes unhandled to the top of the call chain, something has to give—and that's when the .NET runtime terminates the executing thread. To prevent this abrupt termination, one of the callers in the chain has to *trap* the error—which usually means logging it, reporting it to the user, or otherwise correcting the problem.

In a distributed system, exceptions that occur remotely must traverse process or machine boundaries before they reach the client. In an SOA, the boundary is a service boundary, which may be located in the same process or across process or machine boundaries. Beyond these distribution boundaries, there may also be technology and platform boundaries, which require interoperable communication. As discussed in Chapter 1, services imply well-defined boundaries that communicate using serialized messages according to a contract. So, to report an exception from a service to its caller, the exception must be serialized to a known format and wrapped in a message.

In this chapter, I will start by providing you with some background information on SOAP faults and their relationship to service metadata—since they are the standard for propagating exceptions from services. After this, I will discuss different exception handling scenarios in WCF, including how services and clients handle CLR exceptions, how to declare and throw SOAP faults, and how to provide common exception-handling behaviors for a service. I will explain the implications on contract design and implementation and on client exception handling. You'll also complete several labs to gain practical experience with these concepts.

SOAP Faults

A *SOAP fault* is a standards-based format for transferring exceptions between applications. Recall from Chapter 2 that the SOAP specification defines a standard XML format for messages that include a header and body section. The same specification includes a definition for SOAP faults, providing structure for the contents of the message body when errors occur. This makes it possible for different technologies and platforms to provide plumbing to handle faults in a predictable manner. In most cases, this means converting the fault into some form of exception construct representative of the platform. Developers interact with the exception to deal with error conditions.

I discussed in Chapter 2 that the SOAP specification has two versions. In fact, one of the biggest differences between SOAP 1.1 and SOAP 1.2 is in the format for the SOAP fault. Not only do these specifications describe the format for faults, they also supply guidance on the contents of faults (such as error codes) and on the way platforms should process faults.

Fault Versions

SOAP 1.1 and SOAP 1.2 both define a format for faults. Though they essentially contain similar information when serialized, the naming conventions for XML elements were refactored slightly. Table 8-1 compares XML elements described by each specification and describes their purpose.

Table 8-1. Comparison of SOAP 1.1 and SOAP 1.2 elements

SOAP 1.1	SOAP 1.2	Element description
faultcode	Code	Required. Can be one of the specification's predefined codes or a custom code for the application. Predefined codes differ for SOAP 1.1 and SOAP 1.2.
faultstring	Reason	Required. String explanation of the fault. SOAP 1.2 supports multiple reasons for multilingual support.
faultactor	Role	Optional. Required for all SOAP nodes except for the ultimate receiver. A URI describing the source of the fault.
detail	Detail	Optional. Required if the SOAP body could not be processed. Should provide information about the body element(s) that failed.
	Node	Optional. Required for all SOAP nodes except for the ultimate receiver. A URI describing the node that caused the failure.

As you can see, each specification defines similar facets of the SOAP fault, but the structure of the serialized fault changed in SOAP 1.2. To give you some context, a SOAP 1.1 fault is shown in Example 8-1, and a SOAP 1.2 fault in Example 8-2. Like all messages, SOAP faults must also be serialized according to the SOAP supported by the endpoint. This is driven by the binding selection and by default only BasicHttpBinding supports SOAP 1.1.

Regardless of the binding configuration, the same CLR types are used by WCF to represent the SOAP fault at runtime. I'll talk about this later in this chapter.

Example 8-1. SOAP 1.1 Fault

```
<s:Envelope xmlns:s="http://schemas.xmlsoap.org/soap/envelope/">
  <s:Body>
    <s:Fault>
      <faultcode xmlns="">s:Client</faultcode>
      <faultstring xml:lang="en-US" xmlns="">
An invalid operation has  occurred.</faultstring>
    </s:Fault>
  </s:Body>
</s:Envelope>
```

Example 8-2. SOAP 1.2 Fault

```
<s:Envelope xmlns:s="http://www.w3.org/2003/05/soap-envelope"
xmlns:a="http://www.w3.org/2005/08/addressing">
  <s:Header>
    <a:Action s:mustUnderstand="1">
http://www.w3.org/2005/08/addressing/soap/fault</a:Action>
    <a:RelatesTo>urn:uuid:64c5619c-99c3-4a83-9bdc-fcbb6f399f93</a:RelatesTo>
  </s:Header>
  <s:Body>
    <s:Fault>
      <s:Code>
        <s:Value>s:Sender</s:Value>
      </s:Code>
      <s:Reason>
        <s:Text xml:lang="en-US">An invalid operation has occurred.</s:Text>
      </s:Reason>
    </s:Fault>
  </s:Body>
</s:Envelope>
```

 For the most part, you will simply let the service model handle the serialization of SOAP faults according to the correct SOAP version for the binding.

Faults and WSDL

When I discussed contracts in Chapter 2, I mentioned that an operation described in the WSDL document can have <input>, <output>, or <fault> messages associated with it. As with any other message exchanged between applications, fault messages are also described by a formal contract. Example 8-3 illustrates an operation that describes two possible faults.

Example 8-3. WSDL operation with fault elements defined

```
<wsdl:operation name="UploadFile">
  <wsdl:input wsa:Action=
```

Example 8-3. WSDL operation with fault elements defined (continued)

```
"http://www.thatindigogirl.com/samples/2005/12/FileUploadServices/UploadFile"
name="FileUploadRequest" message="tns:FileUploadRequest" />
<wsdl:output wsa:Action=
"http://www.thatindigogirl.com/samples/2005/12/FileUploadServices/
UploadFileResponse"
message="tns:FileUploadServicesContract_UploadFile_OutputMessage" />
<wsdl:fault wsa:Action=
"http://www.thatindigogirl.com/samples/2005/12/FileUploadServices/
FileUploadServicesContract/UploadFileExceptionFault" name="ExceptionFault"
message=
"tns:FileUploadServicesContract_UploadFile_ExceptionFault_FaultMessage" />
<wsdl:fault wsa:Action=
"http://www.thatindigogirl.com/samples/2005/12/FileUploadServices/
FileUploadServicesContract/UploadFileIOExceptionFault" name="IOExceptionFault"
message=
"tns:FileUploadServicesContract_UploadFile_IOExceptionFault_FaultMessage" />
</wsdl:operation>
```

Platforms like WCF supply programming constructs for associating fault messages with operations, and I'll explore this later in this chapter.

WCF Exception Handling

WCF introduces new exception handling concepts to address the differences between traditional component-oriented systems and SOA. While traditional component-oriented systems can share native types for exception reporting and handling, this does not work across service boundaries. Exceptions are serialized as SOAP faults between clients and services. The service model can handle this automatically by converting exceptions into faults, or faults can be explicitly created using new CLR types introduced with WCF for this purpose.

In this section, I'll introduce the concept of fault exceptions and then provide a high-level explanation of the way services and clients deal with exceptions and faults.

Fault Exceptions

WCF introduces several new exception types, most of which derive from a common base type, CommunicationException. Among the types that inherit CommunicationException, FaultException is the most important. Both types are from the System.ServiceModel namespace.

Not surprisingly, FaultException properties are closely related to the SOAP fault—they are Action, Code, and Reason. In addition, FaultException provides access to the entire message associated with the SOAP fault through its Message property. It is through this property that the detail element of the fault can be retrieved, for example.

There is also a generic version of the FaultException: FaultException<T>. This type provides strongly typed access to the detail element of the fault through its Detail property. FaultException<T> is the easiest way to provide a rich set of details to a SOAP fault, beyond just a simple message.

The relationship between these types is illustrated in Figure 8-1. As the figure implies, CommunicationException is the most general form of exception that a client might trap, while FaultException<T> provides the most detailed view of a SOAP fault.

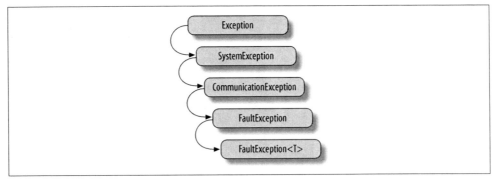

Figure 8-1. Exception hierarchy for FaultException<T>

Although you can throw any exception type from your services or downstream components, you will normally want to throw a fault to communicate problems. You can create a fault in WCF using several techniques including the following:

- You can construct a new instance of the FaultException. To this, you can supply a reason and code, for example.
- You can call the static CreateFault() method exposed by FaultException which returns a FaultException. To this method, you can supply the details section of the fault as well.
- You can construct a FaultException<T> with a strongly typed details section.

Collectively, each of these approaches provides several overrides and opportunities to initialize different parts of the SOAP fault. Your choice of override often depends on the elements of the SOAP fault you want to populate.

Constructing a simple FaultException is an easy way to throw a fault with a simple message, while FaultException<T> is preferred if providing a details section with additional information for the client is important. A FaultException is ultimately used to generate a MessageFault—a runtime representation of a SOAP fault. In fact, FaultException exposes a CreateMessageFault() method to generate a new MessageFault instance. MessageFault is an abstract class that can be overridden to control the serialization of SOAP faults. It is ultimately the MessageFault type that the service model uses to write the SOAP fault to the wire.

I'll provide concrete examples for FaultException, FaultException<T>, and MessageFault later in this chapter.

Service Exception Handling

Services have several options for how they will report exceptions to clients:

- They can allow exceptions to propagate up to the service model. This will result in the service model faulting the channel and returning a less meaningful fault to the client.

- Services can catch exceptions and explicitly throw a fault to the service model. This will not fault the channel and will return better information to the client, in particular if FaultException<T> is used.

- Services can declare known faults for each operation so that the information is part of the service description. This way, clients are informed of the possible fault types that will be thrown.

- Services can catch exceptions globally and decide which exceptions warrant throwing faults instead of uncaught exceptions.

This chapter will explore each of these techniques.

Client Exception Handling

Clients should always wrap calls to a service in a try...catch block in the event there are communication exceptions. Furthermore, clients should always check the state of the channel after each call to see whether the channel has faulted from a communication exception (discussed in Chapter 5). If the channel has faulted, the client will need to recreate the proxy before calling the service again. The decision to notify the user of the problem is specific to the application. For example, the user may need to be informed that session data has been lost because of the failure. Or the user may not care because the session is a secure session that can be restarted without impact to the user (if credentials are cached locally).

To help clients deal with exceptions, it helps to know the type of exceptions that can be thrown from the service. There are several common exception types that clients should be prepared to handle:

CommunicationException

This type is the base type for exception types included with WCF. If you trap this exception, you will trap most exceptions related to service model communications.

EndpointNotFoundException

This exception is thrown when the service endpoint cannot be found, usually because the address is incorrect.

TimeoutException

Timeout exceptions arise when service operations run longer than the allotted receive timeout for the binding, or when the client cannot reach the remote service within the configured send timeout. Since networks can be unreliable, clients should be prepared to handle this type of exception when they invoke remote services.

CommunicationObjectFaultedException

This type of exception results from trying to use the proxy after the underlying channel has been faulted. Clients that use application sessions, reliable sessions, or secure sessions should be prepared to catch this type of exception when they invoke the proxy. Even better, clients should check the communication state of the channel (see Chapter 5) before using the proxy.

ProtocolException

Protocol exceptions are typically thrown by the service model when client and service bindings are not compatible, for example, if the client attempts to flow a transaction to a service that doesn't support it for the operation being invoked (see Chapter 6). These exceptions can usually be avoided if clients are configured according to the WSDL document.

MessageSecurityException

This type of security exception can occur when there is a problem evaluating the security settings of a message. It can also occur at the client when a secure session has expired and the client attempts to send messages within the expired session (see Chapters 5 and 7).

Beyond these types, the service may also declare specific faults for each operation (to be discussed). This information is published with the service description so that client proxies know about those exception types and can reconstruct strongly typed FaultException<T> derivatives. This scenario will be discussed in this chapter.

Exceptions and Debugging

When an exception is thrown by the .NET runtime, the executing thread is aborted if it is not caught somewhere in the call chain. In the case of an executing service operation, an uncaught exception will propagate up to the service model. The service model treats uncaught exceptions as potential indicators of a serious problem and as such will put the channel into a faulted state. If the executing operation is not one-way, the service model will return a fault to the client. The information included in this fault is influenced by the type of exception and by service debugging behaviors.

In this section, I will focus on how the service model handles uncaught exceptions at the service and client. I'll also explore configurable service debugging behaviors. First, you will complete a lab to practice working with exceptions.

Lab: Working with Uncaught Exceptions

In this lab, you will open an existing solution that lets you upload photos to a service, similar to the examples used in Chapter 3. The solution has a faulty configuration setting that will cause the business logic to throw an exception. You will explore how exceptions are reported to the client before and after enabling the service debug behavior to report exceptions as faults.

1. Open the startup solution for this lab, located in *<YourLearningWCFPath>\Labs\ Chapter8\Exceptions\Exceptions.sln*. This solution includes the following projects: ContentTypes, FileManager, LinkItems.Dalc, PhotoManager, PhotoManagerService, Host, and PhotoUploadClient. The PhotoManagerService exposes functionality to upload images and coordinates saving the file and recording the activity to a database. The Host exposes endpoints for this service, and the PhotoUploadClient invokes the service.

2. This lab includes code to call the Photos database, thus you should install the following database script: *<YourLearningWCFPath>\SupportingFiles\DatabaseScripts\ Photos_CreateDB.sql*. See the "Database Setup" section of Appendix A for additional instructions.

3. Compile the solution and run a test to upload a file. Run the Host and then the PhotoUploadClient application in that order. The client interface is shown in Figure 8-2.

Figure 8-2. PhotoUploadClient application interface

4. Try uploading a file from the PhotoUploadClient application. Click the browse ("...") button and select the sample image located here: *<YourLearningWCFPath>\ SupportingFiles\SampleImages\theband.jpg* and select Upload Photo. A ConfigurationErrorsException will be thrown by the service because there is an invalid directory specified in the *app.config* file for the Host. You'll receive a FaultException from the service as shown in Figure 8-3. The information provided in the exception is not related to the original ConfigurationErrorsException. Instead, you are instructed how to enable exception reporting at the service.

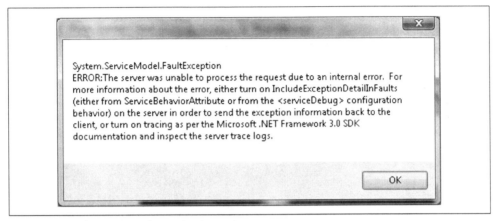

Figure 8-3. FaultException thrown by the service

 If you select an image larger than 16K, the error message will be different since you've exceeded the size limit. See Chapter 3 for more on large-message handling.

5. Go to the Host project and open *app.config*. Add the service debug behavior for reporting exception details by adding the <serviceDebug> element to the existing behavior configuration and setting includeExceptionDetailInFaults to true as shown in Example 8-4.

Example 8-4. Enabling theServiceDebugBehavior for exception reporting

```
<behavior name="serviceBehavior">
  <serviceDebug includeExceptionDetailInFaults="true"/>
  <serviceMetadata httpGetEnabled="true"/>
</behavior>
```

 Enabling includeExceptionDetailInFaults is not a generally recommended practice, but it is helpful during development.

6. Test the solution once again, repeating the same test. This time you receive a FaultException<T> (see Figure 8-4). The message, however, is the correct message originally thrown with the ConfigurationErrorsException.

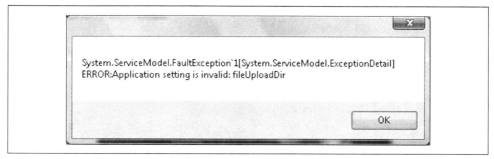

Figure 8-4. A service exception wrapped by FaultException<T>

In this lab, you saw how the exceptions are propagated to the client before and after the service debugging behavior is enabled. Now I'll discuss different ways to enable service debugging and how clients should react to exceptions.

Debugging Behavior

By default, the service model does not return the details of an uncaught exception when it returns a fault to the client. Doing so would present a security risk, since the information contained in an exception could potentially include file paths, database structure, and other proprietary information. During development, exceptions contain useful information for developers that can help them diagnose problems. For this reason, WCF provides an opt-in service debugging behavior. This behavior has a setting for reporting exception details including the stack trace. The exception details are wrapped in a fault returned to the client. This behavior can be enabled in configuration or in code.

ServiceDebugBehavior is the runtime abstraction for this behavior from the System. ServiceModel.Description namespace. It exposes a IncludeExceptionDetailsInFaults property.

As this lab illustrates, you can configure exception handling for ServiceDebugBehavior in configuration as follows:

```
<behavior name="serviceBehavior">
  <serviceDebug includeExceptionDetailInFaults="true" />
</behavior>
```

To set the behavior at the service, set the IncludeExceptionDetailInFaults property of the ServiceBehaviorAttribute to true:

```
[ServiceBehavior(IncludeExceptionDetailInFaults=true)]
public class PhotoManagerService : IPhotoManagerService
```

Another option is to initialize the ServiceHost with this behavior, as shown in Example 8-5. The default setting is false both in configuration and in code.

Example 8-5. ConfiguringServiceDebugBehavior through theServiceHost

```
using (ServiceHost host = new ServiceHost(typeof(PhotoManagerService))
{
  host.AddServiceEndpoint(typeof(HelloIndigo.IHelloIndigoService), new
BasicHttpBinding( ), "HelloIndigoService");

  ServiceDebugBehavior debugBehavior =
host.Description.Behaviors.Find<ServiceDebugBehavior>( );
  if (debugBehavior == null)
  {
    debugBehavior = new ServiceDebugBehavior( );
    host.Description.Behaviors.Add(debugBehavior);
  }

  debugBehavior.IncludeExceptionDetailInFaults = true;
  host.Open( );

  Console.WriteLine("Press <ENTER> to terminate the service host");
  Console.ReadLine( );
}
```

This sample shows how to configure service debug in code: *<YourLearningWCFPath>\Samples\Exceptions\ServiceDebugCode.*

You will normally leave this feature disabled, allowing administrators to enable it only to troubleshoot issues. Avoid hardcoding this feature to the service implementation since this will prevent administrators from disabling the feature, ever. If the behavior is enabled in code, that is assumed to be a dependency of the service. The service model performs an XOR on both settings (code and configuration) to determine the resulting setting.

A sample illustrating this XOR behavior can be found at *<YourLearningWCFPath>\Samples\Exceptions\ServiceDebugXOR.*

Uncaught Exceptions and SOAP Faults

By default, the service model throws a fault when uncaught exceptions are thrown at the service. That's when it faults the service channel. As far as the client is concerned, the message returned always contains a SOAP fault. Recall, however, that if an uncaught exception is thrown at the service, the server and client channels are faulted. So, how does the client channel know the difference between a fault thrown by the service, and a fault that should fault the channel at the client? This is described in the SOAP fault.

Example 8-6 shows a serialized fault message when service debugging is disabled. Notice that the <SubCode> for the fault indicates an InternalServiceFault. When the client channel processes the response, it checks for known fault codes and detects this setting. Thus, it faults the client channel if applicable (for example, if a session is present).

Example 8-6. SOAP Fault with service debug disabled

```
<s:Envelope xmlns:s="http://www.w3.org/2003/05/soap-envelope"
xmlns:a="http://www.w3.org/2005/08/addressing">
  <s:Header>
    <a:Action s:mustUnderstand="1">
http://schemas.microsoft.com/net/2005/12/windowscommunicationfoundation/
dispatcher/fault</a:Action>
    <a:RelatesTo>urn:uuid:09013cb0-71fe-4861-8069-3d5e89f253a4</a:RelatesTo>
    <a:To s:mustUnderstand="1">
http://www.w3.org/2005/08/addressing/anonymous</a:To>
  </s:Header>
  <s:Body>
    <s:Fault>
      <s:Code>
        <s:Value>s:Receiver</s:Value>
        <s:Subcode>
          <s:Value xmlns:a="http://schemas.microsoft.com/net/2005/12/
windowscommunicationfoundation/dispatcher">a:InternalServiceFault</s:Value>
        </s:Subcode>
      </s:Code>
      <s:Reason>
        <s:Text xml:lang="en-US">The server was unable to process the request due
to an internal error.  For more information about the error, either turn on
IncludeExceptionDetailInFaults (either from ServiceBehaviorAttribute or from the
<serviceDebug> configuration behavior) on the server in order to send the exception
information back to the client, or turn on tracing as per the Microsoft .NET
Framework 3.0 SDK documentation and inspect the server trace logs.</s:Text>
      </s:Reason>
    </s:Fault>
  </s:Body>
</s:Envelope>
```

When service debugging is enabled, the fault looks as shown in Example 8-7. The same InternalServiceFault is present; however, the <Detail> section of the fault carries additional information specific to the CLR exception that triggered the fault. You can see from this example that the kind of information included when service debugging is enabled is not desirable to share with clients for the security risk of exposing information about the internal system.

Example 8-7. SOAP Fault with service debug enabled

```
<s:Envelope xmlns:s="http://www.w3.org/2003/05/soap-envelope"
xmlns:a="http://www.w3.org/2005/08/addressing">
  <s:Header>
    <a:Action s:mustUnderstand="1">
http://schemas.microsoft.com/net/2005/12/windowscommunicationfoundation/
dispatcher/fault</a:Action>
    <a:RelatesTo>urn:uuid:ce1f3861-6a5c-463f-aaee-eadec43466ae</a:RelatesTo>
    <a:To s:mustUnderstand="1">
http://www.w3.org/2005/08/addressing/anonymous</a:To>
```

Example 8-7. SOAP Fault with service debug enabled (continued)

```
      </s:Header>
      <s:Body>
        <s:Fault>
          <s:Code>
            <s:Value>s:Receiver</s:Value>
            <s:Subcode>
                <s:Value xmlns:a="http://schemas.microsoft.com/net/2005/12/
windowscommunicationfoundation/dispatcher">a:InternalServiceFault</s:Value>
            </s:Subcode>
          </s:Code>
          <s:Reason>
            <s:Text xml:lang="en-US">Application setting is invalid:
fileUploadDir</s:Text>
          </s:Reason>
          <s:Detail>
            <ExceptionDetail
xmlns="http://schemas.datacontract.org/2004/07/System.ServiceModel"
xmlns:i="http://www.w3.org/2001/XMLSchema-instance">
                <HelpLink i:nil="true"></HelpLink>
                <InnerException i:nil="true"></InnerException>
                <Message>Application setting is invalid: fileUploadDir</Message>
                <StackTrace>
at FileManager.FileUploadUtil.SaveFile(String filename, Byte[] data) in
D:\LearningWCF\Common\FileManager\FileManager.cs:line 28
at PhotoManager.PhotoUploadUtil.SavePhoto(PhotoLink fileInfo, Byte[] fileData) in
D:\LearningWCF\Labs\Chapter8\Exceptions - Copy\PhotoManager\PhotoManager.cs:line 25
at PhotoManagerService.PhotoManagerService.UploadPhoto(PhotoLink fileInfo, Byte[]
fileData) in D:\LearningWCF\Labs\Chapter8\Exceptions -
Copy\PhotoManagerService\PhotoManagerService.cs:line 20
at SyncInvokeUploadPhoto(Object , Object[] , Object[] )
at System.ServiceModel.Dispatcher.SyncMethodInvoker.Invoke(Object instance,
Object[] inputs, Object[]& outputs)
at System.ServiceModel.Dispatcher.DispatchOperationRuntime.InvokeBegin(MessageRpc&
rpc) at System.ServiceModel.Dispatcher.
ImmutableDispatchRuntime.ProcessMessage5(MessageRpc& rpc)
at System.ServiceModel.Dispatcher.
ImmutableDispatchRuntime.ProcessMessage4(MessageRpc& rpc)
at System.ServiceModel.Dispatcher.
ImmutableDispatchRuntime.ProcessMessage3(MessageRpc& rpc)
at System.ServiceModel.Dispatcher.
ImmutableDispatchRuntime.ProcessMessage2(MessageRpc& rpc)
at System.ServiceModel.Dispatcher.
ImmutableDispatchRuntime.ProcessMessage1(MessageRpc& rpc)
at System.ServiceModel.Dispatcher.MessageRpc.Process(Boolean isOperationContextSet)
                </StackTrace>
                <Type>System.Configuration.ConfigurationErrorsException</Type>
            </ExceptionDetail>
          </s:Detail>
        </s:Fault>
      </s:Body>
</s:Envelope>
```

Clients and Faulted Channels

As I discussed in Chapter 5, when sessions are enabled, uncaught exceptions at the service will fault the service channel. If the operation is a request-reply operation, when the client channel processes the response, it will fault the client channel. At this point, the proxy can no longer communicate with the service, and any attempt to invoke operations results in a CommunicationObjectFaultedException. If the operation is a one-way call, although the service channel is faulted, the client channel is not faulted until the next non-one-way call to the service. Subsequent calls will now result in a CommunicationObjectFaultedException.

The client channel has a State property (discussed in Chapters 4 and 5) that is based on the CommunicationState enumeration. Clients should detect the state of the client channel after every call to determine if the channel is still viable. You can do this through the proxy's InnerChannel reference. After an exception, the channel's State property will be set to CommunicationState.Faulted. You can detect this as shown in Example 8-8 and recover by creating a new proxy, and thus a new channel for the client.

> Do not blatantly ignore a faulted channel state. Before starting a new session, try to determine the cause of the fault programmatically through the reported exception details, or at least log the error or present it to the user to make a decision on how to proceed.

Example 8-8. Handling exceptions on the client

```
// proxy scoped to the lifetime of the application
PhotoUploadContractClient m_proxy = new
PhotoUploadContractClient("NetTcpBinding_PhotoUploadContract");
// invoking service operations
try
{
    // other code
    m_proxy.UploadPhoto(fileInfo, fileData);
    MessageBox.Show("File uploaded!");
}
catch (CommunicationException ex)
{
  string s = String.Format("{0}\r\nERROR:{1}", ex.GetType( ), ex.Message);
  MessageBox.Show(s);

  // checking the state of the channel after an exception
  if (m_proxy.InnerChannel.State == CommunicationState.Faulted)
    m_proxy = new PhotoUploadContractClient("NetTcpBinding_PhotoUploadContract");
}
```

> A sample illustrating how clients detect the channel state can be found at *<YourLearningWCFPath>\Samples\Exceptions\DetectingChannelState*.

Fault Contracts

Message exchange patterns describe the direction of messages between clients and services. Recall from Chapter 3 that request-reply, one-way, and duplex (or callback) exchange patterns influence the service description. Specifically, the operation description in the WSDL document for request-reply operations defines an <input> and <output> message, while one-way messages define only an <input> message and callback contracts result in only an <output> message. Declared faults are also documented as part of the metadata for each operation.

When exceptions occur, if they are known, they should be reported as faults instead of letting exceptions propagate up to the service model to fault the channel. Furthermore, known faults should be formal message contracts that describe the type of exception data that will be reported to clients. By declaring known faults in the service contract, you can define schema for each fault so that client applications are aware of the faults for each operation they call and the format of those faults to gather intelligence on the problem. As I mentioned earlier, faults are described as <fault> elements for an operation in the WSDL document. There can be more than one per operation. WCF provides a simple way to declare faults for service operations that ultimately feed the WSDL document.

In this section, you'll learn how to declare fault contracts for your service operations using the FaultContractAttribute and how to throw faults instead of letting exceptions fault the server channel. You'll also learn how to generate useful fault details and how clients can work with declared faults and access those details.

Lab: Throwing Faults and Declaring Fault Contracts

In this lab, you will open an existing solution that lets you upload photos to a service, as in the previous lab. This time, you will explore how to declare a fault contract, how to throw faults, and how to trap faults at the client. You'll achieve this by applying the FaultContractAttribute and by generating faults with FaultException and FaultException<T>.

1. Open the startup solution for this lab, located in <YourLearningWCFPath>\ Labs\Chapter8\FaultContract\FaultContract.sln.

2. Like in the previous lab, the code for this lab also has logic to call the Photos database; thus, you should install the database script <YourLearningWCFPath>\ SupportingFiles\DatabaseScripts\Photos_CreateDB.sql. See the "Database Setup" section of Appendix A for additional instructions.

3. Compile the solution and run the Host and then the PhotoUploadClient project. From the client application, try uploading a file. Click the browse ("...") button and select the sample image located here: <YourLearningWCFPath>\SupportingFiles\ SampleImages\ theband.jpg, then select Upload Photo.

As in the previous lab, a ConfigurationErrorsException is thrown by the service because of an invalid configuration setting in the Host application configuration file. The client receives a FaultException without any useful exception details because the service debug behavior is disabled.

4. You're going to modify the service operation so that it catches the ConfigurationErrorsException from the business tier and throws a fault instead of allowing the exception to propagate.

   Go to the *PhotoManagerService.cs* file and find the implementation for the UploadPhoto( ). Wrap the operation code in a try...catch statement where the catch is typed to the ConfigurationErrorsException. Inside the catch statement, throw a simple FaultException. The modifications are shown in bold in Example 8-9.

Example 8-9. Throwing a simpleFaultException

```
public void UploadPhoto(ContentTypes.PhotoLink fileInfo, byte[] fileData)
{

    try
    {
        PhotoUploadUtil photoUploadUtil = new PhotoUploadUtil( );
        photoUploadUtil.SavePhoto(fileInfo, fileData);
    }
    catch (ConfigurationErrorsException exConfig)
    {
        throw new FaultException(exConfig.Message);
    }
}
```

Compile the solution and run the same test. This time, the client receives a FaultException with the original error message.

> Note that wrapping the error message into the FaultException did not reveal as much information as the service debug behavior enables. Namely, the stack trace is not included.

5. Now you're going to change this so that a declared fault is thrown by the service. Open *IPhotoUpload.cs* and change the service operation definition so that a FaultContractAttribute is applied for the ConfigurationErrorsException, as shown in bold here:

   ```
   [OperationContract]
   [FaultContract(typeof(ConfigurationErrorsException))]
   void UploadPhoto(PhotoLink fileInfo, byte[] fileData);
   ```

   You'll also add a using statement for System.Configuration to the file.

6. Next, open *PhotoManagerService.cs* and modify the UploadPhoto( ) operation implementation to throw a strongly typed fault using FaultException<T>. Replace the previous statement by thowing a FaultException to the following:

```
throw new FaultException<ConfigurationErrorsException>(new
ConfigurationErrorsException(exConfig.Message),
new FaultReason(exConfig.Message),
FaultCode.CreateReceiverFaultCode(new
FaultCode("ConfigurationErrorsException")));
```

Compile the solution and run the same test. You'll see the same results at the client. That's because the client proxy does not yet reflect the new metadata generated by the service with the FaultContractAttribute.

7. Go to the PhotoUploadClient project and open the proxy, *localhost.cs*, to find the definition for the service contract. Find the definition for the PhotoUploadClient interface and add the FaultContractAttribute as in shown bold here:

```
[System.ServiceModel.ServiceContractAttribute(
Namespace="http://www.thatindigogirl.com/samples/2006/06",
ConfigurationName="PhotoUploadClient.localhost.PhotoUploadContract")]
public interface PhotoUploadContract
{
    [System.ServiceModel.OperationContractAttribute(
Action="http://www.thatindigogirl.com/samples/2006/06/PhotoUploadContract/
UploadPho
to", ReplyAction="http://www.thatindigogirl.com/samples/2006/06/
PhotoUploadContract/UploadPhotoResponse")]
    [System.ServiceModel.FaultContract(
typeof(System.Configuration.ConfigurationErrorsException))]
    void UploadPhoto(PhotoUploadClient.localhost.PhotoLink fileInfo,
byte[] fileData);
}
```

You'll also add a reference to the System.Configuration assembly.

 SvcUtil would automatically add FaultContractAttribute to each operation as appropriate based on the service description.

8. Compile and run the solution and run the same test. This time, the client catches the correct exception, FaultException<ConfigurationErrorsException>.

9. Add code to catch the strongly typed fault thrown by the UploadFile( ) operation. Open *Form1.cs* in the code window and find the event handler cmdSave_Click. Modify the code to catch FaultException<ConfigurationErrorsException> as shown highlighted in Example 8-10. The code also inspects the Detail property of the message, which is strongly typed to the ConfigurationErrorsException type.

Example 8-10. CatchingFaultException<T>

```
try
{
  PhotoLink fileInfo = new PhotoLink( );
  // other code
```

Example 8-10. CatchingFaultException<T> (continued)

```
  m_proxy.UploadPhoto(fileInfo, fileData);
  MessageBox.Show("File uploaded!");
}
catch (System.ServiceModel.FaultException
<System.Configuration.ConfigurationErrorsException> exConfig)
{
  string s = String.Format("{0}\r\nERROR:{1}",
  exConfig.GetType( ), exConfig.Detail.Message);
  MessageBox.Show(s);
}
catch (Exception ex)
{
  string s = String.Format("{0}\r\nERROR:{1}", ex.GetType( ), ex.Message);
  MessageBox.Show(s);
}
```

10. Compile and run the solution again to repeat the same test. If you put a breakpoint on the new code block, you'll see that the new catch block traps the message and successfully accesses the details of the exception.

Throwing Faults

Services should not simply allow exceptions to propagate to the service model because this will fault the service channel, which tears down any client application sessions, transport sessions, reliable sessions, or secure sessions. Instead, any exceptions that could be thrown by the business tier to the service should be trapped at the service before making a decision if the problem is fatal or not. If the exception is considered fatal to the service, the channel should probably be allowed to fault. If the exception is something that should be logged, or reported to the client but is not fatal, the service should throw a fault instead of an exception, populating the fault with relevant information for the client. You can throw faults using FaultException or FaultException<T>. You can also use the MessageFault type to initialize the fault with additional details for the SOAP fault.

FaultException

You can throw a fault using the FaultException type from the System.ServiceModel namespace. This type exposes some basic properties related to the SOAP fault (discussed earlier), including Reason and Code. You can throw a simple fault this way:

```
throw new FaultException("An invalid operation has occurred.");
```

This initializes the Reason string and sets defaults for other SOAP fault properties. The resulting serialized fault looks something like Example 8-11.

Example 8-11. SOAP Fault from simpleFaultException

```
<s:Envelope xmlns:s="http://schemas.xmlsoap.org/soap/envelope/">
  <s:Body>
```

Example 8-11. SOAP Fault from simpleFaultException (continued)

```
    <s:Fault>
      <faultcode xmlns="">s:Client</faultcode>
      <faultstring xml:lang="en-US" xmlns="">
An invalid operation has  occurred.</faultstring>
    </s:Fault>
  </s:Body>
</s:Envelope>
```

Throwing a `FaultException` in this way is a quick way to throw a basic fault to prevent faulting the channel for known exceptions and to communicate a basic set of information back to the client.

FaultException<T>

To send a more informative fault to the client, you should use `FaultException<T>`. `FaultException<T>` is a generic derivative of the abstract base type `FaultException`. When you create an instance of `FaultException<T>` you provide a type for the details element of the SOAP fault. This enables strong-typing on the detail element of the fault.

You throw faults with `FaultException<T>` in this way:

```
throw new FaultException<InvalidOperationException>(
new InvalidOperationException(("An invalid operation has occurred."),
new FaultReason(("Invalid operation."),
FaultCode.CreateReceiverFaultCode(
new FaultCode("InvalidOperationException")));
```

The result of throwing this `InvalidOperationException` fault is the serialized SOAP fault shown in Example 8-12. Note that the `<Detail>` element contains a child named for the `InvalidOperationException` type. The client will be able to reconstruct this type only if it knows about it from the service description. That's where fault contracts come in.

Example 8-12. Serialized SOAP Fault fromFaultException<T>

```
<s:Envelope xmlns:s="http://www.w3.org/2003/05/soap-envelope"
xmlns:a="http://www.w3.org/2005/08/addressing">
  <s:Header>
    <a:Action s:mustUnderstand="1">
http://tempuri.org/IFaultExceptionService/
ThrowFaultExceptionInvalidOperationExceptionFault</a:Action>
    <a:RelatesTo>urn:uuid:4b76cee0-dcf4-49f6-bb11-b1d97c2d32f7</a:RelatesTo>
  </s:Header>
  <s:Body>
    <s:Fault>
      <s:Code>
        <s:Value>s:Server</s:Value>
        <s:Subcode>
          <s:Value>s:Server.System.NotImplementedException</s:Value>
        </s:Subcode>
```

Example 8-12. Serialized SOAP Fault fromFaultException<T> (continued)

```
        </s:Code>
        <s:Reason>
          <s:Text xml:lang="en-US">Invalid operation.</s:Text>
        </s:Reason>
        <s:Detail>
          <InvalidOperationException
xmlns="http://schemas.datacontract.org/2004/07/System"
xmlns:i="http://www.w3.org/2001/XMLSchema-instance"
xmlns:x="http://www.w3.org/2001/XMLSchema">
            <ClassName i:type="x:string" xmlns="">
System.InvalidOperationException</ClassName>
            <Message i:type="x:string" xmlns="">
An invalid operation has occured.</Message>
            <Data i:nil="true" xmlns=""></Data>
            <InnerException i:nil="true" xmlns=""></InnerException>
            <HelpURL i:nil="true" xmlns=""></HelpURL>
            <StackTraceString i:nil="true" xmlns=""></StackTraceString>
            <RemoteStackTraceString i:nil="true" xmlns=""></RemoteStackTraceString>
            <RemoteStackIndex i:type="x:int" xmlns="">0</RemoteStackIndex>
            <ExceptionMethod i:nil="true" xmlns=""></ExceptionMethod>
            <HResult i:type="x:int" xmlns="">-2146233079</HResult>
            <Source i:nil="true" xmlns=""></Source>
          </InvalidOperationException>
        </s:Detail>
      </s:Fault>
    </s:Body>
</s:Envelope>
```

 Wrapping an existing CLR exception type in FaultException<T> may be useful for intranet applications where both sides are WCF since the exception type will be meaningful on both ends. This is not very SOA, if you recall the tenets discussed in Chapter 1. For most scenarios, therefore, you should create a few data contracts for some common faults and for corresponding fault contracts. This decouples clients from services and promotes interoperability.

MessageFault

FaultException<T> represents a strongly typed fault exception at runtime, but it is ultimately wrapped in a MessageFault before serialization. MessageFault is a runtime abstraction of a SOAP fault, and its members are mapped to SOAP 1.1 or 1.2 fault formats according to the binding requirements. You can exercise greater control over the contents of the SOAP fault if you use the MessageFault type to initialize the fault. This type exposes a CreateFault() method that generates a FaultException, as shown in Example 8-13.

Example 8-13. UsingCreateFault() to generate a fault

```
InvalidOperationException error = new InvalidOperationException("An invalid
operation has occurred.");
```

Example 8-13. UsingCreateFault() to generate a fault (continued)

```
MessageFault mfault = MessageFault.CreateFault(new FaultCode("Server", new
FaultCode(String.Format("Server.{0}", error.GetType().Name))), new
FaultReason(error.Message), error);

FaultException fe = FaultException.CreateFault(mfault,
typeof(InvalidOperationException));

throw fe;
```

 This sample illustrates different techniques for throwing faults: *<YourLearningWCFPath>\Samples\Exceptions\ThrowingFaults.*

Declared Faults

By applying the FaultContractAttribute to service operations, the service description and thus the WSDL document will include a list of supported faults by operation. This is how WCF services educate clients on the supported fault details. In this lab, you applied FaultContractAttribute to an operation as follows:

```
[OperationContract]
[FaultContract(typeof(ConfigurationErrorsException))]
void UploadPhoto(PhotoLink fileInfo, byte[] fileData);
```

You can stack as many FaultContractAttribute to each service operation as is necessary to include supported faults to the service description.

The FaultContractAttribute indicates to the service model which detail types can be rehydrated from a serialized fault. The client proxy must include the same list of FaultContractAttribute in order to properly construct the FaultException<T> type.

Fault Contracts and Complex Types

When a fault is thrown using FaultException<T>, type T can be any valid data contract or serializable type (discussed in Chapter 2). Likewise, the constructor of the FaultContractAttribute can accept any valid data contract or serializable type. Though it might seem natural to throw an exception type wrapped in a fault exception, it is preferable that you design the fault contract as you would any other data contract for an operation. Every service would likely have at least two fault contracts defined as data contracts: a receiver fault contract for failures related to the payload received to the operation, and a sender fault contract for failures not related to the payload. The fault contract type can be defined, as shown in Example 8-14.

Example 8-14. Custom fault data contract

```
[DataContract(Name="ReceiverFault",
Namespace="http://schemas.thatindigogirl.com/samples/2006/06/Faults")]
```

Example 8-14. Custom fault data contract (continued)

```
public class ReceiverFault
{
  ...private data members

  [DataMember]
  public DateTime Timestamp
  {
    get { return m_timeStamp; }
    set { m_timeStamp = value; }
  }

  [DataMember]
  public string Message
  {
    get { return m_message; }
    set { m_message = value; }
  }

  [DataMember]
  public FailedBodyElement[] FailedBodyElements
  {
    get { return m_failedBodyElements; }
    set { m_failedBodyElements = value; }
  }
}
```

As I mentioned, the type must be a data contract or serializable type. Custom data contracts included in the fault contract are described in schema. During proxy generation, this schema is converted to types with which the client can work, specifically so that clients can construct the details element.

To throw a FaultException<T> with a custom type, simply provide the custom type as type T, as shown here:

```
FaultException<ReceiverFault> fault = new
FaultException<ReceiverFault>(new ReceiverFault("An error has occurred on the
server."), new FaultReason("An error has occurred on the server."),
FaultCode.CreateReceiverFaultCode(new FaultCode("GeneralError")));

throw fault;
```

This sample illustrates the use of data contracts for fault declarations: *<YourLearningWCFPath>\Samples\Exceptions\FaultDataContracts*.

Mapping MessageFault to SOAP Fault

Ultimately, the fault code, reason, and detail element will be serialized by a MessageFault type to a SOAP fault. Table 8-2 lists each SOAP 1.1 fault element and how the MessageFault type maps its properties to those elements. Table 8-3 provides the same list for the SOAP 1.2 specification. When faults are thrown, the appropriate properties of the MessageFault type will be used to build a SOAP fault. You may care about this if you are building web services and are attempting to follow the guidelines provided by each respective SOAP specification.

Table 8-2. SOAP 1.1 elements mapped to MessageFault properties

Fault element	MessageFault equivalent	SOAP 1.1 description
faultcode	Code.SubCode	One of VersionMismatch, MustUnderstand, Client, or Server. Can also extend with custom codes that include a subtype (i.e., Server.NotImplemented).
faultstring	Reason	Free form.
faultactor	Actor	A URI describing the source of the fault. Values can be one of: *http://www.w3.org/2003/05/soap-envelope/role/ultimateReceiver* (for SOAP node), *http://www.w3.org/2003/05/soap-envelope/role/next* (for intermediary nodes), *http://www.w3.org/2003/05/soap-envelope/role/none* (illegal for the receiver), or an extended, custom value.
detail	Detail	Free form. Required if the SOAP body could not be processed. Should provide information about the body element(s) that failed.

Table 8-3. SOAP 1.2 elements mapped to MessageFault properties

Fault element	MessageFault equivalent	Description
Code.Value	Code	Must be one of VersionMismatch, MustUnderstand, DataEncodingUnknown, Sender, or Receiver.
Code.Subcode	Code.SubCode	Custom codes describing the fault.
Reason	Reason	Free form.
Node	Node	A URI describing the node that caused the failure.
Role	Actor	A URI describing the source of the fault. Values can be one of: *http://www.w3.org/2003/05/soap-envelope/role/ultimateReceiver* (for SOAP node), *http://www.w3.org/2003/05/soap-envelope/role/next* (for intermediary nodes), *http://www.w3.org/2003/05/soap-envelope/role/none* (illegal for the receiver), or an extended, custom value.
Detail	Detail	Free form. Required if the SOAP body could not be processed. Should provide information about the body element(s) that failed.

Creating SOAP 1.1 compliant faults

The MessageFault type can be serialized to a SOAP 1.1 or 1.2 compliant fault, however to create truly compliant SOAP 1.1 faults, you should explicitly set some of the MessageFault members by controlling how you create the fault exception.

One of the big differences between SOAP 1.1 and 1.2 faults is in the fault code. For SOAP 1.1, fault codes include "Client" and "Server," but the equivalent in SOAP 1.2 is "Sender" and "Receiver." Using the CreateReceiverFaultCode and CreateSenderFaultCode (see Example 8-15) helper methods on the FaultCode type works for SOAP 1.2 faults—but not for SOAP 1.1 faults.

Example 8-15. Generating a SOAP 1.2 compliant sender and receiver fault

```
FaultException<ReceiverFault> fault = new
FaultException<ReceiverFault>(new ReceiverFault("An error has occurred on the
server."),
new FaultReason("An error has occurred on the server."),
FaultCode.CreateReceiverFaultCode(new FaultCode("GeneralError")));

FaultException<SenderFault> fault = new
FaultException<SenderFault>(new SenderFault("An error has occurred processing message
body."),
new FaultReason("An error has occurred processing message body."), FaultCode.
CreateSenderFaultCode("GeneralError"));
```

Instead, to create a SOAP 1.1 fault, explicitly set the fault code to "Client" or "Server," and include it in the prefix of the fault sub code as shown in Example 8-16.

 Your binding configuration determines the SOAP serialization format, so you are not in control of this when you instantiate the fault exception. You should write code to detect the message version of the incoming request message and format the fault exception accordingly. This information is available through the `OperationContext` (discussed in Chapter 5).

Example 8-16. Generating a SOAP 1.1 compliant client and server fault

```
FaultException<ReceiverFault> fault = new
FaultException<ReceiverFault>(new ReceiverFault("An error has occurred on the
server."),
new FaultReason("An error has occurred on the server."),
new FaultCode("Server", new FaultCode("Server.GeneralError")));

FaultException<SenderFault> fault = new
FaultException<SenderFault>(new SenderFault("An error has occurred processing
message body."),
new FaultReason("An error has occurred processing message body."),
new FaultCode("Client", new FaultCode("Client.GeneralError")));
```

Clients and FaultContracts

The service description and resulting WSDL document describes information about the service, its endpoints and protocol support, and the operations available at each endpoint. When faults are declared for service operations this information is also part of the service description. During proxy generation, any declared faults are also included in the resulting service contracts generated for the client proxy. The `FaultContractAttribute` is applied just as it was at the service so that clients can be aware of the possible faults they should handle for each operation. More importantly, the service model uses this information to deserialize faults into their appropriate runtime representation.

IErrorHandler

Realistically, it is impossible for the service designer to have full knowledge of all the exceptions that may be thrown by downstream business components as the operation executes. I've already established that you shouldn't indiscriminately throw unhandled exceptions as faults. You also don't necessarily want to wrap all uncaught exceptions as faults. You may, however, want to log all uncaught exceptions and, if appropriate, convert some of those exceptions to faults to prevent the channel from faulting.

Adding common error handling code such as this directly to each service operation would be cumbersome and unmanageable. For this reason, WCF provides support for error handler components. Error handlers are types that implement IErrorHandler and are associated with the service behavior. In this section, you will learn how to create and configure a custom error handler. In the process, you'll learn how to dynamically configure the ServiceHost using an IServiceBehavior extension, using a custom attribute, and by extending ServiceHost. You'll do a lab that exercises the basic concepts first.

Lab: Intercepting Uncaught Exceptions with IErrorHandler

The solution for this lab is much the same as the other two in this chapter. Through the client interface, you can upload photos to a service, and the service is currently configured with a bad directory name for file uploads. In this lab, you will explore how to create a custom error handler to process uncaught exceptions and decide which exceptions should be converted to faults. You'll be introduced to a new extensibility feature of WCF, IServiceBehavior, which I will explain after the lab.

Implementing IErrorHandler

In this first section of the lab, you will implement IErrorHandler on a new type to create an error handler component. In the error handler, you will make sure that a proper fault is thrown for specific uncaught exceptions only.

1. Open the startup solution for this lab, located in *<YourLearningWCFPath>\ Labs\Chapter8\IErrorHandler\IErrorHandler.sln*.

2. This lab requires you to install the database script *<YourLearningWCFPath>\ SupportingFiles\DatabaseScripts\Photos_CreateDB.sql*. See the "Database Setup" section of Appendix A for additional instructions.

3. Compile the solution and run the Host, and then the PhotoUploadClient. As in the other labs in this chapter, try uploading a file. A ConfigurationErrorsException is thrown by the service and the client receives a general FaultException.

4. Review the fault types that have been created for this project. Go to the PhotoManagerService project and open *Faults.cs*—you'll see two data contracts,

---

ReceiverFaultDetail and SenderFaultDetail. Currently, the IPhotoUpload contract does not declare these fault contracts.

5. Create a new error handler component in the PhotoManagerService project. Add a new class file named *FaultErrorHandler.cs*. Add a using statement for System.ServiceModel.Dispatcher. On the class file, implement the IErrorHandler interface:

```
using System.ServiceModel.Dispatcher;

public class FaultErrorHandler:IErrorHandler
{
}
```

6. The implementation for ProvideFault( ) will check first to see whether a fault has already been created. If not, it will check to see whether the exception is a ConfigurationErrorsException before wrapping it into a custom FaultException<ReceiverFaultDetail> to report information to the client. In order to report a fault from the error handler, the fault parameter must be initialized.

This parameter is a Message type, which means you must create a FaultMessage. You will use CreateMessage( ) to create a message from a FaultException. The code to add is shown in Example 8-17, including the necessary using statements.

 One of the CreateMessage( ) method overloads supports initializing the Message with a MessageFault. FaultException<T> has a CreateMessageFault( ) method to create such a MessageFault instance.

Example 8-17. HandlingProvideFault( )

```
using System.ServiceModel;
using System.ServiceModel.Channels;
using System.Configuration;

public void ProvideFault(Exception error,
System.ServiceModel.Channels.MessageVersion version, ref
System.ServiceModel.Channels.Message fault)
{
  if (fault == null)
  {
    if (error is ConfigurationErrorsException)
    {
      FaultException<ReceiverFaultDetail> fe = new
FaultException<ReceiverFaultDetail>(new ReceiverFaultDetail(error.Message, true),
error.Message, FaultCode.CreateReceiverFaultCode(new FaultCode("Configuration")));
      MessageFault mf = fe.CreateMessageFault( );

      fault = Message.CreateMessage(version, mf, fe.Action);
    }
  }
}
```

If the fault parameter is not set before ProvideFault( ) returns, the original uncaught exception will propagate to the service model and fault the channel.

7. In the implementation for HandleError( ), add code to log the uncaught exception and to return true to indicate that the exception has been handled. The code should look like this:

```
public bool HandleError(Exception error)
{
    Console.WriteLine("Uncaught exception of type {0} was thrown. Message: '{1}'",
error.GetType( ), error.Message);
    return true;
}
```

Compile PhotoManagerService to verify that the new error handler compiles.

 If the HandleError( ) returns true, other error handlers in the collection will not execute since the error has been handled. If it returns false, another error handler gets a chance to interact with the exception (and fault if any).

Configuring an error handler

In this part of the lab, you will configure the new error handler by adding it to each of the endpoints exposed by the ServiceHost.

1. To configure the error handler, you must interact with the initialization of the ServiceHost channel dispatchers. You can configure an error handler for any endpoint exposed by the ServiceHost. In this case, you will implement IServiceBehavior on the service type. Go to PhotoManagerService and open *PhotoManagerService.cs*. Add IServiceBehavior to the inheritance list on the service type and add a using statement for System.ServiceModel.Descriptions, as shown here:

```
using System.ServiceModel.Description;

public class PhotoManagerService: IPhotoUpload, IPhotoManagerService,
IServiceBehavior
```

2. Implement IServiceBehavior on the service type. There are three methods exposed by this interface: AddBindingParameters( ), ApplyDispatchBehavior( ), and Validate( ). The first and last of these are irrelevant to this discussion and should have no code. Add code to ApplyDispatchBehavior( ) that will traverse the endpoints of the ServiceHost and add an instance of the FaultErrorHandler type to its ErrorHandlers collection. The new methods added to the PhotoManagerService type should look as shown in Example 8-18, including the using statements for System.ServiceModel.Dispatcher and System.ServiceModel.Channels.

Example 8-18. Implementation of IServiceBehavior to add error handling

```
using System.ServiceModel.Dispatcher;
using System.ServiceModel.Channels;


public void AddBindingParameters(ServiceDescription serviceDescription,
ServiceHostBase serviceHostBase,
System.Collections.ObjectModel.Collection<ServiceEndpoint> endpoints,
BindingParameterCollection bindingParameters)
{
}

public void ApplyDispatchBehavior(ServiceDescription serviceDescription,
ServiceHostBase serviceHostBase)
{
  foreach (ChannelDispatcher dispatcher in serviceHostBase.ChannelDispatchers)
  {
    dispatcher.ErrorHandlers.Add(new FaultErrorHandler( )
  }
}

public void Validate(ServiceDescription serviceDescription, ServiceHostBase
serviceHostBase)
{
}
```

3. Compile and run the solution again and run the same test to upload a photo. This time, you will see a FaultException is presented at the client with the configuration error intact. The error handler constructed this fault and also logged the uncaught exception to the console.

Using data contracts as fault contracts

Now you will modify the IUploadPhoto service contract so that SenderFaultDetail and ReceiverFaultDetail are declared faults. The client proxy will be updated so that it also knows about these faults.

1. Go to PhotoManagerService and open *IPhotoUpload.cs*. Add a FaultContractAttribute to the service operation as shown here:

```
[OperationContract]
[FaultContract(typeof(ReceiverFaultDetail))]
[FaultContract(typeof(SenderFaultDetail))]
void UploadPhoto(PhotoLink fileInfo, byte[] fileData);
```

2. Compile the solution and run the Host only so that you can update the client proxy. Go to PhotoUploadClient and update the service reference.

3. Recompile the solution again, run the host and client, and execute the same test as before to upload a photo. This time, the exception received at the client is strongly typed as `FaultException<ReceiverFaultDetail>`.

4. Open the proxy, *localhost.cs*, and note that the `ReceiverFaultDetail` and `SenderFaultDetail` types have been included in the proxy. That's because `FaultContractAttribute` is part of the service description, and any types included in the attribute are defined by schema.

IErrorHandler

Error handlers make it possible to inspect uncaught exceptions and faults in a central location and determine the best course of action. This allows you to decouple exception handling from the service implementation. To create an error handler, you implement `IErrorHandler` from the `System.ServiceModel.Dispatcher` namespace. There are two members on this interface as follows:

ProvideFault
> Gives you an opportunity to control the fault returned from the operation. This method has several parameters:
>
> • The original exception thrown. This may be a standard CLR exception or a `FaultException`.
>
> • The `MessageVersion` for the request. This is important because the message should be formatted according to the correct SOAP version and include the correctly formatted ws-Addressing headers if applicable.
>
> • A reference to a `Message` type that may already be populated if the operation threw a fault or if another error handler was executed prior to this one. Your job is to populate this with the fault you want returned to the client, if so desired.

HandleError
> This method is passed the original exception. Usually you will do work in this method to handle the error, and return `true` if the error has been handled, for example, if you have reported the exception to an administrator. Return `false` if this code doesn't do anything with the exception.

`ProvideFault( )` is called first, within the context of the service operation—thus, the `OperationContext` is available to you. If the fault parameter is `null`, or if you set it to `null` before returning, the original exception will propagate to the service model. If that exception is not a fault, the channel will fault. If a fault has not yet been provided, you should create a fault if the uncaught exception is something that should not fault the channel. You must keep a list of exceptions that are acceptable to convert to faults to achieve this.

During `HandleError( )` you can log or audit uncaught exceptions. The `Exception` type passed in may be a `FaultException` or any other CLR exception type. Most likely, you care only to log CLR exceptions that have not been converted to faults. When HandleError() is called, the OperationContext may not be available since the message is already being returned to the client. Thus, any work you do here to log the exception must be done without relying on this context. If you handle the error, return true so that other error handlers needn't be called (to reduce overhead).

Configuring Error Handlers

To configure an error handler, you add it to the ErrorHandlers collection for an endpoint's channel dispatcher. You can do this by creating an IServiceBehavior implementation or by customizing how the ServiceHost is initialized. The important thing is that the error handler is added to the dispatch behavior before the ServiceHost is opened.

 You'll notice that if you try to add to the ErrorHandlers collection after Open() is called on the ServiceHost, the error handler is not invoked.

Implementing IServiceBehavior

When you implement IServiceBehavior on a service type, it provides you with hooks for service initialization, which implies ServiceHost initialization. There are three points of extensibility provided by IServiceBehavior through its methods:

AddBindingParameters()
> Called before the ServiceHost is initialized, providing you with an opportunity to modify binding configuration prior to generating the service description. You can use this to ensure certain settings are present on a binding.

ApplyDispatchBehavior()
> Called before the ServiceHost is opened, but after the channel dispatchers have been constructed. This is a good place to add extensibility components such as error handlers.

Validate()
> Called after the ServiceHost is opened, so that you can validate the host and service description. You may, for example, check that a particular binding configuration is present.

In this lab, you add an error handler to each and every endpoint as follows:

```
public void ApplyDispatchBehavior(ServiceDescription serviceDescription,
ServiceHostBase serviceHostBase)
{
  foreach (ChannelDispatcher dispatcher in serviceHostBase.ChannelDispatchers)
  {
    dispatcher.ErrorHandlers.Add(new FaultErrorHandler());
  }
}
```

This sample illustrates implementing IServiceBehavior on the service type to add a custom error handler: *<YourLearningWCFPath>\Samples\ Exceptions\ IServiceBehaviorOnService.*

Attributes and IServiceBehavior

You can also easily create a custom attribute that applies an implementation of IServiceBehavior declaratively to a service type. For example, to create a custom error-handling attribute, you can create a type that derives from Attribute and implements IServiceBehavior, as shown in Example 8-19.

Example 8-19. Custom error handling attribute

```
class FaultErrorHandlerAttribute : Attribute, IServiceBehavior
{
  public void AddBindingParameters(ServiceDescription serviceDescription,
ServiceHostBase serviceHostBase,
System.Collections.ObjectModel.Collection<ServiceEndpoint> endpoints,
BindingParameterCollection bindingParameters)
  {
  }

  public void ApplyDispatchBehavior(ServiceDescription serviceDescription,
ServiceHostBase serviceHostBase)
  {
    foreach (ChannelDispatcher dispatcher in serviceHostBase.ChannelDispatchers)
    {
      dispatcher.ErrorHandlers.Add(new FaultErrorHandler());
    }
  }

  public void Validate(ServiceDescription serviceDescription, ServiceHostBase
serviceHostBase)
  {
  }
}
```

Apply the custom attribute to your service type and the error handler will be successfully added to the ErrorHandlers collection:

```
[FaultErrorHandler]
public class PhotoManagerService: IPhotoUpload, IPhotoManagerService
```

 The following sample illustrates a custom attribute that implements IServiceBehavior to add a custom error handler: *<YourLearningWCFPath>\Samples\Exceptions\ErrorHandlerAttribute.*

Extending ServiceHost

You can decouple the configuration of error handlers from the service altogether by extending the ServiceHost type and overriding the InitializeRuntime() method. Example 8-20 shows an example of this custom ServiceHost implementation.

Example 8-20. ExtendingServiceHost to add error handlers

```
class ErrorHandlerHost:ServiceHost
{
  public ErrorHandlerHost(Type t):base(t)
  {
  }

  protected override void InitializeRuntime()
  {
    base.InitializeRuntime();
    foreach (ChannelDispatcher dispatcher in this.ChannelDispatchers)
    {
      dispatcher.ErrorHandlers.Add(new PhotoManagerService.FaultErrorHandler());
    }
  }
}
```

The code to construct the ServiceHost would then change to this in the Host application:

```
using (ErrorHandlerHost host = new
ErrorHandlerHost(typeof(PhotoManagerService.PhotoManagerService)))
{
  host.Open();

  Console.WriteLine("Press <ENTER> to terminate the host application");
  Console.ReadLine();
}
```

 The following sample illustrates extending the ServiceHost to add an error handler: *<YourLearningWCFPath>\Samples\Exceptions\ ExtendingServiceHost.*

Summary

In this chapter, you learned how to deal with exceptions for your WCF clients and services. You learned that the default behavior is to suppress uncaught exceptions to protect the system from sharing proprietary information; you learned how to enable debugging behaviors to share exceptions during development; you learned how throwing any form of FaultException will not fault the service channel and will pass more useful information to clients; and you learned how to create reusable code to control how faults are propagated to clients. Some recommendations you can take away from this chapter are as follows:

- Do not return exceptions as faults except in development. Avoid enabling this on the service type since this will prevent administrators from disabling the feature in configuration.

- Declare just a few meaningful data contracts for the fault detail element, and map known exceptions to those types when you generate faults. Avoid returning CLR exception types in the details element since this is .NET specific. For interoperability, data contracts are preferred. Examples of possible data contracts to create are `ReceiverFaultDetail`, `SenderFaultDetail`, and `VersionMismatchFaultDetail`.

- Always provide an appropriate reason and fault code when throwing `FaultException` or `FaultException<T>`.

- Consider the differences between SOAP 1.1 and 1.2 when generating fault codes. `MessageFault` can serialize to either format according to the binding's envelope version, but there are subtle differences in SOAP 1.1 that are not considered by `MessageFault`. For example, set the fault code to "Client" or "Server" instead of "Sender" or "Receiver". For fault sub codes, supply a dot extension to the fault code as in "Client.InvalidData" or "Server.NotImplemented"—fault sub codes are not included in SOAP 1.1 serialization.

- Provide `IErrorHandler` implementations to handle scenarios where uncaught exceptions can be evaluated, logged and possibly converted to proper faults.

Setup Instructions

This appendix provides detailed setup instructions for labs and sample code referenced throughout this book. Each lab will specifically indicate which sections of this appendix must be completed, if applicable. Code samples for each chapter in the book also rely on you completing the setup instructions for the labs in that chapter. A cross-reference will be provided for samples that require setup, referencing this appendix. The setup instructions discussed in this appendix include:

- Instructions for installing database scripts
- Configuration settings for SQL Server
- Instructions for configuring web applications for the ASP.NET membership and role provider
- Instructions for generating X.509 certificates
- Instructions for installing X.509 certificates
- Instructions for installing an SSL certificate with IIS

Database Setup

Each lab will have its own instructions for installing specific database scripts, or for configuring connection strings. In this section, I'll review some general guidelines for database setup, script installation, and connection string formats.

Choosing a Database Engine

You have to make a decision about the database engine to use for samples that rely on a database or that use ASP.NET membership and roles. Your choice of database engine affects how you configure connection strings for labs and samples.

Your options are as follows:

- Microsoft SQL Server 2000 or 2005
- Microsoft SQL Server 2005 Express Edition (SQL Express)

If you don't have access to SQL Server 2000 or 2005, you can download SQL Express from the following location: *http://msdn.microsoft.com/vstudio/express/sql/download/*.

Installing Database Scripts

To install database scripts for book labs and samples, you'll need a management tool. If you installed SQL Server 2000 or 2005, you can use SQL Server Management Studio to administer any database. Otherwise, you can install SQL Server Management Studio Express from here: *http://msdn.microsoft.com/vstudio/express/sql/download*.

To install a database script, open the database management tool, and then open and run the *.sql* script.

Database Connection Strings

Labs and samples in this book that rely on a database will require a connection string setting in the application or web configuration file.

The following illustrates a connection string for a SQL 2000 or 2005 installation on the local machine:

```
<connectionStrings>
  <add name="PhotosDatabaseConnection" connectionString="data
source=localhost;Initial Catalog=Photos;Integrated Security=True;"
providerName="System.Data.SqlClient" />
</connectionStrings>
```

By comparison, the following illustrates a connection for a SQL Express database:

```
<connectionStrings>
  <add name="PhotosDatabaseConnection" connectionString="data
source=.\SQLEXPRESS;Integrated Security=SSPI;Initial Catalog=Photos"/>
</connectionStrings>
```

Labs and samples are configured to use SQL 2000 or 2005, but you can refer to the differences here if you need to change those settings to work with SQL Express.

Database Security

In this book, you will be working with web site projects that run with the ASP.NET account. That account is either ASPNET (for Windows XP) or NETWORK SERVICE (for Windows Server 2003 and Windows Vista). In some labs and samples, you may be asked to give the ASP.NET account access to a particular database. This section will provide instructions for this based on Microsoft SQL Server 2005.

First, add the ASPNET or NETWORK SERVICE account to the database instance Logins, as shown in Figure A-1. Right-click the Login node and select New Login. Click Search and add the account as the login name. Click OK to complete the process.

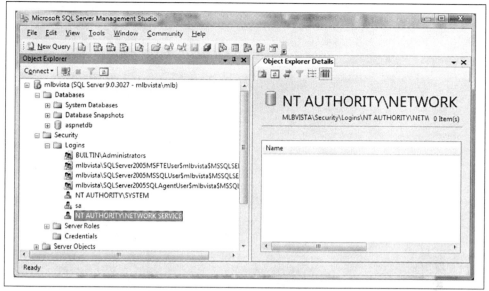

Figure A-1. Adding logins to SQL Server 2005

Now, expand the Databases node and find the database you want to allow this account access to. Beneath the Security node for the database (Figure A-2), right-click the Users node and select New User. Provide a name for the user, and beside Login name, click the browse button ("...") and find the account. In the Database role membership section, check the db_datareader and db_datawriter role members (Figure A-3) and click OK to complete the process.

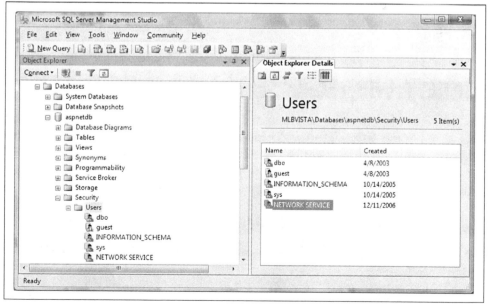

Figure A-2. Account access to a particular database

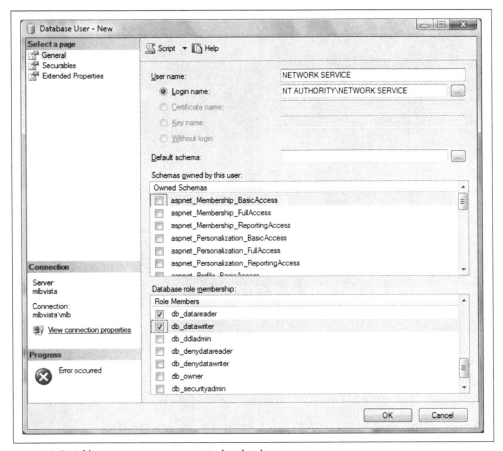

Figure A-3. Adding an account to a particular database

The new user should now appear in the list of users (Figure A-2).

ASP.NET Provider Model Setup

This section summarizes the database configuration settings required to use the ASP. NET membership and roles provider model with your WCF services. You'll learn how to override the default settings in the machine configuration file, how to select the right database connection for your environment, and how to initialize tables for the built-in ASP.NET providers including those for membership and roles.

Generating ASP.NET Provider Tables

For ASP.NET providers to work, the database must be initialized with the ASP.NET provider tables.

If you are using SQL Express, a new database is created for you when you use the ASP.NET web site configuration tool. This database file has an *.mdf* extension and is generated in the web site *\App_Data* directory.

If you are using SQL Server 2000 or 2005, or if you would like to use the central SQL Express database instead of individual files, you must run the ASP.NET SQL registration utility—*aspnet_regsql.exe*—by following these instructions:

1. From the Visual Studio 2008 command line, type *aspnet_regsql.exe*. The wizard will launch; skip to the second page.

2. From the "Select a Setup Option" page, select "Configure SQL Server for application services."

3. From the "Select the Server and Database" page, enter your server name, usually your machine name. If you are using SQL Express, type your machine name followed by "\SQLEXPRESS" (*[machinename]\SQLEXPRESS*). If you forget to type SQLEXPRESS, you will be attempting to connect to a SQL Server 2000/2005 default instance which may or may not be installed on your machine.

   Provide credentials for the database on this page as well. If you installed the database to support Windows authentication (recommended) you can click Next to continue. Otherwise provide your credentials to log in.

4. The summary page will state that it will create a database called aspnetdb for you. This will have numerous tables and supporting code for the ASP.NET provider model. Complete the wizard and you are ready!

To view the aspnetdb tables you just created, use SQL Server Management Studio or SQL Server Management Studio Express. If you're using the former, be sure to connect to the SQL Express instance by supplying the machine name followed by "\SQLEXPRESS," as shown in Figure A-4.

After connecting, you will be able to expand the Databases node to see the provider model tables generated for ASP.NET (see Figure A-5).

ASP.NET Provider Connection Strings

Any lab that uses the ASP.NET provider model will expect you to put a connection string appropriate to the database you are using in your configuration file. The lab will tell you when to do this—this section explains which connection string you should use, and where to put it.

The default connection string in the *machine.config* file for ASP.NET provider is shown in Example A-1.

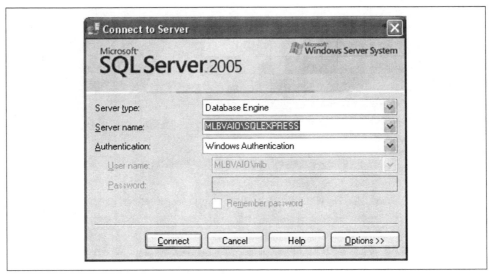

Figure A-4. Connecting to the default SQL Express instance

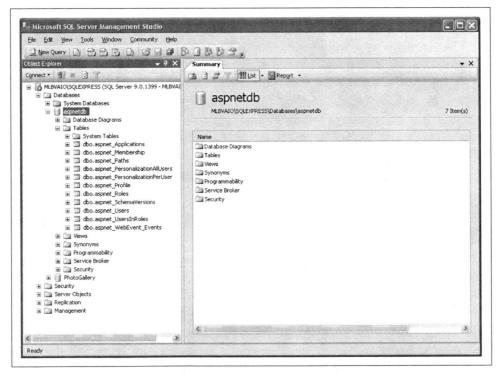

Figure A-5. ASP.NET provider model tables

Example A-1. Default setting for ASP.NET providers in the machine.config

```
<configuration>

  ... other settings

  <connectionStrings>
    <add name="LocalSqlServer" connectionString="data
source=.\SQLEXPRESS;Integrated Security=SSPI;AttachDBFilename=|DataDirectory|aspnetdb.
mdf;User Instance=true"
providerName="System.Data.SqlClient" />
  </connectionStrings>
</configuration>
```

If you have installed SQL Express, this connection string will expect a unique database instance (*.mdf* file) for each web site, beneath the *\App_Data* directory. This will create unnecessary work for you to complete each lab. Instead, if you plan to use SQL Express, I recommend that you override this setting in your application configuration file for the lab by removing and re-adding the LocalSqlServer connection string, as shown in bold in Example A-2.

Example A-2. Using the default Express instance for ASP.NET providers

```
<configuration>
  <connectionStrings>
    <remove name="LocalSqlServer"/>
    <add name="LocalSqlServer" connectionString="data
source=(local)\SQLEXPRESS;Integrated Security=SSPI;Initial Catalog=aspnetdb"/>
  </connectionStrings>
</configuration>
```

If you are not using SQL Express, you'll still need to change this LocalSqlServer setting to a different connection string to support SQL Server 2000 or 2005. Add the bold configuration code from Example A-3.

 You can also configure ASP.NET providers to use a different connection string by a different name, but this requires additional work. The easiest way to go is to remove and re-add the LocalSql1Server connection.

Example A-3. SQL Server 2000 or 2005 setting for ASP.NET providers

```
<configuration>
  <connectionStrings>
    <remove name="LocalSqlServer"/>
    <add name="LocalSqlServer" connectionString="data source=localhost;Initial
Catalog=aspnetdb;Integrated Security=True;" providerName="System.Data.SqlClient" />
  </connectionStrings>
</configuration>
```

The connection string should be set to the correct value before you use the web site configuration tool for a web project—for example, when you are generating new users and roles. Each lab that relies on the ASP.NET provider model will tell you when to update the configuration file to reflect one of these settings.

Creating Sample Users and Roles

Several labs and samples rely on the ASP.NET provider model to provide authentication and authorization. This section will walk you through creating sample users and roles.

1. From Visual Studio, create a new web site.
2. From Solution Explorer, open the *web.config* file and provide a `<connectionStrings>` section for `LocalSqlServer` as discussed in the previous section. Save this change.

 You must do this before you configure users and roles unless you want to use the default SQL Express file-based database.

3. Open the ASP.NET Configuration utility. From the Web Site menu, select ASP.NET Configuration. This launches a browser with the configuration tool.
4. Click on the security link.
5. Configure the application for Internet security and enable roles.
6. Now it's time to create some roles and users. Click the "Create or Manage Roles" link and from this page add three roles: `Administrators`, `Users`, and `Guests`.
7. Return to the main Security configuration page and select the Manage Users link. Click "Create new user" and, from the Create User page, enter values for the first user in Table A-1. Check the roles according to the Roles column in the table. Repeat this for each user in the table.

 The email address is not important to the labs, so feel free to use any email address.

Table A-1. Sample user accounts for labs

Username	Password	Email	Question	Answer	Roles
Admin	p@ssw0rd	admin@thatindigogirl.com	N/A	N/A	Administrators, users
User	p@ssword	user@thatindigogirl.com	N/A	N/A	Users
Guest	p@ssword	guest@thatindigogirl.com	N/A	N/A	Guests

8. Test the accounts by attempting to log in to the application. Add a Login control to the default page and run the web site in a browser instance (F5). Try to log in with one of the accounts. If you created the accounts correctly, you'll be authenticated and no exceptions will be presented. Test each account to be sure it works.

Certificate Setup

This section describes how to install sample certificates to support code samples and labs. Labs that require certificates will include a note requesting that you complete this section before you begin.

Sample Certificates

When you import certificates to the certificate store, you must choose a particular certificate store. In the labs and code samples for this book, I am using the LocalMachine as the "server" store for certificates, and CurrentUser for "client" certificates. Table A-2 provides a list of certificates used by the code in this book and the appropriate location for installation.

Table A-2. List of certificates and locations for installation

Certificate filename	Subject key	Description	LocalMachine	CurrentUser
RPKey.pfx	CN=RPKey	Private key pair for the relying party (target services).	Personal	N/A
RPKey.cer		Public key for target services.	TrustedPeople, Trusted Root Certification Authorities	Personal
IPKey.pfx	CN=IPKey	Private key pair for identity provider services.	Personal	N/A
IPKey.cer		Public key for identity provider services.	TrustedPeople, Trusted Root Certification Authorities	N/A
SubjectKey.pfx	CN=SubjectKey	Private key pair for client applications.	N/A	Personal
SubjectKey.cer		Public key for client applications.	Personal, TrustedPeople, Trusted Root Certification Authorities	N/A
LocalHost.pfx	CN=LocalHost	Private key pair to use import as the SSL certificate in IIS.	Personal, Trusted Root Certification Authorities	N/A

All certificates are located in the *<YourLearningWCFPath>\SupportingFiles\Certificates* directory.

Certificates Console

If you are new to certificates you may also need some instructions on using the Certificates MMC snap-in. Here are some instructions for setting up the snap-in.

1. From the Start menu, select Run and type *mmc.exe*. Click OK to launch the MMC console.

2. From the File menu, select Add/Remove Snap-in. Click Add from the dialog and select Certificates from the Add Standalone Snap-in dialog.

   Click Add, select My user account, and click Finish.

   Click Add, again and select Computer account. Click Next and then Finish.

   Close the Add Standalone Snap-in dialog. Click OK on the Add/Remove Snap-in dialog.

3. Save the Certificates snap-in settings to a file. From the File menu, select Save. Name the file *certificates.msc*. You should see the console shown in Figure A-6.

4. To re-open this console, repeat Step 1 and open the *certificates.msc* file.

You will use this console to import and export certificates.

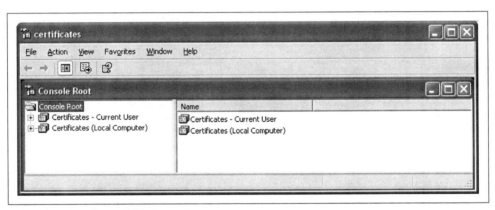

Figure A-6. Certificates MMC console

Importing Certificates

You can use the Certificates console to install certificates listed in Table A-2 to the appropriate certificate stores under LocalMachine or CurrentUser. Each certificate in Table A-2 indicates exactly which stores it must be installed in and you must pay careful attention to complete the installation for each certificate to exactly that list of certificate stores in order for all labs and samples in this book to work properly.

To import certificates do the following:

1. Expand the certificate store and the folder specified in Table A-2.

2. Right-click on the Certificates folder in the hierarchy and select All Tasks → Import (see Figure A-7).

3. Follow the steps in the wizard. Browse for the certificate file in the *<YourLearningWCFPath>\SupportingFiles\Certificates* directory. When browsing for *.pfx* files, change the "Files of type" selection to **.pfx* instead of **.cer*.

Provide the password indigo for private key pairs and do not mark the keys as exportable.

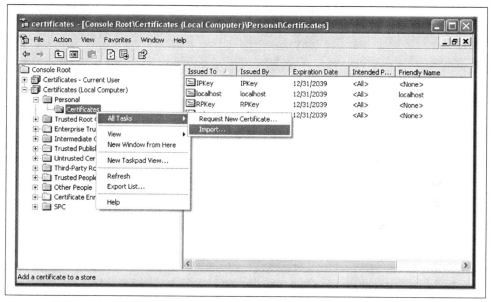

Figure A-7. Importing certificates

Certificate Security

The executing process identity must be given access to private keys installed into a certificate store For example, when hosting services in IIS, the ASP.NET identity (ASPNET or NETWORK SERVICE) must be granted access to the certificate file.

To grant a Windows account access to a particular certificate, follow these instructions:

1. The Windows SDK for .NET 3.0 includes samples for WCF in the ZIP file *WCFSamples.zip*. If you have unzipped this file, you will find sample code for the FindPrivateKey tool in *\WCFSamples\TechnologySamples\Tools\FindPrivateKey*.

2. As an alternative you can download the individual sample from here: *http://msdn2.microsoft.com/en-us/library/aa717039.aspx*.

3. Compile this sample.

4. *FindPrivateKey.exe* is a command-line tool that can be used to find the directory and file that contains a particular key. For example, to find the full path to a key file from the LocalMachine My certificate store, type the following command:

```
Findprivatekey.exe My LocalMachine -n "CN=RPKey" -a
```

Table A-2 includes the subject key name for each certificate.

5. Once you have the path to the file, you can navigate to it using File Explorer as shown in Figure A-8. Right-click the key and select Properties. Select the Security tab from the Properties dialog, as shown in Figure A-9.

6. From this tab, you can add the appropriate users or groups to the list. On Microsoft Vista machines, click Edit and then Add to add new users or groups. On Windows XP/SP2 machines, click Add.

7. After adding ASPNET or NETWORK SERVICE to the list, save the changes.

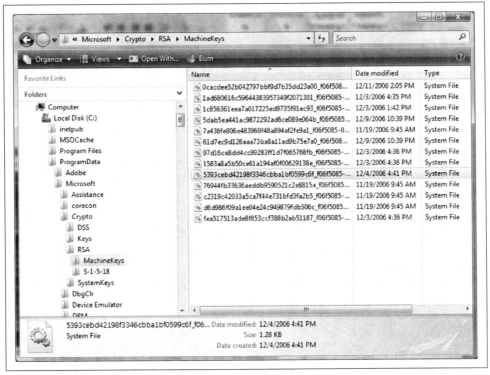

Figure A-8. Using File Explorer to browse certificates

Setting Up an SSL Certificate

Some labs and samples rely on an SSL-enabled web site. This requires you to attach a certificate to your default web site in IIS. This section discusses how to configure the localhost certificate from Table A-2 as the SSL certificate for the default web site. First I'll walk you through instructions for IIS 5.1 and 6.0, followed by instructions for IIS 7.0.

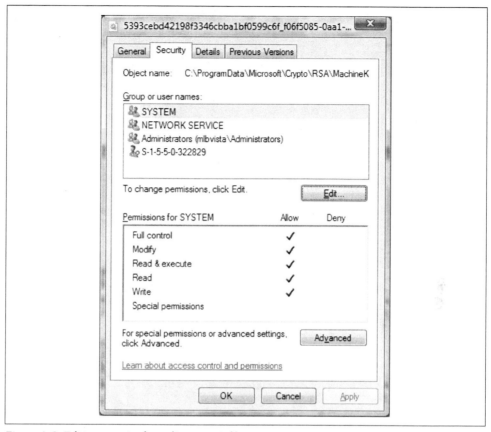

Figure A-9. Editing security for a directory or file

Before you continue, follow the instructions in the earlier section "Importing Certificates" and install the localhost certificate.

Instructions for IIS 5.1 and 6.0

The following are explicit instructions for installing an SSL certificate in IIS 5.1. IIS 6.0 follows similar instructions.

1. Import the *localhost.pfx* certificate as instructed in earlier sections.
2. Open the console for IIS from Control Panel → Administrative Tools.
3. Right-click the default web site node and select Properties.
4. From the Directory Security tab, select Server Certificate (see Figure A-10).
5. Select "Assign an existing certificate" (Figure A-11) and click Next.
6. Certificates installed to the LocalMachine → Personal store will be presented. Select localhost and continue (Figure A-12).

Figure A-10. Directory Security settings for the default web site

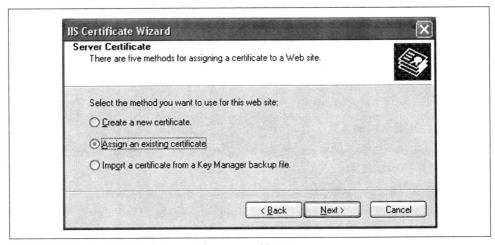

Figure A-11. Assigning an existing certificate to enable SSL support

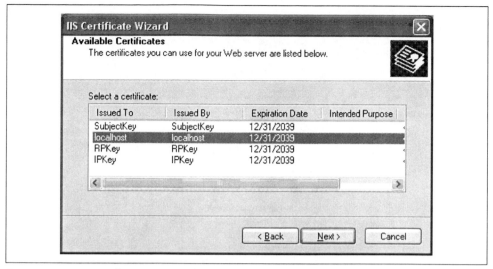

Figure A-12. SSL certificates are installed to the LocalMachine → Personal store

Instructions for IIS 7.0

The following are explicit instructions for installing an SSL certificate in IIS 7.0:

1. Open the console for IIS from Control Panel → Administrative Tools.

2. Select the root node and find the Server Certificates feature shown in Figure A-13. Select this feature, and verify that the localhost certificate is listed, as shown in Figure A-14. If not, import *localhost.pfx* from here—this will import it into the LocalMachine certificate store.

3. Enable HTTPS protocol for the default web site. This is done using the following *appcmd.exe* command line instruction:

   ```
   appcmd.exe set site "Default Web Site"
   -+bindings.[protocol='https',bindingInformation='*:443']
   ```

   I have provided a batch file with this instruction: *<YourLearningWCFPath>\ Samples\Security\enablewashttps.bat*.

4. Now you can associate the localhost certificate with the default web site for HTTPS protocol. Return to the IIS console, select Default Web Site, and find the SSL Settings feature as shown in Figure A-15. From the Actions pane, select Bindings from the Edit Site section.

   In the Web Site Bindings dialog you should see HTTPS protocol listed (see Figure A-16). Select the HTTPS protocol item from the list and click Edit.

   From the Edit Web Site Binding dialog, drop down the list for SSL Certificate— you should see localhost listed if you have installed the certificate per instructions so far. Select localhost and save these changes.

Figure A-13. Server Certificate feature of IIS 7.0

Figure A-14. Importing SSL certificates in IIS 7.0

Generating Certificates

The labs and samples expect you to be using the certificates provided. Still, you may want to create your own certificates for future work, or you may need to create a test certificate for SSL that matches your machine or the domain name of your default web site.

These instructions explain how you can use *makecert.exe* to create test certificates.

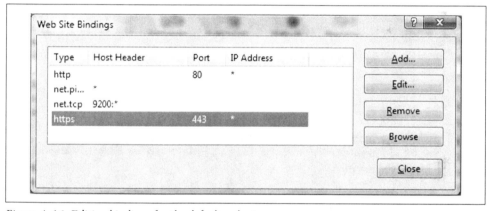

Figure A-15. SSL settings feature for the default web site

Figure A-16. Editing bindings for the default web site

1. Launch the Visual Studio command line and type these instructions to generate a certificate named `localhost`:

```
makecert -r -pe -n CN=localhost -ss my -sr currentuser -sky exchange -sp
"Microsoft RSA SChannel Cryptographic Provider" -sy 12 c:\localhost.cer
```

The certificate will be generated in the `CurrentUser` store, but you will install it in the `LocalMachine` store for SSL.

Naming the certificate `localhost` allows you to use it for local testing on your machine. The SSL certificate must be named the same as the web site. You can rename `localhost` to your machine or domain name if necessary.

2. Since the certificate is generated to enable exporting the private key, you can export it using the Certificates console. Expand the CurrentUser → Personal store, and selecting All Tasks → Export (see Figure A-17).

3. From the wizard, select "Yes, export the private key" (Figure A-18). Click Next.

4. Select "Delete the private key if the export is successful" (see Figure A-19). Click Next.

5. Provide a password to protect the key (Figure A-20). Click Next.

6. Select a filename for the key pair with a *.pfx* extension (Figure A-21).

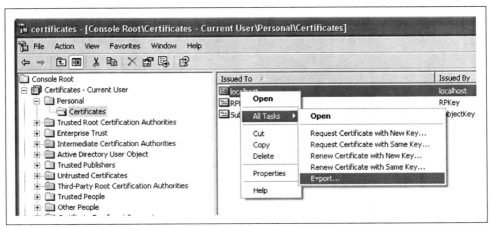

Figure A-17. Exporting a private key certificate

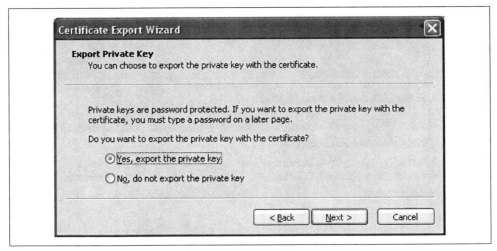

Figure A-18. Export wizard options for exporting private keys

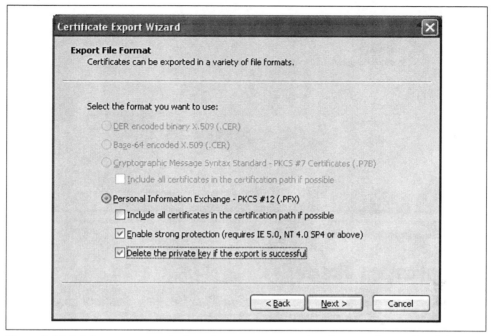

Figure A-19. It is best to remove the key when exporting, in particular since the new key did not have password protection and supports exporting private keys

Certificate Export Wizard

Password
To maintain security, you must protect the private key by using a password.

Type and confirm a password.

Password:
******

Confirm password:
******

< Back   Next >   Cancel

Figure A-20. Private keys require a password

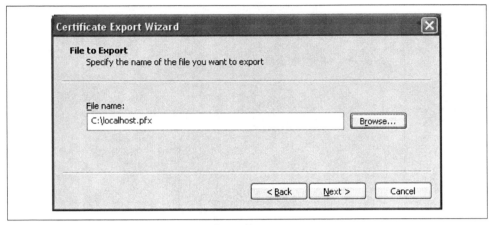

Figure A-21. Selecting the private key certificate file.

IIS Application Directories

Labs and samples that require you to set up an IIS application directory (also called a virtual directory) will provide you with a .vbs script to run, usually in the root of the solution. In some cases, however, you will create a new web site in IIS using Visual Studio. Depending on your default settings in IIS, it is possible that Windows Integrated Authentication may not be enabled for the application directory. This section explains how to accomplish this for IIS 5.1/6.0 and IIS 7.0.

Instructions for IIS 5.1 and 6.0

The following are explicit instructions for enabling Integrated Windows Authentication for virtual application directories in IIS 5.1. IIS 6.0 follows similar instructions.

1. Open the console for IIS from Control Panel → Administrative Tools.
2. Select the web site or application directory to configure and edit its properties.
3. From the properties dialog, select the Security tab.
4. Check the Integrated Windows Authentication checkbox and save the changes.

Instructions for IIS 7.0

Follow these instructions to enable Integrated Windows Authentication for virtual application directories in IIS 7.0.

1. Open the console for IIS from Control Panel → Administrative Tools.
2. Select the web site or application directory to configure and find the Authentication feature.
3. From the Authentication feature, enable Windows Authentication.

ASP.NET Meets CardSpace

This appendix is adapted from *asp.netPRO* magazine (*www.aspnetpro.com*), September 2006, and is reprinted with the express permission of Informant Communications Group, Inc.

Windows CardSpace ("CardSpace") is a client technology that is part of the .NET Framework 3.0—used for creating, managing and sharing digital identities in a secure and reliable manner. You can think of CardSpace as an identity selector that securely stores informational claims about a user, making it easy for that same user to send this information to a trusted web site for authentication purposes. But it isn't just an identity selector—CardSpace also makes it easier for users to identify the target site where claims are sent by authenticating the site and presenting its credentials for user approval. In addition, users can review the claims that the site has demanded, and explicitly allow or disallow sending that information.

In this appendix, I'll provide a very brief introduction to CardSpace. After that, I will jump into the details for how you enable your ASP.NET web sites for CardSpace as a login alternative.

Information Cards and CardSpace: A Brief Tour

Cards refer to informational claims about a subject—the user that is to be given access to a web site, web service, or application (know as the "Relying Party" or RP). Claims might include your name, address, phone number, birth date, or any other information that might prove useful to identify you. Different RP's may demand different sets of claims to authenticate and authorize callers.

Two types of information cards exist: *personal cards* and *managed cards*. Personal cards are self-issued cards that can be created directly in the CardSpace user interface. Managed cards are obtained from a third-party provider who is willing to assert that a set of claims really do relate to *you*. CardSpace can store both types of cards, and creates or obtains a security token containing the claims represented by those cards. That's the ultimate goal: to reliably create a security token that carries claims to identify the user.

The CardSpace user interface is accessible from the Digital Identities icon in the Control Panel shown in Figure B-1.

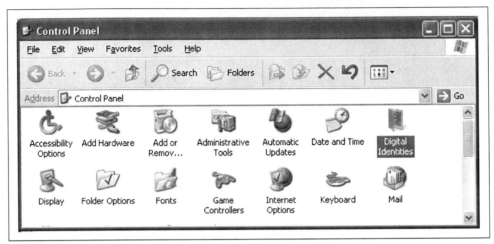

Figure B-1. You can create and manage cards from Digital Identities in the Control Panel; this option is installed with .NET Framework 3.0 on XP/SP2

When you select Digital Identities, it launches a hardened CardSpace user interface where you can safely create personal cards, import and export cards, protect cards with a pin, and perform other functions related to card management.

Personal cards can contain a limited set of claims, most of which are shown in Figure B-2. You may create one or more personal cards based on the type of information you share with different sites. For example, I have two cards—one that contains my business email, web site, and related information; another for my personal email, web log, and related information I might share. Personal cards work well for sites that I would normally identify myself to with a username and password.

When you create a self-issued card using CardSpace, you actually create two things: the information card and a separate record with your actual claims. This distinction is important because the actual information card does not contain the value of each claim. It is the responsibility of the identity provider to store and protect the claims—and to issue tokens for those claims based on a requested information card. In the case of self-issued cards, it just happens that a local identity provider exists inside the CardSpace environment to do just that.

Managed cards may contain similar claims, but most likely have custom claims that are required by the card issuer. For example, a bank may vouch for your account number and an airline may vouch for your frequent flyer number. The card issuer is entirely responsible for defining what claims their managed cards represent.

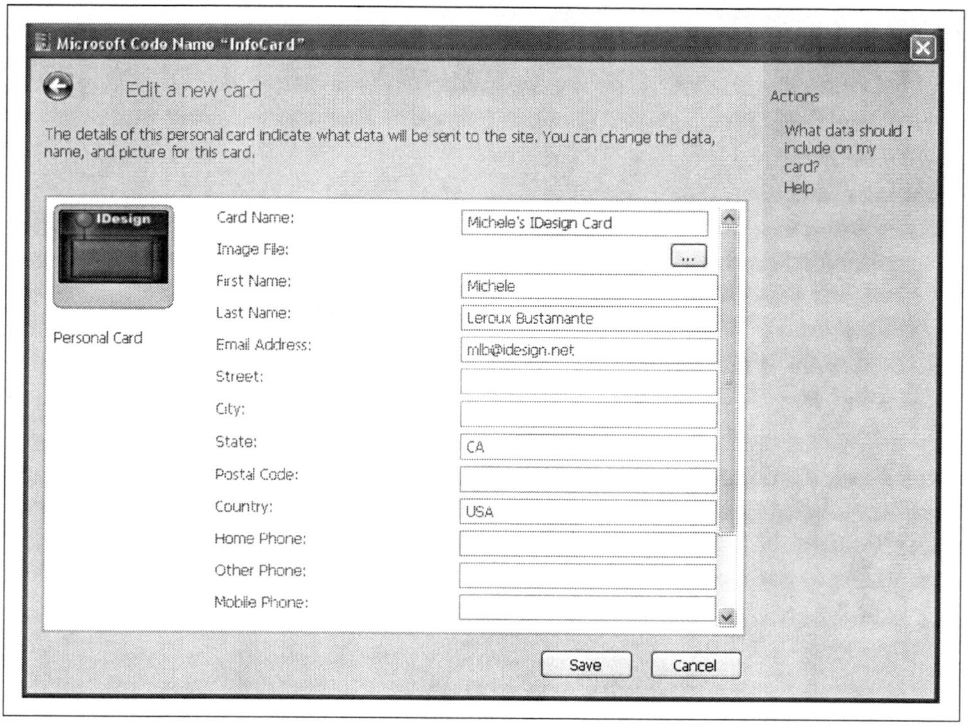

Figure B-2. Creating a new personal card with CardSpace

In the case of managed cards, my bank may issue a card for me to install in Card-Space, but the actual claims are stored remotely with the bank's identity provider. When a managed card is selected in the CardSpace interface, CardSpace makes a call to the managed identity provider to request a token containing the required claims.

Identity Metasystem Participants and Browser Flow

Before I show you how to support CardSpace from your ASP.NET web sites, I'll explain the flow between participants in the Identity Metasystem and the Browser experience.

There are several key participants:

Relying Party (RP)
> This is the target site that relies on a specific set of claims to authenticate calls. In the context of this appendix, your ASP.NET web site would be the RP.

Subject
> This is the user described by a set of claims, for example the user logging in to your web site.

Identity Provider (IP)

This party is responsible for generating a token that includes a set of claims describing the subject. They are the holder of those claims and must keep them secure. They must sign the token to prove that they are the party that supplied the claims.

Windows CardSpace

For Windows machines, CardSpace provides local storage for personal and managed information cards that represent a list of claims. As I mentioned, the card does not contain the actual claim values. For personal cards, CardSpace supplies a local IP that securely stores the actual claims. Thus, in cases where personal cards are supported by the target site, CardSpace acts as both identity selector and IP.

Figure B-3 illustrates the interaction between each participant, assuming personal cards (from CardSpace) are supported. Users browse to a site that returns a login page supporting information cards. When the user clicks the "login using Card-Space" button, IE 7 hands the request off to CardSpace and waits for a signed and encrypted token to be returned.

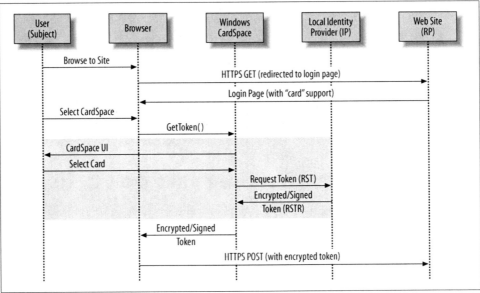

Figure B-3. Interaction between user, browser, relying party, and CardSpace for self-issued cards

The hardened CardSpace user interface appears presenting the user with cards that satisfy the claims required by the target site. If they have selected a card for the site before, that card will be highlighted.

After the user selects a card to send to the site, CardSpace sends a request to its local IP for a token containing the required claims. The token is encrypted and signed by

---

the local IP before CardSpace returns it to the browser. Ultimately the token is posted to the RP via SSL.

The entire exchange with the user for creating or managing their cards through the CardSpace user interface, for requesting the token from the IP, and for encrypting that token is heavily locked down. This is illustrated by the shaded area in the diagram. No malicious code can easily be injected into this exchange.

Let's Log In with CardSpace!

With that brief introduction to CardSpace, let's talk about the requirements for invoking the CardSpace user interface from an ASP.NET page. Here is a list of basic requirements:

1. Your web site must be SSL-enabled.
2. A recent build of IE 7 is required for a browser experience with CardSpace.
3. Your ASP.NET pages can use the <object> tag or XHTML syntax to trigger the CardSpace experience.
4. When the security token is posted to the web site, you are responsible for processing the claims inside the token, and using them to authenticate calls.

Example B-1 illustrates the use of the <object> tag to launch the CardSpace user interface. The <object> tag can be placed inside the header or in the <form> tag. When the ImageButton posts back to the server, the information card object is instantiated, using parameters as input. The Windows desktop is locked down at this point with the CardSpace UI presented. After the user selects a card, Card-Space processes the request and returns a signed and encrypted token to the browser. This token is posted to the server as a form parameter by the name "xml-TokenEncrypted" per the <object> tag name in Listing 1.

Example B-1. Invoking CardSpace with the <object> tag

```
<form name="formCardSpaceLoginOBJECT" method="post"
id="formCardSpaceLoginOBJECT" runat="server">
  ...
  <object type="application/x-informationCard" name="xmlTokenEncrypted"
id="xmlTokenEncrypted">
    <param name="tokenType"
value="urn:oasis:names:tc:SAML:1.0:assertion"/>
    <param name="issuer"
value="http://schemas.microsoft.com/ws/2005/05/identity/issuer/self"/>
    <param name="requiredClaims"
value="http://schemas.microsoft.com/ws/2005/05/identity/
claims/privatepersonalidentifier http://schemas.microsoft.com/ws/2005/05/identity/
claims/emailaddress"/>
  </object>
  ...
  <asp:ImageButton ID="submitInformationCard" runat="server" ImageUrl="CardSpaceLogin.jpg"
/>
</form>
```

Example B-2 illustrates how we achieve the same result with XHTML.

Example B-2. Invoking CardSpace with XHTML

```
<html xmlns="http://www.w3.org/1999/xhtml"
xmlns:ic="http://www.identityselectors.org/2006/10">
...
<body>
  <form name="formCardSpaceLoginXHTML" method="post"
id="formCardSpaceLoginXHTML" runat="server">
...
    <ic:informationCard name="xmlTokenEncrypted"
style="behavior:url(#default#informationCard)"
issuer="http://schemas.microsoft.com/ws/2005/05/identity/issuer/self"
tokenType="http://docs.oasis-open.org/wss/
oasis-wss-saml-token-profile-1.1#SAMLV1.1">
        <ic:add claimType="http://schemas.microsoft.com/ws/2005/05/identity/
claims/privatepersonalidentifier" optional="false" />
        <ic:add claimType="http://schemas.microsoft.com/ws/2005/05/identity/
claims/emailaddress" optional="false" />
    </ic:informationCard>
...
    <asp:ImageButton ID="submitInformationCard"
ImageUrl="CardSpaceLogin.jpg" runat="server" />
  </form>
</body>
</html>
```

In both cases, the syntax of the <object> tag and the XHTML code specified the following:

What format of security token does the web site support?
> The <object> tag requires a SAML 1.0 token, and the XHTML code requires a SAML 1.1 token.

Which claims are required by the site for authentication?
> In both cases, private personal identifier (PPID) and email address claims are required. These are two of the standard set of claims supported by self-issued cards.

Which identity provider (also called a security token issuer) is trusted by the web site?
> In both cases, self-issued tokens are supported—which implies the local Card-Space IP on Windows operating systems. For managed cards, a specific IP might have been required to issue signed tokens.

During postback, you can access the issued SAML token through the Request object like this:

```
string token = Request.Form["xmlTokenEncrypted"] as string;
```

Now, the question is, what do you do with this token?

Processing the Token

The token string is in the form of an `<EncryptedData>` section. It is encrypted with the public key portion of the site's SSL certificate. The code to decrypt it therefore must have access to the site's private key. Specifically, the ASP.NET account will need permissions to access the private key from the certificate store.

The code to decrypt the token is lengthy and a topic in itself, so I'll let you look at the code sample for those details. After the token is decrypted, you'll find that you are working with a SAML token that has a set of claims inside. The claims are exactly those you requested, shown in Examples B-1 and B-2. In this example, the claims include a personal private identifier (PPID) and an email address—but there is a complete list of valid claims in the CardSpace specification, and this can be extended for managed cards.

Once you have decrypted the token and verified that it includes the claims you requested, it is time to authenticate.

Associating Cards with User Accounts

Typically users login with username and password to a web site. Both the username and password are required to authenticate. A site that supports information cards is really stating that it supports authentication against a set of claims. As I have mentioned, those claims might be a username, email address, birth date, or some other information. But anyone can discover this information and create a card with the same data—so before we can authenticate these claims, we need to know that the claims came from a trusted source. If it were a managed card, the token would be signed with the trusted identity provider's private key. In the case of self-issued tokens, we need to look at alternate ways to establish trust.

One approach is to have the card associated with the user account. That implies that the user must log in with her username and password prior to selecting a card to send to the site for the first time. Once logged in, the user can select a card, which sends the security token to the site. If the claims posted with the card include the user's email address, this can be compared to the logged in user to verify the card matches the user. In addition, the personal private identifier of the card can be stored and used to associate that specific card with the user's account:

```
MembershipUser user = Membership.GetUser
  (this.User.Identity.Name);
if (user.Email == emailClaim)
{
  user.Comment = ppidClaim;
  Membership.UpdateUser(user);
}
```

The PPID is a special type of claim. This is a unique identifier for a particular card sent to a particular site. Since a card can be used for multiple sites, CardSpace generates a PPID for every site a card is sent to. In short, the PPID represents the relationship between the relying party and the information card.

With the PPID of the card associated with their account, a user no longer has to provide their username and password to log in. When she logs in with the CardSpace option, instead of processing username and password credentials, you can look up her user account by the email address claim and then verify that the PPID of the posted token matches the PPID stored in her user account:

```
MembershipUser authenticatedUser = null;
MembershipUserCollection matchingUsers =
  Membership.FindUsersByEmail(emailClaim);

if (matchingUsers.Count == 0)
{
  // error
}

foreach (MembershipUser user in matchingUsers)
{
  if (user.Comment == ppidClaim)
  {
    authenticatedUser = user;
  }
}

if (authenticatedUser == null)
{
  //error
}

FormsAuthentication.RedirectFromLoginPage(emailClaim, false);
```

The call to RedirectFromLoginPage( ) handles generating an authentication ticket for the user and redirecting to the originally requested page—just like the ASP.NET Login control would do with the username and password.

Creating a Dual Purpose Login Page

The code sample for this appendix includes a login page that uses the ASP.NET Login control for traditional login and the <object> tag for those who have already associated their information cards with their account. One of the challenges with this is making sure that the <object> tag is only invoked when the user clicks the CardSpace login button. Since we can't have two active <form> tags in an ASP.NET page, I had to learn a little bit more about <object> tags, how they are instantiated, and how to control that instantiation with javascript.

First, I placed the <object> tag declaration in the header section of the HTML page. I also had to use the declare attribute of the tag to indicate this was only a declaration so that the CardSpace object would not be instantiated until it is referenced by the CardSpace submit button:

```
<object declare id="informationCard"
type="application/x-informationCard" name="informationCard" >
...
</object>
```

Next, I created a javascript function, SelectInformationCard( ), that would instantiate the CardSpace object and put the value it returns into a hidden text field:

```
<script type="text/javascript" language="javascript">
  function SelectInformationCard( )
  {
    var infoCardObject =document.getElementById("informationCards");
    var hiddenToken = document.getElementById("hiddenXmlToken");
    hiddenToken.value = infoCardObject.value;
  }
</script>
```

Within the <form> tag, I arranged the Login control and my CardSpace image button, along with the hidden text field (the latter two shown here):

```
<asp:ImageButton ID="cardSpaceSubmit" runat="server" ImageUrl="infocardlogin.jpg"  />
<input id="hiddenXmlToken" type="hidden"  name="hiddenXmlToken" />
```

And then I associated the client-side function, SelectInformationCard( ), to the ASP.NET ImageButton server control:

```
if (!this.IsPostBack)
{
  this.cardSpaceSubmit.Attributes.Add("onclick", "SelectInformationCard( );");
}
```

This last step makes it possible for the server control to invoke a client-side function prior to completing the postback. Of course, the postback includes the hidden text field, which will contain the encrypted token!

Conclusion

Allowing personal cards to be associated with a user's login credentials can simplify their login experience significantly. Instead of trying to remember her username and password every time she visits your site, she can log in once, associate an information card with her account, and in future, go to CardSpace to log in with a few simple clicks. Hopefully, this appendix has provided you with enough of a teaser to inspire you to look at CardSpace for this purpose.

The code for this article and related sample code is based on the July CTP of .NET Framework 3.0.

Index

We'd like to hear your suggestions for improving our indexes. Send email to *index@oreilly.com*.

About the Author

Michele Leroux Bustamante is Chief Architect of IDesign Inc., Microsoft Regional Director for San Diego, Microsoft MVP for Connected Systems, and a BEA Technical Director. At IDesign, Michele provides training, mentoring, and high-end architecture consulting services focusing on web services, scalable and secure architecture design for .NET, interoperability, and globalization architecture. She is a member of the International .NET Speakers Association (INETA), a frequent conference presenter, conference chair for SD West, and is frequently published in several major technology journals. Michele is also on the board of directors for IASA (International Association of Software Architects) and a Program Advisor to UCSD Extension. Contact her at *mlb@idesign.net*, or visit *www.idesign.net* and her main blog at *www.dasblonde.net*. Michele has also provided a blog for this book at *www.thatindigogirl.com*.

Colophon

The animal on the cover of *Learning WCF* is a marine fish commonly referred to as a damselfish (*demoiselle*). Damselfish and clownfish comprise the family *Pomacentridae* and are found in tropical waters throughout the world, though mainly in the Atlantic and Indo-Pacific oceans. The damselfish, of which there are about 250 species, has a deep, compressed body, a small mouth, and an anal fin with two (occasionally three) spines. Its average length in captivity is about 2 inches, but in the wild, the largest member of this subfamily reaches over 14 inches. Coloration varies according to species, location, and age; these fish often lose their brightness as adults.

Because damselfish are extremely hardy, they are often captured and bred in aquariums. They are sometimes used to break in a new aquarium, but this is considered an old-school practice and is frowned upon by advanced aquarists. In captivity, damselfish can become quite aggressive among themselves and toward other tankmates, disrupting an otherwise peaceful environment. In the wild, they tend to stay in small schools while young and eventually break away to become solitary as adults. Some damselfish live with anemones in a comensal relationship, meaning that each party benefits from the arrangement. In its natural habitat, this entertaining little fish can live up to 20 years.

The cover image is from *Lydekker's Natural History*. The cover font is Adobe ITC Garamond. The text font is Linotype Birka; the heading font is Adobe Myriad Condensed; and the code font is LucasFont's TheSans Mono Condensed.